MW00462104

Winner of the Jules and Frances Landry Award for 2003

Published with the assistance of the
V. Ray Cardozier Fund
an endowment created to support
publication of scholarly books

Robert F. W. Allston
Courtesy of Gibbes Museum of Art /
Carolina Art Association, Charleston

WILLIAM KAUFFMAN
SCARBOROUGH

MASTERS
of
THE BIG HOUSE

*Elite Slaveholders of
the Mid-Nineteenth-Century South*

LOUISIANA STATE UNIVERSITY PRESS
BATON ROUGE

DESIGNER: Andrew Shurtz
TYPEFACE: Adobe Caslon
TYPESETTER: Coghill Composition Co., Inc.

LIBRARY OF CONGRESS CATALOGING-IN-PUBLICATION DATA:

Scarborough, William Kauffman.
    Masters of the big house : elite slaveholders of the
mid-nineteenth-century South / William Kauffman Scarborough.
        p.   cm.
Includes bibliographical references (p.   ) and index.
    ISBN 0-8071-2882-1 (alk. paper)
    1. Plantation owners—Southern States—History—19th century.
    2. Slaveholders—Southern States—History—19th century.
    3. Elite (Social sciences)—Southern States—History—19th century.
    4. Slavery—Social aspects—Southern States—History—19th century.
    5. Slavery—Economic aspects—Southern States—History—19th century.
    6. Slavery—Political aspects—Southern States—History—19th century.
    7. Plantation life—Southern States—History—19th century.
    8. Southern States—History—1775–1865.
    9. Southern States—Social conditions—19th century.
    10. Southern States—Race relations.   I. Title.
    F213.S35 2003
    975'.03'08621—dc21   2003007301

CONTENTS

ILLUSTRATIONS

TABLES

ACKNOWLEDGMENTS

Although the final product is mine alone, I am deeply grateful for the assistance of numerous institutions and individuals during the long journey toward the completion of this project. I accumulated some of the manuscript materials for this work as far back as the early 1960s while researching my first book, *The Overseer*. However, the first major step in the project was facilitated by a grant from the National Endowment for the Humanities, which enabled me to spend the summer of 1967 in Baton Rouge, exploring manuscript sources in the Louisiana and Lower Mississippi Valley Collections at Louisiana State University.

For the next twenty-four years, while I was engaged in editing the massive diary of Edmund Ruffin and while I was increasingly occupied with administrative duties as department chair during the 1980s, my work on this project was confined largely to identifying the wealthy slaveholders by perusing the manuscript slave schedules, initially in the original books at the National Archives and later on microfilm. Then, aided immeasurably by two one-semester sabbaticals and by a two-year term as Charles W. Moorman Distinguished Alumni Professor in the Humanities at the University of Southern Mississippi, I was able to spend extended periods of time at various archival sites throughout the South.

Although the list of those who assisted me in my archival travels is too long to enumerate fully here, I wish to express particular appreciation to Richard Schrader and John White of the Southern Historical Collection at my alma mater, the University of North Carolina; C. Patton Hash and Peter L. Wilkerson, both now departed from the South Carolina Historical Society in my favorite city, Charleston; Anne Lipscomb Webster at the Mississippi Department of Archives and History in Jackson; Frances Pollard, archivist at the Virginia Historical Society; Don Carleton of the Center for American History at the University of Texas; and Faye Phillips, who presides over the archival collections at Louisiana State University.

As knowledge of my undertaking filtered out to the general public, I was gratified to receive offers of assistance from a number of descendants of elite slaveholders. Some provided genealogical information and others made available original materials in their possession. Among those to whom I am indebted are Donald G. Linton of Hot Springs, Arkansas, a Linton/Surget descendant; Mrs. Rawdon Blankenstein of Natchez, a Shields descendant; Jonathan H. Ray of Brentwood, Tennessee, who not only clarified relationships in the Conner and Gustine families but also provided me with a photograph of William Gustine Conner; my friend Elmore D. Greaves of Madison County, Mississippi, the great-grandson of S. A. D. Greaves; Mrs. Hart Anderson Banahan of Jackson and John Robinson Anderson of Madison County, descendants of John Robinson; and Russell S. Hall of Germantown, Tennessee, whose persistent contention that slaves listed under the sons of his great-great-great uncle Dr. William E. Hall were actually the property of the elder Hall finally persuaded me that the latter merited inclusion in my list of elite slaveholders. Others were helpful as well. Jessie Poesch of Tulane, my colleague in the St. George Tucker Society, generously shared materials she had gathered relating to John Burnside.

As one whose ignorance of technology almost defies belief in this postmodern era, I could not have completed this project without the help of several of my associates in the Department of History at the University of Southern Mississippi. Chief among those who painstakingly answered my questions and guided me through the labyrinth of computer technology were my colleague Brad Bond; my former doctoral student Glenn Robins, now a professor at Georgia Southwestern University; and, above all, our incomparable department secretary Shelia Smith, who printed the manuscript generated by my ancient word processor and whose knowledge of the computer never ceases to amaze me.

I also benefited immensely from the comments of William W. Freehling, who read the manuscript for the Louisiana State University Press. Although I did not alter the last chapter sufficiently to meet his taste, I did adopt some of his suggestions and can only hope that reviewers of the book will be as generous in their assessment as he was. As always, it has been a pleasure to work with the staff of the LSU Press, an association that now extends through almost four decades. My special thanks go to Leslie E. Phillabaum, who recently announced his impending retirement after twenty-seven years as Director; Associate Director and Editor-in-Chief Maureen G. Hewitt; Acquisitions Editor Sylvia Frank Rodrigue; and my copy editor, Christine Cowan.

Finally, I owe a special debt of gratitude to my wife Patricia, whose patience, understanding, and support during nearly a half-century of marriage to this frequently contentious author must surely qualify her for sainthood.

ABBREVIATIONS

ARCHIVES

ADAH   Alabama Department of Archives and History, Montgomery

CAH   Center for American History, University of Texas, Austin

DU   Perkins Library, Duke University, Durham, North Carolina

GHS   Georgia Historical Society, Savannah

HNO   Historic New Orleans Collection, New Orleans

LSU   Louisiana and Lower Mississippi Valley Collections, Louisiana State University Libraries, Baton Rouge

MDAH   Mississippi Department of Archives and History, Jackson

MHS   Maryland Historical Society, Baltimore

NCDAH   North Carolina Department of Archives and History, Raleigh

SCHS   South Carolina Historical Society, Charleston

SCL   South Caroliniana Library, University of South Carolina, Columbia

SHC   Southern Historical Collection of the Manuscripts Department, University of North Carolina, Chapel Hill

UGA   Hargrett Rare Book and Manuscript Library, University of Georgia, Athens

VHS   Virginia Historical Society, Richmond

JOURNALS

AGH	*Agricultural History*
AHR	*American Historical Review*
JAH	*Journal of American History*
JMH	*Journal of Mississippi History*
JSH	*Journal of Southern History*

MASTERS OF THE BIG HOUSE

INTRODUCTION

T HE GREAT planters of the antebellum South exerted immense influence within their region and profoundly affected the destiny of this nation. They dominated the economy of the South, wielded enormous political power at all levels of government, and set the tone for the society of which they formed the apex. Well-bred, cosmopolitan in background and outlook, intellectually curious, broadly educated, articulate, trained for leadership, and gifted with exceptional entrepreneurial skills, they constituted one of the most significant groups in American history. As contemporary scientist Joseph LeConte once remarked, "nothing could be more remarkable than the wide reading, the deep reflection, the refined culture & the originality of thought & reflection characteristic" of this class.[1] Although many scholars have produced notable studies of the planter class in recent years,[2] no one has yet made a systematic attempt to identify the elite slaveholders—particularly those with multiple holdings, fre-

---

1. MS excerpt from the autobiography of Joseph LeConte, in Langdon Cheves, Jr., Papers, SCHS.

2. A partial list would include the following: James Oakes, *The Ruling Race: A History of American Slaveholders* (New York, 1982), a study of the lesser planters; James L. Roark, *Masters Without Slaves: Southern Planters in the Civil War and Reconstruction* (New York, 1977) and Michael Wayne, *The Reshaping of Plantation Society: The Natchez District, 1860–1880* (Baton Rouge, 1983), on the transition from slave to free labor; Jonathan M. Wiener, *Social Origins of the New South: Alabama, 1860–1885* (Baton Rouge, 1978), and Dwight B. Billings, Jr., *Planters and the Making of a "New South": Class, Politics, and Development in North Carolina, 1865–1900* (Chapel Hill, 1979), on the persistence of planter hegemony in the postwar period; Catherine Clinton, *The Plantation Mistress: Woman's World in the Old South* (New York, 1982), Elizabeth Fox-Genovese, *Within the Plantation Household: Black and White Women of the Old South* (Chapel Hill, 1988), Jane Turner Censer, *North Carolina Planters and Their Children, 1800–1860* (Baton Rouge, 1984), and Joan E. Cashin, "The Structure of Antebellum Planter Families: 'The Ties that Bound Us was Strong,'" *JSH* 56 (February 1990): 55–70, on planter families; Joan E. Cashin, *A Family Venture: Men and Women on the Southern Frontier* (New York, 1991), on the effect of migration on family structure and gender roles; and Laurence

quently extending across both county and state boundaries—and to analyze their characteristics, attitudes, values, and ideology.[3] This is the task upon which I embarked more than thirty years ago and which I have pursued assiduously for the last decade.

Originally conceived as a study of such prominent planter dynasties as the Cockes of Virginia, the Hairstons of North Carolina and Virginia, the Heywards and Hamptons of South Carolina, the Barrows and Bringiers of Louisiana, and the Surgets of Mississippi, the project was subsequently extended to embrace all individual planters in the fifteen slave states who owned 250 or more slaves in 1850 and / or 1860 as determined by the manuscript slave census schedules for those two years.[4] I commenced this project with no preconceived thesis, nor have I been guided by any of the so-called theories, models, and paradigms to which the current generation of historians seems increasingly wedded.

I have chosen, instead, to answer, primarily through manuscript sources, such historically significant questions as the following: Who were these aristocratic slaveholders? What was the structure of their families and the status of women—physically, emotionally, and culturally—within those families? What was their philosophy of education? How did they accumulate their property? Did a significant number invest capital in economic enterprises outside the agricultural sector? What was their role in the sectional crisis of the 1850s and the ensuing Civil War? How does one account for the extreme secessionist position adopted by the South Carolinians in contrast to the staunchly unionist posture of many of their equally affluent counterparts in the Natchez District? How did these once-wealthy elite slaveholders adjust to the postwar environment? And, perhaps most important, did these great planters evince a unique, precapitalist, paternalistic world view, as Eugene D. Genovese and a host of other contempo-

---

Shore, *Southern Capitalists: The Ideological Leadership of an Elite, 1832–1885* (Chapel Hill, 1986), on the capitalistic orientation of large slaveholders.

3. Such an effort was undertaken, in part, by Joseph K. Menn and Chalmers G. Davidson with respect to the states of Louisiana and South Carolina, respectively, but neither author progressed much beyond the mere compilation of interesting data. See Joseph Karl Menn, "The Large Slaveholders of the Deep South, 1860" (Ph.D. diss., University of Texas, 1964) and Chalmers Gaston Davidson, *The Last Foray: The South Carolina Planters of 1860: A Sociological Study* (Columbia, 1971).

4. The Census Bureau aggregated slaveholdings in increments of 100, 200, 300, 500, and 1,000. As my research progressed, it became clear that the most efficacious lower boundary for the cohort being studied would be 250.

rary historians contend, or were their social relations essentially the same as those manifested by northern entrepreneurial capitalists of the period? I shall address the latter issue in the concluding chapter, but it may be remarked here that the ongoing debate between the capitalists and paternalists will yield little fruit unless the contending factions can agree on a common definition of capitalism.

The initial step in establishing the fundamental database for this study was to identify, in systematic fashion, those individuals who owned 250 or more slaves during the decade of the 1850s. This was by no means as easy as it might appear to be at first glance. Passing over the obvious difficulty of conducting a laborious search of the manuscript slave census for every county in each of the fifteen slave states for two successive census years, one was confronted with an even more formidable problem, that posed by multiple holdings. As William Dusinberre has observed, previous writers have "massively" underestimated the number and holdings of the elite planters because they have relied almost exclusively on published census statistics that denote only those slaves held by a proprietor within a single county.[5] In fact, however, slaveholding patterns were exceedingly complex, and many planters, especially those engaged in cotton culture, had multicounty or even multistate holdings. This phenomenon was perhaps most clearly exemplified by Atlantic seaboard families who operated extensive absentee estates in the Lower South and by the wealthy Natchez nabobs, three-fourths of whom had transferred the bulk of their slave forces by 1860 either to the virgin lands of the Yazoo Delta or to the river parishes of northeast Louisiana. The degree to which the concentration of slaveholdings has been understated may be illustrated by figures indicating the ownership of 500 or more slaves. The published census report lists eleven slaveholders in this category in 1850 and fourteen in 1860.[6] When multiple holdings are taken into account, however, the actual numbers are twenty-six and fifty, respectively.[7]

Several examples will suffice to illustrate the problem presented by multiple holdings. Levin R. Marshall, the largest slaveholder in Mississippi on the eve of the Civil War, owned more than 1,000 slaves in six different counties, three

5. William Dusinberre, *Them Dark Days: Slavery in the American Rice Swamps* (New York, 1996), 393.

6. United States Census Office, *Seventh Census of the United States: 1850* (Washington, D.C., 1853); *ibid., Eighth Census of the United States: 1860. Agriculture* (Washington, D.C., 1864).

7. See Appendixes A and B.

in Mississippi and three in Louisiana, but in only one of those six did his slave force exceed the requisite figure of 250. Similarly, Virginia slaveowner Philip St. George Cocke owned 658 slaves in four counties, two in his resident state and two in Mississippi, but in only one of those counties did the slave parcel number more than 250. Another Upper South planter, Peter Wilson Hairston, owned 437 slaves in four different North Carolina and Virginia counties, but the largest number held in any one county was 193.[8] Accordingly, in order to identify those with multiple properties, it was necessary to record *all* significant holdings as the census listings were perused. Even then, some might be missed if the initial number encountered for a particular slaveholder was too small to be deemed significant.

There are other difficulties as well. Some slave parcels were listed under the names of family members even though the latter may not have actually owned them; others were listed under overseers.[9] In addition, although such men as Marshall and Cocke are relatively well known to specialists in southern history, other members of the elite are much more obscure, probably known only to local historians in their state of residence. Those with distinctive names, such as Rice C. Ballard, can readily be identified at each successive mention, but when one repeatedly encounters such common surnames as Jones, Smith, and Williams, the task of identifying owners of multiple holdings becomes much more difficult. Same-name holdings in contiguous counties were assumed to belong to the individual of that name. But when slaves were listed under the same name in disparate areas, it was necessary to confirm the identity of the slaveholder through other sources and, occasionally, by educated guesses. Still, some members of the large slaveholding class, perhaps a dozen, were probably missed.

After identifying members of the population cohort selected for study, the next step in creating a database was to compile extensive biographical and de-

---

8. Unless otherwise indicated, all data concerning the size and location of slaveholdings has been derived from the manuscript slave census returns (Schedule 2: Slave Inhabitants) for 1850 and 1860. See Appendix D for specific details of the various slave parcels owned by Marshall, Cocke, and Hairston.

9. There are two conspicuous examples of the latter. In 1850 slaves on the Butler Estate in Glynn County, Georgia, were listed under Dr. Samuel W. Wilson, who was serving as agent for the absentee owners. Ten years later, the Mordecai-Cameron slaves in Wake County, North Carolina, appeared under the name of overseer Willie Perry.

mographic information on each of the planter aristocrats. These data, essential in identifying characteristics and patterns of behavior, were gleaned from a broad spectrum of sources, beginning with the manuscript population census (Schedule 1) and including the agricultural census (Schedule 4) for Louisiana and Mississippi, plantation records, family correspondence, biographical directories, state and county histories, genealogical works, and various other primary and secondary printed sources. Indeed, the sources are so voluminous that it seems unfeasible to note them in those portions of this book—particularly in this and the following chapter—that delineate statistical aggregations. The reader should consult the bibliography for a comprehensive listing of those works that proved most useful in completing this study. Unfortunately, the information in these sources is uneven in both quality and quantity for each of the individual slaveowners. Thus, the figures on religious and college preferences, presented in Chapter 2, are based on only about 40 percent of the total planter cohort. It can only be regretted that there are not more county histories like that of Georgetown District, South Carolina, by George C. Rogers, Jr., which, in every respect, is a model for works of that genre.[10]

Having established the fundamental database, the next, and by far the most interesting, phase of the research was to examine a multitude of manuscript materials—letters, diaries, business and legal papers—spawned by the large slaveholders, their families, and those closely associated with them. These archival materials are an indispensable source of information concerning attitudes, philosophy, motivation, values, and ideology. In all, I have consulted approximately 125 manuscript collections in fourteen different archival depositories, ranging from Maryland to Texas. It is this research that constitutes the fundamental basis for the conclusions reached in this book. Of course, not all relevant archival materials have been examined. Since members of the elite planter cohort were those most likely to generate papers and to preserve them for posterity, the voluminous quantity of such materials obliges the historian to make judicious selections from the mountain of available manuscripts. I am confident, however, that the archival research for this study has yielded an image of the slaveholding elite that is representative of the whole with respect to size of slave force, geographic location, economic interests, political convictions, and response to the sectional crisis.

10. George C. Rogers, Jr., *The History of Georgetown County, South Carolina* (Columbia, 1970).

The group that constitutes the focal point of this study, those who owned at least 250 slaves during the 1850s, numbered at least 338, of whom 93 (27.5 percent) held that number in both census years. Slightly more than two-thirds of these large slaveholders resided in the three great plantation states of South Carolina, Mississippi, and Louisiana. There were significant but lesser numbers in states like Georgia, Alabama, and North Carolina but only a handful in such peripheral states as Arkansas, Florida, Maryland, and Texas. It will come as no surprise to those familiar with spring pilgrimages and white-columned antebellum mansions to learn that more than a third of the great planters lived in or near the aristocratic citadels of Charleston and Natchez. The elite slaveholders included 22 women, 17 of them residents of South Carolina or Louisiana and all but one widows who had inherited the property of their deceased husbands.[11] Finally, with respect to crop specialization, 131 (39 percent) of the largest planters cultivated rice or sugar, the two staples best suited to large-scale production. Most of the remainder were cotton planters or Upper South grain and tobacco farmers who had transferred most of their slaves to absentee cotton plantations in the Gulf region.

Who were these elite slaveholders? Some, because of their political and / or military reputations, are well known. Examples include Howell Cobb of Georgia; Gideon Pillow of Tennessee; John A. Quitman of Mississippi; and Langdon Cheves, Sr., James H. Hammond, Wade Hampton III, and Robert Barnwell Rhett of South Carolina. The majority, however, are not familiar to the general public or even to historians of the antebellum South. Even as the research methodology described above has succeeded in identifying most of the great slaveholders, it has also called into question some rather extravagant estimates by both contempoary observers and historians of the number of slaves owned by other individuals. Thus, while it is true that the Hamptons of South Carolina had large holdings on their absentee and heavily mortgaged plantations in the Mississippi Delta, the actual number owned in 1860 was about 800, rather than the 1,500 attributed to them by Mary Boykin Chesnut. Nor did Thomas Dabney own 500 slaves in Hinds County, Mississippi, for no combina-

---

11. The single exception was Miss Harriott Pinckney of Charleston, the last surviving daughter of Charles Cotesworth Pinckney. See printed poem dedicated to Miss Pinckney "on her eighty-second birthday," in Harriott Pinckney Papers, SCL.

tion of significant slave parcels in that county would yield a slave force of that size.[12] Perhaps most puzzling is the assertion by at least three historians that another Mississippian, Haller Nutt, owned 800 slaves. Such an estimate is not supported either by Nutt's Araby plantation journal at Duke University for the 1840s or by his correspondence at the Mississippi Department of Archives and History for the following decade.[13]

Whatever the size of their slaveholdings, nearly complete statistics relating to birthplaces of the 339 slaveholders identified in this study indicate that, notwithstanding their cosmopolitan economic and social behavior, the overwhelming majority (85 percent) were born in the slave states. Indeed, their nativity pattern closely approximated that of the general population. Thus, those in the earlier settled Atlantic seaboard states tended to be natives of the states in which they resided, while those in the Southwest came from a much more diverse background (see Table 1). Twenty-one of the elite planters, 16 of whom were domiciled in either Louisiana or South Carolina, were of foreign birth, and 29 were born in the free states, most of them in the Northeast.

If measured by nativity and family background, by far the most diversified regions were the sugar parishes of south Louisiana, where the number of foreign-born elite agriculturalists nearly equaled the number born in Louisiana, and the Natchez District, where nearly two-thirds of the nabobs had migrated to Mississippi from other locales. Of the latter, 3 were of foreign birth, 9 others hailed from the Northeast, and nearly half of the 19 native Mississippians had either spouses or parents from the latter region. An additional 10 members of the Natchez elite, or about 20 percent of the total, were born in the border states of

12. C. Vann Woodward, ed., *Mary Chesnut's Civil War* (New Haven, 1981), 334; Fletcher M. Green, Introduction to Susan Dabney Smedes, *Memorials of a Southern Planter* (New York, 1965). Although Washington County, Mississippi, census records for 1860 have been destroyed, personal tax rolls supply supplementary information. It is from these that I derived the estimate that brothers Wade III and Christopher F. Hampton had 800 slaves in Mississippi on the eve of the Civil War. Dabney had only 154 slaves in Hinds County.

13. This figure was cited initially by D. Clayton James in his *Antebellum Natchez* (Baton Rouge, 1968), 156. It was repeated in Wayne, *The Reshaping of Plantation Society*, 9–10, and Joanne V. Hawks, "Julia A. Nutt of Longwood," *JMH* 57 (November 1994): 293. The Nutt papers in Jackson corroborate the 1860 census report that credits Nutt with 261 plantation slaves—all in Tensas Parish, Louisiana.

TABLE 1 · NATIVITY BY STATE OF RESIDENCE

State of Residence	State(s) of Nativity	Totals
Ala.	Ala.-2, Ga.-6, N.C.-8, N.Y.-2, S.C.-5, Va.-5	(28 of 28)
Ark.	Ky.-1, Tenn.-1	(2 of 2)
Fla.	Ga.-1, N.C.-1, Tenn.-1	(3 of 3)
Ga.	Ga.-22, Northeast-4, South-6	(32 of 36)
Ky.	N.J.-1	(1 of 1)
La. (Cotton)	La.-5, Ala.-1, Ga.-1, Ireland-2, Miss.-5, New England-3, N.C.-2, S.C.-2	(21 of 22)
La. (Sugar)	Foreign-7, La.-8, North-4, South & Border-15	(34 of 38)
Md.	Md.-1	(1 of 1)
Miss. (Natchez)	Foreign-3, Miss.-19 (9 with spouses or parents born outside South), Northeast-9, South & Border-21	(52 of 55)
Miss. (Outside Natchez)	Ga.-1, Ky.-3, Miss.-3, N.C.-4, S.C.-3, Tenn.-1, Va.-1	(16 of 16)
N.C.	Ireland-1, North-1, N.C.-12, Va.-3	(17 of 17)
S.C. (Up Country)	Ireland-1, Scotland-1, S.C.-27, Va.-1	(30 of 30)
S.C. (Low Country)	Foreign-5, North-4, South-2, S.C.-56	(67 of 71)
Tenn.	Ala.-1, N.C.-1, Pa.-1, Tenn.-4	(7 of 8)
Tex.	Ky.-1, Va.-1	(2 of 2)
Va.	Scotland-1, Va.-8	(9 of 9)
TOTALS		(322 of 339)

SUMMARY: Residents of native state were 167 (51.9 percent); southern and border states, 105 (32.6 percent); northern states, 29 (9 percent); and foreign, 21 (6.5 percent). In the Atlantic seaboard states, 126 of 156 (80.8 percent) were residing in their native state.

Delaware, Maryland, Kentucky, and Tennessee.[14] Thus, most of the aspiring planter-aristocrats who migrated to the Natchez region moved along a diagonal line from northeast to southwest rather than along the traditional east-to-west path followed by most white settlers in Alabama or Mississippi. Or, to be more precise, they moved westward until they intersected the Mississippi River and then followed its course south to Natchez. The more traditional pattern is exemplified by the Alabama elite, only 2 of whom were natives of the state. Of those who achieved wealth and status in Alabama, 85 percent hailed originally from the Atlantic seaboard states of Georgia, the Carolinas, and Virginia, a pattern replicated by those members of the Mississippi elite who resided outside the Natchez District.

Although all of the slaveholders in this study could be characterized as wealthy, a few individuals, as well as a larger number of closely knit families, amassed truly extraordinary fortunes through the exploitation of slave labor. At midcentury, the two largest individual slaveowners in the South were Nathaniel Heyward of South Carolina and Francis Surget of Mississippi.[15] At his death in 1851, Heyward left a slave force variously estimated at from 1,829 to 2,340, while Surget held about 1,300 slaves six years before his demise in 1856.[16] In 1860, following the distribution of Nathaniel Heyward's estate, eight members of his immediate family collectively owned more than 3,000 slaves in South Carolina and Georgia.[17] Similarly, four male members of the Surget family held 1,800

14. Statistics on nativity for the Natchez elite are compiled primarily from *Biographical and Historical Memoirs of Mississippi*, 2 vols. (Chicago: Goodspeed Publishing Company, 1891), hereinafter cited as *Goodspeed's*, and from Schedule 1 of the manuscript censuses of 1850 and 1860.

15. The following account of the Surgets and Heywards first appeared in my article entitled "Lords or Capitalists? The Natchez Nabobs in Comparative Perspective," *JMH* 54 (August 1992): 246–50.

16. The 1850 census total of 1,834 for Heyward accords closely with his estate inventory, which listed 1,829 slaves on sixteen plantations. See Charles Heyward Plantation Record Book, SCL. The upper estimate is from Dusinberre, *Them Dark Days*, 33, and probably includes about 500 slaves previously conveyed to three of his children.

17. Family members, their relationship to Nathaniel, and the number and location of their slaves were: William Henry Heyward, grandson (Beaufort-522, Colleton-133, Charleston-16 = 671); Estate Arthur and Maria Louisa (Blake) Heyward, son and daughter-in-law (Colleton-304, Chatham, Georgia-352 = 656); Charles Heyward, son (Colleton-471, Charleston-10 = 481); Daniel Heyward, second cousin (Beaufort-374, Charleston-15 = 389); James Barnwell Heyward, grandson (Colleton-339); William Heyward, second cousin (Beaufort-231); Nathaniel Barnwell Heyward, grandson (Colleton-216); and Edward Barnwell Heyward, grandson (Richland-84) for a total of 3,067 slaves.

slaves in the same year, but if one includes the entire network of families who intermarried with female members of the Surget family, the figure rises to a remarkable 5,287.[18]

To comprehend how such great wealth could be accumulated, it is useful to begin with Pierre (or Peter) Surget, founder of the family's fortune in America. A French sea captain from La Rochelle, Pierre came to New York as a young man, married Catherine Hubbard, a woman of Dutch ancestry, and prospered in the mercantile business. Three children were born to the couple within a span of thirty months, but "long intervals" ensued between a number of subsequent births as a result of Pierre's extended absence in the East Indies and his imprisonment "for a long time among the British." After the Revolution he moved to Baton Rouge and thence, in 1785, just after the birth of his youngest son James, to Adams County, Mississippi, where he settled Cherry Grove plantation. Through the investment of capital derived from his mercantile pursuits, Pierre gradually expanded his holdings until his death in July, 1796, at which time his entire estate passed to his widow.[19]

The union of Pierre Surget and Catherine Hubbard produced six sons and five daughters, of whom the most notable were sons Jacob, Francis, and James and daughter Charlotte Catherine, who married the first Adam Bingaman of Natchez. Jacob, eldest of the three brothers, apparently inherited his father's love of the sea, for he spent some time in seafaring pursuits before settling in New York City, where he resided until his death. Although he retained an interest in several Mississippi plantations, Jacob, who married late in life and left no children, held most of his assets in New York. At his death in March, 1869,

Family demographic information from *South Carolina Genealogies*, 5 vols. (Spartanburg, 1983), II, 352, 367; Duncan Clinch Heyward, *Seed from Madagascar* (Chapel Hill, 1937).

18. This figure includes 1,199 slaves owned by four male members of the Surget family (Francis, Jr.-456; James, Jr.-362; Eustace-258; and Jacob H.-123) as well as 1,211 owned by brothers Alfred Vidal and Samuel Manuel Davis; 1,485 by Stephen Duncan and his children; 444 by Gabriel B. Shields; 310 by Adam L. Bingaman; 294 by Ayres P. Merrill, II; 238 by John S. Minor; and 106 by Hampton Elliott, for a total of 5,287. Information concerning Surget family relationships is drawn primarily from "Copy of the Last Will and Testament and Codicil of Jacob Surget, November 17, 18, 1868" (MS) and from Suit Filed before Supreme Court, City and County of New York, by John I. Brower and James Surget, Executors of Last Will and Testament of Jacob Surget, against Heirs of the Estate, May 2, 1870 (printed copy), both in MacNeil Papers, MDAH.

19. *Goodspeed's*, II, 868; Francis Surget to Catherine Surget Shields, June 30, [1856?], and "Notes from Will Books," Will of Pierre Surget, April 1, 1791, both in MacNeil Papers, MDAH.

Jacob Surget's estate was valued at more than $940,000, much of it in U.S. Government bonds, New York Central Railroad stock, Union Soldiers' Bounty Fund and Substitute Bounty Redemption bonds, and Brooklyn real estate, the last having been acquired during the 1840s.[20]

The youngest brother, James, remained in Mississippi, where he married Catherine Lintot, whose parents had migrated from Connecticut to Adams County a generation before. This union produced only two children who survived infancy, namesake James and daughter Katharine (better known as Kate), who became the wife of John S. Minor. The elder James Surget, in common with neighboring planters of that era, enjoyed considerable success in transforming white fields of cotton into gold. He expanded his operations across the river into Concordia Parish, and by the time of his death in 1855 he had accumulated more than 400 slaves. But it was the third brother, Francis, who was destined to become the grandee of the Surget family, a man termed by J. F. H. Claiborne "the most extensive and successful planter ever known in Mississippi."[21]

Francis Surget combined inheritances from his own and his wife's families with hard work and bold entrepreneurial instincts to erect a plantation empire rivaled earlier only by that of Samuel F. Davis in the Southwest. Like Davis, who had married a daughter of Don Jose Vidal, Spanish commander of Louisiana after 1798, Surget increased his initial assets through a highly propitious marriage to Eliza Dunbar, daughter of Sir William Dunbar. Thus fortified with capital, he purchased additional slaves, added to his properties in Mississippi, and acquired thousands of acres of land in Louisiana and Arkansas. As early as 1840 Francis Surget was the largest slaveowner in Adams County, a rank that he retained until his death. A decade later, he harvested in that county alone 1,600 bales of cotton on 4,000 acres of improved land with a labor force of 600 slaves. A contemporary observer estimated Surget's total annual production on all of his properties at between 3,000 and 5,000 bales during the height of his planting career.[22]

20. "Inventory and Appraisement of the Personal Estate of Jacob Surget," August 31, 1869, and *John I. Brower and James Surget v. Heirs of Jacob Surget Estate,* May 2, 1870, both in MacNeil Papers, MDAH.

21. *Goodspeed's,* II, 868; Paul Wallace Gates, *The Farmer's Age: Agriculture, 1815–1860* (New York: 1960), 149

22. *Goodspeed's,* I, 624; II, 431; MS Census, 1840, Adams County, Mississippi; MS Census, 1850 (Schedule 4: Agriculture), Adams County, Mississippi; Adams County Personal Tax Rolls, 1843,

At his death in 1856 Francis Surget left an estate valued at nearly $2,500,000 to be distributed among his widow and six surviving children. The latter included three sons—Francis, Jr.; Lenox, who died in 1858; and Eustace, who served as a lieutenant colonel on the staff of General Richard Taylor during the Civil War—and a like number of daughters, each of whom married a prominent planter. Catharine, the eldest and clearly her father's favorite, was the wife of Gabriel B. Shields; Jane married Ayres P. Merrill II and inherited Elmscourt, a Natchez residence still owned by a Surget descendant; and Sarah, the youngest, married Alfred Vidal Davis, a son of the other great cotton nabob of the early nineteenth century. At the time of his death Francis owned five plantations in Louisiana, with an appraised value of $717,000, and six more in Mississippi, valued at just over $800,000. Nine of these plantations, the six in Mississippi and three in Louisiana, yielded gross cotton proceeds of $175,000 in the year of his demise. In addition, Surget had previously donated to his five eldest children a like number of Louisiana plantations, valued at $575,000, thus making the total value of his Louisiana property approximately $1,300,000. He also owned the Elmscourt residence in Natchez, appraised at $31,500; some 50,000 acres of land in Arkansas, valued at $250,000; and he had a cash reserve of $67,000.[23]

Like Surget, Nathaniel Heyward began to construct his vast plantation empire on the basis of a modest inheritance, aided shortly thereafter by a financially beneficial marriage. Although the first Heyward migrated to Carolina from Derbyshire, England, shortly after the colony was founded, it was Nathaniel's father, Daniel Heyward, a member of the fourth generation in America, who built the family fortune by reclaiming virgin rice land along the Combahee River. Daniel allegedly owned 1,000 slaves at the time of his death in 1777, but the bulk of his slave property was bequeathed to Nathaniel's older half-brother, Thomas, Jr., Revolutionary War soldier and signer of the Declaration of Independence. Nathaniel inherited only about 200 slaves and two small plantations

1846, 1848, 1852 (microfilm), MDAH; John Hebron Moore, *The Emergence of the Cotton Kingdom in the Old Southwest: Mississippi, 1770–1860* (Baton Rouge, 1988), 117.

23. Last Will and Testament of Francis Surget, May 29, 1856 (TS), and Appraisement and Settlement of Estate of Francis Surget, Sr. [1856] (MS), both in MacNeil Papers, MDAH; Appraisement and Distribution of Estate of Francis Surget, Sr., n.d., and Distribution of Francis Surget Property in Mississippi and Louisiana, January 26, 1857, both in Surget Family Papers (microfilm), MDAH, Roll 3.

from his father, but through additional inheritance, an extremely advantageous marriage, purchase, hard work, and good fortune, he rapidly accumulated a huge estate. His marriage to Henrietta Manigault, daughter of House of Assembly speaker Peter Manigault and granddaughter of wealthy merchant-planter Gabriel Manigault, was especially beneficial, for it is said that his bride contributed $50,000 to his initial rice-planting ventures. He also assumed management at an early age of the plantations of his half-brother Thomas, Jr., as well as those of his brother James, subsequently purchasing the former and inheriting the latter in 1796.[24]

However, it was the premium price commanded by rice in the European market during the Napoleonic Wars that, more than any other single factor, enabled Heyward to multiply his holdings so rapidly. For example, in 1805 he realized a net profit of $120,000 from the sale of an estimated 150,000 bushels of rice; thirteen years later a similar sale netted him $90,000. In true capitalistic fashion, he utilized such handsome profits to purchase additional land and slaves, to say nothing of a string of residences in Charleston. Eventually, Nathaniel Heyward built a plantation empire of seventeen separate units in four Low Country parishes worked by more than 2,000 slaves, only one of whom, according to a descendant, was a mulatto. At his death in April, 1851, his total estate, comprising 45,000 acres of rice land, $1,000,000 worth of slave property, and $180,000 in Charleston real estate, was valued at $2,018,000.[25]

In addition to Nathaniel Heyward and Francis Surget, three other planters—Georgetown District rice planter Joshua John Ward and Natchez nabobs Stephen Duncan and Levin R. Marshall—owned more than 1,000 slaves at some point during the 1850s. Dubbed "the king of the rice planters in Georgetown District" by historian George C. Rogers, Jr., Ward built most of his rice empire by himself, apparently beginning with only one inherited property, Brookgreen. Through estate sales and purchases from neighboring planters, Ward gradually increased his agricultural holdings until they included seven plantations and approximately 1,100 slaves by the time of his death in 1853. The

---

24. Heyward, *Seed from Madagascar*, 46, 54, 62, 65–67; Dusinberre, *Them Dark Days*, 31.

25. Heyward, *Seed from Madagascar*, 71, 81–83, 86; Inventory and Appraisement of the Personal Estate of Nathaniel Heyward, as returned to the Court of Probate by his Executors (TS), in Charles Heyward Plantation Record Book, SCL.

Ward plantations, encompassing 3,500 acres of cultivated land, produced 3,900,000 pounds of rice in 1849, a figure that increased to 4,410,000 pounds six years after his death.[26]

Unlike Ward, who was born at his ancestral estate, both Duncan and Marshall migrated to Mississippi from distant points, Duncan from Carlisle, Pennsylvania, in 1808, and Marshall from Alexandria, Virginia, about 1817. Following his arrival in Natchez, Duncan married successively into the prominent Ellis and Bingaman families and soon began to amass a huge fortune in land and slaves. His slave force increased from a modest 100 in 1820 to nearly four times that number a decade later, all in Adams County. In the late 1840s Duncan began to transfer most of these slaves to Issaquena County in the Delta, where, during the 1850s, his five absentee cotton plantations produced an average of 3,000 bales per year and yielded annual net proceeds of $105,000. At the same time, he had acquired an interest in two lucrative sugar plantations on the Attakapas lands of St. Mary Parish, Louisiana. These units produced an annual average of 1,273 hogsheads of sugar during the same decade, making Duncan one of the top sugar producers in the state. By 1851, according to his own business records, Duncan had increased his slave force to 1,036, situated on eight plantations in four different counties.[27] Perhaps the quintessential capitalist of the Old South, Duncan also held a portfolio of stocks and bonds in the early 1850s that included $210,000 in United States bonds, from which he derived $12,600 in annual interest, and an additional $50,000 in northern railroad bonds.[28]

Duncan's fellow nabob Levin Marshall arrived in Mississippi about the time of statehood and accumulated his initial capital in banking, serving as cashier of the United States Bank, first in Woodville and later in Natchez. About a decade after his arrival, Marshall augmented his resources by marrying into the Chotard family, who had removed to Natchez following the Saint-Domingue slave

26. Rogers, *History of Georgetown County*, 259–60; Charles Joyner, *Down by the Riverside: A South Carolina Slave Community* (Urbana, 1984), 23.

27. *Goodspeed's*, I, 676; MS census returns, 1820 and 1830, Adams County, Mississippi; Stephen Duncan Plantation Journal, 1851–61, in Vol. 3, Duncan (Stephen and Stephen, Jr.) Papers, LSU. Figures on sugar production computed by author from Pierre A. Champomier, *Statement of the Sugar Crop Made in Louisiana, 1844–1861* (New Orleans, 1845–62).

28. Dr. S. Duncan in a/c with Charles P. Leverich, May 28–November 1, 1852, and Stephen Duncan account in C. P. Leverich MS Cash Account Book, 1844–53, both in Leverich Papers, CAH.

insurrection. As early as 1830, four years after his marriage to Maria Chotard, Marshall expressed a preference for a planting career. Within five years he was prospering, harvesting 500 bales of cotton on five plantation units in Mississippi, Louisiana, and Arkansas, and estimating his total worth at $250,000. As the years passed, this slaveholding entrepreneur constructed a financial empire that included numerous cotton and sugar plantations, partnerships in Natchez and New Orleans commission houses, substantial investments in Northern railroad securities, and extensive real estate holdings in Westchester County, New York. On the eve of the Civil War, Marshall, who by then owned slaves in seven counties in three different states, was credited with 1,058 slaves, second in number only to the estate of the deceased Joshua John Ward.[29]

The men discussed above were not the only millionaire slaveholders in the mid-nineteenth-century South. In 1858, after conducting an inventory of Robert Ruffin Barrow's estate, his steward estimated the total worth of his employer at $2,150,000, remarking dryly that "he is in very good circumstances and with economy he has enough to last him & his family for several years to come."[30] David Hunt, one of several Natchez District immigrants from the Northeast, reputedly owned twenty-six plantations and nearly 1,700 slaves at midcentury, but these figures probably include the property of other family members and, even then, seem exaggerated.[31] Two Georgia cotton planters, Turner C. Clanton and Colonel Joseph Bond, reportedly had property valued at $2,500,000 and $1,055,000, respectively, at the time of their deaths. Each had a pretentious residence—Clanton in Augusta and Bond on the outskirts of Macon—and each was operating at least half a dozen plantations.[32] Even more affluent were the Mills brothers, Robert and David G., of Brazoria County, Texas, who com-

---

29. *Goodspeed's*, II, 397–98; Theodora Britton Marshall and Gladys Crail Evans, eds., "Plantation Report from the Papers of Levin R. Marshall, of 'Richmond,' Natchez, Mississippi," *JMH* 3 (January 1941): 46; Maria L. Marshall to sister Eliza, August 2, 1830, and Levin Marshall to Eliza Gould, December 3, 1834, both in Marshall (Maria Louisa Chotard and Family) Papers, LSU; Levin R. Marshall in a/c with C. P. Leverich, October 20, 1851–November 1, 1852, and Levin R. Marshall account in C. P. Leverich MS Cash Account Book, 1844–53, in Leverich Papers, CAH.

30. R. R. Barrow Residence Journal (MS in SHC), February 21, 1858.

31. *Goodspeed's*, I, 989–92; James, *Antebellum Natchez*, 157–58.

32. *The Secret Eye: The Journal of Ella Gertrude Clanton Thomas, 1848–89*, ed. Virginia Ingraham Burr (Chapel Hill, 1990), 232 n. 25; Ralph Betts Flanders, *Plantation Slavery in Georgia* (Chapel Hill, 1933), 109–12.

bined extensive agricultural and commercial interests to build a fortune estimated at $3 million to $5 million on the eve of the Civil War. Older brother Robert, dubbed the "Duke of Brazoria," superintended the commercial side of the business, which included banking as well as partnerships in mercantile firms headquartered in such far-flung cities as New York, Liverpool, and Havana, while David Mills managed the brothers' four sugar and cotton plantations. Unfortunately for the two brothers, their Galveston firm, R. & D. G. Mills & Company, which had been the largest banking and mercantile firm in Texas during the 1850s, was ruined by the war and eventually declared bankruptcy in 1873.[33]

Perhaps even more indicative of the concentration of wealth in the slave South are figures relating to extended family holdings. In addition to the Surgets and Heywards, discussed above, other families had slave parcels that numbered in the thousands at the close of the antebellum period. Among these were the Allstons and their cousins, the Alstons and Pyatts (3,458 or nearly a fifth of all slaves in Georgetown District, South Carolina); the Hairstons (2,529 in three Virginia counties, four in North Carolina, and one each in Alabama and Mississippi); the Barrows (2,008), Pughs (1,381), and Rouths (1,295 in Tensas Parish) of Louisiana; the sons and sons-in-law of the 1840s cotton king, Samuel Davis (1,495, of which 1,307 were situated on nine plantations in Concordia Parish); the Duncans (1,161) and Minors (1,053), Natchez families who employed most of their slaves in Louisiana; the Cockes (1,047 in seven counties in Virginia, Alabama, and Mississippi); and the Adams family of Richland District, South Carolina (1,035).[34] Doubtless there were others as well, but these examples will suffice to illustrate the extent of economic power wielded by the elite slaveholders.

Thus, by means of inheritance, beneficial marriages, profits derived from legal, medical, and mercantile pursuits, application of the Protestant work ethic, bold entrepreneurial instincts, and good fortune, a number of planters amassed

33. Earl Wesley Fornell, *The Galveston Era: The Texas Crescent on the Eve of Secession* (Austin, 1961), 14–15, 45–47; *Dictionary of American Biography*, 21 vols. (New York, 1928–37), XIII, 13–14; Herbert Gambrell, *Anson Jones, the Last President of Texas* (Garden City, N.Y., 1948), 40; Randolph B. Campbell, *An Empire for Slavery: The Peculiar Institution in Texas, 1821–1865* (Baton Rouge, 1989), 194–95.

34. Allston total from Dusinberre, *Them Dark Days*, 287, 512 n. 9; all others are compiled by author from manuscript slave census returns.

great wealth, either individually or as members of extended families. But these wealthiest of the wealthy represented only the tip of the economic pyramid. Their ideology and life-style differed little from the remainder of those in this study; they were merely the most successful. Let us turn now to an examination of some of the specific traits exhibited by all members of the elite slaveholding class.

1

Social and Demographic
Characteristics

This is indeed an afflicting stroke to me—So unexpected!—My most excellent
Son—the ornament of my society—my friend & companion! In silence & tears
I have to lament his death to the end of my days.
    —NATHANIEL HEYWARD, September 6, 1819

About 6 O'clock in the afternoon . . . [Maria] gave Birth to one of the *sweetest*
little daughters that ever was presented to a "Papa." . . . the little stranger is
admired by every one who has seen it, and all concur in its being the "largest and
finest child" in the state.   —LEVIN R. MARSHALL, September 1, 1827

Jimmie Metcalfe was at Auntie's several nights ago, and sent his love to me.
Please tell him, the next time you have the *very extreme pleasure* of seeing him,
"Not to waste his love on the *desert-air*." Between you and myself, I don't believe
Jimmie's love, is worth having. I should not prize it if he were so very generous
as to bestow it upon me.   —GUSSIE PUGH, December 11 [postwar]

WHATEVER their background, geographic location, or extent of wealth, the elite slaveholders shared certain common social and cultural characteristics. Among these were large families; a relatively high infant mortality rate; an extraordinary degree of intermarriage, extending not infrequently to first-cousin unions; a cosmopolitan life-style and outlook; surprisingly close social, economic, and cultural ties with the Northeast; an emphasis upon quality education for both males and females; a catholicity of intellectual interests; and—not least—a confident belief in God as the omnipotent regulator of human affairs.

The structure of elite families mirrored closely the demographic patterns of the general population in the nineteenth-century South. Thus, the overwhelming majority of large slaveholders were or had been married, only rarely did they sever their matrimonial ties through divorce, and most of them fathered numerous children, a significant number of which did not survive to maturity.[1] Although the infant mortality rate was doubtless not as high among elite families as among those of more modest economic circumstances, it was still painfully high, thus bearing eloquent testimony to the ubiquitous incidence of disease in the rural South as well as to the primitive state of medical knowledge in the antebellum period.[2] The specter of death was omnipresent, not only among infants, but among older offspring as well. By no means unique was the experience of Louisiana planter David Barrow, eight of whose twelve children died at an early age. Similarly, his cousin William Ruffin Barrow lost five of his ten children before they attained their majority, as did South Carolina rice grandee Robert F. W. Allston. Thomas Spalding of Sapelo Island, Georgia, fared even worse, losing eleven of his sixteen children in infancy or early youth.[3]

One can only imagine the emotional toll inflicted upon planter families, especially the mothers, by such distressing losses. Levin R. Marshall's first wife,

---

1. Of the 339 slaveholders in this study, only 11 can be positively identified as having never been married.

2. Catherine Clinton has estimated the infant mortality rate among southern planter families at 14 percent, compared to 12 percent for northern farmers (*The Plantation Mistress*, 156).

3. Elrie Robinson, *Early Feliciana Politics* (St. Francisville, La., 1936), 84–85; *Dictionary of Louisiana Biography*, 2 vols., ed. Glenn R. Conrad (1988), I, 44; J. H. Easterby, ed., *The South Carolina Rice Plantation as Revealed in the Papers of Robert F. W. Allston* (Chicago, 1945), 18; Frances Anne Kemble, *Journal of a Residence on a Georgian Plantation in 1838–39*, ed. John A. Scott (New York, 1961), 402.

Maria, was so distraught after the unexpected death of her four-year-old daughter that she followed her "most perfect . . . [and] dearest child" to the grave less than two years later. Maria "never was as cheerful afterwards," observed a close friend at the time of her death.[4] Occasionally, families would be stricken with multiple deaths within a short interval of time. Nathan Bryan Whitfield of Alabama reportedly bore the loss of his two youngest children with "considerable fortitude," but when the specter of death appeared for the third time within a year, he could "hardly realize the death of so lovely a child as his dear little Edith." Not less was the anguish produced by the deaths of successive infants. What must have been the despondency in the family of Gideon J. Pillow when he and his first wife lost the first four of their fourteen children in infancy.[5]

If death took a heavy toll of planter infants, it was no kinder to those who bore them. Elite families were consistently large, thereby subjecting wives to such intense physical and emotional distress that their own health suffered dramatically. This subject will be explored more fully in Chapter 3, but it will suffice to say here that successive pregnancies at short intervals over an extended period of time had an exceptionally debilitating effect upon plantation mistresses.[6] To cite an extreme example, between August, 1827, and March, 1830, a period of less than three years, the youthful bride of Levin R. Marshall gave birth to precisely that number of children.[7] Perhaps more typical was fellow Natchezian Gabriel B. Shields, who produced within a span of twenty-three years no less than fourteen children, most of them at regular two-year intervals. Even more prolific was Judge Edward McGehee of neighboring Wilkinson County, whose three wives bore him a total of nineteen children. In contrast to his spouses, the judge apparently suffered no ill effects from his procreative activities, for he lived to the ripe old age of ninety-four.[8] McGehee's record was

4. Maria L. Marshall to Eliza W. Gould, October 16, 1831, and Jane Riddle to Mrs. William P. Gould, August 19, 1833, both in Marshall Papers, LSU.

5. Mary Ann Whitfield to Sally E. Whitfield, September 28, 1842, in Whitfield and Wooten Family Papers, SHC; *Maury County Cousins: Bible and Family Records* (Columbia, Tenn., 1967), "General Pillow Family Notes," 548.

6. As Catherine Clinton has remarked, "the long months of pregnancy caused both physical discomfort and anxiety" (*The Plantation Mistress*, 151).

7. Levin R. Marshall to Eliza W. Gould, September 1, 1827, Maria L. Marshall to Gould, July 20, 1829; March 4, 1830, both in Marshall Papers, LSU.

8. MS Census, 1860 (Schedule 1), Adams County, Mississippi; Katherine Blankenstein to author, March 18, 1996, citing Journal of Ellen Shields in her possession; *Goodspeed's*, I, 1195–96.

nearly matched by Gideon J. Pillow, who sired fourteen children within the space of twenty-two years with his first wife and three more with a second, who was an eighteen-year-old widow when he claimed her as his bride.[9]

South Carolinians were equally fecund. Like Pillow, Langdon Cheves, Sr., a former congressman and one-time president of the Second United States Bank, fathered fourteen children in twenty-two years, a reproductive effort that ultimately proved fatal to his wife. Three other South Carolina rice barons—William Bull Pringle, Francis Weston, and James B. Heyward—produced at least a dozen children, each with a single spouse, within a span of about twenty years. Robert Barnwell Rhett, himself one of fifteen children, fathered a like number, twelve, by his first wife, Elizabeth, who died two weeks after the birth of her last child.[10] It should be noted that the number of pregnancies may have been greater than these figures indicate, for they do not reflect any miscarriages that may have occurred. For example, Gertrude Thomas of Georgia miscarried in August, 1856, became pregnant again shortly thereafter, and gave birth to a daughter in late May, 1857, only to lose that child before the end of the year.[11]

The obvious question is why these wealthy slaveholders made no apparent effort to limit the size of their families. It was surely not because they needed a plethora of sturdy sons to perform manual labor, as some have speculated was the case with the plain folk.[12] Nor can it be attributed to the desire to produce a male heir, for some planters sired a veritable parade of sons. Rather, it seems reasonable to conclude that knowledge of contraception was minimal, even among the most sophisticated elements of the nineteenth-century population. This is clearly the consensus among a wide spectrum of secondary authorities. Although publications relating to contraception and family limitation appeared in America as early as the 1830s and available methods were employed increasingly by middle-class northern women as the century progressed, such knowledge seems to have had little impact on southern family practices. The

9. "General Pillow Family Notes," 548–49; Nathaniel C. Hughes to author, January 23, 1993.

10. Clinton, *The Plantation Mistress,* 155; *South Carolina Genealogies* (Spartanburg, 1983), I, 380–87; II, 372; III, 332–34; Rogers, *History of Georgetown County,* 274; MS Census, 1860 (Schedule 1), Georgetown District, South Carolina; Rhett Genealogy Notes #2, in Rhett Family Papers, SCHS.

11. *The Secret Eye,* ed. Burr, 150–58.

12. See, for example, Stephanie McCurry, *Masters of Small Worlds: Yeoman Households, Gender Relations, and the Political Culture of the Antebellum South Carolina Low Country* (New York, 1995), 59.

conclusion seems inescapable that families in that region made little, if any, effort, through either abstinence or contraception, to limit the number of their offspring until well after the Civil War.[13]

In choosing a mate with whom to produce such large families, planter aristocrats were usually confined to a relatively small pool of prospects. The result was an exceptional degree of intermarriage, frequently extending to unions between first cousins. There were, to be sure, some exceptions. About one-tenth of the wealthy planters married spouses born outside the slave states, about half of them from the Northeast and the remainder from Europe. The incidence was highest among the Natchezians, many of whom were themselves natives of the Northeast, and among Carolina Low Country planters, several of whom drew their mates from the British Isles.[14] Much more common, however, was the tendency to marry within the elite group. This is scarcely surprising in view of the limited opportunities afforded sons and daughters of great planters to make social contacts with those outside their class. Growing up in rural isolation or in aristocratic citadels like Natchez and Charleston, and carefully chaperoned during their annual treks to such popular watering spots as Saratoga Springs, Newport, or the Virginia springs, they could make few acquaintances outside their closed society. Consequently, within every geographic sector of the plantation South the leading families were bound together inextricably by an intricate web of marriage alliances, which enhanced both wealth and social standing.

The magnitude of this phenomenon may be illustrated by a glance at the family networks in the Natchez District. Within that region there was heavy

13. James C. Mohr, *Abortion in America: The Origins and Evolution of National Policy, 1800–1900* (New York, 1978), 49, 69–71, 210; Nell Irvin Painter, Introduction to *The Secret Eye*, ed. Burr, 32–33; McCurry, *Masters of Small Worlds*, 59, 182; Clinton, *The Plantation Mistress*, 205; Censer, *North Carolina Planters and Their Children*, 25; William W. Freehling, *The Road to Disunion*, Vol. 1: *Secessionists at Bay, 1776–1854* (New York, 1990), 55; Charles Sellers, *The Market Revolution: Jacksonian America, 1815–1846* (New York, 1991), 258–59; Michael P. Johnson, "Planters and Patriarchy: Charleston, 1800–1860," *JSH* 46 (February 1980): 68.

14. Examples of the latter include Henry Middleton, who married Mary Helen Hering of Heybridge Hall, England; Joshua John Ward, whose wife was born in Edinburgh, Scotland; and Plowden C. J. Weston, who wed the sister of a Harrow classmate. *Biographical Directory of the Senate of the State of South Carolina, 1776–1964*, comp. Emily Bellinger Reynolds and Joan Reynolds Faunt (Columbia, 1964), 273; Rogers, *History of Georgetown County*, 257–61, 410 n. 89; Joyner, *Down by the Riverside*, 18.

intermarriage among the Brandons, Hoggatts, and Stantons; among the Marshalls, Hunts, and Chotards; and among the Butlers, Duncans, Ellises, Farrars, and Mercers. Occasionally, these alliances became interregional in scope. Thus, the Minor family, which dated back to the Spanish period, developed ties, not only to the Bingaman, Chotard, Conner, Duncan, Ellis, Surget, and Wilkins families of the Natchez District, but also to the Kenners of Louisiana, the Gustines of Pennsylvania, and the Leveriches of New York.[15]

The latter connection illustrates not only the complexity of these family relationships but their potential economic effect as well. William J. Minor and Dr. Stephen Duncan were the central figures in a close-knit circle of friends, spawned originally by marriage alliances both within the Natchez District and with other families in the Northeast. In addition to Minor and Duncan, other prominent members of the group included Levin Marshall, William N. Mercer, Samuel M. Davis, and the two Francis Surgets. Perhaps a decade before Duncan removed to Natchez in 1808, his sister married Dr. Samuel Gustine, who, like Duncan, was a native of Carlisle, Pennsylvania, and had received his medical training at Dickinson College. Four daughters were born to the Gustines before they removed to Mississippi in the 1830s and settled on a plantation near Natchez. Two of the Gustine sisters married Natchez nabobs William J. Minor and William C. Conner, and the two eldest married, respectively, brothers Charles P. and Henry S. Leverich, who were partners in a leading New York mercantile house. Two other Leverich brothers, James H. and William E., began operating a New Orleans factorage firm about 1840.[16] Additional marriage alliances bound other prominent Natchez families to this group. Thus, the two youngest daughters of Francis Surget, Sr., married, respectively, Ayres P. Merrill II and Alfred Vidal Davis; one of his sisters married the first Adam Bingaman; one of his nieces married the son of William J. Minor, another wed Pennsylvania native Dr. Gustavus Calhoun, and yet another became the second wife of Stephen Duncan. In a continuation of the process into the next generation, Duncan's daughter Charlotte married Samuel Manuel Davis, the brother

15. The Gustine/Leverich connection with Natchez was first noted by Morton Rothstein in his seminal article, "The Antebellum South as a Dual Economy: A Tentative Hypothesis," *AGH* 41 (October 1967): 378–81.

16. *Ibid.*, 378–79; J. H. Leverich to Charles P. Leverich, January 16, 1841, in Charles P. Leverich Papers, MDAH; Conner genealogy in letter from Jonathan Ray to author, February 18, 1996.

of Alfred V.[17] In view of these relationships, it is not surprising that many of the leading Natchez aristocrats conducted most of their business transactions through the Leverich brothers in New York.[18]

More typical of marriage connections among the southern elite was the intraregional pattern that permeated the Carolina Low Country. Such old-line families as the Blakes, Heywards, Izards, Middletons, Pinckneys, and Rutledges comprised one such network; the Westons, Wards, and Tuckers of Georgetown District constituted another. So complicated were the relationships within another Georgetown family, the Allstons, and so frequently were first names repeated in successive generations that a variant spelling of the surname was introduced in the late eighteenth century. Thereafter, the family was divided between single-*l* and double-*l* Allstons.[19] For the most part, the network of marriage alliances in the Charleston area was confined to that relatively closed society. There were, however, a few exceptions. The only direct link between the Carolina and Natchez elite was established in 1849 when John Julius Pringle, son of rice baron William Bull Pringle, married Maria L. Duncan, daughter of Dr. Stephen Duncan. About fifteen years later, there was a similar interregional union between Sallie Rhett, a daughter of fire-eater Robert Barnwell Rhett, and Alfred Roman of Louisiana, son of a former governor and, at the time of his marriage, a colonel on the staff of General P. G. T. Beauregard.[20]

This intricate web of social relationships was by no means confined to the environs of Natchez and Charleston. Perhaps the most notable South Carolina Up Country alliance linked members of the Hampton, Preston, Manning, and Hammond families. In the neighboring state of North Carolina, similar ties bound together the Collins, Cameron, and Warren families, three of the largest slaveholding families in the state. It was the same story in Virginia, where the Wickhams and Carters intermarried, and in Alabama, where Gaius Whitfield claimed as his bride the sister of his North Carolina cousin, General Nathan

17. Surget family relationships are primarily from Surget Family Papers and MacNeil Papers, MDAH.

18. For extensive correspondence over a twenty-year period (1834–54) between the Natchez nabobs and Charles P. Leverich, see the Charles P. Leverich Papers, MDAH; for Leverich account books during an even more extended period, see the Leverich Papers, CAH.

19. Easterby, ed., *South Carolina Rice Plantation*, 11–12.

20. *South Carolina Genealogies*, III, 342–43; Rhett Genealogy Notes #2, in Rhett Family Papers, SCHS.

Bryan Whitfield.[21] Far to the south, the same pattern prevailed in the sugar parishes of Louisiana. Not atypical was the case of Charles Duncan Stewart of Pointe Coupee Parish, whose father had settled in the Mississippi Territory shortly before the War of 1812. Stewart's sister married Judge Harry Cage, a wealthy Terrebonne Parish sugar planter; one niece wed William J. Fort, one of the largest cotton planters in West Feliciana Parish; and another niece and a nephew married children of Judge Edward McGehee of Mississippi, thereby uniting four of the most prominent families in the area.[22]

Even more remarkable was the record of the Bringier family of Ascension Parish, one of the leading sugar producers in the state during the last fifteen years of the antebellum period. The Bringiers intermarried heavily with another French creole family, the Tureauds, and also had close ties with many other prominent south Louisiana families. Michel Doradou Bringier, the principal nineteenth-century progenitor of the family, fathered nine children, three sons and six daughters. The marriage partners of the latter represent a veritable who's who of men with wealth and status in their society. Five of the girls—all of whom wed in their midteens—married, respectively, General Hore Browse Trist, ward of Thomas Jefferson and brother of Nicholas P. Trist of Mexican War fame; Martin Gordon, Jr., a New Orleans commission merchant; Duncan F. Kenner, Ascension Parish sugar planter and Confederate diplomat; Richard Taylor, son of President Zachary Taylor and a lieutenant general in the Confederate Army; and General Allen Thomas, another wealthy sugar planter. The other daughter married a Tureaud first cousin, as did two of her brothers.[23]

The Bringier-Tureaud connection exemplifies the most extreme form of intermarriage—that between cousins. Catherine Clinton has estimated that the rate of cousin marriage among a sample of southern planters was about 12 percent compared to none in a similar sample of northern farmers in the same

21. Charles E. Cauthen, ed., *Family Letters of the Three Wade Hamptons* (Columbia, S.C., 1953), xv; *South Carolina Genealogies*, I, 338–39; Drew Gilpin Faust, *James Henry Hammond and the Old South: A Design for Mastery* (Baton Rouge, 1982), 58; *Dictionary of North Carolina Biography*, 6 vols., ed. William S. Powell (Chapel Hill, 1979–96), I, 404–406; Stella Pickett Hardy, *Colonial Families of the Southern States of America* (2nd. ed.; Baltimore, 1958), 112–13; *Alabama Portraits Prior to 1870* (1969), 384.

22. *Goodspeed's*, II, 833–36.

23. Family relationships are from Louis A. Bringier and Family Papers and Benjamin Tureaud Papers, LSU.

period. Similarly, in her study of North Carolina planter families, Jane Turner Censer found that nearly one-tenth of planter children married either first or second cousins.[24] Whatever the percentage, it is clear that the practice was not uncommon in elite planter families, though not all were comfortable with it. Thus, when counseling his son on prospective marriage partners, R. F. W. Allston asserted unequivocally that "you can never marry a first cousin." Allston was doubtless reminded of such a possibility by his knowledge of the Weston family, his near neighbors in Georgetown District, South Carolina. Francis Marion Weston, father of Plowden C. J. Weston and uncle of fellow Georgetown District rice baron Francis Weston, had married successively two sisters who were also his first cousins.[25]

Such first-cousin unions, however, were no more common in the closed society of the Carolina Low Country than they were elsewhere in the South. Three of the greatest planter dynasties—the Hairstons, Heywards, and Barrows—provide extreme examples of this phenomenon. In the case of the Heywards and Barrows, two male first cousins in each of these families each married a sister of the other, consequently twice becoming brothers-in-law as well as first cousins.[26] Even more extraordinary were the relationships within the Hairston family. When Peter Wilson Hairston took as his first wife his first cousin Columbia Stuart, sister of J. E. B. Stuart, he was merely following the example set by his grandmother, mother, and sister. Moreover, the grandmother, Ruth S. Hairston, was the first cousin, mother-in-law, and sister-in-law of Samuel Hairston, another prominent member of the family.[27]

The Hairston family also illustrates another type of connubial relationship, this one with female slaves. In 1841 Robert Hairston, second husband of the aforementioned Ruth S. Hairston, abandoned his wife and moved from Virginia to Lowndes County, Mississippi, accompanied by his slave mistress Eliza-

24. Clinton, *The Plantation Mistress*, 57–58; Censer, *North Carolina Planters and Their Children*, 84.

25. R. F. W. Allston to Benjamin Allston, May 29, 1856, in Easterby, ed., *South Carolina Rice Plantation*, 134; Rogers, *History of Georgetown County*, 258.

26. William Henry Heyward and James Barnwell Heyward, grandsons of the opulent Nathaniel Heyward, each married the younger sister of the other. In like manner, first cousins William Hill Barrow and William Ruffin Barrow each married the sister of the other. *South Carolina Genealogies*, II, 364–65; Robinson, *Early Feliciana Politics*, 82–83, 86.

27. Cashin, "The Structure of Antebellum Planter Families," 67; Peter Wilson Hairston Papers, SHC.

beth. Shortly before his death in 1852, Hairston made a will leaving his estate to a small mulatto daughter. However, this will was invalid under the laws of Mississippi, and the bulk of his property passed to the wife he had left behind in Virginia.[28]

Although it might be argued that emotional attachments between female slaves and those who exercised absolute power over them are inconceivable, there are several other examples of long-term relationships between members of elite families and their female servants. Robert Stafford of Cumberland Island, Georgia, a bachelor cotton planter, took as his mistress a mulatto nurse, Elizabeth Bernardey, with whom he sired six children over a span of fifteen years. He sent his offspring to the Northeast to be educated, established a second residence in Groton, Connecticut, where his entire family was residing at the outbreak of the Civil War, and at his death in 1877 bequeathed to them an estate valued at nearly $350,000.[29] Just to the north, on St. Helena Island, South Carolina, Clarence A. Fripp, son of wealthy planter William Fripp, Sr., lived openly with his slave housekeeper Rachel, who bore him two children. Two members of prominent Natchez families also enjoyed continuing relationships with slave women. In a will written in 1840, Wilford Hoggatt stipulated that his eight mulatto children by a former slave be freed and that they receive equal shares of his estate upon attaining their majority. A decade later, the noted planter-politician Adam L. Bingaman, who had fathered three children with his Negro mistress, moved to New Orleans, where he reportedly flaunted his mixed family in public.[30]

Somewhat more discreet was another Mississippi planter, Richard T. Archer, who resided in Port Gibson but spent many lonely months attending to the affairs of his absentee plantations in Holmes County. Apparently Archer

28. Will of Major Robert Hairston, September 22, 1841, and Robert A. Hairston to George Hairston, April 13, 1852 (copy), vol. 21, both in Peter Wilson Hairston Papers, SHC; Robert A. Hairston to George Hairston, April 13, October 23, 1852, and Peter W. Hairston to George Hairston, June 8, 1852, July 26, 1854, December 10, 28, 1855, January 15, 23, February 18, 1856, all in George Hairston Papers, SHC.

29. Mary R. Bullard, *Robert Stafford of Cumberland Island: Growth of a Planter* (1986; rpr. Athens, Ga., 1995), 80, 136, 295, and *passim*.

30. Theodore Rosengarten, *Tombee: Portrait of a Cotton Planter* (New York, 1986), 166; John Hebron Moore, *Emergence of the Cotton Kingdom*, 258, 263; James, *Antebellum Natchez*, 127; Interview with Donald G. Linton, a Linton-Surget descendant, Hattiesburg, Mississippi, June 9, 1993.

found solace in the arms of a slave girl named Patty during the long winter nights in Holmes, a dalliance that subsequently became known to his wife. Nevertheless, when he fell ill during the last months of his life while on a visit to Holmes, he begged his wife to permit Patty to nurse him, assuring her that he was then "in such health as to be *impotent*." That Patty consented to nurse Archer though then free and over the strong objections of the other Negroes would seem to indicate some degree of lingering affection, or perhaps simply compassion, on her part.[31]

Much more common, of course, were the instances of blatant sexual exploitation in which masters forced themselves upon slave women who were powerless to resist their unwanted advances. The extent of this activity will never be known, for, with the conspicuous exception of James H. Hammond, such men enveloped their nocturnal encounters with a veil of silence. Hammond, who not only slept with female slaves but also abused four of his nieces, was the most notorious offender among the elite. Other examples of such interracial liaisons have been revealed primarily by female relatives of the guilty parties. Mary Chesnut's disgust with such conduct in general and that of her father-in-law in particular is well documented. Her feelings were echoed by Gertrude Thomas of Georgia, whose father and husband had both apparently committed adultery with slave women. Charging that "the institution of slavery degraded the white man more than the Negro," Thomas advocated a greater emphasis upon the moral education of boys to forestall such alliances.[32] Women were not the only ones to evince strong disapproval of miscegenous relations. Two Virginians, Edmund Ruffin and Benjamin O. Tayloe, privately condemned such conduct, but few other planter aristocrats mentioned the subject at all.[33]

Whomever they took as their marital or sexual partners, the elite slaveholders exhibited a life-style and philosophical outlook that was as cosmopolitan as that of any other group in nineteenth-century America. Although the overwhelming majority of these planter aristocrats were natives of the slave states

31. Richard T. Archer to Ann B. Archer, November 10, 1866, in Richard Thompson Archer Family Papers, CAH.

32. Carol Bleser, ed., *Secret and Sacred: The Diaries of James Henry Hammond, a Southern Slaveholder* (New York, 1988), 17–20, 174–76; Faust, *James Henry Hammond and the Old South*, 241–43; Woodward, ed., *Mary Chesnut's Civil War*, 29, 31; *The Secret Eye*, ed. Burr, 59, 169 (quotation), 322.

33. Edmund Ruffin, Diary (Library of Congress, Washington, D.C.); Benjamin O. Tayloe to William H. Tayloe, January 5, 1852, in Tayloe Family Papers, VHS.

and gave unequivocal support to their peculiar socioeconomic system, they were continually exposed to a variety of external influences. These agricultural capitalists were bound closely to the outside world—particularly the Northeast and, to a lesser extent, Western Europe—through nativity, marriage, residence, travel, education, business, and even by the employment of northern and European tutors and governesses within their households. Whether they resided in Virginia or Georgia, the Carolinas or Mississippi, southern planters sent their sons and daughters to the North for their education; they took extended family excursions to the Northeast and to Europe, frequently in the company of neighboring families within their class; they subscribed to numerous northern journals and newspapers; they purchased clothing, furniture, and luxury items from New York and Philadelphia merchants; and they conducted many of their business operations through New York banking and factorage houses.

One might suppose that the rice grandees of South Carolina, 84 percent of whom were natives of that state and most of whom became ardent secessionists, would be those least likely to fit such a pattern, but examples afforded by three old-line Low Country families—the Blakes, Heywards, and Middletons—belie such a conclusion. Thus, Daniel Blake, born in England and educated at Cambridge, took as his second wife New Yorker Helen Craig. His eldest son received his medical training in Philadelphia. The mother of William C. Heyward, another wealthy Carolinian, was a native of New York City, and his older sister married into the prominent Cutting family of the same city. Notwithstanding these Yankee associations, Heyward, himself a West Point graduate, served as an officer in the Confederate Army.[34] Henry A. Middleton, scion of yet another distinguished Carolina family, was educated at Harvard and at the renowned Litchfield, Connecticut, Law School. He owned extensive property in both Newport, Rhode Island, and Westchester County, New York. Three of his sons were educated in the North, two at Harvard and one at Troy Polytechnic Institute in New York, and his daughter attended school in Northampton, Massachusetts, before marrying a resident of Hunter's Island, New York. Such connections, however, did not alter the political posture of the family. Middleton supported secession, and two of his northern-educated sons were killed in action while serving in the Confederate Army.[35]

34. *South Carolina Genealogies,* I, 94–96 (Blake); II, 358–59, 364 (Heyward).
35. *Ibid.,* III, 65–66, 152–53; Rogers, *History of Georgetown County,* 309, 317, 374, 426–27.

It was among the Natchez nabobs, however, that the conjunction of extra-regional influences was most pronounced, thereby rendering that group unique among aristocratic slaveholders in its response to the sectional crisis at midcentury. They, too, sent their children northward to be educated, traveled widely during the summer months, employed northern teachers, and marketed their crops through New York factors. But there was one additional—perhaps critical—external influence. Unlike their peers on the Atlantic seaboard, most of whom were descended from long-established families in the states wherein they resided, or even their counterparts in Alabama and elsewhere in Mississippi who had followed the traditional east-to-west migration pattern from the south Atlantic states, almost half of the Natchez District elite were not even Southerners, much less Mississippians, by birth. Moreover, nearly half of the native Mississippians in the region had either spouses or parents of non-southern heritage.[36] To cite an extreme example of this phenomenon, William J. Minor, though born in Natchez, was the offspring of parents born, respectively, in Pennsylvania and Connecticut, and he himself married one of the Gustine sisters from Carlisle, Pennsylvania. When one adds to this background the fact that Minor attended the University of Pennsylvania, sent his son to Princeton, spent many of his summers in the North, and conducted his business affairs through the Leverich brothers in New York, it is not difficult to predict what political course he would pursue in the 1860s. Minor was a Southerner by residence only, certainly not by conviction.[37]

Of course, one's birthplace and family connections do not always determine one's ultimate allegiance. A few of the transplanted Natchez Yankees, most conspicuously John A. Quitman, readily adapted to their new environment and embraced the principles of their adopted homeland. A native of Rhinebeck, New York, Quitman migrated first to Ohio and then, in 1821, to Natchez. There he married into a prominent Mississippi family, embarked upon a planting career, entered politics with marked success, performed heroically in the Mexican War, and ultimately became a leading southern fire-eater and apostle of Manifest Destiny.[38] Quitman's transformation from Yankee to Southerner was complete

36. Statistics on nativity are compiled primarily from *Goodspeed's* and from Schedule 1 of censuses of 1850 and 1860.

37. Jack D. L. Holmes, "Stephen Minor: Natchez Pioneer," *JMH* 42 (February 1980): 17–26; *Goodspeed's*, II, 446; Rothstein, "The Antebellum South as a Dual Economy," 378–79.

38. For the details of Quitman's career, see Robert E. May, *John A. Quitman, Old South Crusader* (Baton Rouge, 1985).

and unremitting. But he was an anomaly among the Natchez aristocrats of similar background.

The difficulty of predicting how specific individuals will react to a new milieu is perhaps most vividly illustrated by two members of the Winchester family of Massachusetts. George was the first member of the family to migrate to Natchez, followed in 1837 by his nephew Josiah. Both became prominent lawyers and judges in their new community, George eventually occupying a seat on the state supreme court and Josiah serving as a probate judge. The latter also achieved elite planter status as the long-term administrator of the estate of John Carmichael Jenkins, who died in the yellow fever epidemic of 1855. In letters written almost simultaneously to a relative in Massachusetts just two years after Josiah's arrival in Natchez, the two men presented sharply contrasting appraisals of the city on the bluffs. "No other spot on earth can surpass it if any can equal it," exulted the elder Winchester. "The older I grow in it the more I love it," he continued, "and if it were not for those I hold more dear, than scenery, climate, or air, I would never care to leave it for the dull climes of the North." Quite different were the views of nephew Josiah, who expressed profound dissatisfaction with his new environment. "I am myself heartily sick of southern manners, southern society, and southern life," he wrote, "and if I had this day a fortune I would select almost any other place on this round earth to enjoy it."[39] Not surprisingly, the political course of the two Winchesters diverged as sharply as their perceptions of Natchez. In an essay entitled "The Slavery Question," written in 1849 shortly before his death, George delivered an impassioned defense of slavery and denounced the Washington, D.C., *National Intelligencer* for impugning the motives of those organizing the Nashville Convention, men whom he termed "some of the purest, most patriotic, and most intellectual men of the age in which we live." By contrast, the younger Winchester adopted and consistently pursued a hard-line Unionist position and, together with fellow Adams County delegate Alexander K. Farrar, voted against the secession ordinance in the Mississippi Convention.[40]

Like Josiah Winchester, Stephen Duncan was another northern emigre who never really embraced the principles and values of his new home. After moving to Natchez from his native Pennsylvania during the first decade of the nine-

---

39. E. W. Cook to Josiah Winchester, September 7, 1839, in Winchester Family Papers, CAH.

40. George Winchester, "The Slavery Question," in Winchester Papers, CAH; *Journal of the Mississippi Secession Convention* (1861; rpr. Jackson, 1962), 16.

teenth century, Duncan rapidly began to construct one of the largest slaveholding empires in the Southwest. But he found the South wanting in several
important respects, and despite an early vow to remain in Natchez "for the remainder of my days," he retained close ties, both physically and temperamen-
tally, with the region of his birth.[41] For Duncan, the mild winters and boundless
economic opportunities were the only obvious advantages afforded by the
Natchez region. Chief among its negative features were poor health conditions,
its oppressively hot summers, and the lack of proper educational facilities. The
last was a recurrent theme in Duncan's correspondence with his brother-in-law
and fellow Carlisle native, Judge Thomas Butler of Louisiana. "This business,
of educating our children is an affair that must perplex us much in this country,"
he wrote in 1828, adding that he was inclined to entrust the early education of
his children to "governesses, or private tutors." Five years later, following the
dismissal of Butler's son from West Point for academic reasons, Duncan observed that "New England is the only place, where steady habits are to be acquired. I wish most truly, on my children's acct., I were there. Indeed, I would
be there, were it not for the rascally climate."[42] Accordingly, he sent his daughter Sarah and son John to Philadelphia for their schooling. John later went on
to Yale, and Sarah married a Philadelphia physician and resided in that city
until her premature death in 1839.[43]

Of almost equal concern to Duncan, who lost his first wife after just four
years of marriage, was the unhealthy climate of the Natchez District. There was
a time, he remarked in 1822, "when there was no country, I wd. Prefer to this,
but for the last 5 years we have had scarcely anything to speak of but disease &
death. I don't think I shall ever spend another summer in it, and I am at times,
more than half resolved to purchase a seat near Philada. and call it *my permanent
residence.*"[44] Although he never established his permanent residence in Philadelphia, Duncan made annual summer excursions to the Northeast, beginning at
least as early as 1816.[45] These trips usually lasted from early summer to mid-

---

41. Stephen Duncan to Thomas Butler, August 4, 1816, in Thomas Butler and Family Papers, LSU.

42. Duncan to Butler, August 22, 1828, November 28, 1833, *ibid.*

43. Duncan to Butler, September 29, 1822, July 1, 1823; John Ellis Duncan to Stephen Duncan,
October 31, November 10, 1828; Stephen Duncan to Thomas Butler, September 7, 1833, September
17, 1839; W. A. Irvine to Thomas Butler, October 16, 1833, in Butler Family Papers, LSU.

44. Stephen Duncan to Thomas Butler, September 29, 1822, *ibid.*

45. Duncan to Butler, August 4, 1816, *ibid.*

October and included, in addition to Philadelphia, visits to such sites as New York City, Saratoga Springs, Newport, and Baltimore. Typical was an 1843 summer excursion taken in company with William J. Minor and his family. The party departed Natchez in mid-June on board the steamer *Grey Eagle* and arrived in New York about the first of July. Duncan and his family spent most of their time in Philadelphia, New York, and Saratoga Springs, while the Minor entourage included Boston and Long Branch, New Jersey, in their itinerary before beginning the journey home by way of the "Western train" from Baltimore. The Minors finally returned to Natchez in early October after a pleasant seven-day trip down the Mississippi River.[46]

Such summer excursions were commonplace among wealthy Natchezians, even such second-generation residents as Francis Surget, Jr. According to a Union general who was quartered briefly at Clifton, Surget's palatial mansion, following the fall of Vicksburg, Surget had passed the summers "for almost his lifetime" either "in Europe or at our Northern watering places."[47] Indeed, Surget made one such trip during the heated presidential campaign of 1860. Departing Natchez during the second week in June, Surget, accompanied by his wife and her sister, proceeded to New York City by way of Louisville, Cincinnati, Niagara Falls, and Syracuse. There they established their headquarters at the New York Hotel, paying for their board at the rate of $17 per day. They were in Saratoga Springs during the first half of August, and the following month, they spent a like period at the Fillmore House in Newport, where the weekly boarding cost was $125, about the same as in New York. They then returned to the latter city, where they remained until October 23 before commencing their homeward journey via Louisville. There they boarded the steamer *Woodford* of the Louisville and New Orleans Lightning Line and returned to Natchez on November 3, just three days before the fateful presidential election of 1860.[48]

Of course, such annual treks to the cooler and more healthful climes of the

46. William J. Minor to Charles P. Leverich, May 23, 31, June 30, August 3, September 9 (quotation), October 12, 1843, and Denison Olmsted to C. P. Leverich, August 10, 1843, in Charles P. Leverich Papers, MDAH.

47. General Thomas Kilby Smith to Elizabeth Smith, July 19, 1863, KS 115, Huntington Library, San Marino, California. I am indebted to Donald G. Linton of Hot Springs, Arkansas, for providing me with a copy of this letter.

48. Various bills and receipts, June 18–November 3, 1860, in Surget Family Papers, MDAH.

Northeast were by no means confined to the Natchez elite despite their intimate family ties to that region. Wherever the affluent and socially prominent congregated—whether at Saratoga Springs, Newport, or the Virginia springs—elite slaveholding families could be found. They came from Alabama, Georgia, Louisiana, the Carolinas, from all parts of the land of cotton and magnolias. Examples of these summer excursions are legion, but a few will suffice to illustrate the pattern. During the sixteen-year period from 1843 to 1858, St. Mary Parish sugar planter William T. Palfrey spent a dozen summers away from his plantation, ten in the North and two in Kentucky. The average duration of these trips, which normally began in late June or early July and ended in September, was two and one-half months. Palfrey was prevented from leaving Louisiana in 1852 by his attendance at the State Constitutional Convention and in 1855 when he dislocated his ankle. Another wealthy planter, Paul C. Cameron of North Carolina, embarked in 1857 upon an extended northern excursion in hopes of restoring the health of his teenaged daughter Rebecca. The Cameron itinerary included Philadelphia, New York, Boston, Newport, Cape May, Providence, Quebec, Montreal, and Niagara Falls. Writing to his father-in-law, Judge Thomas Ruffin, shortly after his departure from Newport, Cameron described that resort as "the summer home of the rival nobbs of New York and Boston . . . a place of fast horses, fast women and faster men . . . with poor accomodations [sic] at very high prices." He was particularly disturbed to discover that nearly every male servant at one hotel was a runaway slave from the South.[49]

Thirteen years earlier, two members of the Heyward family, Charles and nephew William H., recorded a much more favorable impression of their sojourn in the Northeast. They were especially enamored of the luxurious lifestyle in Boston. Upon their return to that city from Montreal, William remarked that his uncle was so pleased with their quarters at the Tremont House that he could not persuade him to continue their trip to Saratoga. The living here, declared the younger Heyward, "is *very far superior* to anything of ours." A strong endorsement, indeed, from a member of one of the wealthiest families in Carolina. The family of another South Carolina rice grandee, J. J. Izard Pringle, customarily spent their summers in New York, the native state of Mrs. Prin-

49. Compiled from William T. Palfrey Plantation Diary, 1842–59, 1867, in Palfrey Family Papers, LSU; Paul C. Cameron to Thomas Ruffin, August 28, 1857, in *The Papers of Thomas Ruffin*, 4 vols., ed. J. G. de Roulhac Hamilton (Raleigh, 1918–20), II, 567–68.

gle, and at Newport, where they sometimes rented a house for the summer. By mid-May, 1857, Jane L. Pringle was already settled at the New York Hotel in the city, where daughter Mary, rapidly becoming quite a belle, enjoyed daily walks "every afternoon with various men." Jane's husband remained behind on their plantation in South Carolina until late May, when he too departed for the North. During early summer the various members of the Pringle family divided their time among Manhasset, Sing Sing, where the boys were attending military school, Saratoga, and Niagara Falls before the elder Pringles and daughter Mary proceeded to Newport, which, as wife Jane observed, was "after all the grand centre of civilization."[50]

As a consequence of the deadly, miasmic atmosphere that pervaded the rice swamps from mid-April to mid-October, it was imperative that Low Country planters leave their plantation residences for more extended periods than was common elsewhere in the South. Some, like the Heywards and Pringles, sojourned in the Northeast; others established summer homes at nearby Pawley's Island or interior pineland sites such as Society Hill and Plantersville.[51] But perhaps the most popular summer refuge for Charleston-area rice barons was Flat Rock, North Carolina, situated in the mountains of Henderson County. Established in the late 1820s by Charles Baring, nephew of the founders of the celebrated banking house of that name and husband of one of the Heywards, it soon became the summer colony for a host of prominent South Carolinians. Among its early residents were the Middletons, who established a summer home there as early as 1828, and Judge Mitchell King of Charleston, who constructed a summer place called Argyle and eventually acquired 4,000 acres in the vicinity.[52] As the years passed, other wealthy Low Country and a few Up Country aristocrats, among them the Hamptons and Singletons, built lavish summer residences in Flat Rock. Three of the largest Low Country slaveholders—William Aiken, Walter Blake, and Joshua John Ward—maintained summer homes in this mountain paradise. Ward's residence, built of stone at a cost of $15,000, had a dozen rooms as well as a "very large hall & galleries—billiard

50. William H. Heyward to James B. Heyward, September 1, 1844, in Heyward and Ferguson Papers (microfilm), SHC; Jane L. Pringle to son Julius, May 17, June 28 [1857], Pringle Family Correspondence, in R. F. W. Allston Papers, SCHS.

51. Easterby, ed., *South Carolina Rice Plantation*, 22–23.

52. Louise Howe Bailey, "Flat Rock: 'Little Charleston of the Mountains,'" *Carologue* 11 (Summer 1995): 13–14; Rogers, *History of Georgetown County*, 316.

room ten pin alley and 200 acres of open land."[53] The colony also included an inn, built in the early 1850s when Aiken, Judge King, and eight others contributed $1,000 each toward its construction.[54] As J. D. B. De Bow remarked following a visit to Flat Rock in 1860, the community contained "the summer-seats, many in a style of much costliness and beauty, of some of the wealthiest and most aristocratic families of South Carolina."[55] The Flat Rock colony persisted after the Civil War, and though its population has been augmented in recent years by an influx of retirees from the North, it still attracts a number of affluent Charlestonians during the summer months.[56]

Although the Flat Rock community was unique as a summer refuge for elite planters, other, more traditional, southern resorts, such as the springs of western Virginia, Beersheba Springs, Tennessee, and Biloxi and Pass Christian on the Mississippi Gulf Coast, experienced a growth in their clientele as sectional conflict intensified during the 1850s. Many found the political atmosphere of these popular watering spots more congenial than the increasingly hostile environment to which they were subjected in the Northeast. Thus, Paul C. Cameron encountered very few Southerners during his northern excursion in the summer of 1857. "They have staid away and for a purpose," he explained. Georgia clergyman and rice planter Charles W. Rogers, himself a graduate of Yale but also a strong southern nationalist, reportedly refused to take his family to the North after the rise of the abolition movement, despite the fact that his wife was a native of Connecticut.[57]

Of course, some planters had always preferred the southern resorts, especially the Virginia springs, which attracted principally Virginians and Carolinians. Others made these spas a part of their itinerary as they traveled to and from the watering spots of the Northeast. Among the plantation aristocrats encountered by Edmund Ruffin during his annual visits to White Sulphur and the

53. De Bow's Review 29 (October 1860): 537; John Hammond Moore, *Columbia and Richland County: A South Carolina Community, 1740–1990* (Columbia, 1993), 177; Bailey, "Flat Rock," 28; Davidson, *The Last Foray*, 179; Francis K. Winchester to unknown, n.d. [postwar], in Winchester Family Papers, CAH (quotation).

54. Bailey, "Flat Rock," 28.

55. *De Bow's Review* 29 (October 1860): 537.

56. Bailey, "Flat Rock," 13.

57. *The Papers of Thomas Ruffin*, ed. Hamilton, II, 568; Robert Manson Myers, ed., *The Children of Pride: A True Story of Georgia and the Civil War* (New Haven, 1972), 1662–63.

neighboring Virginia springs in the late 1850s were fellow Virginians Williams Carter and Philip St. George Cocke; James C. Johnston, Paul Cameron, Thomas P. Devereux, and William S. Pettigrew of North Carolina; and R. F. W. Allston, James Chesnut, Jr., John L. Manning, and John N. Williams of South Carolina. Richard Singleton, the largest cotton planter in the last state at midcentury, owned a cottage at White Sulphur Springs and by 1830 had invested $30,000 in that resort. John Perkins, Jr., of Louisiana was an annual visitor to the Virginia spas, but many Deep South planters preferred to summer along the much closer Gulf Coast.[58] In 1851, New Orleans factor Martin Gordon reported that his mother-in-law, Mrs. M. D. Bringier, had engaged a cottage in Biloxi for the summer. Several years later, a visitor to Pass Christian wrote that he had recently dined with General Edward Sparrow, proprietor of munificent Arlington plantation on Lake Providence and later a prominent member of the Confederate Congress. Sparrow, he noted, had "a very comfortable residence for a hot summer, with a Wharf & Bathing House, and a large net in front," by which he was well supplied with fresh fish for dinner.[59]

Wherever they congregated, whether at southern or northern resorts or in the large cities of the Northeast, elite planter families enjoyed a gay and active social life. In a series of letters to her sons, then at school in Europe, Jane L. Pringle described in vivid detail the social activities in Newport during the summer and early fall of 1859. Mrs. Pringle, her husband John Julius, their comely daughter Mary, and their elderly servant Page were quartered at the Bellevue Hotel, where, in addition to two bedrooms and a small dressing room, they had a corner parlor downstairs that she termed "the comfort of our lives." At dinner they had "a small round table" to themselves so that they were "as private as if in a cottage."[60] In mid-August the Newport social season was at its peak. "Newport was never so gay nor so pleasant," exulted Mrs. Pringle. "Balls every night and matinees or breakfasts every day." She reported attending a magnificent recent party where an abundance of soft shell crabs were served at supper amid

58. William K. Scarborough, ed., *The Diary of Edmund Ruffin*, 3 vols. (Baton Rouge, 1972–89), I, 213–14, 228–30, 330–32, 338–40, 442, 448–53; Easterby, ed., *South Carolina Rice Plantation*, 166; Cassie Nicholes, *Historical Sketches of Sumter County: Its Birth and Growth* (Sumter, S.C., 1975), 362.

59. Martin Gordon, Jr., to Benjamin Tureaud, June 28, 1851, in Benjamin Tureaud Papers, LSU; George [torn] to Josiah Winchester, August 29, 1858, in Winchester Family Papers, CAH.

60. Jane L. Pringle to son Lynch, August 1, [1859], Pringle Family Correspondence, in R. F. W. Allston Papers, SCHS.

grounds that were "lighted with colored lanterns" and on which "carpets [were] spread on the grass and seats for flirtation."[61] Daughter Mary, repeatedly characterized by her mother as "the belle of Newport," was being courted by New Yorker Heyward Cutting and was having the time of her life dancing—"decidedly the order of the day & night"—and riding horseback three times a week "with various admirers." By the end of the month, however, the crowd had begun to thin, and by the middle of September none of the "gay birds" were left except the Pringles. Just before their departure on September 22, two female servants, a mother and daughter, belonging to a Kentuckian absconded to Boston. The Pringles' servant Page professed to be "dreadfully shocked" by the incident because, as the perceptive Mrs. Pringle observed, "he is so old & sick that he knows he is better off as a slave than a free black—that's all that keeps him I fancy."[62]

With the exception of such slave elopements, the scene at Newport was repeated on a somewhat smaller and more subdued scale at the southern resorts. Much of the time at the latter was spent in pleasant conversation with friends who returned each year to the same locales. "We are having a very pleasant though quiet summer—going seldom to the ball room but spending the evenings in the parlor with a few friends or at the cottage," reported Mary Ann Conner from the Sweet Springs in western Virginia. At adjacent White Sulphur Springs, another young Mississippi belle declared that, with the exception of "rolling 'ten pins,'" the "task of dressing for dinner, walking in the eve and dancing at night" constituted the sum of their "pleasures and amusements."[63] Perhaps the most popular social events during the summer season at the springs were the fancy dress balls. Edmund Ruffin described the scene at one such ball at White Sulphur Springs in August, 1859. The participants appeared in carefully appointed costumes designed to portray various historical characters, but, according to Ruffin, there was "no pretension to acting the assumed characters"

61. *Ibid.*, August 21, [1859].

62. *Ibid.*, Jane L. Pringle to son Poinsett, August 15, September 12, [1859], and Pringle to son Julius, August 29, [1859], Pringle Family Correspondence, in R. F. W. Allston Papers, SCHS.

63. Mary Ann Duncan Conner to "My dear Sister," September 9, 1860, in Lemuel P. Conner and Family Papers, LSU; Mary to "Ever dear Sister," July 21, 1854, in George Wilson Humphreys and Family Papers, MDAH. For an interesting account of the visitors—among them, General Robert E. Lee—to the Virginia springs shortly after the war, see William C. Rives to William F. Wickham, December 28, 1867, in Wickham Family Papers, VHS.

except in a few cases. There were two of these so-called fancy balls at Sweet Springs the following year. The first was especially impressive, as virtually all the "ladies and gentlemen . . . were in fancy costumes," but at the second, held two weeks later, "the ladies were in simple ball dresses."[64]

On occasion, planter aristocrats were afforded the opportunity to savor the social life of the wealthy and powerful in such cities as New York and Washington, D.C. Near the close of their summer excursion in 1856, the Pringles stopped briefly in New York until the yellow fever abated in Charleston. There, just after the presidential election, they dined with John T. Delane, the charming editor of the London *Times,* accompanied him to Brooklyn after dinner to hear a political sermon by Henry Ward Beecher—"he being beaten we can afford to let him talk"—and attended a concert by Sigismond Thalberg the following evening.[65]

The formal social life associated with government officialdom in Washington was less attractive to some members of the slaveholding elite. Shortly after his election to Congress in 1818, Thomas Butler complained that, despite the formal courtesies exhibited in the nation's capital, there was "nothing like the agreable [sic] social society that we have in Louisiana. There are parties nearly every night where a great deal of splendor & extravagance may be found, but there is not a single home into which I can go without ceremony & spend a social evening." Many years later, Peter W. Hairston described the scene at a presidential levee as something akin to a "menagerie." Guests were ushered through a receiving line where communication was limited to a handshake and a brief greeting and then into the East Room, where the crowd was "so great as to make the atmosphere disagreeable." Former governor John L. Manning of South Carolina had a different complaint. Shortly before the Civil War, he attended an elegant soiree hosted by Mrs. John Slidell and was scandalized by the conduct of the "fast men & women of Washington," who "spent most of their time around the fountains—upon the grass—among the trees—in the Summer houses—untill [sic] each imprudent couple became the theme of gossip in the Saloons." Manning remained only briefly before retiring from this bacchanalian

---

64. Scarborough, ed., *The Diary of Edmund Ruffin,* I, 334; Mary Ann Conner to sister, September 9, 1860, in Conner Papers, LSU.

65. Jane L. Pringle to son Julius, November 9, 1856, Pringle Family Correspondence, in R. F. W. Allston Papers, SCHS.

scene.[66] Clearly, garrulous and refined Southerners did not find the social atmosphere in Washington as congenial as that of Newport or White Sulphur Springs.

Wealthy slaveholders did not confine their travels to the continental limits of the United States. Western Europe was also a favorite destination. The motives for such a long-distance excursion were varied. Frequently, it served as a rite of passage for sons who had completed their formal education and were about to embark upon careers. For others, it was a means of broadening the educational experience of their children, both male and female. Many others, of course, went for the same reasons that still attract Americans to Europe, simply to sight-see and to satisfy their curiosity about the wonders of the Old World about which they had read so much. Illustrative of the first motive was a six-month tour of Europe undertaken in 1853 by Frederick Henry Quitman shortly after his graduation from Princeton and before he assumed the management of his father's sugar plantation in Terrebonne Parish, Louisiana. After several weeks in the British Isles, where his itinerary included many of the sites made famous by Sir Walter Scott and other romantic writers of the period, young Quitman proceeded to Switzerland, where he found the scenery "grander and more magnificent" than he had anticipated, and then to various Italian cities, including Venice and Milan, which he described as "truly a city of palaces and churches." Another recent Princeton graduate, James Chesnut, Jr., traveled to Europe with his brother in the summer of 1839. While in Le Havre, they received a letter from their father counseling them to make the most of their experience. "Notice every thing peculiar to the Institutions of the Countries you visit," advised the elder Chesnut, "& more particularly, the habits, comforts (if they have any) & temperament of the labouring classes." In like manner, R. F. W. Allston urged his son "to keep a Diary journal of . . . interesting events and good thoughts" during his European tour twenty years later.[67]

Another prominent South Carolinian sought to enhance the education of

66. Thomas Butler to Captain Anthony P. Walsh, February 8, 1819, in Butler Family Papers, LSU; Peter W. Hairston to Fanny Caldwell, January 26, 1859, in Hairston Papers, SHC; John L. Manning to Sally B. Manning, May 29, 1860, in Williams-Chesnut-Manning Family Papers, SCL.

67. F. H. Quitman to "My dear Mother," June 29, September 23 (quotations), 1853, in John A. Quitman and Family Papers, MDAH; James Chesnut to James Chesnut, Jr., July 26, 1839, in Williams-Chesnut-Manning Papers, SCL; R. F. W. Allston to Benjamin Allston, May 28, 1859, in Easterby, ed., *South Carolina Rice Plantation*, 158.

the younger children in his extended family through a visit to the Continent. In the spring of 1857, John S. Preston announced that he was going to Europe whether or not he received a rumored diplomatic appointment from the Buchanan administration, and he sought permission to take with him the two youngest children of his brother-in-law John L. Manning. "I go to educate my daughters," explained Preston. "Your child [daughter Mary, age fourteen] will have . . . precisely the same advantages. Here none of them can be educated." As for Mary's younger brother Wade, Preston asserted that "he ought to be in school" and promised that "if you will entrust him to me I will see that he is put at precisely the best place in the World." Manning acceded to Preston's proposal, for in mid-September Mary reported to her mother from London that "our German governess left us last month and as soon as we get back to Paris we will take French and German lessons . . . there." Three years later, Wade H. Manning, then fourteen, returned to Europe, this time with his adult brother, Richard I., Jr., who within the next year would experience the horrible carnage at First Manassas as a captain in the Hampton Legion.[68]

There were other motives that induced wealthy Southerners to venture across the Atlantic. Peter W. Hairston twice visited Europe, the first time in the early 1840s in quest of a cure for the illness of his younger brother George and the second, fifteen years later, on a honeymoon with his second wife. On both visits he was appalled by the poverty he witnessed in Italy, where a multitude of beggars could be found on nearly every street. "You can see more misery in one day here than you could living a life time in the South," he wrote from Leghorn. Even the slaves, he added, "would feel . . . degraded to beg with the importunity they do." It was a desire for fame and glory that led another Carolinian to Italy in the same year that Hairston was enjoying his honeymoon. James Johnston Pettigrew had traveled to Europe to enlist in the Sardinian army during the wars for Italian unification, but his plans were frustrated when an armistice was concluded shortly after his arrival. "I have lost a glorious opportunity of distinguishing myself & seeing the world in its grandest phase," la-

68. John S. Preston to John L. Manning, April 12, 1857, in Williams-Chesnut-Manning Papers, SCL; Mary H. Manning to "Dear Mama," September 15, 1857, Richard I. Manning, Jr., to "My Dear Father," August 6, 1860, Richard I. Manning, Jr., to "My Dear Mother," June 19, August 4, 1861, all in Chesnut-Miller-Manning Papers, SCHS.

mented the disappointed Pettigrew.[69] Yet another Carolinian, Hayne Cheves, the youngest son of Langdon Cheves, Sr., had succumbed in Italy just three years before. Following his graduation from South Carolina College, Hayne contracted tuberculosis and embarked on an extended tour of the Continent in hopes of improving his health. As his condition deteriorated, his brothers back in South Carolina became increasingly concerned. Finally, in the spring of 1856 John R. Cheves announced his intention to go to Europe, which he much preferred to "going to the North," to look after his brother. The trip proved to be in vain, however, as Hayne died in Florence soon after his arrival. The following year, less than two months after the death of his father, another Cheves brother, Langdon, Jr., also traveled to Europe, though he seems to have spent most of his time in Paris.[70]

Normally, elite slaveholders took their families with them on these extended excursions to Europe, frequently in the company of other neighboring planter families, but a notable exception was William F. Wickham of Virginia. In April, 1852, at the age of fifty-nine, Wickham took leave of his magnificent Hickory Hill estate in Hanover County and took passage alone for Europe on board the steamer *Pacific*.[71] In a series of letters to his wife Anne and other family members who remained behind, he recounted in vivid detail his impressions of the various countries he visited during the next six months. His itinerary took him first to England, where at Hyde Park he "beheld a scene that has no parallel in the world."[72] Then, throughout May and early June, he was in Italy, which, in terms of the physical environment, was "the loveliest country" that he had ever seen. Like Hairston, however, he was disenchanted with the "beggary—uncleanliness—and squalid poverty" that he encountered everywhere on the peninsula. Next, he proceeded to Geneva, where he visited various sites "consecrated by their association with the names of Voltaire, Rousseau, De Stael, & Byron," and then to Baden Baden, where he com-

69. Peter W. Hairston to "My Dear Brother," December 20, 1859, in Hairston Family Papers, VHS; J. Johnston Pettigrew to James C. Johnston, July 11, 28 (quotation), 1859, in Pettigrew Family Papers, SHC; Pettigrew to Johnston, November 9, 1859, in Hayes Collection, SHC.

70. Robert Hayne Cheves Receipts, 1853–54, John R. Cheves to Langdon, Jr., April 12, 22 (quotation), 1856, and Paris Bills of Langdon Cheves, Jr., August, 1857, in Langdon Cheves, Jr., Papers, SCHS.

71. William F. Wickham to Anne Carter Wickham, April 3, 1852, in Wickham Family Papers, VHS.

72. *Ibid.*, April 16, 1852.

mented on the gaming tables. After brief visits to Antwerp and Brussels in early July, he moved on to France, where he remained until the end of the month. Returning to the British Isles, he explored England and Ireland during the last six weeks of his European sojourn.[73] Of all the countries he visited, Wickham was most enamored of England, which he characterized as a veritable "fairy land." On the eve of his departure, he wrote: "No tongue can convey the least conception of the beauty of the country. The more I see the more I admire." Yet two weeks later, as the steamer *Pacific* approached New York on his return voyage, he reassured his wife, "I shall like our home better than any place I have seen."[74] Like most aristocratic Virginians, Wickham was manifestly proud of his heritage.

Not only did planter nabobs travel extensively both within and without the United States, but a few of them also established permanent residences in the Northeast, thereby reinforcing their ties to that region. Both George Noble Jones of Savannah and the illustrious Henry Middleton of South Carolina inherited property in Newport, where the latter became a prominent social leader. Another member of the Middleton family, Henry Augustus, summered annually in Newport and reportedly owned $300,000 worth of property there at the end of the Civil War.[75] John Julius Pringle, also a native South Carolinian but later a sugar planter in Louisiana, built a pretentious house in Newport on the same street where the Bellevue was located, "but a good bit nearer the sea." Unfortunately, the new edifice was not completed until the summer of 1860, thus permitting only a brief residence there before the secession crisis. The Pringles spent the war years in Europe, settled briefly in Newport after the war, and then built a splendid villa at Biarritz in 1870.[76]

Other members of the southern elite held property in Westchester County, New York. As early as 1849, Levin Marshall expressed an interest in purchasing

73. Wickham to Anne Willing Carter, June 22, 1852, Wickham to daughters Mary Fanning and Lucy, June 28, 1852, Wickham to Anne Carter Wickham, July 5, 21, 1852, in Wickham Papers, VHS.

74. Wickham to Anne Carter Wickham, September 2, 18, 1852, in Wickham Papers, VHS.

75. Ulrich B. Phillips and James D. Glunt, eds., *Florida Plantation Records from the Papers of George Noble Jones* (St. Louis, 1927), 16–22; *Biographical Directory of the Senate of South Carolina*, comp. Reynolds and Faunt, 273; *South Carolina Genealogies*, III, 152; Rogers, *History of Georgetown County*, 317, 427 n.

76. Jane L. Pringle to son Lynch, December 13, [1859], Pringle Family Correspondence, in R. F. W. Allston Papers, SCHS; *South Carolina Genealogies*, III, 343.

some New York City real estate as an investment. Two years later, he inquired about residential property in the city, as he "might be induced to form a summer residence there." That plan apparently never came to fruition, but sometime before the war, he did acquire an estate in Westchester County and thereafter alternated his residence between Natchez and the estate, where he died in 1870. Another Westchester resident was Dr. Robert J. Turnbull, who owned four absentee cotton plantations and nearly four hundred slaves in the Mississippi Delta. The son of a Charleston nullification pamphleteer of the same name, Turnbull practiced medicine for a time in Charleston, and then, sometime during the late 1830s or early 1840s, he removed permanently to Westchester County, where he resided until his death in 1854. Georgia rice planter William H. Gibbons was yet another elite slaveholder who spent much of his time in the North. Born in New York City, Gibbons inherited most of the estate of his millionaire father, a New Jersey horseman with extensive planting interests in his native Georgia. Following his father's death, the bachelor Gibbons divided his time between his sister's home in Madison, New Jersey, and Savannah, where he lived with his agent. Despite his Yankee associations, Gibbons later served as a major in the Confederate Army.[77]

Whether at home or abroad, elite planters interacted with other family members within a spectrum of emotions that ranged from extreme affection and devotion, on the one hand, to conflict and bitterness on the other. In this respect they differed little from families in any other society or in any age, either before or since. Yet in view of the stigma attached to slaveowners by abolitionists and, more recently, by many contemporary historians, it may come as a surprise to learn that relations among members of these wealthy families were frequently characterized by mutual tenderness, warmth, and affection.

Nowhere was this more evident than in the reaction of nabob fathers to the birth of a child. "The little man is 'a buster,'" exclaimed Paul Cameron as he greeted the birth of his twelve-pound first son. "He looks like a child 3 months old." Equally large was the thirteen-pound nephew of Virginia planter Richard

77. Levin R. Marshall to Charles P. Leverich, February 23, 1849, and April 4, 1851 (quotation), both in Leverich Papers, MDAH; *Goodspeed's*, II, 397–98; Inventory of Estate of Robert J. Turnbull, Issaquena County, Mississippi, April 15, 1856, in Robert J. Turnbull Papers, CAH; *Early Records of Mississippi: Issaquena and Washington Counties*, 2 vols., comp. Alice Wade and Katherine Branton (Jackson, 1982–83), I, 115–16, 125, II, 57; Myers, ed., *The Children of Pride*, 1527.

Baylor, described by his proud father as "the very finest Boy that . . . I or anyone else have as yet seen." In like manner, Ayres P. Merrill, Jr., jubilantly reported the arrival of his first-born, "a beautiful boy," whom he termed "a blessing" descended from "the bounty of Heaven."[78] Such joyous feelings were not limited to the birth of a first child. Absent from home in New York, Thomas Butler eagerly awaited the safe delivery of "a sweet darling infant" back in Natchez. Upon receiving word several weeks later of the birth of "another dear son," he rejoiced to learn that his eldest son, Pierce, was "fond of his brother." Infant daughters were no less welcome. In 1824 Levin Marshall's brother-in-law reported from Tuscaloosa the birth of "one of the most lovely daughters that ever was or ever will be seen." Such expressions of joy and pride were universal among elite planter parents.[79]

As these infants matured into young children, they continued to enjoy the affection showered upon them by doting parents and grandparents. In the midst of his European tour in 1852, an obviously homesick William Wickham expressed a desire for news of his distant two-year-old grandson Henry. "How pleased I shall be to hear Henry say 'I want to stay with grandpapa,'" wrote the proud grandfather. "I suppose he talks quite well by this time & that he has a seat at the table." Two years later, Josiah Winchester, absent in Jackson on court business, described and interpreted for his seven-year-old son the celebration of Washington's birthday in that city. "You know," he explained, "that George Washington was the boy that was not afraid to tell the truth and of course when he became a man, he acted the part of a man and was honored for it."[80] The activities in which these young boys and girls engaged—taking walks, going on picnics, feeding the birds, flying kites, shooting marbles— seem almost amusingly plain to those of us increasingly enthralled by the age of technology. Nevertheless, they afforded great pleasure to the youngsters of that age. What parent could not relate to the childhood games played by the grandchildren of Georgia planter Farish Carter? After expressing gratitude to

78. Paul C. Cameron to "My dear Father," November 23, 1850, in Cameron Family Papers, SHC; Baynham Baylor to Richard Baylor, April 7, 1835, in Baylor Family Papers, VHS; A. P. Merrill, Jr., to William Newton Mercer, February 20, 1852, in William Newton Mercer Papers, LSU.

79. Thomas Butler to wife Nancy, December 21, 1819, January 27, 1820, in Butler Papers, LSU; William Proctor Gould to Maria Marshall, June 15, 1824, in Marshall Papers, LSU.

80. William F. Wickham to Williams Carter Wickham, May 24, 1852, in Wickham Papers, VHS; Josiah Winchester to son Francis, February 26, 1854, in Winchester Papers, CAH.

the elderly Carter for his recent gifts to the children, his daughter-in-law reported that little "Farish still rides on his blanket" and "says he does not wish to ride his sheep skin until next summer." While Farish was so occupied, his brother Colquitt was "driving his marbles over the floor in wild confusion calling them cattle—which he carries daily to market—but never finds sale for them."[81]

In no other elite family was greater warmth and more mutual affection and respect exhibited among family members than in that of Robert Barnwell Rhett, the publicly irascible fire-eater from South Carolina. From early childhood, the Rhett girls, six of whom lived to maturity, wrote lovingly to their father, recounting their daily activities. Thus, in her childish scrawl, four-year-old Elise wrote in the mid-1840s of feeding the birds in the garden before breakfast each morning. On a spring morning a dozen years later, the much more mature teenager walked with two of her younger sisters to a neighboring deserted plantation and tried to climb a large oak, only to find that she "had entirely forgotten how to climb" and that "size & hoops" were "great encumbrances." As she remarked to her father, the spectacle was quite amusing. "I rather think that our town friends would have been much astonished to see Miss Elise Rhett, *sixteen years old* climbing trees."[82] Earlier in the decade, two of her sisters, six and eight years old, respectively, had written excitedly to their father, then a United States Senator in Washington, D.C., about their preparations for a ball in Charleston. "I wish you were here & could see me with all my hair buckled up in paper, to make it curl, for the party to-night," wrote little Claude, who always closed her letters with these words: "I wish I could kiss you." Her sister Sallie expressed like sentiments. "I know if you were here," she wrote affectionately, "we should be a great deal happier tonight."[83]

The deeply religous Rhett enjoyed equally tender relations with each of his two wives. His first spouse, Elizabeth, unequivocally supported her husband's radical political position, and when the South Carolina cooperationists tri-

---

81. Emily S. Carter to Mrs. Farish Carter, October 14, 1858, in Farish Carter Papers, SHC.

82. Elise Rhett to "dear papa," [ca. 1846], and Elise Rhett to "My dear Papa," March 21, [1858], both in Robert Barnwell Rhett, Sr., Papers, SCHS.

83. Claudia Rhett to "dear Papa," February 5, [1852?], and Claude and Sally Rhett to "My dear Papa," February 17, [1852?], both *ibid.* Ages of daughters from Rhett Genealogy Notes #2, in Rhett Family Papers, SCHS.

umphed in the fall elections of 1851, she exploded with anger, vowing to leave "this dishonored state" with him if he so decided. "What you must suffer, I cannot bear to think of," she wrote sympathetically. "May He, who rules the whirlwinds & directs the storm, assuage the bitterness of your distress, my noble Husband, & give you his peace." Throughout this tumultuous period, she repeatedly expressed her deep affection for Rhett. "To think of you, & dream of you, are truly my chief occupations," she confided to him in Febraury, 1851. Less than two weeks later, she reiterated her devotion: "Dear Barnwell it is impossible to tell you, how my heart yearns to be with you—how I think of you, dream of you—miss you continually." Tragically, the debilitating effect of a dozen pregnancies took its toll, and Elizabeth Rhett died at the end of the following year.[84]

Rhett and his second wife, Catharine, whom he married in 1854, were no less devoted to one another. Although she occasionally displayed a temper and was not as religious as his first wife, Rhett remained deeply attached to her as they passed together through the difficult period of war and Reconstruction. Particularly moving is a series of letters from Rhett to his dear "Kate," written in August, 1868, from Flat Rock, where he had gone to recover his health. "Oh! how I wish you were with me," he exclaimed, as he journeyed toward the North Carolina mountains. Depressed by his physical infirmities and the loss of his fortune, he found solace only in the love and support of Kate, "the Companion of my days of adversity," who had stood by him "with unflinching fidelity" and sustained him with her "warm sympathy and ever watchful affection." In a particularly romantic letter, written on the eve of his departure from Flat Rock, the sixty-eight-year-old Rhett playfully alluded to their sexual relationship. "What do you think of an old woman, whom you know, who huffs off her husband, if he interrupts her sleep," he wrote teasingly. "She has passed beyond the heyday of vigorous amenities, and now melds her reciprocities of love, into the enjoyment of tender chucking and sound sleep." But let this woman be provided

84. Elizabeth W. Rhett to R. B. Rhett, October 17, February 13, 22, 1851, in Robert Barnwell Rhett, Sr., Papers, SCHS. For other letters illustrating the affectionate relationship between Rhett and his first wife, as well as the latter's declining health, see E. W. Rhett to R. B. Rhett, November 7, [1850], January 7, 12, 16, February 5, 15, [1851], *ibid.* In her missive of January 7, 1851, Eli gently chided her husband for failing to provide the "loving tenderness" she required when they were first married, but she hastened to add that she did not mean this as a "reproach."

with "a glorious supper . . . crowned with claret," he continued, and she is immediately transformed into a "happy-loving woman!"[85]

Other elite couples also enjoyed the marital bliss exemplified by the Rhetts. For example, in 1822, when Cupid's arrow struck James C. Johnston of North Carolina, his friend Thomas P. Devereux expressed the wish that, if Johnston's suit proved successful, "you may be as happy in married life as I have been & that after being connected for seven years you may find as I have found 'how much the wife is dearer than the bride.'" Raleigh banker George W. Mordecai, who was related by marriage to Devereux, was equally devoted to his wife, Margaret Cameron, whom he married in middle age. In a very affectionate letter written on Thanksgiving Day, 1859, Mordecai thanked God "for having bestowed to [him] that dearest, best of all blessings a good wife!" A year later, he reiterated to his beloved mate, "You have been to me all that a faithful wife could be and far more than I deserved."[86]

Two planter-judges in the Southwest, Thomas Butler of Louisiana and Josiah Winchester of Natchez, also seem to have been blessed with especially happy marriages. Rejuvenated after a visit to Maine in the summer of 1851, the latter returned to his native Massachusetts feeling "as rugged as a bear" and informed his wife, "If I had found you within my reach, after reading your letter, you would have felt the hug of one." So anxious was he to expedite his departure from New England and return to Natchez that he declined several social invitations, including one to "fish and eat chowder" at Marshfield with Daniel Webster. Some months later, while in the Mississippi capital on extended judicial business, he rationalized that such long absences caused him to realize "how much I love you and how necessary to my happiness is your society." But if compelled to be away much longer, he warned, "your greatest fear will be, that, on my return, I may devour you alive." Evidently, after six years of marriage, the wife had not yet superseded the bride with Winchester.[87]

Similar affection was manifested in the correspondence of Judge Thomas

85. R. B. Rhett to wife Kate, August 8, 20, 28, 1868, in Robert Barnwell Rhett, Sr., Papers, SCHS.

86. Thomas P. Devereux to James C. Johnston, April 21, 1822, in Hayes Collection, SHC; George W. Mordecai to Margaret B. Mordecai, November 24, 1859, November 1, 1860, in Cameron Family Papers, SHC.

87. Josiah Winchester to Margaret Winchester, August 17, 1851, April 5, 1852, in Winchester Papers, CAH.

Butler and his wife Ann. Typical was a letter from Butler, written in June, 1838, following a tedious sea voyage to New York. After recounting the harrowing details of the trip, he proclaimed his abiding love by closing with these words: "I have nothing further to say except to tell you what you have heard once or twice before viz. that I love you with all my heart & mind." These tender feelings were reciprocated by Ann less than two weeks later when she assured her beloved husband, "It would be impossible for me to express half the love I bear you." Such affection was truly remarkable in a marriage that had endured for twenty-nine years and had produced a dozen children when these letters were written.[88]

At the opposite end of the spectrum in terms of marital compatibility was another Louisiana couple, Louis A. and Stella Bringier. Their relationship had been a stormy one from the outset and eventually led to a complete break when Louis deserted his wife and moved to Florida after the Civil War. The first sign of trouble appeared in 1855, five years after Bringier's marriage to his sixteen-year-old cousin, when he scolded his young wife for writing too many and too lengthy letters, a curious complaint, indeed! "Your letters are too long," he remarked testily. "I have time to read only one page." Several years later, he needled his wife about a "charming young lady" whom he met at the theater while on a business trip to New Orleans and who invited him to her room the following evening. "Come be generous," he teased. "Don't call me back too soon and promise that you will kick up no fuss If I give her about one third of my time. . . . Variety is the spice of life."[89] One can only imagine Stella's reaction to this missive. During the war, Bringier, who was absent from home in the Confederate Army, berated his wife for neglecting their children and threatened to divorce her if she took the oath of allegiance to the United States.[90] Finally, in 1883, much to the distress of his wife and children, Bringier moved his permanent residence to Florida in order to escape the "*miserable* life" at home, which he termed "no Longer bearable." The distraught Stella responded with a pathetic letter to her husband in which she

88. Thomas Butler to Ann Butler, June 3, 1838, and Ann Butler to Thomas Butler, June 15, 1838, both in Thomas Butler and Family Papers, LSU. Marriage date and children are from Butler Family Tree, in Butler genealogy folder, LSU.

89. Louis Amedee Bringier to wife Stella, December 27, 1855, January 6, 1858, in Louis A. Bringier and Family Papers, LSU.

90. *Ibid.*, November 28, April 23, 1864.

blamed others for the marital break-up and vowed her undying love for her now-departed mate.[91]

Happily, the Bringiers were not typical of the planter families encountered in this study. The high esteem in which many of these wealthy slaveholders were held by family members may be discerned in the eulogies delivered by those whom they left behind. Upon the death of Alabama planter Gaius Whitfield in 1879, his nephew lauded him for "his tenderness of affection, loving nature, & Charitable heart," which evoked love in all who knew him. "No better man than he has died to my knowledge," concluded his North Carolina relative, "and I am old enough to have seen the best of men leave us." The death of Langdon Cheves, Jr., South Carolina intellectual, militant secessionist, and Confederate engineer, who was killed at Battery Wagner on July 10, 1863, by the first shell fired by the attacking Federal fleet, produced an even more emotional response from his widow. Shocked by her husband's sudden and unexpected demise, Charlotte Cheves was almost inconsolable. "I know not how I shall live without him," she wailed. After praising him for his intelligence, modesty, humility, patience, gentleness, and tenderness—qualities she "never knew united in any other man"—she pronounced him "too good & too pure for this world!"[92]

The venerable Edward McGehee of Mississippi received similar approbation from members of his family even before his death. The years had mellowed the patriarchal planter, reported his son and namesake in 1854. "Whereas he formerly secured the respect and awe of his children he now commands their love," explained the younger McGehee, and the youngest of his nineteen offspring could now approach him "with a freedom unknown in former times." Terming his father "a noble man," Edward J. McGehee exhorted his halfbrother to return from California to spend some time with their failing parent before it was too late. Little did he know that the sixty-eight-year-old McGehee was destined to live for another quarter-century. The nobility alluded to by his son was exhibited a decade later when Federal troops burned McGehee's stately residence in Wilkinson County, allegedly assaulting both the

91. L. A. Bringier to daughter Stella, March 18, 1883, and Stella Bringier to husband Louis A., March, 1883, both *ibid.*

92. N. G. Whitfield to "Dear Cousin Nathan," November 13, 1879, in Whitfield and Wooten Family Papers, SHC; Charlotte L. Cheves to cousin Theodore, July 16, 1863, in Langdon Cheves, Jr., Papers, SCHS.

elderly slaveholder and his wife in the process. Many years later, daughter Carrie, who witnessed the event, praised the conduct of her parents during that traumatic experience. "It would be impossible for me to describe the grand, calm, dignity of Father," she recalled, "or the bravery of spirit of our self forgetting Mother."[93] It seems reasonable to conclude that such men as McGehee, Whitfield, and Cheves exemplified to the highest degree those meritorious qualities suggested by the term "southern gentleman."

93. Edward J. McGehee to Micajah McGehee, June 14, 1854, in McGehee Family Papers, MDAH; Aunt Carrie to J. Stewart McGehee, February 7, 1904, in James Stewart McGehee Papers, LSU. Even the Federal officer who commanded the Third U.S. Colored Cavalry, the unit that burned McGehee's Bowling Green plantation residence in October, 1864, conceded that the elderly patriarch's conduct was exemplary on that occasion. "The appearance of Judge McGehee was such as to Command respect any where," he admitted years after the event (J. B. Cook to J. S. McGehee, January 6, 1904, *ibid.*).

2

Religious and Cultural
Characteristics

I believe our cause is righteous & that God will bless it.
— Lemuel P. Conner, March 5, 1861

This has been an anxious day & every one now rejoices—I hope with devout thankfulness for it seems to me clearly that God is on our side.
— Mary Petigru, April 13, 1861 [following surrender of Fort Sumter]

Freedom for whites, slavery for negroes, God has so ordained it!
— Kate Edmondston, December 30, 1864

One object, in parting with John, is to enable him to get a good & *practical* education, & his whole time & energies *must be* devoted to that object.
— William J. Minor, June 15, 1848

ALTHOUGH THE MAJORITY of elite slaveholders, especially those residing in Natchez and along the Atlantic seaboard, were Episcopalians, their religious views accorded closely with those identified by Anne Loveland in her study of southern evangelicals. Philosophical discussions of religious thought and belief do not figure prominently in the correspondence of the group under study. Nevertheless, it is clear that virtually all of them believed in an omnipotent God, were convinced that He sanctioned their peculiar socioeconomic system, and counted on Him to protect them in their hour of crisis. As Loveland has written of the evangelicals, "belief in the sovereignty and omnipotence of God and the dependence of man informed the whole of their thinking."[1] In short, they subscribed to a providential view of the universe.

With respect to denominational preference, there were no surprises. Nearly 80 percent of the 148 members of the planter cohort whose religious affiliation could be ascertained were either Episcopalians or Presbyterians, those denominations that had traditionally catered to the spiritual needs of the well-to-do (see Table 2). Support for the Episcopal Church was almost universal among the South Carolina rice planters, many of whom held memberships in small, rural churches near their plantations as well as in such renowned Charleston congregations as St. Philip's and St. Michael's. Indeed, the only identifiable rice barons who did not adhere to the Episcopalian faith were two Black Swamp planters in Beaufort District, Benjamin R. Bostick and Edmund Martin—the former a Baptist and the latter a Methodist—and French-born Simon Verdier, who was a Presbyterian. There was also a pocket of Presbyterians among the sea island cotton planters who resided on Edisto Island.[2] Episcopalianism was also the dominant religious preference of wealthy slaveholders in Virginia and North Carolina. A somewhat greater range of religious choice prevailed among the Natchez nabobs, though many of the most prominent families adhered to

1. Anne Loveland, *Southern Evangelicals and the Social Order* (Baton Rouge, 1982), 265.

2. Davidson, *The Last Foray*, 179; *Biographical Directory of the Senate of South Carolina*, comp. Reynolds and Faunt, 263, 324–25; Nell S. Graydon, *Tales of Edisto* (Columbia, S.C., 1955), 144. Among the Edisto planters who embraced the Presbyterian faith were Ephraim M. Baynard, William Edings, Isaac Jenkins Mikell, and John F. Townsend. The figures presented here accord with those of Stephanie McCurry, who found that, of the 307 Low Country planters who owned a hundred or more slaves in 1860, two-thirds were Episcopalian and 14 percent were Presbyterian (*Masters of Small Worlds*, 165).

TABLE 2 · RELIGIOUS PREFERENCE

State	Episcopal	Presbyterian	Methodist	Baptist	Catholic	None	Total
Ala.	2	1	4	4			11
Fla.		1	1				2
Ga.	2	3	3	2		1	11
La. (Cotton)	4						4
La. (Sugar)	1				2		3
Md.	1						1
Miss. (Natchez)	15	10	5		3		33
Miss. (Outside Natchez)	6	1					7
N.C.	7	1					8
S.C. (Up Country)	10	7		2			19
S.C. (Low Country)	34	5	1	2		1	43
Tenn.	2						2
Tex.	1						1
Va.	2		1				3
TOTALS	87	29	15	10	5	2	148
PERCENTAGES	58.8%	19.6%	10.1%	6.8%	3.4%	1.4%	

SUMMARY: Based on 43.8 percent of the planter cohort. Episcopal and Presbyterian totaled 116, or 78.4 percent. In Atlantic seaboard states, 72 of 85 (84.7 percent) were of those two faiths.

the Episcopal faith of their Atlantic seaboard counterparts.[3] Only in Georgia and Alabama was there significant religious diversity, with allegiance divided almost equally among the Episcopal, Presbyterian, Methodist, and Baptist churches.

With the notable exception of the sugar planters of south Louisiana, many of whom were Roman Catholic, there were few non-Protestants among the elite slaveholders.[4] Of the 339 members of the group included within this study, only George W. Mordecai of North Carolina was an ethnic Jew, and even he was a practicing Episcopalian. Despite his conversion, however, Mordecai's background proved to be an obstacle when he sought the hand of Margaret Bennehan Cameron, a member of one of the most prominent families in the state. Her father steadfastly opposed the match, in part because of Mordecai's heritage, and it was only after his death in 1853 that the two were wed. Perhaps it was curiosity about her fiancé's ethnicity that had induced Margaret to visit a Jewish synagogue in Philadelphia three years earlier. She emerged with a sympathetic impression of the worshippers coupled with a rather critical view of the service, especially the role of women in it. "Never did I feel more for any people," she declared. "Poor creatures they are to be pitied," she continued. "There was nothing like solemnity in their worship, the whole service was performed in a kind of sing song tone or chant, the men occupied the body of the building, the females the galleries, poor things they seem to have very little to do in the matter."[5] Clearly, both the attendants and the ritual differed dramatically from those to which she was accustomed in the Episcopal church back home.

Margaret Cameron's father was not the only wealthy slaveholder to manifest anti-Semitic sentiments. Many years before, Thomas P. Devereux had sought to assist another Mordecai, presumably a relative of George, in establishing a medical practice in Edenton. Obviously apprehensive about the reception that might be accorded the young physician by James C. Johnston, one of the town's

3. Among the early vestrymen in Trinity Episcopal Church, Natchez, were Benjamin Farrar, William J. Minor, Ayres Merrill, William N. Mercer, George Winchester, Joseph Davis, Stephen Duncan, and John A. Quitman (James, *Antebellum Natchez*, 248–49).

4. Louisiana Catholics are obviously under-represented in Table 2. The data was fragmentary, and only the Bringiers and Duncan F. Kenner, a convert, could be positively identified as Catholic.

5. Censer, *North Carolina Planters and Their Children*, 81; George W. Mordecai to Margaret B. Mordecai, October 20, 1860, and Margaret B. Cameron to Anne Cameron, February 23, 1850, both in Cameron Family Papers, SHC.

most prominent citizens, Devereux praised Dr. Solomon Mordecai as a man of impeccable professional skill and reputation who had rejected the advice of his mentors at the University of Pennsylvania to open a practice in Philadelphia and had chosen instead to settle in Edenton. "I know you do not like some of 'the chosen people' who are his near connections," wrote Devereux, but, he assured his friend, Mordecai was entirely "free from those peculiarities of character" that allegedly distinguished many of his kind.[6] William J. Minor also betrayed more than a hint of anti-Semitism in 1861 when he sought to enlist the support of General T. S. Wells in behalf of Duncan Kenner, who was running for a seat in the Confederate Senate against "the Jew [Judah P.] Benjamin." The previous year, former governor John L. Manning of South Carolina had exhibited no such prejudice, when, after witnessing Benjamin utterly demolish Stephen A. Douglas in a Senate debate on the merits of popular sovereignty, he pronounced the Louisiana senator "beyond all question . . . the ablest man in the Senate."[7]

In contrast to their general view of Jews, the attitude of elite Protestant slaveholders toward Roman Catholics was mixed. Shortly before their marriage in 1859, Peter W. Hairston and Fanny Caldwell engaged in a friendly, yet spirited, debate concerning both the theology and historical contributions of the Catholic Church. Terming himself a "Low Church Episcopalian," Hairston initiated the dialogue by asserting that the Catholic Church was "a truly Christian Church in all the main essentials of religion—its belief in the regeneration of the heart and in being saved through faith in Christ." While objecting to such Catholic beliefs and practices as transubstantiation, veneration of the Virgin Mary, the sale of indulgences, celibacy of the clergy, and the conduct of services in Latin, he, nevertheless, found much to applaud in Catholicism. When his fiancée retorted that the Catholic religion had been primarily responsible for the decline of the Italian states, Hairston mounted an even more vigorous defense. "I have a profound respect for the Catholic Church," he declared, crediting that institution with passing down the Bible "during the darkness of the Middle ages," serving as the "great patron of the fine arts and literature," and

6. Thomas P. Devereux to James C. Johnston, October 21, 1822, in Hayes Collection, SHC.

7. William J. Minor to General T. S. Wells, November 19, 1861, in William J. Minor and Family Papers, LSU; John L. Manning to Sallie B. Manning, May 29, 1860, in Williams-Chesnut-Manning Papers, SCL.

preserving the "monuments of antiquity." If priests exercised excessive power over their members, it was "only what all other ministers would do if they could," and if corruption had crept into the church, it was "but the incident of all things human." Somewhat taken aback, Fanny could only offer this rejoinder: "From the eulogy you pronounce upon the *Roman* Catholic Church, one might suppose you were about to enter into an agreement for its defence—'for life.'"[8]

Like Fanny Caldwell, Elise Rhett found many aspects of Catholicism objectionable, though her complaints related more to ritual than to dogma. Shortly after the war, Elise, the young lady who, as a teenager, had found her hoop skirt an encumbrance in climbing trees, moved to Louisiana to reside with her younger sister Sallie, who had married a native of that state in 1863. Shortly after her arrival, she attended the Catholic church with her sister and brother-in-law and was irritated by what she described as "the stupid little image of the Virgin Mary & the abominable discordant intoning of the priest." She also characterized the choir as "weak" but vowed to lend her vocal talents to the Mass "& help the community for one Sunday, from the hearing of such awful music as disturbed my comfort last Sunday." More than a little surprised to learn that her sister had joined the church of her Roman Catholic husband, Elise hastened to assure her father that he need not fear any similar conversion by her.[9]

Whatever the merits or demerits of Catholicism, most elite planters agreed that, if properly directed, religion in general had a beneficent influence upon humankind. One of the few to address this question explicitly was James C. Johnston, who, while a student at Princeton in the late 1790s, composed an essay on the virtues and evils of religion. In the hands of wise and enlightened men, religion was a blessing. "It teaches us all those virtues without which we should be wicked and miserable," argued young Johnston, "and enables us to approach nearer to the creator and sovereign of the universe." But if directed by misguided men, it could just as easily become a curse, especially when influenced by superstition. After reciting numerous examples of the baneful influence of other religions, Johnston charged that even the Christian religion "has been disgraced by the enormities which some men who pretend to obey it[s] dictates

8. Peter W. Hairston to Fanny Caldwell, December 2, 1858, April [29], 1859, and Fanny Caldwell to Peter W. Hairston, May 9, 1859, in Peter Wilson Hairston Papers, SHC.

9. Elise Rhett to "Dear Papa," February 3, 1866, in Robert Barnwell Rhett, Sr., Papers, SCHS.

have piously committed. Even this holy religion in the hands of superstition has been the cause of wars and bloodshed."[10] Although these words were written by a young college student at the end of the eighteenth century, it seems probable that they reflected accurately the views of most members of the well-read, cosmopolitan, and sophisticated slaveholding elite of the next generation.[11]

The degree of religiosity among the elite varied widely. Some, like Langdon Cheves, Jr., despite his exemplary life, made no formal profession of religion at all. Others were frequently enjoined by friends and relatives to be more devout. Richard Baylor of Virginia, a nominal Episcopalian, was the recipient of impassioned pleas by at least two correspondents to accept Christ as his saviour. "How earnestly do I wish that you were truly a child of God, truly converted & savingly interest[ed] in Christ, that you were safe for eternity," wrote one pastor in 1852. The appeal apparently went unheeded, for several years later another friend sought to address Baylor on "this momentous matter, of your soul's salvation." In yet another communication, the latter writer exclaimed: "O how it would rejoice my heart to visit you *by special invitation*, & join you in the glad praises of a happy convert.[12] Another Virginian, William Wickham, was also slow to embrace the church and was clearly less pious than his wife. Writing from Paris during his European tour in 1852, Wickham admitted that his sabbaths had "not all been spent as you would desire," but he hastened to assure his "dearest love" that he had "enjoyed . . . no amusements, visited no *spectacles*, and in no manner violated it further than I have told you in my letters." Years later, in a letter of condolence to the widow of William C. Rives, Wickham expressed regret that he had not become a member of the church "early in life" as they had. "In affliction," he observed, "it is natural for every thinking being to have recourse to a higher power & to believe we shall be again with those we

10. James C. Johnston, "Essay on Religion," Essays written at Princeton College, 1796–99, in Hayes Collection, SHC.

11. For example, Edmund Ruffin, admittedly more of a religious skeptic than most of his peers, repeatedly denounced the excesses of religion and the alleged misconstruction of Christian tenets by self-styled theologians and preachers. See Scarborough, ed., *The Diary of Edmund Ruffin*, I, 306–307; III, 16–21, 346–47, 348–50.

12. Charlotte L. Cheves to Cousin Theodore, July 16, 1863, in Langdon Cheves, Jr., Papers, SCHS; John Peyton McGuire to Richard Baylor, April 23, 1852, and Arthur Temple to Baylor, September 25, [1856?], June 9, 1856, in Baylor Family Papers, VHS.

love in a happier world." Doubtless the recent death of his own wife had served to confirm his belief that solace could best be found in religion.[13]

Spouses were particularly solicitous about the spiritual welfare of their loved ones. Thus, in the middle of the war, an anxious Fanny Conner inquired whether her husband, then serving as an officer in the Army of Tennessee, was attending church regularly. "Dear Husband do make it a *principle* to do as *little* Sunday work as possible," she admonished, or even better, "*none at all*." Observing the sabbath was not her only concern, however. "We should live strictly by God's commandments, making them the rule of our life," declared the pious Natchez matron, who concluded her brief sermon by expressing regret that her husband had not taken a Bible with him. Of course, it was not always the wife who proved to be more devout. Although he was extremely devoted to his second wife, Robert Barnwell Rhett occasionally chided her for what he deemed to be her lack of piety. After praising her numerous meritorious qualities in a letter written after the two had endured the rigors of war and Reconstruction, Rhett added this single qualification: "There is but one thing you need to make a you a perfect friend—more religion—more trust in God—more patience in his dealings with us all." Nevertheless, he added affectionately, "I thank God he gave you to me; and continually pray for you, a closer communion with him and a more elevated enjoyment of his blessed power."[14]

Perhaps the most deeply committed Christian among all the elite planters included within this study, Rhett had been converted by the noted Presbyterian minister Daniel Baker during the so-called Nullification Revival in the early 1830s.[15] In a lengthy epistle to his son Burnet, written just four years before his death, Rhett recalled his conversion in early manhood and urged his son, then forty years of age, to emulate his course. Although he was prosperous, happily

13. William F. Wickham to Anne C. Wickham, July 21, 1852, Wickham to Mrs. W. C. Rives, April 28, 1868, Mrs. Rives to Wickham, May 14, 1868, in Wickham Family Papers, VHS.

14. Fanny E. Conner to Lemuel P. Conner, June 20, 1863, in Lemuel P. Conner and Family Papers, LSU; R. B. Rhett to "My Dear Wife," August 20, 1868, in Robert Barnwell Rhett, Sr., Papers, SCHS.

15. McCurry, *Masters of Small Worlds*, 151, 153. McCurry argues that there was a relationship between radical religion and radical politics, a contention that seems to be supported by the example of Rhett. According to McCurry, revivalism was strongest in such Nullification strongholds as Beaufort District (*ibid.*, 156).

married, and on the threshold of a promising political career, related the elder Rhett, his "spirit was not satisfied." So he had turned to the Bible to see whether that source could provide "any light—any relief." As he read, his interest increased, but still he "could not *appropriate* his saving grace." Finally, he was able to give himself wholly to Christ and to persuade his brother Ben to follow the like path. Now, in the twilight years of his life, he implored his son to study the New Testament and also to become a follower of Christ. "Do it My Son! Pray for strength to do it," counseled the devout old patriarch, "and you shall receive it."[16]

Whatever their denomination or degree of religious commitment, most elite slaveholders adhered to a belief in the providential universe. Whether in response to epidemics, military and political events, the righteousness of slavery, or the death of loved ones, an omnipotent God was seen as the ultimate arbiter. It was all in His hands, and though they hoped and prayed for a favorable result, they were reconciled to His will, whether for good or ill. Thus, when yellow fever struck Charleston in 1854, claiming as one of its victims the beautiful and talented sixteen-year-old daughter of J. Harleston Read II, neighboring plantation mistress Adele Allston expressed great anxiety for all her friends. "If they all escape we will have great cause for gratitude to a merciful God," she observed with an air of hope. Six years later, when twelve-year-old Fanny Conner, the eldest child of Natchez nabob Lemuel P. Conner, died of scarlet fever, the sister of the grieving mother sought to alleviate her pain with these words: "The lesson of submission to our divine Master you have learned long ere this. Yet how hard it is to say, from our hearts, in the first burst of grief, 'The Lord gave and the Lord taketh away, *blessed be the name of the Lord*'! In this only can we find consolation." A Virginia matron, who had also passed through the painful experience of losing a child, had consoled herself with the belief that such a calamity was not "death but only transition to the beautiful world beyond." On a much brighter note, Margaret Mordecai, whose marriage had been delayed by her father's religious prejudice, later gave thanks to God for his "goodness to me in giving me such a dear husband."[17]

16. R. B. Rhett to Major Burnet Rhett, [1872], in Robert Barnwell Rhett, Sr., Papers, SCHS.

17. Adele Petigru Allston to Benjamin Allston, October 3, 1854, in Easterby, ed., *South Carolina Rice Plantation*, 121; Mary L. McMurran to Mrs. L. P. Conner, October 1, 1860, in Lemuel P. Conner and Family Papers, LSU; Mrs. H. M. Wickham to "Dear Cousin William," July 10, 1873,

In view of their faith in God as the omniscient regulator of human affairs, it is not surprising that southern slaveholders were overwhelmingly convinced that slavery was a divine institution, manifestly sanctioned by God. Typical of their thinking was the argument presented in an essay by Louisa McCord that appeared in the January, 1853, issue of the *Southern Quarterly Review*. In her review of *Uncle Tom's Cabin*, which she termed an "infamous libel upon our people," McCord invoked the authority of the Almighty to justify a system that she characterized as "the best possible for black and white, for slave and master." Southerners, she continued, accepted gratefully "the all-gracious providence of an Almighty God, who has seen fit, so beautifully, to suit every being to the place to which nature calls it." There was no need to apologize for slavery or even to admit that it was a necessary evil, declared McCord. On the contrary, she trumpeted, "we proclaim it . . . a Godlike dispensation, a providential caring for the weak, and a refuge for the portionless." The daughter of wealthy Georgia planter Turner C. Clanton viewed the peculiar institution in a similar light. Although she had occasionally expressed reservations about the morality of slavery, primarily because of its deleterious influence on white males, the final abolition of slavery in 1865 momentarily destroyed her religious faith, for the two institutions were inextricably bound together. "True I had seen the evil of the latter [slavery]," she wrote in October of that year, "but if the *Bible* was right then slavery *must be*—Slavery was done away with and my faith in God's Holy Book was terribly shaken."[18]

It was the sectional crisis of the 1850s and the ensuing Civil War, however, that elicited the most fervent appeals for divine intercession from members of the slaveholding elite. Intense apprehension about the ultimate consequence of sectional division first appeared during the debate over the Compromise of 1850. Remarking that slaveholders were more likely to confine their travel that summer to the southern resorts because they "are not on such amicable terms with the Northerners just now," a Greenville, South Carolina, matron expressed concern about the future and wondered whether her countrymen had not placed more trust in the recently deceased John C. Calhoun than in God. The former

---

in Wickham Family Papers, VHS; Margaret Mordecai to George W. Mordecai, November 27, 1860, in Cameron Family Papers, SHC.

18. Louisa S. McCord, *Selected Writings*, ed. Richard C. Lounsbury (Charlottesville, 1997), 89, 102, 117; *The Secret Eye*, ed. Burr, 276–77.

"was but an arm of flesh, but we looked & trusted too much I am afraid to him & too little to that omnipotent arm who weilds [*sic*] the Sceptre of the Universe." Quite different was the attitude manifested by Elizabeth Rhett following the defeat of her husband's secessionist faction in 1851. "Has God indeed, forsaken our land," she exclaimed. Astonished and bewildered by the triumph of the so-called submissionists, she refused to accept the electoral result "as the will of the Supreme Potentate," though, she conceded, "it *must be*." Five years later, another South Carolinian, the more moderate John L. Manning, invoked the aid of the Almighty in a letter to President Franklin Pierce in which he applauded the leader for the conciliatory tone of his recent annual message to Congress. "True men must rally around you in order to save our institutions from annihilation and our land from bloodshed," he wrote approvingly. "Now may God so dispose of events."[19]

As affairs moved toward a climax at the end of the decade, entreaties to the Supreme Being appeared much more frequently in the correspondence of wealthy Southerners. First there was great anxiety, followed shortly thereafter by thanksgiving for the initial Confederate victory at Fort Sumter. On the eve of the presidential election of 1860, North Carolina banker-planter George W. Mordecai expressed the fear that the omnipotent Creator might punish the South for its transgressions by installing Abraham Lincoln in the White House. "We have in truth been a rebellious & ungrateful people," he admitted contritely, "& deserve nothing but punishment in His hands." As the weeks passed and the crisis deepened, some turned in desperation to God as they sought vainly to arrest the march toward secession. "May God take care of us amid the madness that rages!" exclaimed William S. Pettigrew a week after South Carolina had severed the ties of union.[20] Others relied almost fatalistically on divine guidance to see them through the lowering storm. From Alabama, secessionist William M. Clark placed his confidence in "an all Wise Providence" to direct the rapidly escalating events "for the best." Similarly, as the North Carolina Convention debated what course to adopt, Ellen Mordecai trusted that God

19. Margaret Smith to "My dear Cousin" [Justina L. Walton], June 6, 1850, in Walton Family Papers, SHC; Elizabeth W. Rhett to R. B. Rhett, October 17, [1851], in Robert Barnwell Rhett, Sr., Papers, SCHS; John L. Manning to Franklin Pierce, January 11, 1856, in Williams-Chesnut-Manning Papers, SCL.

20. George W. Mordecai to wife Margaret, November 1, 1860, in Cameron Family Papers, SHC; William S. Pettigrew to James C. Johnston, December 27, 1860, in Hayes Collection, SHC.

would instruct the members of that body to act "wisely."[21] When the die was finally cast with the Confederate attack on Fort Sumter, the initial reaction was to thank God for the bloodless and successful result of that engagement. "God be praised!" cried Catherine Edmondston. "But what a miracle," she added. "The hand of a kind Providence has guarded & guided the cause of the South," exulted Mary Pettigrew four days after the surrender. Less optimistic was a Norfolk factor, who could see only a "dark & gloomy" future. But "we must . . . trust in God for the justice of our cause," he concluded.[22]

Following the outbreak of war, there were many additional allusions to the Supreme Potentate. Some pleaded for an end to the carnage, others credited Him with Confederate successes, and still others found some solace in His divine grace as they sought to cope with military defeat or the loss of loved ones. At home or on the battlefront, appeals to God were almost ubiquitous. Thus, in the spring of 1862, as Fanny Conner prepared to flee with her children to Franklin, Louisiana, and as rumors circulated of an impending bloody conflict at Corinth, Mississippi, where her husband was serving as a staff officer in the Army of Tennessee, she wrote disconsolately that she was on the brink of mental derangement. "Oh! this is a sad sad time," she exclaimed. "You my good noble & most dearly loved Husband gone to the army, and I compelled to leave my home under such painful circumstances. May God grant us brighter days and may He in his infinite mercy preserve you from all harm." Two weeks later, on the eve of what seemed an imminent battle at Corinth, Lemuel P. Conner prayed that his life would be spared. But, "if God wills otherwise," he confided to Fanny, "know that my heart overflows with devotion to you & my dear children. Farewell. May God bless & preserve you all."[23] Fortunately for Conner and others in each army, no major battle materialized at Corinth, as General Beauregard skillfully withdrew his army from that besieged town on the night of May 29.

21. William M. Clark to Lewis Thompson, December 22, 1860, in Lewis Thompson Papers, SHC; Ellen Mordecai to Mildred Cameron, March 16, 1861, in Cameron Family Papers, SHC.

22. *"Journal of a Secesh Lady": The Diary of Catherine Ann Devereux Edmondston, 1860–1866,* ed. Beth G. Crabtree and James W. Patton (Raleigh, N.C., 1979), 48; Mary B. Pettigrew to Carey Pettigrew, April 17, 1861, and Norfolk factor to William S. Pettigrew, April 29, 1861, both in Pettigrew Family Papers, SHC.

23. Fanny E. Conner to "My ever Dearest Husband," May 6, 1862, and Lemuel P. Conner to "My dear Fanny," May 20, 1862, both in Lemuel P. Conner and Family Papers, LSU.

In both triumph and tragedy the hand of God was seen as the ultimate guiding force. When the Union naval assault on Charleston was repulsed in April, 1863, former governor R. F. W. Allston exclaimed: "God be praised!" But, he cautioned, they would doubtless make the attempt again. "May it please God to enable us to repulse them, on every attempt by sea or land." As the war continued and the toll of lives and property mounted, the victims could only turn to God for solace. Thus, in July of 1863, truly a tragic month for the Confederacy, the widow of Langdon Cheves, who had met his death at Battery Wagner, poured out her grief to a family member and observed that "God only can soothe & comfort us!" Equally afflicted was her sister, who had lost "another noble son" at Gettysburg. However, she bore this loss with the "calmness & fortitude of a pure Christian," relying upon her belief that "a merciful God rules all for our good!"[24] A month later, a correspondent in Jackson, Mississippi, described the destruction inflicted upon that city during the Vicksburg campaign and, after recounting his own losses, pleaded for God to end "this cruel war." Confessing that he could yet "see but little light breaking through the dark clouds above & around us," he concluded, nevertheless, that "God is just & merciful & will in due time expel our enemies & give us peace & repose." This prediction proved to be excessively optimistic. Not only did southern whites lose the war, but they were also forced to endure the painful readjustments engendered by Reconstruction. And once again they turned to the Almighty for succor. As another former South Carolina governor, Francis W. Pickens, surveyed the gloomy landscape in the fall of 1867, he could only call on God to save the "country . . . from total ruin." But, like the Mississippian quoted above, he remained hopeful that a brighter day would soon dawn. "I think, by May next," he wrote, "we will begin to see light, and we will at least know what to expect, and to try and adapt ourselves to it."[25]

It should be noted that there is nothing unique, with respect to either social class or chronological age, in these invocations to the deity in times of peril, distress, or triumph. One has only to recall contemporary television interviews

24. R. F. W. Allston to Adele Allston, April 10, 1863, in Easterby, ed., *South Carolina Rice Plantation*, 193–94; Charlotte L. Cheves to Cousin Theodore, July 16, 1863, in Langdon Cheves, Jr., Papers, SCHS.

25. J. C. T. [or F.?] to "Dear Dick," August 20, 1863, in Winchester Family Papers, CAH; Francis W. Pickens to Adele Petigru Allston, November 22, 1867, in Easterby, ed., *South Carolina Rice Plantation*, 236–37.

with survivors of natural disasters or victorious athletes to witness similar expressions of gratitude to God for miraculous escapes or for spectacular deeds on the gridiron or the basketball court. It is a natural tendency of humankind, especially those imbued with religiosity, to credit a higher being with meritorious exploits or the escape from potential disaster as well as to seek solace from the same source when loved ones are suddenly, and sometimes inexplicably, torn from the bosom of a family. In short, the great planters were only manifesting their humanity when they exhibited such behavior.

Although elite slaveholders usually submitted willingly to the dictates of an omnipotent God, they were not entirely fatalistic. They were well aware that they could improve their lot on earth, and that of their families, through their own exertions, most notably through education. Of course, some of the older planters—Nathaniel Heyward and Francis Surget, to mention two of the most prominent—never enjoyed the luxury of a college education. But virtually all of the planter nabobs recognized the value of formal educational training and went to great lengths to ensure that their offspring, both male and female, received the highest quality of instruction that money could buy. Whether it was to prepare sons for careers in agriculture, business, the professions, or the military, or daughters for their roles as wives and as the initial tutors of their young children, the elite deemed a solid educational foundation indispensable to success.

Female members of the elite seemed especially cognizant of the role of education in promoting the future well-being of their offspring. Gertrude Thomas of Georgia characterized "a *good* and *thorough* education" as the "*greatest* of *temporal blessings*" and lamented that girls too often received only superficial training and tended to "leave school *too soon*." But such solicitude by plantation mistresses was not confined only to daughters. Thus, as a Mississippi matron contemplated the educational opportunities available to her son through the benefaction of her friend, John A. Quitman, she expressed the hope that he would receive " a firm, substantial, basis of education . . . a basis that will cling to him through life; and upon which, can be grounded, any profession, or pursuit, that taste, or necessity, may cause him to adopt." Similarly, Jane L. Pringle of South Carolina, a uniquely assertive planter wife who unilaterally directed the educational paths of her three sons, urged eldest son Julius to "seize opportunity by the hair" and "make the most" of the school in Vevay, Switzerland, at which he matriculated in 1856. Four years later, as Julius continued his European schooling, this time in Berlin, his mother asserted unequivocally, "Your education is to be your fortune. . . . Hence the necessity for habits of order industry & frugality." She continued, "With these you must succeed . . . without these you must fail."[26]

Notwithstanding the relentless growth of southern nationalism during the middle years of the nineteenth century, there remained a general perception among Southerners who could afford the best that northern educational facilities were superior to those in the South. This belief was manifested at all levels of the educational edifice, from the choice of private tutors for the very young to the selection of a college for the mature scholar. Not uncommon was the attitude exhibited by South Carolinian William H. Barnwell shortly after enrolling at Harvard in 1834. After describing his new environment with glowing enthusiasm, Barnwell urged his cousin, James B. Heyward, to join him at the Ivy League school, "for they can teach you more here in a year than they can teach you there all your life." Heyward took the advice and soon followed his cousin to Harvard, only to receive a letter from his aunt the following year in which she conveyed news of affairs at South Carolina College, accompanied by a sarcastic remark: "I will presume you so much attached to Carolina as to take some interest in its College although it was not fit for you to be educated in when you left home."[27] Equally patriotic but less enamored of the educational opportunities afforded by southern schools was Mary Munce of Jefferson County, Mississippi. In a letter to General John A. Quitman, who had offered to fund her son's education, Mrs. Munce expressed a preference for the "world-renowned . . . scholastic institutions" of Boston and Cambridge. "I am a Southerner, heart and soul, like yourself," she added, "but experience and observation, have taught me to distrust the permanency, and disapprove the course, of our Southern schools."[28]

In light of such views, it is not surprising that half of the elite slaveholders whose educational background could be determined received their college train-

26. *The Secret Eye,* ed. Burr, 198; Mary C. Munce to John A. Quitman, August 19, 1856, in John A. Quitman and Family Papers, MDAH; Jane L. Pringle to Julius Pringle, December 5, [1856], April 1 [1860], Pringle Family Correspondence, in R. F. W. Allston Papers, SCHS.

27. William H. Barnwell to James B. Heyward, January 15, 183[4], and Mary Barnwell Smith to James B. Heyward, February 27, 1835, both in Heyward and Ferguson Family Papers, SHC.

28. Mary C. Munce to John A. Quitman, August 19, 1856, in John A. Quitman and Family Papers, MDAH.

ing in the North, nearly 30 percent of them at the prestigious Ivy League triumvirate of Harvard, Yale, or Princeton (see Table 3). A handful received their training in Europe, chiefly at Cambridge. For those who elected to remain in the South, South Carolina College and the state universities of Virginia, North Carolina, and Georgia proved to be the most attractive choices. But even in politically conscious South Carolina, twice as many of the Low Country aristocrats attended school in the Northeast as matriculated at South Carolina College.

Whether from Natchez, Charleston, or Savannah, there was a pronounced educational pipeline to the Northeast. Among those from the Natchez District who received their university training in that region were Adam L. Bingaman and Ayres P. Merrill, both of whom graduated from Harvard; Pennsylvania natives Stephen Duncan and John C. Jenkins, who earned medical degrees from Dickinson College and the University of Pennsylvania, respectively; William J. Minor, who also attended Pennsylvania; and brothers Lemuel P. and William G. Conner, both of whom received their college education at Yale. If the list is extended to include children of the Natchez elite, the number becomes even more imposing. For example, Minor's son John graduated from Princeton, as did Frederick H. Quitman, the eldest son of Governor John A. Quitman. One of Duncan's sons, Henry P., was a student at Yale during the same time the Conner brothers were in residence.[29]

Despite the proximity of long-established public institutions of higher learning in their respective states, a number of elite slaveholders along the South Carolina-Georgia rice coast also journeyed to the Northeast to complete their education. Thus, twenty of the thirty-six Carolina Low Country aristocrats whose educational background could be determined received at least part of their university training either in New England or at the United States Military Academy at West Point. Four others, Plowden C. J. Weston and three of the Blakes, received a classical education at Cambridge University in England, and

29. *Goodspeed's*, I, 676 (Duncan, Bingaman), 1020 (Jenkins), II, 430 (Merrill); Mark A. Keller, "Horse Racing Madness in the Old South—The Sporting Epistles of William J. Minor of Natchez (1837–1860)," *JMH* 47 (August 1985): 166–67; May, *John A. Quitman*, 135, 216, 271; Denison Olmsted to C. P. Leverich, October 3, 1842, and Stephen Duncan to Leverich, December 29, 1843, both in Charles P. Leverich papers, MDAH (Conner and H. P. Duncan). The letter from Duncan to Leverich reveals that one of the Conners was involved in a drunken indiscretion at Yale during the fall of 1843.

TABLE 3 · COLLEGE PREFERENCE

State	Harvard	Yale	Princeton	Other Northern Colleges	S.C. College	UNC	UVA	Other Southern Colleges	European Institutions	Total
Ala.					2	2	1	1		6
Ga.	1	2	2	2				3	1	11
La. (*Cotton*)	1	1		3				3		8
La. (*Sugar*)				1			1	1	1	4
Miss. (*Natchez*)	2	2		3			2	2	1	12
Miss. (*Outside Natchez*)						1				1
N.C.	1	1		1		3				6
S.C. (*Up Country*)	1	2	4	3	11		3	3		27
S.C. (*Low Country*)	4	2	5	9	10			1	5	36
Tenn.								1		1
Tex.								1		1
Va.	2		1				1	1	1	6
TOTALS	12	10	12	22	23	6	8	17	9	119

SUMMARY: Based on 35.2 percent of the planter cohort, weighted heavily toward S.C. North totaled 56; South totaled 54; European, 9. The Ivy League (Harvard, Yale, Princeton) totaled 34, or 28.6 percent.

Joshua John Ward apparently attended the University of Edinburgh after graduating from South Carolina College at the age of fourteen.[30] A similar pattern is
discernible in Georgia, where such rice grandees as James Hamilton Couper,
Charles William Rogers, and Joseph L. McAllister enjoyed the benefits of a
New England education. In addition, Savannah lawyer-planter George Welsh-
man Owens was schooled at Harrow and graduated from Cambridge. Yet another Georgian, William B. Hodgson, who became the largest slaveholder in
the state by virtue of his marriage, at age forty-two, into the wealthy Telfair
family, received two honorary degrees from Princeton following a distinguished
career as an oriental scholar.[31]

Southern appreciation for the apparently superior quality of northern educational facilities extended also to schools below the college level. Scores of young
boys and girls from elite planter families were sent northward, either to prepare
for admission to the demanding Ivy League schools, as was frequently the case
with males, or, for the girls, to bring their educational experience to a salutary
conclusion. For example, James C. Johnston, the son of a United States senator
from North Carolina, prepared for his admission to Princeton by attending
school first on Long Island and then at the Woodbury School in New Jersey.
Similarly, after preliminary study in Vicksburg, the younger brothers of Benjamin Roach, Jr., were sent to the College of St. James in Hagerstown, Maryland,
where they remained for two years before they, too, entered Princeton in the
summer of 1859.[32]

Not infrequently, southern students discovered that their initial training
back home had not prepared them adequately for the rigorous course of studies
to which they were exposed in elite northern colleges. Thus, when Judge
Thomas Butler traveled to Connecticut in 1835 to enroll his two eldest sons in
Yale, he decided, upon reflection, that one was not nearly as advanced as the

---

30. *South Carolina Genealogies,* I, 92–96; Rogers, *History of Georgetown County,* 310–11. The
Blakes referred to are Joseph (1769–1865), who apparently never left England, his son Walter (1804–
1871), and his nephew Daniel (1803–1873).

31. James E. Bagwell, "James Hamilton Couper, Georgia Rice Planter" (Ph.D. diss., University
of Southern Mississippi, 1978), 41; Myers, ed., *The Children of Pride,* 1551 (Hodgson), 1601 (McAllister), 1638 (Owens), 1662 (Rogers); William B. Hodgson to President John Tyler, July 3, 1842, in
Telfair Family Papers, GHS.

32. *Dictionary of North Carolina Biography,* ed. Powell, III, 302–304; various receipts, 1856–59, in
Benjamin Roach Family Papers, CAH.

other, and he sent him instead to Philadelphia to be tutored in the classical languages before seeking admission to the sophomore class the following year. The other son, Richard E., was admitted to that class, though, as Professor Benjamin Silliman advised his father, "he will be expected to review his algebra & the four first books of Euclid & on them he may be examined again."[33] Fourteen years later, another son, Robert, was found to be deficient in both Greek and algebra when he, too, sought admission to Yale. Accordingly, he engaged a private tutor in New Haven and shortly thereafter reported enthusiastically that he had "learned more since I have been under Him than I did in the last two years."[34] Presumably, Robert soon became the third of the Butler boys to matriculate at Yale.

Philadelphia proved to be an especially popular educational mecca for southern youth, both male and female. Among those who sent their sons and daughters to that city for their schooling were the Lloyds of Maryland, the Cheves, Pickens, and Singleton families of South Carolina, and the Nutts and Archers of Mississippi. Although he apparently never attended college, Edward Lloyd VI, who was destined to become the largest slaveholder in Maryland, took writing and fencing lessons and occasionally attended lectures on natural philosophy during a sojourn in Philadelphia at the age of nineteen.[35] It is not surprising that Langdon Cheves, Sr., should have chosen a Philadelphia school to prepare his sons for college, for he had earlier resided in that city while serving as president of the Second United States Bank. Another South Carolinian, Richard Singleton, sent his three daughters to Madame Greland's fashionable school in Philadelphia, and some years later, yet another prominent South Carolinian, Francis W. Pickens, took time from his busy political schedule to enroll his "little daughter & her cousin in school" in the same city.[36] Like the senior

33. Thomas Butler to wife Ann (Nancy), August 2, 1835, Benjamin Silliman to Thomas Butler, August 8, 1835 (quotation), Stephen Duncan to Thomas Butler, September 24, 1835, in Thomas Butler and Family Papers, LSU.

34. Robert O. Butler to mother Ann, October 7, 23, November 14 (quotation), 1849, *ibid.*

35. Edward Lloyd [VI] to "My dear Father," November 7, 1817, in Lloyd Family Papers (microfilm), MHS.

36. Langdon Cheves, [Sr.], to A. Bolmar, October 19, 1829, in Langdon Cheves Papers, SCL; Nicholes, *Historical Sketches of Sumter County,* 363, 366; Francis W. Pickens to John L. Manning, December 12, 1856, in Williams-Chesnut-Manning Family Papers, SCL.

Cheves, Haller Nutt also had a previous Philadelphia connection, his father having studied medicine there under the celebrated Dr. Benjamin Rush. In any event, daughters Mary and Carrie were attending a girls' school in Philadelphia in 1860, and shortly after the war, their younger brother Prentiss spent several years at Ury House, a "Select Boarding School for Boys" in the same city, before completing his education at the University of Virginia.[37]

Shortly before Christmas in 1855, another Mississippian, Richard T. Archer of Port Gibson, traveled to Philadelphia to place his two teen-aged daughters in the same school that his wife had attended more than two decades before. Although reluctant to leave his girls so far from home and somewhat disturbed by the expense, estimated at $1,600 for the two, he departed with the hope that the experience might "be profitable to our children." It was not long, however, before Archer became disenchanted with the proprietor of the school, Mrs. J. S. H. Gardell. When the elder daughter became ill and Mrs. Gardell evinced little solicitude for her well-being, Archer withdrew her from the school but acceded to the request of his other daughter to remain for the balance of the year. "Mrs. G. is not now the same in principle or feeling . . . that she was when you were with her," complained Archer to his wife. Not having any children of their own, he continued, she "knows nothing of a Mothers tenderness, and is really a petrification of The School Teacher." As the year progressed, Archer's disenchantment with Gardell gradually turned to rage. Charging that she was neither "truthful or honest," Archer vowed in late September that nothing would induce him "to allow her authority again over a child of [his]." Finally, less than a week later, Archer placed both girls in a Maryland school after launching a parting salvo at the unfortunate Mrs. Gardell. Angered by her demand for additional money, he assailed her as an "utterly dishonest, lying . . . inebriate," whose "principal object" was "to swindle all she can."[38]

Another elite parent who experienced great difficulty locating a suitable

37. Grade reports for Mary and Carrie Nutt, 1860, in Haller Nutt Papers, DU; Mary Ella Nutt to "My dear Pa," April 29, 1860, Jane Crawford to Julia Nutt, October 20, 1866, printed advertisement for Ury House (quotation), in Nutt Family Collection, MDAH; Hawks, "Julia A. Nutt of Longwood," 298.

38. Richard T. Archer to "My dear Wife," December 15, 18 (first quotation), 21, 1855, February 6, 10 (second quotation), September 28 (third quotation), October 3 (fourth quotation), 1856, and Archer to "My Beloved Daughters," October 5, 1856, in Richard Thompson Archer Family Papers, CAH.

school for her children in the Northeast—this time in New York—was Jane Pringle. Apparently all three of her boys began their secondary schooling at the Sing Sing Military Academy in Mrs. Pringle's native state of New York. In the fall of 1856, however, the eldest son, Julius, was sent to Switzerland to continue his education. In letters to her distant son, Pringle soon began to criticize the school in which her younger sons were still enrolled. Thus, after receiving a bill for $600, she remarked that the results were not proportional to the cost. Her youngest son, Lynch, she observed dryly, "spells like a Hottentot and writes like an Egyptian." As time passed, her displeasure increased. Thankful that Julius was now in a proper educational environment, she lamented that instruction in French, music, and German were "as much out of the question" in this country "as if we had the boys at school in the Sandwich islands."[39]

By this time, Pringle was thoroughly incensed by the apparent deficiencies in her younger children's education. Consequently, near the end of her annual summer excursion to the Northeast, she set about to find a quality French school for the boys. The first stop was Lesprincipis, which she described as "a dirty place." Even worse, they "saw a mulatto among the boys," after which the elder boy, Poinsett, flatly refused to consider the school even though the proprietor "promised to send the nigger away." Finally, Pringle settled upon a school run by Monsieur Charlier despite an exorbitant tuition of $400 for six months, to say nothing of an additional $100 for extras. At first, all seemed to go well. In mid-October, Poinsett wrote enthusiastically, "We are now fairly settled at Charlier's, and piling into french and Spanish like a perfect house a fire." His mother, however, was rapidly developing serious misgivings about the schoolmaster. Never had she encountered "a more frivolously tyrannical man than Charlier," she thundered. It was doubtless a good school, but it was "kept by the most odious of human beings." Fearing that Charlier's spartan regimen was too severe for the boys, Pringle took them away "after being only 3 weeks with him" at a cost of $350.[40] The following year, they were sent to Europe to join their elder brother at Sillig's school in Vevay, Switzerland.

There were objections to northern schools quite apart from the problems

39. Jane L. Pringle to son Julius, November 9, 1856, January 13 (first quotation), July 12 (second quotation), October 12, [1857], Pringle Family Correspondence, in R. F. W. Allston Papers, SCHS.

40. Jane L. Pringle to son Julius, September 13, 27, October 12, 27, [1857], Poinsett to Julius, October 11, 1857, *ibid.*

encountered by Archer and the Pringles. As sectional animosity intensified in the late 1840s and 1850s, some wealthy slaveholders began to evince concern about the baneful political influences to which their children might be exposed in the free states. Thus, when asked in 1852 about the quality of an Episcopal girls' school in New York to which an acquaintance was considering sending his daughters, John A. Selden, proprietor of the famous Westover plantation near Richmond, responded that academically it was probably "as good a school as there is in the country." He added, however, that he had refrained from sending his own daughters there because he believed "all of these northern Schools are more or less tinctured with abolitionism." Three years earlier, as the nation moved toward its first serious sectional crisis, John A. Quitman had expressed similar anxiety about the political atmosphere at Princeton, where his son was a student. The latter hastened to reassure his worried father that most of his associates at the college were Mississippians, "so that you need not fear that Northern prejudices can possibly be inculcated into my mind through association." Indeed, declared young Quitman, "I am far more deeply grounded in Southern principles & prejudices now than when I left home."[41]

Perhaps this fear of political contamination in the Northeast explains why so many South Carolinians sent their sons to Europe for their advanced education. Or perhaps it was because many of the fathers had received their schooling there. Whatever the reason, in addition to Jane Pringle's boys, the sons of such prominent Low Country aristocrats as Robert Barnwell Rhett, William Bull Pringle, and John Harleston Read II also studied either in England or on the Continent. Read sent his sons to Switzerland, perhaps to the same school attended by the Pringles. Four other members of the Pringle family of Georgetown District, the sons of William B. Pringle and first cousins of the boys who had studied in Switzerland, were also schooled in Europe, three of them in England in the early 1840s and the other in Dijon, France, in 1858.[42] Jane Pringle sent her sons to the Continent for both academic and moral reasons. "Remember these are the most important years of your life in the formation of your mind habits and character," she admonished her eldest son during his first year at

41. John A. Selden to Richard Baylor, August 7, 1852, in Baylor Family Papers, VHS; F. Henry Quitman to John A. Quitman, November 25, 1849, in John A. Quitman and Family Papers, MDAH.

42. Rogers, *History of Georgetown County*, 274, 310–11; Jane L. Pringle to son Julius, June 21, [1858], Pringle Family Correspondence, in R. F. W. Allston Papers, SCHS.

Vevay. "It was for that reason," she continued, that "I so gladly seized the occasion for you to leave America, where the temptations are so much greater, and the habits so much less simple than where you are." While Julius Pringle was immersing himself in the study of the romance languages, one of the younger sons of Barnwell Rhett was on the Continent, first at Leipzig and later in Paris, for quite a different purpose—that of honing his mercantile skills so that he could return to America and "make money."[43] Unfortunately for young Rhett, that dream never materialized, for he returned home not to enter business but to serve his new country as a lieutenant in the Confederate Army, only to suffer a mortal wound during the Peninsular Campaign of 1862.[44]

South Carolinians were not the only wealthy slaveholders who looked to Europe for the education of their youth. Not surprisingly, some Louisiana sugar planters, attracted by ties of language and ethnicity, sent their sons to France. To cite but one example, one of the Mathers, a family related by marriage to the Bringiers, was studying at the Ecole Centrale des Arts et Manufactures in Paris in the early 1840s. At least three of the Natchez nabobs—Ayres Merrill, Josiah Winchester, and Gabriel B. Shields—also sent their sons to the Continent, though their decision was clearly influenced by the war and, in Merrill's case, by his tenure as minister to Belgium during President Ulysses S. Grant's first term. Thus, two of Merrill's sons received their collegiate education in Brussels after the war.[45] Winchester's two eldest sons were dispatched to Europe in November, 1864, one to Tours and the other eventually to Aberdeen, Scotland. As their father later explained, they went for the specific "benefit of the schools which had been interrupted in this country by reason of the civil war." Frank Winchester, Josiah's eldest son, reported from Tours in October, 1865, that there were about twenty boys from Mississippi there, including three sons of Gabriel Shields. As early as August, 1866, Josiah sought to bring his youngest son home so that he might be "more immediately under my surveil-

43. Jane Pringle to Julius, April 1, [1857], Pringle Family Correspondence, in R. F. W. Allston Papers, SCHS; Robert W. Rhett to R. B. Rhett, Sr., July 1, 1858, November 10, 1859, in Robert Barnwell Rhett, Sr., Papers, SCHS.

44. Rhett Genealogy Notes #2, in Rhett Family Papers, SCHS.

45. Notebook of A. Mather, April 9, 1843, in Benjamin Tureaud Papers, LSU; *Goodspeed's*, II, 430–32.

lance," but it was not until early 1868 that George Winchester finally completed his studies at Aberdeen and sailed for New York.[46]

Notwithstanding the evidence presented in the preceding pages, the majority of elite planters and their families never left the South for their education. But even at home they were exposed to external influences, beginning in early youth through northern or European tutors and governesses. The presence of these alien teachers in planter homes throughout the South is amply documented in the census returns. In the Natchez area, for example, such functionaries were present in the households of Edwin R. Bennett, John N. Helm, George F. Hunt, and John P. Walworth during the last decade of the antebellum period.[47] Across the river in Louisiana, some years before, a cousin of Judge Thomas Butler discussed the merits of two prospective northern tutors, one recommended by Professor Silliman of Yale and the other by a West Point acquaintance. He preferred the latter, a resident of Boston who had received his education in Canada, "on account of his knowledge of French" and noted that he would "come for $400 per annum and his expenses out." The like salary was offered by another Louisianian, William T. Palfrey, when he engaged the services of a teacher for his family in 1848.[48]

Some planters went to extraordinary lengths to procure able instructors for their young progeny. Plowden C. J. Weston was tutored at home by the Reverend Alexander Glennie, who was brought over from England in 1828 solely for that purpose. Four years later, when the Westons went abroad for an extended period, Glennie became the rector of All Saints Episcopal Church in Georgetown District, South Carolina, a position he occupied until the Civil War. Barnwell Rhett also employed a European tutor for his children. Shortly before the war, Lucie Marmier of Burgundy, France, who had previously taught Rhett's children by his first wife, agreed to instruct Rhett's young son Herbert and his granddaughter Lilly for a salary of $600 per year. Before leaving France,

46. Frank Winchester to Josiah Winchester, November 24, 1864, October 5, 1865, August 9, 1866 (quotations), Alex. Anderson to Josiah, January 24, 1868, in Winchester Family Papers, CAH; Journal of Ellen Shields, photocopy in possession of Mrs. Rawdon Blankenstein, Natchez, Mississippi.

47. MS Census, 1850 (Schedule 1), Adams County, Mississippi (Helm, Walworth); MS Census, 1860 (Schedule 1), Adams (Bennett) and Jefferson (Hunt) Counties, Mississippi.

48. Edward G. W. Butler to Thomas Butler, September 17, 1839, in Thomas Butler and Family Papers, LSU; William T. Palfrey Plantation Journal, January 3, 1848, in Palfrey Family Papers, LSU.

however, she implored Rhett to be her "interpreter" toward his second wife. "Please give her my regard and love," she continued, "and make her *promise* that she will not be *too sad* when I will be obliged to punish Herbert."[49] Mademoiselle Marmier was attempting to avert the friction that sometimes marred the relationship between mother and teacher in these situations. Such was the case when twenty-year-old Ruth Hastings of Troy, New York, arrived in Society Hill, South Carolina, in 1852 to tutor the young daughters of John N. Williams. Miss Hastings soon discovered that the mistress of the household was an exceedingly domineering woman who not only tyrannized the slaves and their own adult daughter but also made it difficult for the young tutor to discipline her often unruly pupils. Under these circumstances, it is not surprising that Hastings lasted only a year in her position.[50]

Another South Carolinian who turned to northern and European teachers for the initial instruction of his children was Robert F. W. Allston. During an excursion to Saratoga and Newport in the summer of 1838, Allston engaged the Reverend C. B. Thummel, a German by birth and education but for the past decade a teacher in New York State, to come to Georgetown District and preside over a parish school of twelve to fifteen pupils of both sexes, of which his son Benjamin was one. Thummel was to offer instruction in English grammar, French, the classical languages, and the fine arts, for which he was to receive the handsome salary of $2,000. Thummel agreed to the proposition but encountered an inhospitable reception and apparently did not remain long at his new post.[51] A decade and a half later, the Allstons were relying upon an English governess to tutor their two young daughters, aged eleven and eight. She had already been employed by the Allstons for two years at a stipend of $500 per annum when, in the summer of 1853, the family left for a six-month sojourn in the North and decided to "give the girls a holiday." Accordingly, the governess,

49. Rogers, *History of Georgetown County,* 258; Lucie Marmier to R. B. Rhett, [ca. 1859–60], in Robert Barnwell Rhett, Sr., Papers, SCHS; MS Census, 1860 (Schedule 1), City of Charleston, Ward 6.

50. Christopher J. Gill, "A Year of Residence in the Household of a South Carolina Planter: Teacher, Daughters, Mistress, and Slaves," *South Carolina Historical Magazine* 97 (October 1996): 297–300, 303, 306–307.

51. Robert F. W. Allston to Reverend C. B. Thummel, September 12, 1838, Thummel to Allston, September 18, 1838, Joshua J. Ward to Allston, September 28, 1838, Allston to Adele Petigru Allston, December 15, 1838, in Easterby, ed., *South Carolina Rice Plantation,* 80–83, 86.

Miss Ayme, was engaged to another family in the district during the interim, with the understanding that she would return to the Allstons the following winter. As Mrs. Allston remarked to a friend, Miss Ayme taught "all the branches of an english education": music, drawing, the romance languages, and "the rudiments of latin." The Allstons chose her, explained her employer, because of "her ability to teach correctly what she pretends to teach."[52]

Although the girls who received their first exposure to education through home tutors were never accorded the privilege of attending college with their male counterparts, their further intellectual development was not neglected. After all, as they would have primary responsibility for the early training of their own future sons and daughters, it was imperative that they be exposed to the broadest possible spectrum of knowledge and culture. As has been noted earlier, some were sent to finishing schools in the Northeast, but a larger number continued their education at boarding schools in nearby cities. As Jane Turner Censer has observed, education for planter women was much more than simply "ornamental." Academic subjects such as writing, geography, history, literature, and the romance languages—above all, French—were just as important as the arts in preparing these women for their adult responsibilities.[53]

Accordingly, the daughters of wealthy slaveholders could be found in exclusive girls' schools throughout the South, from Charleston to New Orleans and from Raleigh, North Carolina, to Lexington, Kentucky. Thus, following their home schooling, the Allston girls were sent to Madame R. Acelie Togno's celebrated French boarding school on Meeting Street in Charleston. There, at a cost of $250 per session, they received instruction in French in the following subjects: English, French, history, music, arithmetic, and diction. Among their classmates were the two young daughters of Langdon Cheves, Jr., who were enrolled in the school in January, 1856. Despite their youth, the Cheves girls

---

52. Adele Petigru Allston to Mrs. R. Hamilton, May 19, 1853, *ibid.*, 115.

53. Censer, *North Carolina Planters and Their Children*, 45–46; Clinton, *The Plantation Mistress*, 130–32; Anya Jabour, "'Grown Girls, Highly Cultivated': Female Education in an Antebellum Southern Family," *JSH* 64 (February, 1998): 28, 63. In her recent article, Jabour has argued that there was a significant change in southern female education in the 1830s from paternal to maternal supervision and from classical academic subjects to preparation for courtship, marriage, and domesticity. The author has found little evidence to support this generalization. Formal training in the liberal and fine arts was designed not only to promote their intellectual development but also to prepare them for their future role in society, and there is no indication that this changed over time.

adjusted rapidly to their new environment and, by the third day, seemed "quite cheerful" and were sufficiently at ease to enter their principal's room and bid her an affectionate "good night." Terming herself a member of "the old school," Madame Togno stressed the importance of maintaining "a free & open Intercourse" with the parents of her pupils.[54]

There were female seminaries in many other southern cities as well. In 1851, four years after her father's death, Mary Butler, the youngest daughter of Judge Thomas Butler, was attending a French school in New Orleans directed by Madame Desravaux. Maria Chotard, the first wife of Levin Marshall, was apparently also schooled at a French house in the Crescent City.[55] Ella Ballard, the eldest daughter of wealthy cotton planter and former slavetrader Rice C. Ballard, began her formal education at the age of nine at a Catholic female seminary in Nazareth, Kentucky. Shortly after her arrival, she informed her father that she was especially fond of music and arithmetic, but dancing classes were clearly her favorite. Ella later attended Franklin Female Institute, and she completed her education in Lexington. Several years after the war, the daughter of Mississippi planter George W. Humphreys also attended the school at Nazareth. After a brief visit to the institution, which then boarded three hundred girls, a cousin registered considerable dissatisfaction with the conditions he observed there. "I don't like the place a bit," he reported. "There are one hundred and eighty beds in one room[.] they are not a foot apart, and the girls say they can scarcely breathe in there sometimes." He concluded that study was virtually impossible in such crowded quarters.[56]

Two prominent North Carolina slaveholders, Paul Cameron and Lewis Thompson, sent their daughters to St. Mary's School in Raleigh shortly before the outbreak of the Civil War. The Cameron girls were day students, residing with their uncle, George W. Mordecai and his family. Just the day before the

---

54. Adele Petigru Allston to Benjamin Allston, January 1, 1857, in Easterby, ed., *South Carolina Rice Plantation*, 135; Charles Joyner, Introduction to Elizabeth Allston Pringle (Patience Pennington), *A Woman Rice Planter* (1913; rpr. Columbia, 1992), xvii–xviii; R. Acelie Togno to Langdon Cheves, Jr., January 21, 1856, in Langdon Cheves, Jr., Papers, SCHS.

55. Bill from Maison d'Education pour les Demoiselles, December 31, 1851, in Thomas Butler and Family Papers, LSU; Sarah F. Chotard to Maria Chotard, October 28, 1819, in Marshall Papers, LSU.

56. Ella Ballard to Rice C. Ballard, November 6, [1850?], March 25, 1857, April 2, 1859, Louise C. Ballard to Rice C. Ballard, April 1, 1859, in Rice Carter Ballard Papers, SHC; Leon Humphreys to "Dear Sister," December 29, 1869, in George Wilson Humphreys and Family Papers, MDAH.

firing on Fort Sumter, eight-year-old Pauline Cameron wrote that she and her sister had recently commenced the study of geography. She was pleased that the schoolmaster, Dr. Smedes, had sought to motivate his students by depositing "a great pile" of geography books in the schoolroom with instructions that the girls should study them in the evenings when not otherwise occupied. "I was quite glad," remarked little Pauline, "because I dont think that *I am quite graduated* in that line of education."[57] The year before, Thompson's two daughters, aged fourteen and twelve, had enrolled as boarders at St. Mary's following a period of thorough home schooling. They were soon studying a variety of subjects, including arithmetic, reading, writing, drawing, rhetoric, French, and music. During their second year, the younger sister, Pattie, began taking Latin and pronounced it "perfectly splendid . . . much better than French." As North Carolina moved toward secession in the spring of 1861, the Thompson girls were caught up in the aura of excitement that pervaded the capital city. In July, the older girl reported that her favorite teacher had been dismissed because of her suspected pro-northern sympathies. "I do think it is so silly," she complained to her father. Three months later, her sister wrote that she had recently attended a benefit concert for the soldiers and had subsequently visited a nearby military camp, where she had contracted the measles. Clearly, the war was beginning to impinge upon the educational progress of the young Thompson siblings.[58]

The young women in these nineteenth-century planter families displayed a zeal for learning and an intellectual inquisitiveness that seems sadly lacking in the youth of the present generation. In missives to their fathers and brothers, they eagerly recounted their most recent excursions into the realms of history, literature, and philosophy. Thus, in 1858, sixteen-year-old Elise Rhett informed her father that she was reading "aloud in French every day" and anxiously awaiting the arrival of "Thiers' history." Several years before, her sister Mary, then about the same age, noted that she had been reading "Prescott's 'Ferdinand and Isabella,'" which she pronounced "as delightful as his other works" and, in addition, had been studying "Jouffroy's Introduction to Ethics," which she termed "a beautiful work." No less impressive were the reading habits of young Rose

57. Pauline Cameron to "My darling mother," April 11, 1861, in Cameron Family Papers, SHC.

58. Mary Thompson to Lewis Thompson, July 25, 1860, July 3, 1861 (second quotation), Pattie Thompson to brother Thomas Thompson, April 11 (first quotation), 20, October 4, 1861, in Lewis Thompson papers, SHC.

Quitman, who confided to her brother that she was "reading Plutarch" and took delight in comparing the exploits of the hero Theseus with those of "all of our *worthy* young acquaintances," much to the disadvantage of the latter. So immersed in classical literature was the teenaged Rose that she could not refrain from recounting the simple nocturnal theft of five bushels of corn and a few turkeys in these sophisticated terms: "so deep was every one in the light embrace of Morpheus—that their [the thieves'] proceedings were not discovered, untill [*sic*] the bright face of Apollo again dispersed light over the western hemisphere."[59]

During the Civil War, interest shifted from the classics to the romantic novels of Sir Walter Scott as both adults and children struggled to cope with the vicissitudes of war. In the fall of 1861, when her native Natchez was still far removed from the seat of war, twelve-year-old Louisa Winchester remarked to her brother that she was reading more than she ever had before. "Please send me some books," she pleaded, "and ask ma to send me the Heart of Midlothian." Even more enamored of Scott was Jane G. Conner, the fourteen-year-old daughter of another Natchezian, Lemuel P. Conner. In September, 1864, more than a month before her school reconvened, she announced to her absent father that, after finishing *Waverly*, she had read *Ivanhoe* to her mother. "I liked it very much," she enthused. "We are now reading 'Rob Roy,' and shall read the 'Talisman' next."[60] Whatever they read, these young daughters of elite slaveholders were an impressive lot. It is little wonder that J. Johnston Pettigrew, himself one of the intellectual giants of the Old South, should describe one of the daughters of North Carolina planter Thomas P. Devereux as not only "quite a belle" but also as a "very bright" young lady who seemed "better educated than half the men one meets."[61]

For the male members of planter families who attended distant schools and colleges, there was no dearth of advice. The message was clear and virtually universal. They were expected to cultivate habits of industry, order, persever-

59. Elise Rhett to R. B. Rhett, March 21, [1858], and Mary B. Rhett to R. B. Rhett, December 20, 1851, both in Robert Barnwell Rhett, Sr., Papers, SCHS; Rose Quitman to F. H. Quitman, December 29, May 3, 1857, in John A. Quitman and Family Papers, MDAH.

60. Louisa Winchester to brother Frank, November 30, 1861, in Winchester Family Papers, CAH; Jane G. Conner to "My dearest Father," September 12, 1864, in Lemuel P. Conner and Family Papers, LSU.

61. J. Johnston Pettigrew to James C. Johnston, June 20, 1860, in Hayes Collection, SHC.

ance, frugality, and temperance, which, in turn, would produce achievement and success. Fathers consistently enjoined their sons to improve their minds, hone their communication skills, and excel in all that they undertook. Addressing his son, a student at Princeton in the late 1790s (where, incidentally, the tuition and room charge was $18.66 a session), Samuel Johnston of North Carolina stressed the importance of skillful writing. He urged his son to correspond more frequently, so that he might "acquire a ready and correct method of communicating [his] sentiments in easy and familiar language, on every subject, whether of business, literature, or amusement." A half-century later, John A. Quitman was pleased to learn that his son, also a student at Princeton, had become absorbed in his studies. "It is the spirit with which we should take up every pursuit of life," asserted Quitman. Counseling his son to "become critically accurate in every thing" he took up, he urged him to maintain a daily journal in which he would record "reflections upon [his] studies, and whatever else may appear to [him] worthy of record." In like manner, fellow Mississippian Richard T. Archer emphasized to his son and nephew at the University of Virginia the importance of "excelling." Reminding them that they enjoyed certain inherent advantages by virtue of birth and fortune, Archer admonished them to be studious and diligent and to "always bear in mind the objects of education, and the importance of making good use of [their] time."[62]

The quintessential patriarch, Nathaniel Heyward of South Carolina, closely monitored the progress of his grandson, James B. Heyward, after the latter enrolled at Harvard in 1834. A man notable for the brevity and succinctness of his letters as well as for his fabulous wealth, Nathaniel stated explicitly at the outset the expectations he entertained for his grandson: "I wish to see you return to Ca. a practical scholar, a gentleman, and not a 'book-worm.'" During the next four years, the elder Heyward offered additional advice, occasionally punctuated by a rebuke. When James appeared dazzled by the beauty and intellect of the local belles, his grandfather cautioned him to be wary, for "the Ladies of Boston have very sweet mouths for Southerners." More serious was the question of finances, an issue that engendered conflict between many fathers and their sons

---

62. Samuel Johnston to James C. Johnston, May 26, 1798, and tuition receipt, May 11, 1799, both *ibid.*; John A. Quitman to Frederick Henry Quitman, April 26, 1849, in John A. Quitman Papers, MDAH; Richard T. Archer to Edward S. Archer, January 28, February 27, 1855, in Richard Thompson Archer Family Papers, CAH.

who were away at college. When young Heyward's initial quarterly allowance of $200 proved inadequate, Nathaniel reluctantly increased the amount to $250 while, at the same time, reprimanding his grandson for his extravagance. Observing that "the practice of debt will make it familiar," he admonished the youthful student: avoid debt by embracing "steady habits, with a resolution to deny yourself luxuries, until you have provided resources by professional wit."[63] Clearly, Nathaniel was attempting to encourage his grandson to adopt the same formula that had led to his own success.

Some planter wives were as vocal as their husbands in transmitting advice to their absent sons and in influencing the course of their education. Thus, shortly after the war, the widow of Haller Nutt urged her eleven-year-old son, then in school in Philadelphia, to "study hard so [she] will have it to be proud of." It must be conceded, however, that Julia also had a selfish motive in encouraging her son, for, as she later admitted, she was anxious for her three sons to get their education so that they could "come home & take charge of [her] business." The mother of R. F. W. Allston was instrumental in persuading him to accept an appointment to West Point where he would be exposed to the three D's of "duty, discipline, and diligence"—qualities that would prove especially beneficial in later life.[64]

But it was another South Carolinian, the matriarchal Jane Pringle, who assumed exclusive responsibility for the education of her three sons, first in New York and later in Europe. In addition to the usual moral injunctions against drinking and gambling, Pringle closely supervised the choice of schools, subjects, and even careers for her sons.[65] Shortly after her eldest son, Julius, arrived in Switzerland, she expressed a strong preference for the study of modern rather than classical languages. "It is in your French that I want you pushed," she wrote. "As to Greek I am really very indifferent about your learning it—if you could substitute Spanish I should infinitely prefer it—the one is a matter of vanity the other a means of money making." Occasionally, her advice was more

63. Nathaniel Heyward to James B. Heyward, December 27, 1834, July 23, 1835, February 19, 1838, in Heyward and Ferguson Family Papers, SHC.

64. Julia A. Nutt to "My Darling Son," January 29, April 8, 1866, in Nutt Family Collection, MDAH; Hawks, "Julia A. Nutt of Longwood," 298; Pringle, *A Woman Rice Planter*, 205; Easterby, ed., *South Carolina Rice Plantation*, 13.

65. Jane L. Pringle to son Julius, April 1, September 13, [1857], May 27, [1859], Pringle Family Correspondence, in R. F. W. Allston Papers, SCHS.

general. Thus, after Julius had a slight "quarrel" with his schoolmaster in Berlin, his concerned mother counseled him to keep his mind "well balanced and free from excitement or lectures & studies will fall on arid ground & bring no fruit."[66] But it was the choice of a vocation for her sons that most perplexed Mrs. Pringle. Seemingly obsessed with the need for money, she discouraged her eldest son from becoming a planter and, instead, directed him toward either law or commerce. "I don't know yet which will be the most paying thing for you to do," she wrote in 1857, but she urged him to "study hard so as to command a first place in either." Later, she considered sending her second son, Poinsett, to the Ecole des Mines near Dresden so that he might prepare for a mining career in Sonora and adjacent Mexican provinces, which, she conjectured, would "ultimately be American."[67] In the end, the education of all three Pringle boys was interrupted when they returned to their homeland to serve in the Confederate Army.

Communication between parents and their sons at college in distant environs was by no means unilateral. The boys had much to say about their college experience. In addition to the usual complaints of homesickness and paucity of funds, they wrote of their academic courses and professors, their social life, and, occasionally, of the student misconduct that plagued many campuses in nineteenth-century America. Some discussed their curricula in considerable detail. In the mid-1830s, Benjamin Tureaud of Louisiana was taking courses in moral philosophy, political economy, and general grammar at the University of Virginia, all of them taught by Professor George Tucker. A decade later, Tureaud's cousin and future brother-in-law, Louis A. Bringier, reported that he was enrolled in a more modern course of study, one that included mathematics, modern languages, and physics, the last under the celebrated geologist William Barton Rogers. He had obviously decided to ignore the counsel of his older brother, who had advised him to study medicine, law, music, and ancient languages. Remarking that his sibling had little understanding of the curriculum at Virginia, the younger Bringier explained that both the medical and law schools required five years of study.[68]

---

66. Jane L. Pringle to son Julius, [late November, 1856], February 1, [1860], *ibid.*

67. Jane L. Pringle to son Julius, June 28, [1857] (first quotation), April 1, [1860], Jane Pringle to son Poinsett, February 21, [1860] (second quotation), *ibid.*

68. Notebooks of Benjamin Tureaud, University of Virginia, 1835–36, in Benjamin Tureaud Papers, LSU; Louis A. Bringier to M. S. Bringier, November 8, December 8, 1846, in Louis A. Bringier and Family Papers, LSU. It might be noted that Richard Baylor, one of the largest slaveholders

The eldest son of another Southwestern planter, Alexander K. Farrar, also attended the University of Virginia, but, following his graduation in 1858, he enrolled in the Law Department at Harvard. After consulting with the faculty, he decided to attend "literary Geological anatomical and whatever other lectures I may prefer"—a curious curriculum, indeed, for a law student.[69]

The members of two illustrious slaveholding families, the Johnstons of North Carolina and the Quitmans of Mississippi, had very positive experiences at neighboring Princeton. Shortly after his graduation in 1799, James C. Johnston recalled "with pleasure" his years at "that institution" which he called his "literary mother." He added, "By her, I have been taught the rudiments of literature, the principle of true Friendship and the infinite importance of morality." He particularly enjoyed and benefited from his membership in the Whig Society at Princeton, terming it "an institution which I shall always love, esteem and respect."[70] Fifty years later, Frederick Henry Quitman reported that he was "very much pleased with College life" shortly after his admission to the sophomore class at Princeton. During his first winter in New Jersey, however, young Quitman "found it almost impossible to go to class through the snow & sleet at sunrise every morning." Fortunately, that problem was resolved the following year because morning recitations were not required of juniors. It was in that year, too, that Quitman, son of one of the most notorious fire-eaters in the South, attended a Shakespearean reading by the celebrated actress Fanny Kemble and was captivated by her performance. "I think she is worth more than any corps of actors in the country," he wrote admiringly.[71] During the succeeding year, the political climate at the college began to deteriorate as the students became engrossed in the "all absorbing Slavery Question," and as the time approached for him to leave Princeton in the spring of 1851, Quitman commented wearily, "I have grown exceedingly tired of this place."[72] After more than two years in the Northeast, he was ready to return to his southern roots.

---

in Virginia, had been a classmate of Rogers many years before at William and Mary. William B. Rogers to Richard Baylor, March 17, 1852, in Baylor Family Papers, VHS.

69. George D. Farrar to "My dear Father," December 4, 1858, in Alexander K. Farrar Papers, LSU.

70. James C. Johnston to Edward Watt, January 23, 1800, and Johnston to James Carnahan, January 23, 1800, both in Hayes Collection, SHC.

71. F. Henry Quitman to "My dear Mother," March 15, September 2 (second quotation), October 25 (third quotation), 1849, F. H. Quitman to "My dear Father," April 15, 1849 (first quotation), in John A. Quitman and Family Papers, MDAH.

72. F. Henry Quitman to "My dear Father," March 14, 1850, and F. H. Quitman to "My dear Mother," April 22, 1851, both *ibid.*

There was a social life, as well, in these small nineteenth-century college towns. In the winter of 1831, Daniel Lloyd described a delightful sleigh-ride with "three of the Princeton bells [sic]" and characterized it as "one of the most pleasant evenings" he had spent since he left Maryland. Less fortunate was young Quitman, who, in November, 1849, complained that he had "not visited or spoken to a lady in this place since last June." The like complaint was voiced by a student at the University of North Carolina a decade later. Terming Chapel Hill "this out of the way place," R. W. Anderson informed his cousin, "We have very little going on in our college world likely to interest those abroad." The scene was apparently livelier at the University of Virginia, from which George D. Farrar confided to his uncle that he had "a long story of fun to tell," with this rider: "If you think I can write to you without the women seeing it." If not, concluded Farrar titillatingly, "I must leave the spice out of the pie."[73]

Students of that era were occasionally guilty of both individual and collective acts of misconduct. Paul Cameron, who was destined to become one of the wealthiest slaveholders in North Carolina, was suspended from the University of North Carolina in the 1820s after an altercation with a fellow student. Ironically, one of the principal thoroughfares on the Chapel Hill campus today is named for Cameron, who later served for twenty-six years on the Board of Trustees of that institution. Pierce Butler, the eldest son of Judge Thomas Butler, suffered a like fate in 1833 when he was dismissed from West Point after accumulating the astounding total of 645 demerits by the date of his departure.[74] More typical were incidents involving excessive use of alcohol and sexual transgressions, which were common among college students—both then and now—and which resulted in chastisement rather than expulsion. John Ellis Duncan sought to alleviate his father's concern about such alleged conditions at Yale in the 1820s. "Complainers may say there is dissipation here," he responded heatedly, "but I defy them to point out one single instance where among 320 young men there is less." Perhaps more forthright, if not as polished grammatically, was Stephen D. Farrar after he was admonished by both his father and the su-

73. Daniel Lloyd to Mrs. S. S. Lloyd, January 13, 1831, in Lloyd Family Papers, MHS; F. Henry Quitman to "My dear Father," November 25, 1849, in John A. Quitman and Family Papers, MDAH; R. W. Anderson to Mildred Cameron, July 28, 1860, in Cameron Family Papers, SHC; George D. Farrar to "Dear Dan," December 9, 1857, in Alexander K. Farrar Papers, LSU.

74. *Dictionary of North Carolina Biography*, ed. Powell, I, 312–13; N. S. Harris to Thomas Butler, October 30, 1833, and Butler to Stephen Duncan, November 25, 1833, in Thomas Butler and Family Papers, LSU.

perintendent of the Virginia Military Institute to mend his ways. Conceding that he must stop his "mysbehavior," he promised that he would "change [his] corse and . . . behave [him]self like a man."[75]

Much more serious were the riots and other acts of student violence that sometimes erupted on or near college campuses, though it appears that none of the elite planters or their sons was involved in any of these.[76] In the fall of 1849, F. H. Quitman reported that there was great excitement at Princeton in the wake of a so-called student spree. It seems that while the faculty was in town attending a lecture, the students seized North College, barricaded the building against an apprehended assault by the faculty, broke into the belfry, and began to ring the bell. This incident resulted in a physical confrontation between students and faculty, the outcome of which was not disclosed by Quitman. Even worse was an ugly affair at the University of North Carolina the following year. During a classroom altercation a professor lost his composure and knocked down one of the students with a chair. In retaliation, the students stoned that professor and one of his colleagues, thereby precipitating what Paul Cameron termed "one of the worst riots at Chapel Hill that has ever occurred." Less than a month later, two other students were charged with "entering the Methodist Church some 2 miles from the hill & taking some liberties with the females of the Congregation!" It was some time before the usual tranquility was restored to the campus at Chapel Hill.[77]

What, then, were the fruits of the quality education enjoyed by wealthy

75. John Ellis Duncan to Stephen Duncan, October 31, 1828, in Thomas Butler and Family Papers, LSU; Stephen Duncan Farrar to "My Dear Pa," December 29, 1867, in Alexander K. Farrar Papers, LSU.

76. The most serious offense charged to any of the elite planters in this study was committed not on a college campus but on a plantation near Natchez. According to recently organized Adams County court records, Francis Surget, Sr., destined to become the wealthiest of the Natchez nabobs, was indicted by a grand jury in October, 1808, while he was still a young man of twenty-five, for the alleged rape of spinster Mary Ellis at his plantation the previous July. Apparently the case never went to trial, for there is no further mention of it in the records. See *Territory v. Francis Surget,* October, 1808, Adams County Circuit Court Records, Drawer 24, Old Box 2, New Box 4-90, Adams County Courthouse, Natchez. The author is indebted to Lawrence E. Kight, a former graduate student at the University of Southern Mississippi, for providing him with this information.

77. F. Henry Quitman to "My dear Mother," November 21, 1849, in John A. Quitman and Family Papers, MDAH; Paul C. Cameron to "My dear Father," August 22, September 13, 1850, in Cameron Family Papers, SHC.

slaveholders and their families? Despite their preoccupation with agriculture, a few achieved real distinction in scientific, literary, and intellectual pursuits. Perhaps the most distinguished scholar among all the planters included within this study was William Brown Hodgson of Georgia. After receiving his early schooling in the District of Columbia from the Reverend James Carnahan, later the president of Princeton, young Hodgson pursued the study of oriental languages during sixteen years of residence abroad, principally in North Africa and London. While serving as consul general at Tunis in the early 1840s, Hodgson met Margaret C. Telfair of Savannah during a visit to Paris. After a brief courtship they were married in the summer of 1842, and Hodgson, who had already earned international recognition as an oriental scholar, returned to Georgia to assume direction of the vast Telfair plantation empire.[78] Another Georgian, James Hamilton Couper, achieved distinction not only as one of the foremost scientific agriculturists in the Old South but also as an amateur natural scientist of extended reputation. The nephew of a professor of astronomy at the University of Glasgow and himself a graduate of Yale, Couper made significant contributions in the fields of geology, conchology, herpetology, paleontology, ornithology, and botany. He received his greatest acclaim from the scientific community for his discovery of the entire skeleton of a gigantic prehistoric sloth known as the Megatherium, on which he presented a paper to the Philadelphia Academy of Natural Sciences in 1842.[79]

A quartet of South Carolinians, two men and two women, also deserve recognition for their intellectual achievements. One of the most brilliant Low Country planters was Langdon Cheves, Jr. When Joseph Le Conte engaged Cheves in a spirited debate on the origin of species at Flat Rock, North Carolina, in the summer of 1858, the year before Charles Darwin published his seminal work on the subject, he was confronted, as he later recalled, with an argument that "was exactly what an evolutionist would give today." In short, Cheves had already "cordially embraced the idea of origin of species by transmutation of previous species." During the war, Cheves not only supervised the construction of Battery Wagner on Morris Island, but he also "designed & su-

78. Myers, ed., *The Children of Pride,* 1551; William B. Hodgson to President John Tyler, July 3, 1842, in Telfair Family Papers, GHS.

79. William K. Scarborough, "Science on the Plantation," in Ronald L. Numbers and Todd L. Savitt, eds., *Science and Medicine in the Old South* (Baton Rouge, 1989), 90–92.

perintended the making" of the *Gazelle,* the only hydrogen-gas balloon deployed by the Confederacy during the war.[80] Cheves's sister, Louisa McCord, achieved a considerable reputation as a literary figure, contributing political and social essays to such periodicals as *De Bow's Review* and the *Southern Quarterly Review,* publishing a volume of lyric poetry, and, perhaps "most remarkable of all," composing a five-act verse tragedy entitled *Gaius Gracchus.* Also making her mark as a writer was Elizabeth Allston Pringle, the second daughter of R. F. W. Allston, who, after decades of managing the family's rice plantations in Georgetown District during the postwar era, wrote two books recounting her experiences.[81] Another Georgetown planter, Plowden C. J. Weston, educated at Harrow School and Cambridge University, had two works published in England: the first, a poem entitled "The Pleasures of Music," in 1836, and the second, an edition of early South Carolina historical documents, in 1855. Weston, who has been characterized by William Dusinberre as the "most scholarly of the Georgetown rice planters," was also a member of three state historical societies and had a library valued at $15,000.[82]

Other notable planter intellectuals included James Johnston Pettigrew of North Carolina and Haller Nutt and James A. Ventress of Mississippi. The latter was surely one of the most highly educated members of the planter elite. He reportedly spent nine years in Europe studying at such prestigious institutions as the University of Edinburgh, the *Académie* in Paris, and the University of Berlin. Nutt, son of the famed planter-scientist Dr. Rush Nutt, was proficient in the ancient languages of Greek, Latin, and Hebrew and a frequent contributor to both American and European periodicals. Like his father, he was also a scientific agriculturalist of the first order. Although not himself a large slaveholder, Pettigrew came from one of the most prominent planter families in North Carolina. After graduating first in his class at Chapel Hill in 1847 at the tender age of nine-

80. MS excerpt from autobiography of Joseph Le Conte, MS biographical sketch of Langdon Cheves, Jr., by his nephew Langdon Cheves, 1935[?], Brigadier General Thomas F. Drayton to Captain Langdon Cheves, April 9, 12, 20, May 9, 28, 1862, C. Cevor to Cheves, June 28, September 14, 1862, Mary C. West to "Dear Langdon," May 2, 1896 (quotation), all in Langdon Cheves, Jr., Papers, SCHS.

81. Richard C. Lounsbury, Introduction to McCord, *Selected Writings,* 10–14; Joyner, Introduction to Pringle, *A Woman Rice Planter,* xl–xliv. The other book by Pringle was *Chronicles of Chicora Wood,* published by Scribner's in 1922.

82. Rogers, *History of Georgetown County,* 258–59; Dusinberre, *Them Dark Days,* 410.

teen, he accepted a position with Matthew F. Maury at the recently established Naval Observatory in Washington, D.C. Unfortunately, his life was cut short during the Civil War when, after surviving Pickett's Charge, he was mortally wounded in the Confederate retreat from Gettysburg on July 14, 1863.[83]

Whatever their educational background and intellectual achievements, the vast majority of elite slaveholders lavished the bulk of their energy and attention upon their agricultural operations, a subject that will be discussed in a subsequent chapter. But first, let us examine more closely the status of those "members of the fair sex" who resided in the Big House.

83. *Goodspeed's*, II, 952–56 (Ventress), 519–21 (Nutt); Ebenezer Pettigrew to James C. Johnston, June 24, 1844, June 12, July 19, 1847, in Pettigrew Family Papers, SHC; Ezra J. Warner, *Generals in Gray: Lives of the Confederate Commanders* (Baton Rouge, 1959), 237–38.

3

WIVES, MOTHERS, AND DAUGHTERS

Gender Relations in the Big House

To think of you, & dream of you, are truly my chief occupations; you are never long out of my mind, & almost every thing I do, is done with reference to you.
—ELIZABETH RHETT to R. B. RHETT, February 13, [1851]

You will I know think me very unreasonable, but you will remember it is not a common thing for one *to be as I am three* years in succession, I feel my health—and spirits—have both suffered by it, and I now tell you I *need* rest and quiet.
—ANNE CAMERON to PAUL CAMERON, [May 10, 1850?]

I place my entire business under your management until I return. I know that your judgment and your prudence will do all that can be done under the circumstances.
—PETER W. HAIRSTON to FANNY C. HAIRSTON, May 9, 1861

Mrs. [Levin] Marshall gave me a good laugh by asking me "what was the news in the great world"—I told her my great world was educating children and gathering hen and turkey eggs and the news was very good as well as I could hear.
—MARGARET WINCHESTER, March 16, 1854

Rather than marry Mr. Zanone I would rather have a stone tied around my neck, & be thrown in to the Dead sea. I would like for you to inform your friends . . . I am not so crazy to get married, and am not so fond of the man kind as to even think of a *man* below me in society.
—ELLA BALLARD to her father,
R. C. BALLARD, April 2, 1859

ACCORDING to Catherine Clinton, planter women, in company with all other southern women, rich and poor, black and white, were the victims of oppression. Furthermore, acutely aware of their subordinate status in the patriarchal slave society in which they were entrapped, many of them lashed out at the peculiar institution upon which their world was based. As stewards of the moral conscience of their society, "many southern women viewed bondage as a curse, and some saw slavery as a cruel and unjust system for blacks." To the contrary, Elizabeth Fox-Genovese has argued that slaveholding women did not regard themselves as oppressed, nor did they challenge or oppose the slave system. Rather, the overwhelming majority of them supported slavery "as the necessary price for their own privileged position." Far from sympathizing with the condition of their downtrodden black slaves, concludes Fox-Genovese, these planter women exhibited a virulent form of racism that was "generally uglier and more meanly expressed than that of the men."[1] The evidence in this study of the planter elite strongly supports the latter interpretation. Slaves in the antebellum South were oppressed; the wives and daughters of those who owned them were not.

It is true that planter women lived in a patriarchal society, but in what nineteenth-century society was that not the reality? The militant feminists had not yet unlimbered their heavy artillery, and the women in this study saw no reason to question a system that, in many ways, accorded them preferential treatment. Even after the collapse of the Confederacy, as Drew Faust has noted, elite southern women continued to support the hierarchical and racial order that safeguarded their place in society. In a pair of essays published in *De Bow's Review* in 1852, Louisa McCord contended that both women and Negroes had been consigned to a subordinate position by the laws of nature. To challenge that verity was to oppose "God's eternal law of order." But women need not despair, for their sphere was "higher, purer, nobler" than that of their male counterparts. As McCord phrased it succinctly, "woman was made for *duty*, not for fame."[2] Like McCord, Gertrude Thomas believed that slavery was divinely ordained, though she later exhibited more ambivalent feelings on the subject,

---

1. Clinton, *The Plantation Mistress*, 6, 185, 190 (quotation); Fox-Genovese, *Within the Plantation Household*, 193, 243 (first quotation), 349 (second quotation).

2. Drew Gilpin Faust, *Mothers of Invention: Women of the Slaveholding South in the American Civil War* (Chapel Hill, 1996), 247; McCord, *Selected Writings*, 49, 58 (third quotation), 70, 78 (first quotation), 80 (second quotation).

admitting on one occasion that she could not but think "that to hold men and women in perpetual bondage is wrong." Her reservations about slavery, however, were induced more by what she perceived to be its demoralizing effect on white males than by any humanitarian concern for the Negro. Despite her sometimes equivocal attitude toward slavery, Thomas submitted willingly to the position accorded her gender in southern society. Thus, shortly after her marriage, she thanked God for providing her with "just such a master . . . as suits my woman's nature, for true to my sex, I delight *in looking up* and love to feel my woman's weakness protected by man's superior strength."[3] Did this intelligent, accomplished, college-educated Georgia belle feel oppressed? I think not.

Women were not the only ones who commented about gender roles and alleged gender differences in a patriarchal society. Toward the end of their courtship in 1859, Fanny Caldwell and Peter W. Hairston exchanged letters in which each provided the other with a self-assessment of personal faults and characteristics. The latter then expressed concern for the health of his intended bride. "A woman's nature is different from man's," he wrote. "It is more refined—more sensitive and they have all the petty cares and vexations of life to contend with and their sources of enjoyment depend upon their domestic life."[4] It seems likely that few men or women in the antebellum South would dispute this generalization.

Of course, there were occasional expressions of resentment by planter women against specific abuses and inconveniences that they encountered in their male-dominated world, but as Fox-Genovese has asserted, these rarely extended to a complete "rejection of the system that established their sense of personal identity" within the community. For example, in 1850 Anne Cameron complained bitterly to her husband that she had only received two letters from him in the last four and one-half months, "both of which put together would not make a *good one.*" While conceding that a wife's "first and greatest obligation" was to her husband, she added caustically, "I do not see that a husbands to his wife is any *less.*" Three months later, very depressed and pregnant once

3. *The Secret Eye,* ed. Burr, 122 (second quotation), 236, 239 (first quotation). Gertrude Clanton Thomas graduated from Wesleyan Female College in Macon, Georgia, in 1851, the year before her marriage.

4. Peter W. Hairston to Fanny Caldwell, February, 1858, in Peter Wilson Hairston Papers, SHC.

again, she unburdened herself to her husband. "You know it is not common for me to give way to my feelings, or to express my fears much to *any body*," she wrote, "but *last* year was one of so much *mental* suffering, to say nothing of my bodily ailments, that I have determined to find composure by opening my heart at least to *you*." Nevertheless, she added resignedly, "if you think it wrong for me to express my feelings to you, say so, and I will bury them all in my own bosom." Later in the year, Anne's resentment surfaced once again. Her husband had decreed that she could not visit her father, Judge Thomas Ruffin, during the summer because the ride would be too much for her in her present condition. Instead, she was to remain at home for a time and then spend the latter part of the year in Raleigh with her father-in-law, an arrangement that was communicated to the latter before she was apprised of it. In a letter to her father-in-law, she remarked testily, "It *had* been arranged to suit Mr Cameron's wishes or convenience that I should spend the month of November and part of Dec. in *Raleigh, before* your letters on the subject were received." When Cameron's first male heir was delivered in late November, he was ecstatic; his wife's reaction was not recorded.[5]

Another planter wife who had difficulty adjusting to the subordinate position assigned to women in the patriarchal South was Adele Petigru Allston, the wife of South Carolina governor R. F. W. Allston. Perhaps strength of will was a family characteristic, for her brother was James L. Petigru, the celebrated Charleston lawyer who never relinquished his Unionism despite residing in the most extreme hotbed of secessionism. In any event, when Adele manifested some discontent with her gender role in 1856, her husband responded angrily that her resentment of subordination was merely "an error of belief which must prove fatal to [their] peace unless corrected." He charged, "On the least difference between us you impute to me 'unkindness.' . . . If Providence has endowed me with some judgment & firmness in the management of affairs, you certainly have enjoy'd the benefits, common to my family, derived from their exercise." In closing, Allston chastised his insubordinate mate for complaining of what

5. Fox-Genovese, *Within the Plantation Household*, 193; Anne Cameron to Paul C. Cameron, February 28, May 10, [1850], Paul C. Cameron to Duncan Cameron, October 5, November 23, 1850, Anne Cameron to Duncan Cameron, October 10, 1850, in Cameron Family Papers, SHC. The "mental suffering" referred to by Anne resulted from a miscarriage the previous year.

he termed "the imagined tyranny" of his "arbitrary will," an allegation that he vigorously denied.[6] Perhaps Adele's latent resentment lingered on, but it apparently did not jeopardize what continued to be an essentially happy marriage.[7]

One South Carolina matron who apparently experienced little difficulty with her husband about gender roles was Jane L. Pringle, the wife of Georgetown District rice planter Julius Izard Pringle. Jane was clearly the dominant figure in her household. As was recounted in the preceding chapter, she alone made all decisions concerning the education of her three sons. In addition, she planned family vacations, screened her daughter's suitors, and supervised domestic affairs at the family's Greenfield and White House plantations. Meanwhile, her husband spent much of his time bird-hunting, bagging no less than seventy-one woodcock one month, when not engaged in managing his plantations or attending the races in Charleston. In time, Mrs. Pringle came to rely more on her eldest son Julius than on her husband for counsel and emotional support. As she confided to eighteen-year-old Julius in the spring of 1860, "I begin to talk to you as a friend, and pour out my heart—it is your reward for being a good son that you are early called on to take your share of the care and responsibility which weigh so heavily upon me."[8]

At first, I was quite puzzled by the unique character of the matriarchal Pringle family. How does one explain the existence of such a phenomenon in the heart of one of the most conservative regions in the South? Perhaps Mrs. Pringle, a native of Rome, New York, was simply more self-assertive than the typical southern belle. But Northerners, too, lived in a patriarchal society. To cite but one example, there seems to be little difference between the deferential tone displayed by most of the women in this study and the meek, subservient response of Matilda Leverich when her husband, New York factor Charles P. Leverich, directed her to return home from Philadelphia by a certain date. "[I] am desirous of pleasing my dear husband by showing a desire to gratify his wishes," she wrote. "So I will return on Friday of this week—but how! I leave

6. Charles Joyner, Introduction to Pringle, *A Woman Rice Planter*, xv–xvi, xlix n. 5.

7. See, for example, Adele Petigru Allston to R. F. W. Allston, June 3, 1861, and Adele to Benjamin Allston, May 31, 1864, both in Easterby, ed., *South Carolina Rice Plantation*, 176–77, 198–99.

8. This paragraph is based upon some forty letters from Jane Pringle in the Pringle Family Correspondence, in R. F. W. Allston Papers, SCHS. For reference to the shooting of woodcock, see Jane Pringle to son Julius, January 31, [1857], and Jane to son Poinsett, January 20, 1860, *ibid.* The quotation is from Jane to Julius, April 26, [1860].

you to manage for me."[9] Upon further reflection, I concluded that the explanation for the unusual gender relations in the Pringle family was to be found not in the wife's background but in that of her husband. John Julius Izard Pringle was born several months after his father's untimely death at the age of twenty-three. His mother, the beautiful and accomplished daughter of Senator Ralph Izard, did not remarry until her only son was twenty-five years old. It seems likely, therefore, that, having been raised in a household headed by a dominant female personality, Julius simply deferred to the leadership of a similar figure following his own marriage.[10]

Although few other, if any, elite planter wives enjoyed the virtually autonomous authority within the family exemplified by Jane Pringle, they were by no means second-class citizens. Despite the various legal disabilities to which they were subjected, they and their daughters could receive a quality education; they read widely and exchanged candid opinions on politics, religion, philosophy, and literature with their husbands and / or fathers; they assumed control of their husbands' vast business enterprises when circumstances required such action; and they served as sole executors of their husbands' estates, frequently managing extensive properties conveyed to them by will. This having been said, there *was* one area in which planter women may truly be said to have been oppressed, and that was in their subjection to frequent and often unexpected pregnancies. The reasons for this ordeal have been discussed in Chapter 1, but it should be emphasized here that the birthing of large numbers of children within a relatively short span of time had a profoundly debilitating effect, both mentally and physically, on those who were obliged to undergo this traumatic experience.

Elizabeth Rhett, the first wife of Robert Barnwell Rhett and a woman who absolutely adored her husband, was well aware of the enervating consequences of such frequent pregnancies. In a series of letters to her husband, written two years before her death at the relatively young age of forty-two, she warned that her physical appearance was rapidly deteriorating. "I am looking very old, & begin to feel so," she wrote. Unable to follow her husband's injunction to "go out, ride, & grow fat," she hastened to reassure him: "I am really better now,

---

9. Tilly "your dearly attached little wife" to Charles P. Leverich, December 13, [n.d.], in Charles P. Leverich Papers, MDAH.

10. *South Carolina Genealogies*, II, 331, 448–49, III, 340–41, 352–53; Benjamin Stead, [Jr.?], to John Julius Pringle, Sr., August 23, 1806, John J. Pringle, [Sr.], to Mary Stead Pinckney, November 30, 1807, both in Pringle Family Correspondence, R. F. W. Allston Papers, SCHS.

than before I began to nurse. God, who tempers the wind to the shorn lamb, enables me to endure great fatigue in nursing these little ones, he has committed to my care." But a month later, she returned to the theme of her declining appearance. "Do not expect dear Husband, to see me look *pretty*, that is forever past:—I am in truth *very* ugly, and will never be any thing else again in *this* world. . . . I suspect I suffered more in the last four or five years, than I was aware of at the time. But for your sake I will try & grow young again." Tragically, she was destined to live only another twenty-two months, succumbing on December 14, 1852, just two weeks after the birth of her twelfth child, a son who lived only a day.[11]

There are numerous other examples of the deadly stress imposed upon planter wives by the almost continuous succession of pregnancies and subsequent births. Population census returns confirm the assertion of Elizabeth Fox-Genovese that most slaveholding women bore a child "every year or two during their adult lives." Catherine Ann Devereux, the beloved wife of North Carolina planter Thomas P. Devereux, suffered the same fate as Elizabeth Rhett when she died several months after giving birth to her ninth daughter and eleventh child.[12] Sometimes even an early pregnancy proved fatal. Such was the case with Margaret Washington, the wife of Tennessee planter George A. Washington. She died in 1844 at the age of twenty-one, just nineteen days after giving birth to a son. Similarly, Maria Marshall, the first wife of Natchez aristocrat Levin R. Marshall, passed away in July, 1833, after bearing three children within a period of less than four years. Although she had remained bedridden for five weeks following the birth of her second child and had expressed apprehension on the eve of her third confinement, it was apparently the anguish caused by the tragic death of her eldest child that led directly to Maria's death. As a friend later observed, she never recovered from the death of little Harriet. "She loved her children too much, and sacrificed herself for them." In the end, she could not bear the fatigue she endured for them, "and her feeble body sunk under it."[13]

11. Elizabeth W. Rhett to R. B. Rhett, January 7, 12, 16, February 15, 1851, in Robert Barnwell Rhett, Sr., Papers, SCHS; Rhett Genealogy Notes #2, in Rhett Family Papers, SCHS.

12. Fox-Genovese, *Within the Plantation Household*, 279; Thomas P. Devereux to James C. Johnston, December 21, 1835, in Hayes Collection, SHC; *Dictionary of North Carolina Biography*, ed. Powell, II, 60–61.

13. Silas Emmett Lucas, Jr., comp., *Marriages and Obituaries from Early Tennessee Newspapers, 1794–1851* (Easley, S.C., 1978), 385; Levin R. Marshall to Eliza W. Gould, September 1, 1827, August

Even for those who survived, the physical and mental toll was fearful. As Catherine Clinton has observed, "No hazard was more unrelenting or more ambivalent in its implications for women than pregnancy." In the early 1850s, three prominent Natchez women—two of them daughters of Dr. Stephen Duncan and the other a daughter of Francis Surget—experienced various degrees of physical discomfort either before or after giving birth to a child. In June, 1850, Duncan expressed concern for the health of his daughter Charlotte, the wife of Samuel M. Davis. She "is not well," declared the worried father, "& I think is injuring her health by nursing her child." Two months earlier, another Duncan daughter, this one the wife of Louisiana sugar planter John Julius Pringle, had contracted "a cold in one of her breasts" as a consequence of "riding out too soon" following childbirth. "One cannot be too careful, at such a time," advised a Natchez matron whose sister had also recently borne a child. More serious was the condition of Jane Merrill, who, after undergoing "severe sufferings & bodily afflictions" during her first pregnancy, continued to be plagued with "intermittent fever" after her delivery. In hope of restoring her health, her physician urged the family either to take a sea voyage or to visit the seashore. Apparently the fragile mother suffered no lasting ill effects, for she gave birth to nine more children during the course of her marriage.[14]

The travail experienced by planter wives who sought to cope with a seemingly endless succession of pregnancies is perhaps most vividly illustrated by Gertrude Thomas. The daughter of Georgia cotton planter Turner C. Clanton, Thomas gave birth to ten children and suffered several miscarriages during a period of twenty-two years. In July, 1856, after the birth of two sons, one of whom died after only six weeks, Thomas found herself pregnant once more and expressed ambivalent feelings about the prospect of a third child in as many years. "I do not wish an only child," she confided to her journal, "yet I should not object to long intervals." She miscarried the following month but soon became pregnant again and gave birth in May, 1857, to a daughter who did not

<hr>

3, 1833, Maria L. Marshall to Eliza Gould, July 20, 1829, March 4, 1830, October 16, 1831, Maria to William P. Gould, May 13, 1831, Jane Riddle to Eliza Gould, August 19, 1833 (quotation), in Marshall Papers, LSU.

14. Clinton, *The Plantation Mistress*, 151; Stephen Duncan to C. P. Leverich, June 6, 1850, in Charles P. Leverich Papers, MDAH; M. L. McMurran to Fanny Conner, April 18, 1850, in Lemuel P. Conner and Family Papers, LSU; Ayres P. Merrill, Jr., to William Newton Mercer, February 20, March 25, 1852, in William Newton Mercer Papers, LSU; *Goodspeed's*, II, 430–32.

survive to the end of the year. After the birth of two more children, Thomas faced the prospect in December, 1862, of again becoming a mother, this time in the midst of a war. Severely depressed and "suffering terribly from nausea," she complained that she was "too sick and irritable to regard this circumstance as a blessing *yet awhile*." Her attitude had hardened even further two years later when she admitted candidly that she regretted the "prospect . . . of again becoming a mother." This time she expressed openly her fear of dying in childbirth. "I know I have thought of it this time more than usual," she wrote, "and if I do die I hope that my baby will die with me." Thomas survived, though she was bedridden for three months after giving birth, but the premature infant lasted only a day. Many years later, debilitated by her efforts to keep the family afloat financially and grief-stricken over the death of her seven-year-old son, she commented wearily that she could compare her feelings "to nothing else than the wretched days of early pregnancy." Happily for Thomas, at age forty-six, her child-bearing days were over.[15]

Gertrude Thomas exemplifies another common characteristic of elite women, that of the near deification of their fathers. If there was such great resentment against the subordinate status assigned women in the antebellum South, as some writers claim, one might expect that resentment to be directed against the planter patriarchs. But such was not the case. Most of the daughters in these wealthy slaveholding families literally worshipped their fathers. Thus, when her father passed away, Thomas entered this brief passage in her journal: "I have to record the saddest event which has ever occurred in my history, *the death of my father*." Louisa McCord, who also idolized her father, characterized him, many years after his death, as "the greatest in self poised character and massive intellect that our State has ever given to the country."[16]

When differences between father and daughter occurred, they were painful indeed. Catherine Ann Edmondston, who shared the political beliefs of her husband, a fire-eater from South Carolina, suffered deep emotional distress during the secession crisis early in 1861 when she round herself on the opposite side of the political fence from her father, the staunchly Unionist Thomas P.

15. *The Secret Eye*, ed. Burr, 148 (first quotation), 150, 152, 155, 158, 212 (second quotation), 254 (third quotation), 258 (fourth quotation), 277, 407 (last quotation), 423. Birth dates of children are from Introduction by Nell Painter, 6–7.

16. *The Secret Eye*, ed. Burr, 222; McCord, *Selected Writings*, 6, 295.

Devereux. "It gets almost painful to go to Father's" because "we differ so widely," she remarked sadly in mid-February. The tension continued unabated for two more months. Finally, a week after the fall of Fort Sumter, when her father reluctantly supported the decision of the North Carolina governor to reject President Lincoln's request for troops, the rift between the two began to heal. But the pain still lingered. "This difference of opinion with Father has been very sad to me," she confided to her diary. Never before had she defied the judgment of the man she worshipped. "The admiration, the pride, the earnest warm affection of my heart have all been concentrated on him since my childhood & to differ from him now in so vital a point has been unhappy indeed to me." Happily, the two were soon fully reconciled as a consequence of their mutual support of the Confederacy, and they spent much time together during the war, often playing chess for hours on end.[17]

Only rarely did fathers disappoint their daughters and deny them the affection that they so desperately craved. One who did was the former slavetrader Rice C. Ballard, a man notable for his insensitivity to slaves and family members alike. In the spring of 1857, Ella Ballard reminded her absent father that she would be sixteen years old in less than three weeks and requested a birthday present, preferably a plain little watch, but if that were not possible, she "would like any thing [he] should send to [her]." When no gift was forthcoming, Ella expressed her keen disappointment. Two years later, when her father chastised her after hearing rumors of her impending engagement to a young man of unsuitable social station, she vehemently denied the report. "Rather than marry Mr. Zanone," she fumed, "I would rather have a stone tied around my neck, & be thrown in to the Dead sea." Yet near the end of the letter, as her anger began to recede, she expressed concern for her father's health and urged him to reduce his business obligations. Notwithstanding their differences, she declared that she "would rather have a father than all the money in the world."[18]

Unlike Ballard, most well-to-do planters provided their female offspring with an abundance of both emotional and financial support. It was not uncommon for planters to present their daughters with a plantation, stocked with an

17. *"Journal of a Secesh Lady,"* ed. Crabtree and Patton, 33, 38 (first quotation), 44, 54 (second quotation), 593, 606, 687.

18. Ella Ballard to Rice C. Ballard, March 1, 25, 1857, April 2, 1859, W. Cox to R. C. Ballard, March 22, 1859, Louise C. Ballard to R. C. Ballard, April 1, 1859, in Rice Carter Ballard Papers, SHC.

appropriate number of slaves, on the occasion of their marriage. Natchez nabob Francis Surget, Sr., provides a good example of this practice. Not only did he make generous bequests to his daughters in his will, but he also conveyed extensive properties to them during his lifetime. Thus, following the marriage of his eldest daughter to Gabriel B. Shields in the late 1830s, Surget donated a Lake Concordia cotton plantation to the young couple. Several years later, he made a second donation, this one consisting of seventy-seven slaves and the Basin Place plantation in Madison Parish, Louisiana, to be divided equally between the Shieldses and his eldest son, Francis, Jr. When such a division proved unfeasible, the latter purchased the Shields's half of the property. In the early 1850s Surget purchased yet another plantation for the Shields family. Situated in Adams County, Mississippi, and renamed Montebello, this place became the principal Shields residence in June, 1852.[19] That same year, having already donated a Louisiana plantation to his second daughter, Jane, he purchased Elms Court, a Natchez residence valued at $25,000, for Jane and her husband, Ayres P. Merrill II. Under the agreement, as Merrill reported, the recently married couple were allowed to dwell at Elms Court and "enjoy the usufruct of it—we being his tenants at will." Upon the death of Surget in 1856, the residence was bequeathed to Jane Merrill.[20]

Other planters did not wish to burden their daughters with the responsibility of managing land and slaves. In 1856 two of the Tayloe brothers of Virginia, William H. and Benjamin O., engaged in a lengthy discussion concerning their mutual financial obligations toward their children. William, the wealthier of the two, proposed to give his two daughters, then in their midtwenties and unmarried, an annuity of $1,800 per year and wondered whether that amount was sufficient for "any reasonable lady." His brother responded that it all depended on

19. Information on Catharine Shields compiled from Surget Family Papers, MDAH. For donations in early 1840s, see Gift of Slaves, F. Surget to F. Surget, Jr., and Catharine Shields, January 20, 1841; Act of Revocation & Sale, Francis Surget, Sr., with G. B. Shields & Wife and Francis Surget, Jr., April 26, 1842 (Roll 3); Francis Surget, Sr., Donation to Francis Surget, Jr., Catharine Shields and Gabriel B. Shields, March 12, 1841 (Roll 4); H. B. Shaw to F. Surget, Jr., October 18, 1856 (Roll 1).

20. Francis Surget, Sr., Donation to Jane Surget Merrill, n.d. (Roll 4), and Distribution of Francis Surget Property in Mississippi and Louisiana, January 26, 1857 (Roll 3), both in Surget Family Papers, MDAH; A. P. Merrill, Jr., to William N. Mercer, March 25, 1852, in William Newton Mercer Papers, LSU.

the circumstances. "It seems to me best, while we are able, to make such provisions for our daughters, that they need have none of our servants, except such as are willing to go to them for household purposes and whom they need." Their sons would assume the management of their plantations and slaves when they were deemed competent to accept that responsibility. Even more generous was North Carolina planter Thomas P. Devereux, who sought to bolster the independence of his daughters by providing them with liquid assets in early adulthood. Thus, near the end of the war, he presented each of them with $10,000 in Confederate bonds, a gift much appreciated by at least one of his daughters. "Many fathers would retain the money in their own hands in order that their children might feel & acknowledge their dependance upon him," remarked Kate Edmondston. "Not so with him; he realizes 'the glorious privilege of being Independent'!"[21]

Ironically, one of the most enlightened attitudes toward women in general, and his daughters in particular, was displayed by Mississippi planter Richard T. Archer. A man characterized by an acerbic tongue and a propensity to settle personal disputes with physical violence, Archer was one of the most cantankerous of all the plantation aristocrats. Yet despite these defects and his marital infidelity with the slave girl Patty, alluded to earlier, Archer evinced genuine affection and solicitude for the distaff members of his family. Not only did he seek to provide his daughters with the best available education by sending them to school in the Northeast, but he also went to great lengths to ensure that they had "trusty & experienced" female servants to minister to their needs while in school.[22] Much more important, however, was his progressive view of gender roles. In a remarkable letter, written in 1866, just a year before his death, Archer urged his twenty-four-year-old daughter Jane and her sisters to embrace a vocation that would benefit society. We have reached a time, he asserted, "when it will be well for all to have a useful and profitable vocation." He suggested homeopathy, "the true medical science," which he termed "1000 fold more agreeable, useful and profitable than teaching school." That profession would enable her "to be practical and useful as a lady, a Christian and a member of

21. Benjamin O. Tayloe to "Dear Brother," September 6, 1856, in Tayloe Family Papers, VHS; "Journal of a Secesh Lady," ed. Crabtree and Patton, 623; receipt dated October 13, 1864, signed by Patrick M. Edmondston, in John Devereux Papers, NCDAH.

22. Richard T. Archer to "My Dear Wife," February 13, October 3 (quotation), 1856, Archer to "My Beloved Daughters," October 5, 1856, in Richard Thompson Archer Family Papers, CAH.

society." Some might object that such a vocation would be inappropriate for a woman. "If unusual," he asked, "what is there unladylike in the profession. Is it not an unchristian state to have no vocation to do good? . . . A lady will be a lady in any vocation she may follow."[23] Archer was clearly a man ahead of his time in his conception of woman's place in society.

The daughters of wealthy planters usually had an even more intimate relationship with their mothers. It was the latter who supervised their early schooling, trained them for their future domestic responsibilities, and guided them through the trying period of courtship and the selection of a suitable mate. Then their close relationships tended to recede as the young women became increasingly occupied with their own families. As one disconsolate matron observed, "the worst of it is that frequently just as they finish at School they get married & leave us." Until that time, however, mothers continued to play the role of both counselor and advocate. Thus, when she was unavoidably absent on the birthday of her nine-year-old daughter, Anne Cameron wrote an affectionate letter expressing the wish that "each return of it may be happier than the last, and find [her] growing in the grace of God, as well as all useful knowledge." She continued the moral lesson with an injunction to both of her young daughters to avoid any words of "harshness or anger" toward each other so that they might embark upon a life of mutual "devotion and affection." Quite different were the circumstances that impelled another mother to come to the defense of a much older daughter. When Rice C. Ballard queried his daughter Ella about an alleged romantic involvement with a young ne'er-do-well, Louise Ballard joined her daughter in denouncing the rumor as a palpable falsehood. Louise then added that she had recently noted a dramatic improvement in young Ella. "She seems to be more *reflective* upon all *subjects* and is devoted to her *parents*," Mrs. Ballard assured her husband. "And," she added confidently, "I sincerely hope we will be amply repaid for all our *great* solicitude in raising *her*."[24]

Occasionally, friction developed between mothers and daughters, usually with respect to the choice of marriage partners. Such was the case with the

23. Richard T. Archer to "My Dear Jane," November 11, 1866, *ibid.*

24. Margaret Smith to "My dear Cousin" [Justina L. Walton], August 17, 1849, in Walton Family Papers; Anne Cameron to "My beloved children," July 21, 1849, in Cameron Family Papers; Louise C. Ballard to Rice C. Ballard, April 1, 1859, in Rice Carter Ballard Papers, all SHC.

seemingly ubiquitous Jane Pringle and her daughter Mary. Not only did the former control the education and vocational choices of her three sons, but she also supervised the social life of her daughter, who, in her words, had blossomed into "the belle of belles."[25] The Pringles' annual summer excursions to Newport, Saratoga, and other fashionable northern resorts were designed as much to enhance the matrimonial prospects of their beautiful young daughter as to afford pleasure to other family members. During the late 1850s, as Mary danced her way through cotillions from Charleston to Newport, she was courted by a succession of admirers. One of the first to seek the hand of the twenty-year-old South Carolina belle was Richard Fay, the "very handsome, very nice & very rich" son of a wealthy Boston merchant. Mrs. Pringle seemed quite fond of the young man, and Fay's parents, with whom Mary spent a fortnight in the early fall of 1857, were equally supportive of the match.[26] Within a short time, however, Fay's prospects plummeted sharply when his father was ruined by the financial panic that swept the country in October. Mary's mother now doubted that anything would come of the relationship since Mary had declared frankly that she would "never marry a poor man." Professing to be "not the least committed" to the union, the elder Pringle commented that she would "probably suffer the thing to go by default." But her attitude changed dramatically two weeks later when her daughter suddenly broke off her engagement to Fay, sending him away with "insulting rudeness." Charging that Mary had "lost an earnest sincere love—and a better match than she will ever make," the disgusted mother exclaimed to her son that she could "see no reason short of insanity for her conduct." She predicted, "Mary will live to regret it in sackcloth and ashes or I am much mistaken."[27]

Jane Pringle's anger soon subsided, however, and two years later she was hopeful that another suitor, Heyward Cutting of New York, would win her daughter's heart. In August, 1859, she reported from Newport that Cutting, whom she described as "very handsome . . . very refined and high bred" though "quite young," was "perfectly devoted to Mary and seems as much in love as a

25. Jane L. Pringle to son Julius, April 26, [1860], Pringle Family Correspondence, in R. F. W. Allston Papers, SCHS. In 1857 Mary was, by her own account, five feet, five inches tall, weighed 125 pounds, and had "a very nice small *waist*." See Poinsett Pringle to brother Julius, October 11, 1857, *ibid.*

26. Jane L. Pringle to Julius, August 11 (quotation), September 13, 27, [1857], *ibid.*

27. Jane L. Pringle to Julius, October 12, 13, 27 [1857], *ibid.*

man can be." She added, "I don't know what will come of it, but she is discarding all the others for him." After a glorious summer in Newport, Mary accompanied her parents to New York City, where the flirtation with young Cutting continued. The latter stayed so long in the evenings, recounted Mrs. Pringle, that her husband threatened to "tell him to go" and Mary became "dreadfully frightened" that he would. The following April, with Mary again in New York, Cutting remained "extremely attentive," but Jane worried that if his intentions were not serious, they were "a grave disadvantage," as Edward Carter, among others, seemed to be "only waiting for the decision to advance his own claims." Shortly thereafter, the Pringles sailed for Europe. It was there, apparently, that Mary encountered the French count who subsequently became her husband, a marital choice that doubtless pleased her socially conscious mother.[28]

Just as Mary Pringle selected her mate, so too did the daughters of most wealthy slaveholders. As Jane Turner Censer has observed, marriage was intended to be an affectionate relationship, so planters usually "played only an indirect role in courtship." This is not to say, however, that parents did not display an intense interest in the romantic choices of their offspring or that they were not consulted as the courtship progressed through its successive stages. Thus, when Maria Chotard first apprised her sister of a budding romance with her future husband, Levin Marshall, she remarked that her mother "speaks in raptures of him altho' he has never said any thing to her *yet.*" Two months later, hearing nothing further about the relationship, her mother implored Maria to break her silence. "Your fate perhaps your life is now pending," she wrote, "and, if nothing is yet decided, why not say so."[29] Finally, Maria overcame her doubts and became engaged to Marshall in the summer of 1825. But again she had second thoughts, and after weeks of mental turmoil, she wrote her fiancé a letter declining his proposal. Then, a few weeks later, her widowed mother passed away, placing Maria, as a nineteen-year-old single woman with no living parents, in an exceedingly vulnerable position. Consequently, when Marshall renewed his proposal, she quickly accepted and they were soon wed. As it turned out, she never regretted the decision that had been forced upon her by circum-

28. Jane L. Pringle to son Poinsett, August 15, [1859], Jane to son Lynch, August 21 (quotation); October 16, [1859], Jane to son Julius, April 26, [1860], *ibid.*; *South Carolina Genealogies*, III, 341.

29. Censer, *North Carolina Planters and Their Children*, 68, 72–73; Maria L. Chotard to "My dear Sister" [Eliza W. Gould], January 9, 1825, and Sarah F. Chotard to "My Dear Maria," March 8, 1825, both in Marshall Papers, LSU.

stances beyond her control. Maria was so pleased with her new husband that, as she later confided to her sister, she did "not think he [would] require to be *sent to heaven* for a new moulding."[30]

Like Maria's mother, Richard T. Archer also took a keen interest in his daughter's courtship and eventually granted her permission for the relationship to proceed. While in Virginia on business, Archer became convinced that the amorous attachment between his seventeen-year-old daughter Mary and one Dan Humphreys, which had been developing for some time, was now destined to be "as lasting as life." As he recounted to his wife, "Never did I witness more tenderness and delicacy than he showed or more trustful and abiding love than she returned." A month later, fully satisfied that their relationship would be an "enduring" one, he gave each of the young lovers permission to correspond with one another. He assured his daughter that "there was no impropriety" in her writing to young Humphreys. Still, although Archer himself was "not one of those who think . . . feelings should be repressed when they are rightly placed," he wished that Mary were close enough to consult with her mother, who was back home in Mississippi. As he put it, "A mothers counsels and sympathy are necessary to a delicate mind on such occasions." Contrary to Archer's prediction, the romance between his daughter and Dan Humphreys apparently never progressed to its logical conclusion, for Mary was still single and in ill health a decade later.[31]

When a courtship progressed to the final stage, that of a formal engagement, parental consent was again sought. Although it was customary to consult the parents of each party, the endorsement of the bride's father was deemed most critical. One can only imagine the anxiety and apprehension with which a young lady awaited the outcome of the closed meeting between her father and the prospective groom. Just such a scene, this one in Augusta, Georgia, was described vividly by Gertrude Clanton Thomas. Blinded by love, Clanton had never been fearful about her relationship with Jeff Thomas until the date of that fateful interview arrived. "I had a short conversation with Pa just before he went into the room," she later recalled, "and then commenced my agonised feelings."

30. Eliza W. Gould to "My dear Nephew" [George M. Marshall], October 17, 1868, W[addy] Thompson to "My dear Maria" [his niece], January 26, 1826, Maria L. Marshall to Eliza W. Gould, September 17, 1826 (quotation), in Marshall Papers, LSU.

31. Richard T. Archer to "My Dear Wife," December 26, 1855, January 19, 1856, Archer to daughter Jane, November 12, 1866, in Richard Thompson Archer Family Papers, CAH.

Next, she continued, she hurried up to her own room, where she "gave vent to [her] feelings by prostrating [her]self upon [her] knees and burst into tears and prayers." Happily for young Gertrude, her prayers were answered, albeit somewhat grudgingly. "Although not a direct consent," she noted laconically, "Pa's answer was satisfactory."[32]

The courtship ritual was quite formal even for more mature couples, as is illustrated by the developing romance between Peter W. Hairston and Fanny Caldwell, the daughter of a North Carolina judge. Hairston, whose first wife, Columbia Stuart, had died in 1857, began a relationship with Fanny in December of the following year that culminated in their marriage six months later. At first, the letters between the two were overly stiff, each referring to the other only in the third person. With the passage of time, their communications became less formal as they discussed a variety of topics ranging from religion and politics to slave management. But it was not until March, 1859, three months after the courtship began, that Hairston first addressed Fanny directly.[33] The following month, Hairston traveled to New York to procure a special wedding ring for his bride. There he remained for two weeks waiting for the completion of the ring, which the jeweler promised would be "the finest thing ever got up in the United States." As the time approached for their wedding, the letters between the two became ever more affectionate. Thus, after Peter painted an idyllic picture of their future life together, Fanny responded, less than a week before the scheduled nuptials, that she "could not write or tell the perfect joy" she felt "in loving and being loved by such a man." And later, in closing, she wrote: "I know I cannot tell my tale of love half so eloquently as yours is told, but it comes all the same from a fond devoted heart." To say the least, this passionate letter represented a dramatic change from the stiff third-person missives of just six months before.[34]

The weddings that followed the periods of courtship and engagement were often spectacular affairs. Not only were members of the extended families in attendance, but most of the local social elite were invited as well. The bride's gifts were frequently splendid almost beyond description, as was befitting the

---

32. *The Secret Eye*, ed. Burr, 109–10.

33. Peter W. Hairston to Fanny Caldwell, December 2, 1858, January 26, February [?], March 12, 1859, Fanny to Peter, February 28, 1859, in Peter Wilson Hairston Papers, SHC.

34. Peter W. Hairston to Fanny Caldwell, April [18], [21], 22, [23] (quotation), [29], June 13, 1859, Fanny to Peter, June 17, 1859, *ibid.*

central figure in one of the premier social events in the Old South. In the choice of a wedding date, the Christmas season seemed almost as popular as the more traditional late spring and early summer period. For example, Natchez nabob John A. Quitman was married to the equally wealthy Eliza Turner on Christmas Eve, 1824, in a ceremony attended by "all the grandees in the county." Many years later, two of the largest slaveholding families in North Carolina were united when Anne Cameron wed George P. Collins less than a week before Christmas. One of the most magnificent planter weddings took place in Charleston in May, 1861, a month and a half after the capture of Fort Sumter. As one observer commented disapprovingly, weddings and engagements were flourishing in that city "as if nothing were the matter." On this occasion, the marriage of Louisa Blake and Blake Heyward linked even more closely two of the most prominent rice-planting families in the Carolina Low Country. Among the bride's presents were a "diamond stomacher from her father," a "diamond tiarra . . . such as wd suit a duchess" from the British consul in Savannah, and an assortment of "bracelets brooches & carriages . . . of untold value." The ceremony was held at St. Philip's Episcopal Church at nine o'clock on a Saturday evening, and the bride was given away by her father, Walter Blake, who "kept his place in the pew & only nodded his head at the question of 'who giveth this woman' &c." Such eccentric behavior was apparently typical of the Blakes.[35]

With such fabulous wealth often involved in these matrimonial unions, it is not surprising that some fathers would seek to protect the financial interests of their daughters either through prenuptial agreements or by restrictive provisions in their wills. It was this concern that led some southern states, with Mississippi leading the way in 1839, to pass legislation permitting wives to control their own property after marriage. Illustrative of the prenuptial arrangement is a contract between Alexander C. Keene and Julia Morgan, daughter of one of the largest

35. Maria L. Chotard to "My dear Sister" [Eliza W. Gould], January 9, 1825, in Marshall Papers, LSU; Rebecca Cameron to Margaret Mordecai, December 6, 1860, in Cameron Family Papers, SHC; [Jane Petrigru North] to daughter Carey Pettigrew, May 24, 1861, in Pettigrew Family Papers, SHC. The groom, Daniel Blake Heyward, was the second surviving son of Arthur Heyward and his wife Maria Louisa (Blake) Heyward, both of whom died in 1852. The bride, Louisa, was the daughter of Walter Blake (1804–71), a native of England, who resided at Bonny Hall and managed the vast South Carolina estates of his father, Joseph Blake. See *South Carolina Genealogies*, I, 94, II, 361, 366; Davidson, *The Last Foray*, 179, 209.

cotton planters in Louisiana. This agreement, signed in April, 1845, was designed to preserve for the bride the sole right to her mother's estate, which was to be managed by her father, Oliver J. Morgan, during his lifetime. In addition, Keene renounced his right to any of his wife's property that might ascend to him as the heir of their children. Instead, that property would pass to the proper heirs of Oliver J. Morgan "as if the said Julia Morgan had no descendents." Apparently the elder Morgan survived both his daughter and son-in-law, for the three Keene children, aged five to fourteen, were listed as wards in the household of Oliver T. Morgan, presumably either a cousin or the younger brother of Julia, in the census of 1860.[36]

Much more common was the practice of safeguarding the interests of planter daughters through stipulations in the wills of their fathers. For example, in his last will and testament, John Devereux of North Carolina bequeathed to his daughter Frances, the wife of Bishop Leonidas Polk of Louisiana, one hundred slaves with the proviso that these slaves were to be "free from any controll of her . . . husband, and not liable for any of his debts." It was further specified that if Frances predeceased her father, the slaves were then to be "divided equally amongst her children, the father taking possession of them for their use." In view of Bishop Polk's dubious managerial skills, this provision proved to be a perspicacious one, indeed.[37] In similar fashion, Moorhead Wright of Arkansas decreed in his will that if any of his property should descend to his two very young daughters before they reached the age of majority, it was to be administered by trustees and used for them solely and exclusively. Further, if they should marry, their husbands would have no access to or control over that property.[38]

If planter aristocrats reposed little confidence in the ability of prospective

36. Alexander C. Keene and Julia Morgan Marriage Contract, April 7, 1845, in Natchez Trace Small MSS Collection, CAH; *Goodspeed's*, I, 1029; MS Census, 1850 and 1860 (Schedule 1: Population), Carroll Parish, Louisiana.

37. Last Will and Testament of John Devereux, October 20, 1843, in Leonidas Polk Family Papers, HNO; Sarah E. Devereux to "My dear brother" [Thomas P. Devereux, who was actually her brother-in-law], April 14, June 15, 1854, September 18, 1855, in Devereux Family Papers, DU. Polk reportedly invested $200,000 in a Louisiana sugar plantation, which he was obliged to sell at a loss in 1854.

38. Last Will and Testament of Moorhead Wright, November, 1853, in Gillespie and Wright Family Papers, SHC.

sons-in-law to manage successfully the property of their daughters, they had no such reservation about the administrative abilities of their wives. Not only did they name their spouses to execute their wills, but they also conveyed extensive holdings to them in those documents. Among those who designated their mates as either the sole or principal executors of their vast estates were Haller Nutt and Francis Surget, Jr., of Mississippi, Moorhead Wright of Arkansas, and William Allen of Surry County, Virginia. In addition, the latter willed the bulk of his property to his widow rather than to his eldest son, explaining that his son would have "an ample estate" under the will of Allen's late uncle and that he desired the young man's mother "to have the most ample means for her comfort and enjoyment" and for the property "to be at her absolute disposal."[39] Similarly, Surget bequeathed his entire estate to his wife, Charlotte B. Surget, thereby replicating the course adopted by his grandfather, Pierre Surget. The latter had designated his widow "Mistress of my whole Estate," with the added proviso that "neither sons nor daughters when of age shall be entitled to claim any thing from her." Another Mississippi nabob, the patriarchal John A. Quitman, apparently did not manifest similar confidence in the managerial skills of his wife, choosing instead to place his brother-in-law, Henry Turner, in charge of their jointly owned Palmyra plantation at Davis Bend. In a letter to his mother, written after Quitman's death in 1858, F. Henry Quitman decried that arrangement. Charging that Turner was "not fit to be in charge of property . . . either for himself or others," he declared, "for the interests of all concerned I would greatly prefer to see that you had the entire controul of the place."[40]

Unlike Quitman, some wealthy slaveholders did not hesitate to entrust their wives with heavy administrative responsibilities even before their demise if circumstances required such action. This was most likely to occur when a planter had holdings in widely separated geographic areas. For example, Eliza Carter, with the assistance of an overseer, managed the Baldwin County, Georgia, properties of her husband, Farish Carter, during the latter's extended visits to

39. *Ibid.;* Last Will and Testament of Haller Nutt, April 9, 1861, in Nutt Family Collection, MDAH; Will of William Allen of Claremont, Surry County, Virginia, May 28, 1856, in James Nathaniel Dunlop Papers, VHS.

40. Will of Francis Surget, Jr., September 1, 1862, Will Book 3, p. 294, Adams County Courthouse, Natchez (citation courtesy of Donald G. Linton, Hot Springs, Arkansas); Will of Pierre Surget, April 1, 1791, in "Notes from Will Books," in MacNeil Papers, MDAH; F. Henry Quitman to "My dear Mother," July 28, 1859, in John A. Quitman and Family Papers, MDAH.

Coosawattee, his principal plantation, located in a distant part of the state. Eliza's burden was sometimes difficult to bear. In the summer of 1842, Carter's harried wife admitted that she had had "several little perplexities & trials," but, she assured him, "things are all straight now." On another occasion, she reported that she had returned from town to find a huge fire racing toward their home plantation. She immediately sent "all hands . . . to oppose it" and, after it was under control, "had it watched a great part of the night" to ensure that it did not re-ignite. Shortly after this incident, after her elderly husband became too feeble to write, she took on that additional task, labeling herself "my Husband's Secretary."[41]

In many ways, Ann Archer's experience paralleled that of Eliza Carter. Her husband, Richard T. Archer, also owned properties remote from their Port Gibson residence, and, in addition, he traveled frequently to his native Virginia and to other sites on the East Coast where his children were in school. Consequently, during his extended absences from home in the 1850s, Archer essentially relinquished the management of his Claiborne County properties to his wife. She became responsible for the payment of taxes, supervision of overseers, ordering of supplies, and other duties associated with the oversight of a plantation. Just after the war, Ann Archer's burden increased substantially. Correctly discerning that his death was imminent, Archer conveyed the bulk of his estate to his spouse and then bombarded her with numerous instructions, hastening to add, however, "I write all this as advice and not as dictation."[42] For Fanny Hairston, as for so many other southern women, it was the war that led to the assumption of obligations normally handled by the male head of the family. Thus, when Peter Hairston volunteered for Confederate military service in the spring of 1861, he entrusted his wife with "full powers over all my affairs while I am gone." Four days later, he reiterated that commitment. "I place my entire business under your management until I return," he wrote, adding, "I know that your judgment and your prudence will do all that can be done under the circumstances."[43] Such words provide eloquent testimony, indeed, to the confidence some planters reposed in their wives.

41. Eliza Carter to Farish Carter, June 29, 1840, November 6, 1855, Eliza to "dear Mary" [her niece], January 9, 1857, in Farish Carter Papers, SHC.

42. Richard T. Archer to "My Dear Wife," January 5, 1856, July 25, October 9, 15, 22, 29, November 5, 6 (quotation), 1866, in Richard Thompson Archer Family Papers, CAH.

43. Peter W. Hairston to Fanny C. Hairston, May 5, 9, 1861, in Peter Wilson Hairston Papers, SHC.

It should be emphasized, however, that, prior to the war, few planter wives exercised the degree of authority over business affairs that was displayed by Eliza Carter and Ann Archer. For the most part, their domain rarely extended beyond the house and garden.[44] Much more typical were the activities of North Carolina matron Anne Cameron. On one occasion, for example, she gave explicit directions to her husband on pea-raising and suggested that the landscape of their Fairntosh estate could be improved by planting some large holly trees "between the greenhouse and kitchen." She also customarily took advantage of her husband's absence to put their house in order. As young Margaret Cameron remarked to her aunt in the spring of 1860, "Mother commenced cleaning and whitewashing yesterday as soon as Fathers back was turned as she all-ways does."[45] In like manner, Margaret Winchester informed her absent husband in March, 1855, that she was "gradually getting the house in order, curtains up & c." She also had advice about the garden at their Natchez residence. "I think we could raise fruit enough here to last us all summer," she wrote, "and mustard and turnips enough for the negroes and soup vegetables besides." Domestic life could sometimes be quite taxing. On another occasion, when Mrs. Winchester tried to examine a cow who had given birth to "a fine young heifer calf," the cow became agitated and chased her over the fence. "She gave me a dreadful backache," recounted the shaken Winchester, "but after a good crying fit, I felt much better."[46] The point is that, though slaveholding wives usually focused their attention on the rather mundane concerns of home and garden, their husbands had sufficient confidence in their ability to entrust them with far greater responsibilities when circumstances demanded.

Although they were denied the right to vote or to hold office and, consequently, had no direct influence upon public affairs, the women in slaveholding families were not reticent about expressing their political views. Understandably, planter

---

44. Catherine Clinton grossly exaggerates the role of women in managing southern plantations, claiming, among other things, that the plantation mistress allocated provisions to the slaves. Such a duty must have been exceptionally rare, for I do not recall a single instance of it among elite women whose husbands were still living and were at home. See *The Plantation Mistress*, 22–24.

45. Anne Cameron to "My dear husband," January 30, [1849?], n.d. [1849?], Margaret Cameron to "My dear aunt Maggie" [Margaret C. Mordecai], May 11, 1860, in Cameron Family Papers, SHC.

46. Margaret Winchester to "My dear Husband," March 2, 1855, February 25, 1854, both in Winchester Family Papers, CAH.

wives did not manifest much interest in political affairs until the last decade of the antebellum period, when the sectional controversy over slavery became the overriding topic of interest among all Southerners, both male and female. Only occasionally did references to politics and its practitioners appear in the correspondence of women before 1850. The wife of Mississippian Levin Marshall, however, was sufficiently interested in the presidential campaign of 1828 to offer a sarcastic commentary on Andrew Jackson following the latter's visit to New Orleans to commemorate his glorious victory over the British in 1815. After predicting that despite "all the fine speeches and *Big* dinners" that had marked his visit, Old Hickory would probably not receive the vote of Louisiana "for that office to which he so *modestly* aspires," she added disparagingly: "We in this part of the country, that is my Husband and *me*, altho' always sensibly alive to gratitude are a *little* sceptical upon that little item of qualification."[47] Such an observation doubtless accorded not only with the views of her husband but also with those of all her Whig friends in the Natchez District.

When the first great sectional crisis erupted in 1850, followed two years later by the publication of *Uncle Tom's Cabin,* the women of elite slaveholding families became much more preoccupied with political affairs. No other wife was more supportive of her husband's political stance than Elizabeth Rhett, and no other was more vocal in denouncing his opponents. In this fierce loyalty to her husband, she was merely emulating what she perceived to be the gender role adopted by English wives. As she once wrote admiringly, "an Englishman's wife *seems to be* as she is in truth his second self." In any event, as her husband journeyed to Nashville in November, 1850, to attend the rump session of the convention in that city, she denounced fellow South Carolinian James H. Hammond for offering a lame explanation for not attending the meeting and castigated the state of North Carolina for clinging to "the stupid idea of non-intercourse" as a solution to the crisis. "My mind misgives me sorely, as to *our power* of *resistance,*" she wrote dejectedly, "for with so many cowards, so many simpletons, so many traitors, among us, where are the true, & brave, & enlightened, who are to carry through, so mighty a revolution?" But it was Mrs. Stowe's monumental novel that evoked the most emotional response from southern women. Charg-

47. Maria Louisa Marshall to "My dear Sister," February 7, 1828, in Marshall Papers, LSU; Robert V. Remini, *Andrew Jackson and the Course of American Freedom, 1822–1832* (New York, 1981), 131–33.

ing that Stowe had distorted the true picture of slavery by selecting only the most horrible and exceptional cases imaginable, Louisa McCord declared angrily that her "obscene and degrading scenes are [as] false as the spirit of mischief which dictated them." The novel, she thundered, was "one mass of fanatical bitterness and foul misrepresentation wrapped in the garb of Christian Charity." Equally merciless in her attack on Stowe was Catherine Edmondston, who blamed the New England abolitionist for all of the wartime carnage and vehemently denounced her as a "*murderess, and a murderess for gain!*"[48]

If the events of the early 1850s piqued the political interest of planter women, the secession crisis a decade later engendered an even more intense response. Just after the presidential election of 1860, teenager Cynthia Pugh wrote from New Orleans that if she were a man she would have voted for John C. Breckinridge. "I wish old Lincoln would come here, so I could help salute him with rotten eggs. I would shower them on him with a very good will," she assured her equally young cousin. Such youthful enthusiasm was not altogether typical. Many southern women were apprehensive about secession, doubtless because they were more cognizant than their husbands of the bloodshed that a war could inflict upon their menfolk. One whose commitment to the southern cause superseded her fears was Sallie B. Manning, the second wife of former South Carolina governor John L. Manning. Shortly after the war began, a female friend recalled their mutual patriotism in earlier days and wondered whether Mrs. Manning was "as patriotic now, when the work is to be done." Was she now cutting out "coats & pantaloons with all the assurance of a professional tailor," she asked. "Such is my occupation," remarked the correspondent, "& such is the occupation of every lady in this parish."[49]

Equally patriotic were a trio of sisters from the North family of South Carolina, one of whom had married a Pettigrew and another an Allston. Their correspondence provides a fascinating commentary on the perceptions and attitudes of elite women during the month following the attack on Fort Sumter. Ironically, the three were nieces of James L. Petigru, the noted Charleston lawyer

---

48. Elizabeth Rhett to R. B. Rhett, January 16, [1851], November, 7, [1850], both in Robert Barnwell Rhett, Sr., Papers, SCHS; McCord, *Selected Writings*, 85 (first quotation), 90, 262 (second quotation); *"Journal of a Secesh Lady,"* ed. Crabtree and Patton, 130–31.

49. Cynthia Pugh to "Dear cousin Frank" [Winchester], November 23[?], [1860], in Winchester Family Papers, CAH; E. M. Hatton to Sallie B. Manning, September 30, 1861, in Chesnut-Miller-Manning Papers, SCHS.

who had remained unalterably opposed to secession. On the first day of the Sumter bombardment, Louise North, who resided on a plantation just north of Charleston, leveled her fire at "the unfortunate poor clown at Washington," who "has resolved to initiate Civil war" and wondered how Virginia and North Carolina could "remain supine" as they observed "the coercive action of a government in whose good faith and honour all have lost confidence." The following day, her sister, Carey Pettigrew of North Carolina, outraged by the false assurance given to their uncle by Lincoln crony Ward Lamon that Sumter would be evacuated, expressed her disgust with the "duplicity & cowardly sneaking of Lincoln & his crew." Also upset by the failure of Virginia and North Carolina to cast their lot with the Confederacy, she predicted correctly that a call for volunteers by the Lincoln government would force a decision in those states. From Baltimore, Carey's sister-in-law added her voice to the crescendo of abuse being heaped upon Lincoln by comparing the noble conduct of "our southern brethren" to the "meanness—the falsity—the baseness of the administration at Washington." In early May, as some realization of the long struggle ahead began to dawn, Minnie Allston voiced the fear that Southerners generally might be underestimating their enemy's "strength in courage as well as numbers" and that Virginians, in particular, seemed "ill prepared for what is so soon coming upon them." General Lee, she added perceptively, "is wise and prudent but there will be fearful odds." With the exception of their obviously distorted view of Lincoln, the observations of these Carolina siblings at the outset of the war were remarkably perspicacious and reflect keen insight into a domain usually thought to be reserved for males in the mid-nineteenth century.[50]

As the war continued, the mood of slaveholding women fluctuated between moments of despair in the wake of Confederate defeats and mounting anger against the foe that threatened to destroy their world. Illustrative of the former was Fanny Conner's reaction to the fall of Vicksburg. "All our hopes and fears are now at an end," she wrote somberly to her absent husband. "They have given place to sad reality." Evincing the latter attitude, Catherine Ann Edmond-

50. Louise North to "My dear Carey" [Caroline North Pettigrew], April 12, 1861, Carey Pettigrew to "My dearest Minnie" [Mary North Allston], April 13, 1861, Mary B. Pettigrew to "My Dearest Carey," April 17, 1861, Minnie Allston to Carey Pettigrew, May 8, 1861, in Pettigrew Family Papers, SHC. For more on the Lamon mission, see Kenneth M. Stampp, *And the War Came: The North and the Secession Crisis, 1860–1861* (Baton Rouge, 1950), 277 n.

ston, the daughter of former North Carolina Unionist Thomas P. Devereux, remained bitter and defiant to the end. In 1864 she applauded the alleged massacre of Negro troops at Fort Pillow, Tennessee. "If they will steal our slaves & lead them on to murder & rapine," she fumed, "they must take the consequences." A year later, she was momentarily demoralized by the news of General Lee's surrender. "Good God!" she exclaimed, "We stand appalled at our disaster! What have we done to be thus visited?" But even after this catastrophic event, the fiery Edmondston remained recalcitrant. The submission of the southern people to hated Yankee authority was utterly beyond her comprehension. "We are *crushed!* subjugated! And I fear, O how I fear, *conquered,*" she wailed, "& what is to me the saddest part, our people do not feel it as they ought—like men who have lost their Liberty. . . . O My God, can the very spirit of Freedom die out thus & leave not a trace behind it? . . . Is the very memory of our dead to vanish from our midst?"[51]

Not all planter wives shared either the passionate devotion to the cause or the initial optimism of Catherine Edmondston. Elderly women, in particular, had difficulty adjusting to such wartime privations as the separation from loved ones, the burden of added responsibilities, general financial retrenchment, and the paucity of consumer goods. And always there was the fear of poverty if the war were lost and the slaves emancipated. These were among the concerns of two prominent South Carolina matrons, one the wife of Henry A. Middleton and the other the widow of Langdon Cheves, Sr. Middleton had sent his wife and daughter to the Low Country colony at Flat Rock, North Carolina, while he remained behind on his Weehaw plantation in Georgetown District. There he labored assiduously "to save to the family, as much of the property as [was] possible." The separation was obviously quite distressing to the female members of his family. In July, 1862, Middleton sought to boost their flagging morale and to assuage their concern for his personal welfare. "I can submit, without a murmur, to a very simple state of living," he wrote, and "I cannot but believe that my family would do the same." The present crisis required sacrifices. "The greater part of mankind live in miserable huts," he reminded them. "Why should I shrink from such a fate, if called upon to do so." Declaring that he was

51. Fanny E. Conner to "My ever dearest Husband," July 7, 1863, in Lemuel P. Connor and Family Papers, LSU; *"Journal of a Secesh Lady,"* ed. Crabtree and Patton, 549–50, 694–95, 708.

not prepared to "sacrifice the future, to the comforts of the present," he sought to impress upon them "the necessity," not simply of enduring, but also of remaining cheerful.[52]

Even more disconcerting than flagging morale were the lamentations of Mrs. Cheves. In the fall of 1862, she complained to her son that his absence was having a deleterious effect on the operation of the plantation. Clearly annoyed, Langdon, Jr., replied curtly: "I have never doubted the importance of my presence on the plantation, and am quite aware of the mischiefs that must result from my absence, but the absence is necessary, the mischiefs are inevitable, and the less I bother myself about them the better I can do my work." As Cheves focused his attention on the construction of Battery Wagner, his mother continued to badger him with complaints and with the fear that the war might leave them poverty-stricken. Such a fear was groundless, responded Cheves, who assured her that even "if every negro were lost" on their Savannah and Ogeechee River plantations, they would still have ample financial resources. "Are not folk that shudder at such Poverty a little spoiled by prosperity?" he asked. Reminding her that others had suffered much more severely from the war, Cheves urged his mother to "be thankful that [they] have so little to regret." Little did he suspect that in less than five months he would make the ultimate sacrifice in defense of the fort whose construction he had supervised.[53]

Unlike the repining Middleton and Cheves matrons, most women from wealthy slaveowning families eagerly supported the Confederate war effort. They did so in a variety of ways. In families with men in military service, they were frequently entrusted with primary responsibility for the management of plantations and slaves. Many women made clothing for the soldiers, others volunteered to minister to the sick and wounded, and those who were able made financial contributions. Very early in the war, Peter Hairston reported from Alexandria, Virginia, that the women of that city were even smuggling in guns from Washington City by hiding them under their dresses. More typical was the observation in November, 1861, by young Louisa Winchester that nearly all the women in Natchez were "knitting for the soldiers." The widow Louisa

---

52. Henry A. Middleton to Harriott K. Middleton, [July] 24, [1862], Henry A. Middleton Family Letters, in Cheves-Middleton Papers, SCHS.

53. Langdon Cheves, Jr., to "Dear Mamma," November 12, 1862, February 24, 1863, both in Cheves Family Papers, SCL.

McCord, whose mother had complained so bitterly in her letters to McCord's brother, Langdon Cheves, Jr., proved to be just as patriotic as he was. Passionately devoted to the Confederate cause, McCord outfitted a company of Zouaves commanded by her son, managed a hospital that had been established on the campus of South Carolina College, and served as president of both the Soldiers' Relief Association and the Soldiers' Clothing Association in her hometown of Columbia, South Carolina.[54]

One of the most remarkable female members of the elite class was another South Carolinian, Lucy Holcombe Pickens, whose contributions to the war effort earned for her the appellation "Queen of the Confederacy." The youthful third wife of wartime governor Francis W. Pickens, Lucy possessed feminine charms that made her a favorite of Czar Alexander II and his wife Catherine while Pickens was serving as United States Minister to Russia during the Buchanan administration. The Russian pair accepted the role of godparents to her daughter Eugenia, who was born in the palace at St. Petersburg in 1858. To mark the joyous occasion, they also presented Lucy with a valuable collection of precious stones. Three years later, following the outbreak of the war, Lucy sold her Russian jewels to finance the Holcombe Legion, a unit composed of eight companies, seven of infantry and one of cavalry. Later in the war, her portrait was inscribed on two denominations of Confederate currency, the $100 bills issued from 1862 to 1864 and the $1 bills printed in 1862.[55]

Those women who assumed responsibility for the management of slave plantations during the war often encountered severe difficulties. As Drew Faust has observed, force was the ultimate arbiter on these large agricultural units, yet physical violence simply lay outside women's sphere. Accordingly, slaves took advantage of the absence of their master to test the authority of the plantation mistress, and overseers often resented taking orders from a woman. Thus, shortly after Peter Hairston's departure for military service in the spring of 1861, his wife began to experience trouble with one of his overseers. When apprised of the situation, Hairston vigorously supported his wife. "Of Course if Mr. Mason does not behave himself," he advised, "get your father to turn him off

54. Peter W. Hairston to Fanny C. Hairston, May 10, 1861, in Peter Wilson Hairston Papers, SHC; Louisa Winchester to "My dear Brother" [Frank], November 30, 1861, in Winchester Family Papers, CAH; Richard C. Lounsbury, Introduction to McCord, *Selected Writings*, 8–9.

55. Cynthia Myers, "Queen of the Confederacy," *Civil War Times Illustrated* 35 (December 1996): 72, 76–78; MS Census, 1860 (Schedule 1: Population), Edgefield District, South Carolina.

immediately." Much more serious was a disagreement between J. G. Wilson, who had been hired as the trustee of Louis A. Bringier's Louisiana property during the war, and Bringier's wife Stella. Wilson was angered after the war by Bringier's failure to remit more than $1,000 in back wages due Wilson for his services as trustee. Charging that Bringier's property "was continually interfered with by [his] wife," Wilson asserted that after Stella arrived at Sans Souci plantation in the fall of 1862, she became the *de facto* manager of that property despite the fact that Wilson bore the ultimate responsibility for its effective operation. "You know, from experience," declared the irate trustee, that "Petticoats of that blood [the Tureaud family] are *wilful, and hard to manage.* . . . Would to God, you had left it [your property] in *her* Charge, instead of mine!"[56]

Another Louisiana planter wife, Fanny E. Conner, fared somewhat better, thanks largely to the assistance of her brother-in-law and a more cooperative overseer. Just after the fall of Vicksburg, one of the male slaves asked Fanny to request her absent husband's permission for him to marry a servant on another Conner plantation. Instead, Fanny herself acted immediately and decisively. "I told him I would take the responsibility in this emergency of giving my consent to his wishes before hearing from you," she informed her husband. But when it became necessary to move the Negroes to Texas to prevent their capture by approaching Federal troops, she needed male assistance to enforce the order. First, a trusted slave was sent from home to assist the overseer in getting them off. But that Negro, Dave, feared that some of the plantation slaves might "give trouble" unless their owner or his brother were with them. Accordingly, the brother, Henry Conner, who had been discharged from the army on account of disability, superintended the transfer of the Conner slaves to Texas.[57]

If the war was a traumatic experience for affluent southern women, Reconstruction proved to be much worse. Gender roles changed dramatically, even more than they had during the war. For many, the most immediate concern was financial security. Fanny Conner was confronted with that problem just months after the war's end. Severely depressed by her husband's continuing absence

56. Faust, *Mothers of Invention,* 70; Peter W. Hairston to Fanny C. Harrison, May 5, 1861, in Peter Wilson Hairston Papers, SHC; J. G. Wilson to Louis A. Bringier, May 10, 1866, in Louis A. Bringier and Family Papers, LSU.

57. Fanny E. Conner to "My most dearly loved husband," July 10, 1863; in Lemuel P. Conner and Family Papers, LSU. Information on Henry Conner's military disability is in a letter from Jonathan Ray to the author, February 18, 1996.

from home, she sought to impress upon him the gravity of their current monetary plight. "To provide for a family nowadays requires a continual outlay," she wrote in August, 1865. "The two items for which we never expended a dollar before—servants' hire & meat now cost me about *one hundred dollars per month.*" In addition, money was needed for groceries, shoes for the children, and other essential items. "I hope you will soon be able to send me some assistance," pleaded Fanny. "I dislike *very much indeed* to trouble you," she added apologetically, "but I cannot help it." Fanny's husband, Lemuel P. Conner, responded that she should "leave the money making" to him, assuring her that he would be able to educate their children and support the family "in respectable comfort." Unfortunately for Fanny, Conner's assurance was a bit too optimistic. He was forced into bankruptcy during Reconstruction, and he was obliged to turn from planting to the practice of law before he was finally able to provide the necessary financial security for his family.[58]

Other formerly well-to-do planter women were forced to seek outside employment for the first time in their lives in order to provide sustenance for their families. This unfamiliar burden fell most heavily upon widows, who had now lost all other means of support. For example, Adele Petigru Allston was compelled to open a girls' school in her Charleston residence—now known as the Nathaniel Russell House—in 1866, just two years after her husband's death. In like manner, the widow of Leonidas Polk, the Confederate general who had been killed late in the war during the Atlanta campaign, operated a boarding school in New Orleans in the late 1860s. Other planter wives went to work to supplement the meager resources of their nearly destitute husbands. Such was the case with Gertrude Thomas, whose husband experienced a series of financial reverses during Reconstruction. Finally, after enduring years of economic misery, she began teaching at a county school in Georgia for the paltry sum of $30 per month.[59]

Two prominent matrons, the widows of Haller Nutt of Mississippi and William Allen of Virginia, struggled valiantly but fruitlessly during the postwar period to maintain some semblance of the standard of living they and their

58. Fanny E. Conner to "My ever dearest Husband," August 13, 16, 21, 1865, in Lemuel P. Conner and Family Papers, LSU.

59. Adele Petigru Allston to Adele Vander Horst, December 15, 1865; Adele Allston to Benjamin Allston, October 14, 1866, both in Easterby, ed., *South Carolina Rice Plantation*, 215, 222; Leonidas Polk Family Papers, HNO; *The Secret Eye*, ed. Burr, 318 and *passim*, 379, 424.

families had enjoyed before the war. Julia Nutt, whose husband had lost $1,500,000 worth of property during the war despite his steadfast loyalty to the United States, was faced with the problem of providing for eight children, the youngest only two years old, following her spouse's death in the summer of 1864. She spent most of the remainder of her life trying to collect compensation from the federal government. Although the Court of War Claims eventually upheld an award of $256,000, she never received even half of that amount.[60] Frances Allen was more fortunate than Nutt in that her husband lived until 1875, but less fortunate ultimately because she became the target of a series of lawsuits after his demise that left her virtually penniless. At the beginning of the war, Allen had the largest in-state slave parcel of any planter in Virginia, with 446 slaves domiciled on his extensive properties in Henrico, James City, and Surry Counties. However, as a consequence of the war and emancipation, he lost the bulk of his resources. By the time of his death, his personal property was valued at only $1,500, while the debts owed by his estate in 1877 amounted to $44,000. As a result, his widow was obliged to sell both land and personal effects in an effort to extinguish the debt.[61]

Perhaps even more exasperating to plantation mistresses than the financial woes that confronted them after the war was the prospect of having to assume domestic chores that they would never have dreamed of performing only a few years before. The problem was most acute in 1865–1866, when tens of thousand of blacks, including many house servants, absconded from their former masters. A month and a half after the evacuation of Charleston, Jane Pringle described the state of anarchy that existed just north of the city and urged her friend Adele Allston not to consider an early return to her plantation in Georgetown District. Apart from the general demoralization of the black population, "the question of servants," reported Pringle, "is the pressing one here." According to

60. Claim filed by Sargeant Prentiss Knut on behalf of his mother [ca. 1890] (printed document), and *Samuel Sloan* [Philadelphia architect of Longwood] *v. Julia Nutt, Executrix*, October 2, 1866, both in Nutt Family Collection, MDAH; Hawks, "Julia A. Nutt of Longwood," 296–302.

61. Bill of Complaint, May 1, 1876; Account of Estate Sales at Auction by Thomas W. Keesee for and on Account of Mrs. Fannie Allen, Executrix of William Allen, July 21, August 11, 1875; Appraisal of William Allen Estate by J. Edmund Waddell, Jr., Deputy Clerk of Circuit Court, Henrico County, May 2, 1876; Executrix's Account, William Allen Estate, September 29, 1877; Sales for A/c Mrs. Frances A. Allen, Executrix of William Allen, by James Macdougal, June 24, 1881; et al., in James Nathaniel Dunlop Papers, VHS.

Pringle, a female member of the prominent Trapier family was "cooking and washing," the Charles Alstons, abandoned by their servants, had removed to Columbia, and Mrs. J. Harleston Read was predicting that all the domestics in Plantersville would leave within sixty days.[62]

Although some house servants returned to their former owners after experiencing the initial euphoria of freedom, the servant problem persisted throughout the Reconstruction period. Three years after the cessation of hostilities, another South Carolina matron expressed the fear that the time was "near at hand, if not already here, when most of our accomplished & refined ladies will have to cook"—a task she deemed "the very hardest work they could do" with the exception of field labor. The situation was no better in the Southwest, where, as late as 1874, a daughter-in-law of Judge Edward McGehee reported that a member of the formerly prosperous Metcalfe family was doing the washing for the Barrows in order "to pay the schooling for her little girls." Admirable as that might be, remarked McGehee, "It seems to me I'd rather teach my own children than wash for neighbors." What, she wondered almost incredulously, "is this old country coming to."[63] The cold reality of postwar life was difficult for the women in these elite families to face. The plantation empires that had formed the basis of their opulent life-style had gone with the wind, and they could only look back with romantic nostalgia to those splendid days "befo' the war." It is to that period that we must now turn.

62. Jane Pringle to Adele Petrigru Allston, April 1, [1865], in Easterby, ed., *South Carolina Rice Plantation*, 211.

63. C. S. S. to "Dear Brother" [R. B. Rhett, Sr.], May 6, 1868, in Robert Barnwell Rhett, Sr., Papers, SCHS; Ann B. McGehee to "My dear Hal," March 14, 1874, in McGehee Family Papers, MDAH.

4

AGRARIAN EMPIRES

Acquisition, Production, Profits, Problems, and Management

A desire continually to purchase land and negroes appears to be a characteristic of many of the planters of your state [Louisiana], and is, I think, greatly to be deprecated; as its only tendency is to prevent all ornamental improvements, and to bring upon them pecuniary embarrassment, and its attendent miseries.
—EDWARD G. W. BUTLER, May 5, 1830

I have been smoking & thinking of Texas & thinking of Texas & smoking 'till [*sic*] my nerves have become so much affected that I can scarcely hold my pen. . . . I have thought seriously on this subject. The dice are now in the box. I have shaken them & I hope soon to throw them—death is on one side & *fortune* on the other. As to the result, I am almost indifferent. In either case I shall be happy.   —LEWIS T. WIGFALL, August, 1836

I am tired & disgusted with planting & mean to sell out—lock stock & barrel if the times ever get flush again.   —JOHN B. LAMAR, March 10, 1858

Engaged this day a new overseer by name of Haller Nutt—and will only take him on trust until I can select a better—Rather a poor choice—and cant afford to pay him more than his board & horsefeed.
—HALLER NUTT, July 24, 1848

I regret very much, that our business relations before the rebellion prevent me from having any with you now—There was *no one* to whom I was more attached, in *every way*, than to you, and I showed it by risking a large amount to save you— Your treatment of me was such, that it wounded me in a way, that altho' I trust, God may enable me to forgive, I cannot forget. As far as money was concerned . . . I cared not for it—But the destruction of our friendship could not be healed.
—FACTOR ROBERT L. MAITLAND to
THOMAS P. DEVEREUX, February 21, 1866

A s HAS BEEN NOTED in the initial chapter of this book, the elite slaveholders of the Old South constructed their vast agricultural empires through
various means, usually several of them in combination. Some inherited the bulk
of their wealth, while others utilized advantageous marriages, capital derived
from mercantile and banking enterprises, hard work, aggressive entrepreneurial
tactics, and good fortune to achieve elite status. Age at midcentury and geographic location were important factors in determining those in this study who
acquired large holdings primarily through inheritance. Thus, the numerous
male descendants of Nathaniel Heyward and Francis Surget, Sr., both of whom
died in the 1850s, reaped the benefit of the fortunes accumulated by their fore-
bears. Similarly, the foundations of the great estates of such Atlantic seaboard
families as the Blakes, Izards, and Middletons of South Carolina; the Carters,
Harrisons, and Tayloes of Virginia; and the Lloyds of Maryland had been laid
as early as the seventeenth century. A few used an inheritance derived from
other sources to launch their planting careers. For example, wealthy Belgian
aristocrat Charles Kock immigrated to America about 1830 and, after a brief
residence in New Orleans, began purchasing sugar plantations on Bayou Lafourche with his inherited wealth. Within twenty years he had become one of
the leading sugar producers in the state.[1]

Three members of the elite, John and Pierce Mease Butler, owners of a vast
estate on the Georgia rice coast, and William Allen of Virginia, were obliged
to change their last names in order to secure their inheritance. The founder of
the Butler fortune was Major Pierce Butler (1744–1822), who came to America
as an officer in the British Army before the Revolution, married into the prominent Middleton family of South Carolina, and acquired extensive holdings in
Georgia during the last decade of the eighteenth century. In his will, Butler
stipulated that his Georgia plantations would pass to his grandsons, John and
Butler Mease, provided they changed their surname to Butler. In like manner,
William Allen, head of the fifth generation of one of the wealthiest and most
influential families in Surry County, Virginia, bequeathed the family estate,
Claremont, to his great-nephew William Griffin Orgain on condition that the

---

1. Herman Seebold, *Old Louisiana Plantation Homes and Family Trees*, 2 vols. (1941; rpr. Gretna,
La., 1971), I, 195–97; Champomier, *Statement of the Sugar Crop Made in Louisiana*, 1844–61. Kock
was among the top three sugar producers in the state in 1855 and 1857–59.

latter take the name of Allen. The latter did so and became one of the most prosperous planters in the state during the last decade of the antebellum period.[2]

Because of the extraordinary degree of intermarriage among elite families, most young planters simply augmented their holdings when they took a bride. For a few, however, a profitable marriage proved to be the key to their subsequent opulence. Such was the case with James H. Hammond of South Carolina and, to a lesser extent, with Joseph A. S. Acklen of Tennessee. Hammond, the son of a schoolmaster of modest means, gained not only substantial wealth but also entree into a promising political career by his marriage to Charleston heiress Catherine Fitzsimons in the summer of 1831. Through this salutary union he acquired a 10,800-acre plantation on the Savannah River with nearly 150 slaves, together with a politically powerful brother-in-law in the person of Wade Hampton II.[3] Acklen, already a prominent lawyer and the grandson of the founder of Huntsville, Alabama, was in much more comfortable circumstances than Hammond at the time of his marriage in 1849 to Adelicia Franklin, the widow of former slavetrader Isaac Franklin. That union, however, enabled Acklen to command one of the princeliest fortunes in America. He gained immediate control over a 20,000-acre estate in West Feliciana Parish, Louisiana, that was divided into six lucrative cotton plantations and was termed by one contemporary observer "the finest and best managed" agricultural unit in the entire South. Moreover, with his increased resources he was able to construct a magnificent residential estate in Nashville, which so impressed the visiting James D. B. De Bow that he characterized it as "a perfect paradise." According to De Bow, the grounds were marked by unsurpassed "natural beauties," the buildings were "commodious," and even the greenhouse would "almost compare with that of the government at Washington." Within a decade, Acklen had become the twelfth largest slaveholder in the country.[4]

Isaac Franklin and his one-time partner, Rice C. Ballard, both built their plantation empires on profits derived from the domestic slave trade. Franklin,

2. John A. Scott, Introduction to Kemble, *Journal of a Residence on a Georgian Plantation*, xviii–xix, xxii–xxiii; *Genealogies of Virginia Families: Articles from the William and Mary Quarterly*, 5 vols. (Baltimore, 1982), I, 59–60; James Nathaniel Dunlop Papers, VHS.

3. Faust, *James Henry Hammond and the Old South*, 58–59, 64, 70–71.

4. Thomas McAdory Owen, *History of Alabama and Dictionary of Alabama Biography*, 4 vols. (Chicago, 1921), III, 7; *Southern Cultivator* 10 (August 1852): 227; *De Bow's Review* 29 (August 1860): 248.

the senior partner in Franklin and Armfield, the largest slavetrading firm in the United States, began to acquire his Louisiana property in the mid-1830s, first as a partner of Francis Routh and later, after the latter failed in the Panic of 1837, through purchase at sheriff's auction of Routh's undivided half of the property. Franklin extended his holdings from three plantations with 224 slaves in 1838 to six plantations with nearly 600 slaves shortly after his death in 1846. It was this estate that passed to Acklen following the latter's marriage to Franklin's widow three years later.[5] A native of Virginia, Ballard became associated with the Alexandria-based firm of Franklin and Armfield at least as early as 1831. Four years later, he moved to Natchez, where he entered into a partnership with the Virginia company under the name Ballard, Franklin, and Company. This concern, which became the primary vehicle for the sale of the parent company's slaves in the Natchez market, was dissolved in November, 1841. Then, emulating the pattern established several years before by his partner, Ballard poured the profits generated by his slavetrading activities into land and slaves. At one time or another during the last two decades of the antebellum period, he had an interest in nearly a dozen plantations in Mississippi, Louisiana, and Arkansas. By 1860, either alone or in partnership with Judge Samuel S. Boyd of Natchez, Ballard controlled 500 slaves in those three states.[6]

Other great planters acquired their initial capital through more savory mercantile pursuits. The first Wade Hampton, a man with virtually no formal education, began to make money during the American Revolution by supplying foodstuffs to the patriot forces in South Carolina. At the end of the war he increased his assets by marrying a wealthy widow, and before the end of the century, he had become a prosperous planter with several hundred slaves and numerous commercial interests. Credited with introducing large-scale cotton

5. Wendell Holmes Stephenson, *Isaac Franklin, Slave Trader and Planter of the Old South* (1938; rpr. Gloucester, Mass., 1968), 100–107, 165–86.

6. *Ibid.*, 26, 56, 57, 60, 67; Frederic Bancroft, *Slave Trading in the Old South* (1931; rpr. New York, 1959), 304; Deed of Land from Rice C. Ballard to Samuel S. Boyd, Carroll Parish, Louisiana, July 23, 1860, in MacNeil Papers, MDAH; Rice Carter Ballard Papers, SHC; Plantation Accounts, in Rice Carter Ballard Papers, CAH. In 1860 Ballard's slaveholdings included 120 in Claiborne County, Mississippi, listed under "Ballard & Boyd"; 110 in Carroll Parish, Louisiana, under "S. S. Boyd & R. C. Ballard"; 155 in Madison Parish, Louisiana, under "R. C. Ballard & another"; 76 in Chicot County, Arkansas, under "Rice C. Ballard"; 37 in his residence county of Warren, Mississippi, under "Bay & Ballard"; and 4 at his family's residence in Louisville, Kentucky, under "R. C. Ballard," for a total of 502.

culture into Richland district, he made a profit of $75,000 on his first crop in 1799.[7] The next American war, three decades later, also proved lucrative for some who later became elite planters. Among these were Farish Carter and Benjamin Sherrod, both of whom prospered as army contractors for Georgia troops during the War of 1812 and later ploughed the profits gained from that business into plantations and slaves, Carter in Georgia and Sherrod in Alabama. Another Georgian, James A. Everett, began to build his fortune immediately after the same war when he opened an Indian trading post and married a Creek woman, from whose family he received large parcels of land. He soon developed his trading post into one of the largest mercantile establishments in the Georgia upcountry and used the resulting proceeds to purchase thousands of acres of land and a slave force that numbered 150 by 1839.[8] The progenitors of two other wealthy Atlantic Coast families also founded their agrarian empires on capital derived from mercantile enterprises. Somerset, the family estate of the Collins family in eastern North Carolina, was established in the late eighteenth century by Josiah Collins, Sr., who immigrated to America from England just before the Revolution and soon became a successful merchant and the owner of a rope-walk in Halifax, North Carolina. In like manner, Austin Peay, the father of South Carolina planter Nicholas A. Peay, made his initial money as a Camden merchant. He then established a plantation near the Wateree River in Fairfield District and began to build a landed estate that, at his death in 1841, included more than 300 slaves on ten plantations in four South Carolina counties.[9]

The quintessential example of the transition from commercial to agricultural capitalism occurred just before the Civil War when John Burnside, a wealthy New Orleans merchant, purchased Houmas, the vast Ascension Parish sugar estate of John S. Preston, for a reported $1,000,000. An immigrant from Northern Ireland, Burnside had come to America as a teenager and had started life in this country as a grocer's clerk for Virginia merchant Andrew Beirne. Subsequently, he moved to New Orleans and established a mercantile business

7. Moore, *Columbia and Richland County*, 30–31, 44, 66; Lacy K. Ford, Jr., *Origins of Southern Radicalism: The South Carolina Upcountry, 1800–1860* (New York, 1988), 8.

8. Farish Carter Papers, SHC; Owen, *History of Alabama*, IV, 1547; Joseph P. Reidy, *From Slavery to Agrarian Capitalism in the Cotton Plantation South: Central Georgia, 1800–1880* (Chapel Hill, 1992), 33, 39.

9. *Dictionary of North Carolina Biography*, ed. Powell, I, 404–406; Censer, *North Carolina Planters and Their Children*, 11; Ford, *Origins of Southern Radicalism*, 10.

in partnership with Oliver Beirne, the son of his former employer. After Beirne's retirement in 1847, Burnside assumed full control of the firm, now known as John Burnside and Company, and five years later, he began acquiring sugar plantations. The Houmas estate, which contained 12,000 acres of cultivatable land and 550 slaves, was termed by one observer "the finest property possessed by any single proprietor in America." It became the nucleus of a multimillion-dollar sugar empire that endured long after the end of the Civil War. At his death in 1881, the bachelor Burnside left an estate valued at some $8,000,000.[10]

The Houmas tract was one of many in the Southwest whose origins could be traced to Spanish land grants. Originally granted to the Conway family in the late eighteenth century, it then passed successively to Daniel Clark, Wade Hampton I, Hampton's son-in-law John S. Preston, and finally Burnside. Another Southwestern planter, Samuel F. Davis, received a large Spanish land grant in Concordia Parish following his marriage in the 1790s to the daughter of the Spanish commander in Louisiana and used it as the springboard to one of the greatest cotton empires in the region. Jacques Sorrel, the progenitor of a wealthy St. Mary Parish sugar-planting family also benefited from an early Spanish grant. Sorrel came to Louisiana as a French soldier the year before his native country ceded the province to Spain. Following that cession in 1763, he settled in the Attakapas District and soon received a grant that ultimately enabled him to establish a 4,000-acre cattle ranch. Other immigrants flocked to Louisiana in the closing years of the eighteenth century, doubtless attracted by the generous land policy of the provincial government. For example, under the terms of a proclamation issued in 1793, the authorities promised to give 400 acres of free land to each family of settlers provided they had four or more children or brought with them at least one Negro and remained on the plot for a minimum of three years.[11]

10. *Dictionary of Louisiana Biography,* ed. Conrad, I, 132–33; Roger W. Shugg, *Origins of Class Struggle in Louisiana* (University, La., 1939), 32; J. Carlyle Sitterson, *Sugar Country: The Cane Sugar Industry in the South, 1753–1950* (Lexington, Ky., 1953), 46 n.; *De Bow's Review* 24 (May 1858): 448 (quotation from New Orleans *True Delta*); James B. Lyman to A. K. Farrar, June 26, 1858, in Alexander K. Farrar Papers, LSU.

11. Sitterson, *Sugar Country,* 46 n.; *Goodspeed's,* I, 624–25 (Davis); *Dictionary of Louisiana Biography,* ed. Conrad, II, 754–55 (Sorrel); Proclamation of Baron de Carondelet, New Orleans, October 12, 1793 (MS in French), in Thomas Butler and Family Papers, LSU.

In the early years of the nineteenth century a new wave of settlers arrived in the Southwest, some of whom were destined to achieve wealth and prominence as great planters. For many, it was a combination of factors that resulted in their elevation to elite status. Several examples from the Natchez District will serve to illustrate the process. David Hunt migrated to Natchez from his native state of New Jersey just after the turn of the century to accept employment in his uncle's mercantile firm at an annual salary of only $300. Following the death of his uncle, who was killed in a duel with George Poindexter in 1811, Hunt moved to Jefferson County, married successively into two of the pioneer planter families in the region, and eventually amassed a fortune exceeded only by those of Francis Surget, Levin Marshall, and Stephen Duncan among the nabobs of the Natchez area. By the decade of the 1850s the family reputedly held some 1,700 slaves, though Hunt himself actually owned only about a third of that number.[12]

Also typical were the experiences of two Pennsylvanians, Samuel H. Lambdin and John Carmichael Jenkins, both of whom arrived in Natchez during the second quarter of the nineteenth century. As a teenager Lambdin worked as a clerk in a commission house in his hometown of Pittsburgh. Then, attracted by the more exotic life of steamboating on the Mississippi River, he found employment in that milieu, first as a clerk and later as a steamboat captain. In 1835 he settled in Natchez, where he soon became associated in a plantation supply business with Edwin R. Bennett, a migrant from Delaware and another budding Natchez nabob. Following his marriage into the wealthy Bisland family in 1842, Lambdin abandoned the mercantile business for planting, and by the time of the Civil War, he had accumulated extensive land and slave holdings on both sides of the river.[13] Another immigrant to the Natchez region in the mid-1830s was John Carmichael Jenkins, the son of a Pennsylvania ironmaster and former member of Congress. Educated at Dickinson College and the University of Pennsylvania, from which latter institution he received a medical degree in 1833, Jenkins came to Wilkinson County to assume the medical practice of an uncle who had lost his eyesight. Following the death of his uncle and his marriage in 1839 to Annis Field Dunbar, granddaughter of the celebrated planter-scientist Sir William Dunbar, Jenkins established his residence at Elgin plantation just outside of Natchez. There he prospered and gained a reputation as one of the

12. *Goodspeed's*, I, 989–92.

13. *Ibid.*, I, 377 (Bennett), 1091–92 (Lambdin); Persac's map of "Plantations on the Mississippi River from Natchez to New Orleans," 1858 (1931; rpr. New Orleans, 1967).

foremost scientific agriculturists in the region before succumbing to yellow fever in 1855 at the age of forty-five. After his death his planting interests were administered for more than a decade by Natchez attorney Josiah Winchester, a native of Massachusetts, who had also migrated to the Bluff City in the 1830s.[14]

Following the War of 1812, another migratory movement occurred, this one from the Atlantic slave states to western Alabama and the northern and eastern portions of Mississippi. It accelerated dramatically in the early 1830s when tens of thousands of settlers from the older seaboard states poured into the region to gobble up the former Chickasaw and Choctaw lands that had recently been opened to public sale.[15] By the mid-1830s the speculative mania in the new Southwest had reached frenetic proportions, and it was only ended by the Panic of 1837. Many of these emigrants from the eastern states were young men on the make who brought with them few, if any, slaves and who took advantage of the bonanza conditions to make a fortune almost literally overnight. But others were from well-established Upper South families like the Lloyds of Maryland, the Cockes and Tayloes of Virginia, and the Hairstons, Camerons, and Whitfields of North Carolina. If they did not migrate themselves—and some did—they transferred much of their labor force to Alabama and Mississippi and participated with their less affluent former neighbors in the speculative frenzy in land and slaves. As one North Carolina resident reported enthusiastically from Mississippi in 1836, "capitalists so much believe in the undoubted and irresistible state of prosperity here, that wealth and capital are pouring in and have been, for the last 12 months beyond all former example." Back in South Carolina, crusty old Nathaniel Heyward complained that the "excitement for the West" was ruining his state. Negroes and whites alike were "moving off in great numbers." Although the initial living conditions in their new environment might be rather spartan, observed Heyward, the profits to be made were "immense" and the temptation to relocate "overpowering."[16]

One family that capitalized on the economic opportunities afforded by the

14. *Goodspeed's,* I, 1020; Albert G. Seal, "John Carmichael Jenkins: Scientific Planter of the Natchez District," *JMH* 1 (January 1939): 14–28; Dr. Samuel Grier to Josiah Winchester, November 10, 1855, and H. C. Wright to Winchester, January 6, 1864, both in Winchester Family Papers, CAH.

15. Following two earlier but unsatisfactory treaties, the Choctaws relinquished all their land in Mississippi in the Treaty of Dancing Rabbit Creek, signed in September, 1830. The Chickasaws ceded all their lands east of the Mississippi two years later in the Treaty of Pontotoc Creek.

16. Frederick Norcom to James C. Johnston, January 24, 1836, in Hayes Collection, SHC; Nathaniel Heyward to James B. Heyward, January 5, 1837, in Heyward and Ferguson Family Papers, SHC.

Southwest was the Whitfield family of Lenoir County, North Carolina. As early as the mid-1820s Gaius Whitfield, together with brothers Boaz and William, each of whom had inherited only seven slaves from their father, moved westward and began planting operations in the Black Belt of Alabama.[17] During the following decade Gaius began to prosper, purchasing Negroes at cheap prices in North Carolina, transferring them to Alabama, and placing them on newly cleared canebrake lands. He accumulated much of his early capital speculating in land, an activity that was yielding him "one thousand dollars per week and sometimes more" in 1835.[18] Two years later, another brother, Needham, joined Gaius in the Southwest, eventually settling in Aberdeen, Mississippi. In the meantime, Gaius established his residence in Demopolis, and by the time of the Civil War, he owned three large plantations in Marengo County, Alabama, and another in Lowndes County, Mississippi, which collectively contained nearly 500 slaves and were valued at more than $1,000,000.[19] Another member of the family, Nathan Bryan Whitfield, a cousin and brother-in-law of Gaius, sold his North Carolina property to a brother in 1835 and joined Gaius in Marengo County. There he too amassed a considerable fortune and during the 1840s erected a palatial Greek Revival mansion, Gaineswood, which still stands today near Demopolis.[20] George Whitfield, another brother of Nathan, also decided in the 1830s to "look out for some country" where he could "employ [his] negroes to greater advantage" than he could in North Carolina, but unable to afford the elevated price of land in Alabama, he opted instead for Florida, where he eventually established a plantation in Jefferson County.[21] Thus, within

17. Cashin, *A Family Venture*, 92.

18. Boaz Whitfield to Gaius Whitfield, July 10, 1824, in Gaius Whitfield Family Papers, ADAH; Gaius Whitfield to Needham Whitfield, July 2, 30 (quotation), August 21, 1835, in Whitfield and Wooten Family Papers, SHC.

19. James B. Whitfield to Needham Whitfield, September 30, 1837, Needham Whitfield to Allen W. Wooten, March 5, October 10, 1850, Gaius Whitfield to Wooten, July 29, 1843, in Whitfield and Wooten Family Papers, SHC; James Benson Sellers, *Slavery in Alabama* (University, Ala., 1950), 30; Lowndes County, Miss., Tax Rolls (Land), 1857 (microfilm), RG 29, MDAH.

20. Land Indenture, Nathan Bryan Whitfield to James Bryan Whitfield, April 11, 1835, in Whitfield and Wooten Family Papers, SHC; Carl Carmer, *Stars Fell on Alabama* (New York, 1934), 103–104; W.P.A. Writers' Program, *Alabama: A Guide to the Deep South* (New York, 1941), 153; Caldwell Delaney, *Deep South* (Mobile, 1942), n.p.

21. George Whitfield to Gaius Whitfield, November 1, 1838, in Gaius Whitfield Family Papers, ADAH; George Whitfield to Allen W. Wooten, June 24, 1851, George Whitfield to William D. Cobb, August 23, 1853, both in Whitfield and Wooten Family Papers, SHC.

a span of fifteen years, at least six members of the Whitfield family left the Old North State in quest of a more propitious economic environment.

In contrast to the Whitfields, only one member of the Tayloe family of Virginia removed permanently to Alabama when four brothers in that family began to enter lands in Marengo and Perry Counties in the early 1830s. For a decade, Henry A. Tayloe managed the family properties in Alabama, which were owned principally by his older siblings William H. Tayloe, proprietor of Mount Airy estate in Richmond County, Virginia, and Benjamin Ogle Tayloe, who resided at the Octagon House in Washington, D.C. During the bonanza years of the mid-1830s, Henry sent back exuberant reports of the flourishing conditions in the Alabama Black Belt and encouraged his brothers to speculate in both land and slaves. This they did. Both William and Benjamin shipped a substantial number of their slaves from Virginia to Alabama, some to be sold and others to augment the labor force on the family's growing number of cotton plantations.[22] Henry Tayloe, however, never reaped the profits he continually promised, and in the fall of 1843, unable to pay a $12,600 note, he went bankrupt and was relieved of his managerial responsibilities by his brothers.[23] Under the direction of a hired agent, the Tayloe properties prospered, and by 1851 the family owned at least seven plantations in Alabama, encompassing 13,146 acres and 465 slaves and valued at $334,250. A decade later, the number of Tayloe slaves in Alabama had increased to 768, and William H., the wealthiest member of the family, owned nearly 500 slaves and 7,831 acres of land in the two states of Virginia and Alabama.[24]

Other resident East Coast planters also opened new plantations in the Southwest. Edward Lloyd VI, the master of Wye House on the Eastern Shore of Maryland, established one plantation in Madison County, Mississippi, during the winter of 1836–1837 and another in Tensas Parish, Louisiana, during the 1850s. He made periodic visits to each and reported in 1841 that he had 700 acres under cultivation on his Mississippi place. Lloyd also owned land in Arkansas

22. Henry A. Tayloe to Benjamin O. Tayloe, December 26, 1833, January 7, 1833 [*sic,* 1834], January 5, February 16, September 7, 1835, February 14, 1836, January 28, 1837, February 21, July 20, 29, 1839; May 10, 1840, in Henry A. Tayloe and Family Papers, ADAH.

23. Henry A. Tayloe to Benjamin O. Tayloe, April 1, August 23, November 27, 1843, *ibid.*

24. Valuation of Tayloe Alabama Plantations, January 11, 1851, *ibid.,* MS Slave Census, 1860, Marengo and Perry Counties, Ala.; Mount Airy Plantation Books, Vol. 3, entry for 1860 (microfilm copy *formerly* in SHC).

but apparently never moved any slaves to that state.[25] In similar fashion, Paul Cameron of North Carolina acquired a cotton plantation in Greene County, Alabama, in 1844 and another in Tunica County, Mississippi, about a dozen years later. In time, the latter place proved to be the more lucrative of the two, yielding some 350 bales of cotton in 1860, compared to less than half that amount on the Alabama unit. Doubtless encouraged by this production, Cameron shipped additional slaves from North Carolina to Mississippi in the late fall of that year.[26] Unlike Lloyd and Cameron, who merely supplemented their East Coast operations by opening plantations in the Southwest, another North Carolinian, Alfred Hatch, executed a permanent move with his family and slaves to the wilds of Alabama during the heady atmosphere of the early 1830s. According to Hatch's wife, the entourage made the 460-mile trek to the Alabama Black Belt in just over three weeks, stopping at night in either private homes or taverns while the slaves camped out. Within two decades Hatch was working more than 200 slaves on his Perry County property.[27]

Elite slaveholders were also afflicted with Texas fever during the bonanza decade of the 1830s. Even as the Whitfields were building their plantation empire in Alabama, they were also casting their eyes toward Texas. "We are all here in the notion of buying land in Texas," reported Gaius Whitfield in the summer of 1835. A year later, his brother Boaz announced his intention to go to "Texas and Red River" for the purpose of land speculation.[28] The fever even infected those as far away as South Carolina, where young Nat Heyward was talking of going to Alabama or even of settling in Texas. "He appears not to know his own mind for one day," grumbled his disgusted grandfather. A few months before, twenty-year-old Lewis T. Wigfall declared that he also was thinking of going to Texas. With both parents dead and the family resources

25. Edward Lloyd VI to "My dear Mother," January 2, 1837, February 22, 1839, April 11, 1841, Edward Lloyd VI to his son, Edward VII, December 27, 1860, William Hopkins to Edward Lloyd [VII], June 9, 1864, Sarah A. Dorsey to "Cousin Sam" [Samuel B. Walker], n.d., in Lloyd Papers, MHS.

26. W. T. Lamb to Paul C. Cameron, December 23, 1860, Wilson O'Berry to Cameron, May 2, 1861, H. W. to Cameron, December 29, 1860, in Cameron Family Papers, SHC.

27. Clinton, *The Plantation Mistress*, 168; MS Slave Census, 1850, Perry County, Ala.

28. Gaius Whitfield to Needham Whitfield, July 30, August 21 (quotation), 1835, in Whitfield and Wooten Family Papers, SHC; Boaz Whitfield to Gaius Whitfield, August 18, 1836, in Whitfield Family Papers, ADAH.

exhausted, Wigfall found the lure of Texas irresistible. "I have thought seriously on this subject," he remarked to his friend, Langdon Cheves, Jr. "The dice are now in the box. I have shaken them & I hope soon to throw them—death is on one side & *fortune* on the other. As to the result," concluded Wigfall, "I am almost indifferent. In either case I shall be happy."[29]

Some already in the Southwest were also attracted to Texas, particularly as a venue for land speculation. For example, John A. Quitman used the opportunity afforded by his service in the Texas Revolution to invest in the lands of that nascent republic. Just two weeks after the Battle of San Jacinto, he informed his wife that he had "made some good purchases of land" and was "now contracting for a beautiful site on Galveston Bay."[30] Several other Mississippi nabobs— among them, Levin Marshall, William J. Minor, and Greenwood Leflore— formed the Natchez Land Company for the purpose of speculating in Texas lands. The company became involved in a scheme to purchase some 65,000 acres of patented land in Hopkins and Wood Counties, but the original claim, dating from 1835, was encumbered, thereby resulting in litigation that extended into the Civil War period.[31]

Wherever they resided and however they acquired their initial capital, many of these elite planters made truly extraordinary profits from their exploitation of slave labor. The great fortunes accumulated by such cotton nabobs as Stephen Duncan and the elder Francis Surget and by such rice barons as Nathaniel Heyward and Joshua John Ward have already been discussed, but others fared nearly as well.[32] The decade of the 1850s proved to be especially lucrative for cotton producers in the Southwest. The account books of Rice C. Ballard, the former slavetrader, reveal that during that decade the five plantations he owned in partnership with Samuel S. Boyd produced an annual average of more than 2,500 bales of cotton, yielding gross proceeds of just over $100,000 per annum.

29. Nathaniel Heyward, Sr., to James B. Heyward, January 5, 1837, in Heyward and Ferguson Family Papers, SHC; L. Trezevant Wigfall to Langdon Cheves, Jr., August 1836, in Langdon Cheves, Jr., Papers, SCHS.

30. Receipt from A. L. Burnley "to buy Texas lands," March 29, 1836; John A. Quitman to Eliza Quitman, May 7, 1836, in John A. Quitman and Family Papers, MDAH.

31. Various letters, 1857–58, and William M. Gwin to Levin R. Marshall and William J. Minor, March 31, 1863, in William McKendree Gwin Papers, MDAH; J. S. Capes to Levin R. Marshall, July 12, 1854, in Winchester Family Papers, CAH.

32. See pp. 11–14 of this book.

As a result, Ballard realized a total net profit of more than $330,000 from his planting operations in the ten years immediately preceding the Civil War.[33] The figures for Mississippi planter Benjamin Roach, Jr., are almost identical for the same period. He too harvested an average of 2,500 bales on his five plantations during the 1850s, with average gross sales of $98,000 and a net profit of $90,000 per year.[34]

In neighboring Issaquena County, two absentee owners, Henry R. W. Hill of New Orleans and Dr. Robert J. Turnbull of Westchester County, New York, registered dramatic increases in both the value and yield of their cotton plantations during the 1850s. Turnbull, the son of the South Carolina nullification pamphleteer of the same name, produced only 311 bales with a slave force of 200 on his three Delta plantations in 1849. Shortly after his death five years later, an inventory of his estate disclosed personal assets of nearly $300,000, most of this amount invested in 376 slaves on four plantations. By the end of the decade, the Turnbull slaves, who had doubled in number during the past ten years, were producing almost 2,000 bales of cotton, more than six times the size of the crop harvested a decade before.[35] Equally impressive was the record of Hill, a prominent New Orleans factor who perished in the yellow fever epidemic of 1853 but whose Issaquena cotton empire remained intact under the administration of his son, James Dick Hill. In 1849 the Hill property, comprising four plantations valued at some $115,000, produced 10,500 bushels of corn and a modest 614 bales

33. Figures computed from accounts of Karnac (Claiborne Co., Miss.), Lepine (Warren Co., Miss.), Elcho (Madison Parish, La.), Outpost (Carroll Parish, La.), and Laurel Hill (Warren Co., Miss.) plantations and from Individual Account Book of Col. R. C. Ballard with New Orleans factors, November, 1843–April, 1862, in Rice C. Ballard Papers, CAH. It should be noted that the records are incomplete for some years; the accounts may not show all cotton sold, even in those years for which the data seem complete; and Ballard may have had accounts with other factors not listed in these books. Consequently, it is likely that Ballard's profits were even greater than I have indicated.

34. Computed by author from receipts for sale of cotton, Bachelor's Bend (Washington Co., Miss.), Ball Ground (Warren Co., Miss.), Duck Pond (Yazoo Co., Miss.), Wolf Lake (Yazoo Co., Miss.), and one other plantation, crops of 1852, 1855, 1859, and 1860, in Benjamin Roach Family Papers, CAH.

35. MS Census, 1850 and 1860 (Schedule 2: Slave Inhabitants, Schedule 4: Agriculture), Issaquena County, Miss., MDAH; Inventory of Estate of Robert J. Turnbull, April 15, 1856, Robert J. Turnbull Papers, in Natchez Trace Small MSS Collections, CAH; *Early Records of Mississippi,* comp. Wade and Branton, I, 115–16, 125; Robert James Turnbull Paper, n.d., SHC.

of cotton. Ten years later, the same plantations, now valued at nearly $300,000, yielded 36,000 bushels of corn and 2,600 bales of cotton, more than a fourfold increase in the latter with a slave force whose size had remained relatively static.[36]

Many other plantation patriarchs reaped a golden harvest from their fleecy white fields. Production and profits reached a peak during the 1850s in the river parishes of north Louisiana and in the Yazoo-Mississippi Delta. Thus, after noting that the leading Georgia producer, Colonel Joseph Bond, had marketed 2,100 bales of cotton in 1858, the Vidalia correspondent of a Natchez newspaper remarked that half a dozen planters in Concordia Parish, located just across the river from Natchez, had easily surpassed that figure. Among these were the Davis brothers, Samuel M. and Alfred V., who together produced more than 6,500 bales in 1859; former merchant Frederick Stanton, whose crop of 3,000 bales sold for a gross profit of $122,000 in the same year; Zebulon York and his partner E. J. Hoover, who reportedly made 4,500 bales annually on their six plantations; and Levin Marshall, the Natchez nabob with extensive holdings in three states, who was making 3,500 bales a year on his Louisiana plantations alone at the close of the antebellum period.[37] Other Louisiana cotton barons were equally successful. In Tensas Parish, just above Concordia, four members of the Routh family collectively harvested nearly 5,000 bales of cotton in 1859. Aron Goza of Carroll Parish, identified by one authority as the eighth largest cotton producer in the Deep South, made 2,650 bales in the same year. Even more impressive was the crop of Joseph A. S. Acklen, who produced 3,149 bales on his six West Feliciana Parish plantations with a slave force of about 700.[38]

One did not have to raise such enormous crops as those noted above in order to make handsome profits. On a visit to his family's plantations in the Alabama

36. MS Census, 1850 and 1860 (Schedule 2: Slave Inhabitants, Schedule 4: Agriculture), Issaquena County, Miss., MDAH; Personal Tax Rolls, 1855, 1857, 1858, Issaquena County, Miss., RG 29, MDAH. For the death of H. R. W. Hill, see Rosalie Quitman to F. H. Quitman, September 17, 1853, in John A. Quitman and Family Papers, and John A. Quitman to F. H. Quitman, September 29, 1853, in John A. Quitman Papers, both MDAH.

37. *De Bow's Review* 26 (May 1859): 581; James, *Antebellum Natchez,* 154, 156–57; John Hebron Moore, *Emergence of the Cotton Kingdom,* 117–18, 240; *Dictionary of Louisiana Biography,* ed. Conrad, II, 863–64.

38. MS Census, 1860 (Schedule 4: Agriculture), Tensas, West Feliciana parishes, La., LSU; Menn, "Large Slaveholders of the Deep South," 244.

Black Belt, Benjamin O. Tayloe expressed the hope that "the present crops & price of cotton . . . will make all of us easy in our money matters." Basing his estimate on a price of $60 per bale (or 12 cents a pound for a 500-pound bale), Tayloe predicted that the 1850 crop of 1,200 bales on the seven Tayloe plantations in Alabama would sell for a gross price of $72,180. The following year, Richard T. Archer estimated that his Holmes County, Mississippi, crop of 800–900 bales would bring some $56,000. "I see prosperity ahead," he announced enthusiastically to his wife, "and hope to be able to gratify your every want." A similar profit was recorded by Natchez nabob Haller Nutt when he sold 1,151 bales of cotton for a net profit of more than $52,000, thereby increasing his credit balance with a New Orleans factor to just over $100,000 in the spring of 1860.[39]

Although cotton was indeed king of the staple crops, rice and sugar planters also enjoyed great prosperity. Many of the leading sugar producers in the late antebellum period were situated in Ascension Parish, just below Baton Rouge. Chief among these were Mrs. M. D. Bringier, Henry Doyal, South Carolina absentees John S. Preston and John L. Manning, and, after 1857, John Burnside, by far the wealthiest of them all. During the seventeen-year period from 1829 to 1845, the two principal Bringier plantations in Ascension, Houmas and Hermitage, yielded average annual gross proceeds of $57,000. However, following the death of Michel D. Bringier in 1847, the affairs of the estate were so badly managed that, despite an income of $290,000 in 1847–1848, his widow was still in debt to the tune of some $180,000. Under the capable management of her son-in-law Benjamin Tureaud, the family's fortune improved dramatically in the early 1850s. The Houmas crop of 1852, amounting to nearly 2,000 hogsheads, sold for approximately $100,000, thereby revitalizing the credit of the widow Bringier. Another son-in-law, New Orleans merchant Martin Gordon, Jr., who was handling her financial affairs, exulted: "The Capitalists now *apply to me* for the Bringier paper. What a change . . . from the last four Years, when I had to beg, or treat, and almost supplicate, for renewals." A year later, Gordon wagered $100—correctly, as it turned out—that the Houmas plantation would

39. Benjamin O. Tayloe to William H. Tayloe, January 1, 1851, in Tayloe Family Papers, VHS; Richard T. Archer to Ann B. Archer, January 13, 1852, in Richard Thompson Archer Family Papers, CAH; Haller Nutt in Account with Foley, Avery, & Co., Nett Sales of Cotton, May 4, 1860, in Nutt Family Collection, MDAH.

make "more money, this Year, than any other plantation in Louisiana." Indeed, Houmas was the leading sugar-producing plantation in the state, not only in 1853, when it yielded 2,400 hogsheads, but in 1854 and 1856 as well.[40]

Other Ascension Parish planters consistently produced well over 1,000 hogsheads of sugar per year during the decade and a half before the Civil War. Henry Doyal, proprietor of Mount Houmas Refinery on the left bank of the Mississippi, was the largest sugar producer in Louisiana during the 1850s, leading the state eight years (1850–1855, 1857, 1860) and trailing only John Burnside at the end of the decade. Doyal, who also operated two plantations in Plaquemines Parish, marketed more than 3,600 hogsheads of sugar in the banner year 1853–1854. South Carolina governor John L. Manning and his brother-in-law John S. Preston both averaged nearly 1,500 hogsheads per annum on their Ascension holdings, which were located just above the Houmas plantation of Mrs. Bringier. Twice during the decade, each of the South Carolinians exceeded 2,000 hogsheads in annual production. With the acquisition in 1858 of Preston's three units, together with the contiguous Orange Grove plantation and another in adjacent St. James Parish, John Burnside instantly became the wealthiest sugar planter in the state. With 7,600 acres of improved land and a labor force of nearly 1,000 slaves on his five plantations, Burnside produced an average of 4,000 hogsheads of sugar in the four years before the outbreak of war. His 1861 crop of 7,652 hogsheads was by far the largest ever recorded by an antebellum Louisiana sugar planter.[41]

Like the sugar magnates of south Louisiana, the rice barons of coastal South Carolina and Georgia had enormous investments in land, slaves, and processing equipment. Despite their huge capital investments, many of them continued to prosper during the late antebellum period, though their profits were not as great as they had been earlier in the century when such men as Nathaniel Heyward and Joshua J. Ward took advantage of high prices and other propitious circum-

40. "Les Produit de chaque Recolte," 1826–45, Martin Gordon, Jr., to Mrs. M. D. Bringier, April 21, 1849, both in Louis A. Bringier and Family Papers, LSU; Gordon to Benjamin Tureaud, December 30, 1852; February 3 (first quotation), December 3 (second quotation), 1853, in Benjamin Tureaud Papers, LSU. Rankings computed by author from Champomier, *Statement of the Sugar Crop Made in Louisiana*, 1844–61.

41. All production figures and ranking computations from Champomier, *Statement of the Sugar Crop Made in Louisiana*, 1844–61; Burnside acreage from MS Census, 1860 (Schedule 4: Agriculture), Ascension, St. James Parishes, La., LSU.

stances to erect their vast plantation empires. For example, one of Nathaniel's grandsons, James B. Heyward, earned a relatively modest profit of $35,135 from his 930 acres of rice land in 1859. Terming it "the best crop of rice made at these places," he lamented that a "bad provision crop" had "neutralized" the benefit.[42] Unlike the Heyward empire, which had been divided among more than half a dozen heirs, the Ward estate remained intact following Joshua's death in 1853, and six years later, his slave force of more than 1,100 produced 4,410,000 pounds of rice, which yielded gross proceeds of approximately $140,000. A decade earlier, with the price of rice about the same, another Georgetown District planter family, the Pyatts, had sold 2,010,000 pounds of rice for half that amount. Similar profits were recorded just before the war on the plantations of Stephen C. King and George W. Owens, the two largest rice planters in Camden County, Georgia. Like Ward, Owens died during the mid-1850s, but the estate, administered by his son George S. Owens, yielded an estimated gross profit of $76,800 in 1859 from a crop of 2,400,000 pounds. King's crop of just under 2,000,000 pounds sold for about $62,000 in the same year.[43]

The major staples of cotton, sugar, and rice were not the only sources of revenue for elite planters. Some large slaveholders in the Upper South made handsome, if not exorbitant, profits from the production of grain and livestock. Thus, William Allen of Virginia received more than $40,000 from the sale of grain on his Curle's Neck estate in 1853. Two years before, when grain prices were considerably lower, Robert Bolling earned approximately $23,000 from a wheat and corn crop of similar size on his magnificent Sandy Point estate in Charles City County. With his purchase of Sandy Point in May, 1852, Richard Baylor, who already owned extensive properties in Essex County, undoubtedly became the largest grain producer as well as the largest resident slaveholder in Virginia. Described by neighboring proprietor John A. Selden as "the most valuable and most magnificent estate I ever saw," capable of producing annual crops of 20,000 bushels of wheat and 3,000 barrels of corn, Sandy Point con-

42. James B. Heyward Plantation Book, 1857–60, Vol. VI in Heyward and Ferguson Family Papers, SHC.

43. Production figures from Joyner, *Down by the Riverside*, 20; Rogers, *History of Georgetown County*, 285; Julia Floyd Smith, *Slavery and Rice Culture in Low Country Georgia, 1750–1860* (Knoxville, Tenn., 1985), 226. Estimated gross profits from Table 42 in Lewis C. Gray, *History of Agriculture in the Southern United States to 1860*, 2 vols. (1933; rpr. Gloucester, Mass., 1958), II, 1030. For personal information on Owens, see Owens-Thomas Family Papers, GHS.

sisted of four farms with an aggregate acreage of nearly 4,500, nearly half of which was under cultivation.[44] The premier livestock breeder in the slave South was Mark R. Cockrill, who operated a 5,000-acre stock farm on the Cumberland River near Nashville, Tennessee. Cockrill, who won a prize at the London Exposition of 1851 for the highest quality wool in the world, had 3,500 sheep on the lush, green pastures of his Robertson's Bend farm.[45] But most of his slaves were employed on cotton plantations in Madison County, Mississippi. For it was in cotton that the greatest profits were to be made at the close of the antebellum period.

Although staple-crop agriculture proved to be immensely profitable for many southern planters, they were not immune to the periodic depressions that afflicted the nation's economy during the pre–Civil War years. Since they usually purchased land and slaves on credit and since most of their capital was tied up in those two assets, they had few liquid resources to call upon when prices dropped and notes came due. Consequently, some of these outwardly affluent agriculturists suffered severely in times of economic distress, most notably in the wake of the Panic of 1837 and, to a lesser extent, during the milder recession of 1857. Writing from central Mississippi in 1843, a cousin of North Carolina planter James C. Johnston described the dramatic decline in prosperity that had occurred in that state since the bonanza years of the mid-1830s. "You cannot imagine what a change in things we have had in this country," he exclaimed. Land values had plummeted from $25–$35 to $5–$6 per acre, slave prices had fallen by nearly two-thirds, and cotton had reportedly sold in New Orleans for as little as three and one-half cents a pound. Back in North Carolina, Johnston was having his own problems. The "almost total destruction" of his crops the previous year had left him "without any income" from his farms. Moreover, "the low price of flour & lumber" had resulted in a total loss of income from his mills, leading him to fear that "the coming year [would] bring [him] in debt." Never had he been "more straightened [*sic*]" in his affairs or more troubled in the management of his "Plantation & other business."[46]

44. John A. Selden to Richard Baylor, March 13, 1854, February 21, 1852 (quotation), Robert B. Bolling to Baylor, March 4, April 9, June 2, 1852, in Baylor Family Papers, VHS. Estimated gross profits calculated from Tables 50, 51, in Gray, *History of Agriculture*, II, 1039.

45. Chase C. Mooney, *Slavery in Tennessee* (Bloomington, Ind., 1957), 198–99; Gray, *History of Agriculture*, II, 854; *De Bow's Review* 27 (July 1859): 93.

46. John T. Johnston to James C. Johnston, April 3, 1843, and James C. Johnston to James Iredell, April 3, 1843, both in Hayes Collection, SHC.

Conditions were no better in southern metropolitan centers. When the Panic first erupted in the spring of 1837, Charleston merchant-planter Leroy M. Wiley described the crisis as "an awful One." But unlike many others in his class, he opposed any attempt to resurrect the National Bank. "I hope never to see one in operation again possessing the power of the former ones," he declared. In his capacity as a merchant creditor, Wiley lost heavily in the depression. Several years later, he complained that "the Idea now is to get in debt and cheat Out." He attributed his losses to the "operation of the Bankrupt Law" in Georgia, where he had a number of outstanding loans, and to "the low grade of Morals at present."[47] In New Orleans, where Judge Thomas Butler had gone to seek an extension of credit from the banks early in 1842, the financial distress had reached nearly calamitous proportions. "I never in my life had so gloomy a prospect before me relative to my own affairs," he lamented to his wife in February. Finding that it was "impossible to sell a hogshead of sugar" in the Crescent City, he shipped more than 100 hogsheads to New York, though it could be sold there only "at a very low price." Unable to either sell sugar or borrow money in New Orleans, he was compelled to mortgage twelve Negroes and other unidentified property for $5,000 in order to "raise some money, in these hard times."[48]

Butler's financial difficulties were not attributable solely to the distresses produced by the depression of the late 1830s and early 1840s. Like others of his class, he had not heeded the warning articulated a dozen years before by his cousin, Edward G. W. Butler. The latter had expressed his opinion that one of the "leading characteristics" of Louisiana sugar planters was "an apparent determination to be always in debt, notwithstanding the sufficiency of their ordinary incomes to support them in ease and affluence." Instead of utilizing their profits to enhance the comfort of their families, to improve their grounds, or to support charitable enterprises, they invariably applied their surplus to the purchase of additional land and slaves, thereby bringing upon themselves "pecuniary embarrassment, and its attendent miseries."[49] Unfortunately, Butler fell into the very

47. L. M. Wiley to Farish Carter, May 29, 1837, and March 12, 1842, both in Farish Carter Papers, SHC.

48. Thomas Butler to Ann Butler, January 16, February 20 (first quotation), 23, March 2 (second quotation), 1842, Butler to L. Barras, May 3, 1842 (third quotation), in Thomas Butler and Family Papers, LSU.

49. E. G. W. Butler to Thomas Butler, February 7, May 5, 1830, *ibid.*

pattern described by his younger relative. Already the proprietor of a cotton plantation, he acquired a Terrebonne Parish sugar plantation in 1827 and soon began to stock it with additional Negroes, seeking a loan of $15,000–$20,000 from his brother-in-law, Stephen Duncan, to effect such purchases. In 1833 Butler sold his cotton plantation and, two years later, purchased a second Terrebonne sugar plantation for $30,000, payable in annual notes of $6,000. When the Panic struck in 1837, he owed more than $36,000 to the New Orleans factorage firm of Lambeth & Thompson.[50] Nevertheless, he continued to purchase slaves despite a decline in sugar prices, and in the spring of 1843, Duncan estimated that his friend's total indebtedness was approaching $100,000. As his debts continued to mount, Butler sold his Terrebonne place in December, 1845, for $60,000 but acquired another sugar plantation in Pointe Coupée Parish the following month for $53,500. Shortly before his death in August, 1847, Butler still owed more than $50,000 to various financial establishments in New Orleans.[51] Despite annual net profits of more than $25,000, the Butler estate remained in debt. Noting that the Butler account showed a debit of $25,000, more than $17,000 of which was due in cash, the New Orleans firm of G. W. Burke and Company informed Butler's eldest son and executor in the spring of 1848 that it would not accept "any further drafts." Finally, early in 1850, the administrator of the estate was obliged to sell the Pointe Coupée plantation in order to liquidate much of the debt still owed to New Orleans factors.[52]

Butler was not the only elite planter to die in impecunious circumstances. Thomas Spalding of Sapelo Island, Georgia, was heavily in debt at the time of

50. Thomas Butler to wife Nancy [Ann], April 30, 1830; Stephen Duncan to Butler, September 16, 1830, January 15, 1831; Butler to Duncan, December 11, 1833; Gustavus Calhoun to Butler, November 30, 1833; Act of Sale, Richard G. Ellis to Thomas and William E. Butler, April 17, 1835; Bill of Sale, William E. Butler and wife Patsy to Thomas Butler, April 27, 1837; Lambeth and Thompson to Butler, January 17, 1837, *ibid.*

51. Slave Bills of Sale, March 27, April 12, 1839, April 8, 10, 1841; Thomas Butler to Ann Butler, April 6, 1841; Stephen Duncan to Butler, April 12, 1843; Act of Sale, Ducros Sugar Plantation, Thomas Butler to Van P. Winder, December 27, 1845; Receipt for purchase of Jesse H. Willis Plantation [Raccourci] by Thomas Butler, January 3, 1846; Butler to son Pierce, March 27, 1847; J. W. Maynarel to Pierce Butler, October 13, 1847, *ibid.*

52. Profits computed from invoices for sale of sugar and molasses, 1847–52; G. W. Burke and Company to R. E. Butler, April 18, 1848; Burke and Company to Pierce Butler, April 19, 1848; Receipt for slaves, Pointe Coupée Parish, February 1, 1850; Receipt from Washington Jackson and Company, March 9, 1850, *ibid.*

his death in 1851, despite selling about fifty slaves three years earlier in an effort to reduce his indebtedness. For South Carolina planter Matthew R. Singleton, it was the expense of constructing a palatial mansion together with the simultaneous failure of a Charleston factor for whom he had co-signed notes that brought financial ruin. Following his untimely death in 1854, creditors seized many of Singleton's possessions, including his stable of fine racehorses. Natchez nabob Alexander K. Farrar was another member of the elite class who never seemed able to exorcise his financial woes. Farrar apparently remained in debt before, during, and after the Civil War.[53]

Many planters who had overextended themselves before the war found it impossible to meet their financial obligations during the 1860s. A prime example is afforded by Wade Hampton III, the celebrated Confederate cavalry general from South Carolina. His father, the second Wade Hampton, had established a 2,500-acre cotton plantation, Walnut Ridge, in Issaquena County, Mississippi, in the 1840s. In 1855 he sold this heavily mortgaged property to his sons, Wade, called Jr., and Christopher F., for $175,130, payable in 73 promissory notes at 8 percent interest. The first 32 notes, due between 1857 and 1860 and amounting to $50,000, were paid in a timely manner, but the remaining notes, which came due while the war was in progress, were not paid. Meanwhile, Wade, Jr., had purchased two additional plantations, Wild Woods and Richland, in adjacent Washington County for $170,660, payable in nine installments. Once again, the prewar notes were paid while those that fell due after the war began were not. Most of the notes on the Hampton properties in Mississippi eventually came into the possession of Stephen Duncan and, following his death in 1867, passed to his son, Stephen, Jr. Because of his inability to pay either the principal or the interest on these loans during the war, Hampton's debt to the Duncans, originally about $200,000, was not reduced appreciably either during the war or during the early years of Reconstruction. Finally, burdened with a total debt of nearly $1,000,000, Hampton declared bankruptcy in 1868 and spent much of the remainder of his life trying to negotiate a settlement with the younger Duncan that would enable him to redeem his Mississippi

53. Smith, *Slavery and Rice Culture in Low Country Georgia*, 110; John Hammond Moore, *Columbia and Richland County*, 176–77; George D. Farrar to "My dear father," January 24, 1859, in Alexander K. Farrar Papers, LSU; A. K. Farrar to James O. Fuqua, July 24, 1866, in Winchester Family Papers, CAH. For a description of Singleton's grandiose mansion, completed just weeks before his death, see *Carologue* 13 (Summer 1998): 22.

plantations. Clearly, the war had had a severe impact on the Hampton family fortune, but the initial cause of their misfortune can be traced to the improvident business practices of the two Wade Hamptons during the 1850s.[54]

Economic depressions, rash business decisions, and the disruptive effect of the Civil War were not the only factors that created financial woes for the great planters. Such natural disasters as floods, windstorms, early freezes, and epidemics also took a heavy toll. With only a rudimentary levee system to protect their fields, the cotton and sugar planters of the Lower Mississippi Valley were particularly susceptible to the ravages of the flooding that occurred with distressing regularity during the antebellum years. Floods had long been a problem in that region. Particularly noteworthy were those of 1811, 1815, 1828, and 1840.[55] But it was not until the last two decades of the antebellum period, when cotton planters began to cultivate the fertile lands in the river parishes of Louisiana and across the river in the Mississippi Delta, that these frequent floods had their severest impact on planting interests.

During the 1840s, planters along the Mississippi River and its tributaries were plagued by overflows in 1844 and again in 1847 before confronting the disastrous flood that occurred in the last year of the decade. Following almost incessant rains from late November, 1843, to mid-January of the following year, Stephen Duncan voiced his fear of a "general & unprecedented overflow" of the Mississippi. "I think the prospect is truly alarming," he remarked apprehensively. Duncan's concern proved to be well founded. In late June, as serious flooding began to affect the entire Lower Mississippi Valley, Haller Nutt labored feverishly to bolster the levee protecting his Madison Parish plantation.

54. Cauthen, ed., *Family Letters of the Three Wade Hamptons,* xiii–xviii; Wade Hampton, Jr., to Stephen Duncan, Jr., April 28, 1875, December 4, 8, 1884, in Stephen and Stephen Duncan, Jr., Papers, LSU; Land Indenture, August 27, 1855; "Deed of Conveyance, Samuel W. Ferguson Assignee in Bkptcy of Estate of Wade Hampton to Stephen Duncan," November 23, 1869, and Wade Hampton, Jr., to Stephen Duncan, Jr., May 10, 1874, both in Wade Hampton Papers, Natchez Trace Small MSS Collections, CAH; Memorandum of Notes of W. Hampton, Sr., Wade Hampton, Jr., and C. F. Hampton, April 1, 1863; Stephen Duncan to Josiah Winchester, September 3, October 30, 1866, Wade Hampton, Jr., to Stephen Duncan, Jr., April 18, 1867, Samuel W. Ferguson, Assignee, Deed to Wade Hampton and William C. Patterson, June 12, 1869, Deed of Conveyance, Samuel W. Ferguson, Assignee in Bankruptcy of Est. of Wade Hampton, to Stephen Duncan, November 22, 1869, in Winchester Family Papers, CAH.

55. James, *Antebellum Natchez,* 271; William J. Minor to Charles P. Leverich, May 29, 1840, in Charles P. Leverich Papers, MDAH.

The water was only an inch or two below the level of 1828 and still rising, he reported on June 25. Less than a week later, with 300 acres under water on his Bayou Vidal plantation, he placed the blame for that loss on his neighbor, Francis Surget, whose levee had broken in mid-June. "If Surget had kept out the water from his place," Nutt complained bitterly, "I think we would yet have been entirely free from back water." Duncan later estimated the total loss from the overflow of 1844 at between 175,000 and 200,000 bales.[56] Three years later, the angry waters of the Mississippi threatened once again. In early May, William N. Mercer reported from New Orleans that high water was beginning to affect many plantations north of Natchez. Above the mouth of the Arkansas River, he noted, "the waters are said to be higher by several inches than in 1844." According to Haller Nutt, many levees protecting north Louisiana plantations had been breached, much of Tensas Parish was under water, and the river between Vicksburg and Natchez was six or seven inches higher than in 1844, or about equal to the level of the great flood of 1828. Fortunately, after working sixty hands for nearly a month on his levee, Nutt sustained only minimal damage this time.[57]

As bad as they were, the floods of 1844 and 1847 were not as devastating as the one that struck the Mississippi Valley in 1849. As early as mid-December of the previous year, Stephen Duncan warned, "We are threatened with a flood in the Miss[issipp]i equal to that of '28." He began immediately to shore up the levee protecting his Issaquena cotton plantations, detailing more than two hundred hands to work on a 100-yard segment where a break had occurred the year before. Despite such efforts by Duncan and others, successive floods, beginning in February and continuing throughout the spring, soon took a heavy toll. In mid-March Duncan reported that 3,000 acres of his Issaquena cotton lands were under water, and he doubted that he would make 350 bales on his extensive properties.[58] From New Orleans, the factorage firm of Washington Jackson and

56. Stephen Duncan to C. P. Leverich, December 1, 1843, January 17 (quotations), September 13, 1844, in Charles P. Leverich Papers, MDAH; Araby Plantation Journal, June 25, 28, July 1 (quotation), 1844, in Haller Nutt Papers, DU.

57. W. N. Mercer to C. P. Leverich, May 2, 1847, in Charles P. Leverich Papers, MDAH; Araby Plantation Journal, April 18, 28, 1847, in Haller Nutt Papers, DU.

58. Stephen Duncan to C. P. Leverich, December 15, 20, 1848, March 12, 14, 1849, Levin R. Marshall to Leverich, February 23, 1849, Francis Surget to Leverich, March 12, 1849, in Charles P. Leverich Papers, MDAH.

Company reported that there was "every appearance of a general overflow in the valley of the Mississippi" that would impact the sugar planters even more severely than the cotton producers because they would "lose two crops." As it turned out, one observer estimated that the overflow of the Red River alone had shortened the crop of 1849 by 18,000 hogsheads, and William J. Minor predicted as early as May that the entire sugar crop would be reduced by 50,000 hogsheads as a consequence of the flooding.[59] Some proprietors replanted their cotton and corn crops, only to lose them again as fresh torrents of water poured down from above. In mid-April, the dejected Duncan announced that he had "abandoned all hope of being able to plant [his] overflowed lands." As swollen tributaries continued to dump their waters into the Mississippi, he predicted if there were no runoff before the Missouri came down, *"we will have the greatest overflow, ever known."* Coupled with a killing frost in mid-April, a tornado on May 16, and a severe cholera outbreak that raged throughout the summer, the spring floods rendered the year 1849 one of the most disastrous on record for planters in the Lower Mississippi Valley. As Natchez nabob Samuel M. Davis remarked, it was "one they will long remember."[60]

Flooding continued periodically during the 1850s, culminating in more disastrous losses for both cotton and sugar planters in the closing years of the decade. The latter suffered most heavily in 1851 and 1858. As a consequence of some fifteen to eighteen crevasses in the Mississippi River levee system between New Orleans and the Red River, some planters in Ascension and Plaquemines Parishes lost most of their crop in 1851. Among those most severely affected were William J. Minor, Henry Doyal, and Duncan F. Kenner in Ascension, and Judah P. Benjamin in Plaquemines. Minor, who lost his entire crop at Waterloo, was reportedly "a good deal subdued" as he contemplated the gravity of his financial situation. Seven years later, the mighty Mississippi again wreaked

59. Washington Jackson and Company to C. P. Leverich, March 16, 1849, Stephen Duncan to Leverich, March 12, 1849, William J. Minor to Leverich, May 24, 1849, in Charles P. Leverich Papers, MDAH; Champomier, *Statement of the Sugar Crop Made in Louisiana,* 1849–50, 52; William N. Mercer to Henry Clay, June 3, [1849], in *The Papers of Henry Clay,* Vol. 10: *Candidate, Compromiser, Elder Statesman, January 1, 1844–June 29, 1852,* ed. Melba Porter Hay (Lexington, Ky., 1991), 600.

60. Stephen Duncan to C. P. Leverich, April 18 (first quotation), 23 (second quotation), May 19, 22, 26, 31, June 18, 23, July 10, 1849, Francis Surget to Leverich, May 21, July 9, 1849, Samuel M. Davis to Leverich, June 3, July 6 (quotation), 1849, Levin Marshall to Leverich, June 6, 1849, in Charles P. Leverich Papers, MDAH.

havoc upon those sugar plantations that bordered the river. The "Bell Crevasse" of April 11, 1858, and the "Labranche Crevasse" of May 2 resulted in a complete overflow of the fertile lands between Bayou Lafourche and the Mississippi and destroyed the crops on all Plaquemines Parish plantations within thirty miles of New Orleans.[61]

The following year, many cotton plantations in the northeast portion of the state were inundated by the angry waters of the Mississippi and the back bayous. In mid-March, 1859, the overseer of Rice C. Ballard's Wagram plantation informed his employer that the water was already higher than it had been the previous spring and was rising at the rate of three inches each day. Several weeks later, a neighboring proprietor in Madison Parish notified Ballard that his Elcho plantation was "two thirds under" and the river was "8 or 9 inches above last years water" and still rising. "I wish to god you were at home," he exclaimed, "for if any other levees break, you will all be in my condition, *under water*." Just to the south, in Concordia Parish, Lemuel P. Conner was working desperately at the same time to shore up the levees protecting his Rifle Point plantation. More than two weeks later, he was still battling to contain the flood waters. The river, he reported, "is about 20 inches higher than last year, even higher than 1828." He continued anxiously, "But the front river water is not all the trouble. . . . The back water is rising most rapidly—4 to 6 inches a day!" In the end, it took nearly 10,000 cubic yards of additional dirt to save the levee at Rifle Point.[62]

Flooding was not the only natural phenomenon that affected the fortunes of southern planters. From time immemorial those who cultivate the land have been subjected to the vicissitudes of weather. It is no accident that the two ubiquitous topics in the records and correspondence of antebellum agriculturists were health and the weather. In addition to high water, elite planters, together with their less affluent neighbors, were plagued from time to time by severe windstorms; killing frosts; torrential rains; extended droughts; and infestations

61. Champomier, *Statement of the Sugar Crop Made in Louisiana*, 1851–52, 44–45; *ibid.*, 1858–59, vii; Stephen Duncan to C. P. Leverich, April 3, June 2 (quotation), 1851, Francis Surget, Jr., to Leverich, April 5, 1851, W. J. Minor to Leverich, April 8, 21, 1851, in Leverich Papers, MDAH.

62. H. L. Berry to Rice C. Ballard, March 14, 1859, and George N. Grour [?] to Ballard, April 9, 1859, in Rice Carter Ballard Papers, SHC; Lemuel P. Conner to wife Fanny, April 10, 27 (quotation), 1859, C. H. Lillard to Conner, April 13, 1859, William Morris to Conner, April 19, 1859, William Eustis to Conner, February 20, 1860, in Lemuel P. Conner and Family Papers, LSU.

of worms, lice, caterpillars, and other pests.[63] Thus, as Paul Cameron contemplated the crop prospects on his absentee cotton plantation in Alabama in the summer of 1850, he articulated the uncertainties confronted by all of his fellow agriculturists: "I hope I may make a fine crop & sell it for a fine price—. No telling what is to be the crop as yet—the next [illegible] may blast it—the worm may eat it up—frost may slay it in October—wind & rain may give it to earth to rot—.[64] Such were the tribulations of those who depended on agriculture for their livelihood.

The deleterious effects of weather and insects were often compounded by the appearance of various diseases that decimated the slave forces of wealthy planters. Among the most virulent of these disorders were cholera, yellow fever, and the childhood maladies of whooping cough and the measles. In 1849, the year of the great flood, a severe cholera epidemic wreaked havoc among the slave population on the river plantations of the Lower Mississippi Valley. Hardest hit was Dr. Stephen Duncan, who lost more than 100 slaves on his five cotton plantations in Issaquena County, Mississippi and, later, another 26—"many of them, the best hands on the place"—at L'Argent, his Tensas Parish place.[65] The epidemic first appeared in New Orleans at the beginning of the year and soon spread up the river. By April it had reached Warren County, Mississippi, where John A. Quitman reported 11 deaths on his Palmyra plantation.[66] The following month, it struck Duncan's Issaquena units with a vengeance. At first he tried to treat the disease homeopathically, apparently with some success, but by the end of May it had reappeared in an especially virulent form, frequently leading to a collapse of the victim within "2 or 3 hours after the first complaint." By late June, after a third outbreak, Duncan reported 96 deaths on his Issaquena plantations as the epidemic continued to rage. In July it spread across the river

63. For a systematic recital of the various problems that adversely affected cotton and sugar producers in the Lower Mississippi Valley during the two decades from 1834 to 1854, see the correspondence from Stephen Duncan, William J. Minor, Levin R. Marshall, William N. Mercer, and Francis Surget, Sr. and Jr., to their New York factor, in Charles P. Leverich Papers, MDAH.

64. Paul C. Cameron to [Margaret B. Cameron], July 25, 1850, in Cameron Family Papers, SHC.

65. Stephen Duncan to C. P. Leverich, May 31, June 18, July 10 (quotation), 1849, in Charles P. Leverich Papers, MDAH.

66. S. M. Davis to C. P. Leverich, January 6, 1849, *ibid.;* John A. Quitman to "My dear Son," April 26, 1849, in John A. Quitman Papers, MDAH.

to L'Argent, where the deaths mounted despite the efforts of four physicians, "each treating cases in their own way, & all alike unsuccessful." Before it was over the epidemic had cost Duncan between 125 and 150 Negroes, a calamity, according to his friend William N. Mercer, that depressed their master "not so much from the pecuniary loss . . . as from the loss of human life."[67] Other elite planters who suffered heavy losses in the cholera epidemic of 1849 included Adam L. Bingaman, William G. Conner, Alexander C. Henderson, and Bishop Leonidas Polk. The last lost 80 slaves on his Bayou Lafourche sugar plantation, perhaps the decisive factor in his decision to abandon the sugar-planting business five years later.[68] Wherever and whenever it occurred, Asiatic cholera was one of the most dreaded scourges of the antebellum period. In 1833, about a decade after he settled in Alabama, Gaius Whitfield reported a severe outbreak of the disease "in its most fatal shape" among the slaves in the Demop-olis area. Far to the west, in Iberville Parish, Louisiana, a sugar planter lost a third of his work force within four weeks during the same year.[69] And so it went, year after year throughout the South, as slaveholders and physicians alike remained ignorant of the cause.

The highly contagious diseases of measles and whooping cough also took a heavy toll on southern plantations. Fortunately, these maladies were not nearly as deadly as the most lethal form of cholera. Although children were most sus-ceptible, the two diseases also spread to the adult population on the plantation and frequently resulted in the loss of labor at inopportune times. For example, the overseer of a Plaquemines Parish sugar plantation reported in the early sum-mer of 1859 that an approximately equal number of children and field hands

67. Stephen Duncan to C. P. Leverich, May 19, 22 (first quotation), 26, June 23, July 10 (second quotation), 1849, in Charles P. Leverich Papers, MDAH; Richard E. Butler to Ann Butler, June 23, 1849, in Thomas Butler and Family Papers, LSU; William N. Mercer to Henry Clay, June 3, [1849], in *The Papers of Henry Clay*, ed. Hay, X, 600. In fairness, it should be noted that in making this assessment of Duncan's feelings, Mercer was doubtless trying to impress upon Clay the alleged humanity of the master-slave relationship. In his words, there was a mutual attachment between Duncan and his servants, "which only a slave holder can understand and feel."

68. Stephen Duncan to C. P. Leverich, June 23, 1849, S. M. Davis to Leverich, July 6, 1849, Francis Surget to Leverich, July 9, 1849, in Charles P. Leverich Papers, MDAH; Sarah E. Devereux to Thomas P. Devereux, April 14, June 15, 1854, in Devereux Family Papers, DU.

69. Gaius Whitfield to "My dear Brother" [Dr. Boaz Whitfield], June 1, 1833, in Gaius Whitfield Family Papers, ADAH; E. G. W. Butler to Thomas Butler, September 30, 1833, in Thomas Butler and Family Papers, LSU.

were suffering with the measles. In all, there were more than 150 cases of measles on this plantation during an eighteen-month period, but none of them proved fatal. By contrast, an outbreak of whooping cough the following year resulted in the death of 12 children. In neighboring St. Mary Parish, William T. Palfrey lost 5 children to whooping cough in the same epidemic. In the summer of 1856, whooping cough, clearly the more lethal of the two diseases, claimed the lives of "seven small children" on Windsor, one of the Tayloe family's cotton plantations in Marengo County, Alabama. "I never want to come in contact with it again," wrote the harried overseer, "while ther[e] are as many little ones to have it as is on Windsor." On the rice coast of South Carolina, where the slave mortality rate was higher than elsewhere in the South, 59 slaves, or nearly a fifth of the work force, on Henry A. Middleton's Weehaw plantation died in 1855, most of them from whooping cough and measles. Although such a fatality rate was unusually high, these two childhood diseases were obviously a disruptive force on slave plantations across the South.[70]

Much more deadly to those who had the misfortune to contract it was yellow fever, the most dreaded scourge of the nineteenth-century South. From New Orleans to Charleston, it claimed a frightful toll of victims at periodic intervals during the antebellum period. Fortunately for the large slaveholders, however, it affected primarily working class whites in the urban centers and had little impact on the countryside. The most serious prewar yellow fever epidemic erupted in New Orleans in mid-July of 1853 and soon spread to other towns in the Southwest despite frantic efforts to contain it. Among the communities hardest hit was Natchez, where, despite an extended quarantine and the flight of panic-stricken inhabitants to the country, some 750 persons succumbed to the dreaded disease. Not until late October, following three successive frosts, did the menace finally subside. "You have no idea how much brighter every thing appears to be," sighed a young Louisiana woman with close ties to Natchez. "For the last two months scarcely a day has passed without our hearing of the death of some one of our friends." Other towns severely affected by the epidemic of 1853 included Thibodaux and Baton Rouge in Louisiana and Vicks-

70. Magnolia Plantation Journal, May 25, June 1, 26, 1859, April 21, May 9, October 4, 1860, in Henry Clay Warmoth Papers and Books, SHC; William T. Palfrey Plantation Diary, June 23, 1860, in Palfrey Family Papers, LSU; R. A. Morgan to E. T. Tayloe, June 8–9, 1856, in Henry A. Tayloe and Family Papers, ADAH; Dusinberre, *Them Dark Days,* 412, 415.

burg, Woodville, and Yazoo City across the river in Mississippi.[71] Among the victims were H. R. W. Hill, a prominent New Orleans merchant-planter, and John S. Chadbourne, a Methodist minister and son-in-law of John A. Quitman, who had contracted the disease "in the performance of his duties, visiting the sick and burying the dead." Two years later, the same disease claimed the lives of Natchez nabob John Carmichael Jenkins and his wife.[72]

The terror of yellow fever was by no means confined to the urban centers of the Southwest. In the South Carolina Low Country, where most planter families left their plantations for nearly half the year to escape the miasmic atmosphere of the rice swamps, the city of Charleston and such neighboring coastal towns as Georgetown and Beaufort proved little safer than their counterparts on the lower Mississippi River. Those who lingered too long or returned too early from Flat Rock or the northern resorts ran the risk of exposure to malaria or yellow fever. For example, two of Robert Barnwell Rhett's younger brothers succumbed to the latter disease in Charleston, one in 1824 at the age of seventeen and the other two decades later at the age of thirty-three. In 1854, the year after the great epidemic in the Lower Mississippi Valley, Adele Allston reported that the disease was raging in Charleston and had already claimed the life of the "bright and beautiful" sixteen-year-old daughter of neighboring planter J. Harleston Read II. "I tremble for our friends," Adele remarked apprehensively. "If they all escape we will have great cause for gratitude to a merciful God." Shortly after the end of the war, a daughter of rice baron Henry A. Middleton described the actions being taken to contain an outbreak of yellow fever in Beaufort: "The whole village has been put in Apple pie order—lime sprinkled about in the streets & ditches, all the weeds & trash taken out of the gardens & burnt up, tar burned all night in the town. . . ." Such measures doubtless had some effect in curbing the disease, but it was not until the end of the century that the mosquito was positively identified as the agent of transmission.[73]

71. Mary Butler to brother Edward G. Butler, August 19, November 4 (quotation), 1853, Sarah Butler to Edward G., September 2, 6, 1853, Anna Butler to Edward G., September 6, 1853, in Thomas Butler and Family Papers, LSU; John A. Quitman to "My dear son," September 29, 1853, in John A. Quitman Papers, MDAH; James, *Antebellum Natchez*, 267.

72. Rosalie Quitman to "My Dear Buddie Henrie [brother Frederick Henry], September 17, 1853, in John A. Quitman and Family Papers, MDAH; John A. Quitman to "My dear son," September 29, 1853 (quotation), in John A. Quitman Papers, MDAH; *Goodspeed's*, I, 1020–21.

73. "A Statement of the circumstances of the last illness and death of Albert Rhett . . . ," n.d., and Rhett Genealogy Notes #2, both in Rhett Family Papers, SCHS; Adele Petigru Allston to

Plagued by diseases, deleterious weather conditions, periodic economic depressions, and the mounting external threat to their labor system, a few wealthy planters expressed dissatisfaction with their chosen vocation. Thus, North Carolina planter Ebenezer Pettigrew, whose two eldest sons had already chosen to pursue a life of farming, voiced concern in 1844 that his youngest and brightest male offspring, James Johnston Pettigrew, then standing first in his class at Chapel Hill, might follow suit. "Farming among slaves is a miserable business," declared the elder Pettigrew, "and particularly in this low sickly country, with every indication of the emancipation of labour in a few years." Georgia planter John B. Lamar was even more vociferous in his denunciation of the agricultural profession. Adversely affected by the Panic of 1857 and fearful of the imminent demise of slavery, he advised his nephew to think long and hard before settling upon planting "for a livelihood." In a letter to his brother-in-law, Howell Cobb, Lamar exclaimed: "I am tired & disgusted with planting & mean to sell out—lock stock & barrel if the times ever get flush again. . . ." By investing his money in state and federal stocks at 6 percent interest, he noted, he could make as much income as he derived from the gross amount of his cotton sales. For the young bachelor Henry A. Middleton, Jr., it was the boredom of living alone on an isolated rice plantation that engendered discontent with his station in life. As he confided to his sister one summer evening, "I am only kept alive by visiting Dr Foster [neighboring planter Alexius M. Forster], reading Dr Livingstone, and superintending the carpenters who are carrying out my improvements." Somewhat different was the regret voiced by Mississippi planter Richard T. Archer shortly before his death in 1867. Wearied by the debilitating effects of the war and old age, Archer lamented that he and his sons had not chosen a more beneficent occupation—an occupation that would "do good" for the generality of mankind. Such men as these were the exceptions, however. Despite their numerous trials and tribulations, most elite planters concluded that the benefits that elevated them to the highest echelon of southern society far outweighed any sacrifices they might be obliged to make.[74]

Benjamin Allston, October 3, 1854, in Easterby, ed., *South Carolina Rice Plantation*, 121; Mary Lowndes to "Dear Papa," September 1, 1871, Henry A. Middleton Family Letters, in Cheves-Middleton Papers, SCHS.

74. Ebenezer Pettigrew to James C. Johnston, June 24, 1844, in Pettigrew Family Papers, SHC; John B. Lamar to John A. Cobb, March 10, 1858, Lamar to Howell Cobb, March 10, 1858 (TSS), in Cobb-Erwin-Lamar Family Collection, UGA; Henry A. Middleton, Jr., to "Dear Harriett," July

The success of the wealthy slaveholders was perhaps most vividly exemplified by the grandeur of their residences. If they worked assiduously to construct and retain their agricultural empires, they also cultivated an opulent life-style and sought to erect imperial palaces commensurate with their status in society. Some maintained splendid town dwellings in addition to their ancestral country mansions, while others eschewed urban living altogether in favor of the pastoral beauty and quiet solitude of the countryside. Virtually all filled their homes with lavish furnishings procured in Europe or in the metropolitan centers of the Northeast. These were augmented by magnificent works of art that they had acquired during their extended travels abroad and in the North. The result was a quality of residential life that, in terms of comfort and ostentation, has seldom been surpassed by other Americans of any time or place.

Some of the most impressive plantation homes along the Atlantic seaboard were located in Virginia and South Carolina. Of special note in the former state was Kinloch, the magnificent Essex County country seat of Richard Baylor. Termed "a Palace" by one contemporary observer, Kinloch contained four great halls and twenty-one rooms, eighteen of which had fireplaces. From the observation deck at the top of this four-story Greek Revival mansion, one could see portions of six counties and much of the Rappahannock River Valley.[75] Several hundred miles to the south, in Sumter District, South Carolina, the two-story mansion on Rollindale, George W. Cooper's 2,000-acre estate, featured a dining room large enough to accommodate more than fifty persons. Another magnificent edifice in Sumter was Millford, the country residence of former governor John L. Manning. Described by one architectural historian as the "greatest of all Greek Revival houses in South Carolina," Millford was constructed from 1839 to 1841 under the supervision of Nathaniel F. Potter of Rhode Island. Like other great planters, Manning devoted much attention to landscaping his estate. As a result, Millford became a veritable paradise, especially in the spring. "Millford is looking more lovely than I have ever seen it," Sallie Manning observed cheerfully to her absent husband one bright day in May, 1855.

18, 1858, Henry A. Middleton, Jr., Family Letters, in Cheves-Middleton Papers, SCHS; Richard T. Archer to daughter Jane, November 11, 1866, in Richard Thompson Archer Family Papers, CAH.

75. James B. Slaughter, *Settlers, Southerners, Americans: The History of Essex County, Virginia, 1608–1984* (Essex County, Va., 1985), 105; John A. Selden to Richard Baylor, February 21, 1852, in Baylor Family Papers, VHS. Kinloch was destroyed by fire in the late 1940s.

Several years later, her father termed it "one of the most beautiful places I ever saw." No less impressive was the exterior scenery at Bleak Hall, the Edisto Island estate of sea island cotton planter John F. Townsend. On a visit to the sea islands shortly before the war, James D. B. De Bow described Bleak Hall as one of the most beautiful estates in the South. "It constitutes a complete village in the highest state of improvement," he reported. Perhaps most appealing were its "many acres" of gardens, superintended by a Chinese gardener and containing an abundant variety of "rare and beautiful" plants. Such bucolic scenes were common on the country estates of elite slaveholders throughout the South.[76]

Many great cotton and sugar planters in the more recently settled Southwest also constructed magnificent homes, surrounded by ornate grounds, as a testimony to their affluence and power. Natchez was the site of many of these stately dwellings. Among the most imposing of these was Clifton, the residence in the 1850s of Francis Surget, Jr., and his wife, Charlotte Linton Surget. Situated in the midst of a fairylike melange of exotic flowering plants, winding paths, terraces, grottoes, summer-houses, and a mirrorlike pool, Clifton offered a commanding view of the majestic Mississippi River. The mansion itself was a lofty brick structure with Ionic columns and broad galleries. The furnishings of teakwood, mahogany, and rosewood, together with large mirrors, expensive portraits, marble busts, satin damasks, and specially designed china, were a perfect complement to the exterior of the home. During the Civil War, Clifton served briefly as the headquarters of the general who commanded the Union occupation force before it was demolished by that force, allegedly in retaliation for an unintentional slight to the chief engineer of the Federal contingent. During his short residence at Clifton, Brigadier General Thomas Kilby Smith expressed admiration for both the mansion and its occupants. In a letter to his wife in Ohio, Smith characterized Clifton as "one of the largest & most elegantly appointed mansions in all the South." Indeed, he added, no "description that I can give" could convey the splendor "of its superb appointments." Such an appreciative attitude by the senior Union officer did little, however, to save the

76. Anne King Gregoire, *History of Sumter County, South Carolina* (Sumter, S.C., 1954), 417; *Carologue* 10 (Summer 1994): 16–17; Sallie B. Manning to "My own dearest husband," May 11, 1855, in Williams-Chesnut-Manning Family Papers, SCL; Colin Clarke to grandson [Douglas G. Manning], October 10, 1860, in Chesnut-Miller-Manning Papers, SCHS; *De Bow's Review* 28 (January 1860): 123.

century-old mansion from destruction by the troops under his command three months later.[77]

Louisiana also had its share of palatial plantation homes. South of Natchez, near St. Francisville, stood Catalpa, the opulent residence of William J. Fort, one of the leading cotton producers in West Feliciana Parish. The house was surrounded by exquisitely landscaped gardens that, together with the adjacent grounds, encompassed thirty-eight acres. To the north was a fish pond with a fountain in the center; to the south, a magnificent greenhouse that, among other plants, featured orange and banana trees. Landscaping also attracted the notice of a writer for *De Bow's Review* who visited the Cage family's Woodlawn plantation in 1849. With its lush, green lawn sloping gently toward the edge of Grand Caillou, its two hundred acres of pasture, and its comfortable slave cabins nestled under several rows of shade trees, Woodlawn, he reported, "combined all the qualities of a Tennessee [stock] farm . . . with every quality which characterizes a sugar-planting interest." One of the most imposing homes in the sugar parishes was Ashland, the plantation residence of Duncan F. Kenner. Distinguished by a large gallery around all four sides of the house wide enough to support eight massive square pillars on each side, this two-story brick mansion was bisected by a spacious central hall with three rooms on each side, four of them twenty feet square. Although now in a state of sad disrepair, Ashland still stands on the river road south of Baton Rouge, a forlorn monument to the wealth that it once represented.[78]

For most of the elite slaveholders, the riches that made it possible for them to construct and beautify their splendid homes did not come easily. Whatever their inheritance or good fortune, they could not maintain their position without the sustained application of energy, perseverance, and more than a modicum of managerial skill. In their capacity as agricultural entrepreneurs, these men relied heavily on three important functionaries—factors, overseers, and drivers—to as-

77. "Lost Clifton," MS in Edith Wyatt Moore Collection, LSU; Thomas Kilby Smith to wife Elizabeth, July 19, 1863, in Huntington Library, San Marino, California. Copies of both items furnished to author by Donald G. Linton, Hot Springs, Arkansas. Also author's interview with Linton, a direct descendant of Charlotte Linton Surget, Hattiesburg, Mississippi, June 9, 1993.

78. Seebold, *Old Louisiana Plantation Homes*, I, 284–85; *De Bow's Review* 8 (February 1850): 148–49; MS account of early life of Kenner and horse-trainer George Washington Graves, with a description of Ashland, n.d., in Rosella Kenner Brent Papers, LSU.

sist them in the conduct of their business operations. Because of their extended absences from home during the summer months as well as the magnitude of their business, it was imperative that the great planters find qualified overseers and experienced drivers to superintend the production of the staple crops that generated their income. Those crops were financed and marketed through the agency of a factor, or commission merchant, who typically received a commission of 2.5 percent of the gross proceeds for his services. But the factors assisted their clients in many other ways as well. Not only did they routinely furnish the planters with plantation supplies and personal items, but some, especially those in such metropolitan centers as New York and New Orleans, also filled orders for European imports, made travel arrangements, and even served as surrogate fathers for planter children enrolled in distant schools.[79]

As was noted in an earlier chapter, the Leverich family, which operated factorage firms in both New York and New Orleans, had a particularly close personal and business relationship with a number of elite planters in the Natchez District.[80] Bound by marriage to the prominent Duncan, Conner, and Minor families of Natchez, brothers Henry S. and Charles Palmer Leverich of New York established business relations with Stephen Duncan and other Natchez nabobs as early as 1834.[81] About the same time, two other Leverich siblings, James Harvey, who died in 1844, and William E., began operating a mercantile firm in New Orleans. Ironically, Charles P. Leverich, who served successively as director, vice-president, and president of the Bank of New York, was instrumental in raising $50,000,000 to support the Union war effort, while his brother, William E., became an ardent secessionist and a vigorous supporter of the Confederacy.[82] In addition to the Natchez families noted above, other elite Southwestern slaveholders who conducted their commercial affairs primarily

79. Receipts for Sale of Cotton, Acct. B. Roach, 1852–53, in Benjamin Roach Family Papers, CAH. See, generally, Leverich Papers, and Rice C. Ballard Papers, CAH; Charles P. Leverich Papers, MDAH. The standard account of the factorage system is Harold Woodman, *King Cotton and His Retainers: Financing and Marketing the Cotton Crop of the South, 1800–1925* (Lexington, Ky., 1968).

80. See pp. 23–24 of this book.

81. C. P. Leverich Expense Book, July 26, 1834, in Leverich Papers, CAH; Stephen Duncan to C. P. Leverich, August 2, 23, September 5, 9, 20, December 20, 1834, in Charles P. Leverich Papers, MDAH.

82. Stephen Duncan to C. P. Leverich, June 19, 1844, in Charles P. Leverich Papers, MDAH; Biographical sketch of Charles P. Leverich from Henry W. Domett, *A History of the Bank of New*

through the Leverich brothers in New York included cotton planters William N. Mercer, Levin Marshall, William St. John Elliot, the two Francis Surgets, and Samuel Davis and his son Samuel M., as well as such sugar producers as William T. Palfrey, Mary Porter, and John Julius Pringle.[83]

Calculating the most propitious time to sell one's crop was a collaborative endeavor that involved the planter and his commercial agent. Throughout the year, such capitalist-oriented proprietors as Duncan, Minor, and Mercer kept their New York business associates informed of weather conditions and crop prospects, continually updating estimates of crop production as the harvest progressed. At the same time, both planter and factor closely monitored reports from Europe detailing the consumption of cotton by English textile mills. For example, Duncan estimated early in 1843 that the American cotton crop for that year would amount to 2,200,000 bales, of which 1,300,000 would be shipped to England. At the current rate of consumption, he concluded, the English mills would have a supply of raw cotton sufficient to last them for seventy-two weeks. Only if their consumption increased by a third to 40,000 bales per week would there be a salutary effect on the price of cotton. Less than a year later, however, following a short crop caused by excessive rains during the picking season, Duncan predicted a deficiency of at least 700,000 bales in the supply for Britain, thereby making it "certain" that the price would increase. By contrast, southern sugar production had much less effect on the price of that commodity, which was regulated primarily by production in Cuba and the other Caribbean islands. Still, alert sugar planters kept a close watch on market conditions and advised their factors when to sell. Thus, in the summer of 1849, William J. Minor, noting that sugar was "rising in every market in the world" as a result of short crops in both Cuba and Louisiana, cautioned his New York factor, Charles Leverich, not to "be in a hurry about selling mine." Predicting that "Sugar must go up & keep up till the new Cuba crop comes in," Minor directed his agent to withhold his sugar from the market until "just before the ice closes yr. navigation."[84]

York, 1784–1884 (2nd ed.; New York, 1884), 103–104, in Box 3G130, Folder 4, Leverich Papers, CAH; Rothstein, "The Antebellum South as a Dual Economy," 381 n. 22.

83. Various letters and accounts, 1834–54, in Charles P. Leverich Papers, MDAH, and 1832–73, in Leverich Papers, CAH; A. McWilliams to C. P. Leverich, December 12, 1847, in Charles P. Leverich Correspondence, LSU.

84. Stephen Duncan to Charles P. Leverich, February 13, December 25, 1843, May 19, 1849, W. J. Minor to Leverich, August 17, 1849, in Charles P. Leverich Papers, MDAH.

Cotton planter William Mercer was no less reticent than Minor about specifying the time and conditions under which his crop would be sold. Although he usually deferred to the judgment of Leverich "as to the time of sale and the price," Mercer did not hesitate to make his views known if circumstances warranted. Thus, in May, 1844, with the cotton market severely depressed, he recommended that Leverich suspend further sales until July, but only "if *perfectly convenient* to you," he added diplomatically. Several years later, the Mississippian was more explicit regarding a shipment of Mastodon cotton, a long-staple variety recently introduced into the Southwest from California. After analyzing economic forces in both Europe and America, he became convinced that prices would likely improve later in the season and, consequently, directed his agent not to sell his "good mastodon" for less than fifteen cents a pound. A year later, Mercer elected to retain the last portion of his crop on the plantation "to await better times." He indicated that he would ship it on to New York only when "the state of your market will justify" it. Conversely, in November, 1848, as he prepared to depart for New Orleans for the winter, he ordered Leverich to sell his most recent shipment immediately in order to take advantage of the elevated prices.[85]

In addition to their principal functions of managing the financial affairs, marketing the crops, and supplying the plantations of southern slaveholders, commission merchants provided numerous other services, many of them of a more personal nature. Drawing again from the accounts and prolific correspondence of Lower Mississippi Valley nabobs with the Leverich brothers in New York, a number of examples may be cited to illustrate the close relationship that existed between planter and factor. Representative of the personal and household items procured by the Leverich firm for elite Natchez slaveholders during the extended period of their personal and commercial association were four marble mantels and a like number of grates, a "first rate" billiard table, and two "gold case Hunting watches" that Stephen Duncan intended as gifts for his agent and overseer; a dozen cases of champagne and a pair of pistols for William J. Minor; a gold watch for Levin Marshall's son at Princeton; a musical instrument for the daughter of William N. Mercer; china, several boxes of furniture,

85. William N. Mercer to Charles P. Leverich, May 21, 1844, November 30, 1846, February 24, 1847, February 17, November 1, 1848, in Charles P. Leverich Papers, MDAH; John Hebron Moore, *Emergence of the Cotton Kingdom,* 29–30.

a carriage, two derringer pistols, and a pointer dog for Francis Surget, Jr.; three silver tea sets and a carriage for William St. John Elliot; and a "silver mounted" barouche with "green cloth lining" for Dr. Samuel Gustine.[86]

The Leveriches also assumed responsibility for the welfare of the sons of Natchez nabobs who came north for their education. Such was the case with the Minor brothers, who were sent to preparatory schools and then to Princeton in the late 1840s and early 1850s. When they arrived in the Northeast, it was Charles Leverich who placed them in a suitable school, procured satisfactory accommodations for them, supplied them with appropriate books and clothing, and even took them with his family on summer vacations when their father was unable to leave Natchez. Minor was particularly explicit when he placed his eldest son, John, under the care of Leverich in the summer of 1848. He directed the latter to enroll John in a school that would prepare him, "as soon as possible, to enter the College at Princeton," to ensure that he was "genteel . . . but by no means extravagant" in his dress, and "to see that he [was] comfortably lodged with not more than one roommate." After assuring Leverich that he was "not one of those, who thinks his children perfect & takes offence at any fault found with them," he urged the factor to advise him immediately "of any impropriety" he might "perceive in the conduct of [Minor's] Son" and authorized him to "take the *most prompt & energetick* measures to arrest such conduct," if it occurred.[87]

The Leverich brothers, as well as other factors, also occasionally assumed the role of travel agents by making transportation and lodging arrangements for their clients. One who customarily relied upon the Leverich brothers to perform such services was William N. Mercer. Thus, while visiting Saratoga Springs in the summer of 1845, he notified Charles Leverich that he would soon be in New York City and requested that the latter secure an apartment for his party with

86. Stephen Duncan to C. P. Leverich, November 6, 1843, May 25, 1851, W. J. Minor to Leverich, September 27, 1846, Levin Marshall to Leverich, February 24, 1848, W. N. Mercer to Leverich, July 12, 1848, Francis Surget, Jr., to Leverich, November 14, 1848, in Charles P. Leverich Papers, MDAH; William St. John Elliot a/c with C. P. Leverich, 1851–52, C. P. Leverich MS Cash Account Book, 1844–53, accounts with W. J. Minor and F. Surget, Jr., and Henry S. Leverich Account Book, 1827–37 (Gustine), in Leverich Papers, CAH.

87. W. J. Minor to C. P. Leverich, June 15 (quotations), July 23, September 13, November 6, 1848, August 4, 1851, February 8, 1853, in Charles P. Leverich Papers, MDAH; Minor to Leverich, March 30, 1853, in Leverich Correspondence, LSU.

"a parlour and two adjoining rooms" at the "new hotel" on upper Broadway. Several years later, as he prepared to leave Philadelphia, Mercer again sought the assistance of Leverich in procuring suitable accommodations in New York. This time he requested "a sitting room, and 3 chambers for [his] family, two of the chambers communicating, and all near together—with bed rooms for a maid and two men servants." The following summer, Leverich made arrangements for the transatlantic voyages of both Mercer and the younger Francis Surget and also engaged a stateroom for the homeward passage of Louisiana planter J. J. Pringle on board the steamer *Winfield Scott*, which was scheduled to depart for New Orleans on October 1. Similarly, the New Orleans factorage firm of Nalle & Cox booked a stateroom on the steamer *Sultana* for Rice C. Ballard as he made plans to visit his family in Kentucky in 1846. The factors informed Ballard that they had secured for his comfort a room "in the ladies Cabin . . . on the Starboard side" of the vessel for a fare of $25. The reliance upon factors for such services was quite common among members of the planter elite.[88]

Relations between planter and factor were not always as congenial as those that existed between the Natchez nabobs and their New York agents. For example, several New Orleans business houses provoked the ire of at least two disgruntled planters in the Lower Mississippi Valley. In the midst of the continuing economic crisis of the early 1840s, with sugar selling at less than five cents a pound, Judge Thomas Butler expressed profound dissatisfaction with the manner in which J. H. Leverich & Company was handling his account. Although indebted to that firm for more than $10,000, he elected, nevertheless, to ship his most lucrative lot of sugar to a competing commission merchant, a decision greeted by Leverich with more than a little annoyance. "I am indeed surprized," the latter remarked bitingly, "that you take the only profitable part of the business from us particularly as the Balance due us in Cash when we rendered your account was so large." In the end, however, Butler was compelled by its superior credit resources to return to the Leverich firm, though, as he confided to his wife, "I would infinitely prefer to send my business" to the other house. On another occasion, Butler fulminated against the New Orleans firm

88. W. N. Mercer to C. P. Leverich, July 21, 1845, September 19, 1850, January 15, 1851, F. Surget, Jr., to Leverich, March 31, 1851, J. J. Pringle to Leverich, July 21, 1851, in Charles P. Leverich Papers, MDAH; Nalle & Cox to R. C. Ballard, June 9, 1846, in Rice Carter Ballard Papers, SHC.

of Lambeth & Thompson for charging him compound interest at the rate of 10 percent on a debt incurred for the purchase of a new plantation. Another Southwestern planter, the perennially cantankerous Richard T. Archer, became embroiled in a protracted dispute with J. J. Person & Company of the Crescent City over some $10,000 in notes given to that concern shortly after the outbreak of the war and secured by a Deed of Trust on one of Archer's properties. Both Archer and Person were ruined by the war, but despite intense efforts to settle their differences, the dispute was never resolved to the satisfaction of Archer, who remained convinced until his death that his New Orleans agent had "acted fraudulently" toward him "in this transaction."[89]

Even more acrimonious was the extended conflict between North Carolina planter Thomas P. Devereux and his New York factor, Robert L. Maitland. Their quarrel had personal as well as business ramifications, for Maitland was apparently a close relative of Devereux's second wife. The two men enjoyed a cordial business relationship until December, 1858, when Devereux, who was almost as irascible as Archer, declined to pay what he deemed an excessive commission of $1,665 to Maitland for accepting the North Carolinian's drafts of $30,000 some years before when the latter was in dire financial straits. Maitland responded that he had "maintained [Devereux's] credit, when much more might have been made out of the money advanced to [him], than the paltry commission charged," and pointed out that the commission was lower than that sanctioned by the New York Chamber of Commerce. The disagreement became so heated by the middle of the following year that Maitland refused to have any further intercourse with his client, and notwithstanding the attempt by Devereux's son to effect some sort of reconciliation, the two men were still estranged when the war exacerbated their differences. Following that conflict, in which Devereux suffered losses of between $500,000 and $750,000 "in property of all kinds," he sought to resume communications with Maitland "in an honest endeavor to close the account." However, despite the intercession of a New York attorney, who candidly advised the stubborn North Carolina slave-

89. J. H. Leverich & Company to Thomas Butler, August 31, November 22 (first quotation), 1842, Richard E. Butler to Thomas Butler, November 13, 1842, Thomas Butler to Ann Butler, December 7, 1842 (second quotation), Thomas Butler to Lambeth & Thompson, n.d., in Thomas Butler and Family Papers, LSU; Richard T. Archer to J. J. Person, April 1, 1862, March 8, 1866, Archer to J. D. O'Leary, June 23, 1865 (third quotation), Archer to John Finney, June 26, 1865, Archer to "My Dear Wife," May 3, 1866, in Richard Thompson Archer Papers, CAH.

holder that he was in the wrong, the account was never settled. Finally, with debts of more than $290,000, Devereux was obliged to declare bankruptcy in May, 1868, just ten months before his death.[90]

If the wealthy slaveholders occasionally experienced difficulty with their commercial agents, they had infinitely more trouble with their plantation managers. The friction between planter and overseer has been discussed elsewhere by the author of this book.[91] It will suffice to emphasize here that the relationship between owner and manager was inherently stressful and produced seeds of discord that were seldom entirely muted. Like their less affluent counterparts, the great planters seemed to experience an almost interminable series of problems with their managerial subordinates, who rarely fulfilled the expectations of their employers and, consequently, were subjected to an incessant barrage of criticism. Thus, after receiving what he termed "a sorry account of matters" on his rice plantation, Robert Barnwell Rhett, Jr., seized the occasion to denounce overseers as "a nuisance to be abated as soon as possible." Every planter, concluded Rhett, "should attend to his business closely himself" if he did not wish to "court ruin." Similarly, Francis Surget, Jr., castigated the overseer of one of his Louisiana plantations when he found the place "in a miserable condition" upon his return from an extended excursion to the North. Not only was his superintendent incapable of managing either crops or Negroes, but, according to Surget, "he also gets drunk & abuses the people." Fuming that "he ought to be paid not to go on a place," the incensed proprietor summarily dismissed his unfortunate employee.[92]

Overseers were discharged for a variety of reasons, most commonly for abuse of alcohol, neglect of duties, inability to govern Negroes, general incompetence,

90. Robert L. Maitland to Thomas P. Devereux, February 15, July 26 (first quotation), 1859, January 30, February 21, 1866, E. M. Wright to T. P. Devereux, August 15, 1859, T. P. Devereux to son John, February 16, 1860, R. L. Maitland to John Devereux, March 12, 23, 1860, T. P. Devereux to R. L. Maitland, January 22, 1866 (second quotation), T. P. Devereux to [W. G.] Maitland, February 11, 1868, R. L. Maitland to Henry M. Alexander, March 21, 1868, Alexander to T. P. Devereux, March 21, 1868, in Devereux Family Papers, DU; *"Journal of a Secesh Lady,"* ed. Crabtree and Patton, 729–30.

91. See William K. Scarborough, *The Overseer: Plantation Management in the Old South* (Baton Rouge, 1966), esp. Chap. 5.

92. R. B. Rhett, Jr. to Burnet Rhett, July 17, 1854, in Robert Barnwell Rhett, Sr., Papers, SCHS; Francis Surget, Jr., Overseer Accounts, 1859–66, Account with S. M. Turner, Cholula plantation, November 27, 1860 (Roll 1), in Surget Family Papers, MDAH.

brutality, and undue familiarity with female slaves. The last fault apparently led to the dismissal in 1859 of John Palmer, the manager of Rice C. Ballard's Elcho plantation. In an emotional letter, written shortly after his departure, Palmer accepted full responsibility for the forbidden liaison and begged his former employer to "firgive *Poor Priscellar*" and to allow him to purchase both his paramour and the child that had resulted from their illicit union. Quite different was the reason for the discharge of another Ballard overseer several years before. In that case, the plantation superintendent had packed his cotton so badly that it could only be sold at a much reduced price in New Orleans. "We cannot but conclude that it [the injury to Ballard's cotton] is as much the result of neglect as any thing else," explained the factor, "& we are gratified to find that you have discharged the 'unfaithful steward.'" Another well-to-do cotton planter, Haller Nutt, was plagued by a succession of unsatisfactory managers of his Araby plantation. One worked the hands unnecessarily in standing water, treated the sick improperly, and employed strapping Negroes "to do little simple jobs, which could be done equally as well by some feeble hand or cripple"; another concentrated exclusively on the crop at the expense of stock, equipment, and Negroes alike; and yet another fell victim to "Old Demon Whiskey." Although the last was "industrious, energetic, and anxious to please," albeit "rather foolish when sober," he became "a rampant *Ass*" when drunk, according to his disgusted employer.[93]

It was the first of the Araby overseers, however, who proved to be the most pernicious because of his callous treatment of the slaves. Nutt initially exhibited concern over the disciplinary tactics of his managerial subordinate in April, 1843, shortly after he had acquired his Madison Parish place and while he was still making periodic visits to it from his Natchez residence. During one of those visits, he attributed the recent death of a female slave to the "severe punishment" she had received "for running away" several months earlier. The severity of the overseer's regime was further reflected in the owner's notation less than a month later that no less than five runaways were then "in the woods." Unfortunately, Nutt then became so unwell that he was obliged to take an extended trip to the North to recover his health. Upon his return to the plantation in early

93. John Palmer to R. C. Ballard, December 20, 1859, Cox, Gillis & Boyd to Ballard, October 21, 1854, in Rice Carter Ballard Papers, SHC; Araby Plantation Journal, February 10, 1843, May 23, 1845, February 19, 1849, in Haller Nutt Papers, DU.

November, he was profoundly distressed to hear the "most terrible accounts of the severity, cruelty & bad management" of his overseer. Blaming himself for giving his manager a second chance "after his cruelty last winter," Nutt immediately discharged the brutal operative. Later, in recording the slave deaths on Araby during the year 1843, the proprietor attributed three of the twelve directly to the "ill treatment" and "cruelty" of his overseer. Another example of overseer brutality was reported in 1861 by William T. Palfrey, a St. Mary Parish sugar planter. According to Palfrey, an overseer employed by P. C. Bethell, one of the largest planters in the parish, had accosted and severely beaten one Abram, the slave of an adjacent owner, who was on his way to visit his family on Palfrey's Ricahoe plantation. Then the overseer, in company with the engineer on a neighboring place, had taken the victim and two other unoffending slaves to one of his employer's plantations and placed them in the stocks. Outraged by what he termed this "brutal transaction on the part of these men," Palfrey pursued the perpetrators to the Bethell property, where he found Abram "covered with his own blood, his clothes torn from him, & beaten & swollen in a terrible manner." He immediately secured the release of the two who had not been physically assaulted, but "the release of Abram was refused on the ground that he had *resisted*"—an assertion that Palfrey deemed incredible.[94]

Of course, there were many capable overseers who were temperate in their treatment of the Negroes and who gave complete satisfaction to their employers. Indeed, in view of the greater responsibilities entailed in the management of large estates, together with the capacity of elite slaveowners to pay higher salaries, it is likely that, as a group, the managers of the great rice, sugar, and cotton plantations were more competent than those who superintended the property of lesser planters. If length of service is indicative of owner satisfaction, several overseers performed very well indeed. Among them were Johnson G. Giles, who managed various units for the Hairston family in North Carolina and Virginia from 1843 until his retirement thirty-four years later; Jesse Belflowers, who was, for twenty-five years, an overseer for R. F. W. Allston; Elisha Cain, manager of the Telfair family's Retreat plantation in Georgia for nearly

94. Araby Plantation Journal, April 21, May 16, November 1, 1843, "Births and Deaths," 1843, in Haller Nutt Papers, DU; William T. Palfrey Plantation Diary, June 9, 1861, vol. 18, in Palfrey Family Papers, LSU. For the details of a court case involving cruelty by an overseer to slaves on the Madison Parish plantation of George W. and John C. Humphreys, see Judith Kelleher Schafer, *Slavery, the Civil Law, and the Supreme Court of Louisiana* (Baton Rouge, 1994), 49–52.

as long; and Moore Rawls, who served for fifteen years as a manager for Lewis Thompson, first in North Carolina and later in Louisiana. Peter W. Hairston was especially fortunate in his choice of managers, four of whom served at least fourteen years in that capacity and most of whom lasted nearly a decade.[95]

A more direct expression of appreciation for the merits of a capable overseer was enunciated by South Carolina matron Jane Pringle in the winter of 1860. In a letter to her son, then at school in Europe, she expressed complete satisfaction with the manager of the family's Georgetown District rice plantation. Overseer Pipkin, she wrote, "minds his business and nothing else. He never speaks an unnecessary word and though he makes every negro do his task or take a whipping, they all like him, work well and are never sick." A quiet, diligent manager with productive, healthy, and contented workers, Pipkin would appear to have been the ideal plantation superintendent. But most planters, great and small, encountered a mixture of good and bad as they mined the reservoir of available overseers in their search for the perfect manager. Perhaps typical was a succession of overseers on Henry A. Middleton's Weehaw plantation, also located in Georgetown District. The proprietor lauded Tom Wilson, who managed in the late 1840s, as a "good man & first-rate planter." Two of his successors, apparently brothers, were much less satisfactory. Middleton characterized the first as a "liar & son of a gun" and the second as a "fool" but "good planter." But the last of the prewar Weehaw overseers was clearly the worst. B. J. Bostick, lamented the disgruntled owner, was "the most incompetent planter ever on Weehaw."[96]

Although overseers might come and go with distressing frequency, their subordinates, the Negro drivers, usually provided a measure of stability to plantation operations. Indeed, planters often reposed greater confidence in their drivers than in their overseers. Thus, following the death of a trusted driver on one of Thomas Butler's plantations, his brother-in-law, Stephen Duncan, observed: "This is a serious loss, in as much as, your plantation would never have suffered from the mismanagement of an injurious overseer while Ishmael was the driver." Ishmael, added Duncan, "was the best driver I ever knew." In

---

95. Scarborough, *The Overseer*, 159–60, 163–64, 170–73; Peter Wilson Hairston Papers, SHC.

96. Jane L. Pringle to "Dearest Poss," January 20, 1860, Pringle Family Correspondence, in R. F. W. Allston Papers, SCHS; List of Overseers, 1842–61, Henry A. Middleton, Jr., Plantation Journal, in Cheves-Middleton Papers, SCHS.

recognition of their vital role, drivers were frequently accorded special privileges in the form of better housing, more generous allotments of food and clothing, and cash bonuses at the end of the year. For example, it was customary to reward supervisory slaves on the plantations of Langdon Cheves, Sr., with an annual present of $5 for their "good conduct as drivers." Drivers on Henry Middleton's Weehaw plantation received a like amount at the end of each year. In addition, they received a Christmas allowance of twenty pounds of meat compared to five pounds for each task hand and ten pounds for such specialized workers as nurses, artisans, and herdsmen.[97]

Not only did the owner prescribe special benefits for his drivers, but he also determined which of his male field hands would be most likely to perform capably in that important managerial position. The principal requisites were loyalty to the master and the concomitant qualities of physical strength and leadership ability. It was the last characteristic that resulted in the elevation of Moses to the post of driver on one of the Rhett plantations in the South Carolina Low Country. At first glance, the choice seems a strange one, for the hot-tempered Moses had previously been involved "continually" in "quarrels" of a personal nature with the driver over him. When that driver died, Moses was selected to replace him because, as his owner explained, "being a Negro of resolute will, it was supposed he would make a good Driver." Later, after his sale to a neighboring proprietor, Moses began to claim for himself and several female followers various physical ailments that, if valid, "would have been an effectual obstacle to his appointment" as driver for the Rhetts. Having never seen any indication of such infirmities before the sale, his former owner concluded that "Moses and the women he patronises, are making the usual experiment of Negros on new Masters—that by depreciating their capacity to labour, they might do as little as possible." If the redoubtable Moses manifested little loyalty to his new master, he was clearly exhibiting the forceful leadership that had earned him a promotion to a position of responsibility with the Rhetts.[98]

Infrequently, drivers inspired so much confidence in their owners that the

97. Stephen Duncan to Thomas Butler, October 4, 1831, in Thomas Butler and Family Papers, LSU; Draft for $10, February 22, 1858, signed by Langdon Cheves, Jr., Executor of Estate of Langdon Cheves, Sr., in Langdon Cheves, Jr., Papers, SCHS; Henry A. Middleton, Jr., Plantation Journal, in Cheves-Middleton Papers, SCHS.

98. Robert Barnwell Rhett to Langdon Cheves, March 11, 1858, in Langdon Cheves, Jr., Papers, SCHS.

latter dispensed entirely with overseers, and instead, utilized trusted slaves as plantation foremen. The examples of Edmund Ruffin and Jefferson Davis in this regard are well known and require no elaboration here. But a few other wealthy planters adopted this practice, some on a short-term basis and others for a longer period. For example, in 1856 Robert Barnwell Rhett placed the previously discussed Moses in that position on his Altamaha plantation, with Rhett himself becoming the overseer for that year. Perhaps no other elite slaveholder depended more on slave foremen to manage his absentee properties than James C. Johnston of North Carolina. For more than a dozen years, the Negro Peter superintended affairs on Johnston's Poplar Plains unit in Pasquotank County. Despite the interference of Johnston's cousin, who, on at least one occasion, sided with a recalcitrant slave against Peter, the latter performed his duties in exemplary fashion until the eve of the Civil War. During that conflict, another slave, Ben Johnston, who, like Peter, was sufficiently literate to correspond with his master, managed another Johnston plantation adjacent to Poplar Plains. In a letter to his owner, written when Confederate fortunes were approaching their lowest ebb, Ben reported that the people were well and appeared "to mind their own business," and he assured Johnston that he was trying to control his "fellow servants" in the same way that his master would if he were present.[99]

In the end, however, despite the invaluable contributions of factors, overseers, drivers, and slave foremen to the success of planting endeavors, it was upon the onerous labor of the rank and file slaves that the planters depended for their prosperity, power, and prominence. Consequently, it is appropriate that we focus our attention now on the condition and treatment of those unfortunate human beings on the great landed estates of the slave South.

99. *Ibid.*; Scarborough, *The Overseer,* 16–19; W. J. Hardy to James C. Johnston, July 5, 1847, Peter to J. C. Johnston, October 6, 1850, July 17, 1859, Ben Johnston to "Master Dear Sir Dear master," July 31, 1863, in Hayes Collection, SHC.

William Henry Tayloe
Courtesy of the Virginia Historical Society, Richmond

William Fanning Wickham
Courtesy of the Virginia Historical Society, Richmond

Paul C. Cameron
From Cameron Papers, Southern Historical Collection, University of North Carolina at Chapel Hill

James C. Johnston
From Hayes Papers, Southern Historical Collection, University of North Carolina at Chapel Hill

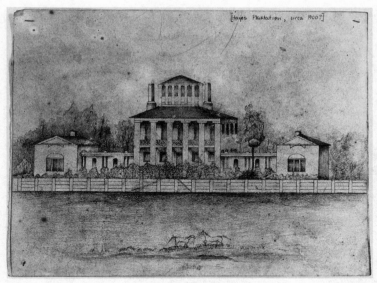

Hayes Plantation ca. 1900

From Hayes Papers, Southern Historical Collection, University of North Carolina at Chapel Hill

Rose Hill, plantation home of Nathaniel Heyward

Courtesy of the Charleston Museum

Chicora Wood, plantation of R. F. W. Allston
From the Collections of the South Carolina Historical Society, Charleston

John L. Manning ca. 1861
From the Collections of the South Carolina Historical Society, Charleston

Louisa McCord, photo of the bust by Hiram Powers
From the Collections of the South Carolina Historical Society, Charleston

Robert Barnwell Rhett
From the Collections of the South Carolina Historical Society, Charleston

William Brown Hodgson
Courtesy of the Georgia Historical Society, Savannah

William Gustine Conner ca. 1858
Courtesy of Jonathan H. Ray, Brentwood, Tennessee

Eliza Turner Quitman at the time of her marriage (1824)

From Special Collections Section, Mississippi Department of Archives and History, Jackson

John A. Quitman in Mexican War uniform

From Special Collections Section, Mississippi Department of Archives and History, Jackson

Edward Sparrow
*From the Louisiana and Lower Mississippi Valley Collections,
LSU Libraries, Louisiana State University*

5

TOILING FOR OLD "MASSA"

Slave Labor on the Great Plantations

It ... would require the wisdom of Solomon, the patience of Job and the strength of Hercules to manage a parcel of negroes and overseers as it should be done to make them profitable and being deficient in all these qualities I can only do the best I can.   —PETER W. HAIRSTON, January [1859]

My New negros are no earthly account at the hoe—and such a set of picklocks, thieves & scoundrels of all kinds never were collected together. I have had a great deal of trouble with them. The hard work has commenced and they run off like partridges. I have now 6 or 8 in chains and will probably be compelled to chain the whole posse before the year is over.
          —WILLIAM G. CONNER, June 12, 1850

I send you [her husband] clothes a pie—a ham biscuits & bread. I also send the dress you asked me to get for Hannah Samson—and the coffee & sugar which I put up for poor old Toby. They tell me he died last week but I still send the articles that you may give them to some of the other infirm old negroes.
          —FANNY E. CONNER, February 7, 1860

I am pained to say that ... poor Lelia died of inflammation of the stomach after five days illness. I felt as if one of the family were dead, so greatly did I regard her. Her family ... have exhibited all the sensibility of refined & educated minds, much more, indeed, than is found in what is called the world. She was a valuable servant, poor Lelia, for her fidelity & trustworthy qualities, and a sad loss it is to my mother.   —JOHN L. MANNING, September 21, 1851

Do you think after all that has transpired between me & the old Man ... that its treating me well to send me off ... to be sold without even my having the opportunity of choosing for my self; its hard indeed and what is still harder [is] for the father of my children to sell his own offspring yes his own flesh and blood My god is it possible that any free born American would brand his character with such a stigma as that.   —VIRGINIA BOYD, May 6, 1853

WHETHER THEY TOILED in the miasmic rice swamps of the South Carolina Low Country or in the broiling heat of the cotton and cane fields of the Southwest, the African American slaves of the antebellum South earned handsome profits for their owners but often at the expense of human suffering almost without parallel in modern times. It should be remembered, however, that the condition of laboring people generally in the nineteenth century was little short of deplorable. It was that condition that impelled Karl Marx to launch his midcentury assault against the exploitation of labor by capital in the rapidly industrializing nations of the Western world. Indeed, with respect to the material conditions of life—food, clothing, shelter, and hours of labor—the chattel slaves of the South did not fare badly compared to their working class counterparts elsewhere on the planet. Rather, it was the absolute denial of freedom that set them apart from other workers and often made their lot unbearable. Slavery rendered them impotent to protect the integrity of their families and frequently exposed them to the erratic behavior of insensitive owners. Some masters, among them R. F. W. Allston and William Aiken of South Carolina, Jeremiah H. Brown of Alabama, and Joseph Davis, elder brother of the Confederate president, treated their servants with genuine benevolence and humanity. Others, such as the former slavetrader Rice C. Ballard and his partner, Natchez judge Samuel S. Boyd, were guilty of a callousness that almost defies belief. Thus, the destiny of every person born a slave in the Old South was determined by chance, and even that was subject to sudden change as a consequence of the death or financial impairment of one's owner.

For their part, the men and women who constituted the upper echelon of the southern slaveholding class had absolutely no compunction about their ownership of human property. They had been born into a society of which slavery was an integral part, many of them had inherited slaves from their forefathers, and virtually all of them believed that slavery was a divine institution, manifestly ordained and sanctified by the omnipotent Creator. William S. Pettigrew gave explicit expression to the sentiments of the overwhelming majority of his fellow slaveholders when he declared, during the tumultuous spring of 1850, that he suffered no pangs of conscience from his ownership of slaves. "The institution of Slavery," he declared, "is unquestionably justified by Scripture, both by precect [sic] & example. The sin does not consist in holding that description of property, but the guilt lies in trespassing on it." Governed by this assumption, it became the principal task of the elite slaveholders to keep their servants relatively contented with their inferior status while at the same time extracting the maximum amount of labor from them. Robert F. W. Allston, one of the most paternalistic slaveholders, stated his position clearly and succinctly. "I like to be kind to my people," he explained to an acquaintance, "but I imperatively require of them honesty, truth, diligence, and cheerfulness in their work, wherever and whatever it is."[1]

The conditions under which the slaves lived and worked were defined, often in the form of explicit, written regulations, by their master. It was he who furnished their housing, determined their allotments of food and clothing, ministered to their health needs, provided for their religious instruction, solemnized their marriages, dictated their holidays, prescribed limits on their punishment, and frequently established incentives to promote the efficiency of their involuntary labor. The responsibilities were onerous and the task often daunting. As Peter W. Hairston once observed, the proper management of Negroes required "the wisdom of Solomon, the patience of Job and the strength of Hercules."[2] Yet the success of the elite planters would seem to indicate that most of them managed to achieve a satisfactory, albeit tenuous, balance between their role as patriarch of their black family and that of an entrepreneur seeking to exploit their human property for the sake of financial gain.

Because of their superior resources, the large slaveholders were better able than their less affluent counterparts to provide material comforts for their chattel laborers. One of their principal obligations was to provide adequate housing for their subservient work force. The typical slave cabin was a two-room structure with a fireplace between the rooms, which housed on average some four to five persons, usually members of a single family. Normally of wood-frame construction, these cabins were quite small, typically containing some 300 to 400 feet of floor space.[3] For example, the slave houses on Gaius Whitfield's Alabama plantation each had about 290 square feet of interior living space. Somewhat larger were the cabins on William G. Conner's Rifle Point estate in Concordia Parish, Louisiana. The seventy Negro cabins on Rifle Point, which

1. William S. Pettigrew to James C. Johnston, March 7, 1850, in Pettigrew Family Papers, SHC; R. F. W. Allston to Sarah Carr, January 17, 1859, in Easterby, ed. *South Carolina Rice Plantation*, 152.

2. Peter W. Hairston to Fanny Caldwell, January, [1859], in Peter Wilson Hairston Papers, SHC.

3. Robert William Fogel and Stanley L. Engerman, *Time on the Cross: The Economics of American Negro Slavery* (Boston, 1974), 115–16.

housed a slave force of 271, measured 19 by 23 feet.[4] Although quite shabby by modern standards, the slave houses of the antebellum period compared favorably with the humble dwellings of poor whites in the South as well as those of both agricultural and industrial workers throughout the Western world in that period.[5]

Occasionally, elite planters provided their black charges with more generous accommodations. Thus, South Carolina planter Plowden C. J. Weston, who was reputed to be a very benevolent slaveholder, installed pane-glass windows in the eighty slave cabins on his Waccamaw River rice plantations. Infrequently, slave dwellings were constructed of brick instead of wood. Visitors to the Charleston area today can still view the now-dilapidated original slave houses on Boone Hall plantation that date from the colonial period. Although more durable, brick was not necessarily the superior mode of construction for slave quarters. The manager of a newly cleared cotton plantation acquired in 1857 by Rice C. Ballard declared his preference for wood housing. The problem with brick quarters, he observed, was that they were "close," and there was a tendency for the Negroes to "have large fires and get too warm" before going out into the cold or rain, thereby becoming more susceptible to "Pneumonia, Colds &c."[6] Whatever the size or construction materials of their slave houses, conscientious proprietors encouraged the occupants to keep their quarters neat and clean. Thus, after visiting the aged Harriott Pinckney's absentee plantation in Beaufort District, South Carolina, a male relative expressed profound dissatisfaction with the general filth of the slave quarters and directed the manager to take immediate steps to whitewash the interior of the cabins and to rake up "all the trash & dirt round the houses, & under them." It was customary for R. F. W. Allston, another member of the Low Country elite, to give his hands half-task on Saturdays and then require that "washing, scouring, raking the yards and burning trash should be done in each household" so that all should be "tidy and clean" on Sunday.[7]

4. Fire Insurance Application, Home Insurance Company of Columbus, Ohio, 1852, in Gaius Whitfield Family Papers, ADAH; MS Slave Census, 1860, Concordia Parish, La.

5. Fox-Genovese, *Within the Plantation Household,* 150; Fogel and Engerman, *Time on the Cross,* 116.

6. Joyner, *Down by the Riverside,* 121, 125; John B. Pelham to R. C. Ballard, March 8, 1857, in Rice Carter Ballard Papers, SHC.

7. C. C. Pinckney, Sr., to William Winningham, January 9, 1858, in Harriott Pinckney Papers, SCL; Pringle, *A Woman Rice Planter,* 112.

Because most of the food was raised on the plantation and there was little need for frequent renovation of slave quarters, the expense of these necessities was usually minimal. On the other hand, elite planters frequently expended substantial sums for slave clothing and medical care. On virtually all plantations, clothing was distributed twice a year, typically in April and October. Because of their ample financial resources, the great planters were perhaps more generous than the lesser slaveholders in their dispensation of slave apparel. For example, during the 1850s, each male slave on Stephen Duncan, Jr.'s, Carlisle plantation in Issaquena County, Mississippi, annually received three cotton shirts, three pairs of pants, one overcoat, and two pairs of shoes. Their female counterparts received three cotton shifts, two gowns—one of linsey and the other of cotton—one petticoat, one overcoat, and two pairs of shoes, while each child was provided with four slips, one of linsey and the others of fine cotton. Two decades earlier, on Maunsel White's Deer Range sugar plantation in Plaquemines Parish, Louisiana, male field hands normally received in the fall two shirts, pantaloons, a jacket or overcoat, one wool cap, and, in alternate years, a blanket, at a cost of approximately $9 for each slave. At the fall distribution of clothing on Deer Range, the women were furnished a robe, chemise, shoes, a shawl or headkerchief, and either an overcoat or blanket, valued together at about $7 for each female slave. Thus, during the two years 1836–1837, White spent nearly $1,350 on winter clothing alone for a slave force of about 80.[8]

With the exception of such items as shoes, hats, headkerchiefs, and blankets, most of the basic articles of slave apparel were usually manufactured on the plantation. Planters purchased the raw materials—osnaburgs, kerseys, flannels, russets, twills, and cotton sheeting—from their factors, who, in turn, procured them from various primary suppliers. A number of prominent cotton and sugar planters in the Southwest regularly ordered such items from the Leverich brothers in New York. For example, in the fall of 1852, eight Natchez District nabobs collectively ordered more than $6,000 worth of clothing materials from the Leveriches to fabricate winter clothing for their respective slave forces. Between

8. Stephen Duncan, Jr., Plantation Journals, Vols. 4 (1856–65), 6 (1861–95), in Duncan Papers, LSU; Maunsel White Plantation Record Book, 1833–43, microfilm copy in Maunsel White Papers and Books, SHC. I am indebted to Stephen E. Wedding, a former student of mine at the University of Southern Mississippi, for allowing me to examine this journal, the original of which is still in private possession, before it was microfilmed for inclusion in the White Papers at Chapel Hill.

January and October of the same year, the Leverich firm shipped to Mary Porter, the proprietor of Oaklawn plantation in St. Mary Parish, Louisiana, various raw fabrics from New York suppliers that cost just under $2,110 and were used to clothe a slave force that numbered between 250 and 300.[9] Shortly after Mrs. Porter's cloth arrived from New York, another Louisiana planter family, the Bringiers, received a similar shipment, at a cost of $1,350, from their New Orleans factor to provide winter clothing for the male field hands on their sugar plantations just below Baton Rouge. Summer clothing was no less expensive. Thus, shortly before the Civil War, Benjamin Roach, Jr., expended nearly $2,500 to provide warm-weather garments for the slaves on five of his Mississippi cotton plantations.[10]

Perhaps the most costly material articles furnished to slaves were shoes and blankets. In 1857 Francis Surget, Jr., purchased footwear for his slaves from a Natchez merchant at the rate of $1.25 a pair for shoes and $2.70 for boots. The following year, he ordered the bulk of his Negro shoes from a firm in Newark, New Jersey, though the cost was slightly higher: $1.35 for shoes and $3.00 for boots. Thus, in one shipment alone in July, 1858, Surget paid $250 for footwear for 161 slaves on two of his plantations and at his Clifton residence in Natchez. Incomplete records indicate that in the final two years of the antebellum period Surget purchased his Negro shoes both through C. P. Leverich in New York and from his old Natchez supplier.[11] Blankets were even more expensive than shoes, but unlike articles of wearing apparel, they were not issued annually to individual slaves. Instead, it was customary to distribute blankets every two or three years. One South Carolina planter, Henry A. Middleton, Jr., gave out blankets in successive years, to men, women, and children, respectively. Thus,

9. Receipts for purchases by C. P. Leverich from Thomson, Quick & McIntosh, September 24, 1852 (Madras headkerchiefs); Waldo, Barry & Company, September 18–30, 1852 (flannels, kerseys, plains); J. G. Dudley & Company, September 21, 1852 (Conestoga sheeting); and Rankin, Duryea & Company, October, 1852 (hats); receipts in Mary Porter Financial Account, January 3–October 14, 1852, all in Leverich Papers, CAH.

10. Martin Gordon, Jr., to Benjamin Tureaud, December 30, 1852, in Benjamin Tureaud Papers, LSU; Benjamin Roach in a/c with Seaman, Peck & Company, March 5–April 27, 1859, in Benjamin Roach Family Papers, CAH.

11. Francis Surget, Jr., in a/c with F. B. Ernest & Company, Natchez, August 29, 1857, April 22, 25, 1859; Bills from Halsey Utter & Company, Newark, April 14, July 24, 1858 (Roll 3); "Invoice of Shoes shipped for a/c F. Surget Esq." from C. P. Leverich, July 2, 1860 (Roll 4), in Surget Family Papers, MDAH.

the members of each segment of the slave population on his Weehaw plantation received a new blanket once every three years. Nevertheless, the cost of blankets was substantial. For example, in 1855 the widow of William St. John Elliot ordered 400 blankets priced at $4 apiece for the slaves on her Black Hawk plantation in Concordia Parish.[12]

Medical care was another major item of expense for elite slaveholders. For both humanitarian and economic reasons, the physical well-being of their slaves was a central concern of masters throughout the South. Unfortunately, because of the primitive state of medical knowledge in the nineteenth century, the collective efforts of slaveowners, overseers, and physicians often proved ineffective in stemming the tide of sickness and disease that swept over the rural estates of the region. As was noted in the previous chapter, such diseases as measles, whooping cough, and, above all, cholera cut a deadly swath through the black population.[13] Slaves were also plagued by hernias, lockjaw, pneumonia, dysentery, scarlet fever, and various diseases of the gastrointestinal tract. Even when such maladies did not culminate in death, not only did they produce severe physical discomfort in those afflicted by them, but they also resulted in the loss of many valuable days of labor to the proprietor. Thus, when summarizing the work accomplished in 1857 on the Terrebonne Parish sugar plantation of Robert R. Barrow, the manager informed his employer that 1,717 days of work had been lost by sickness that year. Three years later, the overseer of a large cotton plantation in the northern part of the same state complained that he had "from 20 to 25 in the Horspitel all the time" with the sore throat just as he was commencing to pick cotton. Yet another Louisianian reported a like number in his hospital, two of them seriously ill with "congestion of the brain."[14] Such was the experience of wealthy slaveholders throughout the South.

Members of the planter elite often went to great lengths to safeguard the health of their black charges. Perhaps no other was more indulgent than Wade Hampton II, father of the Confederate cavalry general of the same name. Ac-

12. Henry A. Middleton, Jr., Plantation Journal, in Cheves-Middleton Papers, SCHS; Estate William St. John Elliot in a/c with Thomas C. Reddy, Natchez Dry Goods Merchant, August 30, 1855, William St. John Elliott Papers, in Natchez Trace Small MSS Collection, CAH.

13. See pp. 147–49 of this book.

14. R. R. Barrow Residence Journal, January 1, 1858, in SHC; Lewis Carter to John Perkins, Jr., September 9, 1860, in John Perkins Papers, SHC; W. G. Conner to Lemuel P. Conner, July 29, 1850, in Lemuel P. Conner and Family Papers, LSU.

cording to Dr. Robert W. Gibbes, who began treating slaves on the Hampton plantations in 1833 and subsequently had "several thousand" South Carolina Negroes under his care, Colonel Hampton was so anxious to alleviate the discomfort of ailing slaves on his estate that he frequently dispensed to them liberal quantities of "Sherry or Madeira of a quality seldom found on sale." Such salutary treatment may account for the unprecedented number of superannuated slaves listed on Hampton's Richland District properties in 1850.[15] Other proprietors spared no expense to recruit the health of injured or diseased members of their so-called black family. Thus, the Cameron family of North Carolina cheerfully paid a Chapel Hill physician $30 to perform an operation on one of their female slaves. Similarly, sugar planter William T. Palfrey sent one of his field hands to a New Orleans hospital in 1855 to be treated for an abscessed arm. Five years later, a cotton planter in the neighboring state of Mississippi paid a Yazoo City physician an astounding $210 for his constant "attention" to a male slave named Charles over a period of more than two months.[16]

Planter nabobs were particularly solicitous about the well-being of young children and child-bearing females. Not long after Edward Jenner developed a vaccine to combat the ravages of smallpox, some knowledgeable slaveholders began to vaccinate their slave children. Young slaves on the plantations of brothers-in-law Thomas Butler and Stephen Duncan were receiving such protection at least as early as 1818. Other slaveowners adopted the practice in later years, both in response to sporadic outbreaks of the dreaded disease in the near vicinity of their plantations and as a regular measure to protect the health of their infant slaves. Thus, after noting the appearance of smallpox within eight miles of his place, a Virginia planter reported that he had "vaccinated every soul on the plantation—tho' only the infants had not been operated on before." Similarly, when the disease erupted in nearby Georgetown on the eve of the Civil

15. Cauthen, ed., *Family Letters of the Three Wade Hamptons*, xiii–xv; Dr. Robert W. Gibbes to R. F. W. Allston, March 6, 1858, printed in *De Bow's Review* 24 (April 1858): 321–22; MS Slave Census, 1850, Richland District, S.C. The Hampton slave force of 309 included a black male listed as 110 years old and blind, a 100-year-old black female, and eleven other slaves between the ages of 90 and 95. I have encountered no other slaveowner with as many superannuated slaves as Hampton.

16. J. B. Jones to Paul C. Cameron, December 19, 1849, in Cameron Family Papers, SHC; William T. Palfrey Plantation Diary, July 3, 1855, in Palfrey Family Papers, LSU; Physician's Bill, Estate Benjamin Roach in a/c with Leake & Barnett, January 6, 1860, in Benjamin Roach Family Papers, CAH.

War, rice planter Henry A. Middleton, Jr., vaccinated thirteen of the smallest children on his Weehaw plantation. Among those who routinely vaccinated the Negro children under their charge were William T. Palfrey of Louisiana and Patrick Edmondston, the son-in-law of North Carolina planter Thomas P. Devereux.[17]

For obvious reasons, elite slaveholders manifested equal solicitude for the welfare of female slaves in their childbearing years, sometimes referred to in the records as "breeding wenches." It was customary to work pregnant women moderately until the time of their confinement, allow them a week or more of complete rest after they gave birth, usually with the assistance of a slave midwife, and then employ them at light tasks while they were nursing their infants. Such was the practice on Eustace Surget's Morville plantation, an absentee unit in Concordia Parish, Louisiana, that was not noted for the benevolent treatment of its black laborers. There, new slave mothers remained in "child bed" for two full weeks after giving birth and were then assigned such light work as spinning and weaving while breast-feeding their babies. Similarly, expectant mothers ("Big belly") on Weehaw plantation in Georgetown District, South Carolina, were placed on half-task until confined, and "sucklers" were continued on that regimen until the child was eight months old. Overseers on the Madison Parish cotton plantation of Haller Nutt were directed not only to give slave mothers a month's respite from labor after their confinement but to nurse even more carefully those who had miscarried, a misfortune that, in the words of Nutt's partner and brother-in-law, should never occur "on a well organized plantation."[18]

Notwithstanding such policies, plantation slaves—young and old, male and female—suffered a variety of maladies and mishaps, many of which required the services of a trained physician. Although a few planters engaged a specific

17. Thomas D. Carson to Thomas Butler, January 15, 1818, in Thomas Butler and Family Papers, LSU; John Taylor to Richard Baylor, March 28, 1856, in Baylor Family Papers, VHS; Henry A. Middleton, Jr., Plantation Journal, January, 1861, in Cheves-Middleton Papers, SCHS; William T. Palfrey Plantation Diary, May 30, 1858, in Palfrey Family Papers, LSU; *Journal of a Secesh Lady,* ed. Crabtree and Patton, 153.

18. Morville Plantation Journal, 1854–55 (Roll 2), in Surget Family Papers, MDAH; Henry A. Middleton, Jr., Plantation Journal, 1855–61, in Cheves-Middleton Papers, SCHS; [Dr.] C. B. N[ew], "Directions &c. in treatment of the *Sick,*" Araby Plantation Journal, in Haller Nutt Papers, DU.

doctor to treat all persons on the plantation at a fixed annual rate, it was more common to pay for medical care on a case-by-case basis. Some proprietors utilized the services of several doctors at the same time to treat their black wards, while others relied entirely on a single physician, usually the same individual who ministered to the needs of the white family. Then, as now, medical care was expensive. Typical charges for a routine visit and prescription ranged from $3 to $10, often depending on the time of day and the distance the physician was obliged to travel. Cases requiring greater attention were more costly. For example, in 1853 a Mississippi physician charged Benjamin Roach, Jr., $3 an hour to attend two slave women "in difficult labour" for four and six hours, respectively. Fellow Mississippian Francis Surget paid his doctor $12 for a night visit to set a fracture.[19] Such costs often reached substantial amounts during the course of a year. Thus, two of the largest slaveholders in the South, Richard Singleton of South Carolina and Benjamin Roach, Jr., of Mississippi, each expended more than $1,000 in a single year for slave medical care on at least two occasions during the 1850s. Medical costs for slaves on the estate of deceased Georgia planter James A. Everett reportedly ran as high as $550 to $650 a year during the same decade.[20] In more general terms, evidence adduced from scattered and incomplete medical accounts throughout the South indicates that, on average, the great slaveholders incurred annual medical expenses of $1 to $2 for each slave that they owned.[21]

19. Medical Account, Estate John Murdoch with Dr. John H. Savage, January 1, 1833, John H. Murdoch Papers, in Natchez Trace Small MSS Collection, CAH; Physician's Bill from Dr. B. F. Holcombe, November 22, 1843, in Thomas Butler and Family Papers, LSU; Estate Benjamin Roach in a/c with Dr. Philip A. Schuyler, July 14, September 19, 1853, Physician's Bill, Estate Benjamin Roach from Leake & Barnett, January 6, 1860, in Benjamin Roach Family Papers, CAH; A[lexander] C. Dunbar Estate in a/c with Dr. James Anyett[?], December 2, 1850–January 10, 1852 (Roll 3), Medical Bill, Dr. E. M. Blackburn to Eustace Surget, December 30, 1860, paid September 18, 1867 (Roll 5), Francis Surget, Jr., in a/c with Dr. C. P. Hornsby, May 1–August 18, 1860 (Roll 6), in Surget Family Papers, MDAH.

20. The Estate of Richard Singleton in Account with Matthew R. Singleton, Executor, November 26, 1852–December 31, 1854, in Richard Singleton Inventory and Estate Book, SCL; Physician's Bill, Estate Benjamin Roach from Leake & Barnett, January 6, 1860, in Benjamin Roach Family Papers, CAH; Flanders, *Plantation Slavery in Georgia*, 115–17.

21. In addition to sources already cited in this paragraph, see Francis Surget Account for Ashwood Plantation with Dr. James Anyett[?], January 14–October 14, 1852, and with Dr. T. B. Baldwin, June 28–July 18, 1852 (Roll 3), in Surget Family Papers, MDAH; Physician's Bill, Dr. J. A. Wragg to Langdon Cheves, Jr., January 1, 1859, in Langdon Cheves, Jr., Papers, SCHS.

Frustrated by the inadequacy of traditional forms of medical treatment, some planters tried alternative methods, the most popular of which was homeopathy. Richard T. Archer, who regularly employed a homeopathic physician to treat the slaves on his plantations in the Yazoo Delta, was so enamored of the practice that he urged his daughters to embrace it as a vocation. Another Mississippi nabob, Stephen Duncan, himself a trained physician, turned in desperation to homeopathy in 1849 in a vain attempt to check the cholera epidemic that was decimating the slave population on his Issaquena County plantations. A decade later, Rice C. Ballard resorted to homeopathic therapy on his Louisiana estates, but at least one of his overseers was not impressed with the results. Apparently the slaves were not either. Less than a week after the Negroes tried to poison him by putting something in his coffee, the harried manager tersely informed his employer that he could not "brake the Chills on these people with homeopathy." He added with an air of finality, "I hav tride suffishantly."[22]

Despite the efforts of physicians, homeopathic or otherwise, the relentless specter of death claimed a heavy toll of victims within the slave population just as it did among those who owned them. Infants and young children of both races were especially vulnerable. Thus, although the birth rate exceeded the death rate on most southern plantations, the long-term survival rate for slave infants was often quite low. For example, even as the overseer of Duncan Kenner's Ascension Parish sugar plantation recorded ten births and only four deaths in the year 1852, he noted that during the previous seven years there had been eighty-six births on the place *"and 47 of them is now dead,"* a mortality rate of 55 percent in that brief period. Fellow sugar planter Robert R. Barrow fared even worse. In a year when deaths exceeded births by a margin of four to one on his Residence plantation, Barrow was obliged to purchase sixty-eight Negroes in three separate lots in the New Orleans slave market in order to replenish his huge labor force. Such extreme mortality rates were not universal on plantations in the Southwest and were certainly uncommon on the more healthful units of the Upper South. For example, on John N. Helm's Beverly plantation near Natchez, there were twice as many births as deaths during the quarter-century

22. Richard T. Archer to daughter Jane, November 11, 1866, in Richard Thompson Archer Family Papers, CAH; Stephen Duncan to C. P. Leverich, May 19, June 18, 1849, in Charles P. Leverich Papers, MDAH; Alexander Hunter to R. C. Ballard, July 10, 1858, S. S. Boyd to Ballard, August 24, 1858, G[reen] B. Wilson to Boyd, August 29, 1858, in Rice Carter Ballard Papers, SHC.

from 1833 to 1857. But even there the death toll was high among infants, and the records do not reflect either miscarriages or stillborn children.[23]

Beyond question, however, the slave mortality rate was highest along the Georgia-South Carolina rice coast. In his study of a limited number of plantations owned by elite slaveholders in that region, William Dusinberre has estimated that two-thirds of the slaves on nineteenth-century rice plantations died before they reached the age of fifteen. Dusinberre, who tends to exaggerate what he perceives to be the "horrific" conditions of slavery, cites as a principal example Butler Island, an absentee Georgia estate with only minimal proprietary supervision, where, he asserts, 61 percent of the Negro children did not survive beyond the age of sixteen. He is compelled to admit, however, that even there the slave force increased at the rate of 14.5 percent per decade. Perhaps more representative was the Middleton family's Weehaw plantation, a well-managed unit in Georgetown District. Despite an unusually large number of fatalities in 1857, many from dysentery, births exceeded deaths on Weehaw by an average of five per annum during the last five years of the antebellum period. Thus, the total slave force on Weehaw rose from 266 in November, 1855, when Henry A. Middleton, Jr., "took charge of the place," to 289 in December, 1860, shortly before he left for the war. Such an increase was slightly higher than the decennial growth rate on the Butler plantations and more than four times as great as Dusinberre's estimate of 4.0 percent per decade for the rice kingdom as a whole.[24]

Disease, unsanitary living conditions, exposure to inclement weather, and inadequate postnatal care were not the only causes of death among plantation slaves. Accidents, many of them work-related, also took a heavy toll. The records are replete with accounts of fatalities resulting from fire, accidental drownings, and equipment mishaps. Thus, Paul Cameron mourned the loss in 1850 of "little Ed," a young boy on his Stagville farm who had succumbed in a house fire when left unattended by his mother. Fire also claimed the life of one of the hands on Haller Nutt's Araby plantation when a burning tree fell on him, killing him instantly. Blaming the mishap on his own carelessness, Nutt

23. Record of Births and Deaths of Negroes, 1852, in Ashland Plantation Record Book, LSU; R. R. Barrow Residence Journal, July 10, 1857, January 1, February 28, March 12, 1858, SHC; List of Births and Deaths, 1833–57, Beverly Plantation Journal, HNO.

24. Dusinberre, *Them Dark Days*, 80, 237–38, 415; Henry A. Middleton, Jr., Plantation Journal, 1855–61, in Cheves-Middleton Papers, SCHS.

expressed the hope that this unfortunate incident would "prove a good lesson" for the future. Another young Negro died from the lingering effects of a fall suffered while trimming trees on a north Georgia estate, and a three-year-old girl was killed when run over by a wagon on John N. Helm's Beverly plantation. Drownings, too, were not uncommon. Another Beverly slave, a prime field hand named Elijah, drowned in Second Creek near Natchez in the summer of 1847. Six years later, a Negro man on William T. Palfrey's Bayou Teche sugar plantation suffered a similar fate when he "fell from his fish wharf."[25]

Other slaves were either killed or maimed as a result of accidents involving farm machinery. Nowhere else were the conditions of labor more hazardous than on Louisiana sugar plantations. For example, William T. Palfrey recorded several mill accidents on his Ricahoe plantation that resulted in painful, yet nonfatal, injuries to the victims. During the rolling season of 1846 his Negro man Jacob escaped with only a dislocated collarbone and "some severe bruises about the head" after he "was caught by the cane carrier of the Mill" and "carried with the drum as far as his shoulder." Some years later, another Palfrey slave "lost his forefinger" when his left hand was "lacerated by the engine." On another Louisiana plantation a female slave got her dress caught in the mill, and "before the engineer could stop the mill her arm had gone under" as well as part of her ear. As a result, she lost the arm, and the engineer suffered a severely "mashed" foot from "stoping the engine so suddenly." Cotton gins could also be dangerous. A young Negro boy on Rosemount plantation in the Alabama Black Belt also had his arm amputated after it was caught in the gin.[26] The slaves mentioned in these examples were the fortunate ones, for they survived; other victims of plantation accidents did not.

Whatever the cause of death—whether disease, accident, or simply old age—many masters exhibited genuine sorrow upon the passing of a faithful

25. Paul C. Cameron to "My dear Father," October 23, [1850], in Cameron Family Papers, SHC; Araby Plantation Journal, February 2, 1846, in Haller Nutt Papers, DU; Benjamin Poore to Farish Carter, April 21, 1840, in Farish Carter Papers, SHC; List of Births and Deaths, February 24, 1840, July 11, 1847, in Beverly Plantation Journal, HNO; William T. Palfrey Plantation Diary, June 26, 1853, in Palfrey Family Papers, LSU.

26. Palfrey Plantation Diary, November 21, 1846, December 11, 1855, in Palfrey Family Papers, LSU; Louisa Winchester to "My dear Brother" [Frank], November 30, 1861, in Winchester Family Papers, CAH; A[melia] T. Glover to "My Dear Mother & Sister, February 23, 1854, Walton Family Papers, SHC.

slave. This was most likely to occur in the case of house servants to whom members of the white family had become emotionally attached during an extended period of loyal service. Thus, upon returning home in the fall of 1851 after a lengthy absence, John L. Manning of South Carolina was greeted with the distressing news that Lelia, a "valuable servant" belonging to his mother, had died of "inflammation of the stomach" after an illness of only five days. As he confided to his wife, "I felt as if one of the family were dead, so greatly did I regard her." Her own family, he added appreciatively, had "exhibited all the sensibility of refined & educated minds, much more, indeed, than is found in what is called the world." The demise of two North Carolina slaves, one without warning and the other from "a complication of diseases," evoked similar expressions of grief from their respective owners. In the fall of 1850, Paul Cameron communicated to his father the sad tidings of the death "in our family of slaves" of "poor Sarah" despite "every effort within our power" to help her "recover her lost health." More shocking was the sudden passing of Essex, a valued servant on Thomas P. Devereux's Connecanara plantation. "[I] can hardly realize I shall never see him again," wailed Devereux's distraught wife. Even more painful was the "melancholy scene" on New Year's Eve, 1834, at Wye House, seat of the Lloyd family on the Eastern Shore of Maryland. Notwithstanding almost daily attendance by a physician, "poor Barnett" succumbed to a combination of influenza, pleurisy, and typhus, only to be followed less than two hours later by his mother, who had seemed "quite well" while ministering to her son on his deathbed. Her death, concluded the distressed Edward Lloyd, "was most singular," and that of the unfortunate Barnett was "a great loss" to the family.[27] It is clear from such examples that many masters developed genuine affection for slaves who had served long and faithfully in that involuntary capacity.

Many elite slaveholders exhibited concern for the spiritual as well as the physical health of their black wards. Some erected elaborate plantation chapels, others employed ministers to conduct services at regular intervals, and still others welcomed missionaries from the leading denominations to their estates. Planter wives, who were frequently more devout than their husbands, partici-

27. John L. Manning to "My dearest Wife," September 21, 1851, in Williams-Chesnut-Manning Papers, SCL; Paul C. Cameron to "My dear Father," October 15, 1850, in Cameron Family Papers, SHC; Anne M. Devereux to Margaret M. Devereux, [April 1, 1853], in Devereux Family Papers, DU; Edward Lloyd [VI] to "My dear Mother," January 1, 1835, in Lloyd Papers, MHS.

pated in the religious instruction of their slaves by holding Sunday School, offering devotions, teaching hymns, and catechizing the children. The motives
were mixed. Obviously, a central objective was that of social control: to encourage good behavior and to render slaves more reconciled to their station in life.
Indeed, Bishop James O. Andrew, whose refusal to divest himself of slave property had led to the formation of the Methodist Episcopal Church, South, in
1845, contended that the slave missions of his church had a mutually beneficial
effect on both servant and master. Exposure to Christianity taught the former
"to regard himself an heir of heaven, and substituted in his heart the fear of
God . . . instead of the fear of punishment as the motive to obedience—thus
making him a good and faithful servant." This salutary consequence, continued
Andrew, produced "a corresponding change" in the master. "The faithfulness
of the servant," he concluded, "increased the kindness of the master."[28] But
there was another, less self-serving, motive as well. As pious Christians themselves, some slaveholders felt a moral obligation to bring the Gospel to members
of their black family. For example, an elderly Mississippi matron was so
conscience-stricken at "keeping her servants from going to preaching" while she
herself was attending that she requested permission from Alexander K. Farrar
to allow three of them to attend services on his Kingston plantation. Kate Edmondston felt a similar responsibility to provide spiritual solace to the Negroes
on her husband's plantation. "It ought to be done & I ought to do it," she declared, adding with some frustration that they seemed to absorb only "the mere
rudiments of Christianity" from her efforts.[29]

In view of their own denominational preference, it is not surprising that
many elite planters sought to encourage their slaves to receive their instruction
in religious doctrine within the confines of the Episcopal Church. That denomination was clearly preferable to the more egalitarian Methodist and Baptist
faiths. Masters tolerated the former, especially after that church divided along
sectional lines, but most refused to countenance any association with the Baptists. Thus, the irascible wife of Society Hill, South Carolina, planter John N.

28. Bishop James O. Andrew, "A Fortnight Among the Missions to the Blacks," in Charles F.
Deems, ed., *Annals of Southern Methodism, 1857* (Nashville, 1858), 309. I am indebted to William
Erwin of the Manuscripts Department in the Perkins Library at Duke University for calling this
source to my attention.

29. Ann Farrar to "Dear Husband," November 3, 1857, in Alexander K. Farrar Papers, LSU;
"Journal of a Secesh Lady," ed. Crabtree and Patton, 21.

Williams, perturbed by her slaves' aversion to Episcopalianism, reluctantly permitted them to attend the Methodist church but not the Baptist, which had "too much of the republican democratic spirit for slaves." Similarly, a Natchez District slaveholder lauded the Episcopal "system of teaching" as "the one most likely, if not the only one, to prevent the religion of the negro, from running into a dangerous and fearful fanaticism." North Carolina planter Josiah Collins III, a staunch Episcopalian, erected a chapel on his Somerset estate in 1836 and then employed a resident clergyman to convert his slaves from Methodism to the Episcopal faith.[30] Of course, there were a few exceptions. A Baptist minister in Alabama who regularly offered religious instruction to the slaves on several Greene County plantations reported the conversion of some thirty to forty servants at a single service. On St. Helena Island, South Carolina, the majority of the Baptists were black. The "Baptist champion" on that island was planter William Fripp, Sr., generally referred to as "Good Billy," who allegedly carried his Bible into the fields, read the law of Moses to his slaves, and whipped them accordingly.[31]

Among those who eventually endorsed the missionary activities of the Methodist Church were some of the wealthiest Episcopalian planters along the South Carolina–Georgia rice coast. When visiting that region in the spring of 1856, Bishop John Early was delighted to find that many rice barons who had previously opposed the "introduction of preaching and catechetical instruction on their plantations" were "now among the most ardent friends of the missions." There had been some difficulty in the past because some regarded the missionaries as intruders, many overseers objected to the practice, planters who were members of other churches preferred to have their servants instructed by their own ministry, and others were hostile to the Methodist ministry "until the Church was divided between North and South, because of the constant agitation on the subject of slavery." Now, however, the attitude of the great planters was much more receptive, and such grandees as James B. Heyward and Daniel Blake were erecting handsome chapels on their plantations. These views were echoed by Bishop Andrew when he visited the same area the following year.

30. Gill, "A Year of Residence in the Household of a South Carolina Planter," 302; *Southern Churchman*, September 26, 1845; *Dictionary of North Carolina Biography*, ed. Powell, I, 404–406; *"Journal of a Secesh Lady,"* ed. Crabtree and Patton, 21 n. 70.

31. Reverend F. M. Crain to John H. Cocke, May 10, 1858 (Roll 4), in Cocke Papers, SHC; Rosengarten, *Tombee*, 114, 146, 647.

After catechizing "a large number of little negroes" in the "commodious chapel" recently completed by Blake, he lauded that proprietor and his wealthy neighbors for their "decidedly friendly" attitude toward the missionary activities of his church.[32]

Whatever their motives, other elite slaveholders in South Carolina and elsewhere in the South took special pains to provide for the religious education of their slaves. Among the Georgetown District planters who manifested a strong interest in the spiritual welfare of their black charges were John H. Tucker, Plowden C. J. Weston, and R. F. W. Allston, all of them staunch Episcopalians. When a new Episcopal church was consecrated in All Saints Parish in 1845, Tucker had the old building removed to his Litchfield plantation for use as a Negro chapel. Weston, who had the reputation of being a "very generous master," built an elaborate Episcopal chapel on his plantation just before the war, and his English-born wife, Emily, taught some of their slaves to read the Bible. Another Georgetown matron, Adele Allston, from the time she came to her husband's plantation as a bride of twenty-two, spent every Sunday teaching the catechism to all the slave children and then rewarded each with a slice of cake when the lesson was over. Just to the north, in Horry District, a transplanted Yankee, Henry Buck, regularly held morning devotional services for his house servants.[33] Similar examples may be cited from the sugar parishes of Louisiana. Three prominent Lafourche Parish planters, Thomas Bibb, Dr. Ebenezer E. Kittredge, and Thomas Pugh, supported the religious instruction of slaves in both word and deed. Members of the Woolfolk family in nearby Iberville Parish were also noted for their benevolent religious concerns. On one occasion, Emily Woolfolk reportedly presided over the baptism of fifty-two Negroes, with her daughter acting as their sponsor.[34]

Despite such efforts by well-intentioned masters to indoctrinate their slaves with the tenets of Christianity, the results were often disappointing. Indeed, for

32. Bishop John Early, "A Fortnight Among the Missions to the Blacks," in Charles F. Deems, ed., *Annals of Southern Methodism, 1856* (Nashville, 1857), 205–207; Andrew, "A Fortnight Among the Missions to the Blacks," 301–303.

33. Rogers, *History of Georgetown County,* 272 (Tucker); Joyner, *Down by the Riverside,* 20–21, 72, 155–56, 216 (Weston, Buck); Pringle, *A Woman Rice Planter,* 309–10; R. F. W. Allston to Adele Petigru Alston, December 1, 1844, in Easterby, ed. *South Carolina Rice Plantation,* 92–93.

34. *De Bow's Review* 8 (February 1850): 150; Louisiana Writers' Project, *Louisiana: A Guide to the State* (New York, 1945), 572.

some, any beneficent effect was barely discernible. Such was the case with William N. Mercer, who erected an Episcopal church on his Laurel Hill plantation in 1839 and for several years thereafter employed a resident clergyman to instruct his slaves in their "religious duties." Although he did not expect to reform the elderly, he did hope to improve the conduct and character of the younger Negroes. After more than a decade, however, he was compelled to conclude that little progress had been made. "Moderate as were my expectations," he remarked sarcastically, "they have scarcely been realized." There was no reason to believe that the morals of his servants had been improved or that they had acquired any "distinct knowledge of the doctrines of our Church, of the Divine Founder of our religion, of the obligations He imposed, or the consolations He offered."[35] Two Carolina women, Kate Edmondston and Elizabeth Allston Pringle, were equally disappointed with the benefit to their Negroes of religious education. The latter, who continued holding Sunday School for black children in her neighborhood long after the conclusion of the war, complained that, despite such instruction, they continued to exhibit almost daily examples of "deceit, faithless work," and the theft of any article that could be "stolen unseen."[36]

Two ministers, one in Louisiana and the other in Alabama, were a bit more sanguine about the influence of their preaching on plantation slaves within their purview. William Phillips, who was conducting biweekly services for slaves on the huge Ascension Parish sugar plantations of South Carolina absentees John L. Manning and John S. Preston in the summer of 1856, reported improved attendance and "greater interest in the Services" than ever before among the people on the Manning properties. "I can truly say that I have much to gratify & encourage me in this work among your people," he concluded optimistically. The outlook was less favorable on Colonel Preston's estate because the hands there had previously been exposed to "negro-preaching" with its consequent "ill-advised courses." However, Phillips was hopeful that he could "do them some good or at least . . . disabuse them of some of their absurd notions of religion." Apparently no such problem impeded the dissemination of the Gospel in the vicinity of John H. Cocke's Hopewell plantation in Alabama. There,

---

35. William Newton Mercer to William Mercer Green, January 22, 1851, quoted in Nash Burger, "A Side-Light on an Antebellum Plantation Chapel," *Historical Magazine of the Protestant Episcopal Church* 12 (March 1943): 72. I am grateful to Glenn M. Robins, one of my doctoral students at the University of Southern Mississippi, for providing me with a copy of this article.

36. *"Journal of a Secesh Lady,"* ed. Crabtree and Patton, 21; Pringle, *A Woman Rice Planter,* 314.

following the conversion of a large number of penitents at the neighborhood chapel, a Baptist minister exulted that he had "rarely seen a larger amo[u]nt of religious feeling & excitement exhibited among a congregation of servants."[37] Of course, one should treat such glowing reports from clergymen ministering to slaves on distant absentee plantations with considerable caution. It was obviously in their interest to portray conditions as favorably as possible in order to justify their continued employment.

While it is likely that the majority of elite slaveholders, for one reason or another, made some provision for the religious instruction of their slaves, there was less uniformity when it came to preserving the integrity of slave families. The forced destruction of such families was manifestly one of the worst features of the peculiar institution, and it occurred with distressing frequency, even among the wealthiest planters. However, some nabobs went to great lengths to keep their black families intact, often stipulating in their wills that family members should not be separated. Others made all reasonable efforts to prevent separation as long as financial circumstances permitted, but a few displayed a callous disregard for family ties among their black wards. Chief among those was the former slavetrader Rice C. Ballard, who followed the pattern of continually buying and selling slaves without regard to marital or parental bonds throughout his planting career. Others who displayed a similar insensitivity to slave family relations included Governor Charles J. McDonald of Georgia, who remarked on one occasion that he allowed his Negroes to marry with the understanding that the union was "to last as long as they live or until it is the pleasure of their owners to separate them," and Henry Tayloe of Alabama, who, in the words of one scholar, bought and sold Negroes in the 1830s "with a stout disregard for family ties."[38]

It is clear that a great many family units were severed, by either masters or professional traders, through the interregional movement of slaves from upper to lower South. We are concerned here, however, primarily with the sensitivity of elite slaveholders toward family relationships among those chattels already in their possession as well as those purchased and sold during the course of their

37. William E. Phillips to John L. Manning, July 31, 1856, in Williams-Chesnut-Manning Family Papers, SCL; F. M. Crain to John H. Cocke, May 10, 1858, in Cocke Papers, SHC.

38. Rice C. Ballard Papers, SHC; Charles J. McDonald to Farish Carter, December 25, 1854, in Farish Carter Papers, SHC; Cashin, *A Family Venture*, 76.

entrepreneurial activities. It should be noted that the manuscript sources upon which this study is based are more likely to yield examples of benevolent concern than instances in which parental and spousal ties were disregarded by owners. Nevertheless, it seems probable that some scholars have exaggerated the extent to which slave families were destroyed by heartless masters. Thus, while conceding that interregional sales had a much more devastating effect on black families than did local sales, Michael Tadman asserts dogmatically that "market forces, rather than sentiment for family, were apparently *always* likely to predominate with slaveowners."[39] In his study of conditions on the estates of several elite families on the South Carolina rice coast, William Dusinberre paints an equally harsh picture. He charges, for example, that though Charles Manigault frequently preserved family units, he also "destroyed family ties when it suited him to do so." Perhaps so, but other evidence suggests that this was far from the norm among Low Country rice barons. Indeed, Henry A. Middleton, scion of one of the most distinguished families in the state, asserted in his application for a pardon from President Andrew Johnson that he had never bought or sold a single slave and that the ancestors of his three hundred slaves had been in his family since 1735.[40] The records are replete with examples of wealthy planters who not only sought to maintain the integrity of their slave families but even went out of their way to unite spouses owned by separate masters, sometimes at the request of the affected parties. Most common were efforts to respect marital ties when owners were obliged to sell some or all of their Negroes. Thus, when instructing slavetrader Rice C. Ballard concerning the disposition of a parcel of Kentucky slaves, the executor of the estate wrote from Louisville: "Bill has a wife here and I would dislike to separate them." Even during the bonanza atmosphere of the mid-1830s when thousands of Negroes were being shipped to Mississippi for sale, a Vicksburg correspondent reported that "the ordinary mode of selling here is man & wife," the couple selling together for an average price of $2,000. Two decades later, when Richard T. Archer was negotiating for the purchase of "a large number of negroes" from a Virginia planter, he noted that the latter did "not wish to seperate [*sic*] them" and had advertised them as "very likely family negroes." Such injunctions

39. Michael Tadman, *Speculators and Slaves: Masters, Traders, and Slaves in the Old South* (Madison, Wis., 1989), 136, 139 (italics mine).

40. Dusinberre, *Them Dark Days*, 107; Rogers, *History of Georgetown County*, 426–27.

against family separation were not unconditional, however. Two years earlier, Archer had been involved in the division of a family estate that had led to the destruction of four slave marriages. "Families are seperated [*sic*] as little as we could help," he remarked, "but it could not be entirely avoided."[41]

A number of elite slaveowners sought to prevent such painful ruptures by inserting restrictive provisions in their wills, but again such injunctions were rarely unconditional. It is difficult to determine how common this practice was, though it is clear that only a small minority of masters included such a clause in their last will and testament. In her study of North Carolina planters, Jane Censer found that only about one-tenth of the large slaveholders in her sample made a specific effort to keep black families intact after their deaths. Among those who did so were Duncan Cameron, Dr. Stephen Davis, John Devereux, and Isaac Wright.[42] The last's son, Moorhead Wright, who became the second largest slaveholder in Arkansas by midcentury, followed the lead of his father and stipulated in his will that if any division of his slaves should take place after his death "such division shall be so made as to *(so far as practicable)* prevent and avoid seperating [*sic*] families—that is, seperating [*sic*] husband wife and children."[43] Other wealthy planters who inserted similar provisions in their wills included Turner Clanton of Georgia and James G. Spann, Jr., of Alabama. The latter directed that in the division of his Negroes among his five sons, "families shall be kept together, and any inequality in value of the different portions, shall be made up in money."[44]

Occasionally, planters received appeals from other slaveowners, and even from the slaves themselves, to reunite families that had previously been separated. Virginia grain producer Richard Baylor received two such requests in the mid-1850s. The first was from a Fredericksburg slaveowner whose female ser-

41. C. A. Moore to R. C. Ballard, February 6, 1844, Rice Carter Ballard Papers, SHC; Frederick Norcom to James C. Johnston, January 24, 1836, in Hayes Collection, SHC; Richard T. Archer to "My Dear Wife," September 28, 1856, February 3, 1854, both in Richard Thompson Archer Family Papers, CAH.

42. Censer, *North Carolina Planters and Their Children*, 140–41; Last Will & Testament of John Devereux, October 20, 1843, in Leonidas Polk Family Papers, HNO.

43. Last Will & Testament of Moorhead Wright, November, 1853, in Gillespie and Wright Family Papers, SHC (italics mine).

44. Nell Irvin Painter, Introduction to *The Secret Eye,* ed. Burr, 30 n. 84; Will of James G. Spann, [Jr.], May 3, 1864 (TS), in Spann Family Papers, ADAH.

vant had been separated from her husband when the latter's neighboring owner emancipated him. This philanthropic act turned out to be a mixed blessing, for Virginia law compelled freed slaves to leave the state. The distraught Negro had been obliged to remove to Baltimore, and his spouse's owner now sought Baylor's aid in securing for the husband a position on one of the steamers running between the two cities in order "to mitigate the hardship" of what he termed "this compulsory divorce." Several years later, Baylor purchased for $400 a male slave named Bob who had requested the transaction so that he could "be with his family." A Georgia slaveholder manifested a like humanitarian concern when he endeavored to honor a commitment made several years before when he purchased a Negro woman and her five children from fellow planter Farish Carter. At the time of the purchase he learned that she had two other boys belonging to Carter, and he promised to buy them when circumstances permitted. Accordingly, six years later, noting that the woman was "still very desirous that I should make a purchase of her Boys," the compassionate master sought to comply with her request "so that all of her family might be brought together."[45]

As illustrated by the case involving the Fredericksburg slaveowner, the practice of permitting slaves to take broad wives—that is, to marry the servant of another master or even a free Negro—often presented special problems for both the owners and the two partners. While masters almost universally encouraged monogamous relationships, they preferred that their slaves choose spouses from within their own black family. Still, most were willing to allow the slaves to select their own mates. Broad wives were most common among house servants and on the smaller units of the Upper South, where the choice was often quite limited. On large plantations the practice was usually discouraged by the owners and sometimes even opposed by the other slaves. Thus, when a slave on one of the neighboring plantations requested permission to take a wife on John H. Cocke's absentee unit in Alabama, Cocke's agent sought his employer's advice, remarking suggestively: "The servants don't wish it." Cocke's response is unknown, but a South Carolina planter, John N. Williams of Society Hill, probably exemplified the attitude of most large slaveholders when he denied a male slave's petition to take a broad wife, counseling him instead to seek a mate on one of his own plan-

45. John Taylor Lomax to Richard Baylor, June 14, 1853, William A. Buckner to Baylor, January 8, 15, 1856, in Baylor Family Papers, VHS; B. S. Morrill to Farish Carter, January 14, 1857, in Farish Carter Papers, SHC.

tations. More compassionate was Eliza Young, the cousin of William N. Mercer, who termed "reasonable" the request of a Laurel Hill Negro to marry a female slave on neighboring Ormond plantation and urged Mercer to consent to the union unless he thought "it would be attended with greater evils."[46]

Two other cases, one from Kentucky and the other from North Carolina, illustrate the difficulties that might confront slaves who elected to take outside spouses. In an especially poignant letter, a house servant for the Ballard family in Louisville begged Ballard to purchase her husband, who had recently been sold out of the city by his previous owner. "If you don't bye him," she pleaded tearfully, "pleas get som body to bye him that will let him com & see me." In view of Ballard's prior record as a slavetrader and his subsequent insensitivity to family members, both black and white, it seems doubtful that he took any action to alleviate this woman's evident distress. Quite different was the dilemma faced by the more compassionate North Carolinian James C. Johnston when a free Negro asked permission to wed the daughter of one of his slaves. Since state law prohibited a "free person of color" from marrying a slave, Johnston would agree to the union only if the couple left the state. "He can marry the Girl as soon as he can carry her away," explained Johnston, "but I can't consent to a break of the laws by letting him marry her here."[47] That he would allow one of his young Negroes to exchange the bonds of slavery for those of matrimony is by itself compelling evidence of Johnston's uncommon magnanimity.

In addition to providing for the material wants, physical and spiritual needs, and family requirements of their slaves, wealthy slaveholders adopted other means to promote the morale and efficiency of their involuntary labor force. One of the most effective was the granting of holidays on Sundays and at other appropriate times throughout the year. Except on Louisiana sugar plantations during the rolling season, it was the universal practice of slaveowners to give their field hands a day of rest on the Sabbath. Even in the sugar parishes at least one great planter, Leonidas Polk, the Episcopal bishop of Louisiana, defied the traditional custom of Sunday work during the long harvest period. Polk, who, according to one authority, was committed to the creation of a biracial Chris-

46. Richard D. Powell to John H. Cocke, January 23, 1864, in Cocke Papers (Reel 4), SHC; Gill, "A Year of Residence in the Household of a South Carolina Planter," 300; E[liza] Y[oung] to "My dear Cousin," December 28, 1853, in William Newton Mercer Papers, LSU.

47. Delia to [R. C. Ballard], October 22, 1854, in Rice Carter Ballard Papers, SHC; James C. Johnston to William S. Pettigrew, January 1, 1861, in Pettigrew Family Papers, SHC.

tian community on his Leighton plantation, insisted upon observing the Sabbath throughout the year "not only because of the essential wrong of Sunday work but because of the necessity to the Negro, as a Negro, of leisure on Sunday for his better instruction & his elevation." The sight of the Leighton slaves parading on the levee in their holiday dress on Sunday afternoons and indulging in "their games up & down the road" so annoyed Polk's son, who was prohibited from engaging in such weekday diversions as hunting and fishing on that holy day, that he complained to his mother. She responded that he had "abundant opportunity for such amusements" during the week, but "working people had no such privileges." Consequently, their Sunday sports were permissible, while his were not.[48] Many planters also gave a half-holiday on Saturdays to enable their hands to tend their gardens, clean their houses, and perform other domestic chores for which they had little time during the week.

Although Christmas was the longest and most festive holiday observed on southern plantations, there were occasional respites from labor at other times during the year. Ironically, the Fourth of July was perhaps second only to Christmas as the most frequently commemorated event. According to Elizabeth Allston Pringle, it was the most celebrated holiday for the Negroes on the plantations of her South Carolina family both before and after the war. Independence Day was also a day of rest for the hands on Magnolia, a large sugar estate located about fifty miles below New Orleans. Even more impressive, however, was the Thanksgiving feast held on that plantation in 1858. Slaves from adjacent plantations together with whites on both sides of the river were invited to a sumptuous barbecue accompanied by such an abundant quantity of claret and champagne that almost "Every Body was tolerable Tite" by nightfall. Fortunately, a "Beatifuly conducted" religious service preceded this bacchanalian carnival, thereby providing ample justification for the event. As the overseer explained, "we feel That it is our Duty To Devote at least one Day in the year in Offering up thank[s] to Our Lord and savior Jesus christ the Giver of all good gifts."[49]

48. Notes by Polk's son on the bishop's attitude toward Negroes, n.d., in Leonidas Polk Family Papers, HNO. For a discussion of Polk's attitude toward the religious instruction of slaves and his alleged dedication to the principle of a biracial Christian community, see Glenn M. Robins, "Southern Episcopalianism: Leonidas Polk and Denominational Identity" (Ph.D. diss., University of Southern Mississippi, 1999), Chap. 3, "The Priest as Planter."

49. Pringle, *A Woman Rice Planter*, 86; Magnolia Plantation Journals, July 4, 1857, October 4, 1858, July 4, 1862, in Henry Clay Warmoth Papers and Books, SHC.

Other proprietors gave holidays at periodic intervals during the growing season, either from custom or as a reward for good work. For example, it was the
policy on the Middleton family's Weehaw plantation to give a day's respite from
labor at the end of each segment of the planting cycle—planting, hoeing, and
harvesting. Similarly, the Devereux family of North Carolina gave their Negroes
a three-day midsummer holiday after the corn crop had been laid by. The overseer of one of the McGehee plantations in Wilkinson County, Mississippi,
proved to be as practical as he was generous. He rewarded his hands for exemplary conduct by twice giving them a full holiday on Saturday during the spring
and summer of 1859, thereby losing only half a day on each occasion. "I think it
the duty of every overseer," he commented appreciatively, "to encourage hands
when they behave so as to deserve it."[50]

It was the yuletide season, however, that afforded slaves their most extended
vacation during the year. Normally lasting from three to seven days, inclusive of
the usual weekend holiday, it was a time of mutual celebration for both masters
and their servants. The latter usually received presents and / or special allowances
of food or clothing, and many were treated to a bountiful dinner followed by
music, dancing, and other forms of merriment. Somewhat surprisingly, scattered
evidence suggests that the holiday tended to be longer on the cotton and sugar
plantations of the Southwest than on the great estates along the South Carolina–
Georgia rice coast, where the norm was three to four days.[51] For example, the
manager of John C. Jenkins's Elgin plantation near Natchez noted on Christmas
Day, 1847: "We shall not have any work done until beginning of New Year." Two
years before, the hands at two other Jenkins plantations had joined those at Elgin
for a grand holiday celebration that lasted from December 24 through 28. Sugar
planter William T. Palfrey was even more generous. During the fifteen-year period from 1845 until the outbreak of the Civil War, the average duration of the
Christmas holiday on Palfrey's Ricahoe plantation was almost nine days. Like

50. Henry A. Middleton, Jr., Plantation Journal, 1855–61, in Cheves-Middleton Papers, SCHS;
"Journal of a Secesh Lady," ed. Crabtree and Patton, 243; Western View Plantation Record Book,
April 9, July 9, 1859, in McGehee Family Papers, MDAH.

51. Three days was the normal Christmas holiday on the plantations of such patriarchal rice barons as R. F. W. Allston, Plowden C. J. Weston, and Henry A. Middleton. Pringle, A Woman Rice
Planter, 274; Joyner, Down by the Riverside, 135; Henry A. Middleton, Jr., Plantation Journal, 1855–
61, in Cheves-Middleton Papers, SCHS. See aso Argyle Plantation Journal, 1828, 1830, in James
Potter Paper, GHS.

other sugar planters, Palfrey usually delayed the full holiday until the end of rolling season, which frequently extended into the new year. However, unlike most of his neighbors, he normally suspended work on Christmas Day, even before the completion of grinding. Thus, in 1858 the Ricahoe hands did not work on Christmas Day and took the balance of their holiday from January 30 to February 9 after they had finished making sugar. Such was apparently not the practice on a Plaquemines Parish sugar estate where in 1862, following the Federal occupation, the Negroes returned from the fields at breakfast on Christmas morning and announced to the overseer that "never having had a chance to keep it before they would avail themselves of the privalege [sic] now."[52]

Christmas was also the occasion for gifts and supplementary allowances to the hands. On Weehaw plantation in Georgetown District, South Carolina, it was customary to dispense extra portions of small rice, molasses, sugar, and fresh meat to each adult Negro, the amount depending upon the individual's position in the slave hierarchy. There were also monetary payments, ranging from $1 to $5, to each specialized hand and to those mothers whose infants had survived for one month and one year, respectively. Many large proprietors also gave presents to their slaves on Christmas morning. For example, in 1854 William B. Hodgson purchased more than $75 worth of headkerchiefs and calicoes for the hands on his three Georgia plantations. Two years earlier, the wife of John N. Williams distributed gifts to each of the four hundred Negroes on his large cotton plantation in Darlington District, South Carolina. The men received tobacco and headkerchiefs; the women, pots and headkerchiefs. Natchez nabob Francis Surget, Jr., opted instead for monetary gifts, dispensing $100 in silver to his slaves in 1860. The servants seemed to appreciate these gratuities from their masters, whether in the form of money or merchandise. Such was the reaction of the slaves at Laurel Hill, another plantation near Natchez. The women "send you a thousand thanks" for their Christmas presents, a female relative informed the absent owner. "They all ask after you," she added, "many with tears" in their eyes.[53] Most scholars would dismiss such expressions of grat-

52. John C. Jenkins Plantation Diary, December 24–28, 1845, December 25, 1847, in John C. Jenkins and Family Papers, LSU; William T. Palfrey Plantation Diary, 1845–61, in Palfrey Family Papers, LSU; Magnolia Plantation Journals, December 25, 1862, in Henry Clay Warmoth Papers and Books, SHC.

53. Henry A. Middleton, Jr., Plantation Journal, 1855–61, in Cheves-Middleton Papers, SCHS; "W. B. Hodgson account Current with R. Habersham & Son," January 15, 1855, in Telfair Family Papers, GHS; Gill, "A Year of Residence in the Household of a South Carolina Planter," 302;

itude as simply part of the typical Negro "put-on," but for some, they may have contained at least a grain of sincerity.

Whatever their inner feelings may have been, the slaves of two paternalistic South Carolina rice barons participated enthusiastically in the events that marked the celebration of Christmas on their Low Country plantations. On R. F. W. Allston's Chicora Wood plantation, all of the slaves trooped to the "Big House" shortly after daybreak on Christmas morning after "setting up" all night because of their belief that they should not be found in their beds on the night that Jesus was born. There, after exchanging greetings with members of the white family, they received their presents. Following a dinner that featured unusually savory fare, they amused themselves in the evening by dancing on the piazza of the mansion "to the music of fiddle, tambourine, bones, drum, and sticks." Christmas of 1856 was an especially joyous occasion for the Chicora Wood Negroes, for their master had just been elected governor. "They made a great noise and drank the Governor's health in many a stout glass of whiskey," recounted Mrs. Allston. Equally festive was the scene that same Christmas at neighboring Greenfield plantation. Jane Pringle reported "the usual scrimmage with the negros, wishing Merry Christmas from round corners and splitting with laughter at the idea of catching *Missus*." There were the usual presents: beads for the women, "a fabulous quantity of shirts" for the men, and headkerchiefs for all. "I hate to refuse the poor creatures," remarked the compassionate mistress of Greenfield.[54]

Quite apart from the merriment of the holiday season, there are many other examples of benevolent treatment by members of the slaveholding aristocracy. Many planters permitted their slaves to earn money by selling poultry and other produce or through overtime work. Others took special pains to care for those too old or infirm to work, and a few even facilitated the manumission of a faithful servant. It was a fairly common practice throughout the South to allow slaves to supplement their rather bland diet by cultivating small vegetable gardens, keeping a henhouse, or fishing during their leisure hours.[55] But some proprie-

Francis Surget, Jr., Account Book, December 24, 1860 (Roll 2), in Surget Family Papers, MDAH; Eliza Young to "My dear Cousin" [William N. Mercer], December 28, 1853, in William Newton Mercer Papers, LSU.

54. Pringle, *A Woman Rice Planter*, 272–74; Adele Petigru Allston to Benjamin Allston, January 1, 1857, in Easterby, ed., *South Carolina Rice Plantation*, 136; Jane L. Pringle to "My dear Son," Christmas night, [1856[, Pringle Family Correspondence, in R. F. W. Allston Papers, SCHS.

55. Representative examples include Joshua J. Ward of South Carolina, James A. Everett of Georgia, and Joseph E. Davis of Mississippi. Dusinberre, *Them Dark Days*, 419; Reidy, *From Slav-*

tors went further and purchased the surplus chickens, eggs, or garden produce raised by their servants, and a few allowed them to sell such items in the local market.[56] Occasionally, wealthy slaveholders permitted their chattels to produce and sell to them small quantities of such basic items as corn, hogs, and cotton. For example, in the mid-1830s a Natchez District planter, John N. Helm, was paying cash to his Negroes for corn and fodder. One recipient used the modest funds thereby accumulated to purchase a "dress pattern" for his wife. The slaves of Georgia planters Howell Cobb and John B. Lamar were allowed to raise cotton on their own account and to sell it with the plantation crop. In 1856 some forty heads of family on the Cobb-Lamar units netted $1,965 in this manner. On another occasion, Lamar purchased the entire lot of Negro hogs in order to achieve self-sufficiency in that important plantation staple. Another Georgian, Alexander Telfair, also permitted his hands to raise hogs, much to the consternation of both his overseer and his neighbors. The former complained that it was "impossible" for him "to tell there [sic] hogs from [Telfair's] stock of hogs," and the latter denounced the practice as an open invitation to theft.[57]

There were other ways for slaves to earn modest cash rewards. Georgia cotton planter James A. Everett, who believed in the efficacy of a reward system, paid his slaves cash for such arduous tasks as cutting shingles and railroad ties. In similar fashion, Joseph E. Davis, elder brother of the Confederate president, allowed his slaves to retain the profits derived from their sale to passing steamboats of wood gathered from adjacent swamplands as well as the usual poultry and garden produce. Another Mississippian, Benjamin Roach, Jr., recorded cash payments to his Negroes for work performed on "their own time." Thus,

ery to Agrarian Capitalism, 44; Janet Sharp Hermann, Joseph E. Davis: Pioneer Patriarch (Jackson, Miss., 1990), 56.

56. Richard T. Archer to Ann B. Archer, January 13, 1852, and Archer to "My Dear Son," February 6, 1855, both in Richard Thompson Archer Family Papers, CAH; Ballard & Boyd in a/c with L. H. Thistle, April 4, 1863, in Rice C. Ballard Papers, CAH; James Gunnells to "the Miss Telfairs," June 27, 1833, in Telfair Family Papers, GHS. Archer afforded his Negroes the privilege of "going occasionally to Port Gibson to dispose of their potatoes &c so long as they abstain from stealing."

57. Slave Accounts, 1835–36, in Beverly Plantation Journal, HNO; [Francis Surget, Jr.] Check Book, W. A. Britton & Co., June 25, 1858 (Roll 2), in Surget Family Papers, MDAH; Reidy, From Slavery to Agrarian Capitalism, 70–71; B. J. Brantley to John B. Lamar, February 23, 1862 [misfiled under 1842], in Cobb-Erwin-Lamar Family Correspondence, UGA; H[amilton] L. Lovett to Alexander Telfair, December 10, 1830, in Telfair Family Papers, GHS.

in the autumn of 1855, Roach paid Tom Knight $5 for cutting five huge cypress logs and hauling them to the sawmill. Another Roach hand received half that amount for "hauling a Waggon load of freight" from the steamer landing to Roach's Warren County plantation "on Sunday."[58] Such monetary payments not only enabled slaves to acquire a few items not normally provided by the master but also gave slave fathers an opportunity to achieve at least a modicum of self-respect by contributing to the support of their families.

Special privileges and small monetary rewards were not the only manifestations of slaveholder benevolence. Some elite planters evinced genuine humanitarian concern for the welfare of their superannuated slaves. For example, when the Savannah merchant-planter Robert Habersham leased one of his plantations to another proprietor shortly before the war, he stipulated explicitly in the contract that his "old crippled woman Peggy" was "to retain possession of the house & ground she occupies." Two plantation mistresses, Jane Pringle of South Carolina and Fanny Conner of Mississippi, exhibited like compassion for aged servants who were about to exchange the travails of their earthly life for the brighter promise of a celestial one. When Tina, the devoted spouse of "poor old Sampson," died just before Christmas on Pringle's Greenfield plantation, the latter predicted correctly that he would "miss her dreadfully." During the ensuing month, the concerned Pringle recounted to her son the steady decline of her faithful servant. He "lies perfectly helpless," she reported in mid-January. "His only enjoyment is his dinner which I send him every day, & making little Bess [?] scratch his back." Finally, at the end of the month, she conveyed the melancholy news of Sampson's death. "He never held up his head after Tina's death," she observed sadly, "but took to his bed and quietly passed away . . . without a struggle." Natchez matron Fanny Conner displayed similar compassion for the elderly Negroes on her husband's Louisiana plantation. Apprised of the death of "poor old Toby" shortly after preparing some sugar and coffee for him, she elected, nevertheless, to send on the articles so that her husband might "give them to some of the other infirm old negroes."[59]

---

58. Reidy, *From Slavery to Agrarian Capitalism*, 44; Hermann, *Joseph E. Davis*, 56; Payments to Negroes for work on their own time, November 22, 1855, in Probate Records, 1854–56 (Folder 2), in Benjamin Roach Family Papers, CAH.

59. Agreement between Robert Habersham and George W. Anderson, February 23, 1858, in George Wayne Anderson Business Papers, Wayne-Stites-Anderson Papers, GHS; Jane L. Pringle to "My dear Son" [Julius], Christmas Night, [1856], January 13, 31, [1857], Pringle Family Correspon-

A few wealthy slaveholders even went so far as to manumit a favorite slave. The practice was not widespread, for there were too many legal impediments to such a charitable act. Thus, when the children of Francis Surget, Sr., sought to carry out their deceased father's wish to emancipate a fifty-year-old slave named Bartlett, they were obliged to send him to Ohio "or some other suitable place" for manumission. Early in the century, another Mississippi nabob, Robert Cochrane, displayed remarkable generosity when he freed without compensation the wife and five children of an emigrant to Liberia so that the family might be reunited in that West African colony. Not only did Cochrane manumit these six slaves, who were valued at $4,000, but he also bequeathed $100 to each of the children.[60] Sometimes the benevolent intent of an elderly slaveholder was frustrated by his heirs. Such was the case with South Carolina rice magnate Langdon Cheves, Sr. Shortly before his death, Cheves indicated his desire to emancipate two faithful house servants, June and Cilla, as well as any children they might have. However, June, who had been conveyed to Cheves's daughter Louisa McCord by a deed of gift, apparently antagonized his new owner. Charging that June was a bad influence on her ailing father, McCord sent him to Charleston to be sold out of the state "in such manner as to prevent his return." Accordingly, after consulting with Langdon, Jr., the family's Charleston factors consigned the unfortunate Negro for shipment by the "first vessel to New Orleans," thereby nullifying the charitable design of his original owner.[61]

There were other examples of benevolent treatment by elite slaveholders. Notwithstanding the general injunction against teaching slaves to read and write, a few wealthy planters provided rudimentary instruction for young Negroes on their estates. The Harrison family of Prince George County, Virginia, actually employed a teacher to conduct a school for children of the servants on

dence, in R. F. W. Allston Papers, SCHS; Fanny E. Conner to "My dearest Husband," February 7, 1860, in Lemuel P. Conner and Family Papers, LSU.

60. "Form of freeing Negroes in Ohio or elsewhere," 1858 (Roll 4), in Surget Family Papers, MDAH; Charles Sackett Sydnor, *Slavery in Mississippi* (1933; rpr. Gloucester, Mass., 1965), 220.

61. Louisa S. McCord to Langdon Cheves, Jr., April 13, 1856, in McCord, *Selected Writings*, 271–74; Capers & Heyward to Langdon Cheves, Jr., January 14, 1857 (first quotation), T. P. Huger to "My dear Langdon," January 14, February 2 (second quotation), 1857, in Langdon Cheves, Jr., Papers, SCHS.

their two Brandon plantations. Several slaves of another Upper South planter, James C. Johnston of North Carolina, were sufficiently literate to correspond with their master. Two of them, Peter and Ben, served as foremen of Johnston's farms on the Pasquotank River and communicated regularly with the absentee owner concerning operations on those units. Johnston's Norfolk factor characterized Peter as "a rare exception to others of his kind" and expressed the hope that other servants of the North Carolina planter would be inspired to emulate his example.[62] In some cases, masters acted as amanuenses for their illiterate slaves, thereby enabling them to communicate with distant relatives. Although useful in mitigating the pain experienced by separated loved ones, letters filtered through slaveowners precluded candor on the part of slave correspondents. Thus, a Virginia mother rebuked her young son in North Carolina for running away to avoid a whipping and admonished him to "do all he can to please his master." The latter, to whom the missive was addressed, was doubtless pleased to relay this motherly advice to his youthful servant.[63]

There were also more singular illustrations of planter beneficence. Joseph E. Davis, one of the most enlightened slaveholders in the Deep South, established a unique plantation court manned by a slave jury to consider allegations of slave misconduct on his Hurricane plantation in Warren County, Mississippi. The largest slaveholder in Arkansas, Elisha Worthington, organized a brass and string band composed of slaves who had received instruction from a white music teacher. Similarly, R. F. W. Allston annually "sent off young lads to learn to play the violin" so that they might lead the music at slave balls on such special occasions as weddings and Christmas.[64] In addition to the customary allocations of clothing, shoes, and blankets, some planters in the Southwest even provided

62. *Genealogies of Virginia Families: Articles from the Virginia Magazine of History and Biography*, 5 vols. (Baltimore, 1981), III, 799–800; Peter to James C. Johnston, September 22, October 6, 1850, Eliza Johnston to James C. Johnston, October 4, 1850, Ben Johnston to James C. Johnston, October 21, 1860, July 31, 1863, W. J. Hardy to James C. Johnston, July 5, 1847 (quotation), in Hayes Collection, SHC.

63. James M. Gilbert to Lewis Thompson, March 14, 1860, and William G. Wright to Thompson, November 20, 1860 (quotation), both in Lewis Thompson Papers, SHC.

64. Hermann, *Joseph E. Davis*, 55; William D. McCain and Charlotte Capers, eds., *Memoirs of Henry Tillinghast Ireys: Papers of the Washington County Historical Society, 1910–1915* (Jackson, Miss., 1954), 352; Pringle, *A Woman Rice Planter*, 274.

their hands with mosquito netting. In this instance, however, the primary concern may have been health rather than comfort.[65]

Indeed, many planters were actuated more by self-serving than by humanitarian motives in extending privileges to their slaves. They believed in the efficacy of rewards rather than punishment as the cardinal principle of labor management. As was noted previously, some slaves received Christmas bonuses, others received money from the sale of produce to their masters, and still others earned cash rewards for overtime or difficult work. In addition, a few wealthy proprietors sought to stimulate more industrious habits among the members of their slave force through a system of rewards for outstanding performances. R. F. W. Allston provides a conspicuous example of this practice. He not only gave annual "prizes for the best workers in the different processes" of ploughing, ditching, and hoeing, but he also rewarded those who had not missed a day of work during the year. A bountiful crop could also yield monetary benefits to those who had been instrumental in making the year particularly successful. Thus, after wagering that "not another plantation in Louisiana" would match the sugar output of the Bringier family's Houmas plantation in 1852, New Orleans factor Martin Gordon suggested that the hands be rewarded with payments of silver. "The boys have no doubt worked well," he remarked, "and a little money given to them, would do good."[66]

There was, of course, another and much darker side of slavery, even on the estates of the great planters. It should never be forgotten that those who labored for old "massa" were entrapped in an often brutal system of forced, involuntary servitude. Nor should one forget that the profit motive was the paramount concern of most large slaveholders. Although some paternalistic planters endeavored to encourage their workers through an array of rewards, a far greater number resorted to harsh physical punishment to keep their chattels in line. While such chastisements were in accord with the penological practices of the age, they nevertheless had a brutalizing effect, not only on those who endured

65. H. L. Berry to Col. R. C. Ballard, April 10, 1859, in Rice Carter Ballard Papers, SHC; William T. Palfrey Plantation Diary (Vol. 17), July, 1844, July, 1847, in Palfrey Family Papers, LSU; Maunsel White Plantation Record Book, 1833–43, in Maunsel White Papers and Books, SHC.

66. Pringle, *A Woman Rice Planter,* 8; Dusinberre, *Them Dark Days,* 324; Martin Gordon, Jr., to Benjamin Tureaud, December 30, 1852, in Benjamin Tureaud Papers, LSU.

them but also on those who witnessed the severe floggings that were ubiquitous on southern plantations.

Elite planters were confronted with a variety of slave transgressions. Some, such as petty theft and malingering, were relatively minor and were often viewed with equanimity by masters and their families. Apart from thievery, running away was probably the most common offense. Induced by a variety of circumstances, these unauthorized absences were usually of short duration, but they could prove costly to proprietors, particularly if they occurred during critical periods of the planting cycle. Much more serious were such infractions as assaults upon masters and overseers or the deliberate burning of plantation structures. Finally, of course, the ultimate manifestation of slave resistance was open rebellion, the fear of which was implanted indelibly within the minds of white Southerners. Although few major slave insurrections materialized in the Old South, the memory of events on the island of Saint-Domingue during the last decade of the eighteenth century plagued planters and overseers alike, and the mere rumor of a slave uprising was enough to send waves of terror through the white community. When such an episode actually occurred, whites frequently became panic-stricken. Thus, Edmund Ruffin described the reaction in Virginia to the Nat Turner insurrection of 1831 as one approaching "very general community-insanity." The fear even spread to distant Mississippi, where Stephen Duncan discounted the rumored "extension of the virginia insurrection." He admitted, however, that his adopted state was susceptible to such threats. "We have here 5 blacks to one white; and within 4 hours march of Natchez there are 2200 able bodied male slaves," he noted ominously. "It behooves [us] to be vigilant—but *silent.*" Many years later during the closing days of the 1860 presidential campaign, when rumors of slave plots reverberated across the South, William S. Pettigrew encountered similar panic among the inhabitants of eastern North Carolina. Ridiculing the notion that slaves had concocted a plot to burn the town of Plymouth and murder its white inhabitants, Pettigrew observed sagaciously that "in case of panic on the subject of insurrectionary designs, the negroes are in more danger from the whites than the whites from the negroes."[67]

67. Scarborough, ed., *The Diary of Edmund Ruffin,* II, 208; Stephen Duncan to Thomas Butler, October 4, 1831, in Thomas Butler and Family Papers, LSU; William S. Pettigrew to James C. Johnston, October 25, 1860, in Hayes Collection, SHC.

Fortunately for the slaveowners, most breaches of slave discipline were much less threatening than the violent uprisings that inspired so much terror. Indeed, acts of petty thievery, particularly of poultry, were regarded so lightly that they frequently evoked expressions of amusement rather than anger from the victims. Such was the case with the women in two Mississippi families. In the spring of 1857, Margaret Winchester playfully remarked to her absent husband that she had been having a bit of "fun" with "Old Minty," who was not only pilfering turkeys but also stealing away each night to imbibe strong spirits. After being queried about two missing turkeys, Minty sought to make amends by bringing "a large yellow gobbler" to her mistress with the further promise to supply a hen within the week. "These turkies have disappeared since you left," observed the young Natchez matron, "did you take 'em?" In similar fashion, Rose Quitman recounted to her brother the nocturnal theft of "an old *turkish* lady, who was quietly at home with her flourishing little brood all at rest under her maternal wings." Added the teenager jocularly, "There is no accounting for the blackness of heart in the human race."[68] Not all minor offenses were treated so lightly. When unidentified Negroes broke into the pork house on a North Carolina plantation, the hands were called together and given thirty minutes to turn in the culprit. When they declined to do so, two of them were chosen by lot and flogged. Another North Carolinian was more ambivalent in his response to the theft of coffee and sugar by two of his house servants in Raleigh. George Mordecai elected not even to mention the incident to one of the suspects "for fear [he] might be provoked to do someting more." But he exiled the other thief to the country because, as Mordecai explained, "it will not do to pass over such an offense." Far to the south, on Duncan Kenner's Ashland sugar plantation, all hands were required to chop wood on a bright May Sunday as punishment for "Stealing wood from [the] wood pile."[69]

Nearly as common as the pilferers of plantation articles were the runaways that plagued virtually all southern slaveholders, both great and small. The frequency of such abscondings varied widely, depending on the conditions that

68. Margaret Winchester to "My dear Husband," March 8, 1854, in Winchester Family Papers, CAH; Rose Quitman to F. H. Quitman, May 3, 1857, in John A. Quitman and Family Papers, MDAH.

69. *"Journal of a Secesh Lady,"* ed. Crabtree and Patton, 220; George W. Mordecai to "My own dear Wife," November 17, 1861, in Cameron Family Papers, SHC; Ashland Plantation Record Book, May 9, 1852, LSU.

prevailed on individual plantations. Two examples from Louisiana during the 1850s represent extreme ends of the spectrum. Runaways were relatively infrequent on the Terrebonne Parish sugar plantations of Robert R. Barrow despite harsh working conditions that caused the natural increase of his slaves to lag far behind the death rate. Records indicate that there were only eleven abscondings from a total slave force of nearly three hundred during a period of eighteen months, and only two of those fled during the rolling season, the period of most arduous labor. Vastly different was the pattern of runaways on Morville, a newly established absentee cotton plantation owned by Eustace Surget and situated in Concordia Parish. There, within the single year 1855, there were thirty-six separate runaway incidents involving half as many slaves, or roughly one-fifth of the entire work force, and resulting in the loss of 543 man-days of labor. Several of the offenders were chronic runaways, one absconding no fewer than nine times during the year, and one Negro, Sam King, eluded capture for almost six months. When they were caught, the typical punishment for runaways on both the Barrow and Surget plantations was whipping and / or incarceration in irons or the stocks.[70] Other proprietors preferred to chain returning runaways, especially if they suspected a recurrence of the offense.[71]

South of the border states, most runaways sought only a brief respite from labor or punishment by hiding out in the near vicinity of their plantations, but a few, even in the Lower South, endeavored to effect a more permanent escape. This was apparently the case with several male slaves belonging to Leroy M. Wiley, a Charleston factor who had extensive absentee holdings in Georgia and Alabama. When these men escaped from his Georgia plantation in the fall of 1844 "they took a due *North direction*," leading their owner to conjecture that "they were trying to get to one of the free states," possibly Ohio, "if they could." Some of the escapees were apprehended at a plantation in the northern part of the state, and Wiley alerted slaveowners in that area "to keep a lookout" for the two who remained at large. If Wiley's supposition was correct, they would "have to cross the Tennessee [River] at one of the Ferries—& there would be a good chance of taking them up." Unfortunately, the records do not reveal whether

70. Data were computed by the author from R. R. Barrow Residence Journal, January 1, 1857– June 13, 1858, SHC; Morville Plantation Journal, 1855 (Roll 2), in Surget Family Papers, MDAH.

71. Araby Plantation Journal, February 4, 1844, in Haller Nutt Papers, DU; W. T. Lamb to Paul C. Cameron, November 4, 1860, in Cameron Family Papers, SHC.

the two fugitives were ever caught. In the neighboring state of Alabama nearly a decade later, a female slave attempted to elude capture by traveling south rather than north. After fleeing from one of Gaius Whitfield's plantations near Demopolis, she made her way by steamboat to Mobile. There, without proper papers, she was soon jailed. However, she attempted to conceal her identity by refusing to disclose either "her own or [her] owners proper name," claiming instead that she belonged "to some person in Mississippi." Fortunately for Whitfield, one of his agents recognized her, and she was soon returned to her rightful owner.[72]

Although troublesome and annoying to owners, runaways could be tolerated; those who committed more serious offenses, such as arson, assault, and murder, could not. Suspicious conflagrations occurred with distressing frequency on slave plantations across the South, but the arsonists were often difficult to identify because they usually committed such acts under the cover of darkness, and many proprietors were reluctant to believe that their own, supposedly faithful, Negroes could be involved in such dastardly deeds. Thus, when a rash of mysterious fires took a heavy toll of barns, stables, and corn-cribs on the farms of Edmund Ruffin in the late 1850s, the veteran agriculturist peremptorily dismissed the suggestion of neighbors that his own slaves might be responsible. Not until the fifth such incident in as many years struck the family properties did he begin to suspect the true identity of the culprits. Much worse was the disaster suffered by another wealthy Virginian, William H. Tayloe. The latter's imposing Mount Airy plantation home, originally constructed in 1755, was burned to the ground by a disgruntled slave woman just before Christmas in 1844 while Tayloe was visiting his holdings in Alabama.[73] Ginhouses were a common target of slave arsonists in the cotton states. Seven years after the burning of Mount Airy, the ginhouse on one of the Tayloe plantations in Alabama was destroyed by fire, resulting in an estimated loss of $4,000. The suspected incendiary was a neighboring Negro who had been whipped for trespassing on the Tayloe property and was thought to have burned the structure "to avenge himself." Following a similar conflagration on a Mississippi cotton plantation,

72. L. M. Wiley to Col. Farish Carter, November 11, 1844, in Farish Carter Papers, SHC; Charles W. Beckley [?] to Gaius Whitfield, May 7, 1852, in Gaius Whitfield Papers, ADAH.

73. Scarborough, ed., *The Diary of Edmund Ruffin*, I, xxv, 111–12, 169, 249–50, 355; Mount Airy Plantation Books, Vol. 3, "Inventory and Crop Book," 1840–60 (Microfilm copy *formerly* in SHC).

the overseer of an adjacent unit decided to post a night watch at his gin. As the worried manager explained to his absentee employer, Paul Cameron of North Carolina, there was "no clue to the perpetrator of this dark and daring act."[74]

Recalcitrant slaves sometimes went far beyond arson and physically assaulted masters or overseers they deemed responsible for real or imagined grievances. While not as terrifying to the white community as the collective threat posed by insurrections, such individual acts of violence could not be tolerated, and the offenders were usually subjected to swift and severe punishment. Thus, when a slave carpenter in Virginia not only defied his supervisor but ran off after receiving "a slight whipping" from his master, the latter sent him to Richmond to be sold out of the state. The owner justified this extreme action on the grounds that the unruly Negro had compounded his initial offense by making "speeches about the hardship of Slavery and his desire to get away North" as well as "corrupting some of my other negroes by other acts too numerous to mention." Overseers frequently bore the brunt of slave hostility. A Louisiana proprietor reported in the fall of 1861 that he had just gone up to his plantation to chastise one of his hands "for insolence to the overseer." The irate planter concluded, "I do not think he will behave so again soon." Across the river, the Negroes on a Mississippi cotton plantation tried to poison their manager by putting "something in his coffee." Even more serious was an incident that occurred near Natchez the previous year. Incensed by a whipping administered to his wife by her master, the woman's husband retaliated by breaking into the slaveowner's house in the middle of the night and assaulting him as he lay "in bed asleep." Although the latter survived the attack, he was described as "badly used up." The assailant fled with his wife but was soon caught and jailed. "He will hang," predicted the Natchez matron who recounted the affair to her husband.[75]

Offenses far less threatening than arson, murder, and mayhem often provoked severe reprisals from exasperated slaveholders. Thus, when misbehavior

74. B. O. Tayloe to "Dear Brother" [W. H. Tayloe], November 8, 1851, Tayloe Family Papers, VHS; W. T. Lamb to Paul C. Cameron, December 9, 1860, in Cameron Family Papers, SHC.

75. John G. Jefferson to Richard T. Archer, October 23, 1856, in Richard Thompson Archer Family Papers, CAH; Alexander Franklin Pugh Plantation Diaries, November 21, 1861, LSU; S. S. Boyd to R. C. Ballard, August 24, 1858, in Rice Carter Ballard Papers, SHC; Ann Farrar to "Dear Husband," November 3, 1857, in Alexander K. Farrar Papers, LSU.

became rampant among a parcel of recently purchased Negroes, William G. Conner resorted to extreme measures. "I have had a great deal of trouble with them," complained the harried owner. "The hard work has commenced and they run off like partridges." Consequently, he reported, "I have now 6 or 8 in chains and will probably be compelled to chain the whole posse before the year is over." R. B. Rhett, Jr., expressed similar dissatisfaction with his house servants. "We get on like the devil with the servants I have," exclaimed Rhett. "The good ones are fools, and the smart, spoilt and unwilling." Until they improve, declared the disgusted South Carolinian, "flogging, driving, and dissatisfaction" will be "the order of the day with me." Another East Coast slaveholder, Paul Cameron, manifested similar feelings while trying to rehabilitate a troublesome male slave belonging to his father. "He is only to be governed by absolute fear," observed the normally placid Cameron.[76]

While such outbursts probably represented aberrant reactions by Conner, Rhett, and Cameron, other wealthy slaveholders exhibited a more general pattern of harsh treatment. Such was the case with Haller Nutt. Although he had earlier castigated an overseer for allegedly brutalizing the slaves on his Araby plantation, Nutt himself was no model of temperance.[77] He routinely punished slave offenders by placing them in chains or incarcerating them in stocks, and he hired professional slave catchers to track his runaways with dogs. On one occasion, after finding conditions on one of his plantations in a deplorable state, not only did the angry proprietor berate the overseer for running out of pork, but he whipped "nearly all the negroes." Henry A. Tayloe, another planter not noted for his paternalistic demeanor, handled the Negroes on the family's Alabama plantations so severely that his older brother sharply rebuked him for his "cruelty." Finally, it was on the Red River estate of Meredith Calhoun, one of the largest slaveholders in Louisiana, that Frederick Law Olmsted witnessed what he termed the "severest corporeal punishment of a negro" that he encountered during his extensive travels throughout the South. Although the beating was administered by the overseer of an absentee estate, the owner was "sojourn-

76. W. G. Conner to "Dear Lemuel," June 12, 1850, in Lemuel P. Conner and Family Papers, LSU; R. B Rhett, Jr., to Burnet Rhett, August 2, 1855, in Robert Barnwell Rhett, Sr., Papers, SCHS; Paul C. Cameron to "My dear Father," September 21, 1850, in Cameron Family Papers, SHC.

77. See p. 162–63 of this book.

ing upon it" at the time and must have been aware of the disciplinary style of his subordinate.[78]

Of all the great slaveholders included in this study, however, no others were more callous or more brutal in the treatment of their human property than Judge Samuel S. Boyd of Natchez and his partner, the former slavetrader Rice C. Ballard. A native of Portland, Maine, Boyd had migrated to Natchez as a young man and married into the prominent Wilkins family. In time, he became "a lawyer of great ability and of widespread reputation."[79] He was related by marriage to such elite Natchez families as the Bingamans, Calhouns, and Duncans, and, following the Civil War, his daughter wed James Surget, Jr.[80] In short, Judge Boyd enjoyed a lofty status in the society of aristocratic Natchez. During the last two decades of the antebellum period he became associated with the less genteel Ballard in the acquisition and operation of a number of plantations in the adjacent states of Mississippi, Louisiana, and Arkansas. By 1860 the two partners had amassed a plantation empire that encompassed more than half a dozen plantations and at least five hundred slaves.

The records indicate that throughout the term of their joint planting venture Ballard and Boyd were constantly buying and selling slaves, apparently in utter disregard of family ties. Purchases clearly predominated as the partners rapidly expanded their holdings. Typical was a communication from Boyd to Ballard in 1844, notifying the latter of the impending sale of eighty-seven Negroes at Vicksburg. "If you have any surplus funds," advised Boyd, "it would probably be well to make a selection of a few choice hands." Similarly, in the spring of 1853, Boyd apprised his colleague of an opportunity to purchase the slaves belonging to a Jefferson County, Mississippi, estate "at a very reasonable rate." He was more cautious, however, about buying in the New Orleans market, where prices had risen recently to $1,550 for men and $1,150 to $1,200 for women.[81]

78. Araby Plantation Journal, February 4, 1844, in Haller Nutt Papers, DU; Haller Nutt to wife Julia, February 25, 1860 (quotation), Nutt to Hamilton Smith, April 26, 1862, both in Nutt Family Collection, MDAH; Cashin, *A Family Venture*, 114; *The Papers of Frederick Law Olmsted*, Vol. 2, *Slavery and the South, 1852–57*, ed. Charles E. Beveridge and Charles Capen McLaughlin (Baltimore, 1981), 220–23 and nn. 2–3.

79. *Goodspeed's*, II, 869.

80. Certificate of Marriage, James Surget, [Jr.], and Catharine C. Boyd, [blank] 18, 1873, in MacNeil Papers, MDAH.

81. Boyd to Ballard, January 14, 1844, April 2, 22, 1853, in Rice Carter Ballard Papers, SHC.

Ballard fared somewhat better three years later when he purchased forty-three Virginia Negroes at an average price of $1,000 for the partners' Elcho plantation in Madison Parish, Louisiana.[82] A Louisville trader, C. M. Rutherford, handled many of these transactions for Ballard and Boyd. On one occasion, Rutherford sought to interest Ballard in a "fine Carriage driver" valued at $1,100. "You Can take him at Cost," offered the generous trader, for "I had you in mind when I bought him." Several years later, Rutherford informed Ballard of the scheduled shipment of a lot of slaves "from the old Country where all the good ones come from" and offered to sell him pairs of male and female hands between the ages of fourteen and twenty-five at the rate of $1,300 a pair.[83] There is no indication from these and other examples that Ballard or Boyd paid the slightest attention to family relationships in their purchase of slave property. Their business transactions were governed entirely by the profit motive.

But trafficking in slaves was not the most egregious of Judge Boyd's sins. His treatment of a female house servant named Maria bordered on sadism. The first inkling of trouble in the Boyd household surfaced in the spring of 1844 when J. M. Duffield, a Natchez attorney, discreetly requested Ballard's assistance in removing Maria from Boyd's control as soon as Boyd's "convenience" would permit. Ballard apparently declined to intercede, and four years later, Maria's situation had become desperate. Duffield, who had fathered a child with the abused slave girl, then informed Ballard that he "had made arrangements to send the child northward, there to be brought up, and educated, and there forever to reside," and he implored Boyd's partner to allow him to purchase Maria in order to save her from the unspeakable cruelties daily being inflicted upon her by the respected judge. The attorney described Maria's treatment in graphic detail. She was, he charged, "lashed . . . like an ox, until the blood gushes from her." Surely Ballard's "kind, humane heart must revolt at the barbarities she is constantly enduring," wrote the distressed Duffield. "I would do any thing on earth," he added, "to relieve her from her present position."[84] Apparently the heartless Ballard was no more responsive to this plea than he had been to the earlier one, and there is no evidence that poor Maria was ever rescued from her temporal purgatory.

82. Elcho Plantation Accounts, February 8, April 14, 1856, in Rice C. Ballard Papers, CAH.

83. C. M. Rutherford to Ballard, August 6, 1853, July 6, 1858, Rice Carter Ballard Papers, SHC.

84. J. M. Duffield to R. C. Ballard, March 20, 1844, May 29, 1848, *ibid.*

Outrageous as was Judge Boyd's abuse of Maria, it was exceeded by his sub-sequent treatment of another female slave, his long-time mistress Virginia. The relationship had evidently been one of extended duration, for by 1853 she had already borne him two children and was pregnant with a third. Apparently fear-ful that the relationship was about to be revealed to his wife, Boyd, in March of that year, directed Ballard, acting through the agency of the slave dealer C. M. Rutherford, to send Virginia and her children—his own children—to Texas to be sold. Accordingly, on April 19, Rutherford notified Ballard that he had "this morning shipped Virginia & children to . . . Houston Texas with special in-structions to sell her not to return to this place [New Orleans] or Miss." The distraught former concubine, clearly a woman of uncommon literacy and high intelligence, did not go quietly.[85] Shortly after her arrival in Houston, she dis-patched a lengthy epistle to Ballard, beseeching him to allow her to earn enough money through "honest work" to enable her to purchase her freedom or at least that of her children. This poignant letter is so remarkable that it merits ex-tended quotation. Virginia began by posing this question to Ballard:

Do you think after all that has transpired between me & the old Man, (I don't call names) that its treating me well to send me off a mong strangers in my situation to be sold without even my having an opportu-nity of choosing for my self; its hard indeed and what is still harder [is] for the father of my children to sell his own offspring   yes his own flesh & blood   My god is it possible that any free born American would brand his character with such a stigma as that, but I hope before this he will relent & see his error for I still beleave that he is possest of more honer than that. . . . is it Possible that such a change could ever come over the spirit of any living man as to sell his child that is his image. I don't wish to return to harras or protest his peace of mind & shall never try [to] get back if I am dealt with fairly. . . . I have written to the Old Man in such a way that the letter cant fail to fall in his hands & none oth-ers   I use every precaution to prevent others from knowing or suspect-ing any thing . . . for I shall not seek ever to let any thing be exposed, unless I am forced from bad treatment &c

Virginia Boyd[86]

85. C. M. Rutherford to R. C. Ballard, April 2, 19, 1853, Boyd to Ballard, April 22, 1853, *ibid.*
86. Virginia Boyd to Ballard, May 6, 1853, *ibid.*

Despite this veiled threat, Virginia's anguished plea fell, as usual, on deaf ears. In early August, Rutherford informed Ballard that he had just received word from Texas that Virginia and her youngest child had been sold. At Ballard's request, the eldest child had been reserved for his own disposition.[87] The callous, insensitive, and even barbaric conduct of Samuel Boyd and his soulless partner depict slavery at its worst. Fortunately, the attitudes of Ballard and Boyd were not representative of the planter class as a whole and certainly not of the elite slaveholders. Nevertheless, the fates of Maria and Virginia Boyd illustrate graphically the greatest iniquity of chattel slavery: the utter powerlessness of slaves to control their own destinies.

87. Rutherford to Ballard, August 8, 1853, *ibid.*

6

CAPITALISTS ALL

Investments and Capital Accumulation Outside the Agricultural Sector

We are all here in the spirit of speculation in the land. . . . I have as much business in the land way as I want and am kept constantly drained of all my funds I get some thing like one thousand dollars pr week and sometimes more.

—GAIUS WHITFIELD, July 30, 1835

On the application of Cap[n]. Eldridge, I have consented to take an interest of 1 / 16 in a large ship now building at N.Y. for the Liverpool tour, provided my share does not exceed $5000.

—WILLIAM NEWTON MERCER, December 17, 1842

[H. A. Willard] is anxious to conclude a bargain at once for a lease of the Hotel [in Washington, D.C.]—with the privilege of buying, when able to do so, at $60,000. . . . If I can *secure* $6000 a year, I would at once close with him. I may have to take less.   —BENJAMIN O. TAYLOE, December 15, 1851

It was fortunate you found no Planters Bank bonds for sale. They would have been a bad purchase at 25 cts on the dollar. The rascals have not only refused to redeem them by taxation—but have refused to apply the funds (80.000$) rec[d]. from the Planters Bank especially for that purpose. This is not only dishonesty— but downright stealing.   —STEPHEN DUNCAN, March 6, 1846

I now think my Texas RR stock will be worth more to our children than the ballance of our property. . . . It will yeald [*sic*] me an annual interest of twenty eight thousand dollars. And possibly other advantages.

—RICHARD T. ARCHER, January 27, 1856

For no man living, can be more indifferent to public opinion than I *now* am, & *ever* have been. I have never sought the *good* opinion of others—& have never taken any extraordinary pains to avoid the bad.

—STEPHEN DUNCAN, April 18, 1866

THE ELITE SLAVEHOLDERS of the antebellum South did not invest all of their capital in land and slaves, nor did they derive their profits exclusively from the sale of staple crops. As was noted earlier, a number of wealthy nabobs had acquired their initial funds by speculating in land or from banking and commercial enterprises. Many abandoned these activities after they began to erect their plantation empires, but a few retained their former ties and others explored these and other investment opportunities outside the agricultural sector. Indeed, as Table 4 indicates, at least one-fifth of the slaveholders included in this study were, or had been, associated with such clearly capitalistic enterprises as banking, commerce, railroading, manufacturing, and land speculation. A considerable number invested heavily in urban real estate and in various corporate, state, and federal stocks and bonds. Finally, a few, such as ironmasters Daniel Hillman of Kentucky and Montgomery Bell of Tennessee, employed all of their slaves as industrial laborers. Indeed, the largest slave force in the latter state during the decade of the 1850s was that of the Cumberland Iron Works in Stewart County.[1]

Of all the economic activities enumerated above, the one most closely related to plantation agriculture was land speculation. An earlier chapter described the carnival of speculation that accompanied the vast Chickasaw and Choctaw cessions in Alabama and Mississippi in the 1830s and the speculative purchases of Texas lands by a company of Natchez nabobs during the same decade. But there are other examples of speculation in land by established planters throughout the late antebellum period. Georgia planter Farish Carter, who had numerous financial interests outside the agricultural sector, participated in the speculative mania of the 1830s, entering former Indian lands from Florida to Arkansas, but he also ranged as far north as Illinois in his quest for land investments.[2] Other wealthy slaveholders acquired substantial amounts of real property in the Midwest. Among these were Wade Hampton II of South Carolina,

1. Harriette Simpson Arnow, *Flowering of the Cumberland* (New York, 1963), 295; Stanley J. Folmsbee, Robert E. Corlew, and Enoch L. Mitchell, *History of Tennessee*, 4 vols. (New York, 1960), I, 475, 478; MS Census, 1850 and 1860 (Schedule 1), Trigg County, Ky., (Schedule 2), Caldwell, Lyon, and Trigg Counties, Ky.; MS Census, 1850 (Schedules 1 and 2), Davidson County, Tenn.; MS Census 1850 and 1860 (Schedule 2), Stewart County, Tenn.

2. L. Atkeson to Farish Carter, [April] 20, [1833], Robert S. Patton to Carter, October 31, 1835, S. Grantland to Carter, April 3, 1836, Charles C. Mills to Carter, September 11, 1836, Grantland to Carter, June 19, 1841, in Farish Carter Papers, SHC.

TABLE 4 · NONAGRICULTURAL ECONOMIC ACTIVITIES

BANKING: Stephen Clay King, Robert Stafford (Ga.); William T. Palfrey (La.); Henry Chotard, Joseph E. Davis, Stephen Duncan, Levin Marshall, William Newton Mercer, William J. Minor (Miss.); William Boylan, George W. Mordecai (N.C.); James Chesnut, Sr., Langdon Cheves, Sr., Wade Hampton II, James Legare, Charles T. Lowndes (S.C.); Montgomery Bell (Tenn.); Robert & David G. Mills (Tex.). TOTAL: 18.

MANUFACTURING: Garland Goode, Joel E. Mathews (Ala.); Farish Carter, Nathaniel F. Walker (Ga.); Daniel Hillman (Ky.); Edward J. Gay, William M. Lambeth, Laurent Millaudon (La.); Cullen Capehart (N.C.); Henry Buck, Wade Hampton II, James H. Hammond, John N. Williams (S.C.); Montgomery Bell, Cumberland Iron Works (Tenn.). TOTAL: 15.

MERCANTILE: James W. Echols, Francis M. Gilmer, Garland Goode, Thomas H. Herndon, John Steele (Ala.); James A. Everett, Robert Habersham, Archibald McDuffy (Ga.); John Burnside, Samuel F. Davis, Edward J. Gay, H. R. W. Hill (La.); Edwin R. Bennett, David Hunt, John D. McLemore, Levin Marshall, Ayres P. Merrill II, Benjamin S. Ricks, Frederick Stanton (Miss.); John R. Donnell (N.C.); David Aiken, James Legare, Leroy M. Wiley (S.C.); Robert & David G. Mills (Tex.); James Galt (Va.). TOTAL: 25.

RAILROADS AND STEAMBOATS: Benjamin Sherrod (Ala.); Robert Williams (Fla.); James A. Everett, Stephen Clay King, Nathaniel F. Walker (Ga.); Henry Boyce, John Compton, Laurent Millaudon (La.); Richard T. Archer, John A. Quitman (Miss.); William Boylan, Paul C. Cameron, George W. Mordecai (N.C.); William Aiken, Wade Hampton III, Allan McFarlan, John S. Preston, Richard Singleton (S.C.); Richard Baylor (Va.). TOTAL: 19.

VARIED (COMMERCIAL, MFG., BANKING): Francis M. Gilmer (Ala.); William Bailey (Fla.); Farish Carter, Stephen Clay King, Robert Stafford, Nathaniel F. Walker (Ga.); Duncan F. Kenner (La.); Edward McGehee, Levin Marshall, John A. Miller, John A. Quitman (Miss.); William Boylan, Paul C. Cameron, James C. Johnston (N.C.); Robert & David G. Mills (Tex.). TOTAL: 15.

LAND SPECULATION: Gaius Whitfield (Ala.); Robert W. Williams (Fla.); Farish Carter (Ga.); Alexander K. Farrar, H. R. W. Hill, Greenwood Leflore, Levin Marshall, William Newton Mercer, William J. Minor, John A. Quitman (Miss.); John R. Donnell (N.C.); Wade Hampton II & III (S.C.). TOTAL: 13.

SUMMARY: Total with economic interests outside agriculture was 72, or 21.3 percent of the entire cohort.

whose Wisconsin lands were a target of litigation by the Duncan family after the Civil War, and Natchez District nabobs William N. Mercer, Edward Mc-Gehee, and James Surget, Jr. Like Farish Carter, Mercer had land in Illinois, while McGehee and Surget owned property in St. Paul, Minnesota. Indeed, when a special tax was levied upon property owners in that town in 1860 to finance a major improvement of Fort Street, Surget was assessed the sum of $2,000 as the second largest property holder along the route.[3]

Of course, elite slaveholders did not have to venture as far north as Minnesota to find attractive municipal real estate opportunities. A number of planters in the Southwest owned property in New Orleans. For example, in 1835 Judge Thomas Butler, who resided near St. Francisville, purchased two lots on St. Joseph Street for $7,200, and fellow sugar planter Michel D. Bringier bought a spacious lot on Canal Street for $8,000. Unfortunately, financial reverses in the wake of Bringier's death in 1847 forced his widow to dispose of this and other New Orleans property.[4] Similarly, William N. Mercer, who normally wintered in the Crescent City, announced to his factor in 1843 that he was "now in treaty for some property in New Orleans, & may draw on [him] ere long for the balance [of funds] in [his] hands." Two members of the Surget family also had investments in New Orleans. Francis, Jr., owned property at three sites in the city during the Civil War, and his brother Eustace, who sought refuge in France after the war, sold his seven city lots for a total of $10,700 in 1866.[5]

Several East Coast planters also had substantial property in such cities as Charleston, Savannah, and Washington, D.C. William B. Hodgson, the largest slaveholder in Georgia on the eve of the war, paid average annual taxes of nearly $2,000 on various properties in Savannah that he owned in conjunction with his wife and his sister-in-law, Mary Telfair. Those properties included several

3. Stephen Duncan, Jr., to [Josiah Winchester], July 17, 1868, in Winchester Family Papers, CAH; William N. Mercer to Henry Clay, April 22, 1845, in *The Papers of Henry Clay*, ed. Hay, X, 217; John Swainson to James Surget, Jr., October 8, 1860, in MacNeil Papers, MDAH.

4. Sale of Property, James Puech and John Davy Bein to Thomas Butler, April 4, 1835, in Thomas Butler and Family Papers, LSU; Sale of Property, Seaman Field to M. D. Bringier, February 3, 1835, in Duncan F. Kenner Papers, LSU; Martin Gordon, Jr., to Benjamin Tureaud, December 9, 1849, January 19, [1850], in Benjamin Tureaud Papers, LSU.

5. William N. Mercer to Charles P. Leverich, May 25, 1843, in Leverich Papers, MDAH; Tax Receipts, New Orleans Property of Francis Surget, Jr., June 7, 1860, May 11, 1865, Eustace Surget in a/c with J. B. Walton & Deslonde, August 11, September 4, 1866 (Roll 5), E. A. Deslonde to Eustace Surget, August 11, 1866 (Roll 1), in Surget Family Papers, MDAH.

homes, a wharf, and a store occupied by the firm of Philbrick and Bell.[6] Although many Carolina Low Country rice planters maintained a residence in Charleston in addition to a plantation mansion, several owned multiple dwellings in the port city. Thus, at his death in 1851, the fabulously wealthy Nathaniel Heyward reputedly owned nine Charleston residences valued with their furnishings at $180,000, though only one of these, situated at the corner of East Bay and Society Streets, served as his personal summer home. Another rice baron, William Algernon Alston, Sr., had four residences in Charleston in 1859, but they were all apparently occupied by family members. Up Country planter Richard Singleton found a different outlet for his surplus capital. Doubtless captivated by the convivial atmosphere at White Sulphur Springs during the summer months, Singleton purchased a cottage there about 1825 and, during the next five years, invested some $30,000 in the popular Virginia resort.[7]

Two members of the prominent Tayloe family, brothers William H. and Benjamin O., enjoyed a substantial income from their ownership of the City Hotel in Washington, D.C., more commonly known as Willard's. Valued at $65,000 in 1827, the property was inherited by the brothers upon the death of their father the following year. In 1850 Benjamin O. Tayloe, who resided at the celebrated Octagon House in Washington, D.C., contemplated selling the hotel, advising his brother "not to ask less than $50,000" for the edifice. The following year, however, noting that the Willard brothers, who were managing the hotel, had cleared $22,000 during the preceding winter, he apparently had a change of heart. Instead of selling the hotel, he now wondered whether they ought to "raise the rent *at least* another thousand?" He further remarked to William, "We ought to make ten per cent on our Capital. Other hotels make more for the landlords, & great profits too for the tenants." At the end of the year, after concluding a bargain with the Tayloes to lease the hotel for a rental that Benjamin hoped would yield $6,000 a year and "with the privilege of buying, when able to do so, at $60,000," the Willards embarked upon a major program of expansion and renovation.[8] As a consequence, Willard's became "the most fa-

6. "Joint Account Hodgson and Telfair" with R. Habersham & Sons, February 9, 1854–February 29, 1864, in Telfair Family Papers, GHS.

7. Ulrich B. Phillips, *American Negro Slavery* (New York, 1918), 250; Heyward, *Seed from Madagascar*, 69; Rogers, *History of Georgetown County*, 524; Nicholes, *Historical Sketches of Sumter County*, 362.

8. Benjamin O. Tayloe to "Dear Brother" [William H.], February 20, 1850, May 14, June 18, December 15, 1851, in Tayloe Family Papers, VHS.

mous of all the hotels" in the nation's capital and served for many years as "the great meeting place" of the city. Ironically, it was at Willard's, a structure owned by two southern slaveholders and managed by two brothers from Vermont, that Abraham Lincoln was quartered following his arrival in Washington, D.C., in February, 1861, and where, later the same year, Julia Ward Howe penned the immortal words to "The Battle Hymn of the Republic."[9] Because of William H. Tayloe's allegiance to the Confederacy, an effort was made late in the war to confiscate the hotel, but "the order of seizure" was revoked after Tayloe received a pardon in August, 1865.[10]

In addition to speculating in land and other real estate, there was another means by which affluent slaveholders could profit from their close association with the plantation system. Utilizing the capital generated by their agricultural operations, some began to lend money to less fortunate planters on a grand scale. Two Mississippians, one a Delta planter and the other a Natchez nabob, were particularly successful in this endeavor. John A. Miller, a native of Georgetown, Kentucky, had migrated southward and prospered, first as a banker in Natchez and later as a coffee merchant in New Orleans, before turning to agriculture after wedding the widow of a wealthy Washington County planter. During the late antebellum period, Miller increased his slave force from 150 to more than 500 and became one of the largest cotton producers in the state. At the same time, he also became an extensive moneylender and, at the outbreak of the Civil War, reportedly held notes totaling at least $1,000,000.[11] Even more lucrative were the moneylending activities of Dr. Stephen Duncan. After amassing a fortune from the production of cotton and sugar on his numerous plantations, Duncan, in true capitalistic fashion, began to explore various other investment opportunities, one of which involved making loans to young planters on the make or to others who had suffered unexpected losses. Typical of the operation was a mortgage agreement concluded between Duncan and John R.

9. Margaret Leech, *Reveille in Washington, 1860–1865* (New York, 1941), 8 (quotations), 36, 114. In 1855 United States Senator Albert Gallatin Brown of Mississippi observed that in contrast to the other two principal hotels in Washington, D.C., the guests at Willard's were "mostly Northerners" (Albert G. Brown to John A. Quitman, November 19, 1855, in John A. Quitman and Family Papers, MDAH).

10. Benjamin O. Tayloe to "Dear Brother," November 23, 1865, in Tayloe Family Papers, VHS.

11. *Goodspeed's*, II, 939; McCain and Capers, eds., *Memoirs of Henry Tillinghast Ireys*, 144–46; Personal Tax Rolls, Washington County, Miss. (Roll 368), RG 29, MDAH.

Bisland in January, 1858. The latter was indebted to Duncan in the amount of $29,436, for which he executed six promissory notes payable January 1, 1859, through January 1, 1864, at 8 percent interest. As security for the notes, Bisland mortgaged his 3,071-acre Richland plantation in Terrebonne Parish, together with the 104 slaves attached to it. During the last five years of the antebellum period, Duncan acquired mortgages on no less than thirty-five properties in Louisiana and Mississippi in this manner.[12]

As long as peace prevailed and times were prosperous, debtors had little difficulty meeting their financial obligations. However, the disruptions resulting from the war and its immediate aftermath prevented most planters from paying their notes when they fell due. Consequently, the relentless Duncan, who, with other members of his family, held the enormous sum of $1,346,486 in notes and "other evidences of Debt" in 1866, threatened to resort to legal action in order to protect his interests.[13] This action was often resented by the harassed debtors and precipitated a particularly acrimonious exchange between Duncan and Charles G. Dahlgren in the spring of that year. Believing that Duncan had already filed suit against him, the beleaguered Dahlgren contended that such action "was in opposition to [his] understanding with [Duncan] . . . that [he] should have five years time from January 1867" to pay off the debt. In a subsequent communication, Dahlgren complained further that a judgment against him "would not only cover the property held by [Duncan's] mortgage: but *all other property* in the Parish." He continued, "This is not fair because it deprives me of the power to give any security for advances to pay the expenses of the plantation and of course paralises all of my efforts." Dahlgren also objected to paying any interest due since the maturity of the notes, arguing that if his last cotton crop of 1,100 bales had not been burned he would have had sufficient funds to pay off all his debts in a timely manner.[14]

In a heated response, Duncan denied that any "*suit had been instituted against [him].*" However, he concurred fully with his attorneys "in the propriety

12. "Certified Copy Act of Mortgage by John R. Bisland favor Dr. Stephen Duncan Agent—January 12th, 1858" (Folder 2), "List of mortgages to S. Duncan by various parties" (Folder 5), Josiah Winchester Professional and Business Papers, 1852–69, in Winchester Family Papers, CAH.

13. "Schedule of Notes & other evidences of Debt belonging to Stephen Duncan Jr. Trustee [for Stephen, Sr.], in the hands of Winchester & North for safekeeping & collection," [1866] (Folder 6), *ibid.*

14. Dahlgren to Duncan, February 20, April 10, 1866, *ibid.*

of bringing suits of an amiable character against all [his] debtors; not with a view to cause payment by forced sales, but to add strength, to [his] security." With respect to the abatement of interest, Duncan agreed to waive all interest prior to January 1, 1866, if Dahlgren paid the balance of his debt by July 1. Finally, although recognizing that Dahlgren's mistaken belief that Duncan had already initiated a suit against him "had created an impression very unfavorable to [him]," the tough-minded Natchez aristocrat offered no complaint. "For no man living," he asserted defiantly, "can be more indifferent to public opinion than I *now* am, & *ever* have been. I have never sought the *good* opinion of others—& have never taken any extraordinary pains to avoid the bad." Shortly after this exchange, Duncan devised a plan that would satisfy the concerns of his debtors while at the same time safeguarding his own interests. He proposed to force the sale of mortgaged property, purchase it himself, and then lease it to the debtor "for a term of years (leaving him in possession) for an amount, which in the term," would pay the debt. After the debt had been retired, Duncan would reconvey the property to the original owner. He also agreed to remit all interest if the debt was paid by January, 1868, and to reduce the interest from 8 to 6 percent if it was paid before 1870. Following Duncan's death in 1867, these arrangements were continued by his son, Stephen, Jr.[15]

Miller and Duncan doubtless benefited from the paucity of commercial banking facilities in Mississippi, especially in the critical Natchez District, after 1840. Duncan and several of his fellow nabobs had actually been instrumental in establishing banking institutions in the Natchez area as early as the 1820s. Duncan served as president of the Bank of the State of Mississippi during that decade, and after its charter was revoked in 1831, he helped to found the Agricultural Bank of Natchez two years later. Another wealthy slaveholder, William J. Minor, succeeded Duncan as president of the latter institution. The other major bank in Natchez during the early 1830s was the Planters' Bank, headed by James C. Wilkins, a well-to-do cotton factor with close personal and business ties to the Surgets, Minors, Bingamans, and other prominent Natchez families. Yet another bank, the Commercial Bank of Natchez, was organized in 1837 with Levin Marshall as president and his brother-in-law Henry Chotard as one of its directors. These banks all fell victim to the Panic of 1837, and by the mid-1840s there were no commercial banks operating in Mississippi. Consequently,

15. Duncan to Dahlgren, April 18, 1866, C. L. Dubuisson to Duncan, May 6, 1866, *ibid.*

the task of advancing credit to support agricultural operations and to facilitate the acquisition of additional land and slaves devolved upon such wealthy slaveowners as Duncan and John A. Miller, as well as upon commission merchants like the Leverich brothers of New York.[16]

Although a number of elite slaveholders supported the banking community by serving as directors or other officers, only a few took an active role in the business after they turned their attention to agricultural pursuits. Three South Carolinians—Wade Hampton II, James Legare, and Charles T. Lowndes—were at one time or another directors of the Bank of the State of South Carolina, and the last was also president of the Bank of Charleston.[17] Georgia rice planter Stephen C. King was associated with his brother, Thomas Butler King, in incorporating the Bank of Brunswick with initial capital assets of $200,000, and another Georgian, Robert Stafford of Cumberland Island, had substantial banking interests in both Georgia and Connecticut.[18] Other large slaveholders who had close ties to the banking industry included William Boylan, who served as president of the State Bank of North Carolina from 1820 to 1828, and Joseph E. Davis of Mississippi, who was appointed to the board of directors of the Vicksburg Commercial and Railroad Bank in 1849.[19]

But the three members of the elite who remained most heavily involved in banking activities after they achieved great planter status were Robert Mills of Texas, William N. Mercer of Mississippi, and George W. Mordecai of North Carolina. Mills was the senior partner in the Galveston firm of R. & D. G. Mills & Company, the largest private bank in the state in the 1850s. The combined banking, commercial, and agricultural assets of this diversified company were estimated to be as high as $5,000,000 on the eve of the war. Mercer, who after 1840 divided his time between New Orleans and his Laurel Hill plantation near Natchez, served for many years as director of the Bank of New Orleans, an office that claimed an increasing proportion of his time during the late antebel-

16. James, *Antebellum Natchez*, 198–203; Richard A. McLemore, ed., *A History of Mississippi*, 2 vols. (Hattiesburg, 1973), I, 291–94; *Goodspeed's*, II, 397–99, 446; Inventory, James Campbell Wilkins Papers, CAH.

17. *Biographical Directory of the Senate of South Carolina*, comp. Reynolds and Faunt, 231; Davidson, *The Last Foray*, 219, 221.

18. Edward M. Steele, Jr., *T. Butler King of Georgia* (Athens, Ga., 1964), 10–13; Bullard, *Robert Stafford of Cumberland Island*.

19. *Dictionary of North Carolina Biography*, ed. Powell, I, 205; Hermann, *Joseph E. Davis*, 92.

lum period. Mordecai, a prominent Raleigh banker who gained most of his slaves through his marriage in 1853 to Margaret Bennehan Cameron, succeeded his father-in-law as president of the State Bank. Of course, the slaveholder who achieved the most distinction in banking was Langdon Cheves, Sr., who presided over the Second Bank of the United States from 1819 to 1822, but that service occurred almost a decade before he embarked upon his rice-planting career in South Carolina and Georgia.[20]

One might suppose that, except in such border states as Kentucky, Tennessee, and Virginia, where there were substantial deposits of coal and iron ore, the large slaveholders would be less likely to invest their surplus capital in manufacturing than in any other economic enterprise outside the agricultural sector. For the most part, that was true, but there were some exceptions. Not surprisingly, cotton textiles proved to be the most attractive manufacturing venture for elite planters in the Deep South. One of the largest slaveholders in the South Carolina Up Country, Colonel John N. Williams of Society Hill, was a cotton mill owner as well as an agriculturist. Indeed, his plantation was called The Factory because of its proximity to the five-story frame mill that he had inherited from his father, former governor David Rogerson Williams. The latter, in shrewd capitalistic fashion, had sought to maximize his profits from slave labor by employing young children and superannuated slaves in the mill.[21] Two Alabamians, Garland Goode of Mobile and Joel Mathews of Dallas County, also had important textile interests. The latter, who had migrated from Georgia in 1831, built one of the first cotton mills in Alabama at Cahaba, and when that burned, he erected another in Selma. Goode, who for nearly forty years was "the leading cotton factor in Mobile," established a cotton factory on Dog River in 1851 and a decade later, was working 21 of his 196 Mobile County slaves at this facility.[22]

20. Fornell, *The Galveston Era*, 14–15, 45–47; *Dictionary of American Biography*, 21 vols., ed. Allen Johnson and Dumas Malone (New York, 1928–37), XIII, 13–14; Rothstein, "The Antebellum South as a Dual Economy," 379–80; Censer, *North Carolina Planters and Their Children*, 81; Billings, *Planters and the Making of a "New South,"* 87; *Biographical Dictionary of the American Congress, 1774–1961* (Washington, D.C., 1961), 687.

21. Gill, "A Year of Residence in the Household of a South Carolina Planter," 296; Woodward, *Mary Chesnut's Civil War*, 196 n. 2; *Biographical Directory of the Senate of South Carolina*, comp. Reynolds and Faunt, 334; Davidson, *The Last Foray*, 128, 264.

22. Owen, *History of Alabama*, IV, 1174–75; *Memorial Record of Alabama* (Madison, Wisc., 1893), II, 539 (quotation); Caldwell Delaney, ed., *Craighead's Mobile* (Mobile, 1968), 105; MS Census, 1860 (Schedule 2: Slave Inhabitants), Mobile County, Ala.

One of the most versatile planter capitalists was Farish Carter of Georgia. Among his many interests was the Coweta Falls cotton factory in Columbus. In partnership with his nephew John B. Baird and two others, Carter began construction of the mill early in 1845. Despite numerous delays, occasioned by the alleged misconduct of Carter's Negroes and constant bickering among the partners, the mill was turning out 1,000 yards of cloth per day by mid-July with the expectation that production could soon be doubled. Two months later, Baird reported that the factory had produced about 90,000 yards of cloth "exclusive of yarns," and he predicted that the debt of $6,000, "incurred for Cotton & wages of operatives," could be entirely retired by December 1 "if no accident happens." By midautumn the debt had been reduced by two-thirds, and Baird, who was managing the enterprise, hoped to employ between thirty-two and forty operatives—eight to ten supplied by each partner—the following year. However, the Coweta Falls mill apparently never proved to be very profitable for Carter and his associates, for Baird complained five years later that though "the Concern may be said to be out of debt," it was also out of cotton, and one uncooperative partner was refusing to purchase his share of new cotton, thereby compelling the remaining partners "to Contract debts which they ought not to do, solely on his account." It is clear from this and other correspondence that Carter's investment in the Coweta Falls factory yielded only modest returns.[23]

Cotton mills were not the only manufacturing enterprises that attracted the interest and capital of wealthy slaveholders. Henry Buck, a native of Maine, developed one of the largest steam-sawmill and lumber businesses in the world after removing to the Waccamaw River region of coastal South Carolina in the mid-1820s. With the profits derived from this business he purchased a recently established rice plantation in Horry District shortly before the war and soon gained a reputation as one of the most benevolent slave masters in the state.[24] Far to the south, in the sugar parishes of Louisiana, where the manufacturing process was already an integral part of plantation operations, several prominent

23. John B. Baird to "My Dear Uncle," February 24, August 16, September 9, 15 (first quotations), October 23, December 18, 1845, June 17, 1850 (second quotations), J. H. Howard to Farish Carter, March 4, June 28, July 15, October 25, 1845, J. C. Leitner to Carter, April 18, 1850, in Farish Carter Papers, SHC.

24. *Biographical Directory of the Senate of South Carolina*, comp. Reynolds and Faunt, 189; Joyner, *Down by the Riverside*, 28–29; Rogers, *History of Georgetown County*, 265–66.

sugar producers also acquired an interest in commercial refineries. Chief among these were Edward J. Gay and William M. Lambeth. The former, who for many years was a merchant in St. Louis, moved his permanent residence to Louisiana in 1856 after inheriting from his father-in-law an Iberville Parish plantation, which he soon renamed for his former hometown. Gay founded the Henderson Sugar Refinery and later served as the first president of the Louisiana Sugar Exchange in New Orleans.[25] Yet another large south Louisiana slaveholder, Laurent Millaudon, the proprietor of two sugar estates in Jefferson Parish, also operated a rum manufacturing business in New Orleans.[26]

Even more attractive than manufactures as an investment opportunity for affluent slaveholders were the railroads that began to open up hitherto inaccessible parts of the South after 1830. For some, the salutary effect that improved land transportation might have on their agricultural operations was the decisive motivating factor, while others simply viewed railroad stocks and bonds as an attractive outlet for their surplus capital. Whatever the motive, a number of elite planters assumed an active role both as railroad promoters and as officers and stockholders in the new companies. For example, in 1832, just two years after the completion of the first leg of the Baltimore and Ohio, the pioneer rail line in the United States, Alabamian Benjamin Sherrod organized a company of fellow cotton planters to build the first railroad in that state, linking Decatur on the Tennessee River with Tuscumbia. When the railroad failed in the Panic of 1837, Sherrod personally assumed responsibility for the entire $500,000 debt of the corporation.[27] Three years after Sherrod initiated his project, John A. Quitman organized the Mississippi Railroad Company with the intention of connecting Natchez with the New Orleans and Nashville line at Canton, but this effort, too, foundered on the shoals of the depression. Over on the Atlantic Coast, rice baron William Aiken was a strong advocate of railroad development during his term as governor of the Palmetto State in the mid-1840s, and Georgia cotton planter James A. Everett reportedly invested $50,000 in the South-

25. *Biographical Directory of the American Congress*, 934; *Dictionary of Louisiana Biography*, ed. Conrad, I, 339–40.

26. Solomon Northup, *Twelve Years a Slave*, ed. Sue Eakin and Joseph Logsdon (Baton Rouge, 1968), 162–63; Champomier, *Statement of the Sugar Crop Made in Louisiana*, 1853–54; MS Census, 1860 (Schedule 1), New Orleans, Ward 5.

27. Owen, *History of Alabama*, IV, 1547; John Witherspoon Dubose, *Alabama's Tragic Decade: Ten Years of Alabama, 1865–1874* (Birmingham, 1940), 140.

western Railroad, which transported the fleecy white gold from the southwestern corner of the state to Macon.[28]

One of the most enthusiastic supporters of railroad development was Richard T. Archer of Port Gibson, Mississippi. Unfortunately, he allowed his unbounded optimism to overwhelm his business sense, and in the end he paid a heavy price for his naive investment in the Southern Pacific Railroad Company. At the urgent invitation of Robert J. Walker and General Nathanael M. Greene, Archer became involved initially with the Texas railroad scheme in January of 1856. On the eve of his purchase of stock in the company, he reported jubilantly to his wife, "I now think my Texas RR stock will be worth more to our children than the ballance of our property. . . . It will yeald [sic] me an annual interest of twenty eight thousand dollars. And possibly other advantages." Three months later, he predicted that his investment would eventually be worth "millions of dollars" to his children. In the fall, with family holdings of nearly 7,000 shares in the company, Archer was elected to the board of directors. "I think the stock will be at $100 per share before the end of 1857," he enthused, "and I shall be able to borrow large sums by hypothecating it, at a much lower rate of interest than I have heretofore paid." To Archer's chagrin, the anticipated pecuniary benefits never materialized. By 1860 the road had already been sold three times, with previous stockholders dispossessed after each sale, and an associate urged Archer to salvage what he could from his investment. The war then intervened, and the projected rail line through Texas to the Pacific Coast was not completed until the early 1880s, some fifteen years after Archer's death.[29]

More satisfactory were the experiences of other large slaveholders who figured prominently in the development of southern railroads. Paul C. Cameron, the wealthiest man in North Carolina on the eve of the Civil War, helped to promote the North Carolina Railroad and was elected its president in the summer of 1861. After the war he served on the board of directors of another North Carolina rail line, the Raleigh & Gaston. The contributions of the Cameron family to railroad development did not end with Paul, however, for his son Ben-

28. James, *Antebellum Natchez*, 191–92; Ford, *Origins of Southern Radicalism*, 219; Reidy, *From Slavery to Agrarian Capitalism*, 52.

29. Richard T. Archer to "My Dear Wife," January 27, April 21, October 9, 1856, M. J. Hall to Archer, February 18, 1860, in Richard Thompson Archer Family Papers, CAH.

nehan was one of the founders of the Seaboard Airline System, one of the three largest railroads in the postbellum South.[30] At least two members of the South Carolina elite were elected to head railroads in that state. In April, 1857, Allan Macfarlan of Cheraw, who was already serving as president of the Cheraw and Darlington road, succeeded Thomas Pinckney Huger as the chief executive officer of the Northeastern Railroad. Noting that the road would be "nearly finished" by the time of his departure, Huger concluded that it was time for him to step down, for he was "worn out and want[ed] a little rest." Before leaving, however, he persuaded his brother-in-law Langdon Cheves, Jr., to purchase some of the company's bonds, which he assured Cheves, were secure and would "yield a handsome interest." Virginia planter Richard Baylor manifested his interest in another mode of transportation by serving as a director of the Old Dominion Steam Boat Company, which operated steamers between Fredericksburg and Baltimore.[31]

In addition to banking, manufacturing, and transportation ventures, some large slaveholders were also associated with mercantile enterprises, usually situated in port cities like Richmond, Charleston, New Orleans, and Galveston. Such was the case with brothers William and James Galt, Scottish immigrants, who inherited a fortune from their adopted father shortly after their arrival in America. For nearly a decade they prospered as partners with John Allan in a highly successful Richmond mercantile firm before turning their attention entirely to their inherited properties in Fluvanna County.[32] Two Charleston entrepreneurs, James Legare and Leroy M. Wiley, parlayed the proceeds derived from their commercial activities into the creation of landed estates while at the same time retaining their business interests in the city. Legare, a partner in the cotton factorage firm of John Colcock & Company, acquired a large rice plantation with more than 300 slaves sometime during the 1850s. Wiley, who was closely allied with Charleston banker Ker Boyce and Georgia planter-capitalist

---

30. *Dictionary of North Carolina Biography*, ed. Powell, I, 312–13; Anne Cameron to [daughter Rebecca], July 19, [1861], J. G. Campbell to Mrs. P. C. Cameron, August 27, 1861, in Cameron Family Papers, SHC; Billings, *Planters and the Making of a "New South,"* 89–90.

31. T. P. Huger to Langdon Cheves, Jr., January 14, 1857, Cheves to J. Fraser & Company, March 9, 1857, both in Langdon Cheves, Jr., Papers, SCHS; John Taylor Lomax to Richard Baylor, June 14, 1853, Franklin Slaughter to Baylor, March 30, 1858, in Baylor Family Papers, VHS.

32. G. Melvin Herndon, "From Orphans to Merchants to Planters: The Galt Brothers, William and James," *Virginia Cavalcade* 29 (Summer 1979): 22–23, 26.

Farish Carter in various speculative enterprises, owned absentee plantations in both Georgia and Alabama. However, they were superintended by his brother, and he visited them so seldom that, as he admitted to Carter on one occasion, "the Negroes at both my plantations seem hardly to know that they belong to me."[33]

Several elite slaveholders in the Southwest achieved great wealth as a result of their dual concentration upon both commerce and agriculture. For example, not only did Henry R. W. Hill of New Orleans head the leading cotton factorage firm in the Crescent City, but he also owned four very profitable absentee cotton plantations in the Yazoo Delta, as well as a sugar plantation in Jefferson Parish. At his death in 1853, his estate was valued at more than $1,000,000 and included lands in Arkansas, Tennessee, and Texas in addition to his slave plantations and his residential property in New Orleans.[34] Two Mississippians, Benjamin S. Ricks and Frederick Stanton, also pursued simultaneous careers in planting and commerce. The former, who resided at Bellevue plantation in Madison County, was a partner with John Carroll in a New Orleans commission house throughout the last two decades of the antebellum era.[35] Stanton, an immigrant from Northern Ireland, got his start in the mercantile business during a brief residence in New York before moving to Natchez in the 1820s. Soon after his arrival, he entered into a partnership with two other entrepreneurs to operate commission houses in New Orleans, Natchez, and Yazoo City, only to lose all of his assets in the Panic of 1837. Undaunted, he reentered the mercantile business following the depression and earned a second great fortune, much of which he invested in land and slaves during the 1850s. His palatial Stanton Hall mansion in Natchez still stands as a testimony to the opulent life-style enjoyed by the nabobs of that historic town before the Civil War.[36]

Some members of the slaveholding elite were heavily involved in a variety

---

33. *South Carolina Genealogies*, I, 422, III, 23; L. M. Wiley to Farish Carter, November 11, 1844, in Farish Carter Papers, SHC; MS Census, 1860 (Schedule 2), Barbour County, Ala., and Macon County, Ga.

34. Woodman, *King Cotton and His Retainers*, 48, 184; Will of Henry R. W. Hill, September 19, 1853, in *Early Records of Mississippi*, comp. Wade and Branton, I, 110.

35. *Goodspeed's*, II, 680; Carol Lynn Mead, *The Land Between Two Rivers: Madison County, Mississippi* (Canton, Miss., 1987), 231–32, 362–63.

36. *Goodspeed's*, II, 818; John Hebron Moore, *Emergence of the Cotton Kingdom*, 239–40; James, *Antebellum Natchez*, 156–57.

of the nonagricultural economic activities discussed above. Among the most notable exemplars of such economic diversification were the Mills brothers of Texas and Farish Carter of Georgia. As noted earlier,[37] the two Texas siblings not only built the greatest plantation empire in the state but they also dominated the economic life of the Brazos River valley for nearly three decades through their control of the commercial, banking, and transportation facilities of the region.[38] Carter, who was identified accurately by Ralph B. Flanders in the index to his book on slavery in Georgia as a "planter and capitalist," had a multiplicity of interests quite apart from his ownership of three plantations and more than 400 slaves. In addition to his extensive speculation in land and his partnership in a Columbus cotton mill (both already mentioned), Carter had an interest in such various enterprises as a tobacco factory, several banks and railroads, the Dahlonega gold fields, a toll bridge at Milledgeville, a ferry, a Tennessee River steamboat, a hotel, and a warehouse and wharf in Macon.[39]

There were other wealthy slaveholders who exhibited a similar degree of economic versatility. In the neighboring state of Alabama, Francis M. Gilmer, who had accumulated his initial capital in the mercantile business, was involved in railroad, banking, and manufacturing pursuits after he became a major planter. In the early 1850s, Gilmer helped to organize a company to construct the South & North Alabama Railroad and later served as the first president of that company. He also organized and was president of both the Red Mountain Iron and Coal Company and the Arms Manufacturing Company, and he was serving as president of the Central Bank of Alabama at the end of the Civil War. Similarly, William Bailey, the largest slaveholder in Florida at midcentury, was active in a variety of enterprises. In 1851 he established at Monticello a small cotton mill that contained 1,500 spindles, employed sixty-five operatives, and continued in operation during the Civil War when it was the only cloth factory in the state. Five years later, he organized the Southern Rights Manufacturing

37. See pp. 15–16 of this book.

38. Fornell, *The Galveston Era*, 15, 45–46; Herbert Gambrell, *Anson Jones, The Last President of Texas* (Garden City, N.Y., 1948), 40.

39. Flanders, *Plantation Slavery in Georgia;* Day & Butts to Farish Carter, June 17, 1831; L. Atkeson to Carter, June 30, 1832, Leroy M. Wiley to Carter, April 16, 1836, May 29, 1837, Stephen H. Long to Carter, February 8, 1838, October 22, 1839, March 1, 1843, Andrew [?] to Carter, June 22, 1843, James Beall to Carter, February 8, 1850, R. A. Holt to Carter, August 30, 1850, et al., in Farish Carter Papers, SHC.

Company near Monticello and the State Bank of Florida in Tallahassee. He also owned stock in two Florida railroad companies, the Tallahassee and the Pensacola and Georgia. Historian Julia Smith has speculated that Bailey was probably the first millionaire in the Sunshine State.[40]

A trio of North Carolinians also had multiple economic interests. Both William Boylan, an ardent supporter of the Hamiltonian-Whig economic philosophy, and George W. Mordecai served terms as president of the Raleigh & Gaston Railroad and also as president of the State Bank of North Carolina. But it was Mordecai's brother-in-law, Paul Cameron, who became the most successful of the three. Indeed, Cameron was the wealthiest man in the Old North State both before and after the Civil War. Although preeminently a planter, with holdings extending from his native state to the Deep South states of Alabama and Mississippi, he was also a banker, industrialist, and railroad developer. Among other interests, he owned stock in two Raleigh banks as well as in textile mills in Rockingham, Rocky Mount, and Augusta, Georgia. So extensive and heterogeneous were the interests of Paul, his father Duncan, and his son Bennehan, that historian Dwight Billings has argued that the history of the Cameron family alone is almost enough to sustain his thesis that "the small landed upper class laid the institutional framework for modern North Carolina."[41] The Camerons were no doubt atypical, but even John A. Quitman, a man more noted for his military exploits and his political extremism, exhibited a similar pattern of economic diversification. In addition to his speculation in Texas lands and his effort to connect Natchez with a major rail line, both of which were mentioned earlier, he was also a director of the Planters' Bank in his hometown and president of the Mississippi Cotton Company. Perhaps in recognition of his diverse economic interests, he was selected as one of the eight vice-presidents of the Southern Commercial Convention for its New Orleans meeting in 1855.[42]

Whether or not they took an active role in the operation and management

40. Owen, *History of Alabama*, III, 656, 659; Julia Floyd Smith, *Slavery and Plantation Growth in Antebellum Florida, 1821–1860* (Gainesville, 1973), 140, 142, 184; William W. Davis, *The Civil War and Reconstruction in Florida* (Gainesville, 1964), 211.

41. *Dictionary of North Carolina Biography*, ed. Powell, I, 205, 312–13; George W. Mordecai Papers, SHC; Billings, *Planters and the Making of a "New South,"* 85 (quotation), 88.

42. May, *John A. Quitman*, 65–67, 87, 94; James, *Antebellum Natchez*, 275; *De Bow's Review* 18 (March 1855): 356.

of the various economic institutions external to the agricultural sector, many large slaveholders invested heavily in securities, both public and private. Of the latter, bank stock and railroad stocks and bonds seemed to attract the most interest. A few examples will suffice to illustrate the extent and diversity of these holdings. Several of the wealthiest planters on the Georgia–South Carolina coast had impressive stock portfolios. The great rice baron Joshua John Ward owned $20,000 worth of bank stock as early as 1828, perhaps an inheritance from his father, who died that year. The James Hamilton estate, administered by James Hamilton Couper, reportedly derived more income from a large block of Schuylkill River bonds, issued by the city of Philadelphia, than from the crops produced by 600 slaves on 1,500 acres of Georgia rice land. Another Georgian, Robert Stafford of Cumberland Island, had huge investments in railroad and bank stock in both Georgia and the Northeast. A northern observer who visited the diehard Unionist just after the war, estimated his total assets at $1,000,000. Yet another Georgian, William B. Hodgson of Savannah, held stock in a wide variety of businesses. Thus, during the decade from 1845 to 1855 alone, he purchased stock in the following enterprises: the Magnetic Telegraph Company, the New York & Savannah Steamship Company, the Floating Drydock Company, the Savannah Gas Light Company, and two railroads—the Augusta & Waynesboro and the Central of Georgia.[43]

North Carolinian Lewis Thompson was also an active participant in the securities market. Since Thompson dealt with several brokers, it is difficult to ascertain the extent of his investments before the war. However, they were clearly very substantial and included, in part, a large quantity of Virginia state bonds and at least five $1,000 bonds issued by the state of Michigan. The latter, which were held by a New York factor, were placed in jeopardy as war clouds descended over the nation in the spring of 1861, but after passing through the hands of two other brokers, they emerged intact at the end of the conflict.[44] Although Thompson, who was a reluctant secessionist at best, purchased Confederate bonds during the war, he gave only grudging support to the Confeder-

43. Rogers, *History of Georgetown County*, 338; Flanders, *Plantation Slavery in Georgia*, 104; Bullard, *Robert Stafford of Cumberland Island*, 265–66, "W. B. Hodgson account Current with R. Habersham & Son," 1845–56, in Telfair Family Papers, GHS.

44. W[illiam] J. Britton to Lewis Thompson, July 31, 1867, De Rosset Brown & Company to Thompson, July 20, 1861, W. H. Wiggins to Thompson, July 14, 1865, Duncan Sherman & Company to Thompson, July 18, 1865, in Lewis Thompson Papers, SHC.

acy, thereby preserving the bulk of his financial assets. Thus, he had ample funds to invest even during the chaotic months immediately following the war. In December, 1866, his Baltimore factor notified Thompson that he was holding funds for the latter's investment and mentioned as possible options Virginia & Tennessee Railroad bonds and Pennsylvania Central Railroad stock, each paying 8 percent, and Pittsburgh & Fort Wayne Railroad stock at 10 percent quarterly. "These are considered good," advised the broker, "but we presume you will prefer Government Securities, at least for the larger portion." That supposition proved to be correct, for, three weeks later, Thompson purchased $45,000 worth of United States coupon bonds. The following year, his stock portfolio in New York, comprised of bank stock, United States bonds, and state bonds from Tennessee, Virginia, and Missouri, was valued at $75,900. Basking in the glow of such prosperity, it is little wonder that Thompson was one of the few members of the elite to support Republican Reconstruction.[45]

Several prominent Natchez slaveholders fared equally well with their investments in stocks and bonds. One of these was the elder Francis Surget, who in 1843 sought to purchase $110,000 worth of bonds issued by the Commercial Bank of New York if they could be procured on reasonable terms. Like fellow nabob Stephen Duncan, Surget also speculated in sterling exchange, converting sterling earned from the sale of cotton in Liverpool to U.S. Government securities when the comparative rates were propitious.[46] Another Natchez planter-capitalist, Levin Marshall, apparently preferred to speculate in railroad bonds. Thus, in October, 1851, he invested $15,000, derived from a recent sale of cotton in New Orleans, in the notes of two northern railroads, the Boston, Concord & Montreal and the Saratoga & Washington. When those notes matured the following April, they yielded Marshall a return of $10,000 and $6,500, respectively, a profit of $1,500 in just six months.[47] But no great planter followed the market more closely or was more knowledgeable about its operation than the

45. James Corner & Sons to Thompson, December 12, 1866, June 27, 1867; Statement, Dowley Corners & Company, January 4, 1867, "Mem[oran]d[um] of Securities belonging to Lewis Thompson," Duncan Sherman & Co., [1867], ibid.

46. Stephen Duncan to Charles P. Leverich, November 17, 1843, November 6, 19, 1847; Francis Surget, [Sr.], to Leverich, April 27, 1848, in Charles P. Leverich Papers, MDAH.

47. Levin R. Marshall in a/c with C. P. Leverich, October 20, 1851—July 1, 1852, C. P. Leverich MS Cash Account Book, 1844–53, Levin R. Marshall Account, October 23, 1851, April 9, 10, 16, 26, 1852, in Leverich Papers, CAH.

ubiquitous Stephen Duncan. It is not surprising, therefore, that five years before the nation was torn asunder by civil conflict, the astute Duncan had already amassed an estate valued at nearly $2,000,000, one-fourth of which was in securities of one kind or another.[48]

Plagued by poor crop years and the effects of the recent economic depression, Duncan apparently had little money to invest in the early 1840s. After a disappointing sugar harvest in 1844, he complained to his New York factor, Charles Leverich, that he would be hard pressed "to meet all [his] engagements this year." However, his financial condition soon improved, and three years later, he expressed an interest in making a substantial investment in U.S. Government securities. For some months, he debated whether treasury notes or government bonds would be the more profitable avenue of investment. At first, he opted for the latter, authorizing Leverich in November, 1847, to sell enough of his sterling to buy $25,000 worth of twenty-year U.S. Government bonds if they could be procured at or below par. Upon subsequent reflection, however, he concluded that "it would be *safest* & *best*, to invest in Treasury notes." As he explained to Leverich, "by holding the notes—I will have the advantage of investing in the stock at par, or demanding the money [in specie]. . . . I wish therefore all investments for me, may be made in Treasury notes."[49] Later in the year, however, he again changed his mind. He had learned from studying newspapers and telegraphic dispatches that the interest on Treasury notes could be added to the principal and government stocks obtained for the aggregate of the two. "If this be so," he informed Leverich, "I wish my Treasury notes *with the accumulated interest*—thus invested." By December of 1848, Duncan's total investment in government securities had reached $210,000, which, during the ensuing years, at 6 percent interest, yielded him a handsome annual income of $12,600.[50]

In addition to government bonds, Duncan also had an impressive portfolio of northern railroad stocks and bonds. In the early 1850s those holdings included

48. James, *Antebellum Natchez*, 150–51.

49. Stephen Duncan to Charles P. Leverich, December 2, 1844, July 19, August 14, November 6, 19, 27, December 11, 1847, January 11, 15, 1848 (quotations), in Charles P. Leverich Papers, MDAH.

50. Duncan to Leverich, September 19, November 23 (quotations), 1848, *ibid.*; C. P. Leverich MS Cash Account Book, 1844–53, Stephen Duncan Account, January 20, 31, February 12, 1848, January 2, July 1, 1850, July 1, 1851, January 2, 1852, Dr. Stephen Duncan in a/c with Charles P. Leverich, July 1, 1852, in Leverich Papers, CAH.

$50,000 worth of 7 percent bonds in the Erie & Kalamazoo, Columbus, Pequa & Indiana, and the Terre Haute & Indiana railroads. Several years later, Duncan had also established an annuity trust account consisting of stock in four other railroads—the New York Central, Michigan Central, Terre Haute & Richmond, and the Panama—amounting in the aggregate to $259,000.[51] In view of such large investments in federal and northern securities, it is not surprising that Duncan would view the gathering war clouds in 1860 with more than a little trepidation. Like Lewis Thompson, he remained a steadfast Unionist during the secession crisis, but unlike the North Carolinian, he subsequently declined to give any support to the Confederate cause. Thus, after fleeing to New York in the middle of the war, he was able to preserve virtually intact a financial empire that was valued in April, 1864, at more than $1,000,000, exclusive of plantations and slaves. More than half of those assets were in northern stocks and bonds.[52] Certainly Duncan was not the typical elite slaveholder in terms of economic behavior, but his career does exemplify the diversity of investment opportunities available to others of his class, whether or not they chose to follow his example.

51. Dr. S. Duncan in a/c with Chas. P. Leverich, July 1–Nov. 1, 1852, C. P. Leverich MS Cash Account Book, 1844–53, Stephen Duncan Account, May 1, September 8, 1852, January 1, March 1, July 19, 27, 1853, Stephen Duncan Annuity Trust Account, ca. 1854–61, in Leverich Papers, CAH.

52. Schedule of Estate, April 15, 1864, in [S. Duncan, Sr.], Plantation and Personal Records, 1861–70 (Vol. 5), in Duncan Papers, LSU.

7

POLITICAL ATTITUDES AND INFLUENCE

The Response of the Elite to the First Sectional Crisis

The result of the Presidential Election has been a most severe disappointment to me. I am really sick & disgusted with our present form of Govt. & have made up my mind, never again to vote for President—while I live.

—STEPHEN DUNCAN, November 23, 1844

It will be [a] melancholy day for North Carolina, when she permits her well tried mode of representation to succumb to the demagogical cry of "free suffrage."

—J. JOHNSTON PETTIGREW, November 3, 1848

There can be no dissolution of the Union with . . . [the border] states against us, it will be folly to dream of it—perfect madness.

—JOHN B. LAMAR, February 27, 1850

There may be a day (I fear there will be) when the institution of Slavery even in the States will be attacked, regardless of Constitutional barriers. . . . Then will be the time for Civil War & Dissolution of the Union; then will be the time to sell our lives for our country. But Heaven be thanked! that day has not yet come.

—WILLIAM S. PETTIGREW, March 7, 1850

S.C. is ripe for disunion. . . . Her glory has departed—& she knows it. That is the rub. But the Union *must* & will be preserved—as I think. Still S.C. may annoy our sisterhood with her old maidish complaints & reproaches. She is proud & poor—having been rich. Poor S.C.!

—BENJAMIN O. TAYLOE, November 11, 1850

I do not and have never concealed the danger of seperate [*sic*] State secession, but great as the future may prove it to be, it cannot possibly equal that of remaining in this union.

—W[ILLIAM] S. LYLES to JAMES CHESNUT, JR., July 1, 1851

T HE VIEWS of Stephen Duncan and Lewis Thompson were by no means representative of the entire cohort of wealthy slaveholders. Indeed, the political opinions of that group were as diverse as those of the general population. Moreover, they were susceptible to change in response to the parade of events that propelled the nation almost inexorably toward civil conflict in the mid-nineteenth century. There was, to be sure, something approaching a consensus on several important issues. Almost without exception, the great planters bitterly resented the mounting abolitionist onslaught against the South and its institutions, most of them believed in the *right* of secession, virtually all distrusted professional politicians in both sections of the country, and many of them were wary of popular democracy because of their conviction that demagogic politicians could easily corrupt the ignorant masses. But there was no general agreement on such specific questions as nullification, the annexation of Texas, the Mexican War, and, above all, the expediency of secession in 1850 or even in 1860–1861.

Just as the views of the elite differed, so too did their degree of political activism. Because of their wealth and social prominence, most large slaveholders exercised considerable authority over local political affairs. But on the state and national levels their participation and influence diminished appreciably in the wake of the constitutional changes that heralded the rise of the common man during the Jacksonian era. In addition, the time-consuming responsibilities associated with the management of extensive agricultural properties and the oversight of other economic interests made it difficult for them to assume an active role in governmental affairs. Only in South Carolina, where the voice of democracy was but faintly heard, did the elite exercise complete political domination throughout the entire antebellum period.

To understand the unique character of South Carolina's political system, one must go back to 1808. In that year a reapportionment compromise was struck between the Up Country and Low Country that gave the latter control over the state senate and the former control over the lower house. However, the Low Country, where the population was 80 percent slave by the time of the Revolution, continued to exercise a disproportionate influence in the state legislature. Although the suffrage was extended to all white adult males in 1810, rigid property qualifications for officeholding remained, and, consequently, slaveholding aristocrats dominated both houses of the legislature. Profoundly affected by the nullification crisis in the early 1830s, an event that Lacy K. Ford has called "the single most important political watershed of antebellum South Carolina," not only did the state decline to embrace the democratizing trends of that decade, but it also became isolated from the new party alignments that developed in every other state during the Jacksonian period. Thus, the planter-dominated legislature continued to wield virtually unlimited power over political affairs in the Palmetto State. In that aristocratic, black majority state, the popular will was reflected only in the election of state legislators, members of the U.S. House of Representatives, and such local officials as sheriffs and tax collectors. The legislature chose the governor, lieutenant governor, U.S. senators, all judges, most other local officers, and even presidential electors. As William Freehling has observed in his provocative analysis of South Carolina eccentricity, "no other southern regime was so committed to eighteenth-century elitist principles or so resistant to nineteenth-century egalitarian republicanism."[1]

In light of this background, it comes as no surprise to find members of the South Carolina planter elite well represented in governmental bodies at the state and national levels. Thus, in the two decades immediately preceding secession and Civil War, no fewer than five members of the elite—James H. Hammond (1842–1844), William Aiken (1844–1846), John L. Manning (1852–1854), R. F. W. Allston (1856–1858), and Francis W. Pickens (1860–1862)—were chosen to lead the state as governor, and all others who occupied that office during this period were substantial slaveholders.[2] Two other planter aristocrats, Joshua John Ward and Plowden C. J. Weston, held the office of lieutenant governor. On the national stage, the fiery secessionist leader, R. B. Rhett, Sr., represented the state in the U.S. Senate in the early 1850s, and the two senators when South Carolina withdrew from the Union a decade later were James H. Hammond and James Chesnut, Jr., son of one of the largest Up Country slaveholders. In addition, as Table 5 indicates, eight members of the South Carolina elite had held seats in the lower house of Congress, nearly forty had served in the state legislature, and seven were members of the secession convention.[3] Thus, at all

---

1. Ford, *Origins of Southern Radicalism*, 101, 106–107, 119 (quotation), 130; Freehling, *The Road to Disunion*, 214 (quotation), 222; McCurry, *Masters of Small Worlds*, 32–33, 35, 241–42, 248–50.

2. Among the latter were John P. Richardson (1840–42), who owned 194 slaves in 1860; John H. Means (1850–52), 127 slaves; James H. Adams, (1854–56), 192 slaves; and William Henry Gist (1858–60), 178 slaves.

3. Compiled from *Biographical Directory of the Senate of South Carolina*, comp. Reynolds and Faunt; John A. May and Joan Reynolds Faunt, *South Carolina Secedes* (Columbia, 1960); and *Biographical Directory of the American Congress*.

TABLE 5 · NATIONAL AND STATE OFFICEHOLDERS

NATIONAL

U. S. SENATE: George M. Troup (Ga.); James H. Hammond, Wade Hampton III, Robert Barnwell Rhett, John Taylor (S.C.). TOTAL: 5.

U. S. HOUSE: Howell Cobb, John B. Lamar, George W. Owens, Thomas Spalding, George M. Troup (Ga.) ; Harry Cage, Edward J. Gay, John Perkins, Jr. (La.) ; John A. Quitman (Miss.) ; William Aiken, Langdon Cheves, Sr., John M. Felder, James H. Hammond, Henry Middleton, Francis W. Pickens, Robert Barnwell Rhett, John Taylor (S.C.). TOTAL: 17.

C. S. CONGRESS: Howell Cobb (Ga.); Duncan Kenner, Henry Marshall, John Perkins, Jr., Edward Sparrow (La.); Robert Barnwell Rhett (S.C.). TOTAL: 6.

OTHER: Howell Cobb (Ga.), secretary of the treasury; Langdon Cheves, Sr. (S.C.), president, Second National Bank. TOTAL: 2.

STATE

GOVERNOR OR LIEUTENANT GOVERNOR: Howell Cobb, George M. Troup (Ga.); Trasimond Landry (La.); John A. Quitman (Miss.); William Aiken, R. F. W. Allston, Wade Hampton III, James H. Hammond, John Doby Kennedy, John L. Manning, Henry Middleton, Francis W. Pickens, John Taylor, Joshua John Ward, Plowden C. J. Weston (S.C.). TOTAL: 15.

CONSTITUTIONAL CONVENTIONS: John S. Hunter (Ala.); J. H. Couper, Francis M. Scarlett, Thomas Spalding (Ga.); Frederick D. Conrad, Duncan Kenner, William T. Palfrey, William W. Pugh (La.); Edward Lloyd VI (Md.); Joseph E. Davis, James A. Ventress (Miss.); Josiah Collins III, Richard H. Smith, Lewis Thompson (N.C.); Alexander R. Taylor (S.C.). TOTAL: 15.

SECESSION CONVENTIONS: Augustus Seaborn Jones, John B. Lamar (Ga.) ; William Ruffin Barrow, Josiah Chambers, Lemuel P. Conner, Henry Marshall, John Perkins, Jr., Edward Sparrow (La.) ; Alexander K. Farrar, Henry Vaughan, Josiah Winchester (Miss.) ; Richard H. Smith (N.C.) ; Langdon Cheves, Jr., Alexius M. Forster, John Izard Middleton, John L. Manning, John S. Preston, Robert Barnwell Rhett, John F. Townsend (S.C.). TOTAL: 19.

LEGISLATURE: Ala. (5), Fla. (1), Ga. (4), La. (9), Md. (1), Miss. (6), N.C. (5), S.C. (39), Tenn. (1), Va. (2). TOTAL: 73.

JUDGES: La. (4), Miss. (1), N.C. (3), Tenn. (1). TOTAL: 9.

levels of government, wealthy slaveholders controlled the destiny of the citizens of the Palmetto State.

Quite different was the degree of political participation by wealthy slave-holders in the state of Mississippi, especially after the adoption of the liberal constitution of 1832. Of the seventy-one elite Mississippi planters included in this study, only one—John A. Quitman of Natchez—served either as governor or as a member of Congress. Quitman, whose political fortunes were enhanced by his reputation as a Mexican War hero, held the office of governor briefly on two occasions and was a member of the House of Representatives at the time of his death in 1858. Only three members of the Mississippi elite were elected to the secession convention, and two of those, Natchez representatives Alexander K. Farrar and Josiah Winchester, cast their votes against the ordinance. Not a single one of the twenty-one Mississippians who served in one or more of the three Confederate congresses was a Natchez area planter.[4] According to Clayton James, the Natchez aristocrats did not even display much interest in local government, only four of them serving on the city council between 1803 and 1860. However, the nabobs, led by Farrar, did dominate a seventeen-man panel that investigated a spectacular case involving the murder of a white overseer by slaves on an Adams County plantation in 1857.[5] Of all the elite Natchez slaveholders aside from Quitman, Farrar seems to have been the most active politically. In addition to service on the board of supervisors and in other county offices, he was for many years a member of the legislature, serving in both houses of that body. But even Farrar found it difficult to reconcile his political responsibilities with his own time-consuming business interests. In the fall of 1859, just before he resigned his seat in the state senate, Farrar complained that his "private business" had "always interfered with [his] duty as a legislator."[6] Another Natchez District cotton baron, Haller Nutt, was also active in local

4. *Journal of the Mississippi Secession Convention*, 5–6, 16; Ezra J. Warner and W. Buck Yearns, eds. *Biographical Registry of the Confederate Congress* (Baton Rouge, 1975), 291–300.

5. James, *Antebellum Natchez*, 94, 98; Michael Wayne, "An Old South Morality Play: Reconsidering the Social Underpinnings of the Proslavery Ideology," *JAH* 77 (December 1990): 845–50.

6. *Goodspeed's*, I, 719–20; James, *Antebellum Natchez*, 134; A. K. Farrar to Col. George H. Gordon, October 14, 1859 (quotation), Farrar to Governor William McWillie, October 14, 1859, in Alexander K. Farrar Papers, LSU. Farrar also served as Natchez Provost Marshal before the city fell to the Federals in 1863. See printed notice from Provost Marshal's Office to Citizens of Adams County, May 2, 1862, Farrar to William Deal, May 3, 1862 (Roll 3), in Surget Family Papers, MDAH.

government, serving several terms as president of the police jury in Tensas Parish, Louisiana, where two of his plantations were located.[7] Farrar and Nutt, however, were clearly the exceptions among elite Mississippi planters in terms of their direct involvement in politics.

The number of great planters who held public office in the other slave states fell somewhere in the middle of the spectrum between oligarchic South Carolina and the much more democratic Mississippi. Next to South Carolina, elite hegemony was most pronounced in Georgia and Louisiana (see Table 5). Perhaps more typical was North Carolina, where several members of the aristocratic class rendered service as judges, legislators, and members of state constitutional conventions. At least four wealthy Tar Heel slaveholders— William Boylan, Josiah Collins, Richard M. Smith, and Lewis Thompson— served multiple terms in the state legislature. Collins was also a member of the state constitutional convention of 1835, and both Smith and Thompson held seats in the postwar convention of 1865–1866. Two other members of the North Carolina elite, John R. Donnell and Josiah O. Watson, made notable contributions in the judicial branch of government before their planting interests began to absorb all of their time. Donnell was one of the six judges on the state supreme court during the 1820s, while Watson served on the Johnston County Court of Pleas and Quarter Sessions from 1816 until at least 1830.[8]

Whether or not they held office in their own right, the elite slaveholders usually exercised considerable influence over political affairs within their respective states as a result of their social and economic prominence as well as their close association with those who were elected to public office. Only in the more progressive states of the Southwest was their influence muted. But even in the seaboard slave states, their power declined in the late antebellum period with the adoption of more liberal state constitutions, such as the one framed by the Virginia Convention in 1851. It is not surprising, therefore, that even beyond the borders of aristocratic South Carolina, a large proportion of wealthy slaveholders displayed profound contempt and undisguised antipathy for the principles

7. *Goodspeed's,* II, 519–21.

8. *Dictionary of North Carolina Biography,* ed. Powell, I, 205 (Boylan), 404–406 (Collins); *The Papers of Thomas Ruffin,* ed. Hamilton, I, 370–71, 422 (Donnell), II, 571 n. (Smith); B. F. Moore to Lewis Thompson, September 3, 1866, in Lewis Thompson Papers, SHC; *Johnston County, North Carolina, County Court Minutes,* transcribed by Weynette Parks Haun, Books VIII–XIII, 1808–30 (Durham, N.C., 1977–81).

of political democracy. Their preference was for representative government dominated by able, propertied men chosen by a severely restricted electorate. Typical was the view expressed by young J. Johnston Pettigrew when, during a visit to New York in 1848, he exclaimed: "It will be [a] melancholy day for North Carolina, when she permits her well tried mode of representation to succumb to the demagogical cry of 'free suffrage.'"[9]

Hostility to universal suffrage, to the popular election of executive and judicial officials, and to other tenets of Jeffersonian democracy was also a constant refrain in the copious writings of Edmund Ruffin. Indeed, it was Ruffin's belief that fellow Virginian Thomas Jefferson was primarily to blame for the demise of republican government in America. While crediting the "Sage of Monticello" with "kindly & benevolent feelings," an "amiable disposition," abundant "private virtues," and a "commanding intellect," he charged that, as "the apostle of the most extreme democratic doctrines," Jefferson had "caused more evil, and done more to destroy free & sound institutions, & to upset all that was stable & valuable in our government" than any other man in the nation's history. To believe in such nonsense as universal suffrage and the popular election of all public functionaries might be "pardonable in boys at school," but for one with Jefferson's political experience and sagacity to embrace such extreme democratic principles was, to Ruffin, utterly incomprehensible. Like many of his fellow planters, Ruffin was convinced that untrammeled democracy tended to place the reins of government in the hands of "demagogues," who were elected and "sustained by the mass of the most ignorant & vicious of the people." In short, extreme democracy led to "a government of the *worst,* instead of the *best* of the people."[10]

Two other members of the Virginia elite expressed similar antidemocratic sentiments shortly after the Civil War as they commented on the parliamentary debate that preceded passage of the English Reform Bill of 1867. While lauding the English for their political skill in choosing the option of reform rather than following the French example of revolution, William C. Rives remarked, never-

9. J. Johnson Pettigrew to James C. Johnston, November 3, 1848, in Pettigrew Family Papers, SHC.

10. Scarborough, ed., *The Diary of Edmund Ruffin,* II, 652–53, I, 420. For other manifestations of Ruffin's antidemocratic bias, see *ibid.,* I, 252–53, 551; II, 167, 169–70, 184, 288, 490; III, 313, 316–17, 549–51, 633–34, 767, 769–71, 915.

theless, that he would deeply regret "to see the old, temperate representative system of England swept away by the wild spirit of modern Democracy." Benjamin O. Tayloe was even more vociferous in his denunciation of the political reforms then being debated on the floor of the House of Commons. "Were I an Englishman," he declared, "judging from my observations of the sad consequences of the extension of the suffrage in our land," a change that had "instituted the rule of demagogues" and "ruined Virginia . . . I sh^d fight reform, as it is called from the first move to the final assault." Of course, there were a few exceptions to the general antidemocratic bias that infected the southern elite. For example, Judge Alfred P. Aldrich of South Carolina, after lamenting the recent defeat of fellow cooperationist James Chesnut, Jr., in his bid for a U.S. Senate seat in 1852, decried the apparent tendency in his state to regard age and experience as virtually the sole prerequisites for elevation to high public office. Consequently, he announced his readiness "to give the election of electors to the people" so that the politicians in Columbia would not "always keep us in ignorance and govern us with old women." He concluded, "If we yield now and work with the tide, we may shape the course of events."[11] Obviously, such a view was not typical among the South Carolina elite. Ever the pragmatist, Aldrich was searching desperately for some means to counter the disturbing strength of the more radical faction within the Palmetto State. Less than a decade later, however, he too joined the ranks of the immediate secessionists, and there was little talk of broadening the electorate.

If the great majority of wealthy slaveholders distrusted democracy, they were no less critical of those elected to office by the untutored masses. Then, as now, there was a strong popular aversion to professional politicians, or demagogues, as they were more commonly labeled. Although criticism of politicians was a general theme in the correspondence of the great planters, it became most pronounced in the last decade of the antebellum period as sectional animosity intensified and increasingly threatened to shatter the bonds of union. Indeed, there is abundant evidence in this study to support the contention of Avery Cra-

11. William C. Rives to William F. Wickham, December 28, 1867, in Wickham Family Papers, VHS; Benjamin O. Tayloe to "My dear Brother" [William H. Tayloe], June 25, 1866, in Tayloe Family Papers, VHS; A. P. Aldrich to [James] Chesnut, [Jr.], December 6, 1852, in Chesnut-Miller-Manning Papers, SCHS.

ven and James G. Randall that inept politicians and fanatical demagogues on both sides were, in large measure, responsible for creating the volatile atmosphere in which civil strife erupted in 1861.[12] For example, in 1850 two members of the elite, one an extremist and the other a moderate, condemned the role of politicians in fanning the flames of discord during the first major sectional crisis. "I am almost as disgusted with *politicians* as I am with lawyers," thundered Benjamin O. Tayloe from his home in the nation's capital. Six weeks later, as the debate over the Compromise of 1850 raged on in Congress, he complained that partisan politics was to blame for the "whole difficulty." At the other end of the political spectrum, secessionist R. F. W. Allston castigated Henry Clay and other southern politicians for their failure to lobby moderate northern members of Congress on behalf of what he termed the "reasonable suggestions" of the Nashville Convention. Without such encouragement northern congressmen dared not support the extension of the Missouri Compromise line to the Pacific because "the masses upon whom they are dependent for political preferment" had previously been inflamed "on the subject of Southern Slavery by designing politicians for their own selfish purposes."[13]

With the passage of time, the denunciation of politicians became even more vituperative, finally reaching a crescendo in the 1860s. Thus, as William S. Pettigrew gloomily surveyed the lowering war clouds in January, 1861, he blamed the politicians for the crisis. "They are radically demoralized both north & south," he charged. "If it is possible to reinstate the Union, it must be accomplished by the people; and they, poor unfortunates, are so entirely in the hands of demagogues as to appear to be . . . powerless for good. The present is dark & the future is black," he concluded pessimistically. Several months later, as both sides moved toward a bloody confrontation at Manassas, a Norfolk factor lamented that "So Much has been caused by Politicians." With the mounting carnage, attacks on the politicians became increasingly vitriolic. In the spring of 1862, as the Confederacy faced one of its darkest hours, one North Carolinian bitterly assailed those responsible for the calamity. "The dark deeds of those

12. Avery O. Craven, *The Coming of the Civil War* (New York, 1942); James G. Randall, "The Blundering Generation," *Mississippi Valley Historical Review* 27 (June 1940): 3–28.

13. Benjamin O. Tayloe to "Dear Brother" [William H.], January 21, March 6, 1850, in Tayloe Family Papers, VHS; "Remarks by Robert F. W. Allston Concerning the Nashville Convention of 1850," in Easterby, ed., *South Carolina Rice Plantation*, 445–46.

who have put us in this situation," he wrote, "ought to assign them to everlasting infamy."[14]

Southerners were not alone in assigning blame to the politicians for the catastrophe that ripped the nation apart in the early 1860s. New York banker August Belmont, who labored assiduously during the summer and fall of 1862 for sectional reconciliation on the basis of the *status quo antebellum,* was equally critical of the politicians. "The misfortune of the Country," he declared in late September, "is that north & south we are in the hands of politicians & under the iron power of party organization." If by some means the crisis could be adjudicated by "*the direct vote of the people,* free from party strife & affinities," he was confident that they "could come to a peaceful reconstruction of the Union with the rights of every section fully guarded & guaranteed." In like manner, Henry K. Winchester of Boston laid the blame for "this bloody and ruinous war" at the door of the politicians. In a letter to his Unionist brother in Natchez, written shortly after the twin Confederate disasters at Gettysburg and Vicksburg, Winchester asserted that all that was needed to restore unity and prosperity to the nation was to "displace a number of wicked demagogues, and politicians who were, and are the sole cause of our troubles."[15] Although they might differ in identifying the most villainous demagogues, it is clear that knowledgeable observers in both sections were convinced that professional politicians bore a major share of the responsibility for the internecine struggle that very few on either side really wanted.

In addition to their general distrust of democracy and politicians, the great slaveholders also shared a common resentment against Northerners, especially the increasingly vocal abolitionist minority among them. Regardless of their position on specific issues, virtually all members of the southern upper class were outraged by the escalating barrage of criticism that rained upon them and their cherished institutions in the waning years of the antebellum period. Always conscious of apparent differences in social, cultural, and personal characteristics between inhabitants of the two sections—a subject that will be addressed

14. William S. Pettigrew to James C. Johnston, January 24, 1861, in Hayes Collection, SHC; P. Henneberry & Co. to Thomas W. Thompson, June 25, 1861, and A[lanson] Capehart to [Lewis] Thompson, March 23, 1862, both in Lewis Thompson Papers, SHC.

15. August Belmont to W. N. Mercer, August 16, September 22, 24 (quotation), November 7, 1862, in William Newton Mercer Papers, LSU; Henry K. Winchester to "My dear Brother" [Josiah], July 27, 1863, in Winchester Family Papers, CAH.

later—their initial dislike of Yankees was intensified by the abolitionist on-slaught against the South that reached a climax in the 1850s. As one South Car-olinian confided to a friend in Connecticut in 1855, "I don't travel about much," for "I am too good a Southerner to feel very comfortable among the Yankees, who either *hate* us or *tolerate* those who do."[16]

But it was the alleged northern hypocrisy toward slavery and the Negro that most incensed southern slaveholders. "Northern people have no more love for negroes than for cattle"; indeed, "not as much," cried Benjamin O. Tayloe. Sim-ilarly, after visiting an antislavery exhibit at the Boston Museum in 1858, Natch-ezian George D. Farrar denounced the hypocritical Yankees for their false charity and philanthropy and charged that their assault against slavery was mo-tivated primarily by envy. Where was the Christian compassion, he asked, in one "who kneels at thy altar and prays that, 'the colored man may be freed from bondage,' while thousands of needy souls perish within his hearing?" He con-cluded righteously, "What sensible master can free his slaves and cast them on the merciful charity of such hypocrisy?" Another who condemned so-called Yankee hypocrisy during a visit to the Northeast was James Johnston Pettigrew of Charleston. After attending a dramatization of *Uncle Tom's Cabin* in Phila-delphia, he noted that the performance had not had any "moral effect" whatever upon the audience, which could scarcely restrain its "mirth" even during the most horrific scenes. "Of course," remarked Pettigrew, "it is perfectly absurd to hear a man declaiming on the stage about the equality of the negro with the white man, and to see at the same time his coloured brethren stowed away in a dark little gallery in the North Eastern corner of the House."[17]

Perhaps no other member of the elite slaveholding class expressed the south-ern point of view more eloquently or more passionately than Virginia patriarch William F. Wickham. If ever there was a southern moderate, it was Wickham. A steadfast Unionist to the end, he categorically rejected the principle of states' rights, asserted that secession had been "a grievous mistake," and condemned Confederate leaders for prolonging the war "when all hope of success was en-

16. Edward Barnwell Heyward to James A. Lord, March 17, 1855 (TS), in Edward Barnwell Hey-ward Letters, SCL.

17. Benjamin O. Tayloe to "Dear Brother" [William H.], March 6, 1850, in Tayloe Family Papers, VHS; George D. Farrar to "My dear Father" [Alexander K.], December 24, 1858, in Alexander K. Farrar Papers, LSU; J. Johnston Pettigrew to James C. Johnston, October 27, 1859, in Pettigrew Family Papers, SHC.

tirely gone."[18] Yet in a retrospective essay on Negro slavery written after the war, this temperate Virginian mirrored perfectly the animosity felt by members of his class toward the abolitionists when he denounced what he termed the hypocritical and self-serving conduct of northern members of Congress during the fateful decade of the 1850s. The southern member of that body, he wrote,

> came from a home where he left his slaves contented & happy, looking up to him as a friend & protector, having no care themselves, because they knew it was for him to provide for their wants, & having as strong an attachment to him as he had to them. Could he bear with composure to be told to his face, in the coarsest terms, that while living in this patriarchal state as his forefathers had done for more than two centuries, his whole conduct was to be held in abhorrence, that he was accursed of God & man, & that slavery ought to be extinguished, [even] if it were done in the blood of the masters & of their wives & children! And this language he knew in nearly every case was used by men who unworthily held a seat in Congress, not from a hatred of oppression or a regard for the slave, but to gain popular favor, & to advance their claims to honors & office. He is to be insulted & tortured that they may gain the price of avarice & ambition. How could he hear such calumny & fail to resent it?[19]

For Southerners, of course, the ultimate redress for such grievances was secession, and unlike Wickham, most large slaveholders supported that option in principle even if not in practice. Some contended that secession was a constitutional right, while others, especially the more cautious cooperationists and conditional Unionists, justified it as a revolutionary right. The constitutional argument for voluntary separation, based on state sovereignty and the compact theory of government, is too well known to require elaboration here.[20] But not

---

18. William F. Wickham, Commonplace Book, "Notes on the U.S. Constitution"; speech entitled "Reconstruction in Virginia" (first quotation); essay on "Political Parties and American Government" (second quotation), undated MSS, Box 10, all in Wickham Family Papers, VHS.

19. William F. Wickham, essay on "Negro Slavery in America," n.d., *ibid.*

20. For a succinct, yet detailed, exposition of this point of view, see William D. Porter, "State Sovereignty and the Doctrine of Coercion," 1860 Association Tract No. 2 (Charleston: Evans & Cogwell's Steam-Power Presses, 1860).

all were convinced that secession was a constitutional right. "I do not believe in secession as a rightful or constitutional remedy," declared a Louisiana cooperationist in January, 1861. Rather, it was simply "another name for revolution." Similarly, North Carolina Unionist Thomas P. Devereux saw only a nominal difference between secession and revolution, though, as he confided to Judge Thomas Ruffin three months after Lincoln's election, he would be willing to concede the principle if execution were delayed for several years. Two months later, following the firing on Sumter, the only debate in North Carolina was between the constitutional and the revolutionary secessionists, and that division soon evaporated as the two groups united to cast a unanimous vote for secession in the convention of that state on May 20.[21]

Whatever their rationale for secession, many large slaveholders, even some who viewed it as a constitutional right, stressed the parallel between their action in 1860–1861 and that of their forefathers in 1776. In both instances, radical measures were required in order to resist the oppressive policies of an allegedly tyrannical government. Such was the argument of Mrs. R. F. W. Allston when she expressed bitterness toward a local Episcopal rector who had elected to side with the North despite a sojourn of fifteen years in the Carolina Low Country. To Mrs. Allston, such apostasy was "inexplicable." How could "anyone who believes in the principles of self government" and "who admits the justice of the principle for which we fought in the war of the Revolution . . . object to our movement now," she asked. "When we left the Government of England," continued the wife of the former governor, "we left an ancient government and a parent country. How much more clear the right to withdraw from a government we assisted in creating when the guarantees which induced us to join it have been violated, ignored, [and] trampled upon." A similar comparison to the patriots of the American Revolution was invoked by the members of the Mississippi Secession Convention when they sought to justify the act of secession by that state. After reciting a long list of alleged grievances, they declared that "for far less cause than this, our fathers separated from the Crown of England."

21. J. G. Campbell to Paul C. Cameron, January 20, 1861, in Cameron Family Papers, SHC; Thomas P. Devereux to Judge Thomas Ruffin, February 4, 1861, in *The Papers of Thomas Ruffin*, ed. Hamilton, III, 118; Robert C. Kenzer, *Kinship and Neighborhood in a Southern Community: Orange County, North Carolina, 1849–1881* (Knoxville, Tenn., 1987), 69–70.

Now, they concluded defiantly, "we follow their footsteps."[22] These are but two of the numerous instances in which southern secessionists sought to validate their radical course of action by citing the example of their ancestors.

As we move now from generalities to more specific political issues, it is clear that there was considerable division among the planter elite in the two decades preceding the crisis of 1850, much of it along party lines. Apart from South Carolina, where the primary political struggle was between the nullifiers and their opponents in the 1830s and between the cooperationists and immediate secessionists in the 1850s, the party allegiance of the great planters appears to have been almost equally divided between the two major parties, with the Whigs holding a slight advantage. The Whigs predominated in the Natchez District, in the seaboard states of Virginia and North Carolina, and in the sugar parishes of Louisiana, where the party's traditional high tariff policy was especially popular. Planters in the interior regions of Georgia and the Gulf South were more likely to support the Democratic Party. One of the most prominent of these was Howell Cobb of Georgia, who was elected five times to the U.S. House of Representatives and served as secretary of the treasury in the Buchanan administration. Another influential Democrat was Edward Lloyd VI of Maryland, who, like Cobb, was an elector for Martin Van Buren in 1836 and later presided over the state senate.[23] Far to the south, several large slaveholders in Mississippi took an active part in Democratic Party politics. Chief among these was Adam L. Bingaman of Natchez, who was the party leader in that area for many years, and Joseph E. Davis, who was a party activist on both the local and state levels from the mid-1840s to the mid-1850s.[24]

Unlike Bingaman, the great majority of the Natchez nabobs were staunch Whigs, attracted by that party's nationalistic, pro-bank, and, in the case of sugar planters like William J. Minor, high-tariff policies. Two of them, Stephen Dun-

---

22. Adele Petigru Allston to Mrs. Joseph Hunter, May 15, 1861, in Easterby, ed., *South Carolina Rice Plantation,* 175; "A Declaration of the Immediate Causes Which Induce and Justify the Secession of the State of Mississippi from the Federal Union," *Journal of the Mississippi Secession Convention,* 5.

23. *Biographical Directory of the American Congress,* 711; [?] to "My Dear Col." [Edward Lloyd VI], February 10, 1852, Horn R. Kneass, William Badger, et al. to Lloyd, August 19, 1852, John Walton to Lloyd, November 13, 1852, in Lloyd Family Papers, MHS.

24. *Goodspeed's,* I, 676; Hermann, *Joseph E. Davis,* 79, 89.

can and John A. Quitman, were founders of the Whig Party in Mississippi, though the latter shifted his allegiance to the Democrats in the mid-1840s in an effort to save his political fortunes. Another Adams County planter, William Newton Mercer, was a close political and personal friend of Henry Clay, often visiting the Kentuckian during his northern excursions and hosting the Whig leader at his winter residence in New Orleans.[25] Another member of the elite with close personal ties to Clay was William B. Hodgson of Georgia. Indeed, the young Hodgson was a protégé of Clay, who procured a position in the State Department for him long before he married into the Telfair family and became the largest slaveholder in the state. Other prominent Whig planters included North Carolinians James C. Johnston, who imbibed Federalist-Whig principles as a member of the Whig Society at Princeton more than three decades before the party was formally established during the Jackson administration, and Lewis Thompson, who switched to the American Party following the demise of the national Whig Party and was still attending local Whig meetings as late as 1860. Yet another prominent Whig planter was John S. Hunter of Alabama, who presided over the Whig state convention at Tuscaloosa in 1840 and published a moving eulogy of Daniel Webster a dozen years later.[26]

The first major political controversy that profoundly affected those who had achieved or would achieve great planter status by midcentury was the nullification crisis, which occurred before the second national party system had become firmly established. Precipitated by the passage of exceedingly high tariffs in the late 1820s and early 1830s, this affair primarily affected South Carolina, creating an emotional atmosphere that propelled that state toward even more radical action in 1860. In what was essentially a battle over tactics—that is, the most efficacious way to oppose the tariff and to defend slavery—the planter aristocrats

25. James, *Antebellum Natchez*, 117–18, 123; William N. Mercer to Clay, December 7, 1844, April 22, November 25, 1845, June 3, [1849], in *The Papers of Henry Clay*, ed. Hay, X, 176, 217, 251, 600. See also a series of letters from Clay to Mercer, 1846–52, in William Newton Mercer Papers, LSU, all of which are printed in Hay's edition.

26. Obituary in Savannah *Republican*, July, 1871, in Telfair Family Papers, GHS; James C. Johnston to Edward Watt, January 23, 1800, Johnston to James Carnahan, January 23, 1800, Johnston to Henry G. Wisner, March 8, 1800, in Hayes Collection, SHC; Kenneth Rayner to Lewis Thompson, February 5, 1860, Whig Executive Committee, Hamilton, N.C., to Thompson, July 13, 1860, Whig Executive Committee, Hertford County, to Thompson, July 19, 1860, in Lewis Thompson Papers, SHC; Owen, *History of Alabama*, III, 872; [Governor] John Gayle to John S. Hunter, August 7, 1853, in Hunter-Milhous Family Collection, ADAH.

in the Palmetto State were badly split. Although the nullifiers carried eighteen of the twenty-one counties with a slave population of more than 40 percent, including thirteen of seventeen Low Country parishes, a number of prominent slaveholding families opposed the movement. Among these were such old-line Low Country families as the Cheveses, Elliotts, Middletons, and Pringles, as well as the equally wealthy Chesnuts, Hamptons, and Prestons in the Up Country.[27] The proponents and opponents of nullification were not divided along either regional or geographic lines. For example, in the Low Country district of Georgetown, rice barons R. F. W. Allston, Thomas Pinckney Alston, and J. J. Ward spearheaded the drive for nullification, while their neighbors William B. Pringle and J. Harleston Read, Sr., led the opposition. Another Georgetown rice planter, Henry A. Middleton, initially opposed nullification but changed his position after reading President Andrew Jackson's strongly worded proclamation of December 10, 1832.[28]

Two of the most conspicuous opponents of nullification were the senior Langdon Cheves and James Chesnut, one from the Low Country and the other from the Up Country. In a letter of August, 1831, to his friend and future son-in-law David J. McCord, Cheves explained why he could not join McCord in supporting the nullification movement. While conceding that he deplored the injustice of the tariff as deeply as any of his fellow Carolinians and believed that "the oppression under which the South labours is one under which a free people ought not to suffer," the veteran statesman, nevertheless, denounced the proposed remedy as "unwise, rash, dangerous and in its effects worse than ineffectual." Instead of the precipitate independent action being advocated by the leaders of his state, he urged the more moderate course of enlisting the aid of other slave states in a concerted response to the discriminatory tariff. "Great questions like this," counseled Cheves, "are never decided wisely, if speedily," and without the cooperation of other interested parties. Even more vociferous in his opposition to the nullifiers was Chesnut, who was outraged to learn in 1836 that his son had accepted a position as an aide to Governor Pierce M. Butler, a leading member of the Nullification party. The seduction of the

---

27. Ford, *Origins of Southern Radicalism*, 125, 128, 134, 168; William W. Freehling, *Prelude to Civil War: The Nullification Controversy in South Carolina, 1816–1836* (New York, 1965), 240, 254; Freehling, *The Road to Disunion*, 276.

28. Rogers, *History of Georgetown County*, 238–46.

youthful Chesnut with "glittering Epaulets," charged the elder Chesnut, was merely a ploy to subvert the influence of "an old man in a district opposed to the Doctrine of Nullification," who had thwarted the designs of the nullifiers in that district. Such tactics had been tried before with great effect and would be "tried again with the same success," declared the irate Chesnut, "but *I still* hope with none of my family." Young Chesnut apparently yielded to his father's objection and declined the proffered post.[29]

Like the South Carolinians, most other southern planters opposed the protective tariff, though they were unwilling to embrace the extreme measure adopted by Palmetto State leaders. Their opposition stemmed from their belief that such high tariffs discriminated against them in order to benefit the manufacturers of the Northeast. No other wealthy slaveholder—perhaps no other Southerner—denounced the protective tariff more bitterly or more consistently than Robert Barnwell Rhett. "How is it possible," he asked, "that in a free Country" where all men are equal under the law, "the Government, under the pretext of levying Taxes can establish a system of rule, by which some citizens are taxed for the benefit of others—and the property of one man is taken and given to another."[30] Such was the general view of the tariff among southern slaveholders. Only the hemp growers of Kentucky and the sugar planters of Louisiana, both of whom depended on the tariff for their economic survival, supported the principle of protection. Representative of the latter was William J. Minor, who, during the battle between President John Tyler and the Henry Clay Whigs in 1842, expressed the fear that if the anti-tariff forces were successful, "the country will be filled with foreign Sugars." Five years later, smarting under the reduced duties imposed by the Walker Tariff, Minor was hopeful that the debt incurred during the Mexican War would "induce the wise men of the nation to put a little more duty on Sugars & keep out some of the rascally Havanas." Minor, however, represented the views of a small minority of Southerners on the tariff question. Thus, when the permanent Confederate constitution was drafted in Montgomery by a committee chaired by Rhett, he had no trouble inserting an article stipulating that tariffs were to be levied solely for revenue

29. Langdon Cheves, Sr., to David J. McCord, August 15, 1831 (copy), in Langdon Cheves Papers, SCL; James Chesnut, Sr., to James Chesnut, Jr., December 25, 1836 (TS), in Williams-Chesnut-Manning Family Papers, SCL.

30. R. B. Rhett MS essay on the "Northern Money Power," n.d., in Robert Barnwell Rhett, Sr., Papers, SCHS.

and prohibiting the use of bounties to promote any branch of industry.[31] At last, the anti-tariff position long held by most Southerners was etched in stone, if only briefly.

In addition to the tariff, banking policy was one of the most volatile political issues during the first half of the nineteenth century. Here again, most Southerners opposed any institution that would enhance the authority of the national government, though there was some division along party lines. Once more, the South Carolinians, ever vigilant against accretions of power at the federal level, were virtually united in their opposition to a national bank. "Congress does not, and never did possess the right to incorporate a Bank of the United States," thundered R. F. W. Allston as he lauded President Jackson for his veto of the recharter bill in 1832. Although receptive to the establishment of an independent treasury that would provide a standard "by which all paper-credits shall be valued," Allston, a self-styled Jeffersonian strict constructionist, remained unalterably "opposed to connecting the Government with Banks or Banking." Two other Georgetown District rice planters, J. Harleston Read, Sr., and John Izard Middleton, also opposed the United States Bank.[32] So, too, did Charleston merchant-planter Leroy M. Wiley. During the financial crisis of 1837, when there was talk of resurrecting the national bank, Wiley declared that he hoped "never to see [another] one in operation again possessing the power of the former ones." Yet another South Carolinian, R. B. Rhett, Sr., added his voice to the chorus of opposition, charging that the creation of national banks had been merely the first in a series of "usurpations on the Constitution" promoted by the malevolent northern states.[33]

Although they reserved their heaviest fire for the National Bank, some planter aristocrats opposed any governmental involvement—federal or state—in banking. Such was the position of sugar planter Edward G. W. Butler, who declared in 1837, "I have ever been opposed to Banks, national & state, upon constitutional grounds." Now, he continued, "I am more than ever opposed to them on the ground of expediency." Not only did such institutions increase the

31. W. J. Minor to C. P. Leverich, July 30, 1842, July 28, 1847, in Charles P. Leverich Papers, MDAH; R. B. Rhett, Sr., to T. Stuart Rhett, [1868], in Robert Barnwell Rhett, Sr., Papers, SCHS.

32. R. F. W. Allston to John A. Allston, September 5, 1838, in Easterby, ed. *South Carolina Rice Plantation*, 78–80; Rogers, *History of Georgetown County*, 231 n., 362.

33. L. M. Wiley to Farish Carter, May 29, 1837, in Farish Carter Papers, SHC; R. B. Rhett, Sr., to T. Stuart Rhett, [1868], in Robert Barnwell Rhett, Sr., Papers, SCHS.

"power or patronage" of government, to which Butler was unalterably opposed, but they could not carry on "the exchanges of the country" as efficiently or as objectively as "individuals or unchartered associations thereof." Two other wealthy slaveholders, John M. Felder and David Hunt, also manifested an antipathy for state banks. The former spearheaded the fight against the Bank of the State of South Carolina while serving as a state senator from Orangeburg District during the decade preceding his death in 1851. Hunt, one of the wealthiest of the Natchez District planters, informed the governor of Mississippi in 1831 that he could not accept an appointment as director of the recently chartered Planters' Bank because he could not "believe that the state in its individual capacity ought to become a Banking Institution."[34]

Unlike Hunt, many other cotton nabobs in the Natchez region, most of them Whigs, supported government banks. Chief among them was that quintessential capitalist, Dr. Stephen Duncan. In the mid-1840s, when cotton prices plummeted to a record low and desperate planters began to blame banks, both public and private, for exacerbating their distress, Duncan came to the defense of the banking community. "They are doing all that can be done & all that they ought to be expected to do," he asserted in 1844. The real fault, contended Duncan, was with the bank customers, who had "no sense of moral honesty—& no regard for punctuality." A month later, in a continuing debate with his brother-in-law Thomas Butler, who had expressed the view that Louisiana would benefit from the demise of ten or twelve banks in that state, Duncan argued heatedly for pro-bank measures then pending in the legislature. "There was never a people, so blind to their own interests," he wrote. "Security to the Banks w^d not only revive your commerce, but make your Banks solvent—and this they cannot be—without indulgence from the Legislature." Fellow Natchez nabob William J. Minor was another strong bank advocate. In the spring of 1840, as the pecuniary difficulties precipitated by the Panic of 1837 struck the Southwest with full force, he noted that the economic distress that had earlier affected Mississippi was now spreading to neighboring states. "The fact is," he observed, "we never shall get right until we get a National Bank." Just a year later, Henry A. Tayloe,

34. E. G. W. Butler to Thomas Butler, September 27, 1837, in Thomas Butler and Family Papers, LSU; Ford, *Origins of Southern Radicalism*, 326; David Hunt to Governor Gerard C. Brandon, January 17, 183[1?], in Abijah and David Hunt Papers, MDAH.

a member of one of the most prominent Whig planter families in the Upper South, denounced President Tyler for his veto of Henry Clay's bank bill. "I had no idea that he would presume to reject it," lamented the disappointed Tayloe, "as certainly a large majority of our citizens must have desired a Bank." Tayloe clearly misjudged the degree of support for the bank, for neither the elite planters nor the public at large was clamoring for a restoration of the controversial financial institution that had earlier been killed by President Jackson.[35]

The bank and the tariff were not the only political matters that generated heated debate within the country during the 1840s. Even more volatile was the question of Texas annexation, which became a central issue in the presidential campaign of 1844 between the veteran Whig leader Henry Clay and the Democratic standard-bearer James K. Polk. The latter's narrow victory led directly to annexation and, subsequently, to the war with Mexico. Not surprisingly, most large slaveholders strongly supported the annexation of Texas. After all, that territory had been settled primarily by Southerners, many of them slaveholders, and a number of wealthy cotton nabobs had already begun to invest heavily in Texas lands. Only the transplanted Yankee planter-capitalist Stephen Duncan seems to have opposed American support for the Texans from the outset. In February, 1836, just a month before the massacre at the Alamo, Duncan complained of the scarcity of specie in both Natchez and New Orleans, attributing the deficit to President Jackson's fiscal policies and to "the suspension of intercourse with the Spanish main." The latter, he charged, had been caused "by our folly in aiding the rebellious movements of the Texans." Not only was such action "unwise & indiscreet," but it was also contrary to both "the dictates of sound patriotism" and "regard for the laws of neutrality." But Duncan was clearly in the minority among his wealthy cohorts in opposing United States designs on Texas. Less than a decade later, elite slaveholders throughout the South, from the Carolinas to Arkansas, were clamoring for the annexation of that republic. Among the most vociferous advocates of annexation were R. F. W. Allston of South Carolina, Joseph E. Davis of Mississippi, Isaac

35. Stephen Duncan to Thomas Butler, December 8, [1844], January 3, 1845, in Thomas Butler and Family Papers, LSU; William J. Minor to C. P. Leverich, May 13, 1840, in Charles P. Leverich Papers, MDAH; Henry A. Tayloe to "Dear Brother" [Benjamin O.], August 21, 1841, in Henry A. Tayloe and Family Papers, ADAH.

Wright of North Carolina and his son Moorhead, the second largest slaveholder in Arkansas, all of them Democrats.[36]

Although southern Whigs were reluctant to oppose the annexation of Texas, they gave their enthusiastic endorsement to Henry Clay in the presidential contest of 1844, a campaign that involved economic issues as well as the question of territorial expansion. Such well-to-do Natchezians as William J. Minor, William N. Mercer, and Stephen Duncan were among the most ardent supporters of the venerable Kentuckian. "We are making great efforts to carry this state for Mr Clay," reported Minor on the eve of the election, "& not without strong hopes of success." When those hopes were dashed shortly thereafter and news of Polk's election reached Mississippi, Duncan pronounced the result "a most severe disappointment" and vowed "never again to vote for President" while he lived. From his winter residence in New Orleans, Mercer tried to console the vanquished candidate. Even in defeat, he assured Clay, the latter remained "the first man in our Country." Such prominent North Carolina Whigs as James C. Johnston and his friend Ebenezer Pettigrew also cast their ballots for Clay in 1844. "I think . . . there can be no doubt of Mr Clays election," Pettigrew observed optimistically several months before the election.[37] On the other hand, those members of the elite with close ties to the Democratic Party were just as outspoken in their support of Polk. A representative, but far from comprehensive, list of these would include John A. Quitman and Joseph Davis of Mississippi, John Izard Middleton and Leroy Wiley of South Carolina, Farish Carter of Georgia, and Edward Lloyd of Maryland, most of whom continued to support the presidential nominees of the national Democratic Party until the fateful election of 1860.[38]

A similar division along party lines occurred with respect to the Mexican

---

36. Stephen Duncan to C. P. Leverich, February 8, 1836, in Charles P. Leverich Papers, MDAH; Rogers, *History of Georgetown County*, 365; Hermann, *Joseph E. Davis*, 91; Moorhead Wright to "My Dear Father" [Isaac], August 7, 1847, in Gillespie and Wright Family Papers, SHC.

37. Minor to C. P. Leverich, October 16, 1844, Duncan to Leverich, November 23, 1844, both in Charles P. Leverich Papers, MDAH; Mercer to Clay, December 7, 1844, in *The Papers of Henry Clay*, ed. Hay, X, 176; Ebenezer Pettigrew to James C. Johnston, May 20, 1844, in Pettigrew Family Papers, SHC.

38. McLemore, ed., *A History of Mississippi*, I, 299; Hermann, *Joseph E. Davis*, 89; Rogers, *History of Georgetown County*, 369; L. M. Wiley to Farish Carter, November 11, 1844, in Farish Carter Papers, SHC; John Walton to Edward Lloyd, November 13, 1852, in Lloyd Family Papers, MHS.

War. Although most Southerners supported that war and such wealthy slave-holders as Quitman and Jefferson Davis played a conspicuous military role in that conflict, some Whig planters bitterly condemned the Polk administration for plunging the nation into war with our virtually helpless neighbor to the south. Thus, in December, 1845, just two weeks before General Zachary Taylor was ordered to proceed to a position near the left bank of the Rio Grande, Natchez planter William St. John Elliot complained to Richard T. Archer, "Your friends are trying hard to get us into a war, which *I* think will pretty well use up the South," then just recovering from the economic depression of the early 1840s. "I still hope," wrote Elliot, that in spite of Polk and his militant associates, "there will be Sense and Virtue enough left in Congress to thwart their plans for President makeing by involving their Country in a nonsensical war." Even more vociferous in his denunciation of Polk's Mexican policy was William S. Pettigrew, who, during the debate over the Compromise of 1850, charged that the Mexican lands had been acquired "by murder & robbery." Now, he concluded, the two sections were quarreling over the spoils, with each seeking to secure "the *lion's share of the plunder.*"[39]

Most wealthy Southerners, however, viewed the conflict with Mexico in quite a different light. Enthusiasm for the war was most pronounced in those slave states with the closest geographic and economic ties to Texas. Thus, as early as mid-May, 1846, a correspondent in New Orleans reported that volunteer companies were pouring into that city from the outlying parishes, "and it is probable that all the present requisition for troops on this State will be made up today or tomorrow." Such patriotic fervor was noticeably absent in distant South Carolina, though the aristocratic leaders of that state were virtually unanimous in their support of the war effort. Just two weeks after the frenzied scene described by the New Orleans observer, Henry A. Middleton, Jr., then a student at Harvard, complained about the apparent lack of patriotism in his native state. "What's become of the chivalry of our state," he asked. "I dont see the report of a single company's having volunteered to go to the Mexican war."[40] In

39. William St. John Elliot to "Dear Archer," [December?] 30, 1845, in Richard Thompson Archer Family Papers, CAH; William S. Pettigrew to James C. Johnston, March 7, 1850, in Pettigrew Family Papers, SHC.

40. Richard Rush [?] to Haller Nutt, May 12, 1846, in Nutt Family Collection, MDAH; Henry A. Middleton, Jr., to [his sister] Harriett, [May 23], 1846, Henry A. Middleton, Jr., Family Letters, in Cheves-Middleton Papers, SCHS.

terms of actual participation in the war by elite slaveholders, Mississippi led the way. Most notable was John A. Quitman, who served with great distinction, first under General Zachary Taylor and later as a major general in the regular army under Winfield Scott. In addition to having a personal interest in Texas lands that he had acquired a decade before, Quitman was motivated, as he confided to his son, by "a sense of duty to [his] country and to [his] character." Two other Mississippians who later achieved elite planter status also saw service in Mexico. Gabriel B. Shields, who married the eldest daughter of Francis Surget, Sr., was a major on General Quitman's staff. Madison County planter S. A. D. Greaves fought with the First Mississippi Volunteer Regiment, commanded by Colonel Jefferson Davis, and was cited by his commanding officer for "outstanding gallantry" at the Battle of Monterrey in September, 1846.[41]

The war with Mexico contained the seeds that germinated a dozen years later when the long-simmering sectional conflict between North and South erupted into a much more costly military confrontation. Acquisition of the Mexican cession lands rekindled the debate over the expansion of slavery that had been allayed for a generation by the Missouri Compromise and led directly to the sectional crisis of 1850. Unlike the debate over the admission of Missouri thirty years before, however, the contest over the disposition of the territory acquired from Mexico took place in an explosive atmosphere generated by the mounting abolitionist onslaught against slavery and slaveholders—indeed, against all things southern. For more than a decade, southern slaveholders had been assailed from all quarters: from the press and the pulpit, in northern schools and in the halls of Congress. Consequently, Southerners were in no mood to accept the admission of California as a free state, thereby fracturing the sectional balance that had been carefully preserved since the time of the Missouri Compromise, without receiving some concessions in return. It was in this atmosphere that the aging Whig leader Henry Clay stepped forward with his last great compromise proposal, a series of resolutions that, in slightly modified form, were adopted in September, 1850, after a bitter debate that consumed the nation for nearly eight months.

41. McLemore, ed., *A History of Mississippi*, I, 300; James, *Antebellum Natchez*, 275; John A. Quitman to "My dear Son" [Frederick Henry], January 11, 1847, in John A. Quitman Papers, MDAH; Excerpts from the Journal of Ellen Shields, 1903, photocopy courtesy of Mrs. Rawdon Blankenstein, Natchez; Elmore Douglass Greaves, Jr., "The Greaves Family and Sunny Place Plantation," 1943 (TS), in possession of Elmore D. Greaves, Madison County, Miss.

Although resentment against the North was almost universal among the large slaveholders in 1850, they were sharply divided in their responses to the crisis. Some, particularly those in South Carolina, were ready to embrace the radical option of secession; others, clearly a majority, might be characterized as conditional Unionists; a few were die-hard Unionists, opposed to secession under any circumstances. Virtually all of the wealthy Whig planters supported the moderate course pursued by the leader of their party. But in South Carolina, the most alienated of the slave states, it was quite a different story. There, rice baron R. F. W. Allston, soon to be elevated to the office of governor, expressed the view of many of his Low Country neighbors when, on the eve of the congressional debate, he declared: "Unless the Northern people now come to be reasonable people, Revolution will be unavoidable It were better to settle the matter now than leave it to our children." Six months later, with the issue still in doubt, his wife Adele, who, like many other prominent Southerners, favored an extension of the Missouri Compromise line to the Pacific, denounced Clay as "a traitor to the South."[42]

South Carolinians were not alone in their denunciation of the Clay proposals and their advocacy of more extreme measures. As the debate over the Compromise of 1850 commenced, F. Henry Quitman, writing from Princeton, where he heard "on all sides nothing but the all absorbing Slavery Question discussed," lauded Calhoun's Senate speech and asserted, if the South could not exact from the North a pledge of peace and security "in the enjoyment of our most cherished institutions to ourselves & future generations . . . then we must in honor to ourselves dissolve" the Union. Other Mississippians expressed like sentiments. Richard T. Archer, who later castigated the moderate William L. Sharkey for his alleged hypocrisy in presiding over the Nashville Convention, declared that "discussion has been exhausted and the time for action has arrived." Declining an invitation to attend a pro-Union rally in Natchez, Archer asked why we should "rally for a Union which no longer exists in fact, and on Constitutional principles when the Constitution and its principles have really been abrogated." Instead of attempting to salvage the present Union, he favored "a Union of Slave States" with the "Proviso that no state shall remain in the Confederacy after abolishing slavery." Across the state, in Aberdeen, Needham

---

42. R. F. W. Allston to Adele Petigru Allston, December 16, 1849, Adele to R. F. W. Allston, June 4, 1850, both in Easterby, ed., *South Carolina Rice Plantation*, 98–99, 101.

Whitfield called for either disunion or an economic boycott of the North "if our Southern rights Cannot be more respected."[43]

The above were some of the more extreme voices among aristocratic slaveholders during the crisis of 1850, but the majority assumed a more moderate posture. Representative of the latter was William S. Pettigrew of North Carolina. In a remarkable letter to staunch Unionist James C. Johnston, written shortly after the congressional debate began, Pettigrew lauded Clay's speech in support of the compromise proposals; rejected the counsel of Calhoun and his South Carolina cohorts, remarking, "I have but little confidence in their love for the Union & almost as little in their judgment"; denounced the plunder of Mexican territory; declared his willingness to allow the inhabitants of the territories to decide the issue of slavery by popular sovereignty; and castigated the political leaders in both sections. Yet he added this ominous qualification to his then-pronounced Unionist stance:

> There may be a day (I fear there will be) when the institution of Slavery even in the States will be attacked, regardless of Constitutional barriers. When that day arrives, the door of hope will be closed, & it will be the duty of the South to go any length in its defense, regardless of consequences. Then will be the time for Civil War & Dissolution of the Union; then will be the time to sell our lives for our country. But Heaven be thanked! that day has not yet come.[44]

That day did come, however, ten years later, and Pettigrew, along with scores of other conditional Unionists within the ranks of the elite slaveholders, reluctantly opted for secession and the establishment of a new confederation.

Other wealthy slaveholders who pursued a moderate course in 1850 only to abandon their Unionist position a decade later included Paul Cameron, a Henry Clay Whig from North Carolina, and Democrats Howell Cobb and John B.

43. F. Henry Quitman to John A. Quitman, March 14, 1850, in John A. Quitman and Family Papers, MDAH; Richard T. Archer to "Gentlemen" [Robert Stanton, William H. Dunbar, John B. Nevitt, et al.], September, 1850, in Richard Thompson Archer Family Papers, CAH; Needham Whitfield to "Dear Cousin Allen" [Allen W. Wooten], October 10, 1850, in Whitfield and Wooten Family Papers, SHC.

44. William S. Pettigrew to James C. Johnston, March 7, 1850, in Pettigrew Family Papers, SHC.

Lamar of Georgia. In early August, already upset by the failure of Whig governor Charles Manly to win reelection—a defeat he attributed to the "Denunciation of the Nashville Convention by Whig orators"—and fearful that the Senate might reject the Clay Compromise, Cameron remarked gloomily: "I fear we have trouble ahead!"[45] In Georgia, the influential Howell Cobb, then serving as Speaker of the U.S. House of Representatives, and his brother-in-law John B. Lamar battled valiantly to stem the tide of disunion that threatened to overwhelm that state. As early as February, Lamar concluded that without the support of the border states, it would be "perfect madness" to even consider a dissolution of the Union. The failure of Tennessee to send delegates to the Southern Convention in Nashville had dealt "a death blow to the whole movement," observed Lamar, and the example of the Volunteer State would "fix the wavering states of Kentucky and Missouri against us." Four months later, as the debate raged on in Congress, Cobb urged Lamar to attend a scheduled public meeting in support of the compromise bill. "The truth is," asserted Cobb, "we are destined to a mortifying and humiliating defeat if the mad counsels" of the extremists "should rule the day." He found it ironic that "the very men who would have ostracised [him] for advocating the Missouri Compromise line" were "now making that their *sine qua non*." Had they united with him "*at the proper time*," continued Cobb, "we could have obtained that line as the basis of settlement." Instead, they had followed the misguided counsel of Calhoun and staked all on the "*constitutional principle of non interference*," a principle they now rejected in favor of the "heretofore repudiated Missouri Compromise." He declared angrily, "I have no patience with such men." In early July, as both sides marshaled their forces in a last-ditch effort to sway public opinion, Lamar reported that "the excitement" in the state was "waxing hot." Cotton nabob Joseph Bond had cast his lot with the pro-compromise forces, but the Democratic press and many prominent members of that party, including former governor Charles J. McDonald, were in the disunion camp. "God damn 'em," exploded Lamar, "how I wish old Jackson was alive & President of the United States for the next twelve months." Happily, Congress approved the compromise mea-

---

45. C. L. Hinton to Paul C. Cameron, August 2, 1850, Cameron to "My dear Father," August 3, 1850, both in Cameron Family Papers, SHC; Cameron to Joseph B. G. Roulhac, August 8, 1850 (quotation), in *The Papers of Thomas Ruffin*, ed. Hamilton, II, 298.

sures two months later, much to the relief of both men, but they, like their North Carolina counterparts, would take a more radical position a decade later.[46]

There were others, however, whose steadfast Unionist stance remained unchanged during the final sectional crisis of 1860–1861. Among these were Josiah Winchester, the lawyer-planter from Natchez, and Benjamin O. Tayloe, the master of Octagon House in Washington, D.C. In 1851 the former received an irate communication from an anonymous correspondent, berating him for his persistent Unionism. "Though the people are still under the charm of that hallowed word 'Union' which you and such as you desecrate to beguile them to their ruin," the secessionist wrote angrily, "the delusions of the day will pass off, and your passionate declarations may meet the execrations of a free and enlightened people." Such inflammatory rhetoric did not faze Winchester, who would be subjected to even more vitriolic criticism a decade later. Nor did such language from the disunionist faction influence Tayloe, who, from his vantage point in the nation's capital, assiduously followed the debate in Congress from late January until passage of the final compromise measures in September. From the outset, he was convinced that the "Cotton Cable" that bound the two sections together would prevent a dissolution of the Union despite the efforts of demagogues on both sides to reap political capital from the crisis. "The Union cannot & will not be dissolved . . . during our generation," he asserted confidently in late January. "It would touch the pocket book too acutely to have a separation." In late autumn, after the passage of the Compromise, Tayloe reiterated his belief that northern abolitionists—"a pitiful minority of scarce 10.000" in the pivotal state of New York—posed little threat to the Union. The real danger, he observed sagaciously, came from the South, especially South Carolina, which was "ripe for disunion." Although adamant in his belief that "the Union *must* & will be preserved," Tayloe was concerned that the "old maidish complaints & reproaches" of the Palmetto State might infect her sister slave states with the germ of secession. No longer a wealthy state, South Carolina was now "proud & poor," clearly a potentially dangerous combination.[47]

46. John B. Lamar to Howell Cobb, February 27, 1850, Cobb to Lamar, June 26, 1850, Lamar to Cobb, July 5, 1850 (TSS), in Cobb-Erwin-Lamar Family Collection, UGA.

47. Isolus to [Josiah Winchester], n.d., [1851?], in Winchester Family Papers, CAH; Benjamin Ogle Tayloe to "Dear Brother" [William H.], January 21, November 11, 1850, in Tayloe Family Papers, VHS.

It was South Carolina, with the collaboration of Mississippi, that had spearheaded the movement for a Southern Convention, which met in Nashville in early June, 1850, to consider a unified response to the proposals then before Congress. The extremists, led by Robert Barnwell Rhett, hoped to use the occasion to rally support for cooperative secession by the aggrieved slave states. Those hopes were soon dashed, however, when only nine of the fifteen slave states sent delegates to Nashville, and even those who did attend adopted a relatively moderate course, endorsing an extension of the Missouri Compromise line to the Pacific and then adjourning to await further developments in Washington, D.C. Only South Carolina sent a full delegation to the Tennessee capital. In addition to Rhett, it included three other elite slaveholders: R. F. W. Allston, James H. Hammond, and Langdon Cheves, Sr.[48] Shortly after his arrival in Nashville, Allston characterized the assembled delegates as "a noble body of intellectual men," leaders of unparalleled virtue and character. Allston's glowing description was surpassed only by that of Mississippi judge George Winchester, whose political views were antithetical to those of his Unionist nephew Josiah. After assailing the *National Ingelligencer* for impugning the motives of those who were about to make the arduous journey to Nashville, the elder Winchester described the members of that body as "some of the purest, most patriotic, and most intellectual men of the age in which we live."[49]

Notwithstanding their exuberant characterization of the Nashville delegates, such ultras as Allston and Winchester were ultimately doomed to disappointment. Already disconcerted by the fiery rhetoric of Virginia delegate Beverley Tucker and by Rhett's radical anti-Compromise address, which had been adopted over the protest of conservatives at the first meeting, a majority of the original delegates elected not to return to Nashville when the convention reconvened in mid-November. Even the vacillating Hammond backed out, pleading sickness in his family as the excuse. "For the first time in his life I'm sure," remarked a disgusted Elizabeth Rhett.[50] At the Second Nashville Convention,

48. Freehling, *The Road to Disunion*, 481, 485; Faust, *James Henry Hammond and the Old South*, 297–98.

49. R. F. W. Allston to Benjamin Allston, June 7, 1850, in Easterby, ed., *South Carolina Rice Plantation*, 102; George Winchester, fragmentary essay entitled the "Slavery Question," [1849–50], in Winchester Family Papers, CAH.

50. Freehling, *The Road to Disunion*, 483–85; Faust, *James Henry Hammond and the Old South*, 298–300; Charles J. McDonald to Farish Carter, June 10, 1850, in Farish Carter Papers, SHC; Eliza-

Langdon Cheves, who had opposed nullification two decades earlier, delivered an impassioned plea for secession, but only if four or more states would secede together.[51] In the end, this rump body denounced the Compromise of 1850, asserted the legality of secession, and called on the individual slave states to convene conventions to consider what further action might be taken to defend southern rights.

Why did the Nashville Convention fail to produce the results sought by those who had promoted it? In a retrospective piece written after his return to South Carolina, Allston assigned primary blame to Clay and the other southern politicians who had supported his proposals. But for their opposition to a settlement based on the Missouri Compromise line, such moderate northern senators as Daniel Sturgeon of Pennsylvania, Daniel S. Dickinson of New York, and Lewis Cass of Michigan might have been persuaded to embrace "the line [Allston and others] proposed." Consequently, "the reasonable suggestions and firm conclusions" of those who had gathered at Nashville were ignored, and the best hope "of saving the Union under the Constitution & reforming the Federal Government" had been lost. Fellow South Carolinian Drayton Nance expressed regret that his state had ever been represented in the Nashville Convention. That body, he charged in a letter to Rhett, had had "a ruinous influence" on what he termed the "true policy, and interests" of South Carolina "by delaying secession" and "giving time to her people to take counsel of their fears," which he feared had "quenched their devotion to principle and patriotism."[52]

As the great slaveholders contemplated the provisions of the final compromise settlement, reaction was decidedly mixed. Although most were relieved that a constitutional crisis had been averted, it was clear to them that the North had gained the most from the historic compromise. The admission of California as a free state had broken the delicate sectional balance that had been so carefully preserved for thirty years. The surrender by Texas of its claim to a large portion of New Mexico in return for a monetary payment of $10 million from

beth Rhett to "Dear Barnwell" [Rhett], November 7, [1850], in Robert Barnwell Rhett, Sr., Papers, SCHS.

51. Langdon Cheves to David J. McCord, August 15, 1831 [copy], in Langdon Cheves Papers, SCL; Freehling, *The Road to Disunion*, 519.

52. "Remarks by Robert F. W. Allston Concerning the Nashville Convention of 1850," n.d., in Easterby, ed., *South Carolina Rice Plantation*, 445–46; Drayton Nance to R. B. Rhett, January 28, 1851, in Robert Barnwell Rhett, Sr., Papers, SCHS.

the federal government could hardly be considered a victory. Moreover, that territory, all of which lay below the Missouri Compromise line, was opened to popular sovereignty. Thus, the only substantive advantage derived by the South from the compromise was a new and more stringent Fugitive Slave Law. As Georgia soon declared, the longevity of the Union would depend upon the faithful enforcement of that law. That sentiment was echoed by many of the elite planters. As he followed events at home while traveling in Europe, William H. Heyward lauded the annual message of Virginia governor John B. Floyd, in which the latter asserted that "everything will depend upon the observance of the Fugitive Slave Law." Even the inveterate Mississippi Unionist Stephen Duncan predicted in November, 1850, that "this state will go for Secession—unless the opposition to the Fugitive slave bill is quieted." On almost the same day, fellow Natchez nabob Francis Surget, Sr., expressed the "firm opinion" that if the North should "attempt at the next session of Congress to repeal or to modify the fugitive slave bill . . . the Slave States would at once secede from the union."[53]

Outraged by a settlement that they regarded as little more than a humiliating capitulation to the North, militant southern rights advocates in three states—Georgia, Mississippi, and South Carolina—responded enthusiastically to the recommendation by the rump Nashville Convention that the individual slave states convene special conventions to consider more appropriate measures of resistance against the mounting onslaught against slavery. Elite slaveholders played a conspicuous role in the ensuing political contests in all three states. For a time, South Carolina delayed taking any action, hoping that one of the other southern states—one less stigmatized by disunion rhetoric—would initiate the process. The hopes of Palmetto State extremists were realized momentarily in the fall of 1850 when Governor George W. Towns of Georgia called for the election of delegates to a convention in his state and John A. Quitman, his counterpart in Mississippi, convened a special session of the legislature to consider a like course of action.[54]

The battle between Unionists and secessionists was soon joined in both

---

53. William Henry Heyward to James B. Heyward, January 5, 1850 [sic, 1851], in Heyward and Ferguson Family Papers, SHC; Stephen Duncan to Charles P. Leverich, November 26, 1850, Surget to Leverich, November 25, 1850, both in Charles P. Leverich Papers, MDAH.

54. Freehling, The Road to Disunion, 521–25.

states, with wealthy slaveholders prominently represented in each camp. In Georgia, those who sought to sever the bonds of union were quickly routed, as the unlikely trio of Democrat Howell Cobb and Whig leaders Robert Toombs and Alexander H. Stephens canvassed the state on behalf of the Compromise and against secession. As a consequence of their efforts, Unionists dominated the convention that met in December and adopted the famous Georgia Platform, in which the delegates accepted the Compromise of 1850 as an honorable and permanent solution to the sectional controversy. As a sop to the disunionists, the convention warned that Georgia would resist any further infringement upon southern rights by the federal government, especially any attempt to weaken the Fugitive Slave Law. Less than a year later, Cobb was elected governor on the Union Democrat ticket.[55]

At first, prospects seemed much brighter for the Mississippi secessionists. Shortly after arriving in Jackson, where the legislature had been called into special session in mid-November, Richard T. Archer, the fiery planter aristocrat from Port Gibson, pronounced himself "so pleased with the progress of events" that he could scarcely "tear [him]self away" from the city. "The legislature will sustain Southern rights by an overwhelming majority," he predicted confidently, "and there is a great concourse of people here from all parts of the State, entertaining my opinions." Governor Quitman, who had earlier assured South Carolina governor Whitemarsh B. Seabrook that Mississippi was prepared to take the lead in the secession movement, delivered a bombastic address to the legislature, denouncing every aspect of the so-called Compromise of 1850 and urging the state to issue an ultimatum demanding substantial concessions from the North on the slavery question. At the same time, however, Mississippi Unionists, led by Judge William L. Sharkey and the unpredictable Henry S. Foote, assembled an informal convention in Jackson in an effort to exert a moderating influence on the legislature. Their strategy was clear. Since they were badly outnumbered in the legislature, their only hope was to submit the issue directly to the people and even then to postpone the decision as long as possible. As one Natchez Unionist advised legislator A. K. Farrar, "the day for testing the question and for the people electing delegates ought to be as late a day as the majority will yield" so that the consequences of disunion could be clarified for every citizen of the state. As a consequence of Unionist pressure, the radical zeal ob-

55. *Ibid.*, 523–24; Allan Nevins, *Ordeal of the Union*, 2 vols. (New York, 1947), I, 355–56.

served just days before by Archer began to dissipate, and the legislature voted to delay the election of delegates to a state convention until the following September.[56]

In the long interim before the convention met in November, 1851, moderates gradually gained the upper hand in the Magnolia State. Capitalizing on the inflammatory rhetoric of Quitman, the Unionists charged with considerable justification that the governor was plotting secretly with the South Carolinians to destroy the Union, a prospect that alarmed a majority of Mississippians despite their dissatisfaction with the Compromise. Matters took a turn for the worse for the impulsive Quitman in February, 1851, when his alleged involvement in the first Lopez filibustering expedition against Cuba forced him to resign the governorship. When charges were dropped following a brief trial before a federal court in New Orleans, Quitman returned to Mississippi to lead the so-called Resistance Party against Senator Henry S. Foote's Unionists. During the next six months, two political campaigns were waged simultaneously: the first for delegates to the state convention, and the second between Quitman and Foote for the office of governor.[57]

As the time for the election of convention delegates drew near, emotions ran high on both sides. From Northampton, Massachusetts, where he was vacationing, cotton nabob William St. John Elliot urged fellow Natchezian Lemuel Conner to exert every influence on behalf of the Unionists "and put down the traitors of the South as the North is doing in regard to her traitors." But for the militant Richard Archer, the real traitors were his submissionist, Union-loving neighbors. In a bitterly worded letter to Judge William Sharkey, whom he had earlier castigated for his hypocritical role at the Nashville Convention, Archer charged that Sharkey, "an opposition candidate for the Convention whose action we hoped to rescue our State from aggression," was "betraying" his country. "For your private worth I have great respect," Archer conceded grudgingly, "but no man more strongly condemns your course on this great issue between con-

56. Richard T. Archer to Ann B. Archer, November 21, 1850, in Richard Thompson Archer Family Papers, CAH; Freehling, *The Road to Disunion*, 521–22, 525–26; Nevins, *Ordeal of the Union*, I, 362, 365–66; J[ohn] T. McMurran to A. K. Farrar, November 24, 1850, in Alexander K. Farrar Papers, LSU.

57. Freehling, *The Road to Disunion*, 526; Nevins, *Ordeal of the Union*, I, 372–73; McLemore, ed., *A History of Mississippi*, I, 304–305.

solidationists and constitutionalists."[58] Unfortunately for Archer and Quitman, the Unionists prevailed in the September convention election, winning 57 percent of the votes. In a desperate effort to save the governorship, Quitman withdrew from the race in favor of Jefferson Davis. But although the latter gained some ground against the controversial Foote during the remaining two months of the campaign, he suffered a narrow defeat at the polls in early November. Less than a week later, the state convention met in Jackson and overwhelmingly adopted an antisecession resolution, thereby following the moderate course established the year before by Georgia.[59]

Thus, South Carolina was left alone to carry the banner of secession. But even there, the ultras, who had enjoyed momentary success earlier in the year, had seen their hopes dashed just a month before the Mississippi convention acted. With die-hard Unionists as scarce as the proverbial hen's teeth in South Carolina, the contest in that state was between the separate-state secessionists, led by Rhett, and the cooperationists, those who favored secession only in concert with other slave states. The elite slaveholders were well represented on both sides. In addition to Rhett, those who favored separate state action included such prominent Low Country planters as John Izard Middleton, John H. Tucker, and Joshua J. Ward.[60] More numerous were the cooperationists, who numbered within their ranks the influential and closely related Chesnut, Hampton, Manning, and Preston families from the Up Country, as well as such wealthy Low Country planters as Langdon Cheves, Sr., William B. Pringle, Henry A. Middleton, Charles Alston, Sr., and John F. Townsend.[61] Another Low Country grandee, R. F. W. Allston, sought to mediate between the two parties in order to restore unity to the state.[62]

The struggle began auspiciously for the immediate secessionists when they

---

58. William St. John Elliot to "Dear Lemuel," August 5, 1851, in Lemuel P. Conner and Family Papers, LSU; Richard T. Archer to William L. Sharkey, October 26, 1850, August 19, 1851 (quotations), both in Richard Thompson Archer Family Papers, CAH.

59. Freehling, *The Road to Disunion*, 526–28; Nevins, *Ordeal of the Union*, I, 373–74; McLemore, ed., *A History of Mississippi*, I, 305–306.

60. Rogers, *History of Georgetown County*, 372–73; Joyner, *Down by the Riverside*, 18.

61. John L. Manning to "My dearest Wife," September 21, 24, 1851, John S. Preston to James Chesnut, Jr., September 27, 1851, Wade Hampton, Jr., to James Chesnut, Jr., June 5, 1852, in Williams-Chesnut-Manning Family Papers, SCL; Rogers, *History of Georgetown County*, 374; Freehling, *The Road to Disunion*, 530; McCurry, *Masters of Small Worlds*, 281.

62. R. F. W. Allston to Adele Petigru Allston, November 29, 1851, in Easterby, ed., *South Carolina Rice Plantation*, 109.

scored a decisive victory in February, 1851, in the election of delegates to a state convention, to be held at a yet-undetermined date. Three months later, some 450 members of the Southern Rights Association met in Charleston and voted for secession either with or without the cooperation of other slave states.[63] Fearful of the consequences of separate state secession, the cooperationists rallied their forces and mounted an effective campaign to turn the tide of public opinion against precipitate action. Especially conspicuous in this effort was James Chesnut, Jr., the son of a large Kershaw District slaveholder and a man who commanded such wide respect within the state that he was elected to the U.S. Senate in 1858. Although he had earlier denounced the Compromise of 1850 as "that *Bill of Surrender,* called a compromise, which proposed to give every thing to the North & take every thing in dispute from the South," Chesnut labored assiduously during the months following the election of convention delegates to counter the extremists.[64] In company with John L. Manning, John S. Preston, and Wade Hampton III, he addressed public meetings, helped to finance a partisan newspaper, and campaigned for cooperationist candidates in the October election to choose delegates to a proposed Southern Rights Congress.[65] As he explained to a group of fellow cooperationists, hasty action by South Carolina at this time, when the other southern states were not yet ready to follow, would likely "result in entire failure, & perhaps in the utter prostration & ruin of the State." If her sister states desired to make one final effort to secure their rights within the Union, then Chesnut believed that it was their "duty to give a fair trial to the experiment," though he did not doubt that such an experiment was doomed to failure and that "the only remaining hope of the South" was "to be found in United Secession, & the formation of a new & adequate government." He looked forward to this end "with bright hope," but for now, he warned, "our passions must be made subservient to our judgments."[66]

63. Ford, *Origins of Southern Radicalism,* 194–95, 199; Freehling, *The Road to Disunion,* 528; McCord, *Selected Writings,* 28.

64. [James Chesnut, Jr.], Reply to Foote "for the Daily Southern Press," [August, 1850], in Chesnut-Miller-Manning Papers, SCHS.

65. John L. Manning to "My dearest Wife," September 21, 24, 1851, John S. Preston to James Chesnut, Jr., September 27, 1851, Wade Hampton, Jr., to Chesnut, June 5, 1852, in Williams-Chesnut-Manning Family Papers, SCL; F. I. Moses to Chesnut, September 30, 1851, in Chesnut-Miller-Manning Papers, SCHS.

66. [James Chesnut, Jr.], to "Gentlemen," July 28, 1851, in Chesnut-Miller-Manning Papers, SCHS.

Other members of prominent South Carolina families, though ultimately committed to secession, echoed Chesnut's relatively cautious sentiments in 1851. Among them was John F. Townsend, one of the largest sea island cotton planters in the state. Described by William Freehling as "the most famous Cooperationist pamphleteer," Townsend argued just as vigorously for disunion as Barnwell Rhett. Yet he was unwilling for the Palmetto State to act alone. As he remarked in one of his most notable pamphlets, he wished to cast his eyes on "the Mighty Nation of the Southern United States" rather than on "the Little Nation of South Carolina." In like manner, Louisa McCord, in a review of the fiery southern rights meeting that had been held in Charleston in May, warned, "We have boasted too much—quite too much—already." For South Carolina to secede alone would be "but a continued boasting" without achieving the desired result. Although convinced that disunion was "the only remedy for [their] ills," McCord adhered to the position earlier espoused by her father, Langdon Cheves, during the nullification controversy and again at the rump session of the Nashville Convention, namely, that separate secession was a *"mischievous folly"* that would only alienate their "true and natural allies." She even invoked the wise counsel of the celebrated Calhoun, who, shortly before his death, had declared that *"concert of action* among the Southern States" was essential to preserve the rights of those states. The issue, she contended, was not "one between resistance and submission." It was "not *whether,* but *how"* to resist.[67]

Although they recognized the dangers inherent in separate state secession, advocates of that course were more fearful of the consequences of delay or inaction. As William S. Lyles of Fairfield District explained to Chesnut, "we are too few committed to secede, and to halt now and wait for new aggressions, will be to fail entirely." Lyles, who had been a "disunionist *per se"* since 1844, called for decisive action before popular emotions had a chance to subside. If South Carolina failed to act now, he warned, "the spirit of our people will never be thoroughly aroused again—the tension of the bow will be lost, the spirit broken down." Whatever the risk associated with separate secession, it could not "possibly equal that of remaining in this union. Out of the union there may be some hope of safety for our institutions, in it there is none." Above all, however, Lyles was concerned about the increasingly bitter division between the two se-

67. *Biographical Directory of the Senate of South Carolina,* comp. Reynolds and Faunt, 323; Freehling, *The Road to Disunion,* 530; McCord, *Selected Writings,* 36–45.

cession parties in the state. Thus, in early July he called on Chesnut to join him in attempting to quell "the passions" that might "lead to a distinct and seperate [*sic*] organization of parties" within the state. For, said Lyles, evoking the memorable expression later used by Abraham Lincoln, "a house divided against itself cannot stand."[68]

Following what Lacy F. Ford has called the most divisive election campaign in the state since the nullification era, South Carolina voters went to the polls in mid-October, 1851, to elect delegates to the proposed Southern Congress. As the results slowly trickled in, it became apparent that a dramatic reversal of popular sentiment had occurred since the election of convention delegates in February. This time, the cooperationists scored a stunning victory. Although the Low Country rice and sea island cotton barons demonstrated that they were still a force to be reckoned with by carrying the coastal districts of Beaufort and Georgetown, the cooperationists overwhelmed their radical opponents in the city of Charleston and in most rural districts elsewhere in the state. Indeed, those opposed to immediate secession received nearly 60 percent of the popular vote and swept six of the seven congressional districts in the state. As she surveyed these shocking returns, Elizabeth Rhett, the devoted wife of fire-eater R. B. Rhett, could only express bewilderment and outrage. "Has God indeed, forsaken our land?" she cried. "After all your noble exertions, your generous self-sacrificing devotion to this ungrateful, cowardly, stupid State," she lamented to her husband, the submissionist leaders and their minions had "disregarded . . . all your warnings & entreaties that they should act like *men*." There was little hope now that the state convention, scheduled to meet the following April, would take any action. Consequently, Rhett would be obliged to resign his seat in Congress as a final act of protest. While others might choose the perilous course of continued life within the Union, the defiant Mrs. Rhett shared the conviction of her husband that death was "preferable to dishonour."[69]

Although it was clear that his cause was lost, at least for the time, Rhett

68. *Proceedings of the State Democratic Convention Held at Columbia, S.C., May 30–31, 1860* (Columbia: Southern Guardian Steam-Power Press, 1860), 40; W. S. Lyles to James Chesnut, Jr., July 1, 1851, in Chesnut-Miller-Manning Papers, SCHS.

69. Ford, *Origins of Southern Radicalism*, 200, 204–206; Freehling, *The Road to Disunion*, 532; Nevins, *Ordeal of the Union*, I, 370; Harold S. Schultz, *Nationalism and Sectionalism in South Carolina, 1852–1860* (1950; rpr. New York, 1969), 30; Elizabeth W. Rhett to "My dear Husband," October 17, [1851], in Robert Barnwell Rhett, Sr., Papers, SCHS.

remained in Washington, D.C., long enough to fire one last salvo against what he regarded as the southern capitulation of 1850. In December he delivered a blistering attack on the compromise settlement, much to the delight of his admirers back home. From Camden, Joseph B. Kershaw, later a major general in the Confederate Army, sent a congratulatory letter expressing gratitude for Rhett's "fearless denunciation of the Grand Dama of political idolatry . . . the Compromise." Kershaw was thankful at least one senator remained "whom neither *fear* nor *interest*" could silence. "I do hope," he concluded bitterly, "that our degradation may be painted in its true colours; that God may yet remove the scales from the eyes of the honest and that Traitors alone may remain at the foot of the Idol." Unfortunately, Kershaw's hopes were not realized when the state convention finally met in late April, 1852. With the cooperationists solidly in command, that body approved overwhelmingly a set of resolutions submitted by a committee chaired by seventy-six-year-old Langdon Cheves. In essence, the convention affirmed the *right* of secession but declared that it was inexpedient for the state to exercise the right at that time. On May 1, the day after the convention adjourned, the disillusioned Rhett resigned his seat in the U.S. Senate, just as his wife had predicted six months before.[70]

Thus, the nation had passed safely over the shoals of the first major sectional crisis, but the future seemed ominous indeed. In South Carolina, a state controlled by the great slaveholders, the secessionists were clearly in the majority. It was simply a question of when, rather than whether, they were prepared to take that revolutionary step. Elsewhere in the slave South, acceptance of the Compromise of 1850 had only been conditional, dependent upon the faithful execution of the Fugitive Slave Law and a cessation of attacks against the most basic institutions of the South. As it turned out, the settlement that many on both sides and in both political parties had hoped would be the final, permanent adjustment of sectional differences proved to be only a temporary and uneasy truce. During the ensuing decade, as sectional strife intensified, the elite slaveholders would again play a pivotal role.

70. J. B. Kershaw to R. B. Rhett, December 22, [1851], in Robert Barnwell Rhett, Sr., Papers, SCHS; Schultz, *Nationalism and Sectionalism in South Carolina*, 37–43; Ford, *Origins of Southern Radicalism*, 211.

8

THE ROAD TO ARMAGEDDON:

The Role of the Planter Elite in the Secession Crisis

It is useless to argue the question of Slavery with the North. Her demagogues have sown the wind—& they cannot control the whirlwind—the contempt which Southern men feel for Northern courage & honor—& the overbearing conduct which that contempt breeds—has produced a rancorous hatred of the South in the breasts of vast members at the North. . . . I have but little faith in the continuance of this Union.

—T. R. R. COBB to HOWELL COBB, May 26, 1858

I cant believe yet, we have madmen enough in the Country to destroy the Union.

—WILLIAM H. TAYLOE, November 11, 1860

The d——d fanatiks are not going to give any guarantees [to the South]. . . . *We* have but *one* choice—to take sides with the North—or with the South? This is all that [is] left us by the logic of Events.

—WILLIAM H. RUFFIN to PAUL C. CAMERON, December, 1860

Xmas was no doubt a very merry one with you in Charleston where every body is drunk or crazy & I hope the new year may be a happy one and that all of you may come to your senses before the end of it.

—JAMES C. JOHNSTON to J. J. PETTIGREW, January 2, 1861

There is no doubt now that Louisiana will cut loose its moorings from a safe and secure harbor to drift God only knows where in the wide water of a tempestuous sea. . . . I am sad and discouraged and feel that I have no choice left but am forced to take my chances on this secession craft.

—KENNETH M. CLARK to LEWIS THOMPSON, January 23, 1861

I have been an obstinate Unionist under the impression that Republicans were not Abolitionists. The mask is removed.

—WILLIAM H. TAYLOE, March 10, 1861

DURING THE DECADE of the 1850s a succession of events coalesced to destroy the fragile compromise settlement of 1850 and propel the divided nation inexorably toward a tragic civil war. Among the most significant of those events were the following: the publication in 1852 of Harriet Beecher Stowe's immensely influential novel *Uncle Tom's Cabin;* northern resistance to the new Fugitive Slave Law; the passage in 1854 of the Kansas-Nebraska Act, which repealed the Missouri Compromise and reopened the controversy over the expansion of slavery; the demise of the national two-party system and the birth of the clearly sectional Republican Party; the brutal caning of Charles Sumner on the floor of the U.S. Senate in May, 1856; the promulgation the following year of the inflammatory Dred Scott decision by a southern-dominated Supreme Court; and, perhaps most important of all, the raid on Harpers Ferry in October, 1859, by the fanatical abolitionist John Brown, an act that led many Southerners to heed the warnings long articulated by the extremists in their midst. The final catalyst, of course, was the election of Republican Abraham Lincoln to the presidency in 1860.

Although the elite slaveholders reacted angrily to certain events—most notably the image of slavery depicted by Mrs. Stowe, the failure of the North to abide by the Fugitive Slave Law, and the efforts of such organizations as the New England Emigrant Aid Society to finance the migration of freesoil settlers to Kansas—they remained divided on an ultimate course of action until the election of Lincoln. Then, most of the former conditional Unionists moved toward secession. However, a few remained loyal to the Union until the firing on Fort Sumter in mid-April, 1861, compelled them to choose one side or the other. Still others, among them some of the wealthiest planters in the Natchez District, never did renounce their allegiance to the United States. Instead, after striving valiantly to avert secession and a war that would likely have catastrophic economic consequences for them, these die-hard Unionists gave little or no support to the Confederacy, and a few even took refuge in New York City during the war.[1]

In South Carolina, where the majority of large slaveholders were committed to secession, either alone or in concert with other slave states, three political

---

1. At least five prominent Natchez District planters—Stephen Duncan, Samuel M. Davis, Levin Marshall, William Newton Mercer, and Ayres P. Merrill, Jr.—found refuge in New York during the war.

factions developed after the bitter internal conflict of 1851–1852. The first and most moderate, led by James L. Orr, sought to work within the framework of the national Democratic Party. The second, which included most of the old separate-state secessionists, worked toward the creation of a new Southern Rights Party. The third and perhaps most important group, spearheaded by such Up Country grandees as John L. Manning, John S. Preston, James Chesnut, Jr., and the third Wade Hampton, was prepared to remain in the Union as long as they were able to exert some degree of influence over events in Washington, D.C. This they were able to do during the Pierce and Buchanan administrations, but with the election of Lincoln in 1860 they finally abandoned all hope of peaceful coexistence within the Union and joined their former intrastate foes to form a united front.[2]

Of all the political events in the early 1850s, no other had more dire consequences for the nation than the Kansas-Nebraska Act of 1854. Not only did that statute destabilize the national political party system; it also led to widespread bloodshed in Kansas and even to violence in the chamber of the U.S. Senate. The southern reaction to this momentous new law was somewhat ambivalent. While slaveholders applauded that portion of the act that repealed the Missouri Compromise, many failed to discern much practical benefit to the slave states from the extension of the popular sovereignty principle to both territories. Thus, as the Nebraska Bill was being debated, South Carolina congressman John McQueen remarked to Barnwell Rhett that though he would be delighted to see the Missouri Compromise repealed, "it is too late to do us much good practically." In like manner, J. L. Claiborne of Mississippi averred that the South should support the measure, "but really," he added, "I cannot see any thing in it, to exult over." Another Mississippian voiced the fear of many Whigs that the controversial bill would reopen old wounds and exacerbate sectional tension. Just two weeks after final passage of the measure, the eldest son of Judge Edward McGehee condemned the

2. Ford, *Origins of Southern Radicalism*, 213–14. For evidence of the cordial relations that existed between the Manning family and the two Democratic presidents, see John L. Manning to President Franklin Pierce, January 11, 1856, President James Buchanan to John L. Manning, January 5, 1857, John L. Manning to Sallie B. Manning, May 18, 29, 1860, in Williams-Chesnut-Manning Family Papers, SCL; Mary H. Manning to "Dear Mama," September 15, 1857, Richard I. Manning, Jr., to John L. Manning, August 6, 1860, both in Chesnut-Miller-Manning Papers, SCHS.

"political vultures" who had promoted it and predicted that the insatiable desire of the Democrats for more territory could only lead to "anarchy and confusion."[3]

McGehee's fears were realized the following year when open warfare
erupted in Kansas in the wake of efforts by both slaveholders and freesoilers to
flood the territory with settlers. Indeed, before the end of July, less than two
months after the act was passed, freesoil emigrants from Massachusetts began
to settle the town of Lawrence. During the ensuing months, both sides financed
the emigration of thousands of settlers into the new territory, seeking to control
the territorial government, which was to be elected by popular vote. Despite the
herculean efforts of Eli Thayer and the New England Emigrant Aid Society,
the proslavery forces, abetted by thousands of fraudulent voters from the neighboring state of Missouri, elected a delegate to Congress in November, 1854, and
the following spring scored an overwhelming victory in the election of the territorial legislature. Undaunted by these blatantly illegal tactics, the freesoilers
drafted their own constitution in Topeka and in January, 1856, elected their own
governor and legislature. With rival governments now contending for hegemony in the territory, the Kansas Question became the all-absorbing topic in the
press and in the halls of Congress.[4]

Although David Atchison and his Missouri confederates were most instrumental in establishing and sustaining the proslavery government in Kansas, several large South Carolina slaveholders participated actively in the campaign to
promote the emigration of young, well-armed Southerners to the troubled territory. Among them were two members of the prominent Heyward family, James
B. and his uncle, Charles. Thus, in the spring of 1856, in response to a solicitation from his nephew, Charles Heyward subscribed $100 to support the activi-
ties of the Kansas Emigration Society and promised "to increase it to a larger
amount" if necessary to attain the objectives of the society. About the same
time, John Rutledge Alston, the son of a wealthy Georgetown District rice
planter, led a body of twenty-three proslavery settlers into Kansas. Although far
removed geographically from the tumultuous events in Kansas, members of the

3. John McQueen to R. B. Rhett, February 3, 1854, in Robert Barnwell Rhett, Sr., Papers, SCHS;
J. L. Claiborne to R. T. Archer, June 24, [1854], in Richard Thompson Archer Family Papers,
CAH; Edward [J.] McGehee to Micajah McGehee, June 14, 1854, in McGehee Family Papers,
MDAH.

4. Nevins, *Ordeal of the Union*, II, 307–13, 384–85, 408–409.

South Carolina elite clearly had an interest in the outcome of the contest for political supremacy in that distant locale.[5]

The violence in Kansas, highlighted in the spring of 1856 by the so-called Sack of Lawrence by proslavery forces, followed two days later by John Brown's retaliatory raid on Pottawatomie, spread to the floor of the U.S. Senate on May 22 when South Carolina representative Preston Brooks viciously battered Senator Charles Sumner of Massachusetts with a gold-headed cane.[6] The assault provoked a storm of protest in the North and seemed to confirm the image long projected by abolitionists that southern slaveholders were little more than barbarians. Not surprisingly, the reaction was quite different south of the Mason-Dixon line. Both publicly and privately, Southerners lauded Brooks for defending the honor of his elderly cousin, Senator Andrew P. Butler, who had been slandered in Sumner's infamous "Crime against Kansas" tirade. Merchants in the port city of Charleston allegedly purchased for the assailant a new cane inscribed with the words "Hit him again." Braxton Bragg, then the proprietor of a large sugar plantation in Lafourche Parish, applauded the act, remarking to a friend that "you can reach the sensibilities of such dogs only through . . . their heads and a big stick."[7] From Aberdeen, Mississippi, one of the Whitfield brothers reported that there seemed "to be a general rejoicing at Brooks giving Sumner a beating." Even the die-hard Unionist Benjamin O. Tayloe defended the South Carolinian. Although he regretted the unfortunate consequences— "northern sympathy & aid to the Black Republican cause"—Tayloe asserted that one could not "blame Brooks, except as to the place, for the thrashing a[nd] sound drubbing, that he gave Sumner—for his insults on Butler & S.C." In short, concluded Tayloe, Sumner "deserved a sound thrashing—& got it."[8]

5. Charles Heyward to James B. Heyward, March 14, 1856, in Heyward and Ferguson Family Papers, SHC; Rogers, *History of Georgetown County,* 377. Another Low Country grandee who supported the Kansas emigrants was R. F. W. Allston. See J. H. Means to Allston, February 8, 1856, E[ugene] B. Bell to Allston, February 11, 1856, both in R. F. W. Allston Papers, SCHS; also printed in Easterby, ed., *South Carolina Rice Plantation,* 129–31.

6. For a superlative description of the assault and of the reaction in both sections to it, see David Donald, *Charles Sumner and the Coming of the Civil War* (New York, 1961), 290–308.

7. Donald, *Charles Sumner,* 305. Bragg, who married the eldest daughter of Richard G. Ellis, a brother-in-law of both Stephen Duncan and Judge Thomas Butler, had 110 slaves on his Bivouac plantation in 1860.

8. Needham Whitfield to "Dear Cousin Allen" [Wooten], June 18, 1856, in Whitfield and Wooten Family Papers, SHC; Benjamin O. Tayloe to "Dear Brother" [William H.], May 26, 1856, in Tayloe Family Papers, VHS.

It was in the volatile atmosphere engendered by the Kansas Question generally and the Brooks–Sumner Affair in particular that the presidential campaign
of 1856 got underway. Veteran southern Whigs faced a dilemma that year as a
three-way contest for the presidency developed. With the demise of their party
on the national level and the emergence of a totally unpalatable alternative in
the form of the new Republican Party, they had only two viable options. They
could either support James Buchanan of Pennsylvania, the nominee of their
long-time Democratic opponents, or they could vote for the Know-Nothing
slate of former president Millard Fillmore and his running mate, Andrew J.
Donelson, who was himself a large slaveholder from Tennessee.[9] As usual, there
was no consensus among the elite planters. Two weeks after Buchanan received
the Democratic nomination in Cincinnati, a north Mississippi planter with
strong southern rights convictions noted approvingly that "both Whigs and
Democrats" in his part of the state were "pleased at the Democratic nomination
. . . particularly the state rights Whigs." Unionist Whigs, however, were not
so enamored with the Democratic candidate. Thus, shortly after attending the
National Whig Convention in Baltimore, which endorsed the Know-Nothing
ticket, Benjamin O. Tayloe was hopeful that Fillmore could be elected. "Fremont [the Republican nominee] is *now* a formidable competitor," he observed
worriedly, and "Buchanan is not as strong as he has been." Six weeks later, however, on the day of the election, he admitted reluctantly that Buchanan was the
likely winner. "The South does not seem to understand its interest," he complained bitterly. "It *ought* to have gone *en masse* for Fillmore. . . . The Country
has an escape from Fremont," he concluded, "but I doubt whether it was ever
intended by the S[eward] clique that he sh^d be elected."[10]

Regardless of party affiliation, the great slaveholders, as well as Southerners
generally, could agree on one point. They could not, under any circumstances,
accept the election of the so-called Black Republican candidate, John C. Fremont. For some, such an eventuality would constitute a sufficient threat to the
slaveholding interests to justify secession, as in fact it did four years later. Such

9. Donelson, a ward of Andrew Jackson, resided in Shelby County, Tennessee, where he only
held 17 slaves, but he also owned 84 slaves in Bolivar County, Mississippi, and another 46 in Lafourche Parish, Louisiana, for a total of 147 in 1860.

10. Needham Whitfield to "Dear Cousin Allen," June 18, 1856, in Whitfield and Wooten Family
Papers, SHC; Benjamin O. Tayloe to "Dear Brother," September 24, November 4, 1856, in Tayloe
Family Papers, VHS.

was the position of John Perkins, Jr., a prominent Democrat and wealthy Louisiana cotton planter who later chaired the committee that drafted the secession ordinance for his state. In response to an invitation in late September to address a meeting of southern rights advocates, Perkins explained his views at some length. The South, he grumbled, had "suffered from two classes of politicians—those who have apologetically confessed slavery to be a great social and political evil . . . and those who have threatened and talked much of resistance to aggression, and yet made none." The present crisis, in his judgment, required more resolute action. Anticipating arguments that would surface again during the next presidential campaign, he contended that the election of a Republican president would lead to repeal of the Fugitive Slave Law, the abolition of slavery in the District of Columbia, interdiction of the interstate slave trade, resistance to the admission of any new slave states, and ultimately to the extinction of slavery where it already existed. Consequently, declared Perkins, "I concur in the sentiment that, if Mr. Fremont be elected, the Union cannot and ought not to continue; and if personally present at your meeting, I should urge that its proceedings look to immediate preparation for a dissolution of the Union as the proper and necessary consequence of that event."[11] Fortunately, Fremont was not elected in 1856, and the Union survived for another four years.

Before the next presidential election, however, an incident occurred that was to have a profound psychological impact on citizens of the slave states and would lead many toward the extreme position already adopted by Perkins and his secessionist cohorts. Despite loud protestations to the contrary, white Southerners had long been cognizant of the potential for bloody slave uprisings in their midst and were terrified by the few that had actually materialized. Indeed, their reaction to the most serious insurrection in the history of the slave South, the Nat Turner rebellion of 1831, bordered on what one observer termed "community-insanity."[12] If that characterization was indicative of the southern mindset at the beginning of the abolition movement, one can only imagine the anger and fear spawned by John Brown's raid on Harpers Ferry, Virginia, nearly three decades later. To make matters worse, several prominent abolitionist leaders were rumored to have been involved in Brown's nefarious plan to precipitate a general slave uprising. The reaction of wealthy slaveholders to this latest attack

11. Printed Broadside, September 28, 1856, in John Perkins Papers, SHC.
12. Scarborough, ed., *The Diary of Edmund Ruffin*, II, 208.

upon their most cherished institution was both sharp and predictable. From Virginia to Mississippi, moderates and fire-eaters alike condemned the raid in the most forceful terms, and many predicted that the incident would drive the nation to the brink of civil war.

The impact of the Harpers Ferry incident on the southern psyche is vividly illustrated by the reaction of two Mississippians, one a longtime secessionist and the other a die-hard Unionist. The usually placid Stephen Duncan was so outraged by the Brown raid and by the nearly simultaneous effort of House Republicans to circulate thousands of copies of Hinton Rowan Helper's inflammatory book *The Impending Crisis* that he vowed, unless he could "see better evidence of a change of feeling in the North" than he could now see, he would bid that section "a *long farewell*."[13] He would "never again visit it—& never again have commercial intercourse with it." When the threat was only to abstract rights, explained Duncan to his New York factor, "there was no unanimity of sentiment, or action," in the South. "But when our *real, tangible rights* are not only threatened in the worst shape, *but absolutely invaded*," there could be only one result: "To make every man owning slave property—a *true Southerner* in *feeling & action*." Even more militant was the response of Richard Archer to the assault on Harpers Ferry. In a letter printed in the Vicksburg *Sun*, Archer called on the people to seize the mantle of leadership from their legislative bodies and to prepare for armed conflict. "'The irrepressible [*sic*] conflict' has begun," he thundered. "The South is invaded. It is time for all patriots to be united, to be under military organization, to be advancing to the conflict determined to live or die in defence of the God given right to own the African."[14]

In Virginia and the Carolinas, areas more directly affected by the Brown fiasco, the reaction was equally bitter. Like the fiery Archer, the much more moderate William S. Pettigrew of North Carolina called for "military instruction and organization" to repel any possible future assaults. "We can only keep these people back by showing that we are prepared to defend ourselves when attacked by their lawless bands," declared Pettigrew. Female members of the

---

13. Although the Helper book was primarily a dull, statistical compendium, it also contained some vitriolic language directed against slaveholders as well as a section entitled "Revolution Must Free the Slaves." See Allan Nevins, *The Emergence of Lincoln*, 2 vols. (New York, 1950), II, 116, 118.

14. Stephen Duncan to [C. P. Leverich], December 22, 1859, in Stephen Duncan Letters, LSU; Richard T. Archer to the Editors of the Vicksburg *Sun*, December 8, 1859, in Richard Thompson Archer Family Papers, CAH.

planter community were particularly terrified by the Brown raid and its implications for the future. Thus, Jane Pringle of South Carolina, predicting that "a dissolution of the Union seems certainly at hand," announced that if the "danger of slave revolts" persisted, she would abandon her South Carolina residence and return to her northern birthplace. "I can't stay here to run the chance of it," she wrote, "and moreover I *wont.*" Pettigrew, however, counseled his female friends not to "regard the matter with such alarm." It would only require "a few more such occurrences as the present," he asserted confidently, "to bring into full bloom that Southern valour, both male & female, which would arouse the admiration of the world. I verily believe there is scarcely a man who would not with alacrity shoul[der] his musket and show that we are not unworthy of our ancestry."[15]

Two members of the prominent Tayloe family of Virginia also registered their reaction to the Harpers Ferry raid and to the resulting escalation of sectional tension. Whigs and Unionists to the core, the Tayloes viewed the recent events with both dismay and apprehension. Just four days after the execution of the martyred Brown, Edward T. Tayloe reported from his Virginia plantation that a "militant spirit pervades the whole state." Northern "indifference" to the "invasion of Virginia by Jno Brown's vile cohort" had awakened "resentment" in many heretofore "calm minds." As a consequence, lamented Tayloe, "the bonds of the Union are fast loosening, and many are looking to the last days of the Republic as near at hand." Such a catastrophe could be averted only by the "creation of a Conservative Party like the old Whigs," but such a creation seemed "hopeless amid the sectional fanaticism" that infected both sections. "We can only pray," concluded the disconsolate Virginian, "that Heaven may interpose to spare us" from the calamity of disunion. A week later, his brother was equally pessimistic as he viewed the beginning of a lengthy partisan battle over the speakership of the House of Representatives from his vantage point in the nation's capital. Remarking that the remaining Brown conspirators, or "the other assassins," as he termed them, would be hanged within the week, thereby meeting the fate that most believed they had "rightly earned," Benjamin O. Tayloe nevertheless expressed disgust at the bickering on Capitol Hill. If only

15. William S. Pettigrew to "My dear Brother" [J. J. Pettigrew], November 29, 1859, in Pettigrew Family Papers, SHC; Jane L. Pringle to "My dear darling Lynch," December 13, [1859], Pringle Family Correspondence, in R. F. W. Allston Papers, SCHS.

the good men of both parties could "throw aside the pernicious & pestiliferous Demagogues," the Union might be saved. But, unfortunately, Tayloe saw "no chance of that" in the foreseeable future.[16]

It was in the immediate aftermath of the Brown raid, the Republican endorsement of the Helper book, and the bitter struggle over the House speakership that the presidential campaign of 1860, the most fateful in the nation's history, got underway. The contest began inauspiciously for the badly divided Democratic Party when the delegates from eight deep South states bolted the national nominating convention in Charleston after losing a platform fight over slavery in the territories to the pro-Douglas faction. In their absence, Douglas was unable to muster the requisite two-thirds of the original number needed for nomination, and the convention adjourned without agreeing on a nominee. When the convention reassembled in Baltimore two months later, the pro-Douglas forces gained control after a bitter credentials fight in which the delegates from Alabama and Louisiana who had bolted the Charleston convention were unseated in favor of rival delegations loyal to Douglas. This controversial decision precipitated another walkout by southern delegates, joined this time by anti-Douglas delegates from California, Oregon, and Massachusetts, and the rump body then proceeded to nominate Douglas on the second ballot. Less than a week later, those disaffected Democrats who had seceded from one or both of the regular conventions met at another site in Baltimore and nominated John C. Breckinridge of Kentucky and Joseph Lane of Oregon on a platform that guaranteed federal protection of slavery in the territories.[17] In the interim between the Democratic meetings in Charleston and Baltimore, two other candidates entered the contest: John Bell, the nominee of the hastily organized Constitutional Union Party, and Abraham Lincoln, the somewhat surprising choice of the Republicans.

As the wealthy slaveholders surveyed this crowded field of presidential contenders, they were united only in their vehement opposition to Lincoln, the nominee of the so-called Black Republican Party. Although it is not surprising

16. Edward T. Tayloe to "My Dear Brother" [William H.], December 6, 1859, B. O. Tayloe to "Dear Brother" [William H.], December 13, 1859, both in Tayloe Family Papers, VHS.

17. Nevins, *The Emergence of Lincoln,* II, 266–72; "Minority Report of Mr. Stevens, of Oregon, Against the Exclusion of the Regular Southern Delegates at the Baltimore Convention," in Breckinridge and Lane Campaign Document No. 7 (Washington, D.C., 1860), 5–8, in the possession of the author.

that they would exhibit hostility toward the standard-bearer of that sectional, antislavery party, it is apparent that many wealthy Southerners perceived Lincoln to be much more radical on the slavery issue than he actually was. Moreover, their dislike of Lincoln was exacerbated by his lowly social status. In short, unlike Republican leader William H. Seward, Lincoln was not a gentleman— not a man with whom they could negotiate in an atmosphere of reason, trust, and honor. Thus, shortly after the Republican Convention adjourned, former governor John L. Manning of South Carolina, a relative moderate amid the ultra-secessionists of his state, expressed astonishment that the Republicans had rejected Seward, "their gifted and talented leader" and "the most gentlemanly of their whole fraternity," in favor of the more radical and uncultured Lincoln. In Manning's eyes, the latter was nothing more than "a wretched backwoodsman" who was "a fanatic in his political policy." Demagogue though he was, Seward was at least "a gentleman" who had promised to respect "the rights of the South" if he were elected president. Manning was not alone in this assessment of the New York Republican. During a visit to Washington, D.C., earlier in the year, North Carolina planter Peter W. Hairston reported that Republican senator Simon Cameron of Pennsylvania had assured a member of the North Carolina congressional delegation that Seward "would not abolish slavery in the district of Columbia or prevent [them] from having any more slave territories" if he were chosen to lead the nation. Clearly, Seward was the more palatable choice for apprehensive Southerners.[18]

Apart from their common detestation of Lincoln, the elite slaveholders were as divided in their support for the remaining three presidential candidates as they had been on other political issues during the turbulent preceding decades. Although most cast their ballots for either Breckinridge or Bell, a few backed Douglas, convinced that only he could check the Republican juggernaut. Some of the most extreme apostles of secession actually longed for a Lincoln victory, believing that such an eventuality would assure the success of their cause. As fire-eater Edmund Ruffin explained on the eve of the election, "I most earnestly & anxiously desire Lincoln to be elected—because I have hope that at least one state S.C. will secede, & that others will follow." Friends and family

18. John L. Manning to Sallie B. Manning, May 29, 1860, in Williams-Chesnut-Manning Family Papers, SCL; Peter W. Hairston to Fanny Caldwell, January 26, 1859, in Peter Wilson Hairston Papers, SHC.

alike were divided as they agonized over the most critical electoral decision they had ever faced. Typical in this regard were the Devereuxs of North Carolina. The patriarch of the family, Thomas P. Devereux, was a Bell supporter and, as late as a month before the election, was still convinced that his candidate would be victorious. However, two of his sons-in-law represented opposite ends of the southern political spectrum. The first, Whig politician Henry Watkins Miller, was a Douglas elector and was just as confident as his father-in-law that his man would be elected. The other, South Carolina native Patrick Edmondston, cast his lot with Breckinridge, though he was "sure" that Lincoln would prevail and that the nation would be plunged into a civil war before the end of the year.[19]

Edmondston was far from alone in his belief that a Republican victory would lead to disunion and civil conflict. Although such extremists as Ruffin welcomed that result, most wealthy slaveholders viewed such a prospect with grave apprehension. As the months passed and Lincoln's election seemed increasingly certain, their anxiety intensified. In response to her husband's prediction of war, Kate Edmondston exclaimed: "God avert it!—and keep him from being a veritable Cassandra!" Other North Carolinians were just as concerned. In mid-October, Paul Cameron, who would shortly cast his ballot for Breckinridge and Lane, expressed his uneasiness about the upcoming election. While clinging to the slim hope that the fifteen slave states together with the two Pacific states of California and Oregon would unite in support of the Southern Democratic ticket, he conceded gloomily that the "Black Republicans" would likely "get the Government into their hands!" His brother-in-law, George W. Mordecai, was equally pessimistic. "God only knows what is to be the result of the approaching Election," he lamented to his wife, then in Philadelphia, where she witnessed a raucous procession of "the miserable Lincolnites" on the eve of the election. Another North Carolinian, contending that a Republican victory, at the very least, would undermine investments in slave property, stated unequivocally that "if Lincoln is elected the beginning of the end is upon us."[20]

19. Scarborough, ed., *The Diary of Edmund Ruffin*, I, 482; *"Journal of a Secesh Lady,"* ed. Crabtree and Patton, 6–10.

20. *"Journal of a Secesh Lady,"* ed. Crabtree and Patton, 6; Paul C. Cameron to Thomas Ruffin, October 12, 1860, in *The Papers of Thomas Ruffin,* ed. Hamilton, III, 99; Battle Noble & Co. to Paul C. Cameron, October 9, 1860, George W. Mordecai to wife Margaret, November 1, 1860, Margaret B. Mordecai to "My dear husband," November 3, 1860, J. N[illegible] to Paul C. Cameron, November 4, 1860, in Cameron Family Papers, SHC.

In South Carolina, the hotbed of secessionism, the mood was quite different in the weeks preceding the election. There, in September a group of prominent Low Country planters had formed a propaganda agency known as the 1860 Association, with the avowed purpose of organizing the South "in the event of the accession of Mr. Lincoln and the Republican party to power." Headed by Robert N. Gourdin, the 1860 Association disseminated 160,000 pamphlets in the two months before the election and was still soliciting funds to continue its activities in support of "Southern Union and Independence" in mid-November. As Gourdin explained in a printed circular directed to such sympathetic members of the elite as R. F. W. Allston and Langdon Cheves, Jr., it was imperative that the association counter efforts by the North "to soothe and conciliate the South" before state conventions were held in several of the slave states. One of the most effective pamphleteers for the association was John F. Townsend, an Edisto Island cotton planter who had opposed nullification in 1832 and separate-state secession in 1851. Following the walkout of the state's delegation at the Charleston Democratic Convention, however, he joined the ranks of the fire-eaters and authored two of the six different pamphlets distributed by the association. In the second of these pamphlets, entitled "The Doom of Slavery in the Union," Townsend delivered an impassioned appeal for the support of the non-slaveholders. "In no country of the world," he argued, "does the poor white man, whether slaveholder or non-slaveholder, occupy so enviable a position as in the slaveholding States of the South. His color here admits him to social and civil privileges which the white man enjoys nowhere else." In the slave states, continued Townsend, "the status and *color of the black race* become the badge of inferiority, and the poorest non-slaveholder may rejoice with the richest of his brethren of the white race, in the distinction of his color."[21]

Even as the 1860 Association sought to marshal support for secession in order to perpetuate the institution of slavery, other South Carolinians debated the legality of that controversial, yet seemingly inevitable, political course of action and the means by which it would be effected. In late October, a correspondent from Columbia chided John L. Manning for not going "far enough" in his

---

21. Robert N. Gourdin to R. F. W. Allston, November 19, 1860 [printed circular], in Easterby, ed., *South Carolina Rice Plantation*, 169–70; identical circular addressed to Langdon Cheves, in Langdon Cheves, Jr., Papers, SCHS; McCurry, *Masters of Small Worlds*, 280–83; *De Bow's Review* 30 (January 1861): 123.

politics. "A Southern Confederacy is the object of us all," wrote A. G. Baskin, and "the only difference between [us] is as to the *modus operandi* of bringing it about." Not only was Manning still reluctant to endorse separate-state action, but he also viewed secession as a revolutionary, rather than a constitutional, right. Baskin disagreed, contending that if one embraced the doctrine of state sovereignty, there could "be no revolution in a political sense." Defining revolution as "insubordination or resistance to authority," he asked Manning how secession could be called revolution if the states were truly sovereign. With respect to the question of whether or not a state should secede alone, Baskin concurred with the former governor that every effort should be made to procure the cooperation of other slave states. Failing that, however, "rather than submit to Northern aggression," he asserted defiantly, "I would raise the banner of resistance, and if we fail 'let us die with our feet to the foe and our face towards heaven.'"[22]

Several weeks earlier, another former South Carolina governor and elite slaveholder, R. F. W. Allston, was in Virginia, where, to his chagrin, he observed overwhelming support for the Bell-Everett ticket in the western and middle portions of the state. "They seem to have no idea of the principles for which we contend," he remarked disgustedly, "and of the disastrous consequences which must flow from a triumph of the Seward party." While attending a Democratic meeting in Richmond, Allston heard Governor Henry A. Wise propose an alternative to secession. His idea, reported the South Carolinian, was "not to secede from the Union, but to take the Union along by taking the Federal City and Treasury." Although sympathetic, Allston doubted the practicality of such a strategy, for it would require the "material and hearty aid and cooperation of both Maryland and Virginia." In the end, he concluded, "our only trust is in the Lord who sees and knows all things." Thus, on the eve of the election, it was clear that many of the most influential figures in the Palmetto State were prepared to take decisive action in the event of a Republican victory.[23]

As the returns began to trickle in on November 6, it soon became apparent

22. A. G. Baskin to John L. Manning, October 27, 1860, in Chesnut-Miller-Manning Papers, SCHS.

23. R. F. W. Allston to Benjamin Allston, October 6, 1860, in Easterby, ed., *South Carolina Rice Plantation*, 167–68.

that the worst fears of the moderate slaveholders and the covert desires of the ultra-secessionists were about to be realized. The dreaded "Black Republican," Abraham Lincoln, was on his way to the White House. The immediate reaction among the slaveholding nabobs ranged from consternation on the one hand to defiant optimism on the other. In South Carolina the response was predictable. On the day after the election, the wife of a North Carolina planter reported from Charleston that all state officials "*under* the [federal] *government*," except for the local postmaster, had resigned their positions and that the banks were expected to "suspend pretty much, today or tomorrow." The shopkeepers looked grim, she continued, and planters were hurriedly shipping their crops to market and "selling for less than *wld* be the case, merely to get cash while it can be obtained." Two weeks later, a grandson of Nathaniel Heyward predicted that the Palmetto State would "take leave of the Union" by "January next," hopefully in concert with her "Sister Cotton States" to the south. As he explained to a boyhood friend in Connecticut, "the condition of affairs at the North since the election of an Abolitionist for president makes it necessary for us to get away as quickly as possible." While agreeing that "the Union ought to be dissolved, as soon as practicable," James Chesnut, Jr., who resigned his U.S. Senate seat just four days after the election, was still reluctant to embrace separate-state action "until the whole field of other honorable remedies shall be exhausted." The best hope for success, argued Chesnut, was the formation of "a Southern Confederacy, consisting of the Cotton growing States."[24]

Outside of South Carolina, the reaction to Lincoln's election was mixed and the immediate course of action less clear. Young Cynthia Pugh of Louisiana, doubtless influenced by her elders, was almost as upset by the election of Lincoln as the South Carolinians. Remarking to her cousin, Frank Winchester, that she would have voted for Breckinridge if she had been able to cast a ballot, she vowed that if "old Lincoln would come here," she would greet him with a barrage of rotten eggs. "I would shower them on him with a very good will," exclaimed the excited teenager. Quite different was the mood of young Frank Winchester's father, Josiah, and many of the latter's Natchez associates. To the

24. Carey North Pettigrew to husband Charles L. Pettigrew, November 7, 1860, in Pettigrew Family Papers, SHC; Edward Barnwell Heyward to James A. Lord, November 20, 1860, in Edward Barnwell Heyward Letters, SCL; James Chesnut, Jr., to "the Editors of the Camden Democrat," [November ?, 1860], in Chesnut-Miller-Manning Papers, SCHS.

elder Winchester, secession in response to Lincoln's election was simply un-
thinkable. It was, said he, akin to "committing suicide for fear we shall die a
natural death." In like manner, fellow Natchezian Stephen Duncan termed secession a "monstrous idea" because of its potential economic impact on the
South. "If the Union is to be dissolved," he remarked shortly before the election,
"I, for one, would be for selling out my possessions immediately." A neighboring planter in Louisiana was much more optimistic in the aftermath of the election. In a letter to a prominent Natchez Unionist, R. J. Bowman speculated that
the election of Lincoln might actually become "a blessing to the Country," for
if it led to the calling of a national convention to propose a "final settlement of
the Slavery question," as he and his conservative friends desired, "it could be
made the means of settling that humbug, abolition, & settling it forever." Bowman was not alone in his call for such a convention, but by December, 1860, it
was too late to hope for any resolution of the sectional controversy from such a
meeting.[25]

In the Upper South, the prevailing mood in the wake of Lincoln's election
was one of apprehension. "The bad passions of men are raging throughout this
once happy America," lamented a deeply troubled William S. Pettigrew in mid-
November. Three weeks later, following a visit to the legislative halls in Raleigh,
he reported that the legislature was sharply divided, "some sympathising with
Southern Sentiment on the subject of disunion, and some of the opposing way
of thinking." However, the former were "gaining ground" and would probably
prevail unless there was "some conciliatory action on the part of the North."
From Washington, D.C., Benjamin Tayloe charged that "men acting like
monomaniacs" seemed "intent on *destroying* the *Country*" simply because the
Democrats had lost control of the government. But from what he could learn,
there was every reason to believe that Lincoln was "disposed to be a conservative
Whig President," just as inclined to "do justice to the South" as the two previous
chief executives. The South could "get what it wants," contended Tayloe, if it
acted with "firmness & dignity" and eschewed extremist rhetoric. Like Louisiana planter R. J. Bowman, he favored a national convention, believing that

25. Cynthia Pugh to "Dear cousin Frank," November 23, [?], [1860], in Winchester Family Pa-
pers, CAH; James, *Antebellum Natchez*, 290–91, quoting Natchez *Courier*, September 19, October 6
(Duncan), November 24 (Winchester), 1860; R. J. Bowman to A. K. Farrar, December 14, 1860, in
Alexander K. Farrar Papers, LSU.

northern economic self-interest would override the abolition "humbug" and render concessions to the South more palatable. As Tayloe put it, "a Henry Clay would settle the whole matter." In the absence of the Great Compromiser, however, he remained concerned. Warning that "the Union is seriously in danger," he urged his brother in Alabama to rally the pro-Union forces in that state.[26]

The fears expressed by Pettigrew and Tayloe soon materialized as South Carolina, the most disaffected of the slave states, moved swiftly to sever its ties to the Union. The Palmetto State was as united as any political entity could be as events approached a dramatic climax. Of its prominent leaders, only Benjamin F. Perry and James L. Petigru remained wedded to the Union. Thus, less than a week after Lincoln's election, a unanimous legislature called for the election of delegates to a state convention that was scheduled to meet in Columbia on December 17. Those delegates, elected on December 6, included such prominent slaveholding nabobs as John L. Manning, John S. Preston, Langdon Cheves, Jr., John Izard Middleton, Robert Barnwell Rhett, and John F. Townsend, and, in the words of one authority, the convention as a whole "comprised the very elite of South Carolina." After adopting a secession resolution at their initial meeting, the delegates, alarmed by an outbreak of smallpox in Columbia, decided to shift the convention to Charleston. There, on Thursday afternoon, December 20, the 170 delegates, without dissent or even debate, approved the Ordinance of Secession. That evening, as the delegates assembled to affix their signatures to the document, the city took on a carnival-like atmosphere. Just a short distance down Meeting Street from Secession Hall, where the signing took place, the bells of St. Michael's Church began to toll. The sound of rockets and firecrackers reverberated throughout the city, mingling with the roar of cannons located on The Battery. Barrels of burning pine rosin illuminated the major streets, and the strains of martial music wafted through the cool night air. It was truly a joyous occasion for the citizens of Charleston. Little did they imagine the carnage that lay ahead.[27]

26. William S. Pettigrew to James C. Johnston, November 15, December 6, 1860, in Hayes Collection, SHC; B. O. Tayloe to "Dear Brother" [William H.], November 27, 1860, in Tayloe Family Papers, VHS.

27. Schultz, *Nationalism and Sectionalism in South Carolina*, 225–30 (quotation, p. 229); Scarborough, ed., *The Diary of Edmund Ruffin*, I, 511–13; E. B. Long, *The Civil War Day by Day: An Almanac, 1861–1865* (Garden City, N.Y., 1971), 11–13.

As South Carolina took the fateful step of asserting its independence, many wealthy slaveholders outside the Palmetto State looked on aghast. They had long feared that the impetuous behavior of the South Carolina hotheads might precipitate a confrontation from which there could be no return. Nowhere was that concern more pronounced than among the slaveholders of her more moderate sister state to the north. Thus, during his brief visit with North Carolina legislators in early December, William Pettigrew found that, despite their differences over the proper course of action to adopt, all were united in their "condemnation" of "the imperious course of South Carolina." Actually, the political animosity between the two Carolinas was of long-standing duration and not merely a product of the secession crisis of 1860–1861. It could be traced at least as far back as the nullification controversy of 1832, when William C. Preston, one of the leading nullifiers, had hurled particularly "offensive epithets" at the Old North State. More recently, the Charleston *Mercury,* the organ of the Rhetts, had abused North Carolina politicians with similar denunciatory rhetoric. Resentful over what they perceived to be the arrogant, supercilious demeanor of the South Carolinians, most North Carolinians were disinclined to follow the political lead of their neighbors to the south. This hostility, predicted Pettigrew in late December, would cause North Carolina "to hesitate long before adopting a course" that would unite her with a state that had "ever treated her so discourtiously [*sic*]." Within a month, however, Pettigrew would begin to modify his position as he moved gradually and painfully toward the secessionist camp.[28]

Of all the great North Carolina planters, no other was more vehement in his castigation of South Carolina than Pettigrew's close friend, James C. Johnston. A die-hard Unionist, the seventy-eight-year-old Johnston was in a surly mood as the year 1861 dawned. Deeply troubled by the storm clouds descending over his beloved country, he began a letter to his namesake, James Johnston Pettigrew, with this sarcastic greeting: "Xmas was no doubt a very merry one with you in Charleston where every body is drunk or crazy & I hope the new year may be a happy one and that all of you may come to your senses before the end of it." He then proceeded to lambaste both South Carolina and the Bu-

---

28. William S. Pettigrew to James C. Johnston, December 6, 1860, in Hayes Collection, SHC; William S. Pettigrew to J. Johnston Pettigrew, December 29, 1860, January 19, 1861, in Pettigrew Family Papers, SHC. See also W. S. Pettigrew to Johnston, January 24, 1861, in Hayes Collection, SHC.

chanan administration, charging that the "revolution" of the former "will be a blot on her history darker than that of the French Revolution" and denouncing what he termed "the corruption & imbecility" of the latter. South Carolina, Johnston continued derisively, reminded him "of an old woman who has been engaged in scoulding all her life until at last she works herself up into a fit of hystericks and has all kinds of fantasies and imaginations . . . & like a wild cat is ready to fly at any person who look[s] at her."[29] For the next month and a half, Johnston sounded the same refrain in a series of letters to William Pettigrew, whose increasing silence on the political crisis finally alerted Johnston to the diverging loyalties of the two close friends. In his last letter to Pettigrew, written in mid-February, Johnston contrasted the motives of the Revolutionary War leaders with those of the present day. "The first," he maintained, had "sacrificed theirself & their interest for their country," while "the latter have sacrificed their country for their own interest & to gratify their vile passion to rule or ruin."[30]

There are others who denounced the rash course of South Carolina. Among them was Thomas P. Devereux, another of the largest slaveholders in the Tar Heel State. Much to the chagrin of his daughter, Kate Edmondston, who was married to a South Carolina fire-eater, the crusty Devereux began to berate South Carolina during the summer of 1860 and continued with his abuse well into the new year. Thus, upon her return to North Carolina in mid-January after a visit to Aiken and Charleston, she "found Father much excited against S C." He could not "say enough of the folly of her conduct," she noted, adding apprehensively: "I hope he will not say so much to Mr Edmondston." There were even a few South Carolinians who criticized the radical course of their native state. A week after the secession ordinance was adopted, Mary Petigru, who apparently shared the moderate views of her brother James, expressed dismay that South Carolina had earned the "unenviable distinction" of being the first to break the bonds of union. "What greavous [sic] wrongs had she to complain of more than all the rest!" she exclaimed.[31] Much more extreme was the reaction of Colonel John N. Williams, wealthy Society Hill planter and mill

29. James C. Johnston to J. Johnston Pettigrew, January 2, 1861, in Pettigrew Family Papers, SHC.

30. James C. Johnston to William S. Pettigrew, January 1, 18, February 18 (quotations), 1861, in Pettigrew Family Papers, SHC.

31. *"Journal of a Secesh Lady,"* ed. Crabtree and Patton, 6, 14, 33 (quotations), 38; Mary Petigru to Adele Petigru Allston, December 27, 1860, in Easterby, ed., *South Carolina Rice Plantation,* 171.

owner. Williams, a staunch Unionist, was so incensed by the secession of his state that when celebrants began firing near his door, "he took what was intended for a harmless Salute, for a personal insult to & triumph over himself" and, seizing a shotgun, fired several volleys in the general direction of the revelers. Mistakenly interpreting the shots as a "friendly response," the visitors departed before Williams could load his more lethal rifles and musket. Still enraged by the incident, the volatile patriarch went to town the following day and announced to all who would listen what he had done and what he had intended to do if the secessionists had not retired. As one commentator remarked, this action doubtless dealt "a death blow to all future pleasant intercourse" between Williams and his neighbors.[32]

At the eleventh hour, a few influential figures outside the South had sought to derail the secession steamroller by appealing to acquaintances within the Palmetto State for restraint. For example, just ten days before South Carolina severed its ties with the Union, Dennis Hart Mahan, a distinguished professor at the U.S. Military Academy and the father of Alfred Thayer Mahan, pleaded with former governor R. F. W. Allston to use his influence to check the secession movement before it was too late. The relationship between Allston and Mahan dated back to the early 1820s when both were cadets at West Point and was doubtless renewed thirty years later when Allston's eldest son Benjamin also attended the academy.[33] Noting that he himself was a Virginian by birth, Mahan alluded to the virulent antislavery sentiment in Europe that he had observed during a trip abroad in 1856 and argued that South Carolina and her sister slave states would be completely isolated if they seceded in defense of "our peculiar institution." Not only would news of the secession of South Carolina "be greeted in Europe as the first step . . . in the downfall of this great Empire, but also one towards the extinction of slavery." Terming disunion "the greatest calamity that could befal [sic] not only this country but Europe," Mahan called on South Carolina to act responsibly in the current crisis so that she might "look back upon the results without remorse." Unfortunately, Mahan's plea fell upon

32. "Journal of a Secesh Lady," ed. Crabtree and Patton, 26.

33. Mark M. Boatner III, The Civil War Dictionary (New York, 1959), 501–502; James I. Robertson, Jr., Stonewall Jackson: The Man, the Soldier, the Legend (New York, 1997), 33; Easterby, ed., South Carolina Rice Plantation, 18. The elder Allston graduated from West Point in 1821, Mahan in 1824, and Benjamin Allston in 1853.

deaf ears, for Allston had long been one of the most ardent secessionists in the state.[34]

Once South Carolina crossed the Rubicon, the spotlight shifted to the other slave states, especially those in the Deep South. Before the end of November, four other states—Mississippi, Alabama, Florida, and Georgia—had already called conventions, and two others, Louisiana and Texas, would soon follow suit. As they had in South Carolina, the elite slaveholders would play a significant role in these assemblages, especially those of Louisiana and Georgia. Despite spirited opposition from conservative forces in the last two states, the result was virtually a foregone conclusion in each of the six Lower South states.[35] Two days after Christmas, Maryland slaveholder Edward Lloyd, then on a visit to his absentee plantation in Tensas Parish, Louisiana, predicted that "these states will all go out of the Union." The opponents of immediate secession would try to extract concessions from the North, but if, as Lloyd thought, "their demands are not acceded to, they are for going out . . . & secession will be almost unanimous in the cotton states." The consequence of such action, he added presciently, "they seem not to have thought of."[36]

Lloyd's analysis proved to be accurate, for during the month of January, secession fever swept across the lower tier of slave states. As elite slaveholders in the Upper South, most of them conditional Unionists, looked on helplessly, the Union began to disintegrate before their eyes. One of these observers was North Carolina planter Lewis Thompson, a staunch American-Whig Unionist who ultimately gave grudging support to the Confederacy. During the critical period from November to the end of January, Thompson received periodic reports on political developments in the Gulf South from two brothers-in-law, one a very reluctant secessionist in Louisiana and the other an enthusiastic disunionist from Alabama. In late November, the former, Kenneth M. Clark, reported gloomily that public opinion had forced the governor to convene the state legislature for the purpose of recommending "the holding of a State Convention." Unless the conservative forces aroused themselves and elected "good men" to the convention, Clark feared that the "demagogues" would prevail and Louisi-

34. D. H. Mahan to R. F. W. Allston, December 10, 1860, in R. F. W. Allston Papers, SCHS.

35. Nevins, *The Emergence of Lincoln*, II, 318–25.

36. Edward Lloyd [VI] to "Dear Edwd" [son Edward Lloyd VII], December 27, 1860, in Lloyd Family Papers, MHS.

ana would join the "feeble list of States that must excite the pity and ridicule of the world." For Clark, the key lay with the border states. "If they are for resistance we can safely count on a United South," but without them and without the "moral force" of favorable world public opinion, secession would be nothing short of "folly and inexcusable madness."[37]

Quite different was the mood of Clark's brother in Alabama. As early as December 10, William Clark predicted that his state would "certainly" withdraw from the Union within a month. Noting that the election of delegates to the state convention was scheduled for Christmas Eve, he asserted confidently that no more than twenty of the one hundred delegates would be "Union men." His county, he added, was "unanimous for secession and separate state action." Two weeks later, Clark reported that "the breaking up of our government" and the formation of a new one had become such an "all absorbing" topic "with us here that . . . business of all kinds is at a stand still." Finally, as the Alabama Convention assembled in early January, Clark defiantly informed Thompson, "Our people are calmly and fully determined never to submit to Lincoln's administration, or to any Compromise with the Northern States." Like many others in the Deep South, Clark could not understand the reluctance of the border states to unite with their sister slave states in a new southern confederation. As he pointed out, they had suffered "so much more from Northern fanaticism, [and] from actual loss in their property," and they were "equally interested in slavery." Before he could complete this letter, Clark received word from a neighbor that the convention had just passed the ordinance of secession, "and Alabama no longer belongs to the United States of America." Somewhat chastened by this intelligence, he expressed the hope that "the Old North State," the land of his birth, would soon follow, and above all, that they would "have no war, nor even rumors of Wars."[38]

On January 7, just as the Alabama Convention opened, voters in Louisiana went to the polls to elect delegates to their convention. On that day, wealthy Bayou Lafourche sugar planter Alexander F. Pugh recorded his thoughts in his plantation journal. "We are bound to secede," he wrote, "and the sooner it is done the better." His entry for the following day was even more belligerent. "Down with the old confederation for the South," he exclaimed. "Let the Yan-

37. Kenneth M. Clark to Lewis Thompson, November 26, 1860, in Lewis Thompson Papers, SHC.
38. William M. Clark to Lewis Thompson, December 10, 22, 1860, January 10, 1861, *ibid.*

kees take care of themselves and ever after this hold their peace about the affairs of Louisiana." Four days later, he noted that state troops had taken possession of federal forts within the state, an action taken several days before by Alabama. "This act will render secession inevitable," observed Pugh. "We cannot retrace our steps."[39] In late January, as members of the Louisiana Convention began their meeting in Baton Rouge, a dejected Kenneth Clark informed his North Carolina kinsman that there was no longer any doubt that Louisiana would "cut loose its moorings from a safe and secure harbor to drift God only knows where in the wide water of a tempestuous sea." Admitting that he was "sad and discouraged," Clark, nevertheless, felt that he had no option but to take his chances "on this secession craft." Thus were the conservative voices silenced within the Pelican State.[40]

The elite slaveholders were well represented in the Louisiana Secession Convention, and they also dominated the delegation that the convention sent to Montgomery when the Provisional Congress of the nascent Confederate States of America met in early February.[41] Indeed, two of them, John Perkins and Lemuel Conner, composed the initial draft of the secession document. At the opening session of the convention on January 23, Perkins was appointed to chair a Committee of Fifteen to draw up the Ordinance of Secession. That afternoon, Perkins and his close friend, Lemuel P. Conner, met in the former's room and prepared a draft that was accepted later in the day by the full committee. Two days later, on Friday, January 25, South Carolina nabobs John L. Manning and John S. Preston, both of whom had long operated huge absentee sugar estates in Ascension Parish, addressed the convention, "urging immediate secession & cooperation" with those states that had already left the Union. At

39. Alexander Franklin Pugh Plantation Diaries, Vol. 2 (TS), January 7, 8, 12, 1861, LSU; William M. Clark to Lewis Thompson, January 10, 1861, in Lewis Thompson Papers, SHC.

40. Kenneth M. Clark to Lewis Thompson, January 23, 1861, in Lewis Thompson Papers, SHC.

41. Slightly more than half of the 127 delegates in the Louisiana Convention were members of the planter class, and 6 of them—William Ruffin Barrow, Josiah Chambers, Lemuel P. Conner, Henry Marshall, John Perkins, Jr., and Edward Sparrow—were among the largest slaveholders in the state. Of the 6 delegates to Montgomery, 4—Marshall, Perkins, Sparrow, and Duncan F. Kenner—were elite planters, and a fifth, Charles M. Conrad, was the brother of wealthy East Baton Parish planter Frederick D. Conrad. *Encyclopedia of Southern History,* ed. David C. Roller and Robert W. Twyman (Baton Rouge, 1979), 743; Warner and Yearns, eds., *Biographical Register of the Confederate Congress,* 291; Craig A. Bauer, *A Leader Among Peers: The Life and Times of Duncan Farrar Kenner* (Lafayette, La., 1993), 174–75.

noon on the same day, the ordinance was presented to the convention, and "after a long exciting debate, not participated in by the Secessionists," it was approved at 1:50 P.M. the following day by a vote of 113 to 17. The Pelican flag was then placed on the Speaker's giant marble desk, and following a blessing by a Catholic priest, it was "taken out & hoisted on the Capitol." The convention thereupon adjourned to meet in New Orleans the following Tuesday.[42]

As had been the case earlier in South Carolina, adoption of the secession ordinance in Louisiana was accompanied by numerous manifestations of joy and approbation. Shortly after the Pelican flag was raised over the Capitol in Baton Rouge, residents rejoiced amid the sounds of "military music" and the "booming of cannon." West of the city, on his Assumption Parish sugar plantation, Alexander Pugh recorded his praise for "the men who had the courage to take this first step to prosperity," which he predicted would "be as permanent as earthly things may be." When the convention assembled again in New Orleans on January 29, the atmosphere rivaled that in Charleston a month before. As the delegates continued their work selecting delegates to the Montgomery Convention and debating whether or not to encumber them with instructions, the celebration continued unabated outside. Lemuel Conner described the scene in the Crescent City in early February, just two days after the Provisional Congress convened in Montgomery. Numerous houses, especially those along Canal Street, were illuminated with "gas & candles & lamps & transparencies in every window & all over the front"; flags fluttered everywhere; soldiers paraded; and the sounds of "drums beating" and "bands of music" could be heard throughout the city. Later, as Conner returned to his hotel following a committee meeting at an office on Canal Street, he "found the street filled with men, women & children—not merely the sidewalks but the entire street." Estimating the crowd at not less than 5,000, he finally made his way back to his room at the St. Charles, where he soon witnessed "a fine display of rockets & fireworks" just across the street. Such scenes were repeated on a smaller scale in cities and towns across the Lower South as citizens celebrated what they hoped fervently would be a peaceful separation from the "Black Republican" North.[43]

42. Draft Copy of Louisiana Ordinance of Secession, with letter of explanation, dated Natchez, March 6, 1936, signed by Lemuel P. Conner, [Jr.], City Clerk of Natchez, in Lemuel P. Conner Papers, HNO; Lemuel P. Conner to wife Fanny, January 25, 26 (quotations), 1861, *ibid.*

43. Alexander Franklin Pugh Plantation Diaries, Vol. 2, January 27, 1861, LSU; Lemuel P. Conner to Fanny Conner, January 26, 29, February 6, 1861, in Lemuel P. Conner Papers, HNO.

In marked contrast to their participation in the Louisiana and South Carolina secession conventions, the large slaveholders did not play a major role in the Provisional Congress of the Confederacy or, indeed, in either of the two subsequent congresses. Apart from the Louisiana delegation, only two members of the elite, Howell Cobb of Georgia and Barnwell Rhett of South Carolina, were members of the Provisional Congress. Cobb was elected to preside over the convention, and Rhett chaired both the standing committee on foreign affairs and the committee that was charged with the task of framing a permanent constitution for the new nation. In his latter capacity, Rhett was instrumental in securing the adoption of a number of changes from the old United States Constitution. Chief among these were the following provisions in the Confederate Constitution: Congress could levy tariffs for revenue only and was prohibited from granting bounties to promote any branch of industry (Art. I, Sect. 8); there were to be no appropriations for internal improvements with the exception of harbor navigational aids (Art. I, Sect. 8, Clause 3); the president and vice-president were elected for a term of six years and were not eligible for reelection (Art. II, Sect. 1), though Rhett would have accepted eligibility for reelection after a one-term interval; the president had the authority to remove civil servants provided he notified the Senate of the reasons for removal (Art. II, Sect. 3, Clause 3); and, finally, upon the request of three or more states, Congress was obliged to call a convention to consider amendments to the Constitution (Art. V). Rhett contended after the war that if the latter provision had been part of the original Constitution, "the vast discontents which preceeded [sic] the War, and made it inevitable, would have been easily arrested and allayed; and the States assembled in Convention, would have settled amicably all their differences."[44]

Cobb and Rhett served only in the Provisional Congress, but three Louisiana planter barons—Duncan Kenner, Perkins, and Edward Sparrow—were elected to both regular congresses, and another, Henry Marshall, was a member of the First Congress. Kenner was chairman of the House Ways and Means Committee but spent most of his time trying to gain European recognition for the Confederacy. Sparrow, who served in the Senate in the First and Second Congresses, headed the important Military Affairs Committee, where he was a

44. Warner and Yearns, eds., *Biographical Register of the Confederate Congress*, 56, 206, 290–93; R. B. Rhett to [nephew] T. Stuart Rhett, [1868], in Robert Barnwell Rhett, Sr., Papers, SCHS.

strong advocate of the centralization of military authority. Perkins, a former U.S. congressman, focused his attention on economic planning and generally supported the policies of President Davis, though he opposed conscription and the arming of the slaves near the end of the war.[45] Despite the contributions of these men, it is clear that the elite planters were not a dominant force in the political councils of the Confederacy. Nor had they been at the national level under the old government.[46] Their financial empires were simply too extensive to afford them the luxury of undertaking laborious and time-consuming public service. In short, the vast majority of them were planter-capitalists, not politicians.

Although most Southerners hoped that secession could be effected peacefully, the evidence suggests that many of the large slaveholders were perceptive enough to realize that this was a vain hope and that war would likely ensue. Thus, on the day the Provisional Congress elected Jefferson Davis to lead the new government, Duncan Kenner confided to former Louisiana governor André B. Roman: "From the news that we receive here, I am sorry to say, that I do not feel as certain of a peaceful solution of our difficulties as I did when I left home." Two leading North Carolina planters had reached the same conclusion the month before. Paul Cameron, who was then moving painfully toward the secessionist camp, pronounced himself "very unhappy" with the present state of political affairs. "I love the Union," and "I love peace," declared the disillusioned Cameron, "[but] I think the Union is gone and we shall have war, if the Military men can get it underway." Even more distraught was die-hard Unionist James C. Johnston, who warned on New Year's Day that the nation might soon be consumed by either "the most wretched anarchy or the most horrible & bloody civil war that ever was recorded in history."[47]

Realizing that war was a distinct probability, some elite slaveholders in the most vulnerable Atlantic seaboard states began to make military preparations

45. Warner and Yearns, eds., *Biographical Register of the Confederate Congress*, 144, 166–67, 192–93, 230.

46. See Table 5. Only twenty-two elite slaveholders in this study, all but one from the three states of Georgia, Louisiana, and South Carolina, served in the U.S. Congress.

47. Duncan F. Kenner to Governor A. B. Roman, February 9, 1861, in Jean Ursin La Villebeuvre and Family Papers, LSU; Paul C. Cameron to Thomas Ruffin, January 21, 1861, in *The Papers of Thomas Ruffin*, ed. Hamilton, III, 114; James C. Johnston to "My dear Friend" [William S. Pettigrew], January 1, 1861, in Pettigrew Family Papers, SHC.

long before the firing on Fort Sumter. Specifically, they procured arms from northern suppliers, raised military companies for home defense, and furnished hands to construct coastal fortifications. Not surprisingly, the South Carolinians were the first to act. Even before his state seceded, R. F. W. Allston equipped two local units with cavalry saber belts and belt plates. Then, on Christmas Eve, just four days after South Carolina proclaimed its independence, he agreed to furnish as many hands as he could spare to build defensive earthworks in his home district of Georgetown.[48] Of all the great Low Country planters, however, no other was more energetic in developing defenses to repel a possible invasion of the unprotected coast between Georgetown and Savannah than Langdon Cheves, Jr., whose rice plantations bordered the Savannah River. In late December, he organized and pledged to pay one-half of the expense of arming the Palmetto Hussars, a sixty-three-man unit designed to protect the plantations on both sides of that river. As Cheves explained to the state Board of Ordnance, the Hussars constituted "the only defence of at least twenty five miles of exposed coast on the mouth & channel of the Savannah River," an area with "a population of much less than ten per cent whites." By mid-January, Cheves had managed to equip his men with Gilbert Smith carbines, procured with the assistance of the Board of Ordnance, and Navy Colt pistols, shipped directly from the Colt factory in Hartford, Connecticut, to the Charleston factorage firm of Gravely & Pringle. The pistols arrived just in time, for, on the very day they were received in Charleston, Colt announced that it was suspending further arms shipments to the South. However, Gravely & Pringle assured Cheves that they could "procure them from another source," and they anticipated "little difficulty in continuing to fill orders." Accordingly, two weeks later, the factors offered to sell Cheves a lot of .44 caliber, twenty-one-inch Colt rifles at a cost of $32.50 each.[49]

Cheves also took the lead in strengthening the fortifications at Fort Pulaski, which guarded the sea approach to the city of Savannah. On January 2, more

48. Receipts for Arms Donations, Citadel Academy, December 8, 1860, Marion Light Troop, December 17, 1860, E. Williams [?] to R. F. W. Allston, December 24, 1860, in R. F. W. Allston Papers, SCHS.

49. Langdon Cheves to Board of Ordnance, December 29, 1860 (first quotation), January 2, 1861, Anthony Barbot, Secy. Ordnance Bureau, to Cheves, December 30, 1860, January 5, 1861, Gravely & Pringle to Cheves, January 11, 18 (second quotation), February 1, 1861, in Langdon Cheves, Jr., Papers, SCHS.

than two weeks before Georgia seceded, Cheves received confidential information from Savannah that, by order of the governor, the unmanned fort would
be occupied the following day by state troops. Immediately after Georgia forces
took control, slaveowners in the near vicinity began to furnish laborers to shore
up the fortifications. In mid-January, in response to a request from his brother,
Chatham County rice planter John R. Cheves, Langdon called upon some of
the large South Carolina slaveholders to assist in the work at the fort. In his
capacity as commissioner of roads in St. Peter's Parish, Beaufort District, he
assured them that "all work that has been contributed or shall now be contributed to the public defences in this state or Georgia will be credited to [them]
as Road work." On the day that Cheves issued this appeal for additional hands,
there were 117 ditchers working at the fort, and his brother estimated that the
defenses could be completed in five days with 100 more hands. Those laborers
were soon forthcoming, as Cheves's neighbors responded unhesitatingly to his
solicitation. Joseph Manigault wrote: "I thoroughly agree with you in the desire
of a fraternal feeling between the poeple [sic] of South Carolina and Georgia,
and would be glad if you would accept the charge of my negroes in aiding to
place fort Pulaski in a state of defense." Even Allen S. Izard, still a committed
Unionist as late as mid-February, expressed complete agreement with Cheves's
views and offered to place "all [his] hands subject to lateral road duty at
[Cheves's] disposal for Fort Pulaski." Buttressed by such cooperation from the
rice planters in both states, the work at Fort Pulaski was soon completed.[50]

As the South Carolinians feverishly prepared to defend their state and as
crowds in the other cotton states celebrated their newly declared independence,
many conditional Unionists in the Upper South began to reassess their position.
This was particularly notable in North Carolina, where, in early January, the
legislature appropriated $300,000 for military defense. One North Carolina
planter who illustrates the gradual transition in political allegiance is William S.
Pettigrew. Just four days before the election of Lincoln, Pettigrew still remained
steadfast in his commitment to the Union. "I think it wisest for the South to
fight her battles in the Union," he wrote. "The Government of the United

50. A[lexander] R. Lawton to Langdon Cheves, January 2, 1861, J. R. Cheves to "Dear Lang,"
January 15, 17, 1861, Langdon Cheves to [Dr. Screven, et al.], January 17, 1861, Joseph Manigault to
[Langdon Cheves], January 26, 1861, Allen S. Izard to Langdon Cheves, January 18, 1861, ibid; Izard
to "My dear Counsellor" [Benjamin Douglas Silliman], February 13, 1861, in Allen Smith Izard
Letter, SCHS.

States," continued Pettigrew, "is ours as much as theirs," so "let us not abandon our rich inheritance to our enemies." During the next two months, however, as the political crisis intensified, he began to waver. By late December he was becoming convinced that there was little hope for the preservation of southern rights within the Union. In a letter, written but never sent, to his more militant brother in Charleston, he declared: "We are, in North Carolina, preeminently a conservative and union loving people; but, when we become convinced that there is nothing but subjugation before us, we will not hesitate to adopt such measures as will be necessary for the security of our rights."[51] Yet the prospect of impending disunion was still deeply troubling to Pettigrew. At the close of the year, he exclaimed to his close friend James C. Johnston: "May God take care of us amid the madness that rages!" However, his lingering hopes for a peaceful reconciliation dissipated during the first two months of the new year as the North rejected the Crittenden Resolutions, which, in the words of Pettigrew, were "unexceptionable & no more than just to both sections." Finally, on March 5, the day after Lincoln's inauguration, Pettigrew angrily cancelled his subscription to the *National Intelligencer* because that paper had agreed to serve as the official organ of the "president of the depraved and revolutionary Black Republican Party."[52] Pettigrew's transformation was complete. He was soon elected to the North Carolina Secession Convention, where, on May 20, he cast his vote for secession. As the church bells rang and cannons roared in honor of the occasion, the reluctant secessionist "felt convinced, indeed," that he was "in the midst of a revolution."[53]

Other elite slaveholders in the Upper South followed essentially the same course as Pettigrew. Paul Cameron, who was defeated in his quest for a seat in the same convention, allegedly because of resentment against his great wealth, had been a die-hard Whig in 1850. "God help us," he exclaimed, after that party

51. William S. Pettigrew to J. Johnston Pettigrew, November 2, December 29, 1861, in Pettigrew Family Papers, SHC.

52. William S. Pettigrew to James C. Johnston, December 27, 1860, January 24, 1861, both in Hayes Collection, SHC; W. S. Pettigrew to J. J. Pettigrew, January 19, 1861, W. S. Pettigrew to E. H. Willis, February 14, 1861, W. S. Pettigrew to "The Editors of the 'National Intelligencer,'" March 5, 1861, in Pettigrew Family Papers, SHC.

53. William S. Pettigrew to William F. Beasley, May 21, 1861, Pettigrew to "My dear Brother" [J. Johnston Pettigrew], May 18 [*sic*, 22], 1861, Pettigrew to "My dear Sister" [Carey?], May 22, 1861 (quotation), in Pettigrew Family Papers, SHC.

suffered what he termed "a perfect Buena Vista defeat" in the state elections of that year.[54] But a decade later, fearful that the "Black Republicans" would gain control of the government, Cameron cast his vote for Breckinridge and Lane, and when those fears materialized, he became an early convert to secession.[55] Yet another conditional Unionist among the North Carolina elite was Peter Wilson Hairston. Two years before the war, he asserted that he was "for the Union so long as it can be maintained on terms of equality and of honour," but he added that, should disunion occur, he would prefer that the slave states seek the protection of Great Britain rather than submit to rule "by the Yankees." When war came, Hairston and other members of his immensely wealthy family gave unequivocal support to the Confederacy. He later remarked: "Every day . . . convinces me" that "we remained in it [the Union] much longer than we ought."[56]

Others were more reluctant to switch their allegiance. Thomas P. Devereux, the largest slaveholder in the Tar Heel State at midcentury, remained loyal to the Union well into the spring of 1861, doubtless influenced by family associations and concern for the preservation of his great fortune.[57] Devereux, a self-styled "old Federalist," was in a state of deep despair as the new year dawned. Terming "the insanity of South Carolina . . . one of the most striking things [he] ever heard or read of," he proposed to counter the projected confederacy of cotton states with a confederation of border states that would include as many free states as would join it, "provided they are . . . homogeneous on the slave question." The attempt by South Carolina and its sister states in the Gulf South "to found a Republic upon negroes & cotton exclusively," he remarked sarcastically, "does not meet my ideas of either strength or durability." A month later, Devereux had a new formula for saving the Union. Declaring that he was

54. William H. Ruffin to Paul C. Cameron, June 4, 1861, Paul C. Cameron to "My dear Father" [Duncan Cameron], August 3, 1850, both in Cameron Family Papers, SHC.

55. Paul C. Cameron to Judge Thomas Ruffin, October 12, 1860, in *The Papers of Thomas Ruffin*, ed. Hamilton, III, 99; Battle Noble & Co. to Cameron, October 9, 1860, in Cameron Family Papers, SHC.

56. Peter W. Hairston to Fanny Caldwell, [April 18, 1859], Hairston to Fanny Caldwell Hairston, April 4, September 26, 1861, in Peter Wilson Hairston Papers, SHC.

57. Devereux's mother was a granddaughter of Jonathan Edwards, and he married, successively, women from Connecticut and New York. *Dictionary of North Carolina Biography*, ed. Powell, II, 60–61.

strongly in favor of the Union "as it is," with guarantees for the security of present institutions, he urged Judge Thomas Ruffin to use his influence to delay secession. Although he denied the right of secession, he was willing to concede the principle if execution were postponed. "Do not plunge us into a state of anarchy without any warning," he pleaded.[58] Not until Lincoln's inaugural address did Devereux begin to waver. "Father does not like it & looks gloomy," noted his daughter on March 6. "Lincoln's intense vulgarity disgusts him," she added. Finally, after the firing on Fort Sumter and Lincoln's subsequent call for troops to suppress the rebellion, Devereux felt obliged to support the Confederacy, though, as he admitted, he was still "excessively down cast by the state of our national affairs." The only hope "of escaping an infinity of troubles," he observed gloomily, was that the miscalculation of aid from the border states by Lincoln, whom he now termed "the stupid blockhead," might lead to "a pause & time for reflection." But, realistically, he had little hope of "reclaiming that prosperity we have so grossly undervalued & so foolishly" squandered.[59] In the end, the war he had sought so desperately to avoid cost him an estimated $750,000 in slaves and other property and forced him to declare bankruptcy in May, 1868, just ten months before his death.[60]

Another reluctant convert to disunion was William H. Tayloe, a Virginia planter with extensive absentee holdings in Alabama. Describing himself as an "obstinate Unionist," Tayloe accepted the election of Lincoln with relative equanimity and urged Buchanan to move decisively against the seceders. "*I cant believe yet*," he exclaimed to his brother a week after the election, that "we have madmen enough in the Country to destroy the Union." But shortly after Lincoln's inauguration, his attitude changed dramatically. Disappointed in the president's cabinet appointments, especially Salmon P. Chase as secretary of the treasury and Montgomery Blair as postmaster-general, and now convinced, as he had not been previously, that the Republicans were indeed "Abolitionists,"

58. Thomas P. Devereux to George W. Mordecai, January 1, 8, 1861, in George W. Mordecai Papers, SHC; Devereux to Judge Thomas Ruffin, February 4, 1861, in *The Papers of Thomas Ruffin*, ed. Hamilton, III, 117–19.

59. *"Journal of a Secesh Lady,"* ed. Crabtree and Patton, 41 (quotation), 54, 60; Thomas P. Devereux to George W. Mordecai, April 22, 1861, in George W. Mordecai Papers, SHC.

60. *Dictionary of North Carolina Biography*, ed. Powell, II, 60–61; Thomas P. Devereux to Robert L. Maitland, January 22, 1866, in Devereux Family Papers, DU; *"Journal of a Secesh Lady,"* ed. Crabtree and Patton, 729–30.

Tayloe vowed that his resources would be used "for self protection & given if necessary to Alabama." Indeed, he added, "I am almost disposed to be a Citizen of Alabama. If Virginia is not with me, I will not be with her."[61] Fellow Virginian Wyndham Robertson, a former Whig governor of the state, also suffered the painful transition from unionism to reluctant support for the new Confederacy. In an amicable exchange with his old friend, fire-eater Richard Archer of Mississippi, in the spring of 1860, Robertson wrote: "Our present difference is mainly that you think disunion (as things are) desirable. I do not. I hope (& only hope) to arrest, & turn back threatened & existing evils. You are hopeless of such a result." Robertson added, however, "We shall certainly be together" when the "honor" and "interests" of our states "are invaded." That time came a year later. On the very day that the Sumter bombardment began, though it was yet unknown to him, the former governor reiterated that his hopes had been for "re-construction and re-union." But now it was apparent that the "division between the South & Black Republicanism" was rapidly becoming "one between South & North," leading inevitably to the formation of two confederacies, which would forever be separate. He could only hope that this unfortunate division could be effected "peaceably."[62]

Surprisingly, at least one prominent South Carolina Low Country rice planter, Allen Smith Izard, was a late convert to the Confederate cause. Perhaps the explanation is to be found in his family background. Born in Philadelphia in 1810, Izard spent the formative years of his life either in the North or in travel abroad. Not until he inherited the property of his widowed mother in the early 1830s did he establish his permanent residence in South Carolina. In any event, Izard made his heretical position crystal clear in mid-February, 1861. In a remarkable letter to New York attorney and Republican stalwart Benjamin D. Silliman, he urged the Republican leaders to make no concessions to the "Southern renegades." "Snub them, grind their noses; mash their toes, & toss them in the gutter," he cried. Despite these sentiments, however, Izard had readily furnished hands to work on Fort Pulaski a month before, and in July, 1861, he pledged his enthusiastic support for a proposed government loan to be

61. William H. Tayloe to "Dear Brother" [Benjamin O.], November 11, 1860, March 10, 1861, in Henry A. Tayloe and Family Papers, ADAH.

62. Wyndham Robertson to "Dear Archer," April 28, 1860, April 12, 1861, in Richard Thompson Archer Family Papers, CAH.

secured by crops. As soon as Secretary Christopher G. Memminger clarified the details of the plan, Izard pronounced himself "not only willing but anxious to aid the Gov^t to the fullest extent in [his] power whether it cost the *present* crop, or *ten* in *succession*." Clearly, Izard's metamorphosis from heretic to patriot was complete.[63]

Despite their huge personal stake in the preservation of slavery, a few elite planters never abandoned their allegiance to the Union and gave little or no support to the Confederacy. Some, like James C. Johnston of North Carolina, could not bring themselves to desert the republic with which they had literally grown up; others, most notably the Natchez nabobs, had unique family and social connections with the Northeast; but most of the die-hard Unionists acted out of economic self-interest. They were convinced that their bountiful assets could best be safeguarded within the Union. The wartime activities of these men will be discussed more fully in the next chapter. It will suffice to say here that none of them ever expressed any reservations about the morality or legality of owning slave property, and, with but few exceptions, they did not collaborate with the enemy during the war. Instead, most displayed a passive, if not active, sympathy for the Confederacy and its people. This was especially true of the native Southerners, who found it difficult to sever the emotional ties to the land of their birth. As William Newton Mercer explained: "Like Desdamona, I have had a divided duty. The strugle [*sic*] was severe, but nature prevailed; when *compelled* to decide, my sympathies were given to the South." Similarly, arch-Unionist James L. Petigru of Charleston, while decrying the carnage wrought by secession, could not refrain from applauding the spirit of the southern people in the fall of 1862. "The spirit that our people have shown in all encounters with the enemy," he remarked, "goes far to redeem the rashness that has ruined so many, and is likely to ruin more."[64]

At least two of the great Unionist slaveholders suffered humiliation and even loss of property at the hands of the Yankees when they stubbornly refused to take an oath of allegiance to the United States. Thus, in February, 1862, follow-

63. *South Carolina Genealogies*, IV, 249–50; Allen S. Izard to "My dear Counsellor" [Benjamin D. Silliman], February 13, 1861, in Allen Smith Izard Letter, SCHS; Izard to Langdon Cheves, January 18, July 19 (quotation), 29, 1861, in Langdon Cheves, Jr., Papers, SCHS.

64. William N. Mercer to Major General Benjamin F. Butler, September 28, 1862, in William Newton Mercer Papers, LSU; James L. Petigru to Adele Petigru Allston, October 31, 1862, in Easterby, ed., *South Carolina Rice Plantation*, 191.

ing the occupation of Edenton, Federal troops threatened to shoot James C. Johnston after he declined to take the oath. Johnston, then in his eightieth year, allegedly responded: "If you do, you cannot cheat me out of much of life." He was subsequently placed under house arrest for a brief time.[65] Even more severe were the consequences for William Mercer after the fall of New Orleans two months later. Among the orders issued by Major General Benjamin F. Butler after he assumed command in the Crescent City was one in late September, 1862, that required the entire population either to take a prescribed oath of allegiance or to declare themselves enemies of the United States. Mercer, who had sworn allegiance to his country earlier in his life, refused to take the oath, contending that since he had never taken an oath to the Confederacy he did "not think it necessary to take an oath of allegiance to the U.S., as he had never forfeited his allegiance!" Infuriated by this act of defiance, however well intentioned, Butler charged that such an example by a man of Mercer's stature was "more dangerous to the interests of the United States than if [as] a younger man [he] had shouldered [his] musket and marched to the field in the army of the rebellion." As a result, Mercer was placed on the enemy list, and his property was immediately sequestered. Not until friends interceded on his behalf later in the war, after he had moved his residence to New York, was his name expunged from "the record of registered enemies" and his property restored.[66]

As the elite slaveholders solidified their respective positions and as new governments were organized in Montgomery and Washington, D.C., the specter of war loomed ever more ominously on the horizon. For some, Lincoln's somewhat enigmatic Inaugural Address proved to be the defining event. "I have read Lincoln's Inaugural," commented Lemuel Conner, "& am pained tho not surprised at its contents." His proposal to "protect Federal property & collect the revenue in the seceding states" means "war & will be so treated by the Montgomery Congress." Much more exuberant was Henry A. Middleton, Jr., who recorded this brief entry in his Weehaw plantation journal on March 5: "Lincoln

65. *"Journal of a Secesh Lady,"* ed. Crabtree and Patton, 119–21.

66. William N. Mercer to "My Dear Doctor" [unidentified], April 10, 1864; "Substantial Copy" of Mercer's original declaration to Butler, October 2, 1864 (first quotation); Major General Benjamin F. Butler to Mercer, September 27, 1862 (second quotation); Mercer to Butler, September 28, 1862; Brigadier General James Bowen to Captain Kilborn, Provost Marshal, July 27, 1863 (third quotation); William C. Cozzens to W. P. Fessenden, secretary of the treasury, December 12, 1864, in William Newton Mercer Papers, LSU.

says in his inaugural that he will enforce laws, collect duties &c So hurrah for war!" For the next month, Middleton sounded the latter refrain, alternating between optimism and despair as rumors of a possible evacuation of Sumter circulated. On March 22 he returned to the subject of Lincoln's Inaugural with this sarcastic synopsis of the address: "He can but he can't; He will but he won't; He'll be damned if he does, He'll be damned if he don't." From his vantage point in Washington, D.C., Benjamin Tayloe offered a markedly different perspective. He was still sanguine of peace as late as mid-March. "The President," said Tayloe, "can do nothing of a hostile character towards the South—he has neither law nor means, *if* he had the disposition, (which I do not believe) to take the forts, or to collect revenue on ship board." Fort Sumter, he predicted, would soon be evacuated, and ultimately the crisis would be resolved peacefully.[67]

Sumter was obviously the key. Consequently, residents of both sections anxiously turned their attention to events in Charleston Harbor during the month after Lincoln's inauguration. In Charleston, where state and Confederate forces had been feverishly rushing military preparations since the beginning of the year, the mood was equally expectant. One of those actively involved in these preparations was Langdon Cheves, Jr. In early January, he reported that 500 Negroes and 1,500 state troops were engaged in constructing earthworks, and heavy cannon were being moved into place around the harbor. However, the threat of an imminent confrontation with Major Robert Anderson, commander of the federal garrison at Fort Sumter, had diminished. Cheves assured his mother that "there will not be any fighting" and predicted that the government in Washington, D.C., was "ready to go to pieces" and would probably not last until Lincoln's inauguration. Shortly thereafter, Robert N. Gourdin, a member of another prominent Low Country family, embarked upon a secret mission to Washington, D.C., allegedly at the "urgent request" of Major Anderson. His goal was to effect some understanding with the authorities in Washington that would forestall a "collision" in Charleston. Upon his return to the latter city in early February, Gourdin reported that President Buchanan and his cabinet were

67. Lemuel P. Conner to "Dear Fanny," March 4, 1861, in Lemuel P. Conner and Family Papers, LSU; Henry A. Middleton, Jr., Plantation Journal, March 5, 7, 11, 12, 22, April 5, 1861, in Cheves-Middleton Papers, SCHS; Benjamin O. Tayloe to "Dear Brother" [William H.], March 16, 1861, in Tayloe Family Papers, VHS.

determined to "avoid any Course which may provoke hostilities" and, consequently, would refrain from sending reinforcements to Sumter, "especially as
Major Anderson has assured the govt. that they are not required." He added,
however, that should the ultimate policy be "to leave the Major where he is,"
then hostilities were "inevitable."[68]

Gourdin's assessment proved to be accurate. Following an unsuccessful attempt in early January to send supplies and reinforcements to the garrison on
the steamer *Star of the West*, the Buchanan administration made no further effort to relieve the fort. However, on the very day of Lincoln's inauguration,
Major Anderson informed the new president that he would be forced to evacu-
ate Sumter unless he received additional supplies before April 15. There followed a month of agonizing indecision in Washington before Lincoln finally
decided on April 6 to send provisions, but not reinforcements, to the belea-
guered garrison. Four days later, as Confederate officials in Montgomery
weighed their options, Langdon Cheves remained convinced that there would
be no violent confrontation at Charleston. "I don't mean that the U.S. won't try
to run in supplies," he said, "but they will fail & probably expect to fail and will
not . . . avenge its failure by any *effective* force." Anderson, continued Cheves,
"will do as little as he possibly can to help them, and it is not probable that a
gun will be fired from the fort nor against it." Little did he know that, even as
he was recording these thoughts, the decision had been made to demand the
evacuation of the fort and, if the ultimatum were rejected, "to reduce it."[69]

At 4:30 A.M. on Friday, April 12, 1861, one hour after emissaries from General Pierre G. T. Beauregard had determined that Major Anderson had not met
the terms of the Confederate demand, a mortar shell from Fort Johnson signaled the beginning of a thirty-four-hour bombardment of Fort Sumter that
miraculously resulted in no casualties to either side. Within fifteen minutes, the
mortar batteries on Morris and Sullivan's Islands began lobbing shells over
the fort according to a prescribed sequence, and after dawn (about 5:00 A.M.)
the heavy siege guns opened up. Not until 7:00 A.M. did Sumter begin returning
the fire, commencing with what General Beauregard termed "a vigorous fire"

68. Langdon Cheves, Jr., to "Dear Mamma," January 4, [1861], in Cheves Family Papers, SCL;
T[heodore] L[ouis] [?] Gourdin to Cheves, January 12, 1861, Robert N. Gourdin to Cheves, February 3, 1861, in Langdon Cheves, Jr., Papers, SCHS.

69. Long, *The Civil War Day by Day*, 23–24, 47–55; Langdon Cheves, Jr., to "Dear Mamma,"
April 10, 1861, in Cheves Family Papers, SCL.

against the Iron Battery on Cummings Point.[70] Thus began the first engagement in what was destined to be a long and bloody civil war. As fire and smoke filled the air, numerous spectators gathered on the rooftops of the splendid mansions overlooking The Battery to view the scene. As Mary Petigru sat down to write a letter to her niece "with the sounds of the cannon booming incessantly" in her ears, she announced: "The war has actually commenced! . . . I fear it is the beginning of a dreadful strife & when it will end who can say." Meanwhile, back in Washington, D.C., the people waited "in feverish anxiety" to "hear the fate of Sumter." An apprehensive Benjamin Tayloe complained that "the diplomacy of Napoleon, of Talleyrand and of Metternich never was more successful than this Cabinet now is in keeping the secrets of Government. To this hour we do not know here if an attack on Sumter is to be expected."[71]

After a dark and windy night punctuated by the luminous traces of mortar shells fired intermittently from the batteries surrounding the harbor, the second day of the bombardment dawned clear and bright. The cannonading resumed at daybreak, and about 8:00 A.M. a shell struck the barracks inside the fort, igniting a fire that burned with increasing intensity throughout the morning. With a strong wind blowing from the west, where the fire had started, the fort was soon enveloped in a thick cloud of black smoke. To Mary Petigru, who observed the scene from the "upper Piazza" of her sister's residence on King Street, it appeared that the entire fort was on fire. Then, about 1:00 P.M., the fort's flagstaff was shot away. The Confederate batteries immediately ceased firing, and after a comedy of errors that consumed most of the afternoon, Major Anderson finally agreed to surrender. At 5:00 P.M., Mary Petigru, who had kept open the letter to her niece, wrote excitedly: "Good news! Fort Sumter has surrendered! . . . This has been an anxious day & every one now rejoices—I hope with devout thankfulness for it seems to me clearly that God is on our side."

70. Scarborough, ed., *The Diary of Edmund Ruffin*, I, 588; *The War of the Rebellion: A Compilation of the Official Records of the Union and Confederate Armies*, 128 vols. (Washington, D.C., 1880–1901), Ser. 1, Vol. I, 31 (quotation), 40, 44, 54, 60, hereinafter referred to as *Official Records*; Henry A. Middleton, Jr., Plantation Journal, April 12, 1861, in Cheves-Middleton Papers, SCHS; Henry A. Middleton, Jr., to "My dear Harriett," [April 12, 1861], Henry A. Middleton, Jr., Family Letters, *ibid.*

71. Mary Petigru to "My dear Carey" [niece Caroline North Pettigrew], April 12, 1861, in Pettigrew Family Papers, SHC; Benjamin O. Tayloe to "My Dear Son" [Edward Thornton], April 12, 1861, in Henry A. Tayloe and Family Papers, ADAH.

From his post on Morris Island, young Ben Allston exulted: "Such a 'bloodless victory' has never yet been recorded in the pages of history."[72]

As Charlestonians celebrated the conquest of Sumter, the ramifications were soon felt elsewhere. Ezekial J. Donnell, a New York merchant and brother of a large North Carolina slaveholder, described the scene in his city three days after the formal surrender of Sumter. "This has been the most extraordinary day ever witnessed in New York," he wrote. "There is no business doing. Every body is running about the streets apparently in a state of intense excitement." According to Donnell, the people were now united politically as never before. "All seem determined to support the government in its present course," and "any thing like open expressions of sympathy with disunion is not tolerated." No lives had been threatened so far, "but some sign of sympathy with the popular feeling is demanded from every body who is at all suspected." In such an atmosphere, Donnell could only conclude painfully, "We have entered upon the most momentous civil war that has ever occurred in the annals of the human family."[73]

In cities throughout the Confederacy, there was an equally frenzied popular response to the fall of Sumter and Lincoln's immediate call for 75,000 state militia to suppress the rebellion. On April 23, less than a week after Virginia severed its ties with the Union, a Norfolk factor reported "all business suspended . . . and all under arms." Corn would soon be needed "to feed our Brave Volunteers—who have determined to defend Va and the South—or die in the attempt." Another factor in the same city promised the "abolition scoundrels a warm reception if they conclude to visit us again." Although his mother-in-law had suffered the loss of a rental house near the Navy Yard when the latter was partially burned by the fleeing Federals on the night of April 20, she was prepared "to give . . . her last cent for the defence of the State." Indeed, she wished "to be one of a hundred to give $500 each as a prize for the body of Lincoln dead or alive." There was also great excitement in the capital of North Carolina

72. Scarborough, ed., *The Diary of Edmund Ruffin*, I, 594–98; Henry A. Middleton, Jr., Plantation Journal, April 13, 1861, in Cheves-Middleton Papers, SCHS; Mary Petigru to "My dear Carey," April 13, 1861, in Pettigrew Family Papers, SHC; T. Harry Williams, *P. G. T. Beauregard: Napoleon in Gray* (Baton Rouge, 1955), 59–61; Benjamin Allston to "My dear Father," April 14, 1861, in R. F. W. Allston Papers, SCHS. Also printed in Easterby, ed., *South Carolina Rice Plantation*, 174–75.

73. E. J. Donnell to "My Dear Bro" [John R.], April 17, 1861, in Donnell Family Papers, SHC.

a month before that state actually seceded. "You ought to be in Raleigh," exclaimed young Pattie Thompson to her brother on April 20. "The secession flag just passed here this morning, and such shouts, and wavings of handkerchiefs you never saw." And in early May, a correspondent from New Orleans informed Pattie's Unionist father, Lewis Thompson, that the war fever in that quarter was almost indescribable. "The whole country is wild & perfectly mad for war," he wrote. "Every where, every body, every thing spoke[n] of [is] only of war." Such enthusiasm soon began to wane as the realities of war became increasingly apparent, but in the beginning both sections of the country were infected by a patriotic fervor that was unparalleled to this point in American history.[74]

Before examining the role of the elite slaveholders in the war that they had done so much to provoke, it might be useful to consider briefly what they believed at the time to be the salient causes of that conflict. Historians have long debated the question without reaching any real consensus, though it is clear to most in the present generation, whatever their ideological perspective, that the division over slavery was the primary causative factor.[75] Most contemporary observers would have agreed with that interpretation. There was, to be sure, much talk then of states' rights, just as there was during the Civil Rights Movement of the 1950s and 1960s and as there is now by conservative white Southerners anxious to preserve the reputation of their beloved Confederate ancestors. But states' rights, both then and more recently, is simply a philosophical justification for the more fundamental institutions of slavery and segregation, respectively. Ironically, there was also much rhetorical emphasis on liberty, by which, of course, the slaveholders meant the republican liberty of the white populace. Thus, Louisa McCord recalled after the war, "We fought for our rights and our liberties." For Richard Archer, the key issues were "Republican Government,

74. K. Biggs & Co. to Lewis Thompson, April 23, 1861 (first quotation), in Lewis Thompson Papers, SHC; McPheeters & Ghiselen [?] to George W. Mordecai, April 24, 1861 (second quotation), in George W. Mordecai Papers, SHC; Pattie Thompson to "My dear bud Toad" [brother Thomas W.], April 20, 1861, William A. Hardy to Lewis Thompson, May 8, 1861, both in Lewis Thompson Papers, SHC.

75. To cite but a few examples, see Shore, *Southern Capitalists,* 83; Ford, *Origins of Southern Radicalism,* 353, 360, 362; Barrington Moore, Jr., *Social Origins of Dictatorship and Democracy: Lord and Peasant in the Making of the Modern World* (Boston, 1966), 141; Shearer Davis Bowman, "Antebellum Planters and *Vormärz* Junkers in Comparative Perspective," *AHR* 85 (October 1980): 794.

State Rights, the liberty of the Citizen," and, perhaps most illuminating, "our own cherished institutions." Obviously, the most "cherished" of those institutions was Negro slavery.[76]

This is not to say that there were not some ancillary contributing factors to sectional division. Chief among these in addition to constitutional issues were the tariff, which had alienated South Carolina as early as the 1820s; economic and cultural differences; and perhaps even different world views, whatever that term may mean. But in the end it was southern concern for the security of slave property above all else that precipitated disunion and the fratricidal war that followed. After that war, fire-eater Robert Barnwell Rhett reflected on the events of the antebellum period and concluded that secession was attributable to "*one cause only*—the usurpations of the Northern States, upon the Constitution of the United States" under the doctrine of implied powers. He then listed those usurpations, "beginning with Banks, alien and sedition Laws, Tariffs, and internal improvements—finally ending with slavery, and in sectionalism." Seventeen years before, however, in a less reflective mood, he was more direct. In a letter to a member of the British Parliament, he wrote: "The Slavery question is still festering in the body politic north & south, and in my opinion, will dissolve the Union."[77]

On the eve of the Civil War, the issue was clear to both the planter aristocrats and their associates. For Virginian Colin Clarke, the father-in-law of former governor John L. Manning of South Carolina, the Constitution was "the root of all evil." But, unlike Rhett, he did not blame the "Black Republicans" for usurping power by misinterpreting that document; rather, it was the southern delegates to the Constitutional Convention, especially those from his own state, who, because of their "miserable, morbid, mawkish sentimentality," had failed to exact specific guarantees for the protection of slave property. Consequently, contended Clarke, if the North refused "to do *now*, what ought to have been done in 1787," the South had no alternative but to "quietly withdraw" from the Union. On the day that Virginia cast its lot with the Confederacy, a member of the Pettigrew family expressed the hope that "we will have a stronger govern-

76. Louisa S. McCord to Hiram Powers, March 20, 1870, in McCord, *Selected Writings*, 284; Richard T. Archer to "Governor [John A.] Quitman," [1850–51?], in Richard Thompson Archer Family Papers, CAH.

77. R. B. Rhett to nephew T. Stuart Rhett, [1868], R. B. Rhett to Matthew Foster, M.P., February 1[?], 1851, both in Robert Barnwell Rhett, Sr., Papers, SCHS.

ment & that all who dare to say one word against the institution *which has been made the cause of all this*—will be made to feel the consequences." Two weeks later, a Norfolk factor also identified slavery as the overriding cause of the war. After admitting that "the odds against us is fearfull [*sic*]," he asserted: "We look upon the question of slavery as having culminated, and it must be defended, or our Country will be over-run and laid waste."[78] However clear their perception of the cause, few could truly envision the horrific road that lay ahead.

78. Colin Clarke to Sallie B. Manning [early 1860], December 5, 1860, in Chesnut-Miller-Manning Papers, SCHS; M[ary] B. P[ettigrew] to "My Dearest Carey" [Carey North Pettigrew], April 17, 1861 (italics mine), Aldridge & Rothy [?] to William S. Pettigrew, April 29, 1861, in Pettigrew Family Papers, SHC.

9

DAYS OF JUDGMENT:

The Demise of a Slave Society

I verily believe the men, women & children—if they had nothing else—would assail Lincoln's army at every point—with bricks & sticks; so great is the determination & so deeply do they feel aggrieved by the accursed invasion.
—JUDGE A. WRIGHT, Tennessee Supreme Court, April 28, 1861

My Whole Soul is in this Conflict—and if I could, I would have my Entire Clan in the field. —ALFRED HUGER, November 5, 1861

We fight for home, for freedom, for independence; they for conquest & tyranny.
—KATE EDMONDSTON, December 16, 1862

This government cannot much longer play a game in which it stakes all and its enemies stake nothing. Those enemies must understand that they cannot experiment for ten years trying to destroy the Government and if they fail, still come back into the Union unhurt.
—ABRAHAM LINCOLN to AUGUST BELMONT, July 31, 1862

From a condition of ease comfort and abundance, I am suddenly reduced to one of hardship, want & privation. The Lord help me & my poor family.—and the Devil may take the authors & originators of this dreadful state of things,—abolitionists & fire eaters together.
—WILLIAM T. PALFREY, January 22, 1863

This is the greatest army in the country—think of infantry surprising cavalry and plundering their camp—it beats 'what Greece or Rome have done or any land beneath the sea' or any other man.
—THOMAS P. DEVEREUX II, September 1, 1864

The events that have lately taken place in Virginia may be said virtually to have ended the war. I never for a moment expected any other final result. Such an instance of insanity as the Southern States exhibited in endeavoring to destroy the Union is I believe with[out] an example in history.

—WILLIAM F. WICKHAM, April 25, 1865

IT HAS OFTEN been said that, on the Confederate side, the Civil War was "a rich man's war and a poor man's fight." Although there is an element of truth in that statement, it is also true that many of the large slaveholders supported the Confederate cause with unremitting devotion and endured hardships equal to those of their less fortunate neighbors. Nevertheless, it is difficult to escape the conclusion that many of them could have contributed more to the war effort. Too many were more concerned with their own economic self-interest than with the ultimate success of the Confederacy. Some resisted government requisitions of hands and provisions, others speculated in cotton and even sold it to the enemy during the war, a few evaded military service by procuring substitutes, and too few were prepared to make a financial commitment to the Confederacy commensurate with their vast resources. Of course, there were many exceptions, particularly among the South Carolinians—those most responsible for causing the war—and it is to those that we will turn first.

Although most of the elite slaveholders were too old to perform active military service themselves, many had sons or other close male relatives in the field. As Table 6 indicates, at least thirty-one (or 11.4 percent) of the wealthy planters served in the Confederate Army, half of them at the rank of colonel or above. The highest ranking officer among them was Wade Hampton III, who organized the famed Hampton Legion at the beginning of the war and rose to the rank of lieutenant general two months before Lee's surrender at Appomattox. Other general officers included Howell Cobb, who, as a major general, commanded the District of Georgia late in the war, and Brigadier Generals John Doby Kennedy and John S. Preston of South Carolina, Gideon J. Pillow of Tennessee, Philip St. George Cocke of Virginia, and Zebulon York of Louisiana. Both Kennedy and Hampton were wounded at First Manassas, and the latter was again wounded at Gettysburg. York, a native of Maine and reputedly one of the wealthiest men in Louisiana, lost an arm leading a gallant charge at

TABLE 6 · CIVIL WAR MILITARY SERVICE

ELITE SLAVEHOLDERS (WITH HIGHEST RANK)

Ala.: James W. Echols (Field Officer, 34th Ala.)

Ga.: Howell Cobb (Maj. Gen.), William H. Gibbons (Maj.), John B. Lamar (aide to Cobb), Joseph L. McAllister (Lt. Col.), Randolph Spalding (Col.)

La.: Louis A. Bringier (Col.), Albert G. Cage (Capt.), Duncan S. Cage (Col.), Josiah Chambers (1st Lt.), James M. Gillespie (Pvt.), Zebulon York (Brig. Gen.)

Miss.: Lemuel P. Conner (Col.), William G. Conner (Maj.), Alfred V. Davis (Capt.), G. Wilson Humphreys (Capt.), Eustace Surget (Lt. Col.)

N.C.: Peter W. Hairston (volunteer aide to Stuart, Early)

S.C.: John R. Cheves (Charleston Harbor defenses), Langdon Cheves, Jr. (Capt.), Wade Hampton III (Lt. Gen.), John Doby Kennedy (Brig. Gen.), John L. Manning (Col.), William C. Heyward, John S. Preston (Brig. Gen.), Alexander R. Taylor (Capt.), Plowden C. J. Weston (Capt.)

Tenn.: Gideon J. Pillow (Brig. Gen.)

Va.: William Allen (Col.), Philip St. George Cocke (Brig. Gen.), George E. Harrison, Jr. (Lt.)

SONS AND OTHER CLOSE MALE RELATIVES (NUMBERS WHO SERVED)

Ala.:	20	N.C.:	14
Ga.:	6	S.C.:	47
La.:	21	Tenn.:	1
Miss.:	50	Va.:	8

SUMMARY: A total of 31 elite slaveholders (11.4 percent of those who held 250+ slaves in 1860) saw active military service; 167 close relatives from 79 elite families (29.2 percent) also served. Families contributing 5 or more men to military service included those of John Routh (La.); Gerard Brandon, William G. Conner, John A. Quitman, and James A. Ventress (Miss.); Thomas P. Devereux (N.C.); Robert Barnwell Rhett (S.C.); James Galt (Va.).

Winchester in September, 1864. The fates were less kind to Cocke, who took his own life in December, 1861, after eight months of debilitating field service.[1]

Much more numerous in terms of actual military service were other members of elite planter families. Nearly 30 percent of the families in this study sent men to the army, and eight of them, including the families of fire-eaters John A. Quitman and Barnwell Rhett, contributed at least five members to the military. The highest ranking officer in this cohort was Lieutenant General Leonidas Polk, brother of Tennessee planter Andrew J. Polk and brother-in-law of the seemingly ubiquitous Thomas P. Devereux of North Carolina. Seven others rose to the rank of brigadier general. Of these, three—Cullen Battle of Alabama, James Chesnut, Jr., of South Carolina, and Williams C. Wickham of Virginia—were the sons of large slaveholders; two, Thomas R. R. Cobb of Georgia and James H. Trapier of South Carolina, were the brothers; and two others, William L. Brandon and Benjamin G. Humphreys of Mississippi, were the uncles of planter nabobs. All but Polk served primarily in the eastern theater. Brandon lost a leg at Malvern Hill, and Battle was severely wounded at Cedar Creek in October, 1864. Both Polk and Cobb made the ultimate sacrifice, the former when struck by a cannon ball at Pine Mountain during the Atlanta campaign, and the latter when he suffered a mortal wound at Fredericksburg. Wickham, like his father a steadfast Unionist, served with J. E. B. Stuart's cavalry until he took his seat in the Second Confederate Congress in 1864. Only Trapier had a notably undistinguished military career.[2]

A few well-to-do slaveholders preferred to serve as volunteer aides to prominent generals, usually relatives, rather than to accept a regular appointment and thus to subject themselves to rigid military rules and regulations. In this way they remained in control of their own lives while still reaping the glory of military service. This attitude was most clearly exemplified by North Carolina grandee Peter W. Hairston. In May, 1861, Hairston volunteered to serve as an aide to his brother-in-law, Colonel J. E. B. Stuart, "for any duty that may be assigned me." Although even this service would be "a trial" for Hairston and his wife, he deemed it necessary in order "to let the poorer classes know that we are

---

1. Warner, *Generals in Gray*, 122–23, 55, 170, 245, 241, 57, 347.

2. *Ibid.*, 20, 32, 48, 56, 145, 242–43, 309–10, 335. Relationships from Owen, *History of Alabama*, III, 115 (Battle); *Goodspeed's*, I, 419–22 (Brandon), 979–87 (Humphreys); Warner and Yearns, *Biographical Register of the Confederate Congress*, 57–58 (Cobb); *Maury County Cousins*, 545–47 (Polk); Rogers, *History of Georgetown County*, 284 (Trapier); Wickham Family Papers, VHS.

willing and ready to set them the example of fighting for our country, our homes and all that men hold sacred and dear." Four months later, however, his initial ardor had cooled. When Stuart, now a brigadier general, offered him the position of aide-de-camp, he declined on the grounds that the new post "would subject [him] to the rules and regulations of war and [he] could not come home when [he] wished." The next day, however, Hairston offered another explanation for his decision to reject Stuart's offer. Whether as a volunteer aide or as a mere captain, he felt unappreciated. Announcing his intention to come home, he declared that he would not return to the Army again unless he received "such an appointment as will comport with [his] dignity and standing at home." He complained further: "The inferior position which I have held here has given me no opportunity to distinguish myself as I could have done had I a command." Accordingly, he soon returned to North Carolina, doubtless somewhat mollified by a letter from Stuart praising him for his "invaluable" services and recommending his appointment to "a much higher grade than that heretofore filled." Two years later, Hairston again entered the field, this time as an aide to General Jubal Early.[3] At least two other prominent slaveholders also acted as volunteer aides during the war. Former senator James Chesnut, Jr., served briefly in that capacity with General Beauregard at Fort Sumter before moving on to President Davis's staff in 1862. Like Hairston, Georgia planter John B. Lamar also assisted a brother-in-law, serving until his death during the Antietam campaign as an aide to Brigadier General Howell Cobb.[4]

Several younger members of the elite, who served as officers of lower rank, also compiled distinguished military records during the war. Among the most notable were William Allen of Virginia and William G. Conner of Mississippi. The latter, the eldest of five brothers who served in the Confederate Army, joined a Natchez company, the Adams Troop, immediately after the war began.[5] Posted to the eastern front, he served, first as a captain and later as a major, with the Jeff Davis Legion, a cavalry unit attached to J. E. B. Stuart's division. He was captured near Williamsburg, Virginia, on May 3, 1862, "while

3. Peter W. Hairston to Fanny Hairston, May 9, September 26, 28, 29, 1861, September 20, 1863, Letter of Commendation from J. E. B. Stuart, October 12, 1861, in Peter Wilson Hairston Papers, SHC.

4. Warner, *Generals in Gray*, 48; *Biographical Directory of the American Congress*, 1186.

5. Conner's mother, Jane E. B. Conner, was dubbed the "Little War Mother" in recognition of the fact that her five sons all fought for the Confederacy. Leverich Papers, Box 3G128, Folder 22, CAH.

detached from his company on picket." Praised by Stuart at that time as one of his "best officers," Conner was exchanged in August and rejoined his unit. He was killed in action at Gettysburg on July 3, 1863, and earned a place on the Confederate roll of honor for his "gallant" performance in that battle.[6]

Allen, a strong supporter of the Confederate cause, erected extensive fortifications on Jamestown Island when hostilities commenced and subsequently armed and fed a company of Virginia volunteers, both at his own expense. Initially a captain of artillery in Major General John B. Magruder's Army of the Peninsula, his exemplary service during the Peninsular Campaign earned him a promotion to major in May, 1862. In a report dated May 3, General Magruder warmly commended Allen for his "self-sacrificing conduct," After alluding to the great personal losses sustained by Allen, who was "endeavoring to remove the public property committed to his charge" even as Federal troops plundered his nearby Claremont estate, Magruder closed his report with these laudatory words: "I cannot commend his conduct as an officer too highly to the Government nor his patriotism as a citizen too warmly to the love and respect of his countrymen." In many respects. Allen's unselfish devotion to the Confederate cause was reminiscent of the patriotism displayed by another Virginian, Governor Thomas Nelson, Jr., during the American Revolution. Like Nelson, Allen, who owned nearly 450 slaves in 1860, lost his entire fortune during the war. In 1875, two years after his death, Allen's widow found his estate encumbered with a debt of $44,000 with only $1,500 in personal assets and minimal real estate to counter this debt. Consequently, she was forced to sell off such personal effects as furniture, paintings, and exquisite bronzes brought from Europe in order to liquidate the debt.[7]

There were others who made important military contributions to the Con-

---

6. *Official Records*, Ser. 1, vol. XI, Pt. 1, p. 445; *ibid.*, Ser. 2, Vol. IV, 442; *ibid.*, Ser. 1, Vol. XXVII, Pt. 2, pp. 698, 776; Fanny E. Conner to "My dear Husband" [Lemuel P.], October 13, 1863, in Lemuel P. Conner and Family Papers, LSU.

7. *Genealogies of Virginia Families: From the William and Mary Quarterly Historical Magazine*, I, 60; *Official Records*, Ser. 1, vol. XI, Pt. 1, p. 410 (quotations), Pt. 3, p. 504, Vol. XL, Pt. 3, p. 798; *ibid.*, Ser. 2, Vol. IV, 807; Estate of William Allen, Box 28, Folder 2, in James Nathaniel Dunlop Papers, VHS; T. R. Fehrenbach, *Greatness to Spare: The Heroic Sacrifices of the Men Who Signed the Declaration of Independence* (Princeton, 1968), 217–34. It was Nelson who ordered American artillerymen to destroy his own mansion, which was being used as a British headquarters, during the siege of Yorktown.

federacy. Few exhibited greater patriotic zeal than Langdon Cheves, Jr., whose activities immediately after the secession of his state have already been recounted in the preceding chapter.[8] For two years after the fall of Sumter, Cheves labored assiduously "without compensation" or rank to develop coastal fortifications in the South Carolina Low Country. During the spring and summer of 1861, he raised the labor for and supervised the construction of the works on Hilton Head Island. Then, as volunteer aide-de-camp to Brigadier General Thomas F. Drayton, commander of the Sixth Military District, he was assigned to engineer duty and constructed fortifications at Red Bluff and several other sites in the area before being placed in charge of the defenses on Morris Island in July, 1862. There he selected the site and superintended the construction of Battery Wagner, a bastion so strong that it withstood a Federal land and naval assault for three months before falling to the enemy in September, 1863. Not until April of that year was Cheves accorded formal military rank. Upon the recommendation of Major William H. Echols of the Confederate Engineer Corps, he was commissioned captain of engineers. Unfortunately, Cheves did not have long to enjoy his well-earned rank, for on July 10 he was killed as he stood at the entrance to his quarters in Battery Wagner "by the first shell fired from the attacking fleet."[9]

Cheves's contributions to the Confederate war effort were not confined to his work on coastal fortifications. In the spring of 1862, he pledged "one half the net proceeds" of his rice crop "to investment in Confederate Bonds." More important, that same spring he designed, procured the materials for, and supervised the construction at the Chatham Armory in Savannah of the *Gazelle*, apparently the only hot-air observation balloon ever deployed by the Confederates. As his daughter later recalled, Cheves teasingly threatened to buy up "all the handsome silk dresses in Savannah" to make the balloon, but it was actually fabricated from imported silk in strips "about 40 feet long, and of various colors . . . yellow, green, black & white." After several delays and considerable skepticism from higher authorities, the *Gazelle* was finally completed and transported

8. See pp. 301–302 of this book.

9. Major William H. Echols to Major D. B. Harris, April 17, 1863 (first quotation); MS Biographical Sketch of Langdon Cheves, Jr., by his nephew Langdon Cheves, 1935 [?] (second quotation), Alfred M. Martin to Langdon Cheves, September 26, 1861, Cheves to Brigadier General Thomas F. Drayton, October 21, 1861, Drayton to Cheves, October 24, 1861, in Langdon Cheves, Jr., papers, SCHS.

to Richmond, where it made several ascents during the Seven Days' battles in June, 1862. Since the only source of gas was in Richmond, "it was the custom to inflate the balloon there, tie it securely to an engine, and run it down the York River Railroad to any point at which we desired to send it up." According to Charles Cevor, who had built the balloon under Cheves's direction, the experiment was a great success. Reporting that he had kept the balloon "suspended the greater portion of the day" on June 27, he informed Cheves, "We could see all that was done" and were continuously within "signal distance of Gen Lee." Unhappily for the Confederates, the *Gazelle* was lost a week later when the steamer on which it was being moved downriver from Richmond was captured.[10]

Other members of the Cheves family made notable contributions to the Confederate cause as well. Even as Langdon was preparing defenses on Hilton Head to counter the Union naval threat that materialized in early November, 1861, with the landing at Port Royal, his brother John R. Cheves, also a large rice planter, was superintending the construction of a system of obstructions and torpedo defenses in Charleston harbor. John's only son, Captain Edward R. Cheves, was killed in Virginia about the time of the Seven Days' battles. Louisa McCord, a sister of the Cheves brothers, also did her part during the war. She equipped at her own expense a company of volunteers from Columbia, managed a hospital, and headed both the Soldiers' Relief Association and the Soldiers' Clothing Association in the South Carolina capital. She too lost a son, Cheves McCord, who was wounded at Second Manassas and died shortly thereafter, following his premature return to duty after a brief convalescence at home.[11]

Many members of elite families recounted their wartime experiences in letters to friends and family. One of the most enthusiastic early volunteers was

10. Langdon Cheves to R. Habersham & Sons, March 10, 1862 (first quotation), Mary C. West to "Dear Langdon" [her cousin], May 2, 1896 (second quotation), Captain W. A. Glassford, "Prolegomenon with historical sketch of The Balloon During the Civil War and The United States Army Aeronautical Corps," n.d. [printed pamphlet], 259–60 (third quotation), Brigadier General Thomas F. Drayton to Langdon Cheves, April 9, 12, 20, May 9, 28, 1862, Charles Cevor to Cheves, June 28 (fourth quotation), September 14, 1862, *ibid.*

11. Biographical Sketch of Langdon Cheves, Jr., 1935, Mary C. West to "Dear Langdon," May 2, 1896, Langdon Cheves to Professor Duane Squires, August 26, 1935, *ibid.*; Richard C. Lounsbury, Introduction to McCord, *Selected Writings*, 8–9.

Henry A. Middleton, Jr., who had shouted "hurrah for war!" upon learning the content of Lincoln's Inaugural Address. Less than a week after the fall of Sumter, Middleton placed the management of his Weehaw rice plantation entirely in the hands of his overseer, remarking, "I am too much absorbed in politics, to attend to anything else, and hope to take a part in the coming fight between North & South." Shortly thereafter, Wade Hampton began organizing his legion, and on May 2 he authorized several prominent Georgetown planters to form a company, with J. Harleston Read as captain and Middleton as third lieutenant. However, recruiting soon lagged, and before the end of the month the camp was broken up and those who had volunteered were paid off and dismissed. Middleton attributed the failure to what he called the incompetence and insincerity of Read. "We have failed in getting up this company," he asserted, "principally on account of Col. J. Harleston Reads personal unpopularity." Charging that Read's "conduct has certainly been most unmanly, & insincere and dishonorable," Middleton vowed to go to Charleston and "if nothing better" could be had, "to join the Legion as a private."[12]

Middleton was as good as his word. In early June, he joined the Legion in Columbia, enrolling as a private in the Washington Light Infantry, one of six infantry companies in the unit. Shortly after his arrival, he reported that "the soldiers to compose the legion are pouring in every day," many of them from Charleston. "All are very fine men," he noted proudly. During the remainder of the month, the green troops drilled steadily, usually five times a day, as they eagerly awaited orders to proceed to Virginia. Finally the orders came, and shortly before daybreak on Saturday, July 6, they arrived in Richmond, where they slept in a tobacco factory before marching through the city to their campsite. Two weeks later, they received the fateful order to move on to Manassas, where the Legion was destined to suffer fearful casualties on July 21 in the first major battle of the war.[13] One of those casualties was the impetuous thirty-two-year-old Middleton, who, according to one officer, was "one of those always at hand when 'rally to the colors' was called." Shot through the lungs, he lingered for nearly a week before succumbing to his wound on July 27. In a letter of

12. Henry A. Middleton, Jr., Plantation Journal, April 17 (first quotation), 22, May 2, 9, 21, 24 (second quotation), 1861, in Cheves-Middleton Papers, SCHS.

13. Henry A. Middleton, Jr., to "My dear Harriett" [his sister], June 7 (quotation), 12, 15, 17, July 7, 19, 1861, Henry A. Middleton, Jr., Family Letters, in Cheves-Middleton Papers, SCHS.

condolence to the grieving father, John Izard Middleton sought to soften the pain. "When we reflect that he died in the discharge of his duty to his country among the brave spirits who established for us an imperishable renown, on the bloody field of Manassas," he wrote, "we cannot but feel that the merit of such a sacrifice deprives it of half its bitterness."[14]

Another member of the Hampton Legion provided a vivid account of the murderous cross fire to which the South Carolinians were subjected on that bloody July day. In an emotional letter to his stepmother and sister, Captain Richard I. Manning, son of former governor John L. Manning, described the carnage that claimed the life of Middleton and so many others in the fighting that raged about Henry House Hill. "It was a terrible day, that 21st July," he began. "It might have made the stoutest heart quail to hear the instruments of death and destruction as they opened their terrible fires upon the devoted heads of the Legion . . . never did men fight more desperately or stand so patiently when they were being mowed down like sheep." With no artillery support on either side, the men of the Legion were exposed to a deadly barrage for twenty minutes before the enemy came within range of their guns. "At length," continued Manning, as "the contest waxed warm and warmer still, the desire to save a friend was absorbed in that of killing the foe." When the Legion's second-in-command, Lieutenant Colonel Benjamin J. Johnson, fell mortally wounded, the men "rallied around their flag, and advanced with redoubled energy." Manning himself did not witness the final Confederate counterattack in the late afternoon, for he was struck by a spent grapeshot that rendered him unconscious for a time. In all, the Hampton Legion suffered a 20 percent casualty rate at First Manassas, including Hampton himself, who was slightly wounded. Several other units on both sides experienced comparable losses. When R. F. W. Allston visited the battlefield two days later, he reported nearly seven hundred bodies "still lying exposed and nearly as many horses." Almost every house within three miles of the battle was filled with wounded, none of whom had received

---

14. "Copy from *Private letter* of Lieut. Logan to his father / 22 July at night / containing full particulars of Hampton's Legion's share in the Battle" (first quotation), Telegram, Theodore G. Baskin to W. Alston Pringle, received Charleston 2 A.M., July 23, Telegram, James Lowndes to Middleton & Co., received Charleston 12 o'clock, July 24, *ibid.*; R. F. W. Allston to Adele Petigru Allston, July 23, 1861, in Easterby, ed., *South Carolina Rice Plantation*, 181; J. Izard Middleton to Henry A. Middleton, August 3, 1861, Henry A. Middleton Family Letters, in Cheves-Middleton Papers, SCHS.

medical attention "until tonight." Two and one-half months later, evidence of the bloody encounter at Manassas was still visible. According to Peter Hairston, the site presented "a horrid spectacle." Many of the bodies had been only "slightly buried," and the combined action of rain and rooting hogs had removed much of the dirt, thereby leaving the bodies "partially exposed." Such scenes would be repeated at many other times and places during the next four years; Manassas was merely the first.[15]

Much later in the war, two other members of elite families provided vivid accounts of their military service. The first was Thomas P. Devereux II, the grandson and namesake of the great North Carolina slaveholder. In the fall of 1863, the eighteen-year-old Devereux left the Virginia Military Institute and enlisted as a private in the Forty-Third North Carolina Infantry. He served for a time as courier to General Junius Daniel until the latter was killed at Spotsylvania Court House in May, 1864. In all, young Devereux participated in more than one hundred skirmishes and battles as a member of the Army of Northern Virginia. He was wounded, apparently in the first month of Grant's campaign against Richmond, and had a horse shot from under him at Stephenson's Station in the Valley in September, 1864. Unlike his grandfather, Devereux was strongly committed to the Confederate cause and exuded optimism until almost the end of the war. Thus, just after the bloody encounter between Lee and Grant at Spotsylvania, he boasted: "We can whip the whole Yankee nation, and we will do it." Several months later, while serving with Early in the Shenandoah Valley, he learned of the fall of Atlanta. "It is a great reverse," he admitted, "but we are not whipped yet."[16]

15. Richard I. Manning, Jr., to "My Dearest Mother" [Sallie B. Manning], August 4, 1861, Chesnut-Miller-Manning Papers, SCHS; Boatner, *The Civil War Dictionary*, 371; R. F. W. Allston to Adele Petigru Allston, July 23, 1861, in Easterby, ed., *South Carolina Rice Plantation*, 181; Peter W. Hairston to Fanny Hairston, October 6, 1861, in Peter Wilson Hairston papers, SHC.

16. Thomas P. Devereux II to "Dear Father" [John], January 3, May 6, 13 (first quotation), September 1, 1864, Devereux to "Dear Mother" [Margaret], March 28, 1864, Devereux to "Dear Kate" [his sister], September 10, 1864 (second quotation), in Thomas P. Devereux II Letterbook, NCDAH. The supposition that Devereux was wounded sometime in May, 1864, is based upon the fact that there is a gap in his letters to the family between May 16 and August 7, when he arrived in Staunton, and upon an undated telegram announcing that he was "wounded & in Richmond" and identifying him as a "Courier to Genl Daniel," who was mortally wounded on May 12 and died the following day. See Telegram, Jas[?] Edmondston to Mr. J. De Rosset[?], n.d., in Devereux Family Papers, DU.

Devereux's confidence wavered momentarily in the wake of decisive victories by Philip Sheridan over Early at Fisher's Hill and Cedar Creek in September and October, respectively. "You people at home—don't know what the war is," he exploded in a letter to his grandfather four days after the defeat at Cedar Creek. Recounting the devastation inflicted upon the Valley by Sheridan, he reported that in the area between Staunton and Strasburg "there have been 2000 barns and [he didn't] know how many dwellings burnt—they burnt every barn that had wheat in it—and drove off every cow—hog and sheep that they could lay their hands on." Nevertheless, in a letter written from the lines at Petersburg on Christmas Eve, he still retained some hope. "We are in a tight place," he conceded, "but I say stick up—and keep a bold front—and we are bound to win. Gen Lee has 60000 of the best soldiers in the world . . . and when he says the word—we will storm Grant in his Breastworks . . . and take them too—or die trying." Devereux remained defiant and optimistic well into the new year. In his last extant letter, dated less than two weeks before Lee's surrender, he told his sister not to look for him "till next winter unless I get a wound."[17]

Edward B. Middleton, another member of one of the first families of South Carolina, viewed the closing days of the war from a different perspective. The son of Thomas and Eweretta Barnwell Middleton, young Edward was a lieutenant in the First South Carolina Artillery stationed at Battery Bee during the Federal siege of Charleston. From that vantage point, he described the intense shelling of the city by the enemy. In late October, 1864, he noted sadly: "Poor old Charleston seems to be gradually going to pieces." At least half a dozen fires had been ignited in the preceding two weeks, the steeple of St. Michael's Church had been struck three times, public buildings at the corner of Broad and Meeting Streets had been damaged, and the streets were virtually deserted. "As far as the eye can reach," he reported, "not a living thing is seen except now & then a stray soldier & not a sound save the screech of the shells as they go crashing through some houses."[18] After the evacuation of Charleston in

17. Thomas P. Devereux II to John Devereux, September 23, 1864, February 20, 1865, Devereux to "My dear Grandpa" [Thomas P., Sr.], October 23, 1864 (first quotation), Devereux to "Dear Kate," December 24, 1864 (second quotation), March 28, 1865 (third quotation), in Thomas P. Devereux II Letterbook, NCDAH.

18. *South Carolina Genealogies*, III, 154: Edward B. Middleton Diary & Journal, August 27, October 1, 23 (quotation), 1864, Eweretta Barnwell Middleton Family Letters, in Cheves-Middleton Papers, SCHS.

mid-February, 1865, Middleton retreated with William J. Hardee's corps into North Carolina. There, on March 16, he was captured during the Battle of Averasboro and sent as a prisoner of war to Johnson's Island near Sandusky, Ohio. Just after his arrival, the atmosphere became very tense when news of President Lincoln's assassination reached the camp. Colonel Hill, the camp commander, addressed the prisoners, urging calm and praising the martyred president. "Many of us thought otherwise," Middleton remarked laconically. In late April, as the last Confederate forces began to surrender, Hill posted a circular offering the prisoners amnesty and informing them that they would not be released until they took the prescribed oath. For more than a week, the imprisoned Confederates heatedly debated whether or not they should accept the offer. By May 4 all but about 400 of the 2,800 prisoners had applied for the oath. Middleton was one of the last hold-outs, refusing to take any step "until some official intelligence is received of Kirby Smith's surrender or of a proclamation from J[efferson] D[avis] absolving us from allegiance to the C.S." Not until June 5 did he finally capitulate and submit his formal application for amnesty. Two weeks later, he bade "this 'dear spot' adieu" and after a brief interlude in New York, where he was introduced to Admiral David G. Farragut, he returned to South Carolina.[19]

While the sons of wealthy slaveholders risked their lives on distant battlefields, the war took a heavy emotional toll on those who remained behind. After each battle, they anxiously scanned the casualty lists, fearful lest they find the name of a loved one. The battle deaths suffered by members of elite planter families are summarized in Table 7. Although the human losses were frightful among all classes of the population, the well-to-do bore their share of the heartache. Edward Middleton survived his ordeal at Johnson's Island and returned home after the war, but his older brother, Thomas, Jr., did not. The latter contracted fever while stationed at Battery Wagner and died in January, 1864. Their uncle, Henry A. Middleton, lost two sons in the war. So, too, did another Georgetown planter, William B. Pringle. Wade Hampton lost his brother Frank at Brandy Station, Virginia, in June, 1863, and his son Preston, a member

19. Edward B. Middleton Diary & Journal, March 16, April 10, 14, 15 (first quotation), 25, May 3, 4 (second quotation), 30, June 6, 19 (third quotation), July 4, 7, 10, Eweretta Barnwell Middleton Family Letters, in Cheves-Middleton Papers, SCHS.

TABLE 7 · CIVIL WAR CASUALTIES KILLED IN ACTION

ELITE SLAVEHOLDERS KILLED IN ACTION

Ga.:   John B. Lamar, Crampton's Gap, September 14, 1862
            Joseph L. McCallister, Trevilian's Station, June 11, 1864

Miss.:   William G. Conner, Gettysburg, July 3, 1863

S.C.:   Langdon Cheves, Jr., Battery Wagner, July 10, 1863

ELITE SLAVEHOLDERS WHO LOST SONS AND OTHER CLOSE MALE RELATIVES

Ala.:   Thomas H. Herndon (son, Wilderness)
        William Robinson (son, Wilderness)
        James G. Spann (son, Petersburg)

La.:   John Julius Pringle (2 brothers, S.C.)

Miss.:   Richard T. Archer (nephew, Malvern Hill), William L. Balfour (son)
        Edwin R. Bennett (2 sons, Shiloh), Thomas G. Blewett (son)
        Gerard Brandon (2 brothers, Chancellorsville, Fredericksburg)
        Nathaniel Jefferies (son, Second Manassas), John A. Quitman (son-in-law)
        James A. Ventress (nephew, Spotsylvania C.H.)
        Henry Vaughan (2 sons, Gettysburg, Vicksburg)

N.C.:   Thomas P. Devereux (grandson, Bristoe Station)
        Thomas D. Warren (brother-in-law, Mechanicsville)

S.C.:   Charles Alston, Sr. (son, Battery Wagner), John R. Cheves (son, Seven Days')
        Wade Hampton III (son, Petersburg; brother, Brandy Station)
        Charles Heyward (son), James B. Heyward (son, Second Manassas)
        Henry A. Middleton (2 sons, First Manassas, Hawes Shop, Va.)
        Oliver H. Middleton (only son, Matadequin Creek, Va.)
        William B. Pringle (2 sons, Battery Wagner)
        Robert Barnwell Rhett (youngest son, Seven Days')

Va.:   James Galt (2 nephews, Winchester)

SUMMARY: A total of 34 were killed from 28 elite families (10.3 percent of those who held 250+ slaves in 1860).

of his own cavalry corps, the following year near Petersburg.[20] The Rhetts, denounced as "miserable creatures" by one North Carolinian in late January, 1861, because it was said that not one of them had joined the army despite the fact that they had played "so prominent a part" in precipitating the crisis, actually contributed four brothers to the service, all of them officers. The youngest, Robert Woodward Rhett, a lieutenant in the First Regiment, South Carolina Volunteers, was mortally wounded at Cold Harbor on June 27, 1862. Of course, South Carolinians were by no means the only ones who experienced the pain of battlefield deaths. Henry Vaughan of Mississippi, himself a native of the Palmetto State, lost two sons within a month's time, one at Vicksburg and the other at Gettysburg. Another Mississippian, Richard T. Archer, had "three brave sons" when the war began and lost two of them early in the conflict. The first, whom Archer had adopted following the death of his brother, "fell in the first rank at the battle of Malvern Hills [sic]" when ordered to charge a "Battery of fifty guns." The other, only sixteen when he joined an infantry company "temporarily because our Country was invaded," succumbed as a consequence of three days and three nights of "hard service" in pursuit of deserters. And so it went in slaveholding families throughout the Confederacy.[21]

Yet another prominent South Carolina family, the Heywards, suffered a particularly heart-wrenching loss during the war. Not only was a beloved son killed at Second Manassas while serving with the First Regiment, South Carolina Volunteers, but his body was never recovered. Young Nathaniel Heyward, the eldest son of James B. Heyward and namesake of his immensely wealthy great-grandfather, died "instantly" at sundown on the first day of the battle when a shell exploded about fifteen feet from where Heyward and several others were resting and discussing "the actions of the day." Family and friends were devastated. "We feel as if we too had lost a brother," lamented a female cousin in a letter of condolence to the victim's younger brother. "The War," she continued, "has really come home to us & desolated our fireside like that of many other afflicted families. Your poor mother is dreadfully distressed & of course looks

20. *South Carolina Genealogies,* III, 152, 154, 333–34; Cauthen, ed., *Family Letters of the Three Wade Hamptons,* xvii.

21. William S. Pettigrew to James C. Johnston, January 24, 1861, in Hayes Collection, SHC; Rhett Genealogy Notes #2, Rhett Family papers, SCHS; *Goodspeed's,* I, 309–310, II, 952; Richard T. Archer to General Joseph E. Johnston, [August, 1863?] in Richard Thompson Archer Family Papers, CAH.

very badly & careworn." Shortly after receiving word of his son's death, James Heyward set out for the battlefield in an attempt to locate Nat's body and bring it home. Sadly, his search proved to be futile. Despite exhaustive efforts by the family over a period of nearly forty years, young Heyward's remains were never recovered.[22]

Apart from direct military participation, wealthy slaveowners made numerous other contributions to the Confederate war effort. Many offered financial support, most commonly by purchasing Confederate bonds and equipping local military units. Consistent with their sense of noblesse oblige, they provided assistance to soldiers' families, either with direct monetary support or through the donation of provisions. They also bore a disproportionate share of the special war taxes imposed by the national and state governments. At the beginning of the war, a great many large slaveholders who were too old for military service made generous donations to military companies being organized in their immediate vicinity. For example, Paul Cameron gave $500 to support Company C of the Sixth North Carolina Regiment when it was organized in his home county of Orange in May, 1861. Other prominent North Carolinians made similar contributions about the same time. Josiah Collins, Sr., and William S. Pettigrew gave $1,000 and $500, respectively, for "the use of the military companies of Washington County who had enlisted or may hereafter enlist." Several members of the Hairston family made like donations.[23]

Elsewhere in the South, the story was much the same. Jeremiah H. Brown, the largest slaveholder in Alabama, is said to have equipped and maintained "perhaps more than a regiment of soldiers" during the war. Another Alabamian, Joel E. Mathews, equipped several companies of volunteers and donated $15,000 in gold for the state's defense shortly after secession.[24] Many who had

22. *South Carolina Genealogies*, II, 364, 372; John W. Chambers [1st Lt commanding Co. L, 1st S.C. Volunteers] to James B. Heyward, September 6, 1862 (TS), Mary [Barnwell Heyward] to cousin Frank, September 11, 1862, R. B. Rhett to [James B. Heyward], October 1, 1862, Sue M. Monroe to Mattie Hayne Heyward [niece of Nat], May 26, 1899, in Heyward and Ferguson Family Papers, SHC.

23. Kenzer, *Kinship and Neighborhood in a Southern Community*, 73, 89; Note dated April 30, 1861, and signed by Josiah Collins and William S. Pettigrew, Series 2.1.2, Folder 461 in Pettigrew Family Papers, SHC; Peter W. Hairston to Fanny C. Hairston, April 4, 1861, in Peter Wilson Hairston Papers, SHC.

24. Owen, *History of Alabama*, III, 231–32, IV, 1174–75.

opposed secession also contributed liberally to the Confederate cause. Thus, in the spring of 1861, Benjamin Roach, Jr., made modest donations to military forces in three of the four Mississippi counties in which he held slaves. Fellow Natchezian Francis Surget, Jr., was even more generous. In addition to monetary gifts totaling nearly $1,000 to three local companies—the Adams Troop, Adams Light Guards, and Natchez Fencibles—he also donated "one large Fat Beef" to the Natchez Rifles in August, 1861, $100 for the "Soldiers going to Columbus" two months later, and a horse to the Macon Cavalry early the following year.[25] Similarly, William B. Hodgson of Georgia subscribed $50 to the Chatham Light Infantry in June, 1861, and, two years later, gave $200 to benefit the "wounded soldiers of Bragg's army" following the battle of Chickamauga.[26]

Very early in the war, some members of the elite began to manifest concern for the welfare of their less fortunate neighbors, especially those families whose male members had volunteered for military service. In the fall of 1861, noting that the rice crop lay unpounded and unmarketable because of the blockade, Benjamin Allston suggested to his father that after ample provision had been made for the slaves, the balance of the crop should be given to the poor. "We must support these men and the families of those who are fighting," he declared. Several planters whose contributions to military units have already been mentioned also helped to support soldiers' families. Among these were Joel Mathews, Paul Cameron, and several members of the Hairston family. Even before the bombardment of Sumter, Samuel Hairston of Virginia donated 300 bushels of wheat to the volunteers and their families. During the war, Cameron made loans totaling more than $13,000 to assist the families of soldiers from his home county of Orange.[27] Another North Carolinian, Thomas P. Devereux,

25. Receipts dated March 27 (Washington Horse Guards), April 15 (Yazoo City), May 27 (Adams Light Guard Battalion), 1861, Folder 6, in Benjamin Roach Family Papers, CAH; "F. Surget a/c with Charles P. Leverich," December 24, 1860 (Roll 1), [Francis Surget, Jr.] Account Book, February 26, April 15, 25, May 6, 1861, [Francis Surget, Jr.] Checkbook, W. A. Britton & Co., Natchez, November 26, 1861 (second quotation), [Francis Surget, Jr.] checkbook, Bank of Louisiana, New Orleans, March 19, 1862 (Roll 2), Receipt dated Natchez, August 26, 1861, F. Surget to John B. Nevitt (first quotation) (Roll 6), in Surget Family Papers, MDAH.

26. "Joint Account Hodgson and Telfair" with R. Habersham & Son, June 8, 1861, W. B. Hodgson a/c with R. Habersham & Son, October 12, 1863, Box 9, Folder 75, both in Telfair Family Papers, GHS.

27. Benjamin Allston to "My dear Father," November 24, 1861, in R. F. W. Allston Papers, SCHS; Owen, History of Alabama, IV, 1174–75; Peter W. Hairston to Fanny C. Hairston, April 4,

gave 800 bushels of his ample supply of salt to poor families in his district in exchange for socks, which he then donated to the Confederate Quartermaster for distribution to the troops. "In this way," explained his daughter, "he prevented an amount of suffering which it is difficult to estimate & became a benefactor to the poorer class" throughout the region. Turner C. Clanton of Georgia was another wealthy slaveholder who sought to ameliorate the plight of the poor. In the spring of 1862, when meal was selling for $2 a bushel, Clanton offered it to families of volunteers from Richmond and Columbia counties at half that price. He had previously contributed several thousand dollars "to aid the soldier's cause."[28]

Clanton's son-in-law Jefferson Thomas was one of many slaveowners who supported the war effort by purchasing Confederate bonds. Thus, after selling his cotton crop in Augusta in July, 1863, Thomas invested $15,000 in Confederate States bonds paying 8 percent interest. During a single month the following year, seventy-four-year-old Theodore L. Gourdin, an ardent South Carolina secessionist, purchased a like amount of Confederate 4 percent bonds. In addition, as late as February, 1865, Gourdin donated 7,000 pounds of fodder "for use of" a South Carolina cavalry battalion.[29] Even more generous in his financial contributions to the Confederate cause was Thomas P. Devereux, the reluctant secessionist from North Carolina. In October, 1864, he held at least $27,000 in Confederate bonds bearing 6 percent interest, of which he transferred $10,000 to his son-in-law Patrick M. Edmondston to be held in trust for the latter and Devereux's daughter Kate. Another North Carolinian, Raleigh banker George W. Mordecai, invested heavily in Confederate bonds during the war, both for himself and for his clients at the Bank of North Carolina. In January, 1863, Mordecai exchanged some state bonds for $9,000 in Confederate coupon bonds, and six months later, following somewhat ambivalent advice from his Richmond stockbroker, he purchased $100,000 worth of newly issued cotton bonds

1861, in Peter Wilson Hairston Papers, SHC; Kenzer, *Kinship and Neighborhood in a Southern Community*, 89.

28. *"Journal of a Secesh Lady,"* ed. Crabtree and Patton, 100; *The Secret Eye*, ed. Burr, 203 and 203 n. 20.

29. *The Secret Eye*, ed. Burr, 217; *Biographical Directory of the Senate of South Carolina*, comp. Reynolds and Faunt, 224; T. L. Gourdin, C.S.A. 4 percent bonds, March 11, 23, 31, 1864, Receipt dated February 27, 1865, signed M. J. Kirk, Captain commanding 19th Batt. S.C.C., Folder 15 in Theodore L. Gourdin Plantation and Personal Papers, SCHS.

bearing 6 percent interest. Although he had subscribed $500 toward the construction of an ironclad gunboat the year before, the evidence suggests that Mordecai, who speculated in cotton throughout the war, was probably more interested in preserving his own capital assets than in aiding the Confederacy. William B. Hodgson, the largest slaveholder in Georgia at the beginning of the war, also gave some financial support to the Confederacy, but considering his great wealth, one wonders whether he could have done more. Records indicate that he subscribed $1,000 to a Confederate loan less than a week after the fall of Fort Sumter and, a year later, purchased a single Confederate bond yielding a paltry 2 percent interest.[30]

The wealthy planters also contributed to the war effort in several involuntary ways, most notably through taxes and labor requisitions. In August, 1861, the Provisional Congress of the Confederacy levied a war tax of one half of 1 percent on various kinds of property including land and slaves, but collection proved to be largely ineffective. Following the adoption of the permanent constitution, which followed the United States Constitution in requiring that direct taxes be apportioned among the states according to population, the subsequent Confederate congresses were precluded from levying a national war tax on property.[31] Many state and local governments, however, did enact such taxes, both to support military units and to provide relief for soldiers' families. For example, in mid-June, 1861, the Board of Police in Adams County, Mississippi, imposed a 50 percent surcharge on the state tax for 1860 to be used "for military purposes." Both Mississippi and Louisiana levied special war taxes on property holders within their boundaries. Thus, Francis Surget, Jr., paid county and state taxes totaling $246.39 on his Natchez mansion in 1861. Of that total, $67.60 was the tax on real property; $58.95, that on personal property (excluding slaves); $74.90, the state war tax; and $44.94, the county war tax. That same year, his brother Eustace paid $939.13 in taxes on his Palmetto plantation in Adams County and

30. M. McMahon to Thomas P. Devereux, October 12, 1864, Receipt dated October 13, 1864, signed P. M. Edmondston, Folder 2, both in John Devereux Papers, NCDAH; John A. Lancaster & Son to George W. Mordecai, January 30, July 7, August 1, 5, 1863, William A. Wright to Mordecai, April 14, 1862, in George W. Mordecai Papers, SHC; "Joint Account Hodgson and Telfair" with R. Habersham & Son, April 18, 1861, W. B. Hodgson a / c with R. Habersham & Son, April 3, 1863, both in Telfair Family Papers, GHS.

31. E. Merton Coulter, *The Confederate States of America, 1861–1865* (Baton Rouge, 1950), 174–77; Emory M. Thomas, *The Confederate Nation, 1861–1865* (New York, 1979), 137.

$2,347.42 on his Morville plantation in Concordia Parish, Louisiana. The latter included a 1 percent war tax levied by the state, and approximately one-fourth of the Palmetto tax was in the form of county and state war taxes. The tax on Palmetto was about $200 higher the following year, with a portion now designated for "military relief."[32]

Another form of taxation was the tax in kind, which ultimately proved more onerous than the relatively modest taxes noted above. As the war continued and the financial needs of the Confederacy became increasingly critical, there was a demand for tax legislation of some kind to alleviate the mounting economic distress caused by the printing of huge quantities of unsecured treasury notes and bonds. Congress responded in April, 1863, with the passage of a comprehensive tax law so severe that historian Emory Thomas has termed it almost "confiscatory." Among other provisions, the act imposed an 8 percent ad valorem tax on agricultural products, a tax of 1 percent on money on hand on July 1 of that year, and, most important, a 10 percent tax in kind on a wide array of agricultural products and livestock.[33] The effect on the great planters was immediate and significant. For example, in September, 1863, George W. Mordecai paid the Confederate government a tax of nearly $7,000 on 87,000 pounds of cotton that he had purchased during the war for speculative purposes. Two months later, Theodore L. Gourdin paid the tax-in-kind tithe on the agricultural products grown on his South Carolina plantations. These products included corn, rice, sweet potatoes, cured fodder, cotton, and peas. On his Charleston District plantation alone, the tax amounted to 14,560 bushels of corn, 13,200 bushels of sweet potatoes, 4,000 pounds of fodder, 600 bushels of peas, and 337 bushels of rice.[34]

Another burden that fell most heavily upon large slaveholders was the gov-

32. Tax Receipt, Natchez, July 31, 1861, Francis Surget, Jr. (quotation) (Roll 1); Tax Receipt, Adams County [1862], Francis Surget, Jr.; Tax Bill, Adams County, June 12, 1862, Eustace Surget; Tax Receipt for Morville Plantation, Concordia Parish, January, 1862, Eustace Surget (Roll 4); Tax Receipt, Adams County, February 23, 1863, Eustace Surget (Roll 5), in Surget Family Papers, MDAH.

33. Thomas, *The Confederate Nation*, 198; Coulter, *The Confederate States of America*, 177–78.

34. "Joint Account Hodgson and Telfair," November 17, 1863, in Telfair Family Papers, GHS; D. Malloy & Son to George W. Mordecai, September 8, 1863, in George W. Mordecai Papers, SHC; "Form of the Estimate and Assessment of Agricultural Products," Williamsburg District, November 26, 1863, Charleston St. Stephen's, November 27, 1863, Folder 15, in Theodore L. Gourdin Plantation and Personal Papers, SCHS.

ernment impressment of laborers and draft animals to work on fortifications. Although planters were sometimes compensated for the use of their slaves and stock, this practice interfered with the plantation work routine and frequently provoked complaints from owners and overseers alike. Thus, when Confederate authorities requisitioned mules and hands to construct coastal defenses in North Carolina following the fall of Roanoke Island in February, 1862, Thomas P. Devereux grumbled that their absence would seriously impede work on the next crop. The manager of an Alabama plantation became even more irate when the government took a dozen of his hands to work on the fortifications at Mobile in the winter of 1863–1864. "I wish our own Government may not ruin us, before the Yankees get a Chance at us up here," he remarked caustically. Three of these Negroes died while in government service, and the remainder were not returned to their plantation until early May, long after the planting season had commenced.[35]

In exposed port cities throughout the South, from Charleston to New Orleans and from Wilmington to Mobile, slaves were impressed by the government to erect fortifications. For example, in early April, 1862, General Mansfield Lovell requisitioned 105 slaves from sugar plantations in Plaquemines Parish to work on Forts Jackson and St. Philip, the two forts guarding the river approach to New Orleans. Two weeks later, additional hands were taken to complete work on an ironclad ram. These feverish labors were in vain, however, for the city surrendered to the naval forces of David G. Farragut on April 26. Over on the East Coast, some 300 slaves were employed for ten months constructing Battery Wagner and other defensive works on Morris Island. These hands were accompanied by overseers (one for each 100), who were paid by the state at the rate of $50 per month. Owners who supplied hands to work on the fortifications at Wilmington in the spring and summer of 1863 were compensated at the rate of fifty cents a day for each slave. Although smaller slaveholders were also affected by these government requisitions, it is clear that in most areas the bulk of the hands were furnished by those who owned the most slaves.[36]

35. Thomas P. Devereux to George W. Mordecai, February 13, 1862, in George W. Mordecai Papers, SHC; Richard D. Powell to John H. Cocke, December 10, 1863 (quotation), January 23, May 5, 1864 (Roll 4), in Cocke Papers, SHC.

36. Magnolia Plantation Journals, April 3, 21, 1862, in Henry Clay Warmoth Papers and Books, SHC; Major A. L. Dearing to Captain Langdon Cheves, September 10, 1862, Major W. H. Echols to Cheves, June 25, 1863, both in Langdon Cheves, Jr., Papers, SCHS; Receipt signed W. C. Pace,

Some elite planters were also incensed by the frequently arbitrary conduct of the Confederate Commissary Department. One of the most unlikely critics was Langdon Cheves, Jr., whose numerous contributions to the Confederate war effort have already been discussed. Outraged by the unauthorized killing of three of his "working oxen" to provide meat for the soldiers of a regiment stationed near his Savannah River rice plantation, Cheves dispatched a blistering letter of protest to Major General John C. Pemberton, commander of the Military Department of South Carolina, Georgia, and Florida. Charging the commissary department with gross "incompetence or mismanagement," he predicted that such destruction of working stock could only lead to "famine for army & people" alike during the following year. Much more catastrophic than his own loss, however, was that of his equally wealthy neighbor, Allen Izard, whose *"entire stock"* had been plundered by commissary agents. With some 300 "people" to feed, declared Cheves, Izard had "used the prudence & energy which the commissary dept. *did not*. He bought cattle from a distance and provided for the future." Now, continued the irate South Carolinian, "his entire provision is swept away, he is paid a mere fraction of its money value, and he dare not . . . provide for his negroes' necessary subsistence at the market price, lest another raid should be made upon him." If such "systematic contempt" for "personal rights" continued, he warned, planters would be obliged to remove their Negroes "to some place where [they] may be allowed to feed them." Thus, even those most committed to the Confederate cause were not reticent about criticizing government policies when their own interests were adversely affected.[37]

Despite occasional complaints about government requisitions of men and provisions, the wealthy slaveholders discussed thus far actively supported the Confederacy. A few die-hard Unionists, however, did not. This was particularly true of the Natchez nabobs, who were influenced not only by the desire to safeguard their economic interests but also by their close family and social connections with the Northeast. There were, to be sure, a number of elite families in the Natchez District who did give unconditional support to the war effort.

Lt. Col. Commanding 118 Regiment, North Carolina Militia, March 17, 1863, John A. Winder to George W. Mordecai, July 10, 1863, both in George W. Mordecai Papers, SHC.

37. Langdon Cheves to "General" [John C. Pemberton], May 17, 1862, in Langdon Cheves, Jr., Papers, SCHS.

Chief among these were the Conners, Quitmans, and Brandons. As was noted earlier, five members of both the Conner and Quitman families served in the Confederate Army. The Brandons were even more patriotic. At least eight near relatives of Natchez aristocrat Gerard Brandon, the son of former governor Gerard C. Brandon, performed the like service.[38] Apart from John A. Quitman, perhaps the most rabid prewar secessionists in the district were Richard T. Archer and George Wilson Humphreys, both of Claiborne County. Despite a feud between the two families that resulted in a violent encounter between the hot-headed Archer and one of Humphreys's brothers in late 1859, both men eventually found common cause in their mutual support of the Confederacy. Humphreys served as a captain of cavalry during the war and remained an unreconstructed rebel until the end of his life.[39] In all, the sons or close relatives of at least a third of the largest slaveholders in the Natchez District fought in the Confederate Army, and members from at least six of these families paid with their lives.[40]

Among those at the apex of the social hierarchy in Natchez, however, these families were the exception. More representative was Haller Nutt, who, unlike the old North Carolina Federalist James C. Johnston, was motivated almost entirely by concern for his economic interests. Nutt, one of several Natchezians with Philadelphia connections, was the son of the celebrated planter-scientist Dr. Rush Nutt and proprietor of the unfinished Longwood mansion near Natchez. Notwithstanding his political posture, he reputedly suffered property losses amounting to more than $1,500,000 during the war. As a consequence of Nutt's well-publicized loyalty to the Union, his widow was able to recover nearly $100,000 in compensation from the federal government during the two

38. Letter from Conner descendant Jonathan Ray to author, February 18, 1996; May, *John A. Quitman*, 352; *Goodspeed's*, I, 419–22.

39. Richard T. Archer to George Wilson Humphreys, October 10, 1859, Archer to the "Editors of the Sun," December 18, 1859, Archer to D. G. Humphreys, December 21, 1859, in Richard Thompson Archer and Family Papers, CAH; Lt. Col. George Moorman to Capt. Wilson Humphries [*sic*], July 2, 1864, in Weekly Time Book, George Wilson Humphreys and Family Papers, MDAH. For evidence that Humphreys remained hostile to Yankeedom long after the war's end, see A. C. Wharton to G. W. Humphreys, July 2, 1894, *ibid.*

40. See Table 7. The Archer, Bennett, Brandon, Conner, Jefferies, and Quitman families were all from the Natchez District.

decades following the war.[41] That Nutt opposed secession because of the apprehended impact on his financial fortunes is apparent from his activities during the war. Despite the voluntary Confederate embargo on the shipment of cotton abroad, Nutt sold 551 bales of cotton through a New Orleans factor just weeks before the fall of that city.[42] Undeterred by the latter event, which he dismissed as merely "unpleasant news," he was making plans to resume cotton shipments to New Orleans as early as September, 1862, a prospect that his friend John Routh correctly labeled optimistic. Nevertheless, after successfully evading both Yankee incursions and Confederate orders to burn cotton by storing it under sheds and in swamps, Nutt was again shipping the white staple out of New Orleans by the spring of 1864. One can well imagine the opprobrium experienced by Nutt and his family, especially among his Louisiana neighbors, as a consequence of his steadfast Unionism. In his last letter to his wife, Julia, written in June, 1864, while he was in Vicksburg waiting to testify before a U.S. military commission, Nutt reminded her of their delicate situation. "Do try & bear in mind our present condition—and what a volcano we are resting on," he counseled. "Nothing to cheer us but our own calm, reasonable good sense & steady exertions—relying on none but ourselves—letting all others alone."[43]

Another Natchezian whose wartime conduct was apparently governed more by economic self-interest than by concern for the fate of his homeland was Benjamin Roach, Jr. As the executor of his late father's estate, Roach was administering properties in eight Mississippi counties yielding annual net profits of $90,000 when hostilities commenced.[44] Although he made modest contributions to several local military units in the spring of 1861, he was soon seeking

41. Claim filed by Sargeant Prentiss Knut on behalf of his mother, Julia A. Nutt [ca.] 1890 (printed document), Dispatch of James F. Latham to New York *Herald,* October 16, 1863 (MS copy), both in Nutt Family Collection, MDAH; Hawks, "Julia A. Nutt of Longwood," 299.

42. Freeman C. Holmes to Haller Nutt, January 25, February 1, 1862, "Account Sales of . . . Cotton sold on plantation for a/c of Haller Nutt Esq.," March 11, 1862, in Nutt Family Collection, MDAH.

43. John Routh to Haller Nutt, September 16, 1862, Nutt to Hamilton Smith, April 26, July 17, 1862, Smith to Nutt, May 2, September 16, 1862, April 20, 1864, Haller Nutt to Julia Nutt, June 3, 1864, *ibid.*

44. Computed by author from receipts for sale of cotton, 1852, 1855, 1859–60, in Benjamin Roach Family Papers, CAH. Roach's 1860 crop amounted to 2,413 bales, which yielded gross proceeds of $109,055 and a net of $100,488.

market outlets for his bountiful cotton crop. Like Nutt, he resumed shipments to New Orleans shortly after the Federals occupied that city, and by the spring of 1864 he was sending cotton to New Orleans, paying the federal excise tax and then shipping it on to New York.[45]

Of all the Natchez nabobs, no other had a more illustrious heritage than William J. Minor. Indeed, the original town of Natchez was situated on land purchased by the Spanish government from his father, Stephen Minor, in 1788. A native Pennsylvanian, the latter had enlisted in the Spanish army during the Revolutionary War after migrating to the Southwest and had served briefly as the Spanish governor of Natchez.[46] Although born in Mississippi, William never relinquished the ties to the Northeast that he had inherited from his father. Educated at the University of Pennsylvania, he married into the Gustine family of that state and conducted his business affairs through the Leverich brothers of New York. Thus, his persistent Unionism should come as no surprise. In testimony before the Smith-Brady Commission in New Orleans shortly before the end of the war, Minor explained that he had opposed secession because he "didn't perceive the right or necessity for it."[47] Indeed, he did all in his power to thwart what he later termed "the great secession blunder," urging governors of the slave states and public officials in both Mississippi and Louisiana to pursue a moderate course. During the war, Minor became such a high-profile Unionist that General Benjamin F. Butler tried to persuade him to go to Washington, D.C., to confer with President Lincoln. Minor declined the invitation, however, on the grounds that such a mission might "tend still more to injure his family around Natchez."[48]

Another prominent Natchezian who remained loyal to the Union throughout the war was Massachusetts-born Josiah Winchester, who had expressed

45. Est. B. Roach decd. In a/c with B. Roach executor, March 15, 1863, Steamship Morning Star in a/c with Est. Roach, April 29, 1864, both in Benjamin Roach Family Papers, CAH.

46. Holmes, "Stephen Minor," 17–26.

47. Testimony of William J. Minor, Plantation Affairs, E. 736 RG 94, Testimony before Smith-Brady Commission, Box 4, National Archives, Washington, D.C. I am indebted to Thomas Scarborough, a doctoral candidate at the University of California at Santa Barbara and a distant cousin of mine, for providing me with a copy of this item.

48. W. J. Minor to Dr. Stephen Duncan, August 6, 1865, quoted in Wayne, *The Reshaping of Plantation Society*, 58 (first quotation); Frank W. Klingberg, *The Southern Claims Commission* (Berkeley, 1955), 111–12 (second quotation).

such great disenchantment with his new surroundings shortly after his arrival in 1837.[49] Although he soon warmed to the social life of the city and became the legal advisor to many of its most distinguished citizens, he never embraced the political principles of his adopted state. Consequently, his allegiance to the United States never wavered during the war. He, too, sold cotton to the enemy;[50] he took the oath of allegiance after Union troops occupied Natchez; and during the last two years of the war he acted as an intermediary between Federal authorities and local citizens still loyal to the Confederacy.[51] For Winchester, the war was merely an annoying distraction. In November, 1864, as Sherman's army began to cut its destructive swath through Georgia, Winchester's two sons were in New York preparing to embark for Europe, and he was investing funds in gold in the same city.[52]

New York was apparently a popular destination for disaffected Natchez District Unionists during the war. Even before Winchester's sons departed for Europe, at least four of the most prominent members of that group—Stephen Duncan, Samuel M. Davis, Ayres P. Merrill, Jr., and William Newton Mercer—had already taken refuge in that city. A fifth, Levin Marshall, also settled in New York, though it is not clear whether or not he did so while the war was still in progress.[53] Upon his departure for the North in the spring of 1863, Duncan left behind a bill for the Confederate government in the amount of $185,801.59, allegedly to compensate him for losses and impressments by the Confederates as well as depredations committed by the enemy, all of which he attributed to the act of secession.[54] Merrill, Harvard-educated and the son of a Massachusetts-born physician, apparently moved to New York about the same time as Duncan. At the end of 1864, he had so lost touch with affairs on his Mississippi and Louisiana plantations that he had no idea how many of his

49. See p. 31 of this book.

50. W. C. Daugherty to Thomas Henderson & Co., November 18, 1863, H. S. Buckner & Co. to Josiah Winchester, April 26, 1864, both in Winchester Family Papers, CAH.

51. J. Alexander Ventress to Josiah Winchester, February 22, 1864, Lt. Cdr. James A. Green[?] to Winchester, March 14, 1864, Ann M. Farrar to Winchester, January 23, 1865, *ibid.*

52. George W. Koontz[?] to Josiah Winchester, November 20, 1864, *ibid.*

53. Account with S. M. Davis, 1863, in Stephen Duncan, Jr., Plantation Journal, 1861–95, volume 6 in Duncan Papers, LSU; Wayne, *The Reshaping of Plantation Society*, 53.

54. "Debited to Govt. of C.S.A.," March 26, 1863, Stephen Duncan Plantation Journal, 1861–70, volume 5 in Duncan Papers, LSU. Of the total losses incurred, Duncan attributed $147,911.09 to "Losses & Impressments" by the Confederates and $37,890 to "Depredations by the enemy."

"own former negroes," as he called them, were left on his places. Merrill remained in New York after the war as a partner in the factorage firm of Goodman and Merrill, becoming sole owner of the business following the death of Goodman in April, 1866. He was subsequently appointed minister to Belgium by President Grant.[55] Mercer, the Adams County planter who resided much of each year in New Orleans, arrived in New York early in 1863. Despite his heated dispute with General Butler over the oath of allegiance several months before, Mercer was treated with uncommon solicitude by Federal authorities after his removal to New York. In May, the provost marshal in New Orleans authorized the passage to New York of Mercer's longtime companion Eliza H. Young and a female servant with the added stipulation that their baggage was to be passed "without examination." Six months later, Rear Admiral David D. Porter arranged to send "an old faithful body servant" from Mercer's Laurel Hill plantation to New York to wait on his old master.[56]

Although Natchez remained the hotbed of Unionism among members of the elite slaveholding class during the war, there were several other wealthy planters elsewhere in Mississippi and throughout the South who gave little or no support to the Confederate cause. Some were openly defiant in their opposition to the Confederacy, while others were more circumspect. Conspicuous among the first group was Mississippi cotton nabob Greenwood Leflore, former chief of the Choctaw and the largest Indian slaveholder in the South. Leflore reportedly flew a United States flag over his palatial Malmaison residence throughout the war, an action that led to his ostracism by neighboring whites. Robert Stafford of Cumberland Island, Georgia, contended in a claim submitted after the war that "from the beginning of hostilities against the United States to the end thereof his sympathies were constantly with the cause of the United States." He gave no aid to the Confederacy and was allegedly "uniformly kind" to Federal soldiers both during and immediately after the war.[57] Although

55. *Goodspeed's,* II, 430–32; Merrill to Josiah Winchester, December 19, 1864, in Winchester Family Papers, CAH; Merrill to Eustace Surget, November 8, 1865, April 30, 1866 (Roll 1), both in Surget Family Papers, MDAH.

56. William Cozzens to Dr. Mercer, February 20, 1863, Pass, Office of the Provost Marshal of Louisiana, New Orleans, May 20, 1863, Rear Admiral David D. Porter, commanding Mississippi Squadron, to Lieutenant John Pearce, commanding USS Fort Hindman, November 16, 1863, in William Newton Mercer Papers, LSU.

57. *Mississippi: The WPA Guide to the Magnolia State* (1938; rpr. Jackson, 1988), 403–405; Bullard, *Robert Stafford of Cumberland Island,* 238–39, 266.

James C. Johnston's Unionist views were well known, he was a bit more discreet than Leflore or Stafford. Thus, when he became concerned about the economic plight of the Confederacy in the spring of 1863, he instructed his banker to convert $6,500 in Confederate 8 percent bonds into state bonds or other safer securities and to make no further "investment for me in Confederate Bonds." The latter directive, he added, should be kept "in confidence as it might be considered treasonable." Equally cautious in revealing his "true sentiments" was Ascension Parish sugar magnate John Burnside. According to one observer, Burnside's neighbors were not aware of his Unionist views until the Federals occupied New Orleans. Thereafter, "he associated with the Union officers, and they dined with him at his [New Orleans] residence every day."[58]

The intense animosity felt by some members of the elite toward those whom they held responsible for precipitating the calamitous war was reflected in their private correspondence. Their comments ran the gamut from mild sarcasm to extreme bitterness. Representative of the former was a communication in late 1861 from Charleston lawyer James L. Petigru to his brother-in-law R. F. W. Allston, speculating on possible Federal military movements. "Let us hope for the best," began Petigru. "But what is the best? Perhaps that Beauregard may whip McClellan, and overrun the whole North, and make Jef Davis Emperor. If he and McClellan stand face to face eating up the substance of the country," he concluded disgustedly, "it will not be long before famine is added to insolvency."[59] Much more severe were the comments of Virginia Unionist William F. Wickham following the fall of Richmond. "I never for a moment expected any other final result," he remarked bitterly. "Such an instance of insanity as the Southern States exhibited in endeavoring to destroy the Union is I believe

58. James C. Johnston to George W. Mordecai, February 4, April 20 (quotation), 1863, in George W. Mordecai Papers, SHC; *Daily Picayune* (New Orleans), August 5, 1881. I am indebted to Jessie Poesch, Professor of Art History at Tulane University, for providing me with a copy of the latter source. The independent-minded Burnside also angered neighboring planters in Ascension Parish during Reconstruction when he refused to cooperate with them in resisting payment of what were deemed outrageous state and parish taxes. Despite being the largest property holder in the parish, he declined "to make any arrangement or have any understanding with his neighbors on this or any other subject," thereby thwarting "united action" by the planters "on the subject of taxation." See Duncan F. Kenner to William J. Minor, December 10, 1868, in William J. Minor and Family Papers, LSU.

59. James L. Petigru to "My dear Governor," December, 1861, in R. F. W. Allston Papers, SCHS. Also quoted in Easterby, ed., *South Carolina Rice Plantation*, 186.

with[out] an example in history." Nevertheless, Wickham had the highest respect for General Lee, whom he encountered "repeatedly" in the weeks after
the latter's surrender. However, as befitted gentlemen of their class, "not a word
. . . passed between [them] on public affairs." Another who remained loyal to
the Union throughout the war was Natchez planter-merchant William J. Britton. His position, as he explained to a sympathetic North Carolina Unionist
after the war, was "the only one [he] thought it possible for an honest man, who
loved his country, his family and himself to occupy." Although he estimated his
losses from both Confederate and Federal forces at not less than $750,000, he
saw "no reason to regret the course [he] felt it [his] duty to pursue." Still, he
could not conceal his anger against those he deemed most responsible for reduc-
ing the South to ruin. "I often *feel*," he admitted, "that I would like to see some
of the political mad caps, who have destroyed our once prosperous & happy
people Swing at the end of hemp—and I do not think my tears w^d flow if our
great man Davis was among the number." Such were the sentiments of a small
minority of the great slaveholders.[60]

One of the most tragic consequences of the sectional conflict between North
and South was the divided allegiance within families. Although this was most
common in the border states, it also affected some families in the Deep South,
especially those with close personal ties to the Northeast and those with relatives
in the military. The case of Edward Middleton, a member of one of South Carolina's most prominent families, illustrates the dilemma faced by those in
United States military service at the beginning of the war. Less than two weeks
before the attack on Fort Sumter, Middleton, then serving as a lieutenant in the
U.S. Navy, urgently solicited the advice and opinion of his brothers "in regard
to the permanency of the existing separation." If the separation continued, he
would have no choice but to resign his commission, as he had "no intention of
serving any other government than that acknowledged by [his] native state."
Nevertheless, such a step would be "a painful one," as he explained to his older
brother, Edisto Island planter Oliver H. Middleton, "for it is a great sacrifice to
give up a commission for which I have been toiling all my life." In the end,
Edward did not resign. Perhaps in deference to his delicate situation, he was

60. William F. Wickham to Charles Carter, April 25, May 8, 1865, both in Wickham Family
Papers, VHS; William J. Britton to Lewis Thompson, July 31 (first two quotations), August 10 (last
quotation), 1867, both in Lewis Thompson Papers, SHC.

posted to the Pacific Coast during the war and eventually rose to the rank of rear admiral before retiring from the naval service in the 1870s. Other members of the family were not so fortunate. His nephew, Oliver H., Jr., joined the Charleston Light Dragoons and was killed in action at Matadequin Creek, Virginia, in May, 1864.[61] Like Edward Middleton, a North Carolina naval officer was faced early in the war with the agonizing decision of whether to abandon his career or to side with his native state. "He was when I last heard from him clinging to the old Ship," reported his brother, an enthusiastic Alabama Confederate, "but since Virginia has come to us, & N.C. certainly will I most Sincerely hope that he will no longer hesitate." Unfortunately, the records do not reveal the final choice made by this ambivalent Tar Heel.[62]

For those with close relatives in the North, the political separation and ensuing war were especially painful. Family members in the North often evinced great concern for those residing behind the curtain of war and hastened to assure their southern relatives that their affection for them had not diminished. Thus, in late 1863, a young New York relative of South Carolina matron Eweretta Middleton lamented the separation imposed by the conflict and emphatically rejected the notion that "any change of heart towards [her] family could have come with all this unhappy war." Indeed, she continued emotionally, "I feel like folding you in my arms— & kissing that dear pale cheek— & being all a daughter would be." In like manner, Benjamin O. Tayloe, who resided in Washington, D.C., and remained loyal to the United States throughout the war, expressed great "anxiety" about his "relatives at the South," especially his eldest son Thornton, who was managing family property in Alabama. "I pray of you to take care of him," Benjamin implored his brother in 1862, and "to give him judicious counsel." Despite their divided political loyalties, the war seemingly had little effect on the personal relationship between Benjamin and his brother William. The former protected the assets of their joint business ventures in Washington, D.C., and, after the war, was instrumental in securing an early amnesty for his brother so that the latter could reclaim possession of the Willard Hotel in the capital.[63]

61. Edward Middleton to Oliver H. Middleton, April 1, 1861, in Middleton-Blake Papers, SCHS; South Carolina Genealogies, III, 142–43.

62. V. M. Murphey to Paul C. Cameron, May 3, 1861, in Cameron Family papers, SHC.

63. F.[?] to "My dear Aunt," December 7, [1863], Eweretta Barnwell Middleton Family Letters, in Cheves-Middleton Papers, SCHS; South Carolina Genealogies, III, 154; Benjamin O. Tayloe to

One wonders whether relations within the Palfrey family remained as harmonious as those within the Tayloe family during the war. Four sons had followed John Palfrey, the family patriarch, from Massachusetts to Louisiana in the early nineteenth century. Two soon died of yellow fever and one went bankrupt, but the other, William T. Palfrey, became a successful sugar planter in St. Mary Parish. His eldest brother, John Gorham, however, followed quite a different path. The latter remained in Massachusetts, where he served for eight years as editor of the *North American Review* and subsequently became active in the antislavery movement. Relations between the Palfrey brothers surely must have become strained, for in the midst of the war a disconsolate William Palfrey bitterly condemned both "abolitionists & fire eaters" as "the authors & originators" of the "dreadful state of things" then existing.[64] The Winchesters, another Massachusetts family with southern connections, also experienced some emotional turmoil during the war. During a visit to Boston in the summer of 1864, young Frank Winchester, the pro-Confederate son of Natchez Unionist Josiah Winchester, reported that there was such an acrimonious disagreement between his grandfather and aunt over the conduct of the war that they had "not spoken for a whole year." According to Frank, the elder Winchester was "not an abolitionist at all" and cursed "the government all the time," while his aunt was "very strong about the war" and thought "it all for the best."[65]

A few elite families in the heartland of the Confederacy were afflicted with similar divisions. Among these were two prominent and closely related families in the South Carolina Low Country, the Allstons and Petigrus. As with the Tayloes, however, their political differences do not appear to have undermined the personal relationships within the two families. Certainly that was the case with ardent secessionist Robert F. W. Allston and his maverick brother-in-law, Charleston attorney James L. Petigru. Relations between the two remained cordial after the beginning of hostilities. Ironically, both died during the war, Petigru in 1863 and Allston the following year. At least two of Petigru's female

William H. Tayloe, May 8, 1862 (quotations), August 20, November 23, 1865, in Tayloe Family Papers, VHS.

64. Ulrich B. Phillips, *Life and Labor in the Old South* (New York, 1929), 292–300; *Biographical Directory of the American Congress*, 1421; William T. Palfrey Plantation Journal, January 22, 1863, in Palfrey Family Papers, LSU.

65. Frank Winchester to "Dear Pa" [Josiah], July 12 (quotations), August 17, 1864, both in Winchester Family Papers, CAH.

siblings, Mary Petigru and Jane Petigru North, shared their brother's Unionist views. In December, 1860, Jane admitted to her sister Adele, the wife of Allston, that her political opinions might be considered "demoralizing" to the Allston clan. "I must ever regard with amazement," she wrote, "the temerity which could break up this august government, and not recoil from an act involving the well being of Millions, and the glory of the nation." Four months later, following the bombardment of Sumter, she still lamented "the folly" that had "rushed the country" into war. "But I hope our side will *Beat*," she added. Her belated conversion to the Confederate cause elicited this comment from her much more militant daughter: "Pray say to mamma that I am quite shocked [by] her patriotism—flags so soon—Does not every event prove the South right."[66] The most recalcitrant member of the family was James Petigru's daughter Caroline. Reportedly fearing scenes reminiscent of the French Revolution in the North and of the Saint-Domingue slave insurrection in the South, she fled first to the North and then to Europe. On the eve of her departure for the North, a cousin expressed doubt that Caroline would find her Yankee friends very friendly, though, she added sarcastically, "assuredly she has done and felt nothing to forfeit their regard."[67]

Another family whose members followed separate paths during the war was the Surget family of Mississippi. Francis, Sr., the patriarch of that family, had viewed the prospect of disunion with relative equanimity when he predicted in November, 1850, that "unless the north ceases to agitate the slave question," disunion "will occur at a much earlier period than is generally supposed." Should secession become general among the slave states, he continued, "it would be folly" for the "general government to oppose it as they never could be forced back into the union and it would only be agrevating [*sic*] matters to attempt it." Surget died five years before the outbreak of hostilities, but his two surviving

66. Mary Petigru to Adele Petigru Allston, December 27, 1860, Jane G. North to Adele, December 29, 1860, both in Easterby, ed., *South Carolina Rice Plantation*, 171–72; J[ane] P[etigru] N[orth] to daughter Carey North Pettigrew, May 7, 1861, Carey Pettigrew to sister Louise, May 28, 1861, both in Pettigrew Family Papers, SHC. For further evidence of the later commitment of the Norths to the Confederate cause, see J[ohn] G. N[orth] to "My dear Brother" [brother-in-law R. F. W. Allston], September 15, 1863, in R. F. W. Allston Papers, SCHS.

67. Mariana [last name unknown] to Carey North Pettigrew, May 6, 1861, Minnie [Mary North Allston] to sister Carey North Pettigrew, May 8, 1861 (quotation), in Pettigrew Family Papers, SHC; Easterby, ed. *South Carolina Rice Plantation*, 240n.

sons followed divergent courses. The youngest, Eustace, revealed his allegiance as early as January, 1861, when he resigned his membership in the prestigious New York Club. Apparently energized by the conquest of Sumter, he purchased a Sharps rifle and cavalry saber from a New Orleans supplier just four days after the fall of the Charleston fort and, shortly thereafter, departed for Pensacola, where he served briefly as a volunteer aide to General Braxton Bragg. Subsequently, he saw active service as a lieutenant colonel on the staff of General Richard Taylor. After the war, disillusioned by the prospect of Federal occupation, he moved his residence to Bordeaux, France.[68] By contrast, his older brother, Francis, Jr., remained a staunch Unionist, though his loyalty must have been sorely tested when the Yankees, on a flimsy pretext, blew up his Natchez mansion in 1863. Yet another member of the family, Katharine Surget Minor, a niece of the two brothers and the daughter-in-law of William J. Minor, was even more open in her support of the Union during the war. According to testimony before the Southern Claims Commission after the war, Kate, as she was called, took the oath of allegiance immediately after the Federals occupied Natchez. Indeed, Kate herself testified that she was "an abolitionist in principle" and had remained "loyal to the flag of the Union throughout the rebellion." Her testimony was apparently persuasive, for the government awarded her $13,072 in 1879.[69]

Many of those who did not openly oppose the Confederacy found ways to evade their military obligation entirely or to perform only grudging service if forced into the army. Others took advantage of the war to promote their own economic interests by speculating in cotton or even by selling the precious commodity to the enemy. Not surprisingly, men from Unionist families seemed especially anxious to avoid any lengthy military commitment. Thus, while serving

68. Francis Surget to Charles P. Leverich, November 25, 1850, in Charles P. Leverich Papers, MDAH; Edward A. Bibb, Treasurer New York Club, to Henry P. Duncan, February 4, 1861, Braxton Bragg to Eustace Surget, June 21, [1861] (Roll 1), Receipt dated February 8, 1862, from Hyde & Goodrich for arms purchased April 17, 1861 (Roll 4), in Surget Family papers, MDAH; Eustace Surget service record courtesy Donald G. Linton, Hot Springs, Arkansas. Shortly after his return from Pensacola, Eustace purchased for $120 a pair of ivory-handled Navy pistols from another New Orleans firearms dealer. Receipt dated July 3, 1861, from George Folsom (Roll 5), in Surget Papers, MDAH. Mary Linton, Eustace's cousin and later wife, was also an early secessionist. See Lemuel P. Conner to "Dear Fanny," March 18, 1861, in Lemuel P. Conner and Family Papers, LSU.

69. "Lost Clifton," MS in Edith Wyatt Moore Collection, LSU, copy kindly provided to author by Donald G. Linton; Klingberg, The Southern Claims Commission, 222–23.

with the Adams County Light Infantry at Bowling Green, Kentucky, in the winter of 1862, young Stephen Duncan, Jr., hastened to assure a Natchez matron that she was quite "mistaken about his being in for the war." On the contrary, "he is tired of it already," reported a member of a cavalry unit attached to the same regiment. When Duncan and Stephen Minor, the son of another prominent Natchez Unionist, learned that they had been granted a furlough, they were described as "the most delighted persons . . . you ever saw." A fellow soldier added: "we could hardly hold them when here." Some members of another Natchez unit, the elite Adams Troop, evinced a similar aversion to the hardships of camp life. In early July, 1861, William H. Ker reported from Virginia that one member of the Troop had initially and inexplicably "refused to take the oath to obey all officers in the Confederate Army for the time of the war" and that even Henry Conner had vowed "never to leave home again" if he were fortunate enough to get back to Natchez. Indeed, remarked Ker, "if he could with honor do so, he would be willing to walk all the way home." Several months later, as winter approached, Ker noted that several members of his unit were trying to escape service: two "on the plea they are *under age*" and another on the grounds "of having had his arm broken once upon a time." If the last used such a weak excuse, concluded Ker disapprovingly, "I think it would look rather badly for him."[70]

Natchezians were by no means the only ones who sought to avoid military service. One of the most common ways to evade such service was to procure a substitute from the pool of men not liable for induction into the army. Thomas W. Thompson, the eldest son of North Carolina Unionist Lewis Thompson, did so on two occasions. At the beginning of the war, Thompson enlisted for twelve months in a North Carolina company, but he soon expressed dissatisfaction with his life in the field. "I am willing to try to do my duty," he informed his father, "but I want my rights, and will try to get them." The following year, when he became subject to the Confederate Conscription Act, he paid $600 to an illiterate exempt "to act as a substitute for him . . . for the war." For some reason, that poor fellow served only a year, and, in May, 1863, Thompson was obliged to obtain another substitute—this one a seventeen-year-old Virgin-

70. "Your affection[ate] Uncle" to Carrie Nutt, January 15, [1862], in Nutt Family Collection, MDAH; William H. Ker to his mother, July 1, October 19, 1861 (Roll 1), both in Surget Family Papers, MDAH.

ian—to take his place in "the military service of the Confederate States" until such time as the "said substitute" attained "military age."[71]

Starke Hunter, the son of a Dallas County, Alabama, planter who had moved to Kentucky in 1857, displayed even less enthusiasm for active military service than Thompson. In late March, 1862, Hunter enlisted for ninety days in an Alabama company that remained in camp for a month and a half before proceeding to Mobile. Initially, he gave his qualified endorsement to the conscription law enacted by the Confederate Congress in mid-April because it would "make a great many go [to the army] that would not otherwise." But a week later, apparently now cognizant that the new legislation might affect *him*, he reported that the act was causing "much dissatisfaction" among my troops. "It is hard to be torn from the buusom [*sic*] of my family without my consent," he lamented to his wife, "but we are under military despots, and have to do as they say, not as we wish." Hunter spent the remainder of his enlistment castigating the Conscription Act, denouncing what he called the despotic character of the government ("Despotism prevails, and . . . Liberty has flown"), ridiculing Confederate efforts to defend Mobile, charging his colonel with incompetence, and desperately trying to secure a substitute. In mid-May, a "stout able bodied man" dispatched by his father arrived to take his place, but he could not use him until his time expired because to do so would render Hunter subject to conscription at the conclusion of his ninety-day term. Therefore, he sent the man to the family plantation to await his call. Accordingly, when he was mustered out of service in late June, the substitute took his place and Hunter returned home. As he explained to his wife, "there is no man who is more willing to do his duty than I am, but I think I am worth more to my family and their interest at home than I would be in the Army." So much for southern nationalism![72]

71. Thomas W. Thompson to "Dear Father," June 2, 1861, Receipt for substitute, May 22, 1862, signed with his mark by George Casper, Certificate of Exemption, May 25, 1863, signed by Lieutenant T. J. Stewart, Enrolling Officer, Northampton County, North Carolina, in Lewis Thompson Papers, SHC.

72. Owen, *History of Alabama*, III, 872; Starke Hunter to "My Dear Wife" [Laura Milhous], April 18 (first quotation), 24 (second quotation), May 2, 5, 12, 13 (last quotation), June 21, 1862, in Hunter-Milhous Family Collection, ADAH. In fairness to Hunter, it should be noted that he had been married little more than a year and was the proud father of an infant daughter, circumstances that might account, at least in part, for his anxiety to return home.

Other members of the planter elite had more valid reasons to seek relief from field service. In January, 1863, Thomas Middleton Jr., then serving as an artillery lieutenant at Battery Ramsay in Charleston Harbor, informed his sister that he had received certificates from two physicians recommending him for "Bureau duty" and that, as soon as his health permitted, he intended to petition the Board of Surgeons for an exemption from field service. "My head throbs so and at times am so giddy," complained the suffering young officer, that "I hardly know what I write." As it turned out, Middleton was not malingering. A victim of typhoid fever, he endured a worsening condition after his battalion was ordered to Battery Wagner in August, and on Sunday morning, January 31, 1864, he passed away at the age of thirty.[73] Somewhat different was the case of Abram B. Archer, eldest son of fire-eater Richard T. Archer of Mississippi. Young Archer became so disenchanted with his company commander, Major Joseph M. Magruder, during the summer of 1863 that he sought permission from his father to sell a parcel of land in order to pay for a substitute. Abram's chief complaint was that he had been compelled "to perform arduous service when too sick for service," thereby debilitating his health. After counseling his son to consider a transfer to another command if he could not obtain a suitable substitute, the elder Archer dispatched an angry letter of protest to General Joseph E. Johnston. Charging that Magruder was "a confirmed sot" who owed his promotion solely to family influence, Archer implored the general "to give [his] soldiers protection from drunken officers." Ironically, just a month before the Archers lodged their complaint, Magruder had praised Abram's performance, asserting that he was "now universally regarded by officers and men, as one of the best [soldiers] in [their] Battalion." It is not known whether Abram secured a substitute, but he did survive the war only to become estranged from his dying father.[74]

Even more injurious to the Confederate cause than efforts to avoid military

73. Thomas Middleton, Jr., to "My dear little Sister [Eweretta], January 10, 1863, printed obituary of Thomas Middleton, Jr., n.d., H[arriott] M[iddleton] to "My dear dear Aunt [Eweretta B. Middleton], February 2, [1864], Eweretta Barnwell Middleton Family Letters, in Cheves-Middleton Papers, SCHS.

74. Richard T. Archer to "My Dear Son Abram," August 22, 1863, Archer to General Joseph E. Johnston, [August, 1863], J. M. Magruder to R. T. Archer, July 29, 1863, Archer to "My Dear Wife," November 10, 1866, Archer to "My Dear Jane" [his daughter], November 12, 1866, in Richard Thompson Archer Family Papers, CAH.

service was trafficking with the enemy. Yet some Unionist planters did so in the last years of the war. Reference has been made above to the activities of Haller Nutt and Benjamin Roach, Jr., in this regard.[75] Other Natchez nabobs who were heavily involved in this illicit trade included Stephen Duncan and Josiah Winchester. During the last two years of the war, these two die-hard Unionists regularly purchased cotton from neighboring planters and, in collusion with Federal officials in both Natchez and New Orleans, shipped that cotton as well as their own to the latter city. As early as May, 1863, New Orleans factor George S. Mandeville, "who had made his arrangements with the Federal authorities to resume his business as Commission Merchant," was buying cotton stored on various plantations in the Natchez area for the account "and risk" of Duncan and several other speculators. Following the Union occupation of Natchez in mid-July, it was relatively easy for loyal planters to obtain a permit to ship their cotton directly to the New Orleans market. For those in outlying areas still under Confederate control, however, the problem was more difficult. Thus, more than a year after Mandeville had purchased for Duncan 82 bales of cotton on Levin Marshall, Jr.'s, Wilkinson County plantation, the precious staple had not yet been moved. A congressional act of July 2, 1864, provided one alternative by authorizing agents of the Treasury Department to purchase products from citizens in insurrectionary states and to pay them three-fourths of the market value of the product in New York at last quotation. Obviously, the most profitable choice was direct shipment to markets when circumstances permitted.[76]

The loyalist Duncan was also the instrument by which fellow planter and former Confederate provost marshal Alexander K. Farrar was able to avoid a significant loss after the Federals occupied Natchez. A month after Union troops arrived, an expedition commanded by the colonel of an Illinois regiment seized a large quantity of cotton on Farrar's outlying Kingston plantation and hauled a portion of it to Natchez. Undaunted by this distressing event, Farrar, who was heavily in debt to Duncan and others, proposed that these creditors

75. See pp. 339–40 of this book.

76. "*Invoice of 614* Bales Cotton purchased for a/c and risk of D^r S Duncan agent for Martin of L'pool, England," May 2, 1863, in Duncan Papers, LSU; A. K. Farrar to James O. Fuqua, July 24, 1866 (quotation), George E. Payne to Josiah Winchester, August 12, 30, 1864, both in Winchester Family Papers, CAH. I am indebted to William Ashley Vaughan, a doctoral graduate of the University of Southern Mississippi, for providing me with a copy of the invoice from the Duncan Papers.

assume those debts and "arrange with the federal authorities for the recovery of the Cotton," which would then be "shipped and sold in his name" in order to satisfy both his own debt and those which Duncan had assumed. Duncan immediately accepted this mutually beneficial proposition, and Farrar was able to liquidate his indebtedness through the sale of 1,100 bales of cotton consigned to the Mandeville firm in New Orleans. After the war, Farrar brought suit in Duncan's name against Mandeville to recover what he termed the "exorbitant unjust and inexcusable" commission charged by the latter on this shipment.[77]

There were others who profited from the sale of cotton to the enemy. Like Duncan, Josiah Winchester made numerous shipments of cotton to New Orleans after Union forces occupied the city. From the fall of 1863 through the spring of 1865, Winchester sold cotton through several New Orleans factors, principally H. S. Buckner & Co. Not surprisingly, in view of the blockade and consequent shortage of cotton in Europe, the fleecy staple brought increasingly high returns during this period. Thus, in April, 1864, with the better grades selling for 76 to 80 cents on the New Orleans market, Winchester sold 196 bales for a gross profit of $52,681.61. A month later, the price had risen to between 82 and 90 cents a pound, and by January of 1865, middling cotton was selling for $1.08 in New Orleans and $1.20 in New York. Thus, there was a strong incentive for Winchester and the Unionist clients he represented to participate in this trade, especially since they felt little or no allegiance toward the Confederacy in the first place. New Orleans was not the only center of this illicit cotton trade, nor were the Natchez nabobs the only ones involved in the traffic. In February, 1864, a correspondent in northeast Louisiana reported great demoralization among the people there because of the general belief that local officials were selling cotton beyond enemy lines "for their own private benefit." This "unfortunate sale of cotton to the enemy," he declared bitterly, "will do more to stain our cause than anything which has yet been done."[78]

The desire to promote one's own economic self-interest during the war was also evident among some members of the elite on the eastern border of the

77. A. K. Farrar to James O. Fuqua, July 24, 1866 (quotations), Stephen Duncan authorization to Richard Mason, September 22, 1863, both in Winchester Family Papers, CAH.

78. W. C. Daugherty to Thomas Henderson & Co., November 18, 1863, H. S. Buckner to Josiah Winchester, April 26, May 28, 1864, J. Winchester in a/c with H. S. Buckner, 1864, J. Norman Jackson to Winchester, January 11, 1865, in Winchester Family Papers, CAH; E. D. Farrar to "Dear Col." [Lemuel P. Conner], February 18, 1864, in Lemuel P. Conner and Family Papers, LSU.

Confederacy. Two members of the Mordecai family, Raleigh banker-planter George W. and his half-brother Samuel in Richmond, turned to cotton speculation as an investment during the second year of the conflict. Acting through agents in Cheraw, South Carolina, and Columbus, Georgia, respectively, the two brothers began buying up cotton from farmers near those locations in the spring of 1862. Unlike the speculators in the Southwest, they did not collude with the enemy to ship their cotton abroad but instead stored it either in warehouses or on the plantations, anticipating that the escalating price would yield a handsome profit when circumstances enabled them to market it. Between April, 1862, and April of the following year, the price of good middling cotton soared from 7 to as much as 35 cents a pound, an increase of 500 percent in a single year.[79] Consequently, in early April, 1863, D. Malloy & Son of Cheraw advised George Mordecai to sell a portion of his cotton, then amounting to more than 600 bales and "scattered all through the Country" where "much of it" might "get more or less damaged by remaining so long time." Such a sale at this time, counseled Malloy, would "pay you a large profit, and save a great deal of trouble in collecting it to gether hereafter." Mordecai agreed, and by the end of June the Cheraw firm had collected nearly 200 bales of his cotton, presumably for sale to their parent company, the Charleston commission house of Colcock, McCalley, and Malloy.[80] Finally, in early September, Malloy sold more than 200 bales of Mordecai cotton, on which the North Carolina speculator paid the 8 percent ad valorem tax levied on agricultural products by the Confederate Congress in its comprehensive tax law of April, 1863. Although the tax amounted to almost $7,000, it is apparent that Mordecai realized a liberal return from his investment in cotton.[81]

Whatever their political posture and however they conducted themselves during the war, all elite slaveholders eventually felt the impact of the changing behavior of their laborers as Federal troops increasingly penetrated the heartland

---

79. Charles Rogers & Company to Samuel Mordecai, April 15, May 26, September 23, December 10, 1862, April 17, 1863, D. Malloy & Son to George W. Mordecai, May 6, 13, 17, 31, June 11, 28, July 9, August 19, 1862, January 3, April 4, 1863, Samuel Mordecai to Charles Rogers & Company, January 10, 1863, in George W. Mordecai Papers, SHC.

80. D. Malloy & Son to George W. Mordecai, January 3, April 4, June 24, 1863, May 13, 1862, *ibid.*

81. D. Malloy & Son to George W. Mordecai, September 8, 1863; *ibid.;* Thomas, *The Confederate Nation,* 198; Coulter, *The Confederate States of America,* 177.

of the plantation South. Living under the misapprehension that their slaves were attached to them by mutual "ties of affection," some slaveholders predicted at the beginning of the war that most of their chattels would remain loyal to their masters during the military confrontation with the North. Thus, a judge on the Tennessee Supreme Court expressed the view in April, 1861, that "a majority of the negroes will be with us in the conflict." Several months later, the eldest son of R. F. W. Allston voiced a similar opinion. While conceding that "there are many of our negroes that will prove unfaithful to us," he, nevertheless, could not yet believe that this would be "the case with the great majority." About the same time, aware that the recent Union landing at Port Royal might induce a general flight of slaves in the South Carolina Low Country, military authorities suggested that Savannah River rice planters abstain from "extreme coercive measures with the negroes except in cases of dire necessity" in order to "quell the uneasy feeling at present existing among that class of our population."[82]

As the war progressed and Federal troops began to overrun the southern countryside, a few Negroes did remain loyal to their owners. But they were very much the exceptions. One who had little reason to criticize the conduct of his slaves was Duncan F. Kenner, wealthy Ascension Parish sugar planter and a prominent member of the Confederate Congress. When soldiers from an Indiana regiment suddenly raided Kenner's Ashland plantation in late July, 1862, an elderly field hand warned his master, who was out riding with a neighboring planter, and Kenner made good his escape. As Kenner and his companion rode leisurely toward the river, the faithful servant allegedly ran toward them and cried out: "Marse Duncan, for God's sake don't go to the river—dat boat is full of soldiers—& dey is all landing." After stripping the plantation of all movable articles during a three-day occupation, the Federals finally departed, taking with them all the white men on the place and leaving Mrs. Kenner and her three children alone among a sea of blacks. That night, two trusted slaves, each armed with a pistol, stood guard over the family and prevented any harm from coming to them before they left to rejoin Kenner the following day. As his thirteen-

---

82. Scarborough, ed., *The Diary of Edmund Ruffin*, II, 471; Judge A. Wright to Paul C. Cameron, April 28, 1861, in Cameron Family Papers, SHC; Ben Allston to "My dear Father," November 24, 1861, in R. F. W. Allston Papers, SCHS; Edward Lynah to Langdon Cheves, November 16, 1861, in Langdon Cheves, Jr., Papers, SCHS.

year-old daughter later recalled, "Some of the negroes went with the Federals when they left, but the Majority remained at home." Because the soldiers had treated them rather harshly, she added, "the negroes were not tempted to join them & encounter the fortunes of war." The neighboring Bringier family was equally fortunate during the same raid. A relieved Stella Bringier reported to her absent husband that "not one of [their] negroes" had left their Hermitage plantation, though 5 had absconded from another family estate. Kenner's slaves apparently remained relatively quiescent throughout the war despite the proximity of Federal gunboats on the river. Thus, after receiving an account of affairs in Ascension early in 1864, he remarked: "I am glad to learn that so many of my negroes, if I can still call them *mine* are at home."[83]

There were other slaves who elected to remain with their masters rather than to subject themselves to an uncertain future with the Yankees. In some cases their apprehension was warranted. In the summer of 1863, Richard T. Archer reported that 11 of his Negroes had returned to his Claiborne County, Mississippi, plantation after being impressed into service by the Federals during the Vicksburg campaign. They brought with them "their good U.S. mules," but the slaves themselves were so debilitated that they were "not fit for work." Another 40 of Archer's Negroes had died of various causes during their absence from home. According to their master, the remainder wished to come home but they could not yet "get over the river." Some slaves remained on their home plantations and continued to perform their usual tasks even after the end of hostilities. For example, a month after General Lee's surrender at Appomattox Court House, William F. Wickham, who had assumed control of the Virginia estates of Williams Carter following the latter's death in 1864, reported that more than 340 of Carter's original complement of 420 slaves remained on his two plantations and were working "better than we could have hoped for in their present ambiguous position."[84]

83. "The Federal Raid Upon Ashland Plantation in July 1862" (quotations), in Rosella Kenner Brent Recollections, LSU; article recounting Federal raid on Ashland in July, 1862, and Duncan Kenner's escape to Bayou Lafourche, n.d., in Rosella Kenner Brent Papers, LSU; Stella Bringier to husband Amedee, July 28, 1862, in Louis A. Bringier and Family Papers, LSU; Duncan F. Kenner to Lemuel P. Conner, February 11, 1864, in Duncan F. Kenner Letter, HNO.

84. Richard T. Archer to "My Dear Son Abram," August 22, 1863, in Richard Thompson Archer Family Papers, CAH; William F. Wickham to Charles Carter, April 25, May 8, 1865, both in Wickham Family Papers, VHS.

Such examples were clearly the exception, however. The general pattern of slave conduct during the war was similar throughout the South. There was little disruption of the normal work routine until Federal troops actually penetrated the immediate neighborhood of the slaves. Then the slaves manifested their long-suppressed *true* feelings toward both their masters and the oppressive system in which they had been entrapped throughout their lives. They did so by resorting to various acts of defiance and insubordination. Large numbers fled to the enemy, others refused to work, and still others pillaged the property of their owners. Somewhat surprisingly, there were very few instances of rape, murder, or even physical assaults against members of planter families, though they were occasionally subjected to humiliating treatment. The response of slaveowners to these acts of resistance and independence was one of near-universal astonishment, disappointment, and ultimately anger. They could scarcely believe that those whom they regarded affectionately as members of their "black family" could exhibit such ingratitude. As one North Carolina planter exclaimed, after a formerly trusted slave "accompanied the Yankees in their excursions" through his neighborhood: "He was once a faithful man; but the times have changed him. What a change! What a change!"[85] Indeed so. For the first time in their lives, the slaveholders were made aware of the true sentiments of the men and women whom they had held in bondage.

The flight of slaves from their home plantations commenced in earnest during the spring of 1862 as Federal forces began to make significant inroads in both the Upper and Lower South. Occasionally, the abscondings resulted from the decision of owners to transfer their most valuable hands to more remote sites in the interior, often at the expense of separating families. Thus, following the capture of New Berne in mid-March, 1862, many large slaveholders in eastern North Carolina began to send their slaves inland. When Charles S. Pettigrew announced his intention to move his male slaves immediately, leaving the women and children behind for the present, virtually all of the men on his two plantations "took to the woods" in protest. Pettigrew retaliated by withholding provisions from those left behind, an action that soon produced the desired result. The men returned the next morning "humbled & subdued" and resumed their normal work routine. Shortly thereafter, however, when Pettigrew was absent, a body of armed white men raided his plantation after hearing a rumor that his Negroes "were in open insurrection." The frightened slaves, who reportedly were *"quietly* in *their houses,"* again fled the plantation in a panic. When their master returned, they all poured out of the woods and, according to Pettigrew, "flocked about him as their friend & protector," begging him never to leave them again. Such was the volatility of conditions on slave plantations during the early stages of the war.[86]

Two months later, additional Federal incursions into Virginia and North Carolina provoked a series of slave defections in both states. Shortly after the fall of Yorktown, one observer reported that the Negroes were fleeing in droves as General George B. McClellan's huge army advanced up the peninsula toward Richmond. "The negroes in this quarter are demoralized," he declared, "and from the present aspect, it looks as if all the large plantations of this Neck are broken up." From his vantage point near the Virginia capital, Edmund Ruffin observed that "the number, & general spreading of such abscondings of slaves" was "beyond any previous conceptions." To the south near Edenton, North Carolina, which was also threatened by Yankee invaders, the house of Aletha Collins, sister of wealthy slaveholder Josiah Collins III, was "plundered . . . shamelessly" by trusted elderly servants whom she had left in charge during her absence. "They have taken what they wanted," remarked Kate Edmondston. Even ultra-Unionist James C. Johnston had become disgusted with the conduct of the Negroes by the summer of 1863. "They now are at large roaming about as free as if they were in Yankee land," he commented bitterly. "They are . . . totaly [*sic*] worthless and if I could hire white labour would send away our Share here to the Yankees."[87]

The story was much the same in South Carolina. In October, 1862, slaves began to flee plantations in several Low Country districts. Near the end of the month, the Francis Westons were surprised to learn that "their head carpenter and 18 others of his finest, most intelligent and trusted men had taken his family boat . . . at an early hour after dark and made their escape to the enemy." About the same time, Colleton District planter Charles T. Lowndes, described by James L. Petigru as "a model of a good master," was equally astonished when

86. Carey North Pettigrew to "My dearest Mama" [Jane Petigru North], March 22, 1862, in Pettigrew Family Papers, SHC.

87. Benjamin O. Tayloe to "My dear Brother" [William H.], May 8, 1862, in Tayloe Family Papers, VHS; Scarborough, ed., *The Diary of Edmund Ruffin*, II, 307; *"Journal of a Secesh Lady,"*

his Negroes began deserting by the "scores."[88] More than two years later, as General William T. Sherman's mighty army ploughed through the Carolinas, conditions in the rice districts deteriorated rapidly. Many planters fled to the interior, but those who remained were subjected to humiliating treatment by insubordinate slaves and marauding Yankee troops alike. Only five adult males on the Weston plantation remained faithful to their master, thereby incurring the "ill will" of their fellow bondsmen. The remainder divided up the land, pulled down the fences, refused to submit to a driver, and drove off the overseer. At Chicora Wood, the residential plantation of the Allstons, Federal troops encouraged the Negroes to join them in plundering the mansion. A distraught Jane Pringle, who had remained in Georgetown District during the occupation, informed Adele Allston that her former slaves were behaving "like devils." She warned Adele that if she should return, "all [her] servants who have not families so large as to burthen them and compel a veneering of fidelity, will immediately leave [her]. The others will be more or less impertinent as the humor takes them and in short will do as they choose." Such was the scene along the rice coast as the war drew to a close.[89]

Elite planters in the Gulf states experienced similar massive slave defections as Federal forces began to penetrate the Lower Mississippi Valley during the second year of the war. After the Federals gained effective control of the Mississippi River with the capture of New Orleans and Memphis during the first half of the year, plantations bordering the river became especially vulnerable to Yankee incursions. Thus, following one such raid into the Lake St. Joseph region of north Louisiana in July, slaves on many Tensas Parish cotton plantations either absconded on their own or were seized by the invaders. Among the wealthy planters who suffered losses on this occasion were John Routh, Dr. Allen T. Bowie, Samuel Dorsey, and Anna F. Elliot. The last, the widow of wealthy Natchezian William St. John Elliot, lost twenty-nine Negroes from her Bal-

---

ed. Crabtree and Patton, 173; James C. Johnston to C. W. Hallowell, July 28, 1863, in Hayes Collection, SHC.

88. Adele Petigru Allston to Benjamin Allston, October 30, 1862, James L. Petigru to Adele Allston, October 31, 1862, both in Easterby, ed., *South Carolina Rice Plantation*, 190, 192.

89. Elizabeth Weston to Adele Allston, March 17, 1865, Adele Allston to Colonel Brown, Commander, U.S. forces in Georgetown, [March, 1865], Adele Allston to Captain Morris, Commanding Officer, USS *Chenaugh* in Georgetown Harbor, [March, 1865], Jane Pringle to Adele Allston, April 1, [1865], *ibid.*, 206–11.

moral plantation, many of whom subsequently died of camp fever apparently contracted while they were with the Yankees. Hearing that Federal troops were in the neighborhood, all of the Dorsey Negroes, "both Men, Women & children," absconded to the enemy. The Yankees, however, wanted only the able-bodied men and, after selecting them out, "drove all the balance back." When Sarah Dorsey "went out to talk to them and reason with them, they Cursed her & Mr Dorsey, and then threatened" to take "their lives." Faced with this insubordinate behavior, the Dorseys were obliged to abandon their home temporarily until some semblance of order could be restored by neighboring planters, who threatened to hang the ringleaders.[90]

Defections continued to mount during the fall, both along the river and in south Louisiana where the tide of war swept back and forth across the sugar parishes. In mid-September, as the Union gunboat *Essex* threatened Natchez, Haller Nutt's overseer reported the flight of a valuable slave from Nutt's Evergreen plantation in Tensas. "I suppose it was his intention to get to [the] Yankee fleet above Vicksburg," surmised the overseer, but it was not likely that he would succeed because patrols had been established along the river to prevent such escapes. Skilled artisans were among those most likely to defect. In November, nearly a dozen Negroes, including a bricklayer and a carpenter, absconded from the Conner plantations in Concordia Parish.[91] In the southern part of the state, where opposing forces alternated in their control of contested territory, conditions were even more chaotic. In April, 1863, following an engagement on Bayou Teche and the subsequent occupation of Franklin, sugar planter William T. Palfrey observed that the slaves in his neighborhood were "demoralized, refractory, leaving their women & going to the enemy, who receive them with open arms." He remarked dejectedly, "Many of my negroes

90. John Routh to Haller Nutt, July 6, 1862, Julia Nutt to "Dear Irene" [her sister], July 9, 1862 (quotations), in Nutt Family Collection, MDAH; Fanny E. Conner to "My ever dearest Husband," November 11, 1862, in Lemuel P. Conner and Family Papers, LSU. This is the same Sarah Dorsey who befriended Jefferson Davis after the war and sold him her Beauvoir home in Biloxi, Mississippi, for the nominal price of $5,500. See Clement Eaton, *Jefferson Davis* (New York, 1977), 264–65. Beauvoir is now the site of the recently constructed Jefferson Davis Presidential Library.

91. John Routh to Haller Nutt, September 16, 1862, Hamilton Smith to Nutt, September 16, 1862, both in Nutt Family Collection, MDAH; Fanny E. Conner to "My ever dearest Husband," November 11, 1862, in Lemuel P. Conner and Family Papers, LSU.

have left me, & some of them I have dismissed owing to [their] refusing to work as usual."[92]

Slave recalcitrance escalated sharply during the last two years of the war as the Federals tightened their noose around the Lower Mississippi Valley. The Vicksburg campaign, in particular, affected plantations on both sides of the river. During the sieges of Port Hudson and Vicksburg, large numbers of slaves fled to the Yankees, and it was reported that some neighborhoods were "almost depopulated of negroes." Commenting on the defections from a neighboring plantation, Lemuel P. Conner, with an obtuseness characteristic of the members of his class, remarked: "There is something magical about the word 'Freedom'—which the poor deluded creatures cannot resist." Not until July 11, a week after the fall of Vicksburg, did Conner's own slaves begin to desert, four of them succumbing to the enticement of sailors on a passing gunboat. A week later, the hands on Francis Surget's Chiripa plantation in Concordia Parish began threatening to leave. By the end of the month they were refusing to work, claiming that there was plenty to eat and Negroes on other plantations in the vicinity had already ceased their labors. The harried overseer predicted that all of them would decamp shortly.[93]

Six months later, slaves belonging to the John C. Jenkins estate in Wilkinson County, Mississippi, exhibited similar refractory behavior. They too refused to work until they received some unspecified promise from Josiah Winchester, the administrator of the estate. In the meantime, they were behaving in an impudent manner toward their overseer and his wife and were even threatening to divide the land among themselves. Forced to utilize a cart driver to do his cooking after his regular cook refused to perform that task any longer, the tormented manager complained to his employer: "Thare must be a chang for the beter or I cant stay on the [place] much longer." Conditions were even worse in St. Mary Parish, Louisiana, as the Red River campaign began in March, 1864. Thousands of Federal troops streamed through the parish, looting plantations,

92. Long, *The Civil War Day by Day*, 338; William T. Palfrey Plantation Diary, April 25, 1863, in Palfrey Family Papers, LSU. For additional examples of slave defections and rebelliousness in the sugar parishes during 1862–63, see Scarborough, *The Overseer*, 152–55.

93. Fanny E. Conner to "My ever dearest Husband," June 20 (first quotation), July 11, 1863, Lemuel P. Conner to "My dear Fanny," June 28, 1863, in Lemuel P. Conner and Family Papers, LSU; J. A. Briley to Francis Surget, July 19, 29, 1863 (Roll 1), in Surget Family Papers, MDAH.

driving off livestock, and conscripting Negroes into the army. Those servants who remained behind, remarked one disgusted planter, were "insolent & refractory, and . . . are more trouble & vexation than they are of use. Their laziness and impertinence is beyond belief." Clearly, by the closing months of the war, the much-vaunted paternalistic relationship between master and slave had been shattered beyond repair.[94]

Before slave resistance became ubiquitous, some slaveowners retaliated against rebellious Negroes by selling either the offenders or members of their families. Occasionally, they resorted to even more extreme measures. Thus, when slaves began deserting plantations in Georgetown District, South Carolina, in the fall of 1862, three male slaves, who were captured when they returned from enemy lines to retrieve their wives, were tried by the provost marshal's court and hanged the next day so that "no executive clemency might intervene." One prominent planter, Henry A. Middleton, applauded the action. Blacks were encouraged to attend the execution, and Middleton predicted that "the effect will not soon be forgotten." The provost marshal, he added, had "acted with great decision & judgment."[95]

Slaveowner retribution against those who fled to the enemy usually took a less severe form, however. More typical was the reaction of Edmund Ruffin, Jr., who, in June, 1862, sold twenty-nine Negroes from families whose male members had absconded during the Peninsular Campaign. As the elder Ruffin explained, these family members had been "passive" participants in the defections, "knowing well the intentions of the others, & keeping their secret." Similarly, when several slaves, including the close relatives of a trusted female servant named Mary, fled to the Yankees from Adele Allston's Chicora Wood plantation in the summer of 1864, Mrs. Allston suggested that Mary be held accountable and punished for the actions of her family. There were "too many instances in her family for me to suppose she is ignorant of their plans and designs," reasoned the South Carolina matron. Also typical was the response of North Carolina planter Thomas P. Devereux when two of his Negroes were caught trying to escape to the enemy. He immediately dispatched the two defectors, along

94. H. C. Wright to Josiah Winchester, January 6, 1864, in Winchester Family papers, CAH; William T. Palfrey Plantation Diary, March 14, 16, 1864, in Palfrey Family Papers, LSU.

95. Henry A. Middleton to Harriott Middleton, November 5, 1862, Henry A. Middleton, Jr., Family Letters, in Cheves-Middleton Papers, SCHS.

with several others whom they had implicated, to Richmond to be sold. Despite such punitive measures, many slaves continued, whenever circumstances permitted, to pursue the freedom that they had never enjoyed.[96]

Even more exasperating to elite slaveholders than the conduct of refractory slaves were the depredations against property committed by advancing Federal troops. Never before or since have American civilians been subjected to the ravages of an invading army on the scale experienced by Southerners during the Civil War. The first to bear the full brunt of the war were the Virginians, whose state became a battleground throughout the war, and those in the coastal region of the Carolinas, where the Federals established enclaves early in the conflict. Shortly thereafter, civilians in the Lower South, especially those bordering the Mississippi River, were exposed to the physical hardships of war. As Union forces steadily encroached upon Confederate territory, many planter families fled to interior sites in an effort to escape the clutches of the advancing enemy. Ultimately, of course, few safe havens remained, and most Southerners were forced to endure the hardships of Union occupation.

Long before General William T. Sherman began to cut his destructive swath through Georgia and the Carolinas, Federal troops had inaugurated a systematic policy of property destruction in the state of Virginia. Some of these depredatory acts were sanctioned by higher military authorities, while others were committed by undisciplined, marauding soldiers. For the victims, however, the effect was much the same. As early as August, 1861, Peter W. Hairston complained of the "wanton destruction of property and the desolation" inflicted upon Fairfax County by the invading Federals. "Many families are completely ruined," he observed bitterly, "and have had to take refuge elsewhere." But it was the Peninsular Campaign of 1862 that most exposed the inhabitants of eastern Virginia to the ravages of war. Among the families affected by this incursion were the Tayloes and the Ruffins. After Edward T. Tayloe abandoned his Powhatan Hill plantation in King George County and fled to Danville in late April, 1862, his house remained relatively unscathed while Union regimental officers were quartered there. But after the regiment departed, "a marauding party of soldiers" plundered the house of "everything they could carry off—the

---

96. Scarborough, ed., *The Diary of Edmund Ruffin*, II, 351, 353; Adele Petigru Allston to Colonel Francis Heriot, [July, 1864], in Easterby, ed., *South Carolina Rice Plantation*, 200; *"Journal of a Secesh Lady,"* ed. Crabtree and Patton, 529.

clothing—such ladies dresses as were left, the blankets, sheets &c." After the Federal tide receded, the owners resumed occupancy only to endure a repetition of such destruction in the fall of 1863. Some eight thousand to ten thousand Yankees "poured down upon us," reported Tayloe, and "stole everything they could find": clothing, silverware, fruit, and livestock. He was "saved from general pillage" only "by the interposition of officers, to whom [he] appealed for protection, which they gave [him] readily & effectively."[97]

Perhaps because of the notoriety of the family patriarch, the Ruffin plantations—Beechwood on the James River and Marlbourne on the Pamunkey—fared even worse. The first Federal occupation of the latter, which occurred during the Seven Days' battles in June, 1862, resulted in relatively minor damage. Apart from the elder Ruffin's valuable collection of rare fossil shells, "the most beautiful & precious" of which were stolen from two locked cabinets, the losses were confined largely to slaves, livestock, and provisions. However, the work of destruction continued during subsequent raids and occupations until, by the summer of 1864, the Yankees "had destroyed everything not effectually destroyed before, including the windows of the mansion." Indeed, by early fall, the entire country within a ten-mile radius of Richmond had been "robbed of everything portable" and, in the words of Edmund, Sr., "left a desert & barren waste."[98]

Bad as it was, the damage at Marlbourne did not compare with that inflicted upon Beechwood. The latter was also abandoned by the family in late June, 1862, after the senior Ruffin took a last nostalgic look at the residence that brought so many "tender recollections" to his mind. When he returned in mid-August to survey the damages after a two-week occupation by Federal troops, he could scarcely believe the extent of destruction. The yard was littered with broken furniture, shredded bedding, and shattered crockery. Every room in the mansion was "covered, still more thickly than the yard, with the rubbish & litter produced by the general breakage & destruction of everything that could not be conveniently stolen & carried off." Agricultural implements had been either broken or pilfered, all of the farm buildings were seriously damaged, and even

97. Peter W. Hairston to "My Dear Fanny," August 23, 1861, in Peter Wilson Hairston Papers, SHC; Benjamin O. Tayloe to "My dear Brother" [William H.], May 8, 1862, Edward T. Tayloe to "My Dear Brother" [William H.], September 8, 1863, both in Tayloe Family Papers, VHS.

98. Scarborough, ed., *The Diary of Edmund Ruffin*, II, 337–38, 368 (first quotation), 472, III, 37, 364–65, 441, 461, 469 (second quotation), 475 (third quotation), 565.

the slave quarters had been ransacked. The abandoned plantation was subjected to further pillaging later in the war by marauding bands of Negroes as well as by a Union regiment that stripped the mansion of virtually all wooden appurtenances except the framed walls, thereby exposing the interior to severe damage from the weather. It is little wonder that the victim of these outrages castigated the hated Yankees with his last "writing & utterance" just moments before he took his own life in June, 1865.[99]

Residents in the Carolinas were also confronted with the harsh realities of war after the Federals established beachheads along the coast during the first year of the conflict. Thus, following the Union landing at Port Royal in November, 1861, many Low Country families began to seek sanctuary in such inland sites as Columbia, Greenville, Aiken, and Augusta, all within relatively close proximity to Charleston.[100] Several Edisto Island planters—among them, Isaac J. Mikell, James Legare, and Mrs. James Hopkinson—exhibited their patriotism by burning their cotton before fleeing to the interior. Mikell refugeed in Aiken, as did rice planter William Lucas, while another Edisto cotton planter, John F. Townsend, chose Orangeburg as his place of refuge.[101] Early the following year, rice planters along the Savannah River began to remove family clothing, household effects, and other valuables from their plantation residences. "I am only sorry of the necessity for your having to remove them," commiserated an Augusta correspondent, as he acknowledged receipt of several trunks containing such items from Mrs. Langdon Cheves.[102] Later the same year, when Union gunboats ventured up the Waccamaw River in Georgetown District, Mrs. Plowden Weston, whose husband was then in the army, fled first to a farm in Horry District and, subsequently, to her native England. Neighboring planter Daniel W. Jordan abandoned his Laurel Hill estate in July, 1862, and spent the remainder of the war in Camden. Other Georgetown planters fol-

99. *Ibid.*, II, 353, 358 (first quotation), 416–20 (second quotation, p. 418), 426, 430, 511, 591, III, 807, 899, 901, 949 (third quotation).

100. Thomas Middleton, Jr., to "Dear Mother," November 30, 1861, Eweretta Barnwell Middleton Family Letters, in Cheves-Middleton Papers, SCHS.

101. Scarborough, ed., *The Diary of Edmund Ruffin*, II, 176; Graydon, *Tales of Edisto*, 40–43; Rogers, *History of Georgetown County*, 403; *Biographical Directory of the Senate of South Carolina*, comp. Reynolds and Faunt, 323.

102. William P. Carmichael to Mrs. Charlotte L. Cheves, February 5, 1862, in Langdon Cheves, Jr., Papers. SCHS.

lowed suit early in 1863, many of them purchasing expensive homes in the interior. "Should there be peace tomorrow," observed one proprietor who remained behind, "they will be left a deadweight upon their hands," for "in ordinary times, they are places of little or no value."[103]

The war affected the lives of wealthy slaveholders on the North Carolina coast in the early months of 1862 when a massive Federal land and sea expedition commanded by Brigadier General Ambrose E. Burnside defeated an inferior Confederate force at Roanoke Island and soon extended its sway over several of the eastern counties where most of the large plantations in the state were located. The town of Edenton fell to Union naval units on February 12, and a month later, Burnside captured New Berne, thereby establishing another base from which to launch inland expeditions.[104] One of those driven from his home by the occupation of New Berne was Judge John R. Donnell, who fled to Raleigh, where he remained for the duration of the war. Donnell later complained that it had been his "peculiar misfortune" to have had nearly all his business interests in the "most endangered" locations: New York, New Orleans, New Berne, and, above all, Hyde County, North Carolina, "where a large and valuable plantation with more than 300 slaves" was "now behind the lines of the Enemy or entirely beyond [his] control." Other elite Tar Heel slaveholders who experienced substantial losses during the war included Josiah Collins, William and Charles Pettigrew, and even the steadfast Unionist James C. Johnston. The devastation inflected upon Somerset, the Collins plantation in Washington County that was abandoned by the family in August, 1862, rivaled that suffered by the Ruffin plantations in Virginia the same year. When William S. Pettigrew visited Somerset in the summer of 1864, he found that the house had been stripped entirely of furniture; shutters, doors, and even the front steps had been ripped off; papers were scattered all over the grounds; and most of the owner's 3,000-volume library had been stolen. Indeed, a Union soldier admitted that "they had taken from Mr. Collins house eighteen thousand dollars worth of

---

103. Joyner, *Down by the Riverside*, 82; Rogers, *History of Georgetown County*, 402–403, 410, 422; Adele Peitigru Allston to Elizabeth Allston, January 11, 1863, in Easterby, ed., *South Carolina Rice Plantation*, 192; Henry A. Middleton to Harriott Middleton, January 5, 1862 [*sic*, 1863], Henry A. Middleton Family Letters, in Cheves-Middleton Papers, SCHS.

104. Long, *The Civil War Day by Day*, 159–60, 168–70, 184–85.

articles." It is little wonder that Judge Donnell characterized the invading Yankees as "Vandals."[105]

Many of the great planter families of the Southwest were also subjected to the dislocations and ravages produced by the war. After the fall of New Orleans in late April, 1862, cities and plantations along the Mississippi River were increasingly exposed to the threat of attack from Union gunboats plying the river. Thus, in early May, with a Yankee gunboat rumored to be approaching from the south, Fanny Conner prepared to leave her Natchez residence for a more secure site in the interior. "I am all packed, even the servants' bedding has been sent out," she reported disconsolately to her absent husband. "God grant we may *all* return to our homes in peace & happiness." But it was the campaigns against Vicksburg and Port Hudson a year later that produced the most severe turmoil on both sides of the river. For example, Federal troops overran cotton-rich Tensas Parish in the spring of 1863, "throwing Every thing in[to] a state of Confusion." One absentee planter was informed that most of his Negroes had been sent to Texas, where they were "hired out in Families," while others were with the overseer in Franklin Parish, about sixty miles from the river. Neighboring planter Samuel Dorsey had also fled to Texas "with nearly all of his Negroes."[106]

To the south, the war spread to sugar plantations in the Teche country in November, 1862, when Union gunboats entered Berwick's Bay and began to engage in periodic skirmishes with Confederate land forces. Damages were inflicted by friend and foe alike. Thus, when a Louisiana brigade departed William T. Palfrey's Ricahoe plantation after an encampment of more than a month, they left, in the words of the proprietor, "devastation & desolation behind them." After removing his hands to a safer locale and sending his family briefly to the town of Franklin, Palfrey remained on his plantation until mid-April. Then, as the fighting escalated, the entire family moved permanently to Franklin, where Palfrey rented a house for $25 a month. A year later, as General Nathaniel Banks began his Red River Campaign, Palfrey lamented that his

105. John R. Donnell to Messrs. Keys and Gunter, April 28, 1863, in Donnell Family Papers, SHC; *Dictionary of North Carolina Biography*, ed. Powell, I, 406; William S. Pettigrew to James C. Johnston, August 9, 1864, Johnston to Henry J. Futrell, August 10, 1864, both in Hayes Collection, SHC.

106. Fanny E. Conner to "My ever Dearest Husband," May 6, 1862, in Lemuel P. Conner and Family Papers, LSU; William Hopkins to Edward Lloyd [VII], June 9, 1864, in Lloyd Papers, MHS.

once-beautiful parish had been reduced to a veritable wasteland. "Plantations abandoned [,] fences & buildings destroyed, mules, horses & cattle driven off by the federals, the negroes conscripted into the army or wandering about without employment or support, & stealing for a living. . . . The Lord help us," he exclaimed, but "such is war, civil war." Across the river in Wilkinson County, Mississippi, J. A. Ventress complained that in a nocturnal raid upon his plantation in February, 1864, the Federals had stripped him of "nearly every horse & mule that [he] possess[ed] in the county," carried off twenty-three male slaves, had broken into his house and stolen "a few articles," and robbed his overseer "of two gold watches and . . . a good portion of his wife's clothing."[107]

Two other elite Mississippi families were the victims of particularly abusive treatment by the invading soldiers. One of these was the family of Natchez planter Gabriel B. Shields, a strong supporter of the Confederacy. Shortly after the Federals occupied Natchez in mid-July, 1863, a small body of Union marauders, led by a notorious lieutenant who had earned a reputation for "committing atrocities on the defenseless" since the occupation, galloped up to Montebello, the Shields's residence, and demanded that they be admitted to the house and that all the men in the household be surrendered to them. When Shields refused both demands on the grounds that "even in the laws of the United States every man's house is his castle," the enraged Yankees returned with increased numbers and began to batter the heavy oaken doors of the mansion with axes and staves. As the assault continued for nearly two hours, Shields and his sixteen-year-old son fired periodically at the intruders while other family members cowered in an upstairs room. Finally, after a Unionist neighbor interceded, Shields agreed to surrender to his assailants, and father and son were escorted to town, where they were charged with firing upon United States troops and incarcerated. Efforts by Shields's two adult daughters to gain their father's release proved futile, and the two young women were ordered to "leave town & go home" after being threatened and verbally abused by a group of Federal soldiers. It is not clear how long Shields and his son languished in jail, but the family attributed the deaths soon thereafter of three of the youngest

107. William T. Palfrey Plantation Diary, November 2, 3, 4, 6, 12, 16, 17, December 10, 19 (first quotation), 1862, January 2, 14, 22, April 12, 25, August 22, 1863, March 9, 10, 14, 16 (second quotation), 1864, in Palfrey Family Papers, LSU; J. Alexander Ventress to Josiah Winchester, February 22, 1864, in Winchester Family Papers, CAH.

Shields children to the "terrible fright" induced by what they termed "the Yankee atrocity."[108]

In the fall of 1864, the family of seventy-eight-year-old Judge Edward McGehee of Wilkinson County was subjected to even more egregious treatment by troops of the Third United States Colored Cavalry. On October 6, this unit, commanded by Major J. B. Cook, raided Judge McGehee's Bowling Green plantation; ransacked the mansion; ordered the judge, his wife and their three daughters to vacate the house within twenty minutes; and then burned it to the ground. The pretext for this vindictive act was simply that McGehee had been providing food to Confederate troops in the vicinity. Alerted by a pal of smoke rising over Bowling Green and by the tearful pleas of a faithful McGehee servant, a neighbor rushed to the scene and found "the House in ashes & the family sitting in the yard with a small pile of wearing apparel," virtually the only items saved from the house. During the course of the incident, according to family members, both the judge and his wife were physically abused by the Negro soldiers. Major Cook, however, categorically denied that any of his men had struck either of the elderly residents. "I would have shot any one on sight had I witnessed such a thing," he declared vehemently. By all accounts, McGehee behaved with exemplary dignity and restraint throughout the entire ordeal. Whatever the truth concerning the alleged assaults, Major Cook later conceded that the order from his superior to burn Bowling Green was "very cruel and very unjustifiable."[109]

Such orders became more common the following year as General William T. Sherman began his destructive march through the Carolinas. Because of its perceived role in causing the war, South Carolina was a particular target of Yankee venom, and the inhabitants of that state probably suffered greater losses,

108. Journal of Ellen Shields, 1903, photocopy in possession of Mrs. Katherine Blankenstein of Natchez, who was kind enough to provide the author with excerpts from the journal. Ellen Shields was the daughter of Gabriel Shields and Catherine Surget and was twenty-two years old at the time of the alleged incident. The three young children, aged nine, six, and three, died within the span of a single week in the fall of 1863.

109. J. B. Cook to J. S. McGehee, January 6 (second quotation), April 4, 1904, "Aunt Carrie" [Caroline E. McGehee, daughter of Edward] to "Dear Stewart" [J. S. McGehee], February 7, 1904, Eve Brower to J. S. McGehee, February 22, 1904 (first quotation), W. H. Chapin to McGehee, March 20, 1904, printed letter, George T. McGehee to J. B. Cook, in *Independent Venture* (Woodville, Miss.), April 6, 1904, in James Stewart McGehee Papers, LSU.

proportionately, than those in any other Confederate state. One of the first country mansions to fall victim to Sherman's vengeful troops was Ingleside, the Beaufort District residence of Benjamin R. Bostick. As one Union soldier recounted, after the troops had helped themselves to whatever books and paintings attracted their fancy, the "grand homestead" was left "in ashes, the chimneys alone remaining to mark another mile of 'country subjugated.'" Other mansions torched by Sherman's army as it continued its itinerary through the Palmetto State included Melrose, the magnificent home of Nicholas A. Peay in Fairfield District; Weehaw, the Georgetown plantation residence of Henry A. Middleton; and the handsome country homestead of Charles Heyward in Colleton District. In addition, Heyward's Charleston residence was sacked and the most valuable furniture stolen, and all of the buildings on his five Combahee River rice plantations were destroyed. In the words of his son, the entire country between Savannah and Charleston "is now a howling wilderness."[110]

Another South Carolinian, Catharine Rhett, the second wife of Barnwell Rhett, provided a dramatic account of the midnight flight of her family from their Low Country home in the spring of 1865. Awakened in the dead of night by a Confederate soldier pounding on the door to alert the Rhetts that an enemy gunboat had passed the obstructions on the Combahee and was coming up the river, Catharine hastily threw on her clothes and collected some silver and a few other "precious articles" before fleeing the home that contained "so many loved and precious memories." Her husband immediately ordered the two buggies and every available wagon to be readied for the evacuation of the family and slave children. As she set out in one of the buggies with her maid, she surveyed the tranquil, pastoral scene before her, inhaled the "perfume of the magnolia blossoms" that was "almost overpowering" in its "midnight fragrance," and cast one "long and mournful look around" before departing her beloved home. After riding for several hours through the pitch black night and passing through several friendly picket lines, she finally crossed the bridge over the river just as a new day began to dawn. Her husband, who had become sepa-

110. Thomas O. Lawton, Jr., "The Life and Death of Robertville," *Carologue* 16 (Winter 2000): 13 (first quotation); *Biographical Directory of the Senate of South Carolina*, comp. Reynolds and Faunt, 287; Rogers, *History of Georgetown County*, 421; Elizabeth [Blyth Weston?] to Adele Petigru Allston, March 17, 1865, in Easterby, ed., *South Carolina Rice Plantation*, 206; E. B. Heyward to James A. Lord, January 22, 1866 (TS) (last quotation), in Edward Barnwell Heyward Letters, SCL.

rated from her during the night, then hurried back on horseback "to hasten on" the adult Negroes, who were proceeding on foot. Thus did one of the most notorious southern fire-eaters narrowly escape the clutches of the enemy during the closing days of the war.[111]

Although North Carolina largely escaped the ravages inflicted by Sherman on its sister state, damage to the property of large slaveholders was still extensive. The piedmont region of the state, which had been spared during the first four years of the war, lay directly in the path of Sherman as he entered the state with his massive army in early March, 1865. By mid-April, Raleigh had fallen, and the opposing commanders, Sherman and Joseph E. Johnston, prepared to enter into surrender negotiations at nearby Durham's Station. As the two armies faced one another, planters in the region suffered heavy losses from marauding soldiers on both sides. Among the unfortunate proprietors was Paul C. Cameron, the wealthiest slaveholder in the state. On April 16, a party of bummers from Sherman's army raided Fairntosh, Cameron's 30,000-acre estate located about two miles north of Durham's Station. They invaded the dwelling house, rifled through trunks, stole the family's clothing, burned a number of personal papers, and even plundered the slave cabins. In the end, the mansion and other farm buildings were spared, but the losses in livestock and provisions were immense. Cameron estimated that the vandals had taken more than sixty horses and mules as well as "nearly *all* [their] food and bacon, flour, lard, [and] molasses." The story was much the same on other plantations in the vicinity of the North Carolina capital. Cameron's brother-in-law, George W. Mordecai, reported that the farms near Raleigh "have been completely despoiled of everything in the shape of provisions & forage," and, in many cases, "the houses have been either burned or torn to pieces."[112]

With Rebel armies reeling before the advancing Federals while those at home were increasingly subjected to both rebellious slaves and the depredations inflicted by occupying forces, it would seem that most Southerners would be reconciled to defeat. Yet a few members of the elite remained defiant to the end.

111. Catharine Rhett's Account of Flight from Yankees, n.d., in Robert Barnwell Rhett, Sr., Papers, SCHS.

112. Mark L. Bradley, *This Astounding Close: The Road to Bennett Place* (Chapel Hill, 2000), 189–90; Paul C. Cameron to Thomas Ruffin, May 11, 1865, in *The Papers of Thomas Ruffin,* ed. Hamilton, III, 452. The last quotation, Mordecai to David L. Swain, May 15, 1865, from Walter Clark Papers, NCDAH, is quoted in Bradley, *This Astounding Close,* 190.

Peter W. Hairston, who had earlier vowed to go to Chile before submitting to Yankee rule, settled instead in Baltimore because he "could not live in North Carolina" under postwar conditions. Shortly after Lee's surrender, another North Carolinian, Kate Edmondston, lamented that "our people do not feel it [defeat] as they ought—like men who have lost their Liberty. . . . O My God, can the very spirit of Freedom die out thus & leave not a trace behind it? . . . Is the very memory of our dead to vanish from our midst?"[113]

Another diehard Confederate was Charles Alston, Sr., reputedly the last of the great Georgetown rice planters to take the oath of allegiance and the last to emancipate his slaves. But perhaps the most unyielding of all the wealthy slaveholders was Louis A. Bringier. A member of one of the great sugar-planting families of Louisiana, Bringier was serving as colonel of the Seventh Louisiana Cavalry in the closing months of the war. In December, 1864, he vowed to "fight it out to the bitter end," employing guerrilla tactics if necessary. Several months later, he rejoiced in the assassination of Lincoln and directed his wife to name their next child, if a boy, "B. Booth Bringier" in honor of the assassin. Finally, as rumors circulated in May of General Edmund Kirby Smith's impending surrender, the fiery Creole angrily disowned "this cowardly people" and announced his intention to depart for Brazil as soon as the last Confederate army surrendered. In the end, however, Bringier did not leave the country. Instead, he and the other slaveholding nabobs were compelled to accept the reality of defeat and military subjugation and to confront a new world—a world that saw them stripped of the economic and political power they had wielded before the first shells exploded over Charleston harbor in the spring of 1861.[114]

113. Peter W. Hairston to Fanny Hairston, July 11, 1861, September 19, 1865, both in Peter Wilson Hairston Papers, SHC; *"Journal of a Secesh Lady,"* ed. Crabtree and Patton, 708.

114. Joyner, *Down by the Riverside,* 227; L. A. Bringier to Stella Bringier, December 7, 1864, April 23, May 11, 1865, in Louis A. Bringier and Family Papers, LSU.

10

POSTWAR ADJUSTMENT:
The Legacy of Emancipation and Defeat

What a change has come over our land. From being the happiest & most prosperous people on the face of the globe after years of slaughter & desolation, we are now trodden down under the iron heel of military despotism.
—WILLIAM F. WICKHAM, July 9, 1865

Our negroes in the cotton region will be forced to work—tho' free. Cotton must be made—& our New England brethren must have cotton—or their losses will be immense—incalculable. —BENJAMIN O. TAYLOE, November 23, 1865

The negros will not do. Coolies or some other labour we must substitute.
—CHARLES D. HAMILTON, November, 1865

I feel now that I have *no country*. I *obey* like a subject, but I cannot love such a government. —EDWARD BARNWELL HEYWARD, January 22, 1866

The truth is I am thoroughly disgusted with free negro labor, and am determined that the next year shall close my planting operations with them. There is no feeling of gratitude in their nature. —HOWELL COBB, December, 1866

Ours is no Constitutional government now. It is a fierce democracy & the will of the Majority Stands for Law. —WILLIAM T. MARTIN, March 7, 1867

If you find yourself able I would advise you never to return to this Godforsaken & oppressed Country.
—DANIEL M. ADAMS to EUSTACE SURGET
in Bordeaux, France, March 10, 1867

The war has made a great change in Virginia—indeed "*Old Virginia*" no longer exists. We make the best of it, as repining is useless—but the change is a sad one.
—WILLIAM F. WICKHAM, March 3, 1874

IN THE WAKE of Confederate defeat and the loss of the most valuable portion of their property, the elite planters were forced to adjust to a society that, in many respects, was turned upside down. Many reacted with bitterness, anger, and pessimism, while others did their best to adapt to the new social order. Their most immediate task was to bring some semblance of order to the labor system so that they could resume agricultural production. The old master–slave relationship had been shattered by the war, and landed proprietors were now confronted with unprecedented demands from their laborers. No longer could they maintain discipline merely by the threat of the lash. Moreover, in the months immediately after the war, any agreement they reached with the freedmen was subject to review by federal authorities. Weakened by the staggering economic losses sustained during the war and by the loss of their political power after the end of hostilities, they struggled to regain some measure of control over their own destiny. Some, like John Burnside of Louisiana and Paul Cameron of North Carolina succeeded in recovering the lofty position they had enjoyed before the war; many others did not.

At the conclusion of the conflict, conditions were in a state of turmoil in plantation districts throughout the South. From Virginia to Texas, Negroes seized the opportunity to exploit their newly won freedom. Some roamed aimlessly over the countryside, many who remained on their plantations refused to work, and others openly defied their overseers and former masters. As a result, agricultural operations came to a virtual standstill in 1865, much to the consternation of the planters. The latter complained bitterly that, although they were compelled to continue their support of the women, children, aged, and infirm, they could not force the able-bodied freedmen to work. As Kate Edmondston put it, the Negroes were "endeavouring to be both slave & free at the same moment—a slave on the food, shelter, & clothing question but free where labour is concerned." Paul Cameron, who began trying to reach some accommodation with his people in August, 1865, declared flatly: "They must go to work or they must leave the places." Two months later, however, his hands were still idle. "At Fairntosh and Stagville," he reported gloomily, "all are going to the devil or dogs as fast as they can—wont work—and destroying stock—out houses, enclosures! No reliance can be placed in any contract. . . . Nothing but want will bring them to their senses." In Virginia, William F. Wickham complained that despite repeated requests to the Freedmen's Bureau for some measure "to relieve [them] from the maintenance of the negros who remain on the plantations," no assistance had been forthcoming. Consequently, he lamented, "I am at a loss how to proceed with regard to the plans for next year."[1]

The situation was no better further down the coast. The overseer on one of the Cobb plantations in Georgia informed his employer in July, 1865, that the Negroes were in a state of quiet rebellion. "Some of them" he reported, "go when tha pleas and wher tha pleas and pay no attention to your orders nor mine." In Georgetown District, South Carolina, where blacks were in the overwhelming majority, they were, in the words of one discouraged plantation mistress, "masters of the situation." Many had absconded, others were stealing meat and other provisions from their former owners, and still others were destroying property throughout the district. "I see no hope," declared Adele Allston at the end of the year. "[The Negroes] are so numerous and we have no redress. There are not any who are willing to engage for another year. They still wait for some great thing 1st Jan." Another Georgetown rice baron, William B. Pringle, fared even worse. Not only did his Negroes refuse to sign their contracts for the next year, but they also burned down his house. Those who did agree to work demanded what their former masters deemed extortionate wages: as much as $15 a month on the rice plantations near Savannah. William H. Heyward predicted that some would soon insist on *weekly* wages, payable each Saturday night. "It makes the planter *a slave*, far worse than his slave used to be," Heyward remarked bitterly.[2]

Similar conditions prevailed on the great cotton and sugar plantations in the Southwest. Blacks in the region manifested little inclination to sign labor contracts for the year beginning in January, 1866. "I have heard of one or two planters making contracts for next year," reported a Rapides Parish landowner, but most Negroes "don't like to contract yet as they believe they are to have lands next year." Even those who agreed to work did so grudgingly. "Sometimes these

1. William F. Wickham to Charles Carter, July 9, September 25 (quotation), 1865, in Wickham Family Papers, VHS; *"Journal of a Secesh Lady,"* ed. Crabtree and Patton, 713; Paul C. Cameron to Thomas Ruffin, August 11, October 4, 1865, in *The Papers of Thomas Ruffin,* ed. Hamilton, III, 464, IV, 35.

2. J. D. Collins to John A. Cobb, July 31, 1865 (TS), in Cobb-Erwin-Lamar Family Collection, UGA; Jane Pringle to Adele Allston, April 1, [1865], Adele Allston to Adele Vander Horst, December 15, 1865, both in Easterby, ed. *South Carolina Rice Plantation,* 209–11, 216; Rogers, *History of Georgetown County,* 432–33; William Henry Heyward to James B. Heyward, April 17, 1866, in Heyward and Ferguson Family Papers, SHC.

Freedmen work quite well," observed a Mississippian, "& then again they do almost nothing." The explanation, he concluded, was that most entertained "a deep hatred to[ward] white people" that might erupt at any time. A Louisiana planter expressed a desire to sell his place in the spring of 1866 if he could obtain "a fair price for it" because "the Labor is too uncertain" and he was "not able to go through the toil & perplexity of working Freedmen."[3] Later the same year, one of the Conner brothers complained of what he called the "determined obstinacy" of the hands on his Rifle Point plantation in Texas. All of the women had "just discovered" that they were pregnant and thus unable to do any work because of their "delicate situation." According to Conner, the men were even worse. "I have offered every inducement for them to work," he remarked dejectedly, but "still it has no effect." Similarly, a harried Richard Archer reported from his plantation in the Mississippi Delta that only about half of his cotton had been ginned and pressed because "the negroes would not work." In the face of such adversity, many agriculturists did not even make an attempt to resume operations during the first year after the war. For example, the Concordia Parish planters who had abandoned their places during the war did not begin cultivation again until the spring of 1867.[4]

Despite the volatile labor situation, a number of wealthy planters in areas not severely affected by military operations were successful in contracting with their former slaves to continue working on their old plantations. The terms of these labor agreements varied considerably from planter to planter and from one locality to another. During the year of the surrender, arrangements between employer and laborer were rather haphazard, usually differing little from their pre-emancipation relationship except for the payment of minimal monthly wages to the hands. Thereafter, formal written contracts became the rule. These involved renting land to the freedmen, compensating them with a share of the

3. William C. Thompson to "Dear Father" [Lewis Thompson], November 26, 1865 (first quotation), in Lewis Thompson Papers, SHC; C. L. Dubuisson to Dr. Stephen Duncan, May 19, 1866 (second quotation), Zenas Preston to Duncan, May 2, 1866 (third quotation), both in Winchester Family Papers, CAH.

4. Farar B. Conner to "Dear Brother" [Lemuel P.], September 27 (first quotations), November 30 (last quotation), 1866, in Lemuel P. Conner and Family Papers, LSU; Richard T. Archer to "My Dear Wife," December 28, 1866, in Richard Thompson Archer Family Papers, CAH; A. H. Harris [agent for George S. Mandeville] to Eustace Surget, August 24, 1867 (Roll 1), in Surget Family Papers, MDAH.

crop, paying them monetary wages, or some combination thereof. These terms changed over time, but in the initial postwar years they had to be approved by agents of the Freedmen's Bureau, who usually endeavored to protect the interests of the freedmen. For example, in 1866 the Bureau established a wage scale ranging from $12 to $15 a month for males and $8 to $10 for females in the state of Georgia. As planter and laborer struggled to reach an accommodation in the postemancipation world, there was much grumbling and dissatisfaction on both sides. Eventually, however, they reached some kind of detente, though neither party was ever fully satisfied with its new status.[5]

Despite efforts by the Freedmen's Bureau to ameliorate the lot of the freedmen, the latter generally fared poorly in their initial year of freedom. After Federal troops overran his Wilkinson County, Mississippi, plantation in the spring of 1864, Francis Surget, Jr., began paying his Negroes at the rate of $4 a month for men and half that amount for women. These wages remained the same the following year except for those hands with special skills. Thus, Hannah Scott was engaged as a cook for a monthly wage of $12. Surget furnished all of his workers with food, shelter, clothing, and medical care, just as he had before they were emancipated. In the same year, Fanny Conner reported that freedmen on the family's plantations were unhappy with their $3 monthly wage. In compliance with a directive issued by Federal military authorities, the workers on one sugar plantation in St. James Parish, Louisiana, were divided according to age, gender, and ability into four classes, with wages ranging from $3 per month for the lowest class to $8 for the highest. But not even the Federals could persuade the newly freed blacks on Oliver H. Middleton's Edisto Island plantation to resume their labors. After recovering his plantation in January, 1866, Middleton offered to contract with his people on what a Union lieutenant termed "very fair terms," but "they refuse[d] to contract on any terms."[6]

5. E. Merton Coulter, *The South During Reconstruction, 1865–1877* (Baton Rouge, 1947), 74–79; Eric Foner, *Reconstruction: America's Unfinished Revolution, 1863–1877* (New York, 1988), 104–108; Reidy, *From Slavery to Agrarian Capitalism,* 147.

6. Miscellaneous Accounts with Negroes, 1864 (Roll 5), Freedmen Contracts, 1865 (Roll 1), in Surget Family Papers, MDAH; Fanny E. Conner to "My ever dearest Husband," October 21, 1865, in Lemuel P. Conner and Family Papers, LSU; Payroll of Laborers Employed by D. Tureaud on Union Plantation, St. James Parish, February 4, 1865, in Benjamin Tureaud Papers, LSU; "Restoration Papers for Edisto Lands," January 23, 1866, Certificate signed by R. L. Clark, Lieutenant, 35th U.S.C.T. and Assistant Provost Marshal, February 10, 1866, Middleton Family Letters, in Middleton-Blake Papers, SCHS.

Other planters elected to pay their freedmen by giving them a share of the crop rather than paying them a specific wage. Thus, as Sherman's army ploughed through piedmont North Carolina in the spring of 1865, Paul Cameron proposed to compensate his remaining Negroes with one-fourth of the crops of wheat, sweet potatoes, and peas, and one-third of the corn and molasses. The following year, Cameron increased the freedmen's share of all farm produce to one-half, but they were required to feed and clothe themselves. In addition, the hands were enjoined to be "perfectly respectful in language and deportment to the proprietor and his agent or agents." Those who violated this injunction or who refused to perform any work required of them were subject to immediate banishment from the plantation. Another North Carolinian, Lewis Thompson, employed a combination of crop shares and wages to compensate the workers on his Bertie and Northampton County farms. For example, in 1866 Thompson's hands received one-fourth of the cotton, corn, peas, and fodder, which they divided among themselves in any manner they chose. The owner controlled the management of the units, pitched the crop, and housed and fed the Negroes. In other instances, Thompson entered into wage agreements with individual freedmen. Thus, Jacob Spelman, who was hired as a laborer, servant, and farm hand on Thompson's Bertie County farm in 1866, was paid $108 in addition to his maintenance expenses. Spelman's contract also specified that he was to "behave himself respectfully and orderly, be peaceable and quiet . . . entertain no bad Company, and be subject to such general directions in his labor as the said Lewis Thompson may give."[7]

Similar restrictions, strikingly reminiscent of plantation rules and regulations before emancipation, were incorporated into the freedmen contracts of South Carolina grandee Theodore L. Gourdin. Like Cameron, Gourdin agreed to share the crops equally with the freedmen, with the exception of the net proceeds from the sale of cotton, two-thirds of which were retained by the owner. Gourdin allowed his Negroes to remain in their houses, but they were obliged

7. Contract Proposed by Paul C. Cameron for Negroes on Family Farms in Orange County, North Carolina, [April, 1865], in *The Papers of Thomas Ruffin*, ed. Hamilton, III, 449–50; Labor Contracts, Lewis Thompson, Dwelling House and Farm, Bertie County, North Carolina, January 1, 1866, Collective Agreements, Lewis Thompson with seventeen hands on Roanoke River plantation, with sixteen hands on Hickory Neck tract [Bertie County], January 1, 1866, Folder 61, in Lewis Thompson Papers, SHC. For other freedmen contracts on the Thompson plantations, see folders 60–61, 66 of Lewis Thompson Papers, SHC.

to furnish their own food and clothing "of every kind." They were also required to "submit at all times" to the control of the proprietor, to "behave in a respect-full [*sic*] and orderly manner," and to "do a reasonable days work," defined by their employer as ten hours or "such as was formerly done on the plantation." Those found to be neglectful or idle were fined fifty cents for each day lost, and those absent without leave from the plantation were subject to immediate re-moval, forfeiture of their share of the crops, and possible punishment by the nearest military authorities. Finally, the hands were prohibited from entertain-ing company, possessing firearms or liquor, and bringing animals of any kind to the plantation without the permission of the owner. One could scarcely blame the freedmen if they perceived little difference between these restrictions and those contained in the antebellum slave codes. Consequently, it comes as no surprise to learn that a Freedmen's Bureau official was summoned by Gourdin in the summer of 1866 to investigate what the officer termed "the difficulties on your plantation."[8]

In addition to wages and crop shares, another method utilized by planters to attract laborers in the immediate aftermath of the war was to rent land to them in return for some form of personal service or for a share of the crop. Many Negroes preferred this arrangement because it afforded them a greater degree of autonomy and freedom from scrutiny than either of the other plans. The aging Richard Archer entered into such an agreement with his hands in the fall of 1866 to cultivate a ninety-acre field planted in provision crops near his residence in Port Gibson, Mississippi. Concerned about the welfare of his wife after what he believed to be his imminent death, he initially instructed her to rent the land and cabins to the Negroes for half the crop. After further re-flection, he advised his spouse to rent the land at $8 per acre "if [she] can get it" and to hire the Negroes three days a week to work for her. The proprietor would furnish the necessary working stock and would feed the hands, but the latter were obligated to clothe themselves. In addition, the freedmen agreed to perform all the "usual and necessary [work] outside of the crop every day and every night, such as feeding & taking care of the stock." Archer also rented some good cotton land in the same county to a few select Negroes. Thus, in the

8. Memorandum of Agreement between T. L. Gourdin of Charleston, St. Stephen's and Freed-men, 1866, Freedmen Contract, July 7, 1865, F. W. L. [Freedmen's Bureau agent] to Gourdin, June 22, 1866, Folder 16, in Theodore L. Gourdin Plantation and Personal Papers, SCHS.

spring of 1867 he had two six-man squads working the place, from which he anticipated a yield of forty-eight bales. The first squad paid the owner one-third of the crop, while the other, to which Archer furnished mules, gave one-half. In addition to the land, the proprietor furnished housing and basic provisions to the renters.[9]

Although these contracts brought some stability to postwar relations between planters and freedmen, former slaveowners continued to complain about the labor supply throughout the Reconstruction period. Only occasionally does one encounter positive comments about the work habits of the freedmen. For example, the son of Natchez planter Charles G. Dahlgren reported in April, 1869, that affairs on the family's plantation were going well. The servants, enthused young Dahlgren, "have behaved just the same as though they never heard of freedom." Much more typical, however, was the attitude of Jacob Surget, who declared it "a pity [that] the blacks were not all driven out of the country." Another Mississippian, former Confederate general Samuel G. French, noted at the beginning of 1869 that a Negro who picked 312 pounds of cotton in 1856 was now picking only half that amount. "Why is it," he asked, "that the little children then picked more per day than any man or woman has picked this year for me?" Similarly, a Louisiana planter, heavily indebted to Stephen Duncan, complained that "the New System of Labor, controlled and guided . . . by Fanatics," had turned out to be even worse than he had predicted.[10]

Some planters became so disgusted with the behavior of the freedmen that they simply expelled them from their property, while others were forced to cope with periodic turmoil among the laborers on their estates. North Carolina planter Richard S. Donnell encountered considerable resistance from the freedmen on his Hyde County farm when he ordered them to vacate the property by the end of 1866. In February of the following year, Donnell's agent reported that the former slaves had defied both the overseer and the sheriff and were still

9. Coulter, *The South During Reconstruction,* 78–79; Richard T. Archer to "My Dear Wife," October 9, 15, November 5 (quotations), 1866, Archer to [New Orleans factor], May 18, 1867, in Richard Thompson Archer Family Papers, CAH.

10. B. Dahlgren to "Dear Father," April 13, 1869, in Nutt Family Collection, MDAH; Jacob Surget to James Surget, Jr., January 18, 1869, in MacNeil Papers, MDAH; Gen S. G. French to A. K. Farrar, January 17, 1869 (Xerox copy), in Alexander K. Farrar Papers, LSU; [Zenas Preston] to Col. L. V. Reeves or Josiah Winchester, September 10, 1867, in Winchester Family Papers, CAH.

refusing to leave. "Their association with Yankees and Buffaloes," he concluded, "has fixed very mischeivous [sic] notions in their heads, which must be eradicated." Those notions apparently were soon dispelled, for three weeks later, the agent informed Donnell that he had "succeeded in expelling the last of the negro trespassers from [Donnell's] Hyde farm." After being confronted with the threat of force by a posse comitatus, he explained, "they *vamosed the Ranch.*" Those proprietors who elected to employ black laborers on their plantations continued to experience problems well into the 1870s. For example, in the fall of 1874 South Carolina rice baron William Aiken was almost obliged to terminate a visit to New York after learning of the "difficulties among the Negroes" on his Jehossee Island estate. The foreman had "had some of them imprisoned" and had momentarily restored order, but Aiken still felt "rather uncomfortable" about the situation.[11]

Labor problems also plagued some Louisiana sugar producers in the years immediately preceding the end of Reconstruction in that state. On March 1, 1875, Benjamin Tureaud entered into a contract with approximately 150 male hands on his Ascension Parish plantations that provided for a daily wage of $1.00 without rations, one-half payable "after Grinding," from which the worker's debt to the plantation store would be deducted, and the other half payable on March 1, 1876. The payment of said wages was contingent upon the laborer fulfilling his contract "fully," and any man who left the plantation or in any manner broke "his bargain" would "forfeit his back wages." The freedmen apparently grew disenchanted with this arrangement, for in January of the following year in the midst of the rolling season, Tureaud complained that he was having difficulty getting the hands to work. "Only 3 or 4 want to work in the field," he grumbled, "and it was with difficulty I could get enough to run the sugar house." Nor could he do any plowing, he continued, because "there was no one to take a plow." Perhaps in response to such resistance, Tureaud increased wages the following year to $1.15 a day for men and $.85 for women.[12]

Some prominent Natchez District planters became so discouraged about the

11. D. M. Carter to "My dear Donnell" [Richard S.], February 3, 23, 1867, in Donnell Family Papers, SHC; William Aiken to [daughter] Henrietta [Rhett], September 15, 1874, in Robert Barnwell Rhett, Sr., Papers, SCHS.

12. Labor Contract, [March 1, 1875], Folder 60, Benjamin Tureaud to Benjamin Tureaud, Jr., January 18, 1876, Folder 51, Pay Scale, 1877, vol. 83, in Benjamin Tureaud Papers, LSU. Number of workers computed from Time Books, 1873–78, vols. 82–83, *ibid.*

labor situation after the war that they launched an elaborate scheme to import Chinese coolies to replace black laborers on their plantations. Tureaud also employed about 25 Chinese laborers on his sugar plantations in 1875, but he was apparently not directly associated with the plan developed by the Natchez nabobs.[13] The idea of utilizing Chinese coolies as an alternative labor supply began to circulate shortly after the end of the war. As early as November, 1865, a Mississippi planter expressed an interest in importing such laborers. "The negros will not do," he declared flatly. "Coolies or some other labor we must substitute." Less than two years later, following the expulsion of the freedmen from Richard Donnell's North Carolina farm, an associate urged Donnell to replace them with Chinese. "The sooner we can get things under way there with *Chinese* I think, the better," he advised. "In *Louisiana* the experiment succeeds *admirably* in *all respects*," he concluded enthusiastically. Others pointed to the example of Cuba, where it was reported that one planter had "sold off all his slaves and substituted Chinamen for them much to his satisfaction."[14]

Doubtless influenced by such glowing reports, a group of Natchez nabobs led by former Unionist Josiah Winchester began to formulate a plan to import thousands of Chinese coolies to work the cotton and sugar plantations of the Southwest. Winchester, who was described by a fellow Natchezian as "being so absorbed in the Chinese question" that he could think of little else, began to enlist support for the project during the summer of 1869. As he explained in a letter apparently written to Wade Hampton, who owned several heavily mortgaged cotton plantations in the Delta, Winchester was convinced that Negroes would not work without coercion and that Europeans and white Americans could never be induced to cultivate tropical crops. The obvious solution was Chinese labor, which he argued would be "cheaper and far more efficient than negro labor ever was." A plan to procure up to 10,000 laborers from Chinese companies in California to cultivate the crop of 1868 had been thwarted by the opposition of northern Republicans, who contended that European immigrants, white laborers from the North, and freed blacks could provide ample

13. Plantation Payrolls for Houmas and Brulé plantations, January–December, 1875, Folders 40–41, *ibid.*

14. C. D. Hamilton to C. Beltherford [?], November, 1865, in Richard Thompson Archer Family Papers, CAH; Thomas M. Keerl to Richard S. Donnell, March 1, 1867, in Donnell Family Papers, SHC; W. S. Capers [?] to "Dear Ellick" [A. K. Farrar], September 15, 1869, in Alexander K. Farrar Papers, LSU.

labor to restore southern cotton and sugar fields to their former prosperity. Two years later, however, that opposition had dissipated, and Winchester was hopeful that there would no longer be "any serious opposition in the North to the introduction of Chinese labor." After they studied the matter further, it became apparent to Winchester and other members of the Natchez elite that they would have to import coolies directly from China rather than from California, where Chinese laborers were being paid $15 to $25 a month in gold. As one nabob observed, "as long as these laborers get such wages there they will not emigrate to the South or any where else."[15]

Accordingly, in the early 1870s, Winchester, with the collaboration of Vernon Seaman, a venture capitalist from New York, and Charles E. Hill, who was dispatched to China as their resident agent, embarked upon a plan to import thousands of Chinese laborers to work on plantations in the Natchez District. In addition to solving the labor problem, Winchester and his associates expected to reap a handsome profit from their joint enterprise. On August 1, 1872, Seaman sailed from San Francisco on board the steamer *America* en route to Shanghai, where, together with Hill, he hoped to arrange with Chinese officials for the emigration of 1,000 laborers for a term of five years. Unfortunately, there were difficulties from the outset of his mission. Seaman's journey began most inauspiciously when the *America* "was totally destroyed by fire on the night of the 24th in the harbor of Yokohama," resulting in the loss of all his belongings and very nearly his life.[16]

As the shaken Seaman resumed his trip to Shanghai on board another steamer, Hill reported from that city that Chinese officials had agreed in principle to the proposal he had presented to them on behalf of the partners. That proposal required an initial capital outlay of $184,000 to cover the cost of transporting 1,000 Chinese to the South and paying their wages for the first year at the rate of $84 per head. Hill assured his cohorts that the risk to the planters would be minimal because "the mandarins insist upon every man signing his agreement in the presence of himself & the Consul." Should the laborer abscond before the end of his term of service, "the Consul could easily enforce the

15. James Surget to A. L. Bingaman, 1869, in MacNeil Papers, MDAH; Josiah Winchester to [Wade Hampton III?], June 11, 1869; Samuel M. Davis to Winchester, July 29, 1869, in Winchester Family Papers, CAH.

16. Vernon Seaman to Josiah Winchester, July 24, August 28 (quotation), 1872, in Winchester Family Papers, CAH; Winchester to S. M. Davis, October 2, 1872, in Duncan Papers, LSU.

penalty here, as the emigrants whole family would be made to suffer." It was imperative, Hill emphasized, that the planters assume some risk if the plan were to succeed. Noting that he had already expended two years and $10,000 of his own money on the project, the disillusioned agent charged that "the South do not want labor bad enough to run one dollar's risk & we cannot offer sufficient inducement to Capitalists to have them touch it." If the capital were available, continued Hill, he could supply 5,000 men immediately and 20,000 eventually from near Swoton. But, he added, if neither the planters nor transportation providers would agree to furnish the requisite capital, "let us drop it [the plan] altogether."[17]

During the ensuing months, Winchester and Seaman labored frantically but unsuccessfully to attract the financial support of both planters and capitalists. In December, Winchester reported from New York that he had "met with little encouragement from Capitalists here," and he would "have to rely upon the assistance" he might "get from our planters at home." Among those who had expressed an interest in the project were members of the Duncan family, Samuel M. and Alfred V. Davis, Alexander K. Farrar, Gabriel B. Shields, William N. Mercer, and, above all, Colonel Edmund Richardson, who reputedly became the largest planter in the country after the war. While trying to raise capital, Winchester also had to protect his political flank. He sought the assistance of Secretary of State Hamilton Fish in order to counter a threat from the British consul at Hong Kong, who was trying to enforce an informal convention of 1866 designed to suppress the Chinese coolie trade. He charged that Britain was attempting "to prevent the Emigration of laborers from China into the sugar & cotton regions of the U.S." because she desired "to monopolize this labor, in her own tropical possessions." If all went well, however, Winchester estimated that the three partners, who had taken the name Hill, Seaman & Company of Natchez, could earn a net profit of nearly $60,000 by importing 500 Chinese for sixteen months of labor, commencing August 1, 1873. One-half of the profits would go to the planter and his agent, and the other half would be shared equally by the partners—a division rejected by Hill on the grounds that it "was asking too much" to expect him to share the burden of expenses for two years

17. Charles E. Hill to Vernon Seaman, September 10, 1872, Seaman to Winchester, August 6, 1872, both in Winchester Papers, CAH; Josiah Winchester to S. M. Davis, October 2, 1872, in Duncan Papers, LSU.

before receiving any compensation. The question of how to divide the spoils soon became a moot point, however, for by the summer of 1873 the scheme was temporarily abandoned, largely because Winchester and his associates could not persuade enough planters and capitalists to assume the financial risk necessary to implement it.[18]

After a hiatus of five years, the Chinese labor scheme was revived briefly in the late 1870s. Upon learning that the "question of Chinese labor for the South" was again being "agitated," Seaman expressed the hope to Winchester that they might "yet be able to atone for the misfortunes of the past." A year later, Winchester was invited to address a labor convention in Vicksburg on the subject. Alarmed by "the exodus of Negro labor" from the region, many of the largest landowners had reached "a determination to import their labor from China" if it could be accomplished at a "reasonable rate." That summer, Seaman unveiled a new proposal to Winchester, this one involving the procurement of up to 1,000 laborers in San Francisco through the agency of his friend Chin Poo. Under this plan the employer would pay the cost of transportation from California at $40 per head, furnish the workers with housing, provisions, and free medical care, and pay wages at the rate of $14 a month. For their part, the Chinese were obligated to work twenty-six days a month for ten hours a day with a three-day holiday for New Year's. Lost time would be deducted from wages. "*The prompt payment of wages is the main point,*" asserted Seaman, "this being secured, all the rest is comparatively easy." Seaman proposed for themselves a commission of $10 to $15 per laborer, to be divided equally among Winchester, Chin Poo, and himself. Apparently Winchester was not receptive to the proposition, for by the end of the year Seaman was back in New York speculating in mining ventures. Thus, after a decade, the plan to import Chinese coolies into the Natchez District was finally abandoned. Although some Chinese were employed on cotton and sugar plantations in the Southwest during the postbellum years, the massive importation envisioned by Winchester and his associates never materialized.[19]

18. Josiah Winchester to Charles E. Hill, December 21, 1872 (first quotations), Hill to Winchester, June 10, 1873 (last quotation), Samuel M. Davis to Winchester, July 29, 1869, Hill to Vernon Seaman, September 10, 1872, Seaman to Winchester, January 20, 1873, A. K. Farrar to Winchester, January 21, 1873, in Winchester Papers, CAH; blank contract attached to letter from Winchester to S. M. Davis, October 2, 1872, in Duncan Papers, LSU.

19. Seaman to Winchester, April 6, 1878, July 14, December 22, 1879, E. D. Farrar to Winchester, April 17, 1879, in Winchester Family Papers, CAH.

Labor was not the only problem faced by elite planters in the immediate aftermath of the war. Most of them suffered enormous financial losses as a consequence of the war and emancipation. Natchez merchant-planter William J. Britton, a staunch Unionist before the war, estimated his losses at not less than three-quarters of a million dollars, much of which he attributed to actions by the "so-called Confed Authorities & armies." He lamented that he had not been able to resist business pressures and, instead his "own judgment, formed while at the Vᵃ Springs & Old Point [Comfort] in 60," to place the bulk of his assets in the Bank of England prior to secession. Similarly, Thomas P. Devereux, another prewar Unionist, lost between one-half and three-quarters of a million dollars "in property of all kinds" despite the fact that his plantations "were not ravaged" and his farm machinery remained intact. Devereux never did recover, and in May, 1868, just ten months before his death, with debts totaling more than $290,000, he was forced to declare bankruptcy.[20] Many other formerly wealthy slaveholders followed Devereux into bankruptcy. Some took in northern partners, others leased their plantations to those better able to weather the acute postwar economic exigencies, and all experienced the shock of adjusting to a world with which they had scant familiarity.

Particularly distressing were the financial difficulties that plagued the elite immediately after the cessation of hostilities. Thus, in the summer of 1865 Fanny Conner complained, "The two items for which we never expended a dollar before—servants' hire & meat now cost me about *one hundred dollars per month*." That expense coupled with the cash required to purchase fresh foodstuffs and shoes for the children had placed her in dire circumstances. Desperately seeking advice from her absent husband, she asked: "When I am again in want of any thing in the grocery line what shall I do? . . . I am as economical as possible . . . but it takes a great deal to supply so many—family & servants . . . for those so impoverished as we are." Across the river in Louisiana, an embittered Louis A. Bringier returned from the war to find his abandoned sugar plantation under the control of the Freedmen's Bureau. The only means of recovering his property from those he termed "Bald-faced thieves" was by bribery, and that he

20. W. J. Britton to Lewis Thompson, July 31 (first quotation), August 10 (second quotation), 1867, in Lewis Thompson Papers, SHC; T. P. Devereux to R. L. Maitland, January 22, 1866 (third quotation), in Devereux Family Papers, DU; *"Journal of a Secesh Lady,"* ed. Crabtree and Patton, 729–30.

could not undertake, he explained sarcastically, for "want of the main ingredient: Money!" Consequently, this scion of one of the great planter families in the Pelican State was obliged to seek employment as an overseer in order to support his family.[21]

The situation was no better along the Atlantic seaboard. Virginia Unionist William F. Wickham also found Freedmen's Bureau officials less than helpful in the fall of 1865 when he sought assistance "to relieve us from the maintenance of the negros who remain on the plantations." He even went to Washington, D.C., to confer personally with General Oliver O. Howard, head of the bureau, in hopes of obtaining a favorable ruling. Although better off than most of his compatriots, Wickham still required an advance of $7,000 to $8,000 to meet his obligations for the year. He also hoped, rather naïvely, that loyal slaveholders would eventually be compensated for the loss of their chattel property. Although he later recouped his immense fortune, Paul Cameron was in much worse circumstances than Wickham in the autumn of the year the war ended. In November, he prepared an advertisement offering his entire property for sale and declared that he "would gladly get off with *a half of its value* to some new field of industry and hope."[22] Some of the most prominent South Carolina families faced similar hardships. Fire-eater Barnwell Rhett was obliged to swallow his pride and journey to New York in a futile search for credit. He found the bankers there suspicious, cold, and heartless, unwilling to invest or even lend money in the South "on any Southern Securities, personal or material." Perhaps, he concluded bitterly, "God has sent me here, to humble my pride." Even more humiliating was the experience of the Pinckneys, who were forced to sell many of their precious family relics, including a portrait of George Washington that had been painted by the celebrated artist Gilbert Stuart for General Charles Cotesworth Pinckney. Especially galling was the fact that most of these family heirlooms were purchased by Yankees![23]

21. Fanny E. Conner to "My ever dearest Husband," August 13 (first quotation), 21 (second quotation), 1865, in Lemuel P. Conner and Family Papers, LSU; Louis A. Bringier to Stella Bringier, August 20, 1865, in Louis A. Bringier and Family Papers, LSU.

22. William F. Wickham to Charles Carter, September 25 (quotation), October 5, 1865, Carter to Wickham, September 29, 1865, in Wickham Family Papers, VHS; Paul C. Cameron to Thomas Ruffin, November 27, 1865, in *The Papers of Thomas Ruffin*, ed. Hamilton, IV, 42.

23. R. B. Rhett to "My Dear Kate," June 9, 1867, in Robert Barnwell Rhett, Sr., Papers, SCHS; Harriott Middleton to "Dear Papa," September 9, [1868], Henry A. Middleton Family Letters, in Cheves-Middleton Papers, SCHS.

Painful as was the disposal of family relics, it was a kinder fate than the bankruptcy suffered by many formerly wealthy planters. Some, like Madison County, Mississippi, planter Stephen A. D. Greaves, were able to retain a portion of their estate even after declaring bankruptcy. After defaulting on a loan of $80,000 from the Bank of New Orleans, Greaves lost two of his five plantations but saved the others by arguing successfully that he had held them in trust for his now-deceased wife. Through complex litigation that continued until his death in 1880, Greaves was able to preserve most of his estate for his heirs.[24] Other Mississippians were not so fortunate. Among these were three Natchez District planters—Samuel H. Lambdin, Frederick Stanton, and Henry S. Metcalfe—all of whom declared bankruptcy between 1867 and 1869. The last, together with his brother James, had incurred a debt of $48,000 with a New Orleans factor during the war. After borrowing an additional $46,000 from various relatives and friends in 1866, Henry Metcalfe was still unable to meet his financial obligations and sued for bankruptcy three years later. The courts awarded his five plantations, totaling more than 7,000 acres, to the heir of his former factor.[25]

Members of the elite in other states were also ruined economically by the war. Tennessee lawyer-planter Gideon J. Pillow, who had served without distinction as a brigadier general in the Confederate Army, was another economic casualty of the war. Perhaps the most spectacular reversals of fortune are exemplified by the Allstons of South Carolina and the Mills brothers of Texas. Reportedly worth between $3,000,000 and $5,000,000 and by far the largest slaveholder in the Lone Star State before the war, the Galveston commercial, banking, and planting firm of Robert and David G. Mills went bankrupt during the Panic of 1873.[26] Although rice baron R. F. W. Allston, the fourth largest

24. Elmore D. Greaves, Jr., "The Greaves Family and Sunny Place Plantation," Summer, 1943, "Abstract of Lands of Elmore D. Greaves, Peyton R. Greaves, & Mrs. Delia Whitesides," January 12, 1939, TSS in possession of Elmore D. Greaves, Jr., Madison County, Mississippi. Elmore Greaves is the great-grandson of S. A. D. Greaves.

25. Samuel H. Lambdin Bankruptcy Petition, U.S. District Court for the Southern District of Mississippi, March 6, 1869, James Surget Legal Papers (Folder 3), in MacNeil Papers, MDAH; Frederick Stanton to Eustace Surget, September 3, 16, 1867 (Roll 1), in Surget Family Papers, MDAH; Ronald L. F. Davis, *Good and Faithful Labor: From Slavery to Sharecropping in the Natchez District, 1860–1890* (Westport, Conn., 1982), 125–26.

26. Warner, *Generals in Gray*, 241; *Dictionary of American Biography*, XIII, 14.

slaveholder in his state, died in 1864, his family was plagued by severe financial woes after the war. Already heavily encumbered by a debt of some $200,000 incurred in the late 1850s by the purchase of a plantation for his son Benjamin, more than 200 additional slaves, and a handsome residence on Meeting Street in Charleston, the Allston estate became insolvent following emancipation. For three years immediately after the war, Allston's widow Adele operated a boarding school for girls at her residence in Charleston. By the third year, however, enrollment had declined to such an extent that the school scarcely made enough to pay its teachers, one of whom was Adele's daughter Bessie. Consequently, in 1869 mother and daughter moved back to Chicora Wood, their residence plantation in Georgetown District and the only property the family was able to save. Another daughter lived for a time with her husband in a "negro house" on their plantation because the dwelling house had been burned by Federal troops. Finally, son Benjamin, who had returned from the war to assume the management of the family's crumbling estate, filed for bankruptcy in 1867 and moved briefly to Texas before returning to enter the ministry. Thus did the fortunes of one of the great Low Country families wane in the aftermath of war and emancipation. Yet, as Adele remarked to her niece in 1868, "The birds sing as sweetly, and the flowers bloom as gaily as ever, and those who are very young, will not, I hope, feel the dreadful ruin as elderly people must feel it."[27]

William Allen of Surry County, Virginia, one of the largest slaveholders in the state before the war, lived a decade longer than Allston, but his widow, like Adele Allston, was faced with almost insurmountable financial problems following her husband's death in 1875. Allen, who served with great distinction as a major in the Confederate Army during the Peninsular Campaign, committed his personal resources to the benefit of his country and, according to Major General John B. Magruder, sacrificed "almost the whole of his immense possessions in endeavoring to remove the public property committed to his charge" during that campaign. As a result of these losses, together with the emancipation of his 450 slaves, Allen's estate was decimated. Two years after his death, his forty-five-year-old widow found herself encumbered with a debt of $44,000 with only $1,500 in personal assets and minimal real estate to liquidate this debt

27. Dusinberre, *Them Dark Days*, 359–60; Pringle, *A Woman Rice Planter*, xxi, xxiv–xxix; Adele Petigru Allston to Caroline Carson, April 13, 1868, in Easterby, ed., *South Carolina Rice Plantation*, 241.

as well as to support her three minor children. Consequently, she was forced to sell off such personal effects as furniture, oil paintings, and even small bronze figurines that had been brought from Europe by her deceased husband, a melancholy process that continued until the mid-1880s.[28]

In contrast to such zealous supporters of the Confederacy as the Rhetts, Allstons, and Allens, some members of the elite planter class, especially those who gave little or no support to the new government, actually benefited from the war despite the loss of their slaves. Chief among these was Natchez nabob Stephen Duncan. During the war many planters who had been in comfortable circumstances before secession found themselves unable to pay the notes that came due on their mortgaged property. Duncan held some of these mortgages before the commencement of hostilities and, with almost unlimited assets, acquired others during the war. Thus, in 1869 the Duncan estate held mortgages on sixteen properties in Tensas Parish alone, a number that remained constant throughout the next decade.[29] Postwar conditions exacerbated the plight of these debtors, and Duncan and his sons were obliged to bring suit against the insolvent planters in order to avoid the payment of taxes and other expenses. As he explained to one irate debtor, these suits of what he termed "an amiable character" were designed not "to cause payment by forced sales, but to add strength, to my security." The usual arrangement was for Duncan to compel the sale of mortgaged property, purchase it at sheriff's auction, lease it to the debtor for a period sufficient to enable the latter to satisfy his debt, and then reconvey it to the original owner when the entire debt was paid. This offer was satisfactory to some but not to all. As one insolvent planter remarked, "Many persons are disposed to Complain at your bringing Suit, but I am satisfied & have to tel [sic] them it is

28. On Allen, see p. 321 of this book. *Official Records*, Ser. 1, Vol. XI, Pt. 1, p. 410; Deposition of Mrs. F. A. Allen, Richmond, May 29, 1877 (Box 27, Folder 7), Frances A. Allen to James N. Dunlop, April 28, 1876 (Box 28, Folder 1), Appraisal of William Allen Estate by J. Edmund Waddell, Jr., Deputy Clerk of Circuit Court, Henrico County, May 2, 1876, William Allen's Estate: Executrix's Account, September 29, 1877, Sales for a/c Mrs. Frances A. Allen, Executrix of William Allen, by James MacDougal, June 24, 1881 (Box 28, Folder 2), Newspaper notice of sale, Surry County tract known as "The Meadow," August 25, 1885 (Box 28, Folder 6), Affidavit of Henry Tyler, March 10, 1879 (Box 28, Folder 9), in James Nathaniel Dunlop Papers, VHS.

29. "Special Parish or 'Marshall Tax' on Lands of the Est. of S. Duncan in the Parish of Tensas State of Louisiana Paid by Judge Winchester June 7th 1869," Josiah Winchester Professional & Business Papers (Box 2E921, Folder 7), in Winchester Family Papers, CAH; State and Parish Taxes, 1878 (Folder 3), in Duncan Papers, LSU.

best for them in the end and is the best guarantee they can have to work out of debt." Perhaps so, but it was also the most efficacious way for the ultra-capitalistic Duncan family to safeguard its own financial interests during the dark days of Reconstruction.[30]

By far the largest debtor to Duncan and his heirs was another member of the elite slaveholding class, Wade Hampton III, the celebrated Confederate cavalry commander. In 1854, four years before his death, the second Wade Hampton had conveyed his already heavily mortgaged Mississippi plantations, Walnut Ridge in Issaquena County and Wild Woods and Richland (or Bayou Place) in Washington County, to his sons Wade III and Christopher F. At the time of this conveyance, the mortgage on the Issaquena plantation amounted to $175,130, payable in seventy-three promissory notes at 8 percent interest, while the Washington properties served as security for nine notes totaling $170,660 and payable from 1856 through 1864. The Hamptons had no difficulty meeting these notes as they came due until the war intervened. Then the payments ceased. The notes were held principally by Duncan, though some came into the possession of fellow Natchezians Samuel M. Davis and William T. Martin. After unsuccessful efforts to raise money in New Orleans and elsewhere following the war, General Hampton was forced to petition for bankruptcy in 1868. In accordance with the bankruptcy proceedings, Stephen Duncan, Jr., then head of the family following the demise of his father in 1867, gained possession of the Hampton plantations in each county for the nominal sum of $500. He then allowed Hampton to remain on the property and cultivate it for five years, with the privilege of redemption if the balance of the notes was paid within that time; if not, the property would either be turned over to the Duncans or retained by Hampton on payment of two-thirds of its assessed value.[31]

30. Stephen Duncan to Charles G. Dahlgren, April 18, 1866 (first quotation), Zenas Preston to Duncan, May 2, 1866 (second quotation), C. L. Dubuisson to Duncan, May 6, 1866, Dahlgren to Duncan, February 20, April 10, 1866, in Winchester Family Papers, CAH. For an account of the bitter exchange between Dahlgren and Duncan over the former's mortgaged property, see pp. 223–24 of this book.

31. Cauthen, ed., *Family Letters of the Three Wade Hamptons*, xiv–xv; Indenture dated August 27, 1855, "Deed of Conveyance, Samuel W. Ferguson Assignee in Bkptcy of Estate of Wade Hampton to Stephen Duncan," filed November 23, 1869, Wade Hampton Papers, in Natchez Trace Small MSS Collections, CAH; Stephen Duncan, Jr., to [Josiah Winchester], January 22, 1868, Samuel W. Ferguson, Assignee, Deed to Wade Hampton and William C. Patterson, June 12, 1869, Deed of Conveyance, Samuel W. Ferguson, Assignee in Bankruptcy of Estate of Wade Hampton, to Ste-

During the 1870s and 1880s Hampton labored assiduously in the face of poor crop years and declining land values to reduce his debt and to recover his properties. Despite these efforts, however, his debt to Duncan was still $90,000 in May, 1874.[32] The following year, he was able to redeem Walnut Ridge and half of Bayou Place by paying Duncan $35,000 to supplement the $60,000 already paid for the two places. Almost another decade passed before Hampton was also able to reclaim Wild Woods, his residence plantation in the Yazoo Delta. He did so by disposing of his moiety in Bayou Place to co-owner, Edmund Richardson for $5,000 and agreeing to pay Duncan that sum and an additional $5,000 by January 1, 1886.[33] Thus, after more than three decades, the Hampton debt to the Duncan family, which originally totaled $200,000, had finally been adjusted to the satisfaction of both parties, and the former Confederate general had at last been enabled to redeem his extensive, though now unproductive, Mississippi properties.[34]

Southern Unionists were not the only ones who sought to capitalize on the misfortune of formerly wealthy planters. Even before the war ended, some Northerners began to make plans to exploit the crumbling plantation system for their own benefit. As early as January, 1864, Henry Winchester, brother of Natchez Unionist Josiah Winchester, reported from Boston that companies were being formed to purchase southern cotton and sugar plantations at low cost and to cultivate them with free labor and "all the modern improvements in Agriculture." Boasting that these plantations would be managed much more profitably than they had been under slavery, he predicted that the prospect of such profits would induce "an immense migration south after the war." After lamenting that he had lost "a great opportunity of making a fortune" through wartime profiteering, he now hoped to reap that fortune in the South. "If there should be a chance to invest profitably," he wrote enthusiastically, "I should

phen Duncan, [Jr.], November 22, 1869, in Winchester Family Papers, CAH; Bills Receivable, Notes due by Wade Hampton, Jr., 1856–64 (Volume 3), in Duncan Papers, LSU.

32. Wade Hampton to Stephen Duncan, Jr., May 10, 1874, Wade Hampton Papers, in Natchez Trace Small MSS Collections, CAH; Account of Receipts and Expenditures, Stephen Duncan, Jr., 1870–95 (Volume 6), in Duncan Papers, LSU. The latter records remittances from Hampton dated May 7, 1870 ($7,000), January 18, 1882 ($1,500), April 2, 1885 ($7,500).

33. Hampton to Duncan, April 28, 1875 (Folder 3), December 4, 8, 1884 (Folder 4), in Duncan Papers, LSU.

34. Hampton to Stephen Duncan, Jr., April 18, 1867, in Winchester Papers, CAH.

like to be counted *in.*" The following year, a Natchez native then residing in Massachusetts sounded a similar refrain in a letter to his father. "Speculators are running south to buy lands," he reported disapprovingly. "People here think that the tremendous fortunes of the South will be acquired in almost as little time as it took to lose them." Indeed, he added with more than a touch of sarcasm, three-quarters of the population of Massachusetts "would move south tomorrow if they had the money to start with." About the same time, Virginian Charles Carter observed bitterly that the chief object of the "Yankee Satraps" regulating the condition of labor immediately after the war was "to force the land into the Market to be sacrificed, so that the Yankees May buy it for a song."[35]

Although the bonanza envisioned by northern speculators never fully materialized, many Yankees did acquire southern plantation lands following the war, and others entered into partnerships with southern owners, thereby enabling the latter to retain partial title to their properties. One elite family that lost all of its property to northern speculators was the Fripp family of St. Helena Island, South Carolina. Already forfeited to the United States Government for nonpayment of taxes, the Fripp property encompassing some twenty plantations on 11,000 acres, was sold at public auction in March, 1863. More than half of this land was purchased by a New England syndicate headed by Edward S. Philbrick. In contrast to the Fripps, Mississippian Richard T. Archer seemingly found a Yankee savior shortly after the war. In the summer of 1866, "a very wealthy Northern Man who wished to buy a plantation for his son" reportedly offered to pay $200,000 in cash for Archer's Juno Albena plantation in Holmes County. "If I can sell at this price," enthused Archer, "it will pay me out of debt." Unfortunately, the transaction was apparently never consummated, for Archer continued to struggle financially until his death the following year. Wade Hampton experienced a similar disappointment. After filing for bankruptcy in 1868, Hampton entered into a partnership with William C. Patterson of Philadelphia in order to pay off the mortgages held by the Duncan family and their associates on his Washington County properties. However, the available

---

35. Henry Winchester to "Dear Brother" [Josiah], January 4, 1864 (quotations), Henry to [nephew] Frank Winchester, January 11, 1864, both in Winchester Family Papers, CAH; George D. Farrar to "My Dear Father" [Alexander K.], July 9, 1865, Ben Swayze to A. K. Farrar, October 9, 1865, both in Alexander K. Farrar Papers, LSU; Charles Carter to William F. Wickham, September 29, 1865, in Wickham Family Papers, VHS.

evidence suggests that Patterson never did provide the necessary financial assistance. Other planters indebted to Duncan fared somewhat better. Faced with chaotic labor conditions in the spring of 1866, a Louisiana proprietor who owed Duncan $15,000 notified the latter that he had taken in "a Yankee officer" as a partner to "furnish & keep 90 hands" on his cotton plantation for the balance of the year. The choice of such a partner was particularly appropriate because, as he explained to Duncan, most of the hands procured "were discharged Soldiers & floating population."[36]

Some members of the elite, who, for one reason or another, could not personally superintend the resumption of operations on their plantations, elected to lease their properties to men who were willing and able to confront the chaotic conditions that prevailed in the immediate aftermath of the war. This practice was especially prevalent in the Southwest, and those most likely to adopt this option were aged male proprietors, widows, and expatriates. For example, Ayres Merrill, a Natchez Unionist who had fled to New York during the war, leased his two Louisiana cotton plantations for the sum of $30,000 in 1866. The lessee apparently proved to be incompetent, for, the following year, a neighboring planter reported that Merrill's places were "going to wreck." Another Natchezian, Eustace Surget, who sought refuge in France after the war, also leased his plantations, one of them for one-fifth of the cotton produced on the place.[37] Among the widows who were compelled to lease their property were Julia Nutt, Adelicia Acklen, and Isabella Cheves. The last speculated in the fall of 1868 that she could earn $4,000 to $5,000 a year by leasing her Savannah River rice plantation for three years. "I think I had better do so," she remarked to her father.[38] Other formerly wealthy planters who leased or contemplated leasing their plantations after the war included the elderly Richard T. Archer of Missis-

36. Rosengarten, *Tombee,* 261; Richard T. Archer to "My Dear Wife," July 25 (quotations), September 29, October 22, 29, December 28, 1866, in Richard Thompson Archer Family Papers, CAH; Samuel W. Ferguson, Assignee, Deed to Wade Hampton and William C. Patterson, June 12, 1869, S. M. Davis to [Josiah Winchester], July 29, 1869, Zenas Preston to Stephen Duncan, May 2, 1866, in Winchester Family Papers, CAH.

37. A. P. Merrill, Jr., to Eustace Surget, December 11, 1865, William G. Deal to Surget, February 16, 1867 (quotation), Roll 1, both in Surget Family Papers, MDAH.

38. Mary E. Nutt to "My Dear Prentiss," March 15, 25, 1866, in Nutt Family Collection, MDAH; John F. Gunkel to Josiah Winchester, December 17, 1865, in Winchester Family Papers, CAH; Isabella Cheves to "Dear Papa" [Henry A. Middleton], September 4, [1868], Henry A. Middleton Family Letters, in Cheves-Middleton Papers, SCHS.

sippi, Judges Josiah Winchester and Samuel Boyd of Natchez, and Lewis Thompson of North Carolina. One of those who expressed an interest in leasing Thompson's distant Red River sugar plantation was J. Madison Wells, who served as governor of Louisiana during the period of Presidential Reconstruction. However, Thompson's death just three months after Wells had inquired about lease terms probably precluded this transaction, and one of Thompson's sons inherited the property shortly thereafter.[39]

Not only were formerly wealthy slaveholders plagued by labor problems, the loss of their fortunes, and a political world that was literally turned upside down, but they were also forced to adjust to a profoundly different life-style and to circumstances that seemed hardships to them if not to others. As was discussed in Chapter 3, many female members of elite families found themselves in unaccustomed roles after the war. Some entered the teaching profession, others were obliged for the first time in their lives to perform a variety of distasteful household chores, and still others, usually widows, struggled valiantly to secure sufficient financial resources to sustain their families.[40] A number of their male counterparts, thoroughly disillusioned with postwar conditions in the agricultural sector, chose to pursue other vocational options. Thus, Peter W. Hairston moved from his rural North Carolina homestead to Baltimore immediately after the war. Estimating that it would cost $6,000 a year to live in the Maryland metropolis, he entered into a partnership with a Baltimore commission merchant and purchased a house on prestigious Charles Street. "I think living is cheaper here," he remarked, "& society better." His only regret was giving up his horses, but, as he confided to his wife, he had to "cease to be a gentleman now & go to work." Similarly, George Winchester, son of the prominent Natchez Unionist, leased his share of the family plantations and moved to New Orleans, where he became a cotton broker. Another Natchezian, Lemuel P. Conner, after struggling unsuccessfully to retain his extensive properties, resumed his study of the law in the early 1880s

39. Fred G. Smith to Richard T. Archer, October 2, 1866, in Richard Thompson Archer Family Papers, CAH; John F. Gunkel to Josiah Winchester, December 17, 1865, Frank Winchester to "Dear Father," November 21, 1871, in Winchester Family Papers, CAH; J. H. D. Bossman [?] to Judge Boyd, February 16, 1866, in Rice C. Ballard Papers, CAH; J. Madison Wells to Lewis Thompson, September 6, 1867, in Lewis Thompson Papers, SHC.

40. See pp. 118–21 of this book.

and, after being admitted to the Louisiana bar, opened a practice in Vidalia.[41] Sugar planter Louis A. Bringier, beset by personal and financial woes for nearly two decades after the war, finally abandoned his wife and his Louisiana plantations in 1883 and moved to Florida, where he became first a citrus grower and later the general manager of the Florida Sugar Manufacturing Company. Eventually he was joined in Florida by three of his sons, doubtless motivated by the desire to escape the clutches of their bitter, severely depressed mother.[42]

Of course, not all elite families were ruined either financially or psychologically by the war. Indeed, some historians in recent years have emphasized the persistence of planter hegemony and wealth in the postwar South, though they differ over the question of whether the former slaveholders impeded or promoted economic modernization.[43] Dwight Billings, who argues that the persistent planters in North Carolina spearheaded the industrialization of that state, has asserted that the Cameron family "alone" is almost enough to prove the validity of his thesis. Although Paul Cameron, the head of that family in the mid-nineteenth century, complained bitterly of his impoverishment in the immediate aftermath of the war, he soon rebounded and, between 1870 and 1875, tripled the value of his assets in his home county of Orange. His son, Bennehan, emulated the practices of his father and invested not only in agriculture but also

41. Peter W. Hairston to Fanny Hairston, September 19 (first quotation), 26 (second quotation), both in Peter Wilson Hairston Papers, SHC; Business Card, George Winchester and F. W. Quackenboss, n.d., George Winchester Correspondence, 1864–80, in Winchester Family Papers, CAH; Lemuel P. Conner and Family Papers, LSU.

42. L. A. Bringier to daughter Stella, March 18, 1883, Bringier to son [Dubourg], October 2, 1883, June 21, 29, 1884, June 15, 1890, Bringier to son Browse, April 26, 1885, December 5, 1886, April 1, 1889, Stella Bringier to son Browse, May 11, June 3, July 3, 1889, Browse to mother Stella, July 10, 1889, Trist Bringier to mother Stella, August 28, 1889, Dubourg to brother Browse, December 17, 1889, Stella to son Trist, December 17, 1889, in Louis A. Bringier and Family Papers, LSU; ? to [Fanny Tureaud?], 1892, in Benjamin Tureaud Papers, LSU. In a letter written just before Christmas in 1889, twelve-year-old Dubourg pleaded with his brother: "Tell Father I say *please for goodness sake let me come*" for a visit. Life with their mother in Louisiana had clearly become unbearable for the children.

43. For a useful analysis of the debate, see James C. Cobb, "Beyond Planters and Industrialists: A New Perspective on the New South," *JSH* 54 (February 1988): 45–68. See also Billings, *Planters and the Making of a "New South"*; Wiener, *Social Origins of the New South*; and Shore, *Southern Capitalists*, 162–67.

in railroads, banks, and textile mills.[44] Another wealthy North Carolina family that survived the war in relatively comfortable circumstances was the Hairston family. When Peter Wilson Hairston entered the commission merchant business in Baltimore after the war, he retained possession of his extensive agricultural holdings in North Carolina. Most of these properties remained in the family for generations. His son and namesake resided on the family's 4,000-acre Cooleemee plantation until his death in 1943, at which time he was described as one of the largest landowners in the state.[45] Another North Carolinian, Lewis Thompson, lived only two years after the conclusion of hostilities, but he too weathered the financial storm by retaining northern bonds in New York during the war and investing heavily in United States Government securities after the conflict.[46]

Members of the elite in other former slave states fared equally well. Robert Stafford of Georgia, who like Cameron and Thompson had a diversified investment portfolio before the war, left an estate valued at nearly $500,000, much of it in Connecticut real estate and northern securities, when he died in 1877. John S. Preston, who had the good fortune to sell his Louisiana sugar plantations to New Orleans merchant John Burnside shortly before the war, was able to preserve the million dollars he received from that sale. He was paid $400,000 before the outbreak of hostilities, and Burnside deposited the remainder with a Liverpool firm during the war, thereby enabling the Prestons to move their residence to Europe in the fall of 1865. Several major sugar planters were also able to recoup their fortunes after the war. Among them was the Woolfolk family of Iberville Parish. Although the patriarch of the family died in 1856, his son and

44. Billings, *Planters and the Making of a "New South,"* 85, 87–90; Kenzer, *Kinship and Neighborhood in a Southern Community,* 104. For a discussion of Paul Cameron's prewar economic diversification, see p. 233 of this book.

45. Clippings from Greensboro *Daily News,* September 24, 1939, Salisbury *Sunday Post,* April 3, 1938, Salisbury *Evening Post,* November 15, 1943, in Peter Wilson Hairston Papers, SHC.

46. De Rosset Brown & Co. to Lewis Thompson, July 20, 1861, W. H. Wiggins to Thompson, July 14, 1865, Duncan Sherman & Co. to Thompson, July 18, 1865, Statement, Dowley Corners & Co., January 4, 1867, James Corner & Sons to Thompson, June 27, 1867, W. J. Britton to Thompson, July 31, August 10, 1867, Memorandum detailing location of assets, November 1, 1867, in Lewis Thompson Papers, SHC. For a more detailed account of these transactions, see pp. 234–35 of this book.

namesake, Austin Woolfolk, still owned two Iberville plantations at the turn of the century and was reportedly one of the leading sugar producers in the state.[47]

But the two sugar barons who achieved the greatest prosperity in the postwar era were John Burnside and Duncan Kenner. After regaining possession of his Ascension Parish sugar plantations from agents of the Freedmen's Bureau, the latter resumed planting operations, and during the course of the next two decades, he acquired several adjacent plantations and began cultivating rice as well as sugar. Because of the huge expenses involved in producing these two crops, Kenner's income from his agricultural properties diminished over time. However, like other successful planter-capitalists of that era, he invested heavily in both real estate and stocks and bonds. Consequently, at his death in 1887, Kenner's total worth was estimated at $1,500,000, though his Ascension Parish plantations were valued at little more than one-fifth of that sum. In addition to a large quantity of securities, he owned an entire block of buildings on Carondelet Street in New Orleans, and he was president of the New Orleans Gas Light Company, two oil companies, the Louisiana Cotton Manufacturing Company, and the Louisiana Sulphur and Mining Company.[48]

Fellow Ascension Parish planter John Burnside fared even better than Kenner after the war. An immigrant from Northern Ireland and longtime New Orleans merchant before he turned to planting, Burnside gave neither financial nor moral support to the Confederacy. Instead, he carefully husbanded his resources and quickly resumed his place as the state's leading sugar producer immediately after the war. Indeed, in 1868, when Burnside refused to cooperate with neighboring planters in resisting what they deemed to be unjust taxes levied by the Reconstruction government, he reportedly owned at least one-seventh of the property in Ascension. By the time of his death in 1881, Burnside had amassed an estate variously estimated at between $6,000,000 and $8,000,000. He resided in a palatial mansion in the garden district of New Orleans and held assets in that city alone of more than $360,000. Eight years later,

47. Bullard, *Robert Stafford of Cumberland Island*, 295–96; Adele Vander Horst to Adele Petigru Allston, September 20, 1865, in Easterby, ed., *South Carolina Rice Plantation*, 214; William E. Clement, *Plantation Life on the Mississippi* (New Orleans, 1952), 173–74.

48. Plantation Accounts, Ashland-Bowden, Houmas, Hermitage, 1880–86, James Fahey to Mrs. Alexander, July 7, 1887, "Inventory of Property in Ascension Parish belonging to Succession of Duncan F. Kenner," July 29, 1887, Printed Obituary of Duncan F. Kenner, July 4, 1887, in Duncan F. Kenner Papers, LSU.

when the contents of the Burnside residence, including a magnificent art collection purchased from banker James Robb, were auctioned off, one reporter described the scene at the mansion as one "fit . . . for a festival." In view of the princely fortune accumulated by the bachelor planter-merchant from Belfast, it would seem that the war was only a minor distraction in his quest for power and riches.[49]

Whether or not they recovered economically after the war, virtually all of the former elite slaveholders were consumed by feelings of bitterness and resentment following the cessation of hostilities. For some, those emotions never subsided. Their rancor was directed principally toward the Reconstruction process, the freedmen, and Northerners generally, though a few former die-hard Unionists also leveled some of their wrath at those within the South who had been most instrumental in leading the section along a path that culminated in death and destruction. It should be emphasized that the resentment over Reconstruction was by no means confined to the ranks of the elite. However benign current historians may characterize that period in our nation's history, it was the painful memory of their experiences during Reconstruction that caused white Southerners of all classes to give their overwhelming electoral support to the Democratic Party for nearly a century after the last gun was fired.

Initially, some leaders counseled moderation as President Johnson implemented his relatively mild Reconstruction plan in the summer and fall of 1865. As might be expected, former Unionists such as William F. Wickham of Virginia were those most likely to adopt this position. After characterizing the postwar condition of his state as one of unexampled "poverty & humiliation," he nevertheless urged his fellow Virginians to govern their conduct by "reason & cool reflection" rather than by "impulse & feeling," to which latter he attributed the "evils" of the past. Yet a decade later even Wickham still mourned the passing of the life-style that had existed in *Old Virginia* before the war. "We make the best of it," he wrote dejectedly, "but the change is a sad one." Former Unionists were not the only ones to offer constructive advice to their despondent countrymen in the dark days immediately following their defeat on

49. Duncan F. Kenner to William J. Minor, December 10, 1868, in William J. Minor and Family Papers, LSU; *Dictionary of Louisiana Biography*, ed. Conrad, I, 132–33; New Orleans *Daily Picayune*, August 2, 4, 1881, December 1, 3 (quotation), 1889, February 12, 1892. I am indebted to Jessie Poesch, Professor of Art History at Tulane, for providing me with copies of the articles in the *Picayune* relating to Burnside.

the battlefield. Thus, in a communication published in the press in the fall of 1865, former Confederate general Wade Hampton urged his compatriots to take the oath of allegiance to the United States, remain in the South, "participate in the restoration of civil government," and help to rehabilitate their war-ravaged country. "To save any of our rights" and "to preserve any thing more from the general ruin," he counseled, would "require all the statesmanship and all the patriotism of citizens." In a characteristic allusion to the classics, the aristocratic South Carolinian called on all ex-Confederates to "emulate the example" of an unnamed Roman general who had received the thanks of the Senate "because in the darkest hour of the Republic he did not despair."[50]

As the months passed, however, despair was increasingly accompanied by bitterness. In January, 1866, Edward Barnwell Heyward, who, together with his father, had owned nearly seven hundred slaves before the war, vowed to leave the country rather than face "the storm . . . which must soon burst upon *the whole* country, and break up everything which we have so long boasted of." In a letter to a boyhood friend in Connecticut, Heyward wrote despondently: "I feel now that I have *no country*. I *obey* like a subject, but I cannot love such a government. Perhaps the next letter you get from me, will be from England." From Mississippi, Joseph E. Davis, elder brother of the imprisoned Confederate president, pointed to the "cowed and humiliated condition of the people" and complained bitterly that "the voice of the South is not heeded." A New Orleans correspondent warned another Mississippian, one who had fled to France after the war, not to come home. "If you find yourself able," he wrote, "I would advise you never to return to this Godforsaken & oppressed Country."[51]

The despair and outrage deepened in the spring of 1867 as the Radical Republicans imposed their harsh Reconstruction program on an already downtrodden South. In North Carolina several prominent Unionists sought to mitigate the severity of Congressional Reconstruction by organizing a conservative faction within the Republican Party. While admitting that it was against

50. Essay entitled "Reconstruction in Virginia," n.d., W. F. Wickham to [cousin] Harriet M. Wickham, March 3, 1874, both in Wickham Family Papers, VHS; Wade Hampton "To the Editor of the Phoenix," copied Raleigh, N.C., October 28, 1865, in George W. Mordecai Papers, SHC.

51. E. B. Heyward to James A. Lord, January 22, 1866 (TS), in Edward Barnwell Heyward Letters, SCL; J. E. Davis to J. H. Van Evrie, May 23, 1866, Joseph Emory Davis Papers, in Natchez Trace Small MSS Collection, CAH; Daniel M. Adams to Eustace Surget, March 10, 1867 (Roll 1), in Surget Family Papers, MDAH.

his nature to affiliate with a party whose aim was "confiscation and a division of the lands among the negroes," William A. Smith argued nevertheless that they "must except [sic] the reconstruction bill in good faith, and form a state Constitution in conformity to the views of congress." It was imperative that the conservative Union men organize and restrain the demagogues and Negroes lest the latter "runaway with the wagon, and vote themselves other peoples property." Unfortunately, he continued, the Conservative Unionists could not count on the support of the poor whites, who were too prejudiced to vote with the Negroes. Despite their efforts, such Unionists as Smith, Lewis Thompson, and John Pool were unable to control the state party convention that met later in the year. As Pool summarized the meeting, "the spirit & conduct of the convention was disgusting & alarming to all who saw it." He dared not even speak "for fear of being insulted." The die-hard Unionists were in a difficult position. They refused to cooperate with their old political enemies, "the secessionists and traitors," as Smith called them, yet they were not at all comfortable in the party of Stevens, Butler, and Sumner—the party that threatened to confiscate their property and institute Negro rule.[52]

Other members of the elite counseled patience in the face of adversity. In November, 1867, former governor Francis W. Pickens of South Carolina surveyed the bleak horizon and perceived a glimmer of hope amid the "hopeless poverty and ruin" that then prevailed. Predicting that the present state of affairs could not long continue, he asserted that "our only policy" should be "to keep quiet and *silent*, and be ready to take advantage of circumstances as they arise." He concluded hopefully, "I cannot but think that Providence has [something] better in store for us." Shortly before the advent of Congressional Reconstruction, two of the Tayloe brothers had advised a similar course. The South, they argued, should disregard "the doings at Washington," wait "calmly on events," and do all in her power "to recover her prosperity."[53] In the end, the strategy advocated by Pickens and the Virginia siblings proved to be the most efficacious way to end the reconstruction process and restore white Democratic rule over the defeated and blighted region. It soon became clear that the northern public

52. W. A. Smith to Lewis Thompson, April 18, 25, 1867, John Pool to Thompson, September 31 [sic], 1867, in Lewis Thompson Papers, SHC.

53. Francis W. Pickens to Adele Petigru Allston, November 22, 1867, in Easterby, ed., *South Carolina Rice Plantation*, 236–37; Edward T. Tayloe to "My Dear Brother" [William H.], January 25, 1867, in Tayloe Family Papers, VHS.

would not continue indefinitely to support federal interference in the social and political affairs of the states that comprised the late Confederacy. When that support collapsed, the brighter future envisioned by Pickens could and did become a reality.

Some members of the former master class were not as forgiving as those Northerners who soon turned their attention to other matters. The legacy of sectional bitterness engendered by the war and exacerbated by Reconstruction consumed many Southerners for years to come, and some never became reconciled to their bitter defeat at the hands of the hated Yankees. Not surprisingly, Yankeephobia was especially rampant during the immediate aftermath of the war. Thus, in the fall of 1866, Virginia planter Wyndham Robertson denounced what he termed the "spirit of vengeance & hate in disregard of promised immunity—that has no modern parallel for inhumanity & ill faith." Shortly thereafter, a young Natchezian enrolled in the Virginia Military Institute expressed outrage at the rumored passage by Congress of a bill to close all military schools in the rebellious states. "They have deprived us of money, lands, and every other property & rights and now they strive to take from us our very minds [and] our education," he protested. "Let them pass every bill, take away every privilege, & bar us from every right, but while the sun shines they cannot by coercion bridge the gulf between us," he concluded defiantly. From New York, where he had gone to seek a loan from the banking establishment, arch-secessionist Robert Barnwell Rhett wrote: "I am disgusted beyond expression, at the wretched business I have here been engaged in. . . . They seem here to look upon the South, as one vast . . . Bog, where all who enter it, will be submerged." Female members of the elite were equally bitter. "I must confess," declared Gertrude Thomas shortly after the end of hostilities, "that I do most heartily dispise [sic] Yankees, Negroes and everything connected with them." Six years later, her rancor had not abated. After meeting Jefferson Davis, for whom she had named her second son, she declared that she had had no president since the war, "and until a Southern man, not a radical presides in the White House" she would "acknowledge none." It was not until 1881, when a New York banker generously donated $50,000 to her alma mater, Wesleyan Female College in Macon, Georgia, that Thomas was finally able to eradicate "the last faint *gleam of hostility* to the *North, conquered* by *kindness* after *near sixteen years resistance*"[54]

54. Wyndham Robertson to "Dear Archer," November 15, 1866, in Richard Thompson Archer Family Papers, CAH; Henry K. Farrar to "Dear Father," March 1, 1867, in Alexander K. Farrar

Others were not as forgiving as Thomas. After expressing disbelief that Hiram Powers had not sympathized with "the heroic struggles of our recent lost but glorious cause," Louisa McCord proceeded to vent her feelings of rage and despair in a letter to the famed sculptor in the spring of 1870, a time when her beloved South Carolina was still under military occupation. "We *are* destroyed," she declared succinctly. "Now, ground down, and writhing beneath the heel of a brutal conqueror," the people of her native state—"as noble a people as ever trod *God's* earth"—must inevitably lose their "higher characteristics," she feared. Another member of the elite who could never adjust to the postwar world was Louisiana planter-politician John Perkins, Jr. Immediately after the Confederate surrender, Perkins fled to Mexico City. Then, in 1866, he removed to Paris and thereafter traveled extensively on the Continent and in Canada before returning to the United States. At his death in 1885, his grieving widow remarked that he was never "the same person after we lost '*our cause.*'" She explained, "He never felt himself a citizen of the *United States*," but only "of *Louisiana* which he loved with his whole heart." But perhaps the most extreme manifestation of persistent Yankeephobia encountered by the author was recorded in a letter from an elderly Virginia matron who resided on a portion of the Manassas battlefield. "I hate the U.S. flag with all my heart soul & body & will die hating it," she exclaimed at the end of the century. "I hope to live to see it hauled down by some other nation." Such was one legacy of this bitter internecine conflict.[55]

A final legacy of the Reconstruction period was racial animosity, an emotion that affected all classes of white Southerners and that, sadly, persists to this day. It was engendered initially by the perceived disloyalty of slaves during the war and then reinforced by their political activism and labor demands after the war. The conflict between planters and freedmen over labor contracts in the postwar South was discussed earlier in this chapter. The typical white attitude toward the newly freed blacks may be illustrated by the comments of Paul Cameron

---

Papers, LSU; R. B. Rhett to "My Dear Kate," June 9, 1867, in Robert Barnwell Rhett, Sr., Papers, SCHS; *The Secret Eye*, ed. Burr, 275, 373, 423–24.

55. Louisa McCord to Hiram Powers, March 20, 1870, in McCord, *Selected Writings*, 284; Clipping from the *Mexico Times*, September 16, 1865, Petition from John Perkins, Sr., to Edgar Farrar, Judge of the Thirteenth Judicial District, State of Louisiana, December 18, 1865, both in John Perkins Papers, SHC; Evelyn M. Perkins to L. P. Conner, December 21, 1885, in Lemuel P. Conner Papers, HNO; Sue M. Monroe to Mattie Hayne Heyward, May 26, 1899, in Heyward and Ferguson Family Papers, SHC.

and Howell Cobb in the fall of 1866. After suffering through two years of turmoil with his labor force, the former thundered: "If any one want[s] the negro . . . take him!" After a like experience, Cobb vowed never again to employ free black labor on his plantations. "Nothing satisfies them," he complained. "Grant them one thing and they demand something more, and there is no telling where they would stop. . . . There is no feeling of gratitude in their nature." Although many proprietors eventually reached some kind of accommodation with their workers, neither was ever really satisfied, and racial enmity continued to infect both parties.[56]

The wounds opened by the dispute over labor conditions soon worsened when the Negro became a political pawn of the Radical Republicans in the states of the late Confederacy. It was utterly inconceivable to the great planters that their former slaves would be granted the suffrage at the same time that they themselves were being disfranchised, yet that became a reality in 1867. A year before, Edward B. Heyward had predicted a race war if the North persisted in its determination to give blacks "a place in the councils of the Country and make them the equal of the white man." That prophecy seemed about to come to fruition in the summer of 1868 when there were threats of Negro violence in such South Carolina cities as Charleston and Greenville as the fall elections approached. A matron in the latter city reported in late August that the Negroes there were all armed and "said they intended to kill all the white people." Her fears were somewhat assuaged when a trusted servant assured her that he would let no harm come to the family. Still, there was much resentment over the Negro suffrage issue. North Carolina Unionist William A. Smith expressed chagrin at the idea of "associating with Negroes Politically." Although he was eventually persuaded to join the Republican Party, he found it very difficult "to Join a party and Hurra for those who had put me Politically below a negro."[57] Not surprisingly, former secessionists were even more outspoken in their de-

56. Paul Cameron to George Mordecai, September 1866, quoted in Kenzer, *Kinship and Neighborhood in a Southern Community,* III; Howell Cobb to "My Dear Wife," December, 1866 (TS), in Cobb-Erwin-Lamar Family Collection, UGA.

57. E. B. Heyward to James A. Lord, January 22, 1866 (TS), in Edward Barnwell Heyward Letters, SCL; Isabella Cheves to "Dear Papa" [Henry A. Middleton], August 15, 26, [1868], Mary E. Lowndes to "Dear Papa," August 30, 1868 (quotation), Henry A. Middleton Family Letters, in Cheves-Middleton Papers, SCHS; William A. Smith to Lewis Thompson, April 18, 1867, in Lewis Thompson Papers, SHC.

nunciation of Negro suffrage. For example, when former governor Francis W. Pickens learned that the South Carolina Black and Tan Convention had passed such a measure, he immediately organized a public meeting in his home district of Edgefield to consider an appropriate response. Those in attendance condemned the new constitutional provision and informed officials in Columbia "that they would not consent to it." It was not long, however, before such conservative politicians as Wade Hampton began to court the black vote, much to the disgust of many of their fellow conservatives.[58]

Thus, the former slaveholders emerged from the war and Reconstruction an embittered class. Many were ruined financially, while others persevered and managed to recover much, if not all, of their prewar prosperity. But virtually all were angered by what they perceived to be the vindictive policies of their conquerors and by the new status accorded their former chattels. That rancor receded somewhat in the years following Reconstruction as southern whites regained control of their sociopolitical system and, with the acquiescence of the North, once again placed southern blacks in a subordinate position. Nevertheless, the racism born under slavery and nurtured during Reconstruction persisted for generations to come. That racism was vividly reflected in a letter written in 1894 by the editor and proprietor of the Port Gibson *Reveille* to a Mississippi planter who had denounced the New York *Post* for its condemnation of "mob law." Displaying a rather enlightened attitude for the time and place, the Mississippi journalist expressed grave concern over the growth of unrestrained lynch law in the South. Yet he closed his communication by reassuring the irate planter that he was of a like mind concerning the general Negro question. "I am perfectly aware of the inferiority of the negro race," he wrote, "& for my part wish the last one of them were back in Africa. Then our country could work out its destiny undisturbed by race conflicts & all the evils that spring therefrom." Unfortunately, such sentiments would not soon die in the South or, indeed, elsewhere in this country.[59]

58. Harriott Middleton to "Dear Papa," August 31, [1868] (quotation), Isabella Cheves to "Dear Papa," August 15, [1868], both in Henry A. Middleton Family Letters, SCHS.

59. A. C. Wharton to G. W. Humphreys, July 2, 1894, in George Wilson Humphreys and Family Papers, MDAH.

11

LORDS AND CAPITALISTS:

The Ideology of the Master Class

I came here to make money & it I must have by any means it can be made in an honest way. —HENRY A. TAYLOE, February 6, 1836

If I can ever regain my health I shall devote the remnant of my days to making money. There was a great difference between Calhoun & Kerr Boyce, but the children of the latter would hardly exchange name & condition with those of the former. —JAMES H. ADAMS, January 14, 1859

I understand you said in Petersburg that I had made a bad bargain & bought a very poor farm. You forget that poor people are not able to buy rich farms. —THOMAS G. BAYLOR to RICHARD BAYLOR, February 23, 1856

"Is that man a christian who kneels at the altar and prays that, 'the colored man may be freed from bondage,' while thousands of needy souls perish within his hearing, and still regardless of their wants he throws his charity beyond them? What sensible master can free his slaves and cast them on the merciful charity of such hypocrisy? —GEORGE D. FARRAR from Cambridge, Mass., December 24, 1858

To constantly see before you the maimed, the lame and the blind causes you to come to sympathise with their miseries as you feel the impossibility of relieving them. You can see more misery here than you could living a life time in the South. One of our slaves would feel himself degraded to beg with the importunity they do. —PETER W. HAIRSTON from Leghorn, Italy, December 20, 1859

NEARLY FORTY YEARS AGO, Eugene Genovese advanced the debate over the fundamental nature of the southern social order to a new level when he argued that the planter class of the Old South embraced a paternalistic, antibourgeois ideology antithetical to the value system of the capitalistic North. While admitting that the slaveholders were imbued with an acquisitive spirit and that, as a production unit, the plantation responded to the demands of the world market, he contended that the paternalistic master-slave relationship uniquely shaped interpersonal relations within the family, community, and region. The result was the development of a set of values and customs that emphasized family, status, honor, public service, and the accumulation of wealth for pleasure rather than as an end in itself.[1] Although Genovese has somewhat modified his thesis in recent years, other historians, most but not all of them Marxists, have joined him in stressing the paternalistic, precapitalist character of antebellum southern society.[2]

At the same time, the Genovese school has been challenged by an equally imposing array of historians who contend that the slaveholders were indeed capitalists and that their fundamental values differed little from those of their northern counterparts. The planters have been described variously as agrarian capitalists, slaveholding capitalists, and entrepreneurial capitalists. Chief among the proponents of this capitalistic interpretation is James Oakes, though he, like Genovese, has become somewhat less intransigent over time. In his initial book, *The Ruling Race,* Oakes contended that the emergence of a market economy in the postcolonial South tended to push the slaveholders away from a paternalist ideology and "toward an acceptance of liberal democracy and free-market com-

1. Eugene D. Genovese, *The Political Economy of Slavery: Studies in the Economy and Society of the Slave South* (New York, 1961), 28–29; Billings, *Planters and the Making of a "New South,"* 13.

2. In their more recent book, *Fruits of Merchant Capital: Slavery and Bourgeois Property in the Rise and Expansion of Capitalism* (New York, 1983), Genovese and Elizabeth Fox-Genovese admit that "the slaveholders functioned like ordinary capitalists in many respects," but they could not be classified as either seigneurial or capitalist. Instead, they operated within what the authors term "a unique socioeconomic formation," whatever that means (p. 161). For examples of other historians who support the prebourgeois thesis, see Cashin, *A Family Venture,* 6; Fox-Genovese, *Within the Plantation Household,* 53, 55–56, 82; McCurry, *Masters of Small Worlds,* 70; Reidy, *From Slavery to Agrarian Capitalism,* 32, 80, 138, 242–47; Douglas R. Egerton, "Markets Without a Market Revolution: Southern Planters and Capitalism," *Journal of the Early Republic* 16 (Summer 1996): 207–208, 211, 220–21; Steven Hahn, "Capitalists All!" *Reviews in American History* 11 (June 1983): 219–25; and Johnson, "Planters and Patriarchy," 46, 55.

mercialism." In his view, the planters became increasingly acquisitive and obsessed with material success. Nearly a decade later, while still contending that the slaveholders exhibited a capitalist spirit, Oakes conceded that the slave South was not totally a liberal capitalist society because slavery itself negated the values of such a society. Nevertheless, he concluded, "southern slave society emerged within rather than apart from the liberal capitalist world." This may be contrasted with the Genoveses' assertion that "the South was in but not of the bourgeois world." Thus, although the gap has narrowed somewhat, the debate continues.[3]

Unfortunately, there can be no definitive resolution of the conflict between these two schools as long as there is no common definition of capitalism. Those who support the Genovese interpretation define capitalism in such a way that free labor is an integral part of the definition. In other words, without free labor, there can be no capitalism. If one accepts that definition, then obviously the slaveholders, whether great or small, were not capitalists, and the antebellum South was not a bourgeois society.[4] But that is not the only possible definition of capitalism, a word that did not even enter the vocabulary until the nineteenth century. As Edward Pessen and others have pointed out, capitalism is a constantly changing, flexible system "susceptible of diverse definitions." Charles Sellers defines planter capitalism as "production for a competitive world market with commodified slave labor." William Dusinberre, who notes correctly that the classical economists were not thinking of slavery when they offered their definition of capitalism, found the rice barons to be a distinctive breed of ag-

3. Oakes, *The Ruling Race*, xii–xiii (quotation), 6, 69–73, 191; Oakes, *Slavery and Freedom: An Interpretation of the Old South* (New York, 1990), xiv, 53, 79 (quotation); Fox-Genovese, *Within the Plantation Household*, 55; Edward L. Ayers, "The World the Liberal Capitalists Made," *Reviews in American History* 19 (June 1991): 194–99. For a representative sampling of other historians who argue that the slaveholders were essentially capitalists, see Censer, *North Carolina Planters and Their Children*, 13, 18–19, 53–54, 117, 152–53; Dusinberre, *Them Dark Days*, 6, 202–203, 289, 299, 368, 404–407; Ford, *Origins of Southern Radicalism*, 64–65, 275; Charles Sellers, *The Market Revolution*, 279, 408, 472 n. 15; Shore, *Southern Capitalists*, 13–14, 122, 200–201 n. 29; and Bowman, "Antebellum Planters and *Vormarz* Junkers," 783.

4. For explicit statements of this Marxian definition of capitalism, see Fox-Genovese and Genovese, *Fruits of Merchant Capital*, vii, 21; Egerton, "Markets Without a Market Revolution," 207–208, 211. Like this author, Stephanie McCurry has remarked on the futility of attempting to reconcile the disagreement over the definition of capitalism and, more particularly, over whether free labor is central "to any society historically called capitalist." *Masters of Small Worlds*, 71 n. 61.

ricultural capitalists, operating a system that, though not as "dynamic as the wage-labor variant," was still "far from economically stagnant." Even Douglas Egerton, a zealous champion of the Marxian definition, has admitted that the sugar planters were "businessmen in the northern sense," or, to put it another way, capitalists, at least in their economic outlook.[5]

As a non-Marxist historian, I cannot accept either the Marxian definition of capitalism or the characterization of wealthy slaveholders that flows from that definition. Nor do I believe that the great planters of the slave South were devoid of the bourgeois values attributed to free labor capitalists. I submit that capitalism is simply an economic system in which individuals invest capital, from whatever source and by whatever labor system derived, with the hope and expectation of generating additional capital. If measured by this standard, the elite slaveholders were clearly capitalists. It should be emphasized that I make no claim that small slaveholders and yeomen who had only a marginal association with the market economy fall within the parameters of this definition. That is for others to debate. But the evidence presented in this book confirms the contention of Oakes and the findings of Jane Turner Censer in her study of North Carolina planter families that the large slaveholders, both in their economic motivation and behavior and in their family and inheritance practices, exhibited values little different from their free-state counterparts. As the precapitalist scholars concede, these staple producers were acquisitive entrepreneurs who were closely tied to the market economy on both the national and international levels. Moreover, they personally subscribed to and imbued their children with such bourgeois values as industry, self-discipline, frugality, self-reliance, and the importance of a quality education.[6] Finally, many of the great planters, especially those from the Natchez District, were themselves products of the Northeast and retained close personal and economic ties to that region. Are we to believe that their migration to the slave South suddenly produced a revolutionary transformation of their so-called world view? If men such as Ste-

5. Edward Pessen, "How Different from Each Other Were the Antebellum North and South?" *AHR* 85 (December 1980): 1146–47; Paul A. Gilje, "The Rise of Capitalism in the Early Republic," *Journal of the Early Republic* 16 (Summer 1996): 160; Charles Sellers, *The Market Revolution*, 6 n. 19; Dusinberre, *Them Dark Days*, 404–407; Egerton, "Markets Without a Market Revolution," 214 n. 12.

6. Oakes, *The Ruling Race*, 69, 72, 127–28; Oakes, *Slavery and Freedom*, 89–92; Censer, *North Carolina Planters and Their Children*, 18–19, 41, 48, 53–54, 117, 119, 152–53.

phen Duncan, David Hunt, John Burnside, Farish Carter, and the Mills brothers of Texas were not capitalists, what mid-nineteenth-century American was?

This is not to deny that paternalism was a cardinal feature of slave society,
but paternalism and capitalism are not inherently contradictory. One has only
to look to the paternalistic mill villages of the New South or to George Pull-
man's model town in Illinois or even to such modern corporations as Kodak
to discover examples of capitalistic enterprises that practiced paternalism. One
further point should be made. There has been a tendency among both contemporary observers and historians to use the terms *patriarchy* and *paternalism* inter-
changeably, but the two are not precisely the same. It is particularly important
for Marxist historians to draw a distinction between the two concepts, for one
of their leading theoreticians, Eric Hobsbawn, clearly characterized the structure of the bourgeois family as patriarchal. Thus, Elizabeth Fox-Genovese,
while readily admitting the male-dominated orientation of slaveholder households, prefers to label the society of which they were a central part "paternalistic," a word that "invokes a specific metaphor of *legitimate* domination."[7] the
nineteenth century was quite obviously a patriarchal age, whether one refers to
the slave South, the freesoil North, or even to Western Europe. But the unique
master-slave relationship probably did endow the antebellum South with a
more generous dose of the brand of paternalism defined by Fox-Genovese.

The slaveholder version of this paternalism was most evident in the plantation regions of the older, longer-settled Atlantic Coast states such as Virginia
and the Carolinas. Perhaps the most explicit support for the precapitalist, antibourgeois thesis was provided by Charlestonian Thomas J. Withers, uncle of
famed diarist Mary Boykin Chesnut, during a visit to New York in the summer
of 1848. In a letter to James Chesnut, Sr., Withers conceded that the material
progress of that great city was impressive, but he found the social relations of
its inhabitants "palpably in the rear of ours. They are artificial—cold-blooded,
full of mutual suspicion & jealousy between classes." Indeed, he doubted that
there was one person in "this great Babel of 400,000 noisy, busy, pie-bald creatures . . . who finds that scope for the exercise of the truly delicate & delightful—the tender and Christian-like Sympathies and charities of our nature
which may be and are daily exercised by [Chesnut] & Mrs. Chesnut in [their]

---

7. Eric J. Hobsbawm, *The Age of Capital, 1848–1875* (New York, 1975), 237–39; Fox-Genovese,
Within the Plantation Household, 64 (italics mine).

Negro-Cabins." After lambasting the New Yorkers for their supposedly hypocritical assault on slavery, Withers concluded that "the patriarchal relation of
Master & Slave is the natural & enduring one," and that, as a consequence, the
slave commonwealths were destined to survive long after the glitzy exterior "of
those around [him] now" had succumbed to "the mistress of decay." Similarly,
in a piece written five years later as a rebuttal to *Uncle Tom's Cabin,* another
South Carolinian, Louisa McCord, vigorously defended the hierarchical structure of southern society. Under their system of government, she contended, the
upper classes were more elevated, the lower classes more comfortable, and all
worked together without bitterness in "the genial spirit of Christian love and
charity."[8]

Yet despite these manifestations of a paternalistic world view, even the
South Carolinians exhibited the same acquisitive economic behavior and the
same bourgeois values as their counterparts in both the slave and free states.
Three of the largest slaveholders in the Palmetto State—Nathaniel Heyward,
Joshua John Ward, and Robert F. W. Allston—were essentially self-made men,
each converting a modest inheritance into a vast plantation empire. Moreover,
although all exhibited quintessential paternalistic qualities, they did not eschew
bourgeois values. For example, in his role as family patriarch, Allston began to
instruct his young wife on her child-rearing and educational responsibilities
when his first-born son was only five years old. He emphasized the cultivation
of such habits as self-control, self-denial, and independence of both thought
and action. Such qualities must be inculcated in their children, he counseled, so
that when they attained their majority, they could "take their own stand against
men, choose their own principles of action, and think, & act and manage for
themselves." Nor were the female children to be ignored. It was his wife's "sacred duty," asserted Allston, to make their young daughter "submit to what is
right & to deny her in any habit that is wrong." I would suggest that such injunctions were strikingly similar to those issued by heads of household in the
free-labor states to members of their families.[9]

8. Thomas J. Withers to James Chesnut, Sr., August 19, 1848, in Williams-Chesnut-Manning
Papers, SCL; McCord, *Selected Writings,* 91.

9. Heyward, *Seed from Madagascar,* 65; Dusinberre, *Them Dark Days,* 31; Rogers, *History of
Georgetown County,* 259–60; Easterby, ed. *South Carolina Rice Plantation,* 19–21; Allston to wife
Adele, November 29 (quotations), December 4, 1838, November 30, 1843, in R. F. W. Allston Pa-
pers, SCHS.

Those historians who emphasize the economic and cultural similarities between North and South prior to 1865 generally agree that the most significant difference between the two sections was the existence of racial slavery in the South. For example, Jane Censer, who found that elite North Carolina planters were similar to their northern counterparts in their values, their family attitudes, and their emphasis upon education, independence, and material success, concluded that the great difference between the two sections was slavery. Similarly, Thomas P. Govan, who asserted that cultural distinctions within the country as a whole were "minor and inconsequential," contended that the only real conflict was over slavery and that emancipation removed that divisive factor. However, it was not simply slavery as a labor system that divided the two sections, but a slave system based on race. As Oakes has pointed out, the ideology of the slaveholding class was based upon a marriage between "racism and the gospel of prosperity." Perhaps the most vociferous proponent of the view that sectional differences were minimal is Edward Pessen. In an article published in the *American Historical Review* in 1980, he argued that the two sections were fundamentally alike in their hierarchical social structure, profit-driven economy, inequitable distribution of wealth, and political system based on republicanism and limited democracy. However, Pessen was on less solid ground when he professed to see striking sectional similarities in such areas as intellectual achievement, racial and gender attitudes, and materialism.[10]

Whatever the verdict of historians, it is apparent that many wealthy slaveholders perceived significant differences between themselves and their northern counterparts. A Mississippian explained those differences quite succinctly. After predicting that the South would be obliged to secede no later than the presidential election of 1860 in order to protect slavery, he declared: "The decendents [*sic*] of the narrow minded, sanctimonious, biggots, who landed at Plymouth Rock from the 'Mayflower,' and the decendents of 'the Cavaliers of Virginia' who landed at Jamestown are *two peoples*—and they must ever so remain. The hightoned gentlemen decended from the 'cavaliers,' and the 'round head' Mugginses, decended from the psalm-singing pharasees of New England can never really become '*one people*.'" James Johnston Pettigrew also employed

---

10. Censer, *North Carolina Planters and Their Children*, 119, 152–54; Thomas P. Govan, "Was the Old South Different?" *JSH* 21 (November 1955): 450 (quotation), 451, 454; Oakes, *The Ruling Race*, 138; Pessen, "How Different from Each Other," 1127, 1130–31, 1135–36, 1144, 1147, 1149.

the Cavalier-Roundhead dichotomy in his assessment of the characteristics of the two peoples. In a letter extolling the virtues of die-hard Charleston Unionist James L. Petigru, the North Carolinian Pettigrew, who was on the opposite side of the political spectrum from Petigru, nevertheless praised the latter for his courageous attachment to principle. Petigru's views, he averred, proceeded "from an elevated tone of heart and the habit of surveying an extended intellectual horizon." This was in marked contrast to "the Yankee pig-headed, puritanic obstinacy of the Round heads," which was "founded upon prejudice" and "accompanied . . . by narrow views and limited susceptibilities." Thus, because the Charlestonian exhibited the demeanor of a southern gentleman, his unpopular views were tolerated. Of course, southern perceptions of Yankee traits were not always negative. For example, in the midst of the war, another South Carolinian expressed serious reservations about the "pertinacity and endurance" of the southern populace. If the South were defeated, he asserted, it would be because of a deficiency in perseverance, a "quality in which as a people, we are inferior to the Northern feinds [sic]."[11]

Perhaps the most balanced commentary on the differences between the two regions of the country was offered by Virginia planter William F. Wickham in an essay written just after the war. In an attempt to explain the tragic, fratricidal war that he had deplored from the beginning, Wickham cataloged the sectional perceptions that had been exacerbated by the growing animosity engendered by the dispute over slavery. First, he characterized the people of the northern states as "shrewd, laborious, persevering, remarkable for their inventive genius, devoted to the acquisition of wealth, colder & more distant in their manners," less sensitive in their feelings, and "more careless of giving or receiving offence." By contrast, southern society was more hierarchical, deficient in its emphasis upon education, and marked by a clear aversion to manual labor. In addition, New Englanders "looked on the Southerner as indolent, dissolute, wasteful & proud," impractical, "fond of political abstractions, & unfit . . . to conduct the affairs of State." In short, observed Wickham, "like the cavaliers & Roundheads of former days," the two peoples "felt a mutual contempt for each other." But

11. R. J. Fitz to John A. Quitman, January 3, 1857, in John A. Quitman and Family Papers, MDAH; J. Johnston Pettigrew to R. F. W. Allston, November 21, 1852, in R. F. W. Allston Papers, SCHS; Allston to Adele Petigru Allston, November 11, 1863, in Easterby, ed., *South Carolina Rice Plantation*, 197.

had they viewed one another "with unprejudiced eyes," he continued, "they would have recognized the good parts that belonged to each." Thus, in addition to the traits already noted, Southerners would have discerned in their Yankee cohorts "kindness, hospitality, generosity," charity, and good fellowship, while Northerners would have recognized that the inhabitants of the slave states were equally industrious and frugal and no more prone to dissipation and extravagance than their neighbors to the north. Unfortunately, the bitter controversy over slavery blinded the inhabitants of both sections to their many common, positive characteristics.[12]

Not surprisingly, it was New York, a city viewed by elite slaveholders with a mixture of awe and revulsion, that seemed to evoke the most vivid comparisons between the worlds of Yankees and Southerners. As we have already seen, it was a visit to that city that prompted Charleston lawyer Thomas Withers to contrast its crass materialism with the more courtly patriarchal society of his native South Carolina. Other southern visitors to New York also commented on the distinctive characteristics of that city and its inhabitants, but, unlike Withers, they did not emphasize the dichotomy between bourgeois and paternalistic features. Peter W. Hairston was perhaps more impressed than Withers with the majestic splendor of the city, and he too was struck by the cold, impersonal nature of human relations. On the crowded streets, each person seemed to be "hurrying on so that he has no time to take thought for his neighbors." A North Carolina expatriate who, for ten years, had lived next to Cornelius Vanderbilt remarked that he did not even know the steamboat magnate by sight. Yet even more than the unfriendliness of New Yorkers, it was the urban environment that most distressed Hairston. There was "no green grass—no flowing streams nor trees with their graceful boughs—none of that country air so fresh and pure which makes me so wedded to the country life."[13]

For Barnwell Rhett, in New York seeking to obtain credit after the war, it was the demeanor of the women that most attracted his attention. From his lodging in an aristocratic part of the city, Rhett was astonished to see women of the highest class sitting at their windows "looking out or sewing, exactly like

12. William F. Wickham, "Essay on Negro Slavery in America," n.d., in Wickham Family Papers, VHS.

13. Peter W. Hairston to Fanny Caldwell, [April 18 (first quotation), 21, 23 (second quotation), 1859], in Peter Wilson Hairston Papers, SHC.

Milliner Girls," who, when catching sight of a male at an opposite window, would appear at their window seemingly receptive to "intriguery." More than a decade earlier, Rhett's eldest son had also been critical of New York women during a summer visit. "One cant even see pretty and well dressed women at this season," he complained. Clearly, they did not measure up to the elegantly coiffured belles of his native state. Another South Carolinian, like other southern visitors, was struck by the obsessive materialism of New Yorkers. "Money—money is the topic, the pursuit, the motive power," declared R. F. W. Allston. "Little else is thought of—little else is cared for."[14]

If New York defined elite perceptions of sectional differences, New England, because of its alleged supercilious, arrogant demeanor and its warm embrace of abolitionism and all the other hated isms, was the particular target of southern ire. The attitude that Southerners found so offensive was reflected in a letter written by a Boston resident to his brother in Natchez in the fall of 1868. Reflecting on the current condition of the country, the former asserted confidently that the "industry, enterprise, will, and perseverance" of the North, especially New England, would ensure the prosperity of the country. Even the South should prosper, he added condescendingly, "when her people engage in some more laudable purpose than murdering ignorant and helpless negroes, and enterprising Yankees or 'Carpet baggers.'" Shortly before the war, a Natchez student in Massachusetts encountered the same smug attitude, much to his disgust. After listening to a preacher speak "about how glad the New Englanders ought to be" because they were "so superior to any other persons of the United States in respect to virtue," young Henry Conner asked rhetorically: "Now where will you find ladies more virtuous than those in the sunny south." Above all, he continued, "I . . . hate to see a Yankee Preacher get up and slander the customs and people of the south—when they themselves are much more deficient in the same custom."[15]

Other members of the southern elite were equally vocal in their denunciation of the supposedly hypocritical New Englanders. Commenting on the presi-

14. R. B. Rhett to Catharine Rhett, June 9, 1867, R. B. Rhett, Jr., to "My dear Burnet," July 17, 1854, both in Robert Barnwell Rhett, Sr., Papers, SCHS; R. F. W. Allston to "My Dear Adele," October 23, 1850, in R. F. W. Allston Papers, SCHS.

15. Henry Winchester to "Dear Brother" [Josiah], November 9, 1868, in Winchester Family Papers, CAH; Richard E. Conner to "Dear Brother" [Lemuel P.?], January, 1865 [sic, probably 1859], in Lemuel P. Conner and Family Papers, LSU.

dential campaign of 1852, one of the Virginia Tayloes was especially critical of Franklin Pierce's New Hampshire background. "*You* know the Yankees of *that ilk*," he remarked to his brother. "They are not the most straightforward people in the world—& are somewhat selfish & contracted [?]. They are brought up to be so." In the midst of the secession crisis, another Virginian exclaimed: "God grant it may end by our getting rid of New England & make the Hudson & the lakes the *new line*, instead of Masons & Dixons." Several months after the war began, a Louisiana planter echoed that sentiment. Although he was willing to resume friendly commercial relations with states in the Northwest after the cessation of hostilities, he adamantly rejected any suggestion of a reconciliation with the New England states or with New York and Pennsylvania. "I would not be willing on any arrangement that they could make to us, to be again united with them under the same government," he asserted bitterly. Yet another elite slaveholder, Peter W. Hairston, while engaging in a playful dialogue about religion with his fiancée, vigorously defended Catholicism and declared that he would much "prefer it to the sour Puritanism of New-England—which does not relieve its austerity by the virtues which it professes." On all counts, then, New England was anathema to most Southerners.[16]

But the factor that most infuriated Southerners about New England was that region's commitment to the abolition of slavery, an institution that constituted the very heart of the South's socioeconomic system. Two members of the Winchester family, ironically both natives of Massachusetts who had removed to Natchez, clearly articulated the centrality of slavery to the southern social order. In an essay written shortly before the first sectional crisis in 1850, George Winchester declared that the institution of slavery, by virtue of "the political and social and natural inequalities, moral, mental, and religious of the white and Black races," had become "so incorporated into the existence of slave holding States as social communities" that it could not be "destroyed but by the destruction of their social existence as Communities, and with it their destruction as civil & political States, and as equal members of the Union." More than two decades later, his nephew, the outspoken Unionist Josiah, invoked the writ-

16. Benjamin O. Tayloe to "My dear Brother" [William H.], November, 1852, in Tayloe Family Papers, VHS; Colin Clarke to Sallie Manning, December 5, 1860, in Chesnut-Miller-Manning Papers, SCHS; B[enjamin] Ballard to Lewis Thompson, September 17, 1861, in Lewis Thompson Papers, SHC; Peter W. Hairston to Fanny Caldwell, April [29], 1859, in Peter Wilson Hairston Papers, SHC.

ings of Samuel Pufendorf and Aristotle, who had stressed the hierarchical nature of society, to support his defense of the slave system that then lay in
shambles. The "commercial wealth" of the entire country, he asserted, had been
based upon the staple crops produced by slave labor. Now, however, with "the
restraints of slavery" removed and the Negroes "left to their own guidance," they
would prove incapable of "that continuous labor" he deemed essential to produce those crops. This belief led the younger Winchester to inaugurate his postwar scheme to import Chinese coolie laborers.[17]

Other members of the elite sounded a similar refrain. Writing on the eve of
secession, Virginian Colin Clarke declared that it was imperative for the South
to protect "a property upon which depends our social & domestic happiness,
our [indu]strial wealth, & which is itself worth some $200,000,000." Another
Virginian, William F. Wickham, pointed to climate as one of the principal ra-
tionales for southern slavery. "Nature," he said, "seems to have decreed that a
tropical climate should be occupied by the Ethiopian & a temperate one by the
Caucasian race." Members of the latter, reasoned Wickham, were not constitu-
tionally suited to cultivate "the crops of the South under its burning sun," hence,
the necessity for African slavery. However it had materialized, slavery, declared
William S. Pettigrew in 1850, was an institution that the South should go to any
length to defend should it ever be directly threatened by the North.[18]

Not only did the elite slaveholders emphasize the vital importance of slavery
to the society of which they formed the apex, but they had no doubt about the
morality of the institution. Because the concept of one man holding another in
bondage is so alien to the values of the modern world, many historians have
concluded that southern planters *must* have felt guilty about owning slaves. For
example, James Oakes claims that the slaveholders' alleged obsession with death
"exposed patterns of behavior and systems of belief which indicated deeply troubled consciences." Few masters, he argues, failed to experience some degree of
guilt. There is little evidence in the writings of the large slaveholders to support

17. George Winchester, Fragmentary Essay entitled the "Slavery Question," [1849], in Winchester Family Papers, CAH; Josiah Winchester to S. M. Davis, October 2, 1872, in Duncan
Papers, LSU.

18. C[olin] C[larke] to daughter Sallie [Manning], [early 1860], in Chesnut-Miller-Manning Pa-
pers, SCHS; William F. Wickam, Essay on Political Parties and American Government, n.d., in
Wickham Family Papers, VHS; William S. Pettigrew to James C. Johnston, March 7, 1850, in
Hayes Collection, SHC.

such an interpretation. To the contrary, why should they have felt guilty? They believed that slavery was a divine institution sanctioned by God. Although the Bible condemns a host of mankind's sins and vices, there is no explicit injunction against slavery. Moreover, like most other nineteenth-century Caucasians, they believed that Africans were of an inferior order, capable of surviving only if placed in a subordinate station. As William Wickham observed, "different orders of men have their different pursuits & different objects of interest." Although it was difficult for the "educated & refined" to conceive that a "degraded race held in servitude" could derive much pleasure from life, Wickham speculated that one might "find as much happiness among the African slaves as elsewhere." Perhaps William S. Pettigrew articulated the moral position of the slaveholders most succinctly. After stating that the institution of slavery was "unquestionably justified by Scripture," he asserted unequivocally that his conscience was clear.[19]

There were, to be sure, a few who expressed doubts about the morality of slaveholding. One of those was Gertrude Thomas of Georgia. Throughout her life, Thomas exhibited an ambivalent attitude toward the "peculiar institution." On the one hand, she recognized the financial benefits that she and her family derived from the exploitation of slave labor, but on the other, she abhorred the sexual temptations to which white boys and men were exposed. As Nell Painter has suggested, her concern was probably induced by the belief that both her husband and her father had entered into liaisons with slave women.[20] Shortly after her marriage, she seemed unperturbed when her husband sold a male slave, remarking dryly that the bondsman had been "the cause of a great deal of trouble and expense." But later on, as her beloved Confederacy entered its darkest hours, she began to express reservations about the morality of owning slaves. "I have sometimes doubted on the subject of slavery," she confided to her journal in mid-September, 1864, "but of late I have become convinced the Negro *as a race* is better off with us as he has been than if he were made free." Nevertheless, she conceded that the whites might benefit from emancipation. A week later, Thomas admitted that she was no longer "certain" that slavery was right. In an

19. Oakes, *The Ruling Race*, III (quotation), 122; William F. Wickham, Essay on Negro Slavery in America, n.d., in Wickham Family Papers, VHS; William S. Pettigrew to James C. Johnston, March 7, 1850, in Hayes Collection, SHC.

20. Nell Irvin Painter, Introduction to *The Secret Eye*, ed. Burr, 59.

attempt to assuage her doubts, she began reading a proslavery tract, but even that did not dispel her growing realization "that to hold men and women in perpetual bondage is wrong." After the war, despite the property loss resulting from emancipation, Thomas expressed no regrets. Indeed, she wrote in 1871, "if one word of mine would restore the institution I would not utter it." Thus did one plantation mistress struggle with the moral ramifications of human bondage, but her mental anguish over the subject seems to have been the exception rather than the rule among members of the slaveholding elite.[21]

As was noted above, southern support for slavery was grounded in large measure upon a belief in the inherent inferiority of those they held in bondage. Expressions of this viewpoint are too legion to belabor the obvious. It will suffice to say that this view was ubiquitous among the large slaveholders regardless of their political position during the sectional crisis. Slaveholders frequently cited the examples of Haiti and Jamaica to support their contention that Negroes were incapable of self-government or even of laboring without coercion. The typical view of Haiti was reflected in an article that appeared in *De Bow's Review* in 1858. After recounting the allegedly deplorable conditions that had existed in that black-ruled island nation since the successful slave insurrection in the 1790s, the writer asserted that "the present condition of the island" was "a sad commentary upon the capacity of the negro race for progressive civilization." Anyone who expected significant improvement in the future, he concluded, "belongs to that happy class which learns nothing from the past." Similarly, a South Carolinian who had recently visited Jamaica and Central America described the Negro and Indian half-breed inhabitants of those areas as "worthless, beggarly devils." Declaring that nothing good "will ever come out of these colored races," he predicted that in North America "the whole colored race that is not enslaved will soon disappear before the restless progress of the white man."[22]

Two men at opposite ends of the political spectrum vividly illustrated the universality of white racism. In an essay on slavery apparently penned shortly before the war, fire-eater Barnwell Rhett contemptuously dismissed the suppos-

21. *The Secret Eye*, ed. Burr, 131 (first quotation), 168–69, 236 (second quotation), 238–39 (third quotation), 265, 276–77, 321–22, 364 (fourth quotation).

22. "The Model Negro Empire," *De Bow's Review* 24 (March 1858): 211; Edward J. Pringle to "My dear Cousin" [Jane Pringle], December 29, [1853], Pringle Family Correspondence, in R. F. W. Allston Papers, SCHS.

edly barren historical record of the Negro. "The history of the Negro Race," he wrote, "is simply a page of natural history. It has no intellectual history, because God has not endowed it with the faculties necessary." Indeed, he continued, "from the 'Great Desert' to the 'Cape of Good Hope' the true land of the negro, not a vestige of civilization [is] to be found." Nor would education or any other improvement elevate the lot of the Negro. In Rhett's view, "the intellectual & physical characters of the differing races were the same five thousand years ago as they are now." After the war a man with quite different political views, Massachusetts-born Josiah Winchester of Natchez, echoed the racist sentiments of the South Carolina ultra-secessionist. "If the Negroes are not of that class of human beings, who if left to their own guidance will 'either do mischief or do nothing,'" declared Winchester, "then we may admit that the experience of past ages is no guide for this progressive age and for the future." God himself, explained the Natchezian, had established "the relation of superior and inferior, of master & slave, between the White and Black races."[23]

Such malignant racism was by no means confined to male members of the elite. As Elizabeth Fox-Genovese has noted, "the racism of the women was generally uglier and more meanly expressed than that of the men." Like Barnwell Rhett, Louisa McCord maintained that "the negro alone has, of all the races of men, remained entirely without all shadow of civilization." That deficiency, she argued, could not be attributed to "his want of opportunities and instruction," for the white man had neither of those advantages "when the power of mind guided him to the destiny for which Heaven created him." In short, contended McCord, "if ever God's seal was set upon the brow of any race with the stamp of inferiority . . . it is upon that of the negro." In like manner, Kate Edmondston, who believed that God had ordained slavery for Negroes, described the latter variously as "a degraded race" and as "ignorant children at best." Even Gertrude Thomas, who did not mourn the demise of slavery and who manifested some sympathy for her former chattels, was not immune from the virulent racism that infected most elite families. Commenting after the war on a photograph of the noted black abolitionist Frederick Douglass, she re-

23. R. B. Rhett, Essay on Slavery, n.d., in Robert Barnwell Rhett, Sr., Papers, SCHS; Josiah Winchester to S. M. Davis, October 2, 1872 (quotations), in Duncan Papers, LSU; Winchester to [Wade Hampton III?], June 11, 1869, in Winchester Family Papers, CAH. Winchester's quotation is from Pufendorf, the seventeenth-century law writer and political philosopher.

marked: "he looks as if he was two degrees removed from the ape creation. I do not believe he has the talent with which he is credited." Thus, relying upon their distorted perceptions of history, ethnology, and religion, both male and female members of wealthy slaveholding families used the alleged inferiority of the Negro to justify their enslavement of untold thousands of persons of African descent.[24]

Of course, racism was not an exclusive characteristic of southern whites during the nineteenth century, nor were all members of the elite as extreme in their attitudes toward blacks as those cited above. One prominent Northerner who betrayed his inherent racism after the war was Oliver H. Kelley, principal founder of the National Grange. In a series of letters to the son of a South Carolina rice grandee, Kelley counseled patience during the tumultuous early days of Radical Reconstruction. "The *people* at the North," he assured Benjamin Allston, "are not more desireous [*sic*] of being *ruled* by the nigger than you are in the South." He predicted that immigration and disease would soon reduce the Negro population in the South to manageable numbers. "The enterprising ones will go to California if they learn of its inducements, and if you are anxious to get rid of them," he added sarcastically, "you can tell them of the *blissful abode* in store there for them!" Happily, there were a few elite families, even in South Carolina, who displayed a more enlightened attitude toward race. Chief among these was the prominent Read family of Georgetown District. Apparently a political moderate during the secession crisis, John Harleston Read II, a rice planter with more than five hundred slaves, opposed efforts to limit the rights of free blacks before the war. Later, his son was one of only two whites to vote against the "understanding clause" in the state constitution of 1895. Such progressive views, however, were clearly the exception among the men examined in this study.[25]

Let us turn now from race to class, another element in the pantheon that seems to hold so much fascination for contemporary historians. The relationship between classes in the antebellum South, while marked by condescension

---

24. Fox-Genovese, *Within the Plantation Household,* 349; McCord, *Selected Writings,* 115–16 (first quotations), 122 (last quotation); *"Journal of a Secesh Lady,"* ed. Crabtree and Patton, 651, 653, 709; *The Secret Eye,* ed. Burr, 305.

25. Oliver H. Kelley to Benjamin Allston, October 10 (first quotation), November 30 (second quotation), 1867, in Easterby, ed., *South Carolina Rice Plantation,* 234, 238; Rogers, *History of Georgetown County,* 480–81.

on the one hand and mild resentment on the other, never signaled class conflict in the Marxist sense. The great planters took pride in their exalted status as "gentlemen" and clearly regarded themselves as superior to whites of lower socioeconomic rank. That pride was reflected in the correspondence of young Thomas P. Devereux, who faced unaccustomed hardships after enlisting as a private in a North Carolina regiment at the age of eighteen. Reminding his father that he had joined the army against the latter's advice, he remarked, "I am willing to do my duty—but don't want to go where I will be eaten up with vermin. I am a gentleman, and wish to remain one." Several months later, that wish appeared to be near fruition. Anticipating a promotion to first lieutenant, he wrote proudly, "I will put on bars and be a gentleman once more." A Louisiana planter who found himself in financial difficulty also cherished the importance of being a gentleman. Seeking a buyer for his place, he advised Paul Cameron that he was willing to sell at a sacrifice, but he would "prefer that a gentleman should lord it over my acres" rather than "a low bred upstart." Upper-class snobbery was also apparent in the comments of other members of the elite. Thus, while a student at Harvard, Henry A. Middleton, Jr., described a fellow South Carolina classmate as not "exactly a country-cracker but not a most civilized person" either. "I had rather that he came from any other state," admitted young Middleton with more than a trace of shame. Another South Carolinian was disgusted by the vulgar society he encountered in the interior of Mississippi during the bonanza years before the Panic of 1837. "I had hoped to find blackguardism and vulgarity confined here as in older states to prescribed [?] classes of the community," he remarked. "But here," he continued disgustedly, "all society seems to participate in one common degeneracy. All seems ignoble, low, rowdy to the last extreme."[26]

The pretentious demeanor of the elite understandably provoked considerable resentment among the ranks of the plain folk, though that resentment was usually muted. A desire for respect on the part of the less privileged was perhaps revealed most clearly in correspondence between overseers and their employers.

26. T. P. Devereux II to "Dear father" [John], October 25, 1864, Devereux to "Dear Kate," February 8, 1865, in Thomas P. Devereux II Letterbook, NCDAH; George Mason Long to Paul C. Cameron, May 7, 1849, in Cameron Family Papers, SHC; H. A. Middleton, Jr., to [sister] Harriett, October 4, [1845], Henry A. Middleton, Jr., Family Letters, in Cheves-Middleton Papers, SCHS; [Joseph W. Lesene?] to Langdon Cheves, Jr., December 31, 1836, in Langdon Cheves, Jr., Papers, SCHS.

Thus, after detailing various grievances resulting from the unwanted presence of several white visitors on Lewis Thompson's Rapides Parish sugar plantation, overseer Moore Rawls threatened to leave if conditions did not improve. "Its not altogether in a pecuniary view that causes me to speak thus," he wrote. But "I am entitle[d] to elbow room, or what might be call[ed] Respect, or I am not a fit Subject to fill the place of a Steward." Another Louisiana plantation manager, who had been invited to dine on Christmas Day with his employer's family, expressed gratitude for the thoughtful gesture but admitted that he would have preferred to spend the holiday at home. "Poor folks always has poor ways," he remarked, "and I am unfortunately one of that class." In like manner, a Virginia overseer revealed his understanding of the social and economic chasm that separated the privileged class from the less fortunate. Miffed by a report that his wealthy cousin had ridiculed him in Petersburg for striking a bad bargain in purchasing "a very poor farm," he responded tartly: "You forget that poor people are not able to buy rich farms." The latent resentment of poor whites surfaced in other ways. For example, while in Raleigh on Thanksgiving Day in 1850, Paul Cameron was informed that "some of the Country people coming to town [had] complained much to find all the Stores & Shops closed" and had attributed it to "the doings of a 'Whig Governor'!"[27]

The jealousy and resentment of the common folk sometimes emerged in popular elections involving members of the elite. Among the victims of lower-class animosity was Cameron, who was defeated in a state senate race in 1858 when his opponent ridiculed him for wearing gold spectacles and again three years later in his bid for a seat in the state secession convention when his wealth again proved to be an impediment to election in the democratic state of North Carolina. A friend and supporter charged that Cameron's defeat was a consequence of "that mean jealousy" that had lately "*tabooed* the *rich*." While conceding that the government should bestow no special favors on that or any other class, he nevertheless found it appalling that "ones fellow citizens should *black ball* him because of his wealth—never mind how obtained or how ernd [*sic*]." Fellow North Carolina secessionist William S. Pettigrew suffered a like fate in

27. Moore Rawls to Lewis Thompson, October 28, 1860, in Lewis Thompson Papers, SHC; R. R. Barrow Residence Journal, December 25, 1857, SHC; Thomas G. Baylor to "Dear Cousin" [Richard Baylor], February 23, 1856, in Baylor Family Papers, VHS; Paul C. Cameron to "My dear Father" [Duncan Cameron], November 15, 1850, in Cameron Family Papers, SHC.

his race for a convention seat in 1861. Charging that his opponent was elected "by the most shameless means," he asserted that he had been depicted as the "property-holders candidate" and his opponent as the "poor man's candidate." In the days immediately preceding the election, it was even said, declared Pettigrew angrily, "that [he] would not permit the poor to enter [his] house, but would send a servant to meet them at the gate & ask their business." Such tactics resulted in Pettigrew's defeat by a margin of 120 votes. Class resentment might even affect a legal as well as an electoral contest. Thus, when Richard T. Archer became embroiled in a lawsuit over the disposition of his sister's estate, he expressed concern that his own wealth might redound to his disadvantage. The other litigant was poor, and "I am esteemed rich," observed Archer. "The sympathy felt for poverty," he added, "I think colours testimony, and indisposes person[s] to act as freely in rendering justice as should be."[28]

As the sectional crisis reached a climax in 1860–1861, many wealthy slaveholders became acutely aware that measures had to be taken to enlist the support of the plain folk in the impending conflict. As noted earlier, John F. Townsend of South Carolina was one of those who sought to convince the nonslaveholders that the status they enjoyed by virtue of their race would be lost if slavery were extinguished.[29] "In no country of the world," declared Townsend, "did the poor white man . . . occupy so enviable a position" as in the slave South. Such arguments proved persuasive as tens of thousands of lower-class whites flocked to the colors early in the war. Indeed, it was this segment of the population that constituted the backbone of the Confederate Army throughout the four years of war. Another wealthy planter who recognized the importance of courting the nonslaveholders was William Pettigrew. The day after North Carolina seceded, Pettigrew broached the delicate subject of tax reform to his brother. "Perhaps it will be best to act, at an early day, on the subject of taxation," he wrote, "as it will have a tendency to unite our people—the nonslaveholders—more closely with us in this contest with the north for our existence."[30]

28. Kenzer, *Kinship and Neighborhood in a Southern Community,* 58–59; William H. Ruffin to Paul C. Cameron, June 4, 1861, in Cameron Family Papers, SHC; William S. Pettigrew to "My dear Friend" [James C. Johnston], March 12, 1861, in Pettigrew Family Papers, SHC; Richard T. Archer to "My Dear Edward" [nephew Edward S.], May 20, 1856, in Richard Thompson Archer Family Papers, CAH.

29. See p. 287 of this book.

30. *De Bow's Review* 30 (January 1861): 123; William S. Pettigrew to "My dear Brother" [J. Johnston Pettigrew], May 18 [*sic,* 22], 1861, in Pettigrew Family Papers, SHC.

One other aspect of the slaveholder psyche merits comment. To put it candidly, Southerners harbored a general feeling of mistrust and animosity toward Northerners, quite apart from the understandable hostility spawned by abolitionist activity before the war and exacerbated by their experiences during the war and Reconstruction. As was noted earlier in this chapter, most Southerners perceived themselves as being different from their Yankee counterparts, especially New Yorkers and New Englanders, whom they found particularly obnoxious.[31] But the antagonism toward Northerners was not confined to political or even cultural matters. It extended also to legal and business practices. Thus, while visiting Philadelphia during the summer of 1838, Judge Thomas Butler, himself a native Pennsylvanian, remarked that his daughter was then "traversing Chesnut & Second Streets," where she was "no doubt being cheated by the shopkeepers as all persons from the south are more or less." A decade later, Butler's son registered a similar complaint when he purchased winter clothing while a student at Yale. "Every southerner who comes here," he charged, "is cheated by these people for the first year." I suppose, he concluded disgustedly, that "in the course of time . . . I shall learn [from] experience."[32]

Another member of the slaveholding elite who criticized northern business ethics was Benjamin O. Tayloe. Embroiled in a dispute with H. A. Willard, lessee of a Washington, D.C., hotel owned by Tayloe and his brother, he grumbled that Willard had recently "backed out" of a verbal agreement with the Tayloes. "A *northern* man does not consider a contract made, until signed by the parties," he complained bitterly. Southern ideas of honor were seemingly "obsolete" when dealing with money-grubbing Yankees. "You and I," he observed to his brother, "are bound by our verbal engagements," but that was not the case with northern business associates "unless it seems for *their* interest." Tayloe was equally critical of Yankee lawyers. After a long period of litigation over the estate of his first wife, the daughter of a New York congressman, the Virginia Unionist exploded: "If *all* of the North were like the New York lawyers, I should go at once for *disunion,* rather than attempting to hold to a compact with such Knaves." A South Carolinian who had moved to Mobile and accepted an invitation to enter the practice of law with a northern partner ex-

31. See pp. 412–16 of this book.
32. Thomas Butler to Ann Butler, June 20, 1838, Robert O. Butler to Ann Butler, December 9, 1849, both in Thomas Butler and Family Papers, LSU.

pressed similar disenchantment with the latter. "Fisher is a *Yankee*," he confided to a friend in the Palmetto State, "and some of the most important elements of his character are so revolting to him, that the gradual discovery of them is daily extinguishing my respect and esteem for him." Thus, it is clear that slaveholder hostility toward Northerners extended well beyond the political arena.[33]

In summary, then, the ideology—or world view, as some prefer to call it—of the wealthy slaveholders included a number of diverse components. Although the elite planters exhibited many paternalistic characteristics by virtue of their dual role as family patriarchs and as patrons and regulators of the lives of their slaves, they were also capitalists in the classical, if not the Marxian, sense of the word. Some used the capital generated by their agricultural enterprises to purchase additional land and slaves, but others developed extremely diversified economic portfolios. In their personal lives as well as in the education of their children, they differed little from their northern counterparts in their emphasis upon such bourgeois values as industry, frugality, self-discipline, and acquisitiveness. It is true that they placed greater stress than the latter on such qualities as honor, gentility, generosity, courtliness, and the importance of the extended family, but these cannot be attributed solely or even primarily to their peculiar labor system. Indeed, many of these characteristics persist in elite southern families today, more than 135 years after the demise of slavery. Many of the great slaveholders, even some with northern antecedents, also harbored a latent dislike for Yankees, especially those from New England. That animus, of course, reached a peak in the period immediately preceding, during, and following the Civil War. Within their own region, they tended to view their white social inferiors with an air of condescension, if not contempt, a demeanor frequently resented by the plain folk. But, above all else, it was their unqualified endorsement of slavery, their belief in the importance and morality of that institution, predicated upon their conviction that slavery was ordained by God and the only natural condition for persons of African descent, that made their world view unique among the civilized societies of the mid-nineteenth century.

33. Benjamin O. Tayloe to "Dear Brother" [William H.], July 27, 1851 (first quotation), March 22, 1851 (second quotation), both in Tayloe Family Papers, VHS; J. W. L. to Langdon Cheves, Jr., September 24, 1837, in Langdon Cheves, Jr., Papers, SCHS.

APPENDIX A

SLAVEHOLDERS WITH 500 OR MORE SLAVES, 1850

	Planter	Birthplace	State of Residence	Subdivision	Subtotal	Total
1	Nathaniel Heyward (1766–1851)	S.C.	S.C.	Beaufort-Prince William	286	
				Beaufort-St. Helena	16	
				Colleton-St. Bartholomew	1,487	
				*Chastn-St. Philip & St. Michael	45	1,834
2	Francis Surget, Sr. (ca. 1783–1856)	La.	Miss.	*Adams, Miss.	596	
				Wilkinson, Miss.	183	
				Concordia, La.	430	
				Madison, La.	89	1,298
3	Joshua John Ward (1800–1853)	S.C.	S.C.	Georgetown-Lower All Saints		1,092
4	Stephen Duncan (1787–1867)	Pa.	Miss.	*Adams, Miss.	198	
				Issaquena, Miss.	470	
				St. Mary, La.	181	
				Tensas, La.	92	941
5	William Aiken (1806–1887)	S.C.	S.C.	*Chastn-St. Philip & St. Michael	7	
				Colleton-St. John, Jehossee Island	897	904

	Planter	Birthplace	State of Residence	Subdivision	Subtotal	Total
6	Est. John Butler (1806–1847) & Pierce Mease Butler (1810–1867)	Pa. Pa.	Pa.	McIntosh, Ga. Glynn, Ga. (listed under Samuel W. Wilson)	524 319	843
7	Richard Singleton (1776–1852)	S.C.	S.C.	Orangeburg Richland Richland (listed under son Matthew R.) *Sumter	212 248 281 89	830
8	James Hamilton Couper (1794–1866)	Ga.	Ga.	Glynn		765
9	John Smith Preston (1809–1881)	Va.	S.C.	*Richland, S.C. Ascension, La.	39 701	740
10	Meredith Calhoun (ca. 1805–)	S.C.	La.	Natchitoches *Rapides	169 550	719
11	William Algernon Alston, Sr. (1782–1860)	S.C.	S.C.	Georgetown–Lower All Saints		690
12	Est. Henry Middleton (1770–1846)	England	S.C.	Beaufort–Prince William		686
13	Mrs. Michel Doradou Bringier (1798–1878)		La.	*Ascension St. James	599 74	673

	Planter	Birthplace	State of Residence	Subdivision	Subtotal	Total
14	Henry R. W. Hill (–1853)	N.C.	La.	Issaquena, Miss.	447	
				Yazoo, Miss. (1848 tax rolls)	95	
				Jefferson, La.	155	667
15	Levin R. Marshall (1800–1870)	Va.	Miss.	*Adams, Miss.	218	
				Wilkinson, Miss.	56	
				Madison, La.	213	
				Jefferson, Ark.	142	629
16	Joseph Blake (1769–1865)	England	England	Beaufort-Prince William		
	Agt. Walter Blake (1804–1871)	England	S.C.			610
17	Henry Doyal (–1859)	Va.	La.	*Ascension	390	
				Plaquemines	205	595
18	Thomas Pollock Devereux (1793–1869)	N.C.	N.C.	*Halifax	273	
				Northampton	307	
				Wake	3	583
19	Ephraim Mikell Baynard (1797–1865)	S.C.	S.C.	Beaufort-St. Luke	203	
				Colleton-St. Bartholomew	34	
				*Colleton-St. John, Edisto Island	339	576

	Planter	Birthplace	State of Residence	Subdivision	Subtotal	Total
20	Pierre M. Lapice (1798–)	St. Domingo	La.	Concordia	319	
				*St. James	254	573
21	Est. Isaac Franklin (1789–1846)		Tenn.	West Feliciana, La.		567
22	Robert Ruffin Barrow (–1875)	N.C.	La.	Ascension	60	
				Assumption (Martin & Barrow)	75	
				Lafourche	54	
				*Terrebonne	364	553
23	James Cathcart Johnston (1782–1865)	N.C.	N.C.	*Chowan	126	
				Halifax	272	
				Pasquotank	144	542
24	William John Minor (1807–1869)	Miss.	Miss.	*Adams, Miss.	319	
				Ascension, La.	216	
				Terrebonne, La.		535
25	Samuel F. Davis	Mass.	La.	Concordia		523
26	David Hunt (1779–1861)	N.J.	Miss.	Issaquena, Miss.	52	
				*Jefferson, Miss.	374	
				Concordia, La.	81	507

*Denotes county of residence

APPENDIX B

SLAVEHOLDERS WITH 500 OR MORE SLAVES, 1860

	Planter	Birthplace	State of Residence	Subdivision	Subtotal	Total
1	Est. Joshua John Ward (1800–1853)	S.C.	S.C.	*Georgetown–Lower All Saints	1,131	
				Charleston–Ward 5	15	1,146
2	Levin R. Marshall (1800–1870)	Va.	Miss.	*Adams, Miss.	188	
				Claiborne, Miss.	96	
				Wilkinson, Miss.	164	
				Concordia, La.	248	
				Jefferson, La.	91	
				Madison, La.	271	1,058
3	John Burnside (ca. 1810–1881)	N. Ireland	La.	*Ascension	753	
				St. James	186	939
4	Stephen Duncan (1787–1867)	Pa.	Miss.	*Adams, Miss.	11	
				Issaquena, Miss.	706	
				Tensas, La. (listed under son Saml P.)	173	890

	Planter	Birthplace	State of Residence	Subdivision	Subtotal	Total
5	John Izard Middleton (1800–1877)	S.C.	S.C.	Beaufort–Prince William	520	
				*Georgetown–Lower All Saints	211	
				Georgetown–Prince George	107	838
6	Zebulon York (1819–1900) & E. J. Hoover (ca. 1828–)	Maine La.	La.	Concordia		782
7	John Hendricks Horne (1795–1864)	N.C.	Miss.	Wayne		751
8	William Aiken (1806–1887)	S.C.	S.C.	*Charleston–Ward 5	19	
				Colleton–St. John, Jehossee Island	700	719
9	Meredith Calhoun (ca. 1805–)	S.C.	La.	Rapides		709
10	Gerard Brandon (1818–1874)	Miss.	Miss.	*Adams, Miss.	512	
				Concordia, La.	113	
				Tensas, La.	81	706
11	Ruth Stovall Hairston (1784–1869)	Va.	Va.	Henry, Va.	121	
				*Pittsylvania, Va.	93	
				Forsyth, N.C.	49	
				Stokes, N.C.	438	701
12	Joseph Alexander Smith Acklen (1816–1863)	Ala.	Tenn.	*Davidson, Tenn.	32	
				West Feliciana, La.	659	691

	Planter	Birthplace	State of Residence	Subdivision	Subtotal	Total
13	Paul Carrington Cameron (1808–1891)	N.C.	N.C.	*Orange, N.C.	358	
				Person, N.C.	114	
				Greene, Ala.	116	
				Tunica, Miss.	83	671
14	William Henry Heyward (1817–1889)	S.C.	S.C.	Beaufort-Prince William	386	
				Beaufort-St. Peter	136	
				*Charleston-Ward 2	16	
				Colleton-St. Bartholomew	133	671
15	Philip St. George Cocke (1809–1861)	Va.	Va.	Brunswick, Va.	158	
				*Powhatan, Va.	125	
				Lowndes, Miss.	259	
				Yazoo, Miss.	116	658
16	Edward Lloyd VI (1798–1861)	Md.	Md.	*Talbot, Md.	412	
				Madison, Miss.	92	
				Tensas, La.	154	658
17	Est. Arthur (1805–1852) & Maria Louisa Blake (1816–1854) Heyward	S.C.	S.C.	Colleton-St. Bartholomew	304	
				Chatham, Ga.	352	656
18	Joseph Blake (1769–1865)	England	England	Beaufort-St. Peter	74	
	Agt. Walter Blake (1804–1871)	England	S.C.	*Beaufort-Prince William	545	
				Henderson, N.C. (Walter)	36	655

	Planter	Birthplace	State of Residence	Subdivision	Subtotal	Total
19	Alfred Vidal Davis (ca. 1827–)	La.	Miss.	*Adams, Miss.	14	
				Concordia, La.	637	651
20	John Laurence Manning (1816–1889)	S.C.	S.C.	*Clarendon, S.C.	27	
				Ascension, La.	616	643
21	Est. Frederick Stanton (1798–1859)	N. Ireland	Miss.	*Adams, Miss.	180	
				Concordia, La.	458	638
22	Robert Francis Withers Allston (1801–1864)	S.C.	S.C.	Georgetown-Prince George Winyah		631
23	Ephraim Mikell Baynard (1797–1865)	S.C.	S.C.	Beaufort-St. Luke	197	
				Colleton-St. Bartholomew	32	
				*Colleton-St. John, Edisto Island	370	
				Colleton-St. Paul	26	625
24	William John Minor (1807–1869)	Miss.	Miss.	*Adams, Miss.	42	
				Ascension, La.	223	
				Terrebonne, La.	357	622
25	Est. Henry Doyal (–1859) & Henry R. Doyal (ca. 1840–)	Va.	La.	*Ascension	271	
				Plaquemines	349	620

	Planter	Birthplace	State of Residence	Subdivision	Subtotal	Total
26	William Brown Hodgson (1800–1871)	D.C.	Ga.	Burke	240	
				*Chatham	72	
				Jefferson	284	596
27	Leonidas A. Jordan		Ga.	Baldwin	62	
				Dougherty	185	
				Lee	346	593
28	Daniel Blake (1803–1873)	England	S.C.	*Colleton-St. Bartholomew	527	
				Henderson, N.C.	59	586
29	Est. John Ashby Colclough (1799–1850) & Eliza Maria Cantey Colclough (1813–1886)	S.C. S.C.	S.C. S.C.	Clarendon	102	
				*Sumter	468	570
30	William Algernon Alston, Sr. (1782–1860)	S.C.	S.C.	Georgetown-Lower All Saints	567	567
31	Mrs. Michel Doradou Bringier (1798–1878), Marius Ste. Colomb Bringier (1814–1884), Louis Amedee Bringier (1828–1897)	La.	La.	*Ascension (M. S. & L. A.)	530	
				St. James	26	
				New Orleans-Ward 1 (Mrs. M. D.)	11	567
32	David Hunt (1779–1861)	N.J.	Miss.	Issaquena, Miss.	82	
				*Jefferson, Miss.	386	
				Concordia, La.	99	567

	Planter	Birthplace	State of Residence	Subdivision	Subtotal	Total
33	Samuel Manuel Davis (ca. 1827–1878)	Miss.	Miss.	*Adams, Miss. Issaquena, Miss. Concordia, La.	15 159 386	560
34	James Cathcart Johnston (1782–1865)	N.C.	N.C.	*Chowan Halifax Pasquotank	103 271 181	555
35	Benjamin Roach, Jr. (–1820) Adm. Est. Benjamin Roach, Sr. (–1848)	Ky.	Miss.	*Adams Warren Washington Yazoo	10 176 100 + 266	552 +
36	John Robinson IV (1822–1879)	Miss.	Miss.	Madison		550
37	Edward McGehee (1786–1880)	Ga.	Miss.	*Wilkinson, Miss. West Feliciana, La.	471 74	545
38	Charles Heyward (1802–1866)	S.C.	S.C.	*Charleston-Ward 3 Colleton-St. Bartholomew	10 **532	542
39	Jeremiah H. Brown (1800–1868)	S.C.	Ala.	Sumter		539
40	Arthur Middleton Blake (1812–1881)	England	S.C.	Charleston-St. James Santee		538

	Planter	Birthplace	State of Residence	Subdivision	Subtotal	Total
41	John Harleston Read II (1815–1866)	S.C.	S.C.	Charleston-Ward 4	20	
				*Georgetown-Prince George	511	531
42	Elisha Worthington	Ky.	Ark.	Chicot	529	529
43	John Basil Lamar (1812–1862)	Ga.	Ga.	Baldwin (trustee for Howell Cobb)	137	
				*Bibb (to as trustee for Mary Cobb)	90	
				Sumter	193	
				Worth (trustee for Mary Cobb)	56	
				Leon, Fla. (listed under T. B. Lamar)	47	523
44	Richard Baylor (1803–1862)	Va.	Va.	Charles City	180	
				*Essex	340	520
45	Robert Ruffin Barrow (–1875)	N.C.	La.	Ascension	40	
				Lafourche (Barrow & Pittman)	75	
				*Terrebonne	397	512

	Planter	Birthplace	State of Residence	Subdivision	Subtotal	Total
46	Est. John (1806–1847) & Pierce Mease Butler (1810–1867)	Pa. Pa.	Pa. Pa.	McIntosh, Ga.		505
47	Rice Carter Ballard (1800–1860) & Samuel S. Boyd	Va. Maine	Ky. Miss.	*Jefferson, Ky. (Louisville–Ward 3)	4	502
				Claiborne, Miss. (Ballard & Boyd)	120	
				Carroll, La. (Ballard & Boyd)	110	
				Madison, La. (Ballard & "another")	155	
				Chicot, Ark. (Ballard)	76	
				Warren, Miss. (Bay & Ballard)	37	
48	James Dick Hill (ca. 1831–)	Ky.	La.	Issaquena, Miss.		502
49	Elgee & Chambers			Wilkinson, Miss.		501
50	John A. Miller (ca. 1797–1875)	Ky.	Miss.	Washington		500 +

*Denotes county of residence

**Figure from Charles Heyward Plantation Record Book, South Caroliniana Library

APPENDIX C

ELITE SLAVEHOLDERS BY STATE OF RESIDENCE, 1850

	Slaveholder	Birthplace	County	Major Crop	Subtotal	Total
			ALABAMA (10)			
1	Gaius Whitfield (1804–1879)	N.C.	*Marengo	cotton	350	399
			Lowndes, Miss.		49	
2	Est. Benjamin Sherrod (1786–1847)	N.C.	Lawrence	cotton		394
3	William Robinson (1799–1882)	N.C.	*Lowndes	cotton	188	371
			Marengo		183	
4	Dr. Cullen Battle (1785–1879)	N.C.	*Barbour	cotton	243	353
			Russell		110	
5	James Asbury Tait (ca. 1790–)	Md.	Wilcox	cotton		316
6	Henry Lucas (ca. 1777–)	Va.	Montgomery	cotton		309
7	W. P. Molett (1791–)	S.C.	Dallas	cotton		299
8	James Wright (ca. 1800–)	N.Y.	Russell	cotton		286

	Slaveholder	Birthplace	County	Major Crop	Subtotal	Total
9	Dr. Robert J. Ware (1801–1866)	Ga.	Montgomery	cotton		279
10	Jeremiah H. Brown (1800–1868) Listed under Abraham Bird	S.C.	Sumter	cotton		271
	FLORIDA (1)					
1	William Bailey (1790–1866)	Ga.	Jefferson	cotton		330
	GEORGIA (20)					
1	Est. John Butler (1806–1847) & Pierce Mease Butler (1810–1867)	Pa. Pa.	McIntosh Glynn (listed under Samuel W. Wilson)	rice sea i. cotton	524 319	843
2	James Hamilton Couper (1794–1866)	Ga.	Glynn	rice		765
3	William Brown Hodgson (1800–1871)	D.C.	Burke *Chatham–City of Savannah Jefferson (Hodgson & Telfair)	cotton	135 69 246	450
4	Farish Carter (1780–1861)	S.C.	*Baldwin Murray	cotton	55 355	410
5	Hartwell H. Tarver (–ca. 1853)	Va.	Twiggs	cotton		378
6	Francis M. Scarlett (ca. 1785–)	England	Glynn	rice		368
7	Robert Stafford (1790–1877)	Ga.	Camden Glynn	sea i. cotton	349 5	354

	Slaveholder	Birthplace	County	Major Crop	Subtotal	Total
8	George Michael Troup (1780–1856)	Ga.	*Laurens	cotton	280	345
			Montgomery		65	
9	William Heyward Gibbons (1831–1887)	N.Y.	Chatham	rice		342
10	George Noble Jones (1811–)	Ga.	*Chatham	cotton	118	328
			Jefferson		129	
			Jefferson, Fla.		81	
			Leon, Fla.			
11	John Basil Lamar (1812–1862)	Ga.	*Bibb	cotton	97	300
			Sumter		92	
			Lowndes, Ala.		111	
12	Daniel Heyward Brailsford Troup (ca. 1825–)	Ga.	Glynn	rice		300
13	Thomas Spalding (1774–1851)	Ga.	McIntosh	rice		293
14	George Welshman Owens (1786–1856)	Ga.	Camden	rice	183	292
			*Chatham		109	
15	John Richardson Cheves (1815–)	S.C.	Chatham	rice		291
16	Est. Charles William Rogers (1780–1842)		Bryan	rice		277

	Slaveholder	Birthplace	County	Major Crop	Subtotal	Total
17	Joseph Bond (–1859)	Ga.	Baker	cotton	83	
			*Bibb–City of Macon			
			Lee		190	273
18	Stephen Clay King	Mass.	Camden	rice	116	
			Glynn		107	
			Wayne		40	263
19	Robert Habersham (1783–1870)	Ga.	Chatham	rice		261
20	Est. James Abington Everett (1787–1848)		Houston	cotton		254
			KENTUCKY (1)			
1	Daniel Hillman	N.J.	Caldwell	iron mfg.	98	
			*Trigg		155	253
			LOUISIANA (22)			
1	Meredith Calhoun (ca. 1805–)	S.C.	Natchitoches	cotton	169	
			*Rapides		550	719
2	Mrs. Michel Doradou Bringier (1798–1878)		*Ascension	sugar	599	
			St. James		74	673
3	Henry R. W. Hill (–1853)	N.C.	Jefferson	sugar	155	
			*Orleans			
			Issaquena, Miss.	cotton	417	
			Yazoo, Miss.	cotton (tax rolls)	95	667

	Slaveholder	Birthplace	County	Major Crop	Subtotal	Total
4	Henry Doyal (–1859)	Va.	*Ascension	sugar	390	595
			Plaquemines		205	
5	Pierre M. Lapice (1798–)	St. Domingo	Concordia	sugar	319	573
			*St. James		254	
6	Robert Ruffin Barrow (–1875)	N.C.	Ascension	sugar	60	553
			Assumption (Martin & Barrow)		75	
			Lafourche		54	
			*Terrebonne		364	
7	Samuel F. Davis	Mass.	Concordia	cotton		523
8	Thomas Pugh (1796–1852)	N.C.	*Assumption	sugar	273	367
			Lafourche		94	
9	Laurent Millaudon (ca. 1785–)	France	Jefferson	sugar	272	357
			*Orleans–N.O., Ward 5		3	
			St. Bernard		82	
10	William Ruffin Barrow (1800–1862)	Miss.	West Feliciana	cotton		349
11	Daniel Turnbull (1796–1861)	La.	West Feliciana	cotton		347
12	Mrs. Adelia E. Flint	La.	Rapides	sugar		335
13	James (ca. 1775–1853) & Harry (ca. 1795–1859) Cage	N.C. Tenn.	Terrebonne	sugar		299

	Slaveholder	Birthplace	County	Major Crop	Subtotal	Total
14	John Compton (1779–1855)	Md.	Rapides	sugar		299
15	Martial Sorrel (ca. 1800–)	France	St. Mary	sugar		296
16	Thomas Bibb (ca. 1802–)	Tenn.	Lafourche	sugar		286
17	William Hill Barrow (1808–1870)	N.C.	West Feliciana	cotton		283
18	John Routh (1791–1867)	Miss.	Tensas	cotton		276
19	Widow Edmond Fortier (1784–1849)	La.	Jefferson	sugar	132	271
			*St. Charles		139	
20	Duncan Farrar Kenner (1813–1887)	La.	Ascension	sugar		264
21	Josiah Chambers (1820–1917)	La.	Rapides	cotton & sugar		258
22	Oliver J. Morgan (1784–)	N.H.	Carroll	cotton		253
	MARYLAND (1)					
1	Edward Lloyd VI (1798–1861)	Md.	*Talbot		355	466
			Madison, Miss.	cotton	111	
	MISSISSIPPI (22)					
1	Francis Surget, Sr. (ca. 1783–1856)	La.	*Adams	cotton	596	1,298
			Wilkinson		183	
			Concordia, La.		430	
			Madison, La.		89	

	Slaveholder	Birthplace	County	Major Crop	Subtotal	Total
2	Stephen Duncan (1787–1867)	Pa.	*Adams	cotton	198	
			Issaquena	cotton	470	
			St. Mary, La.	sugar	181	
			Tensas, La.	cotton	92	941
3	Levin R. Marshall (1800–1870)	Va.	*Adams	cotton	218	
			Wilkinson		56	
			Madison, La.		213	
			Jefferson, Ark.		142	629
4	William John Minor (1807–1869)	Miss.	*Adams		319	
			Ascension, La.	sugar	216	
			Terrebonne, La.	sugar		535
5	David Hunt (1779–1861)	N.J.	Iasaquena		52	
			*Jefferson	cotton	374	
			Concordia, La.		81	507
6	Benjamin Roach, Jr. (1820–) Adm. Est. Benjamin Roach, Sr. (–1848)	Ky.	*Adams	cotton	19	
			Warren		130	
			Washington		78	
			Yazoo		261	488
7	John A. Sanderson	Va.	*Adams	cotton	171	
			Concordia, La.		243	414
8	Edward McGehee (1786–1880)	Ga.	*Wilkinson	cotton	333	
			West Feliciana, La.		77	410

	Slaveholder	Birthplace	County	Major Crop	Subtotal	Total
9	James Surget, Sr. (1785–1855)	La.	*Adams	cotton	234	
			Jefferson		36	
			Concordia, La.		136	406
10	Philip Hoggatt (ca. 1795–)	Ky.	Adams	cotton		383
11	John A. Miller (ca. 1797–ca. 1875)	Ky.	Washington	cotton		345
12	William Newton Mercer (1792–1874)	Md.	Adams	cotton		342
13	Richard Thompson Archer (1797–1867)	Va.	*Claiborne	cotton	219	
			Holmes		104	323
14	Nathaniel Hoggatt (–1853)	Ky.	*Adams	cotton	125	
			Madison, La.		197	322
15	William St. John Elliot (ca. 1800–1855)	Md.	*Adams	cotton	19	
			Wilkinson		131	
			Concordia, La.		143	293
16	James Metcalfe		Adams	cotton		290
17	John Anthony Quitman (1799–1858)	N.Y.	*Adams		46	
			Hinds		11	
			Warren	cotton	134	
			Terrebonne, La.	sugar	85	276
18	Henry Johnson (–1865)	Ky.	Washington	cotton		274

	Slaveholder	Birthplace	County	Major Crop	Subtotal	Total
19	Alexander C. Henderson (ca. 1795–)	Miss.	*Adams Concordia, La.	cotton	138 128	266
20	James Railey (ca. 1797–)	Ky.	*Adams Claiborne	cotton	85 181	266
21	Nathaniel Jefferies (1802–)	Tenn.	*Claiborne Jefferson	cotton	108 150	258
22	Alexander King Farrar (1814–1878)	Miss.	Adams	cotton	150	250
			NORTH CAROLINA (11)			
1	Thomas Pollock Devereux (1793–1869)	N.C.	*Halifax Northampton Wake-City of Raleigh	grain & cotton	273 307 3	583
2	James Cathcart Johnston (1782–1865)	N.C.	*Chowan Halifax Pasquotank	grain & cotton	126 272 144	542
3	Lewis Thompson (1808–1867) & Adm. Est. William M. Clark (–1836)	N.C.	*Bertie Rapides, La.	cotton sugar	120 354	474
4	Josiah O. Watson (ca. 1790–)	N.C.	*Johnston Wake-City of Raleigh		408 21	429

	Slaveholder	Birthplace	County	Major Crop	Subtotal	Total
5	Thomas Davis Warren (ca. 1818–)	Va.	Chowan			353
6	Paul Carrington Cameron (1808–1891)	N.C.	*Orange Greene, Ala.	tobacco & wheat cotton	218 128	346
7	Josiah Collins III (1808–1863)	N.C.	Washington	corn		288
8	William Faison	N.C.	Sampson			285
9	John Robert Donnell (1789–1864)	Ireland	*Craven Hyde		64 220+	284+
10	Thomas Amis Dudley Cameron (1806–1870)	N.C.	Orange	tobacco & wheat		283
11	Stephen Davis (ca. 1786–)	N.C.	Warren			275
	SOUTH CAROLINA (62)					
1	Nathaniel Heyward (1766–1851)	S.C.	Beaufort-Prince William Beaufort-St. Helena Colleton-St. Bartholomew *Chastn-St. Philip & St. Michael	rice	286 16 1,487 45	1,834

	Slaveholder	Birthplace	County	Major Crop	Subtotal	Total
2	Joshua John Ward (1800–1853)	S.C.	Georgetown–Lower All Saints	rice		1,092
3	William Aiken (1806–1887)	S.C.	*Chastn–St. Philip & St. Michael		7	
			Colleton–St. John, Jehossee Island	rice	897	904
4	Richard Singleton (1776–1852)	S.C.	Orangeburg	cotton	212	
			Richland		248	
			Richland (listed under son Matthew R.)		281	
			*Sumter		89	830
5	John Smith Preston (1809–1881)	Va.	*Richland	sugar	39	
			Ascension, La.		701	740
6	William Algernon Alston, Sr.	S.C.	Georgetown–Lower All Saints	rice		690
7	Est. Henry Middleton (1770–1846)	England	Beaufort–Prince William	rice		686
8	Joseph Blake (1769–1865)	England	Beaufort–Prince William	rice		610
	Agt. Walter Blake (1804–1871)	England				
9	Ephraim Mikell Baynard (1797–1865)	S.C.	Beaufort–St. Luke	rice	203	
			Colleton–St. Bartholomew		34	
			*Colleton–St. John, Edisto Island		339	576
10	Est. Joseph Cunningham		Kershaw	cotton		495
11	Daniel Blake (1803–1873)	England	Colleton–St. Bartholomew	rice		491
12	Arthur Middleton Blake (1812–1881)	England	Charleston–St. James Santee	rice		484

	Slaveholder	Birthplace	County	Major Crop	Subtotal	Total
13	Wade Hampton II (1791–1858)	S.C.	*Richland	cotton	309	
			Issaquena, Miss.	cotton	166	475
14	William Clarkson (1807–1858)	S.C.	Richland	cotton		450
15	Charles Alston, Sr. (1796–1881)	S.C.	Georgetown–Lower All Saints	rice		441
16	William Cruger Heyward (1808–1863)	S.C.	Colleton–St. Bartholomew	rice		438
17	James Chesnut, Sr. (1773–1866)	S.C.	Kershaw	cotton		430
18	John Laurence Manning (1816–1889)	S.C.	Horry		41	
			*Sumter		27	
			Ascension, La.	sugar	357	425
19	John Nicholas Williams (1797–1861)	S.C.	Darlington	cotton		424
20	Mrs. Harriett Pinckney Rutledge (ca. 1780–1858)	S.C.	*Charleston–St. James Santee	rice	117	
			Georgetown–Prince George Winyah		302	419
21	Mrs. Sarah Taylor (ca. 1775–) Widow John Taylor (1770–1832)	S.C.	Lexington	cotton	205	
			*Richland		212	417
22	Hugh Wilson, Sr. (1786–1864)	S.C.	Colleton–St. John, Wadmalaw Island			408
23	Langdon Cheves, Sr. (1776–1857)	S.C.	Beaufort–St. Peter	rice	284	
			Chatham, Ga.	rice	121	405

	Slaveholder	Birthplace	County	Major Crop	Subtotal	Total
24	Robert Francis Withers Allston (1801–1864)	S.C.	Georgetown-Prince George Winyah	rice		401
25	Richard O. Anderson (–1852)	S.C.	Georgetown-Prince George Winyah	rice		384
26	Thomas Fuller (ca. 1790–)	S.C.	Beaufort-Prince William	rice	130	383
			*Beaufort-St. Helena		253	
27	Simon Verdier (1780–1853)	France	Colleton-St. Bartholomew	rice		375
28	Samuel Porcher (1768–1851)	S.C.	Colleton-St. Stephen	rice		369
29	Richard Richardson Singleton (1840–1900), held in trust by John C. & Richard Singleton	S.C.	Richland	cotton		360
30	Edward Charles Whaley (1826–1887)	S.C.	Colleton-St. John, Edisto Island			356
31	Charles Tidyman Lowndes	S.C.	Colleton-St. Bartholomew	rice		342
32	William Staggers (1780–1862)	S.C.	Williamsburg	cotton		340
33	William Fripp, Sr. (1788–1861)	S.C.	Beaufort-Prince William	provisions &	36	337
			*Beaufort-St. Helena	sea i. cotton	301	
34	Cornelius M. Huguenin	S.C.	*Beaufort-Prince William	rice	269	329
			Beaufort-St. Luke		60	

	Slaveholder	Birthplace	County	Major Crop	Subtotal	Total
35	John Francis Pyatt (1817–1884)	S.C.	Chastn-St. Philip & St. Michael	rice	20	
			Georgetown-Prince George Winyah		309	329
36	John Ashby Colclough (1799–1850)	S.C.	Sumter	cotton		324
37	Arthur Heyward (1805–1852)	S.C.	*Chastn-St. Philip & St. Michael	rice	323	323
			Chatham, Ga.			
38	John Harleston Read (1788–1859)	S.C.	Georgetown-Prince George	rice	323	323
39	Miss Harriott Pinckney (1776–1866)	S.C.	Beaufort-St. Luke	rice &	294	
			*Chastn-St. Philip & St. Michael	sea. i. cotton	20	314
40	William Lucas (1790–1878)	S.C.	Chastn-St. James Santee	rice	238	
			Georgetown-Prince George		72	310
41	Robert Barnwell Rhett, Sr.	S.C.	Colleton-St. Bartholomew	rice		306
	(1800–1876), né Smith					
42	Alexander Ross Taylor (1812–1888)	S.C.	Orangeburg	cotton	156	
			*Richland		150	306
43	Henry Augustus Middleton	S.C.	Georgetown-Prince George	rice		303
	(1793–1887)					
44	William Heyward (1800–1871)	S.C.	*Chastn-St. Philip & St. Michael		13	
			Charleston-St. Thomas & St. Dennis		92	
			*Beaufort-Prince William	rice	194	299

	Slaveholder	Birthplace	County	Major Crop	Subtotal	Total
45	William Elliott (1788–1863)	S.C.	Colleton–St. Paul	rice		296
46	Joseph Benjamin Pyatt (1820–1910)	S.C.	Chastn–St. Philip & St. Michael		5	296
			Georgetown–Prince George Winyah	rice	291	
47	John Raven Matthewes (1788–1867)	S.C.	Colleton–St. Bartholomew	rice		290
48	William Edings (1809–1858)	S.C.	Colleton–St. John, Edisto Island	rice		288
49	John McPherson DeSaussure (1807–1883)	S.C.	Sumter	cotton		285
50	John Myers Felder (1782–1851)	S.C.	Orangeburg	cotton		285
51	William Bull Pringle (1800–1881)	S.C.	Georgetown–Prince George Winyah	rice		281
52	Matthew Richard Singleton (1817–1854)	S.C.	Richland	cotton		281
53	Thomas Pinckney Alston (1795–1861)	S.C.	Georgetown–Lower All Saints	rice		274
54	James U. Adams (1812–)	S.C.	Richland	cotton		271
55	Ralph Stead Izard, Jr. (1815–1858)	S.C.	Georgetown–Prince George Winyah	rice		271
56	George Edwards (1776–1859)	S.C.	Beaufort–St. Luke	rice		264

	Slaveholder	Birthplace	County	Major Crop	Subtotal	Total
57	Christopher Fitzsimons Hampton (1821–1886)	S.C.	*Richland Issaquena, Miss. Washington, Miss.	cotton	51 211	262
58	Solomon Clark (ca. 1796–ca. 1851)	S.C.	Charleston–St. John Berkley	rice		257
59	James Kirk, Sr. (ca. 1781–)	S.C.	Beaufort–St. Luke	rice		257
60	James Henry Hammond (1807–1864)	S.C.	Barnwell	cotton		252
61	George William Cooper (1817–1875)	S.C.	Sumter	cotton		250
62	Edmund Martin (1794–1871)	S.C.	Beaufort–St. Peter	rice		250
	TENNESSEE (4)					
1	Est. Isaac Franklin (1789–1846)		*Davidson West Feliciana, La.	cotton		567
2	Woods, Stocker & Co. (Cumberland Iron Works)—Marimus Stocker	Pa.	Stewart	iron mfg.		444
3	Montgomery Bell (ca. 1769–ca. 1855)	Pa.	Davidson	iron mfg.		322
4	Mark R. Cockrill (1788–)	Ireland	*Davidson Madison, Miss.	livestock cotton	28 227	255
	VIRGINIA (6)					
1	Richard Baylor (1803–1862)	Va.	Essex	grain		480

	Slaveholder	Birthplace	County	Major Crop	Subtotal	Total
2	Philip St. George Cocke (1809–1861)	Va.	Brunswick	grain	96	
			*Powhatan	grain	118	
			Lowndes, Miss.	cotton	196	410
3	Williams Carter (1782–1864)	Va.	*Caroline	grain	206	
			Hanover		133	339
4	William Henry Tayloe (1799–1871)	Va.	*Richmond	grain	166	
			Prince William		22	
			Marengo, Ala.	cotton	133	321
5	Samuel Hairston (1784–1880)	Va.	Patrick	corn, tobacco & cotton	50	
			*Pittsylvania		246	296
6	Ruth Stovall Hairston (1784–1869)	Va.	*Pittsylvania	corn, tobacco & cotton		
			Stokes, N.C.		278	

*Denotes county of residence

Total slaveholders with 250+ in 1850 were 160, of whom 62 (39 percent) were domiciled in South Carolina.

APPENDIX D

ELITE SLAVEHOLDERS BY STATE OF RESIDENCE, 1860

	Slaveholder	Birthplace	County	Major Crop	Subtotal	Total
			ALABAMA (25)			
**1	Jeremiah H. Brown (1800–1868)	S.C.	Sumter	cotton		539
**2	Gaius Whitfield (1804–1879)	N.C.	*Marengo	cotton	383	466
			Lowndes, Miss.		83	
**3	James Wright (ca. 1800–)	N.Y.	Russell	cotton		390
4	Francis Merriwether Gilmer, Jr. (1810–1892)	Ga.	Lowndes	cotton	232	366
			*Montgomery		134	
5	John Collins (1798–1867)	Va.	Marengo	cotton		361
6	John W. Walton (1817–)	N.C.	Greene	cotton		360
**7	W. P. Molett (1791–)	S.C.	Dallas	cotton		351
**8	Robert J. Ware (1801–1866)	Ga.	Montgomery	cotton		346
9	John Peters (ca. 1802–)	Va.	Lauderdale	cotton		313

	Slaveholder	Birthplace	County	Major Crop	Subtotal	Total
10	Dr. Anderson? Saltmarsh (ca. 1794–)	N.Y.	Dallas	cotton		300
11	Alfred Hatch (ca. 1800–)	N.C.	*Marengo Perry	cotton	174 123	297
12	Est. Thomas Hord Herndon (1793–1842)	Va.	*Greene Sumter	cotton	159 131	290
13	Est. James G. Spann	S.C.	Lowndes	cotton		290
14	John Starke Hunter (ca. 1796–1866)	S.C.	Dallas	cotton		285
15	Leroy M. Wiley [S.C. absentee]		Barbour Macon, Ga.	cotton	190 95	285
16	Joel Early Mathews (1809–1874)	Ga.	Dallas	cotton		284
17	John Steele (1796–1863)	Va.	*Autauga Wilcox	cotton	130 153	283
**18	Est. Henry Lucas (ca. 1777–)	Va.	Montgomery	cotton		275
19	Garland Goode (1811–1887)	S.C.	*Mobile Jackson, Miss.	cotton mill	196 78	274
20	Nathan Bryan Whitfield (1799–1868)	N.C.	*Marengo Lenoir, N.C.	cotton	249 23	272

	Slaveholder	Birthplace	County	Major Crop	Subtotal	Total
21	George W. Mathews (1807–1880)	Ga.	Montgomery	cotton		266
22	Gideon E. Nelson (1824–)	Ala.	*Greene	cotton	145	264
			Marengo		119	
23	Virginia Mathews (1824–)	Ala.	*Dallas	cotton	76	255
			Wilcox		179	
24	Duncan Dew, Sr. (ca. 1797–1864)	N.C.	Greene	cotton		253
25	James Walter Echols (ca. 1815–1869)	Ga.	Macon	cotton		250
	ARKANSAS (2)					
1	Elisha Worthington	Ky.	Chicot	cotton		529
2	John A. Jordan		Arkansas	cotton		298
	FLORIDA (3)					
1	Robert W. Williams (ca. 1809–)	Tenn.	*Leon	cotton	48	477
			Carroll, La.		429	
2	Frederick R. Cotten (1820–)	N.C.	Leon	cotton		337
**3	William Bailey (1790–1866)	Ga.	*Jefferson	cotton	185	260
			Leon		75	
	GEORGIA (26)					
**1	William Brown Hodgson (1800–1871)	D.C.	Burke	cotton	240	596
			*Chatham–Savannah		72	
			Jefferson		284	

	Slaveholder	Birthplace	County	Major Crop	Subtotal	Total
2	Leonidas A. Jordan		Baldwin	cotton	62	
			Dougherty		185	
			Lee		346	593
**3	John Basil Lamar (1812–1862)		Baldwin (trustee for Howell Cobb)		137	
			*Bibb (to as trustee for Mary Cobb)	cotton	90	
			Sumter		193	
			Worth (trustee for Mary Cobb)		56	
			Leon, Fl. (listed under T. B. Lamar)		47	523
**4	Est. John Butler (1806–1847) & Pierce Mease Butler (1810–1867)	Pa. Pa.	McIntosh	rice		505
5	James Potter (1793–1862), exctr. Est. Thomas F. Potter	S.C.	Chatham	rice		440
**6	Est. James Abington Everett (1787–1848)		Crawford	cotton	83	
			*Houston		343	426
7	Turner C. Clanton (1798–1864)	Va.	Columbia	cotton	213	
			Dougherty		79	
			Richmond		88	
			*Richmond-city of Augusta, Ward 4		24	404
**8	Farish Carter (1780–1861)	S.C.	*Baldwin	cotton	42	
			Murray		345	387

	Slaveholder	Birthplace	County	Major Crop	Subtotal	Total
**9	William Heyward Gibbons (1831–1887)	N.Y.	Chatham	rice	320	371
			*Chatham–city of Savannah, Dist. 1		51	
10	Mrs. Elizabeth Luke Lamkin (ca. 1807–)	Ga.	Columbia	cotton		362
11	P. L. Wade	Ga.	Screven	cotton	266	328
			Whitfield		62	
**12	Est. George Welshman Owens (1786–1856)	Ga.	Camden	rice	256	327
			Chatham		71	
**13	George Noble Jones (1811–)	Ga.	*Chatham–city of Savannah	cotton		318
			Jefferson		124	
			Jefferson, Fla.		130	
			Leon, Fla.		64	
**14	Stephen Clay King	Mass.	Camden	rice		309
15	George Washington Walthour (1799–1859)	Ga.	Liberty	rice & sea i. cotton		300
16	Archibald McDuffy	S.C.	Chatham	rice		291
**17	Est. Hartwell H. Tarver (–ca. 1853), Extr. William H. Tarver	Va.	Twiggs	cotton		290

	Slaveholder	Birthplace	County	Major Crop	Subtotal	Total
18	Nathaniel F. Walker (1787–1879)	Ga.	Taylor	cotton	96	290
			*Upson		194	
19	Lodowick Meriwether Hill (ca. 1804–)	Ga.	Oglethorpe	cotton	46	286
			*Wilkes		240	
20	Augustus Seaborn Jones (1795–1869)	Ga.	*Chatham–Savannah, Dist. 4	rice	97	285
			Screven		168	
			Whitfield		20	
21	Jacob Waldburg	Ga.	*Chatham–Savannah, Dist. 2		26	281
			Liberty	sea i. cotton	255	
22	George W. Persons (1804–)	Ga.	Crawford	cotton	127	275
			*Houston		148	
23	Howell Cobb (1815–1868)	Ga.	Baldwin (see also J. B. Lamar)		137	271
			*Clarke–town of Athens		9	
			Houston	cotton	30	
			Sumter		95	
24	Joseph Longworth McAllister (1820–1864)	Ga.	Bryan	rice		271
**25	Robert Habersham (1783–1870)	Ga.	Chatham	rice	213	271
			*Chatham–Savannah, Dist. 2		55	
26	Randolph Spalding (1822–1862)	Ga.	McIntosh	rice		252

	Slaveholder	Birthplace	County	Major Crop	Subtotal	Total
			KENTUCKY (2)			
1	Rice Carter Ballard (1800–1860) & Samuel S. Boyd	Va. Maine	*Jefferson-Louisville, Ward 3	cotton	4	
			Chicot, Ark. (Ballard)		76	
			Carroll, La. (Ballard & Boyd)		110	
			Madison, La. (Ballard & "another")		155	
			Claiborne, Miss. (Ballard & Boyd)		120	
			Warren, Miss. (Bay & Ballard)		37	502
**2	Daniel Hillman	N.J.	Lyon (Hillman Bros.)	iron mfg.	121	
			*Trigg		255	376
			LOUISIANA (49)			
1	John Burnside (ca. 1810–1881)	N. Ireland	*Ascension	sugar	753	
			St. James		186	939
2	Zebulon York (1819–1900) & E. J. Hoover (ca. 1828–)	Maine La.	Concordia (York & Hoover)	cotton	479	
			Concordia (E. J. Hoover)		236	
			Concordia (Z. York)		67	782
**3	Meredith Calhoun (ca. 1805–)	S.C.	Rapides	cotton & sugar		709
**4	Est. Henry Doyal (–1859) & Henry R. Doyal (ca. 1840–)	Va. La.	*Ascension (Henry R.)	sugar	271	
			Plaquemines (Est.)		349	620
**5	Mrs. Michel Doradou Bringier (1798–1878), Marius Ste. Colomb Bringier (1814–1884), Louis Amedee Bringier (1828–1897)	La.	*Ascension (M. S. & L. A.)	sugar	530	
			St. James		26	
			New Orleans–Ward 1 (Mrs. M. D.)		11	567

	Slaveholder	Birthplace	County	Major Crop	Subtotal	Total
**6	Robert Ruffin Barrow (-1875)	N.C.	Ascension	sugar	40	
			Lafourche (Barrow & Pittman)		75	
			*Terrebonne		397	512
7	James Dick Hill (ca. 1831-)	Ky.	*Orleans			502
			Issaquena, Miss.	cotton		
**8	Oliver J. Morgan (1784-)	N.H.	Carroll	cotton		476
**9	Duncan Farrar Kenner (1813-1887)	La.	Ascension	sugar		473
10	William Johnson Fort (ca. 1819-ca. 1861)	La.	West Feliciana	cotton		461
11	Est. Juan Ygnacia de Egana (-1859)	Spain	Jefferson	sugar	144	
			*Lafourche		306	450
12	Duncan Stewart Cage (1825-)	Miss.	Terrebonne	sugar		445
**13	Daniel Turnbull (1796-1861)	La.	West Feliciana	cotton		444
14	H. Clement Millaudon (ca. 1825-)	La.	Jefferson	sugar		440
15	Alfred A. Williams (1820-)	N.Y.	East Baton Rouge	cotton	102	
			*West Baton Rouge		213	
			Terrebonne	sugar	124	439
16	Oliver T. Morgan (ca. 1828-)	La.	Carroll	cotton		430
**17	Adelia E. (Mrs. John) Casson (Adelia E. Flint in 1850)	La.	Rapides	sugar		417

	Slaveholder	Birthplace	County	Major Crop	Subtotal	Total
18	Mary (Mrs. James) Porter		St. Mary	sugar		397
19	Edward Sparrow (1810–1882)	Ireland	*Carroll Concordia	cotton	277 115	392
**20	Est. John Compton (1779–1855)	Md.	Rapides	sugar		377
21	Mary C. Stirling (1812–) (widow of Ruffin G. Stirling)	La.	*West Feliciana Pointe Coupée	cotton sugar	127 246	373
22	Martial Sorrel (ca. 1800–) Paul Corwin, Agt.	France	St. Mary	sugar		362
23	John Perkins, Jr. (1819–1885)	Miss.	Madison	cotton		340
24	Pierre Adolphe Rost (1797–1868)	France	New Orleans–Ward 8 *St. Charles	sugar	5 332	337
**25	Josiah Chambers (1820–1917)	La.	Rapides	cotton & sugar		335
26	Henry Boyce (1797–1873)	Ireland	Rapides	cotton		332
27	W. H. Pugh & Co. (heirs of Col. Augustin Pugh, 1783–1853)	N.C.	Assumption	sugar		329
28	John Julius Pringle (1834–1901)	S.C.	Pointe Coupée	sugar		324
29	William Taylor Palfrey, Sr. (1800–1868)	Mass.	St. Mary	sugar		320
30	Trasimond Landry (1795–1873)	La.	Ascension	sugar		316

	Slaveholder	Birthplace	County	Major Crop	Subtotal	Total
**31	Eliza Foley Pugh (ca. 1807–), Widow of Thomas Pugh (1796–1852)	La. N.C.	Assumption	sugar		312
32	Ebenezer Eaton Kittredge (1799–1867)	N.H.	*Assumption Lafourche	sugar	219 89	308
33	Charles Kock (ca. 1814–)	Germany	Ascension *Assumption New Orleans–Ward 3	sugar	124 176 6	306
**34	John Routh (1791–1867)	Miss.	Tensas	cotton		300
35	William B. Whitehead		St. Charles St. John the Baptist	sugar	119 169	288
36	David Barrow (1805–1874)	N.C.	*West Feliciana Pointe Coupée	cotton	103 184	287
37	Henry Marshall (1805–1864)	S.C.	Bossier *De Soto	cotton	86 201	287
38	Edward James Gay (1816–1889) (Est. Andrew Hynes)	Va.	Iberville	sugar		279
39	Madam Emily Woolfolk (1816–) Widow of Austin Woolfolk (–1856)	Md.	Iberville	sugar		274
40	James M. Gillespie (ca. 1833–)	Miss.	Tensas	cotton		269

	Slaveholder	Birthplace	County	Major Crop	Subtotal	Total
41	Bradish Johnson		Jefferson (Johnson & Gossett)		60	
			*Plaquemines	sugar	214	
			Plaquemines (Johnson & Lawrence)		40	314
42	Aron Goza (1805–)		Carroll	cotton		260
43	Elvira N. Stewart (ca. 1802–), Widow of Noland Stewart (ca. 1797–before 1858)	N.C.	West Baton Rouge	sugar		259
44	Gustave Sabatier		Lafourche	sugar		256
45	Charles Duncan Stewart (ca. 1813–1886)	Miss.	Pointe Coupée	sugar		255
46	J. M. Bateman (ca. 1797–)	N.Y.	St. Mary	sugar		254
47	Est. William M. Lambeth, Extr. William L. Pitts (ca. 1820–)	Ireland	Avoyelles	sugar		251
48	Joel (or E. P.?) Tatum (ca. 1826–ca. 1861) & John T. Simmons (1825–1867)	Ala. Ala.	Caldwell	cotton		251
49	Frederick Daniel Conrad (ca. 1800–)	Va.	East Baton Rouge	sugar		250
**1	Edward Lloyd VI (1798–1861)	Md.	MARYLAND (1)			
			*Talbot		412	
			Madison, Miss.	cotton	92[1]	
			Tensas, La.	cotton	154	658

MISSISSIPPI (59)

Slaveholder	Birthplace	County	Major Crop	Subtotal	Total
**1 Levin R. Marshall (1800-1871)	Va.	*Adams	cotton	188	
		Claiborne		96	
		Wilkinson		164	
		Concordia, La.	cotton	248	
		Jefferson, La.	sugar	91	
		Madison, La.	cotton	271	1,058
**2 Stephen Duncan (1787-1867)	Pa.	*Adams	cotton	11	
		Issaquena		706	
		Tensas, La. (listed under son Saml. P.)		173	890
3 John Hendricks Horne (1795-1864)	N.C.	Wayne			751
4 Gerard Brandon (1818-1874)	Miss.	*Adams	cotton	512	
		Concordia, La.		113	
		Tensas, La.		81	706
5 Alfred Vidal Davis (ca. 1827-)	La.	*Adams		14	
		Concordia, La.	cotton	637	651
6 Est. Frederick Stanton (1798-1859)	N. Ireland	*Adams	cotton	180	
		Concordia, La.	cotton	458	638
**7 William John Minor (1807-1869)	Miss.	*Adams		42	
		Ascension, La.	sugar	223	
		Terrebonne, La.	sugar	357	622

	Slaveholder	Birthplace	County	Major Crop	Subtotal	Total
**8	David Hunt (1779–1861)	N.J.	Issaquena	cotton	82	
			*Jefferson		386	
			Concordia, La.		99	567
9	Samuel Manuel Davis (ca. 1827–1878)	Miss.	*Adams	cotton	15	
			Issaquena		159	
			Concordia, La.		386	560
**10	Benjamin Roach, Jr. (1820–) Adm. Est. Benjamin Roach, Sr. (–1848)	Ky.	*Adams		10	
			Warren	cotton	176	
			Washington		100+	
			Yazoo		266	552 +[2]
11	John Robinson, IV (1822–1879)	Miss.	Madison	cotton		550
**12	Edward McGehee (1786–1880)	Ga.	*Wilkinson	cotton	471	
			West Feliciana, La.		74	545
13	Elgee & Chambers (formerly David Dunham Withers)		Wilkinson	cotton		501
**14	John A. Miller (ca. 1797–1875)	Ky.	Washington	cotton		500+
**15	Richard Thompson Archer (1797–1867)	Va.	*Claiborne	cotton	221	
			Holmes		227[3]	
			Amelia, Va.		25[4]	473

	Slaveholder	Birthplace	County	Major Crop	Subtotal	Total
16	John D. McLemore (ca. 1813–)	Tenn.	*Carroll Tallahatchie	cotton	436 26	462
17	Francis Surget, Jr. (1813–1866)	Miss.	*Adams Wilkinson Concordia, La. Madison, La.	cotton	22 125 145 164	456
**18	William Newton Mercer (1792–1874)	Md.	Adams	cotton		452
**19	Anna F. Elliot (ca. 1805–), Widow of Wm St. John Elliot (ca. 1800–1855)	Miss. Md.	*Adams Concordia, La. Tensas, La.	cotton	12 297 140	449
20	Gabriel Benoist Shields	Miss.	*Adams Concordia, La.	cotton	91 353	444
21	Est. John Carmichael Jenkins (1810–1855), Adm. Josiah Winchester (1817–1887)	Pa. Mass.	Wilkinson	cotton		424
22	George Wilson Humphreys (1819–1907)	Miss.	Bolivar (G. W. & John C.) *Claiborne Lafayette Madison, La.	cotton	25 285 13 85	408
**23	James Railey (ca. 1797–)	Ky.	*Adams Carroll, La.	cotton	78 324	402

	Slaveholder	Birthplace	County	Major Crop	Subtotal	Total
24	Est. Robert James Turnbull (1804–1854)—N.Y. absentee	S.C.	Issaquena	cotton		401
25	James Surget, Jr. (1836–1920)	Miss.	*Adams / Concordia, La.	cotton	13 / 349	362
26	John Murdock (ca. 1814–1860)	Miss.	*Claiborne / Tensas, La.	cotton	166 / 195	361
27	John Newton Helm (1798–1861?)	Va.	*Adams / Tensas, La.	cotton	170 / 189	359
28	Joseph Emory Davis (1784–1870)	Ga.	Warren	cotton		355
**29	Alexander C. Henderson (ca. 1795–)	Miss.	*Adams / Concordia, La.	cotton	77 / 280	337
30	Andrew M. Payne (ca. 1806–)	Ky.	*Carroll / Yazoo / St. Landry, La. (G. U. & A. M. Payne)	cotton	123 / 115 / 193	335
**31	Alexander King Farrar (1814–1878)	Miss.	*Adams / Wilkinson / Catahoula, La.	cotton	204 / 34 / 84	322
**32	James Metcalfe		Adams	cotton	150	315
33	Smith Coffee Daniell II	Miss.	*Claiborne / Tensas, La.	cotton	164	314

	Slaveholder	Birthplace	County	Major Crop	Subtotal	Total
34	Evan Shelby Jefferies (ca. 1813–)	Tenn.	*Claiborne	cotton	203	314
			Jefferson		111	
35	Est. William L. Balfour (–1857)	N.C.	Bolivar	cotton	61	311
			*Madison		77	
			Yazoo		70	
			Carroll, La.		103	
36	Adam Lewis Bingaman (1793–1869)	Miss.	Adams	cotton		310
**37	Est. John Anthony Quitman (1799–1858) & Henry Turner (1810–)	N.Y. Miss.	Warren	cotton		308
38	Tobias Gibson (ca. 1801–)	Miss.	*Adams	cotton	18	297
			Concordia, La.		75	
			Terrebonne, La.	sugar	204	
39	Ayres Phillips Merrill II	Miss.	*Adams	cotton	92	294
			Concordia, La.		202	
40	Henry Vaughan, Sr. (1800–1870)	S.C.	Yazoo	cotton		293
41	Benjamin Sherrod Ricks (1802–)	N.C.	*Madison	cotton	151	290
			Yazoo		139	
42	Francis N. Hooke (1816–1865)	Miss.	Wilkinson	cotton		285
43	John Taylor Moore (ca. 1819–)	Miss.	Claiborne	cotton		283

	Slaveholder	Birthplace	County	Major Crop	Subtotal	Total
44	Lemuel Parker Conner (1827–1891)	Miss.	*Adams		26	282
			Concordia, La.	cotton	256	
45	Levi L. Babers (ca. 1826–)	S.C.	Wilkinson	cotton		280
46	Edwin R. Bennett (1811–1876)	Del.	*Adams	cotton	177	277
			Madison, La.		100	
47	Henry E. Chotard (1787–1870)	St. Domingo	*Adams		35	275
			Issaquena		86	
			Concordia, La.	cotton	154	
48	Samuel H. Lambdin (1811–)	Pa.	*Adams (listed under James H.)		120	275
			Concordia, La.	cotton	155	
49	William Gustine Conner (1826–1863)	Miss.	*Adams		271	271
			Concordia, La.	cotton		
50	Greenwood Leflore (1800–1865)	Miss.	Carroll	cotton	271	267
51	John P. Walworth (1799–1883)	N.Y.	*Adams		13	263
			Chicot, Ark.		158	
			Carroll, La.	cotton	92	
52	Haller Nutt (1816–1864)	La.	*Adams		261	261
			Tensas, La.	cotton		
53	James Alexander Ventress (1805–1867)	Tenn.	Wilkinson	cotton		261[5]

	Slaveholder	Birthplace	County	Major Crop	Subtotal	Total
54	Stephen Arne Decatur Greaves (1817–1880)	S.C.	Madison	cotton		260
55	John C. Patrick		Wilkinson	cotton		260
56	Eustace Surget (ca. 1830–)	Miss.	*Adams	cotton	143	258
			Concordia, La.		115	
57	Joseph W. Sessions (ca. 1817–)	Miss.	*Adams	cotton	62	257
			Concordia		195	
58	Thomas Garton Blewett, Sr. (1789–1871)		*Lowndes	cotton	78	255
			Noxubee		177	
59	John S. Chambliss (ca. 1797–)	S.C.	*Jefferson	cotton	107	251
			Carroll, La.		144	
	NORTH CAROLINA (12)					
**1	Paul Carrington Cameron (1808–1891)	N.C.	*Orange	tobacco & wheat	358	671
			Person		114	
			Greene, Ala.	cotton	116	
			Tunica, Miss.	cotton	83	
**2	James Cathcart Johnston (1782–1865)	N.C.	*Chowan	grain & cotton	103	555
			Halifax		271	
			Pasquotank		181	
**3	Thomas Davis Warren (ca. 1818–)	Va.	Chowan			475

	Slaveholder	Birthplace	County	Major Crop	Subtotal	Total
4	Peter Wilson Hairston (1819–1886)	Va.	Davidson	tobacco & grain	74	
			*Davie		193	
			Stokes		50	
			Henry, Va.		120	437
5	Isaac Wright (1780–1865)	N.C.	*Bladen		306	
			Duplin		13	
			Sampson		39	358
**6	Lewis Thompson (1808–1867)	N.C.	*Bertie	cotton	153	
			Rapides, La.	sugar	198	351
**7	Josiah Collins III (1808–1863)	N.C.	Washington	corn		328
**8	John Robert Donnell (1789–1864)	Ireland	*Craven		13	
			Hyde		292	305
9	George W. Mordecai (1801–1871) & Margaret Cameron Mordecai (1811–1886) (Wake slaves listed under overseer Willie Perry)	N.C.	*Wake–city of Raleigh	tobacco & wheat	15	
			Wake		277	292
10	Richard Henry Smith (1810–1893)	N.C.	Halifax	cotton		280
11	William Boylan (1777–1861)	N.J.	Johnston		61	
			*Wake–city of Raleigh		25	
			Yazoo, Miss.	cotton	193	279
12	Cullen Capehart (ca. 1789–)	N.C.	Bertie	cotton		258

Slaveholder	Birthplace	County	Major Crop	Subtotal	Total
		SOUTH CAROLINA (75)			
**1 Est. Joshua John Ward (1800–1853)	S.C.	Charleston-Ward 5		15	
		*Georgetown-Lower All Saints	rice	1,131	1,146
2 John Izard Middleton (1800–1877)	S.C.	Beaufort-Prince William	rice	520	
		*Georgetown-Lower All Saints		211	
		Georgetown-Prince George		107	838
**3 William Aiken (1806–1887)	S.C.	*Charleston-Ward 5		19	
		Colleton-St. John, Jehossee Island	rice	700	719
4 William Henry Heyward (1817–1889)	S.C.	Beaufort-Prince William	rice	386	
		Beaufort-St. Peter		136	
		*Charleston-Ward 2		16	
		Colleton-St. Bartholomew		133	671
**5 Est. Arthur Heyward (1805–1852) & Maria Louisa Blake Heyward (1816–1854)	S.C. S.C.	Colleton-St. Bartholomew	rice	304	
		Chatham, Ga.		352	656
**6 Joseph Blake (1769–1865) Agt. Walter Blake (1804–1871)	England England	Beaufort-Prince William	rice	545	
		Beaufort-St. Peter (Walter)	rice	74	
		Henderson, N.C. (Walter)		36	655
**7 John Laurence Manning (1816–1889)	S.C.	*Clarendon		27	
		Ascension, La.	sugar	616	643
**8 Robert Francis Withers Allston (1801–1864)	S.C.	Georgetown-Prince George	rice		631

	Slaveholder	Birthplace	County	Major Crop	Subtotal	Total
**9	Ephraim Mikell Baynard (1797–1865)	S.C.	Beaufort–St. Luke	rice	197	
			Colleton–St. Bartholomew		32	
			*Colleton–St. John, Edisto Island		370	
			Colleton–St. Paul		26	625
**10	Daniel Blake (1803–1873)	England	*Colleton–St. Bartholomew	rice	527	
			Henderson, N.C.		59	586
**11	Est. John Ashby Colclough (1799–1850) & Eliza Maria Cantey Colclough (1813–1886)	S.C. S.C.	Clarendon (Est. John A.)	cotton	102	
			*Sumter		468	570
12	William Algernon Alston, Sr. (1782–1860)	S.C.	Georgetown–Lower All Saints	rice		567
13	Charles Heyward (1802–1866)	S.C.	*Charleston–Ward 3		10	
			Colleton–St. Bartholomew	rice	532[6]	542
**14	Arthur Middleton Blake (1812–1881)	England	Charleston–St. James Santee	rice		538
15	John Harleston Read II (1815–1866)	S.C.	Charleston–Ward 4		20	
			*Georgetown–Prince George	rice	511	531
16	Wade Hampton III (1818–1892)	S.C.	*Richland	cotton	30	
			Issaquena, Miss.		249	
			Washington, Miss.		ca. 210[2]	ca. 489
17	Theodore Louis Gourdin (1790–1866)	S.C.	Charleston–St. John Berkeley	rice	100	
			*Charleston–St. Stephen		229	
			Williamsburg		135	464

	Slaveholder	Birthplace	County	Major Crop	Subtotal	Total
**18	James Chesnut, Sr. (1773–1866)	S.C.	Kershaw	cotton		448
**19	William Fripp, Sr. (1788–1861)	S.C.	*Beaufort-St. Helena Beaufort-St. Luke	provisions & sea i. cotton	326 116	442
**20	Charles Alston, Sr. (1796–1861)	S.C.	*Charleston-Ward 1 Georgetown-Lower All Saints Georgetown-Prince George	rice rice	18 209 199	426
**21	Christopher Fitzsimons Hampton (1821–1886)	S.C.	*Richland Issaquena, Miss. Washington, Miss.	cotton	61 88 ca. 260[2]	ca. 409
22	Daniel Heyward (1810–1888)	S.C.	*Beaufort-Prince William Beaufort-St. Peter Charleston-Ward 1	rice	130 244 15	389
**23	Catherine B. Verdier (1799–) Widow of Simon Verdier (1780–1853)	S.C. France	Charleston-St. Andrew *Colleton-St. Bartholomew	rice	65 321	386
**24	George William Cooper (1817–1875)	S.C.	Sumter	cotton		374
25	Benjamin Robert Bostick (1791–1866)	S.C.	Beaufort-St. Peter	rice		371
**26	Charles Tidyman Lowndes (1808–1884)	S.C.	Colleton-St. Bartholomew	rice		370
**27	Thomas Fuller (ca. 1790–)	S.C.	Beaufort-Prince William *Beaufort-St. Helena	rice	143 220	363

	Slaveholder	Birthplace	County	Major Crop	Subtotal	Total
28	James Sinkler Moore (1831–)	S.C.	*Sumter Yazoo, MS	cotton	210 153	363
**29	John Francis Pyatt (1817–1884)	S.C.	Charleston-Ward 5 *Georgetown-Prince George	rice	5 357	362
30	Est. Nicholas Adamson Peay (1811–1857)	S.C.	Fairfield	cotton		361
**31	John Nicholas Williams (1797–1861)	S.C.	Darlington	cotton		357
**32	Miss Harriott Pinckney (1776–1866)	S.C.	Beaufort-St. Luke *Charleston-Ward 3	rice & sea i. cotton	342 12	354
**33	Est. Ralph Stead Izard, Jr. (1815–1858)	S.C.	Georgetown-Prince George	rice		353
**34	Joseph Benjamin Pyatt (1820–1910)	S.C.	Georgetown-Prince George	rice		352
35	Est. John Hyrne Tucker (1780–1859)	S.C.	Georgetown-Prince George	rice		347
36	Stephen Duvall Doar (1805–1872)	S.C.	*Charleston-St. James Santee Georgetown-Prince George	rice rice	236 109	345
37	James Barnwell Heyward (1817–1886)	S.C.	*Charleston-Ward 2 Colleton-St. Bartholomew	rice	339	339
**38	James Henry Hammond (1807–1864)	S.C.	Barnwell *Edgefield	cotton	294 44	338
39	Est. John Coles Singleton (1813–1852)	S.C.	Richland	cotton		338

	Slaveholder	Birthplace	County	Major Crop	Subtotal	Total
40	Plowden, Charles Jennet Weston (-1864)	S.C.	Georgetown-Lower All Saints	rice		334
41	Francis Weston (1811–1890)	S.C.	Georgetown-Prince George	rice		332
42	Alan Macfarlan (1819–1869)	Scotland	*Chesterfield Marlborough	cotton	238 90	328
43	Daniel W. Jordan (1810–1883)	N.C.	*Georgetown-Lower All Saints Horry	rice	261 58	319
**44	William Bull Pringle (1800–1881)	S.C.	*Charleston-Ward 2 Charleston-St. Andrews Georgetown-Prince George	rice	32 58 226	316
45	Henry Buck (1800–1870)	Maine	Horry-Kingston	rice		312
**46	James U. Adams (1812–)	S.C.	Richland	cotton		309
**47	Edmund Martin (1794–1871)	S.C.	Beaufort-St. Peter	rice		305
48	James Legare (1805–1883)	S.C.	*Charleston-Ward 2 Colleton-St. Paul	rice & sea i. cotton	304	304
49	Joseph Alston Huger	S.C.	Beaufort-St. Peter	rice		303
50	Thomas William Porcher (1808–)	S.C.	Charleston-St. John Berkeley	rice		302
**51	John McPherson DeSaussure (1807–1883)	S.C.	Sumter	cotton		301

	Slaveholder	Birthplace	County	Major Crop	Subtotal	Total
**52	Hugh Wilson, Sr. (1786–1864)	S.C.	Colleton–St. John, Wadmalaw Island			300
**53	William Lucas (1790–1878)	S.C.	*Charleston–Ward 6		13	
			Charleston–St. James Santee	rice	201	
			Georgetown–Prince George		84	298
54	Langdon Cheves, Jr. (1814–1863)	Pa.	Beaufort–St. Peter	rice		289
55	Francis Wilkinson Pickens (1807–1869)	S.C.	Edgefield	cotton		275
56	Mary Goodwyn (Hopkins) Adams (1789–1867), widow of Joel Adams, Sr. (1784–1859)	S.C.	Richland	cotton		273
57	Alexius Mador Forster (1815–1879)	S.C.	Georgetown–Prince George	rice		273
58	John (Ferrars) Townsend (1799–1881)	S.C.	Colleton–St. John, Edisto Island	sea i. cotton		272
59	John J. Ragin (ca. 1818–)	S.C.	Clarendon	cotton		271
60	Andrew Turnbull (1801–1870)	S.C.	*Charleston–Ward 6 Issaquena, Miss.	cotton	271	271
**61	John Raven Matthewes (1788–1867)	S.C.	*Charleston–Ward 1 Colleton–St. Bartholomew		270	270
**62	Henry Augustus Middleton (1793–1887)	S.C.	Georgetown–Prince George	rice		270

	Slaveholder	Birthplace	County	Major Crop	Subtotal	Total
63	Martha Hayes Allston Pyatt (1789–1869)	S.C.	*Charleston–Ward 5		16	
			Georgetown–Lower All Saints	rice	213	
			*Georgetown–Prince George		41	270
64	John Doby Kennedy (1840–1896)	S.C.	Kershaw	cotton		267
65	William Heyward Trapier (1805–1872)	S.C.	Georgetown–Lower All Saints	rice	87	
			*Georgetown–Prince George		179	266
66	Isaac Jenkins Mikell (1808–1881)	S.C.	Colleton–St. John, Edisto Island	sea i. cotton		265
67	Allen Smith Izard (1810–1879) (né Joseph Allen Smith)	Pa.	Beaufort–St. Peter	rice		263
68	Mrs. Mary (Pyne) March (–1861)	S.C.	Colleton–St. Bartholomew	rice		260
69	Oliver Hering Middleton (1798–1892)	S.C.	Colleton–St. Bartholomew	rice	122	
			*Colleton–St. John, Edisto Island	sea i. cotton	138	260
70	David Aiken (1786–1860)	Ireland	Fairfield	cotton		257
71	Joseph Glover (1830–1895)	N.J.	Beaufort–St. Luke	rice		257
72	James Hopkinson (ca. 1811–)	N.J.	Colleton–St. John, Edisto Island	sea i. cotton		257
**73	William Elliott (1788–1863)	S.C.	Beaufort–St. Helena	rice	103	
			Colleton–St. Bartholomew		39	
			*Colleton–St. Paul		114	256

	Slaveholder	Birthplace	County	Major Crop	Subtotal	Total
74	William Ellison Hall (1801–1864)	S.C.	*Fairfield	cotton	191	
			Echols, Ga.		48	
			Stewart, Ga. (listed under son John T.)		17	256
75	Thomas Aston Coffin (1795–1863)	S.C.	Beaufort-St. Helena	sea i. cotton		253[7]
	TENNESSEE (6)					
1	Joseph Alexander Smith Acklen (1816–1863)	Ala.	*Davidson		32	
			West Feliciana, La.	cotton	659	691
**2	Woods, Lewis & Co. (Cumberland Iron Works)		Stewart	iron mfg.		418
3	Gideon Johnson Pillow (1806–1878)	Tenn.	*Maury		81	
			Phillips, Ark.	cotton	221	302
4	Andrew Jackson Polk (1824–1867)	N.C.	*Maury	corn & livestock	96	
			Tunica, Miss.	cotton	200	296
5	James Hazard Wilson II (1800–1869)	Tenn.	*Williamson		55	
			Carroll, La.		169	
			Madison, La.	cotton	70	294
6	George Augustine Washington (1815–1892)	Tenn.	Robertson	tobacco & grain		274

Slaveholder	Birthplace	County	Major Crop	Subtotal	Total
TEXAS (2)					
1 David G. Mills (ca. 1820–)	Ky.	Brazoria	cotton & sugar		344
2 Abner Jackson (1810–)	Va.	Brazoria	sugar		286
VIRGINIA (10)					
**1 Ruth Stovall Hairston (1784–1869)	Va.	Henry	corn, tobacco & cotton	121	701
		*Pittsylvania		93	
		Forsyth, N.C.		49	
		Stokes, N.C.		438	
**2 Philip St. George Cocke (1809–1861)	Va.	Brunswick	grain	158	658
		*Powhatan		125	
		Lowndes, Miss.	cotton	259	
		Yazoo, Miss.		116	
**3 Richard Baylor (1803–1862)	Va.	Charles City	grain	180	520
		*Essex		340	
**4 William Henry Tayloe (1799–1871)	Va.	*Richmond (listed under son Henry A. Tayloe)	grain	169	494
		Bertie, N.C.		48	
		Marengo, Ala.	cotton	125	
		Perry, Ala.		152	
5 William Allen of Surry (1828–1875) (né William Griffin Orgain)	Va.	Henrico	grain	232	446
		James City		57	
		*Surry		157	

	Slaveholder	Birthplace	County	Major Crop	Subtotal	Total
**6	Williams Carter (1782–1864)	Va.	*Caroline	grain	216	
			Hanover		211	427
**7	Samuel Hairston (1784–1880)	Va.	Henry	corn, tobacco	34	
			Patrick	& cotton	58	
			*Pittsylvania		187	279
8	William Fanning Wickham (1793–1880)	Va.	Hanover	grain		269
9	George Evelyn Harrison, Jr. (1837–1880)	Va.	Prince George	grain		255
10	James Galt (1805–1876)	Scotland	Fluvanna	grain		251

*Denotes county of residence

**Denotes those slaveowners who held 250+ in 1850

1. Figure from Madison County Personal Tax Rolls, 1859.
2. Estimated from tax rolls; Washington County census destroyed.
3. Figure from Holmes County Personal Tax Rolls, 1861.
4. Figure from Richard T. Archer Family Papers, University of Texas–Austin.
5. Figure from Wilkinson County Personal Tax Rolls, 1859.
6. Figure from Charles Heyward Plantation Record Book, South Caroliniana Library.
7. Figure from Theodore Rosengarten, *Tombee*, 67, 718–19.

Total slaveholders with 250+ in 1860 were 270, of whom 93 (or 34 percent) held that number in 1850.

BIBLIOGRAPHY

PRIMARY SOURCES

MANUSCRIPT COLLECTIONS

Alabama Department of Archives and History, Montgomery
Hunter-Milhous Family Collection, 1828–1924. 8 folders.
Spann Family Papers, 1850–1962 (ts). 1 folder.
Henry A. Tayloe and Family Papers, 1833–80 (photostat copies). 3 folders.
Gaius Whitfield Family Papers, 1713–1922. 2 boxes.

Center for American History, University of Texas, Austin
Richard Thompson Archer Family Papers, 1790–1919. 5 ft., 4 in.
Rice C. Ballard Papers, 1843–72. 20 items.
Leverich Papers, 1827–97. 7 boxes.
Natchez Trace Small MSS Collections
 Joseph Emory Davis Papers, 1865–66.
 William St. John Elliot Papers, 1855–56.
 Wade Hampton Papers, 1855–74.
 Alexander C. Keene and Julia Morgan Marriage Contract, 1845.
 John H. Murdoch Papers, 1826–34.
 Francis Surget Papers, 1856–57. 4 items.
 Robert J. Turnbull Papers, 1855–56.
Benjamin Roach Family Papers, 1831–67. 5 in.
Winchester Family Papers, 1783–1902. 17 ft.

Perkins Library, Duke University, Durham, North Carolina
Josiah Collins Papers, 1819–50. 3 items.
Devereux Family Papers, 1776–1936. 454 items and 4 vols.
Haller Nutt Papers, 1846–1911. 722 items and 4 vols.
 Araby Plantation Journal, 1843–50.

Georgia Historical Society, Savannah
    Benjamin Palmer Axson Papers, 1907, 1926–27. 5 boxes.
    R & J Habersham Papers, 1806, 1823. 28 items.
    Owens-Thomas Family Papers, 1837–1954. 278 items.
    James Potter Paper, 1828–31. 1 item (Argyle Plantation Journal).
    Telfair Family Papers, 1751–1875, 1909. 19 boxes.
    Wayne-Stites-Anderson Papers, 1756–1957. 8,490 items.

Historic New Orleans Collection, New Orleans
    Benjamin-Millaudon Collection, 1845–81. 30 items.
    Beverly Plantation Journal, 1826–57. 1 item.
    Lemuel P. Conner Papers, 1861–1936. 13 items.
    Duncan F. Kenner Letter, 1864. 1 item.
    Leonidas Polk Family Papers, 1843–1959. 25 items.

Louisiana and Lower Mississippi Valley Collections, Louisiana State University Libraries, Baton Rouge
    Ashland Plantation Record book, 1852. 1 vol.
    Robert Barrow Manuscript, 1858. 1 item.
    W. M. Barrow and Family Papers, 1847–74. 31 items and 1 vol.
    Rosella Kenner Brent Papers, 1902–15. 5 items.
    Rosella Kenner Brent Recollections [1862]. 1 vol.
    Louis A. Bringier and Family Papers, 1786–1901. 599 items and 13 vols.
    Thomas Butler and Family Papers, 1663, 1793–1950. 8,333 items, 74 printed vols., 52 MS vols.
    Lemuel P. Conner and Family Papers, 1818–1953. 5,982 items.
    Stephen Duncan Letters, 1855, 1859–60. 72 items.
    Duncan (Stephen and Stephen, Jr.) Papers, 1846–99. 255 items and 11 vols.
    Nathaniel Evans and Family Papers, 1791–1932. 3,475 items, 45 MS vols., 42 printed vols.
    Alexander K. Farrar Papers, 1804–1931. 2,304 items.
    John C. Jenkins and Family Papers, 1840–1900 (ts). 89 items, including 13 vols.
    Duncan F. Kenner Account Book, 1887–88. 1 vol.
    Duncan F. Kenner Executor's Account Book, 1887–88. 1 vol.
    Duncan F. Kenner Memorandum, 1854, 1858. 1 item.
    Duncan F. Kenner Papers, 1838–94, 1905. 306 items and 2 MS vols.
    Roswell King, Jr., Plantation Journal, 1838–45. 1 vol.
    Leverich (Charles P.) Correspondence, 1843–53. 12 items.
    James Stewart McGehee Papers, 1878, 1903–1904. 25 items.
    Marshall (Maria Louisa Chotard and Family) Papers, 1819–68. 48 items.
    William Newton Mercer Papers, 1789–1936. 1,624 items, including 64 vols. and 2 rolls of microfilm.

William J. Minor and Family Papers, 1748–1898. 410 items, including 37 vols.

Palfrey Family Papers, 1776–1918. 377 items and 21 vols.

Alexander Franklin Pugh Plantation Diaries, 1850–65. 7 vols.

H. M. Seale Diary, 1853–57. 1 vol.

Lewis Stirling and Family Papers, 1797–1933. 2,651 items, 38 MS vols., 2 printed vols.

Benjamin Tureaud Papers, 1805–1932. 3,411 items, 87 vols.

Jean Ursin La Villebeuvre and Family Papers, 1806–1917. 1,022 items, 39 vols.

Mississippi Department of Archives and History, Jackson

Aventine Plantation Diary, 1857–60. 1 vol.

Daniel (Smith Coffee) Collection, 1809–67 (photostat and TS). 1 box.

Ellet-Jefferies Papers, 1842–92. 14 items.

Gwin (William McKendree) Papers, 1856–63. 17 items.

Humphreys (George Wilson and Family) Papers, 1823–98, 1910–13. 382 items and 1 vol.

Hunt (Abijah and David) Papers, 1797–1840. 99 items and 1 vol.

Killona Plantation Journals, 1836–44. 2 vols.

Leverich (Charles P.) Papers, 1833–54. 966 items.

McGehee Family Papers, 1854–74. 4 items and 1 vol.

MacNeil (Grace M. S.) Papers, 1806–1980. 62 boxes.

Nutt Family Collection, 1810–1896, 1937. 319 items.

Quitman (John A.) Papers, 1847–53. 3 items.

Quitman (John A. and Family) Papers, 1820–1931. 252 items.

Surget Family Papers (microfilm). 6 rolls.

Maryland Historical Society, Baltimore

Lloyd Family Papers (microfilm).

North Carolina Department of Archives and History, Raleigh

John Devereux Papers, 1712–1886. 13 boxes.

Thomas P. Devereux II Letterbook, 1863–65. 1 vol.

South Carolina Historical Society, Charleston

R. F. W. Allston Papers

Incoming Personal Letters, 1856–64. 150 items.

Outgoing Personal Letters, 1820–64. 250 items.

Pringle Family Correspondence, 1806–1807, 1853–65. Ca. 200 items.

Chesnut-Miller-Manning Papers, 1744–1900. 5 ft.

Langdon Cheves, Jr., Papers, 1835–39, 1855–59. Ca. 200 items.

Cheves-Middleton Papers, 1770–1906. 11 ft.

Eweretta Barnwell Middleton Family Letters, 1830–64.

Henry A. Middleton Family Letters, 1862–64.

Henry A. Middleton, Jr., Family Letters, 1842–61. 55 items.

Henry A. Middleton, Jr., Plantation Journal, 1855–61. 1 vol.

Theodore L. Gourdin Plantation and Personal Papers, 1822–66. 60 items, 2 vols.

Allen Smith Izard Letter, 1861. 1 item.

Middleton-Blake Papers, 1794–1903. 2 boxes.

Rhett Family Papers. 11 folders.

Robert Barnwell Rhett, Sr., Papers, 1825–1968. Ca. 400 items and 2 vols.

Simons-Siegling-Cappelmann Collection. 300 boxes.

Joshua John Ward Plantation Account Book, 1831–69. 1 vol.

South Caroliniana Library, University of South Carolina, Columbia

Cheves Family Papers, 1808, 1819-1934. 74 items.

Langdon Cheves Papers, 1800–57. 30 items.

Charles Heyward Plantation Record Book, 1858–65. 1 vol.

Edward Barnwell Heyward Letters, 1855–66. 4 items.

Harriott Pinckney Papers, 1854–61. 26 items.

John Smith Preston Letters, 1854, 1861. 2 items.

Richard Singleton Inventory and Estate Book, 1852–55. 1 vol.

Williams-Chesnut-Manning Family Papers, 1682–1929. 1,048 items.

Southern Historical Collection of the Manuscripts Department, University of North Carolina, Chapel Hill

Rice Carter Ballard Papers, 1822–88. Ca. 5,000 items.

R. R. Barrow Residence Journal, 1857–58. 1 vol.

Cameron Family Papers, 1757–1978. 33,000 items.

Farish Carter Papers, 1806–68. 2,800 items, including 2 vols.

Cocke Papers, 1804–83 (microfilm). 798 items, including 22 vols.

James Hamilton Couper Plantation Records, 1818–54. 4 vols.

Donnell Family Papers, 1795–1868. 469 items.

Gillespie and Wright Family Papers, 1720–1877. 701 items.

George Hairston Papers, 1779–1922, 1950. 480 items.

Peter Wilson Hairston Papers, 1773–1965. 550 items, including 22 vols.

Hayes Collection, 1694–1874. 20,000 items, including 158 vols.

Heyward and Ferguson Family Papers, 1806–1923 (microfilm). 238 items.

George W. Mordecai Papers, 1776–1898. 4,500 items, including 44 vols.

Mount Airy Plantation Books, 1805–60 (microfilm). 3 vols.

John Perkins Papers, 1822–85. 550 items.

Pettigrew Family Papers, 1685, 1776–1930s. 9,230 items.

Skinner Family Papers, 1705–1900. 466 items and 3 vols.

Lewis Thompson Papers, 1723–1895. Ca. 4,650 items.

Robert James Turnbull Paper, n.d. 1 item.

Walton Family Papers, 1811–1910. 250 items.

Henry Clay Warmoth Papers and Books, 1798–1931. 120 folders and 82 vols.
Maunsel White Papers and Books, 1802–1912. 92 items, including 11 vols.
Whitfield and Wooten Family Papers, 1796–1918. 158 items, including 10 vols.

Hargrett Rare Book and Manuscript Library, University of Georgia, Athens
Cobb-Erwin-Lamar Family Collection, 1842–66.

Virginia Historical Society, Richmond
Baylor Family Papers, 1662–1962. Ca. 3,000 items.
James Nathaniel Dunlop Papers, 1840–88. Ca. 5,900 items.
Hairston Family Papers, 1816–64. 22 items.
Tayloe Family Papers, 1650–1970. 27,925 items.
Tayloe Family Papers Addition, 1841–1920. 152 items.
Wickham Family Papers, 1754–1977. Ca. 11,500 items.

PUBLIC DOCUMENTS

Adams County Circuit Court Records. Natchez, Mississippi. October, 1808. Drawer 24, Box 4-90.
Journal of the Mississippi Secession Convention. 1861. Reprint, Jackson: The Mississippi Commission on the War Between the States, 1962.
Manuscript Census Returns. Eighth Census of the United States, 1860. Schedule 1 (Population) and Schedule 2 (Slave) for all counties in the fifteen slave states and the District of Columbia.
Manuscript Census Returns. Schedule 4 (Agriculture) for selected counties in Mississippi and Louisiana, 1850 and 1860.
Manuscript Census Returns. Seventh Census of the United States, 1850. Schedule 1 (Population) and Schedule 2 (Slave) for all counties in the fifteen slave states and the District of Columbia.
Mississippi Personal Tax Rolls, 1842–1864 (microfilm). RG 29, Mississippi Department of Archives and History, Jackson.
Proceedings of the State Democratic Convention Held at Columbia, South Carolina, May 30–31, 1860. Columbia: Southern Guardian Steam-Power Press, 1860.
The War of the Rebellion: A Compilation of the Official Records of the Union and Confederate Armies. 128 vols. Washington, D.C.: U.S. Government Printing Office, 1880–1901.

EDITED WORKS AND OTHER PUBLISHED SOURCES

Andrew, Bishop James O. "A Fortnight Among the Missions to the Blacks." In Charles F. Deems, ed., *Annals of Southern Methodism, 1857.* Nashville: J. B. McFerrin, 1858.
Bleser, Carol, ed. *Secret and Sacred: The Diaries of James Henry Hammond, a Southern Slaveholder.* New York: Oxford University Press, 1988.

Cauthen, Charles E., ed. *Family Letters of the Three Wade Hamptons 1782–1901.* Columbia: University of South Carolina Press, 1953.

Champomier, Pierre A. *Statement of the Sugar Crop Made in Louisiana, 1844–1861.* New Orleans: Cook, Young and Company, 1845–62.

De Bow's Review. 43 vols. New Orleans, 1846–80.

Early, Bishop John. "A Fortnight Among the Missions to the Blacks." In Charles F. Deems, ed., *Annals of Southern Methodism, 1856.* Nashville: Stevenson and Owen, 1857.

Easterby, J. H., ed. *The South Carolina Rice Plantation as Revealed in the Papers of Robert F. W. Allston.* Chicago: University of Chicago Press, 1945.

House, Albert Virgil, ed. *Planter Management and Capitalism in Ante-Bellum Georgia.* New York: Columbia University Press, 1954.

"Journal of a Secesh Lady": The Diary of Catherine Ann Devereux Edmondston, 1860–1866. Edited by Beth G. Crabtree and James W. Patton. Raleigh, N.C.: Division of Archives and History, 1979.

Kemble, Frances Anne. *Journal of a Residence on a Georgian Plantation in 1838–39.* Edited by John A. Scott. New York: Alfred A. Knopf, 1961.

Marshall, Theodora Britton, and Gladys Crail Evans, eds. "Plantation Report from the Papers of Levin R. Marshall, of 'Richmond,' Natchez, Mississippi." *JMH* 3 (January 1941): 45–55.

Mathew, William M., ed. *Agriculture, Geology, and Society in Antebellum South Carolina: The Private Diary of Edmund Ruffin, 1843.* Athens: University of Georgia Press, 1992.

McCord, Louisa S. *Selected Writings.* Edited by Richard C. Lounsbury. Charlottesville: University Press of Virginia, 1997.

Myers, Robert Manson, ed. *The Children of Pride: A True Story of Georgia and the Civil War.* New Haven: Yale University Press, 1972.

Northup, Solomon. *Twelve Years a Slave.* Edited by Sue Eakin and Joseph Logsdon. Baton Rouge: Louisiana State University Press, 1968.

The Papers of Frederick Law Olmsted. Vol. 2: *Slavery and the South, 1852–57.* Edited by Charles E. Beveridge and Charles Capen McLaughlin. Baltimore: Johns Hopkins University Press, 1981.

The Papers of Henry Clay. Vol. 10: *Candidate, Compromiser, Elder Statesman, January 1, 1844–June 29, 1852.* Edited by Melba Porter Hay. Lexington: University Press of Kentucky, 1991.

The Papers of Thomas Ruffin. 4 vols. Edited by J. G. de Roulhac Hamilton. Raleigh: Edwards and Broughton Printing Company, 1918–20.

Phillips, Ulrich B., and James D. Glunt, eds. *Florida Plantation Records from the Papers of George Noble Jones.* St. Louis: Missouri Historical Society, 1927.

Pringle, Elizabeth Allston (Patience Pennington). *A Woman Rice Planter.* 1913. Reprint, Columbia: University of South Carolina Press, 1992.

Robinson, Solon. "Agricultural Tour South and West." *American Agriculturalist* 8 (October 1849): 314–15.

Scarborough, William K., ed. *The Diary of Edmund Ruffin.* 3 vols. Baton Rouge: Louisiana State University Press, 1972–89.

The Secret Eye: The Journal of Ella Gertrude Clanton Thomas, 1848–89. Edited by Virginia Ingraham Burr. Chapel Hill: University of North Carolina Press, 1990.

Woodward, C. Vann, ed. *Mary Chesnut's Civil War.* New Haven: Yale University Press, 1981.

SELECTED SECONDARY SOURCES

BIOGRAPHICAL DIRECTORIES AND REFERENCE WORKS

Biographical Directory of the American Congress, 1774–1961. Washington, D.C.: U.S. Government Printing Office, 1961.

Biographical Directory of the Governors of the United States, 1789–1978. 5 vols. Edited by Robert Sobel and John Raimo. Westport, Conn.: Meckler Books, 1978.

Biographical Directory of the Senate of the State of South Carolina, 1776–1964. Compiled by Emily Bellinger Reynolds and Joan Reynolds Faunt. Columbia: South Carolina Archives Department, 1964.

Biographical Directory of the South Carolina House of Representatives. 5 vols. Edited by Walter Edgar, N. Louise Bailey, Elizabeth Ivey Cooper, and Alexander Moore. Columbia: University of South Carolina Press, 1974–84; South Carolina Department of Archives and History, 1992.

Boatner, Mark M., III. *The Civil War Dictionary.* New York: David McKay, 1959.

Dictionary of American Biography. 21 vols. Edited by Allen Johnson and Dumas Malone. New York: Charles Scribner's Sons, 1928–37.

Dictionary of Georgia Biography. 2 vols. Edited by Kenneth Coleman and Charles Stephen Gurr. Athens: University of Georgia Press, 1980–83.

Dictionary of Louisiana Biography. 2 vols. Edited by Glenn Conrad. Louisiana Historical Society, 1988.

Dictionary of North Carolina Biography. 6 vols. Edited by William S. Powell. Chapel Hill: University of North Carolina Press, 1979–96.

Encyclopedia of Southern History. Edited by David C. Roller and Robert W. Twyman. Baton Rouge: Louisiana State University Press, 1979.

Long, E. B. *The Civil War Day by Day: An Almanac, 1861–1865.* Garden City, N.Y.: Doubleday, 1971.

May, John A., and Joan Reynolds Faunt. *South Carolina Secedes.* Columbia: University of South Carolina Press, 1960.

Wakelyn, Jon L. *Biographical Dictionary of the Confederacy.* Westport, Conn.: Greenwood Press, 1977.

Warner, Ezra J. *Generals in Gray: Lives of the Confederate Commanders.* Baton Rouge: Louisiana State University Press, 1959.

Warner, Ezra J., and W. Buck Yearns, eds. *Biographical Register of the Confederate Congress*. Baton Rouge: Louisiana State University Press, 1975.

BOOKS

Allmendinger, David F., Jr. *Ruffin: Family and Reform in the Old South*. New York: Oxford University Press, 1990.

Bagwell, James E. *Rice Gold: James Hamilton Couper and Plantation Life on the Georgia Coast*. Macon: Mercer University Press, 2000.

Bancroft, Frederic. *Slave Trading in the Old South*. 1931. Reprint, New York: Frederick Ungar Publishing Company, 1959.

Bauer, Craig A. *A Leader Among Peers: The Life and Times of Duncan Farrar Kenner*. Lafayette: Center for Louisiana Studies, University of Southwestern Louisiana, 1993.

Bell, Malcolm, Jr. *Major Butler's Legacy: Five Generations of a Slaveholding Family*. Athens: University of Georgia Press, 1987.

Billings, Dwight B., Jr. *Planters and the Making of a "New South": Class, Politics, and Development in North Carolina, 1865–1900*. Chapel Hill: University of North Carolina Press, 1979.

Bradley, Mark L. *This Astounding Close: The Road to Bennett Place*. Chapel Hill: University of North Carolina Press, 2000.

Bullard, Mary R. *Robert Stafford of Cumberland Island: Growth of a Planter*. 1986. Paperback reprint, Athens: University of Georgia Press, 1995.

Campbell, Randolph B. *An Empire for Slavery: The Peculiar Institution in Texas, 1821–1865*. Baton Rouge: Louisiana State University Press, 1989.

Cashin, Joan E. *A Family Venture: Men and Women on the Southern Frontier*. New York: Oxford University Press, 1991.

Censer, Jane Turner. *North Carolina Planters and Their Children, 1800–1860*. Baton Rouge: Louisiana State University Press, 1984.

Claiborne, J. F. H. *Mississippi, as a Province, Territory and State*. 1880. Reprint, Baton Rouge: Louisiana State University Press, 1964.

Clinton, Catherine. *The Plantation Mistress: Woman's World in the Old South*. New York: Pantheon Books, 1982.

Coulter, E. Merton. *The Confederate States of America, 1861–1865*. Baton Rouge: Louisiana State University Press, 1950.

———. *The South During Reconstruction, 1865–1877*. Baton Rouge: Louisiana State University Press, 1947.

Davidson, Chalmers Gaston. *The Last Foray: The South Carolina Planters of 1860: A Sociological Study*. Columbia: University of South Carolina Press, 1971.

Davis, Ronald L. F. *Good and Faithful Labor: From Slavery to Sharecropping in the Natchez District, 1860–1890*. Westport, Conn.: Greenwood Press, 1982.

Dixon, Nancy. *Fortune and Misery: Sallie Rhett Roman of New Orleans: A Biographical*

Portrait and Selected Fiction, 1891–1920. Baton Rouge: Louisiana State University Press, 1999.

Donald, David. *Charles Sumner and the Coming of the Civil War.* New York: Alfred A. Knopf, 1961.

Dusinberre, William. *Them Dark Days: Slavery in the American Rice Swamps.* New York: Oxford University Press, 1996.

Edmunds, John B., Jr. *Francis W. Pickens and the Politics of Destruction.* Chapel Hill: University of North Carolina Press, 1986.

Faust, Drew Gilpin. *James Henry Hammond and the Old South: A Design for Mastery.* Baton Rouge: Louisiana State University Press, 1982.

———. *Mothers of Invention: Women of the Slaveholding South in the American Civil War.* Chapel Hill: University of North Carolina Press, 1996.

Flanders, Ralph Betts. *Plantation Slavery in Georgia.* Chapel Hill: University of North Carolina Press, 1933.

Fogel, Robert William, and Stanley L. Engerman. *Time on the Cross: The Economics of American Negro Slavery.* Boston: Little, Brown, and Company, 1974.

Foner, Eric. *Reconstruction: America's Unfinished Revolution, 1863–1877.* New York: Harper & Row, 1988.

Ford, Lacy K., Jr. *Origins of Southern Radicalism: The South Carolina Upcountry, 1800–1860.* New York: Oxford University Press, 1988.

Fornell, Earl Wesley. *The Galveston Era: The Texas Crescent on the Eve of Secession.* Austin: University of Texas Press, 1961.

Fox-Genovese, Elizabeth. *Within the Plantation Household: Black and White Women of the Old South.* Chapel Hill: University of North Carolina Press, 1988.

Fox-Genovese, Elizabeth, and Eugene D. Genovese. *Fruits of Merchant Capital: Slavery and Bourgeois Property in the Rise and Expansion of Capitalism.* New York: Oxford University Press, 1983.

Freehling, William W. *Prelude to Civil War: The Nullification Controversy in South Carolina, 1816–1836.* New York: Harper & Row, 1965.

———. *The Road to Disunion.* Vol. 1: *Secessionists at Bay, 1776–1854.* New York: Oxford University Press, 1990.

Gates, Paul Wallace. *The Farmer's Age: Agriculture, 1815–1860.* New York: Holt, Rinehart, and Winston, 1960.

Gray, Lewis C. *History of Agriculture in the Southern United States to 1860.* 2 vols. 1933. Reprint, Gloucester, Mass.: Peter Smith, 1958.

Hermann, Janet Sharp. *Joseph E. Davis: Pioneer Patriarch.* Jackson: University Press of Mississippi, 1990.

Heyward, Duncan Clinch. *Seed from Madagascar.* 1937. Reprint with new introduction by Peter A. Coclanis. Columbia: University of South Carolina Press, 1993.

Hobsbawm, Eric J. *The Age of Capital, 1848–1875.* New York: Charles Scribner's Sons, 1975.

James, D. Clayton. *Antebellum Natchez.* Baton Rouge: Louisiana State University Press, 1968.

Joyner, Charles. *Down by the Riverside: A South Carolina Slave Community.* Urbana: University of Illinois Press, 1984.

Kenzer, Robert C. *Kinship and Neighborhood in a Southern Community: Orange County, North Carolina, 1849–1881.* Knoxville: University of Tennessee Press, 1987.

Klingberg, Frank W. *The Southern Claims Commission.* Berkeley: University of California Press, 1955.

Kolchin, Peter. *American Slavery, 1619–1877.* New York: Hill and Wang, 1993.

Leech, Margaret. *Reveille in Washington, 1860–1865.* New York: Harper and Brothers, 1941.

Loveland, Anne. *Southern Evangelicals and the Social Order.* Baton Rouge: Louisiana State University Press, 1982.

Mathew, William M. *Edmund Ruffin and the Crisis of Slavery in the Old South: The Failure of Agricultural Reform.* Athens: University of Georgia Press, 1988.

May, Robert E. *John A. Quitman, Old South Crusader.* Baton Rouge: Louisiana State University Press, 1985.

McCurry, Stephanie. *Masters of Small Worlds: Yeoman Households, Gender Relations, and the Political Culture of the Antebellum South Carolina Low Country.* New York: Oxford University Press, 1995.

Mohr, James C. *Abortion in America: The Origins and Evolution of National Policy, 1800–1900.* New York: Oxford University Press, 1978.

Mooney, Chase C. *Slavery in Tennessee.* Bloomington: Indiana University Press, 1957.

Moore, Barrington, Jr. *Social Origins of Dictatorship and Democracy: Lord and Peasant in the Making of the Modern World.* Boston: Beacon Press, 1966.

Moore, John Hebron. *Agriculture in Ante-Bellum Mississippi.* New York: Bookman Associates, 1958.

———. *The Emergence of the Cotton Kingdom in the Old Southwest: Mississippi, 1770–1860.* Baton Rouge: Louisiana State University Press, 1988.

Nevins, Allan. *The Emergence of Lincoln.* 2 vols. New York: Charles Scribner's Sons, 1950.

———. *Ordeal of the Union.* 2 vols. New York: Charles Scribner's Sons, 1947.

Numbers, Ronald L., and Todd L. Savitt, eds. *Science and Medicine in the Old South.* Baton Rouge: Louisiana State University Press, 1989.

Oakes, James. *The Ruling Race: A History of American Slaveholders.* New York: Alfred A. Knopf, 1982.

———. *Slavery and Freedom: An Interpretation of the Old South.* New York: Vintage Books, 1990.

Phillips, Ulrich B. *American Negro Slavery.* New York: D. Appleton and Company, 1918.

———. *Life and Labor in the Old South.* New York: Grosset and Dunlap, 1929.

Reidy, Joseph P. *From Slavery to Agrarian Capitalism in the Cotton Plantation South: Central Georgia, 1800–1880.* Chapel Hill: University of North Carolina Press, 1992.

Robertson, James I., Jr. *Stonewall Jackson: The Man, the Soldier, the Legend.* New York: Macmillan Publishing, 1997.

Rosengarten, Theodore. *Tombee: Portrait of a Cotton Planter.* New York: William Morrow and Company, 1986.

Rowland, Dunbar. *Mississippi.* 3 vols. Atlanta: Southern Historical Publishing Association, 1907.

Scarborough, William K. *The Overseer: Plantation Management in the Old South.* Baton Rouge: Louisiana State University Press, 1966.

Schafer, Judith Kelleher. *Slavery, the Civil Law, and the Supreme Court of Louisiana.* Baton Rouge: Louisiana State University Press, 1994.

Schultz, Harold S. *Nationalism and Sectionalism in South Carolina, 1852–1860.* 1950. Reprint, New York: De Capo Press, 1969.

Sellers, Charles. *The Market Revolution: Jacksonian America, 1815–1846.* New York: Oxford University Press, 1991.

Sellers, James Benson. *Slavery in Alabama.* University: University of Alabama Press, 1950.

Shore, Laurence. *Southern Capitalists: The Ideological Leadership of an Elite, 1832–1885.* Chapel Hill: University of North Carolina Press, 1986.

Shugg, Roger W. *Origins of Class Struggle in Louisiana.* University: Louisiana State University Press, 1939.

Sitterson, J. Carlyle. *The Secession Movement in North Carolina.* Chapel Hill: University of North Carolina Press, 1939.

———. *Sugar Country: The Cane Sugar Industry in the South, 1753–1950.* Lexington: University of Kentucky Press, 1953.

Smith, J. Frazier. *White Pillars.* New York: Bramhall House, 1941.

Smith, Julia Floyd. *Slavery and Plantation Growth in Antebellum Florida, 1821–1860.* Gainesville: University of Florida Press, 1973.

———. *Slavery and Rice Culture in Low Country Georgia, 1750–1860.* Knoxville: University of Tennessee Press, 1985.

Smith, Mark M. *Debating Slavery: Economy and Society in the Antebellum American South.* New York: Cambridge University Press, 1998.

Starobin, Robert S. *Industrial Slavery in the Old South.* New York: Oxford University Press, 1970.

Steele, Edward M., Jr. *T. Butler King of Georgia.* Athens: University of Georgia Press, 1964.

Stephenson, Wendell Holmes. *Alexander Porter, Whig Planter of Old Louisiana.* Baton Rouge: Louisiana State University Press, 1939.

———. *Isaac Franklin, Slave Trader and Planter of the Old South.* 1938. Reprint, Gloucester, Mass.: Peter Smith, 1968.

Sydnor, Charles Sackett. *A Gentleman of the Old Natchez Region: Benjamin L. C. Wailes.* Durham: Duke University Press, 1938.

———. *Slavery in Mississippi.* 1933. Reprint, Gloucester, Mass.: Peter Smith, 1965.

Tadman, Michael. *Speculators and Slaves: Masters, Traders, and Slaves in the Old South.* Madison: University of Wisconsin Press, 1989.

Taylor, Joe Gray. *Negro Slavery in Louisiana.* Louisiana Historical Association, 1963.

Taylor, Orville W. *Negro Slavery in Arkansas.* Durham: Duke University Press, 1958.

Thomas, Emory M. *The Confederate Nation, 1861–1865.* New York: Harper and Row, 1979.

Thornton, J. Mills, III. *Politics and Power in a Slave Society: Alabama, 1800–1860.* Baton Rouge: Louisiana State University Press, 1978.

Wayne, Michael. *Death of an Overseer: Reopening a Murder Investigation from the Plantation South.* New York: Oxford University Press, 2001.

———. *The Reshaping of Plantation Society: The Natchez District, 1860–1880.* Baton Rouge: Louisiana State University Press, 1983.

Weaver, Herbert. *Mississippi Farmers, 1850–1860.* Nashville: Vanderbilt University Press, 1945.

Wiencek, Henry. *The Hairstons: An American Family in Black and White.* New York: St. Martin's Press, 1999.

Wiener, Jonathan M. *Social Origins of the New South: Alabama, 1860–1885.* Baton Rouge: Louisiana State University Press, 1978.

Williams, T. Harry. *P. G. T. Beauregard: Napoleon in Gray.* Baton Rouge: Louisiana State University Press, 1955.

Woodman, Harold. *King Cotton and His Retainers: Financing and Marketing the Cotton Crop of the South, 1800–1925.* Lexington: University of Kentucky Press, 1968.

ARTICLES

Ayers, Edward L. "The World the Liberal Capitalists Made." *Reviews in American History* 19 (June 1991): 194–99.

Bailey, Louise Howe. "Flat Rock: 'Little Charleston of the Mountains.'" *Carologue* 11 (Summer 1995): 12–15, 28.

Bowman, Shearer Davis. "Antebellum Planters and *Vormärz* Junkers in Comparative Perspective." *AHR* 85 (October 1980): 779–808.

Carrison, Henry. "A Businessman in Crisis: Col. Daniel Jordan and the Civil War." *South Carolina Historical Magazine* 102 (October 2001): 335–61.

Cashin, Joan E. "The Structure of Antebellum Planter Families: 'The Ties that Bound Us was Strong.'" *JSH* 56 (February 1990): 55–70.

Clifton, James M. "Jehossee Island: The Antebellum South's Largest Rice Plantation." *AH* 59 (January 1985): 56–65.

Cobb, James C. "Beyond Planters and Industrialists: A New Perspective on the New South." *JSH* 54 (February 1988): 45–68.

Egerton, Douglas R. "Markets Without a Market Revolution: Southern Planters and Capitalism." *Journal of the Early Republic* 16 (Summer 1996): 207–21.

Gilje, Paul A. "The Rise of Capitalism in the Early Republic." *Journal of the Early Republic* 16 (Summer 1996): 159–81.

Gill, Christopher J. "A Year of Residence in the Household of a South Carolina Planter: Teacher, Daughters, Mistress, and Slaves." *South Carolina Historical Magazine* 97 (October 1996): 293–309.

Govan, Thomas P. "Was the Old South Different?" *JSH* 21 (November 1955): 447–55.

Hahn, Steven. "Capitalists All!" *Reviews in American History* 11 (June 1983): 219–25.

Harlow, Jeanerette. "Surget Name Legend in Homes at Natchez." Jackson (Miss.) *Clarion-Ledger*, 6 April 1969.

Hawks, Joanne V. "Julia A. Nutt of Longwood." *JMH* 57 (November 1994): 291–308.

Herndon, G. Melvin. "Agricultural Reform in Antebellum Virginia: William Galt, Jr., A Case Study." *AH* 52 (July 1978): 394–406.

———. "From Orphans to Merchants to Planters: The Galt Brothers, William and James." *Virginia Cavalcade* 29 (Summer 1979): 22–31.

Holmes, Jack D. L. "Stephen Minor: Natchez Pioneer." *JMH* 42 (February 1980): 17–26.

Jabour, Anya. "'Grown Girls, Highly Cultivated': Female Education in an Antebellum Southern Family." *JSH* 64 (February 1998): 23–64.

Johnson, Michael P. "Planters and Patriarchy: Charleston, 1800–1860." *JSH* 46 (February 1980): 45–72.

Keller, Mark A. "Horse Racing Madness in the Old South—The Sporting Epistles of William J. Minor of Natchez (1837–1860)." *JMH* 47 (August 1985): 165–85.

Kulikoff, Allan. "The Transition to Capitalism in Rural America." *William and Mary Quarterly* 46 (January 1989): 120–44.

Lawton, Thomas O., Jr. "The Life and Death of Robertville." *Carologue* 16 (Winter 2000): 8–13.

May, Robert E. "Southern Elite Women, Sectional Extremism, and the Male Political Sphere: The Case of John A. Quitman's Wife and Female Descendants, 1847–1931." *JMH* 50 (November 1988): 251–85.

Merrill, Michael. "Putting 'Capitalism' in Its Place: A Review of Recent Literature." *William and Mary Quarterly* 52 (April 1995): 315–26.

Myers, Cynthia. "Queen of the Confederacy." *Civil War Times Illustrated* 35 (December 1996): 72–78.

Pease, William H., and Jane H. Pease. "Traditional Belles or Borderline Bluestockings? The Petigru Women." *South Carolina Historical Magazine* 102 (October 2001): 292–309.

Pessen, Edward. "How Different from Each Other Were the Antebellum North and South?" *AHR* 85 (December 1980): 1119–49.

Rothstein, Morton. "The Antebellum South as a Dual Economy: A Tentative Hypothesis." *AGH* 41 (October 1967): 373–82.

Scarborough, Thomas A. H. "The Bislands of Natchez: Sugar, Secession, and Strategies for Survival." *JMH* 58 (Spring 1996): 23–62.

Scarborough, William K. "Lords or Capitalists? The Natchez Nabobs in Comparative Perspective." *JMH* 54 (August 1992): 229–67.

Seal, Albert G. "John Carmichael Jenkins: Scientific Planter of the Natchez District." *JMH* 1 (January 1939): 14–28.

Sitterson, J. Carlyle. "Lewis Thompson, a Carolinian, and His Louisiana Plantation, 1848–1888: A Study in Absentee Ownership." In *Essays in Southern History*, edited by Fletcher M. Green, pp. 16–22. Chapel Hill: University of North Carolina Press, 1949.

———. "The William J. Minor Plantations: A Study in Ante-Bellum Absentee Ownership." *JSH* 9 (February 1943): 59–74.

Wayne, Michael. "An Old South Morality Play: Reconsidering the Social Underpinnings of the Proslavery Ideology." *JAH* 77 (December 1990): 838–63.

DISSERTATIONS AND THESES

Bagwell, James E. "James Hamilton Couper, Georgia Rice Planter." Ph.D. diss., University of Southern Mississippi, 1978.

Baxter, Anne Brady. "The Forgotten Aristocracy: Plantation Society in Jefferson and Claiborne Counties." Master's thesis, University of Southern Mississippi, 1986.

Boucher, Ann Williams. "Wealthy Planter Families in Nineteenth Century Alabama." Ph.D. diss., University of Connecticut, 1978.

Menn, Joseph Karl. "The Large Slaveholders of the Deep South, 1860." Ph.D. diss., University of Texas, 1964.

Owen, Christopher H. "Sanctity, Slavery, and Segregation: Methodists and Society in Nineteenth-Century Georgia." Ph.D. diss., Emory University, 1991.

Robins, Glenn M. "Southern Episcopalianism: Leonidas Polk and Denominational Identity." Ph.D. diss., University of Southern Mississippi, 1999.

STATE, LOCAL, AND SELECTED GENEALOGICAL SOURCES

Alabama

Gandrud, Pauline Jones, comp. *Alabama Records.* Easley, S.C.: Southern Historical Press, 1981.

———. *Marriage, Death, and Legal Notices from Early Alabama Newspapers, 1819–1893.* Easley, S.C.: Southern Historical Press, 1981.

Memorial Record of Alabama. Madison, Wis.: Brant and Fuller, 1893.

Owen, Thomas McAdory. *History of Alabama and Dictionary of Alabama Biography.* 4 vols. Chicago: S. J. Clarke, 1921.

Arkansas

Shinn, Josiah H. *Pioneers and Makers of Arkansas.* Little Rock, 1908.

Florida

Griffin, Patricia C. *Mullet on the Beach: The Minorcans of Florida, 1768–1788.* Jacksonville: University of North Florida Press, 1991.

Georgia

Rocker, Willard R. *Marriages and Obituaries from the Macon Messenger, 1818–1865.* Easley, S.C.: Southern Historical Press, 1988.

Swiggart, Carolyn Clay. *The Clay & McAllister Families of Bryan County, Georgia.* Darien, Conn.: Two Bytes Publishing, 1999.

Louisiana

Louisiana Writers' Project. *Louisiana: A Guide to the State.* New York: Hastings House, 1945.

Robinson, Elrie. *Early Feliciana Politics.* St. Francisville (La.) *Democrat,* 1936.

Seebold, Herman de Bachelle. *Old Louisiana Plantation Homes and Family Trees.* 2 vols. 1941. Reprint, Gretna, La.: Pelican Publishing Company, 1971.

Maryland

Footner, Hulbert. "The Lloyds of Wye." Chap. 18 in *Rivers of the Eastern Shore: Seventeen Maryland Rivers.* Cambridge, Md.: Tidewater Publishers, 1944.

Mississippi

Biographical and Historical Memoirs of Mississippi. 2 vols. Chicago: Goodspeed Publishing Company, 1891.

Callon, Sim C., and Carolyn Vance Smith. *The Goat Castle Murder.* Natchez, Miss.: Plantation Publishing Company, 1985.

Early Records of Mississippi: Issaquena and Washington Counties. Compiled by Alice Wade and Katherine Branton. 2 vols. Jackson: Mississippi Department of Archives and History, 1982–83.

Gillis, Irene S., and Norman E. Gillis, comps. *Adams County, Mississippi, Marriages, 1802–1859.* N.p., 1976.

Headley, Katy McCaleb. *Claiborne County, Mississippi: The Promised Land.* Port Gibson, Miss.: Claiborne County Historical Society, 1976.

Marriages and Deaths from Mississippi Newspapers. Compiled by Betty Couch Wiltshire. 4 vols. Bowie, Md.: Heritage Books, Inc., 1987–90.

McCain, William D., and Charlotte Capers, eds. *Memoirs of Henry Tillinghast Ireys: Papers of the Washington County Historical Society, 1910–1915.* Jackson: Mississippi Department of Archives and History and Mississippi Historical Society, 1954.

McLemore, Richard A., ed. *A History of Mississippi.* 2 vols. Hattiesburg: University and College Press of Mississippi, 1973.

Mead, Carol Lynn. *The Land Between Two Rivers: Madison County, Mississippi.* Canton, Miss.: Friends of the Madison County-Canton Public Library, 1987.

Mississippi Index of Wills, 1800–1900. Compiled by Betty Couch Wiltshire. Bowie, Md.: Heritage Books, Inc., 1989.

Mississippi: The WPA Guide to the Magnolia State. 1938. Reprint, Jackson: University Press of Mississippi, 1988.

North Carolina

Bizzell, Oscar M., ed. *The Heritage of Sampson County, North Carolina.* Winston-Salem: Hunter Publishing Company, 1983.

Ingmire, Frances T., comp. *Chowan County, North Carolina, Marriage Records, 1742–1868.* St. Louis: Ingmire Publications, 1984.

———. *Craven County, North Carolina, Marriage Records, 1780–1867.* St. Louis: Ingmire Publications, 1984.

Johnston County, North Carolina, County Court Minutes. Books VIII–XIII, 1808–30. Transcribed by Weynette Parks Haun. Durham, N.C., 1977–81.

South Carolina

Brewster, Lawrence Fay. *Summer Migrations and Resorts of South Carolina Low-Country Planters.* 1947. Reprint, New York: AMS Press, 1970.

Glover, Beulah. *Narratives of Colleton County, South Carolina.* 1962. Reprint, Spartanburg: The Reprint Company, 1984.

Graydon, Nell S. *Tales of Edisto.* Columbia, S.C.: The R. L. Bryan Company, 1955.

Green, Edwin L. *A History of Richland County.* Baltimore: Regional Publishing Company, 1974.

Gregoire, Anne King. *History of Sumter County, South Carolina.* Sumter: Library Board of Sumter County, 1954.

Holcomb, Brent H., comp. *Marriage and Death Notices from Columbia, South Carolina Newspapers, 1838–1860.* Columbia: n.p., 1988.

———. *Marriage and Death Notices from the Charleston Observer, 1827–1845.* Greenville, S.C.: A Press, Inc., 1980.

———. *Marriage and Death Notices from the (Charleston) Times. 1800–1821.* Baltimore: Genealogical Publishing Company, 1979.

———. *Marriage, Death, and Estate Notices from Georgetown, South Carolina, Newspapers, 1791–1861.* Easley, S.C.: Southern Historical Press, 1979.

McMaster, Fitz Hugh. *History of Fairfield County, South Carolina.* Columbia: The State Commercial Printing Company, 1946.

Moore, John Hammond. *Columbia and Richland County: A South Carolina Community, 1740–1990.* Columbia: University of South Carolina Press, 1993.

Nicholes, Cassie. *Historical Sketches of Sumter County: Its Birth and Growth.* Sumter: Sumter County Historical Commission, 1975.

Rogers, George C., Jr. *The History of Georgetown County, South Carolina.* Columbia: University of South Carolina Press, 1970.

South Carolina Geneaologies: Articles from the South Carolina Historical (and Genealogical) Magazine. 5 vols. Spartanburg: The Reprint Company, 1983.

Wilson, Teresa E., and Janice L. Grimes, comps. *Marriage and Death Notices from the Southern Patriot.* Vol. 1, 1815–30. Easley, S.C.: Southern Historical Press, 1982.

Tennessee

Arnow, Harriette Simpson. *Flowering of the Cumberland.* New York: Macmillan Company, 1963.

Federal Writers' Project. *Tennessee: A Guide to the State.* New York: Viking Press, 1937.

Folmsbee, Stanley J., Robert E. Corlew, and Enoch L. Mitchell. *History of Tennessee.* 4 vols. New York: Lewis Historical Publishing Company, 1960.

Lucas, Silas Emmett, Jr., comp. *Marriages and Obituaries from Early Tennessee Newspapers, 1794–1851.* Easley, S.C.: Southern Historical Press, 1978.

Maury County Cousins: Bible and Family Records. Columbia, Tenn.: Maury County Historical Society, 1967.

Whitley, Edythe Rucker, comp. *Marriages of Davidson County, Tennessee, 1789–1847.* Baltimore: Genealogical Publishing Company, 1981.

Virginia

Genealogies of Virginia Families: Articles from the *Virginia Magazine of History and Biography.* 5 vols. Baltimore: Genealogical Publishing Company, 1981.

Genealogies of Virginia Families: Articles from the *William and Mary Quarterly.* 5 vols. Baltimore: Genealogical Publishing Company, 1982.

Hardy, Stella Pickett. *Colonial Families of the Southern States of America.* 2nd ed. Baltimore: Southern Book Company, 1958.

Slaughter, James B. *Settlers, Southerners, Americans: The History of Essex County, Virginia, 1608–1984.* Essex County Board of Supervisors, 1985.

Wingfield, Marshall. *A History of Caroline County, Virginia.* 1924. Reprint, Baltimore: Regional Publishing Company, 1975.

INDEX